The Java™ Language Specification

Third Edition

The Java™ Series

Ken Arnold, James Gosling, David Holmes
The Java™ Programming Language, Third Edition

Cynthia Bloch, Annette Wagner
MIDP 2.0 Style Guide for the Java™ 2 Platform, Micro Edition

Joshua Bloch
Effective Java™ Programming Language Guide

Mary Campione, Kathy Walrath, Alison Huml
The Java™ Tutorial, Third Edition: A Short Course on the Basics

Mary Campione, Kathy Walrath, Alison Huml,Tutorial Team
The Java™ Tutorial Continued: The Rest of the JDK™

Patrick Chan
The Java™ Developers Almanac 1.4, Volume 1

Patrick Chan
The Java™ Developers Almanac 1.4, Volume 2

Patrick Chan, Rosanna Lee
The Java™ Class Libraries, Second Edition, Volume 2: java.applet, java.awt, java.beans

Patrick Chan, Rosanna Lee, Doug Kramer
The Java™ Class Libraries, Second Edition, Volume 1: java.io, java.lang, java.math, java.net, java.text, java.util

Patrick Chan, Rosanna Lee, Doug Kramer
The Java™ Class Libraries, Second Edition, Volume 1: Supplement for the Java™ 2 Platform, Standard Edition, v1.2

Kirk Chen, Li Gong
Programming Open Service Gateways with Java™ Embedded Server

Zhiqun Chen
Java Card™ Technology for Smart Cards: Architecture and Programmer's Guide

Maydene Fisher, Jon Ellis, Jonathan Bruce
JDBC™ API Tutorial and Reference, Third Edition

Li Gong, Gary Ellison, Mary Dageforde
Inside Java™ 2 Platform Security, Second Edition: Architecture, API Design, and Implementation

James Gosling, Bill Joy, Guy Steele, Gilad Bracha
The Java™ Language Specification, Third Edition

Doug Lea
Concurrent Programming in Java™, Second Edition: Design Principles and Patterns

Rosanna Lee, Scott Seligman
JNDI API Tutorial and Reference: Building Directory-Enabled Java™ Applications

Sheng Liang
The Java™ Native Interface: Programmer's Guide and Specification

Tim Lindholm, Frank Yellin
The Java™ Virtual Machine Specification, Second Edition

Roger Riggs, Antero Taivalsaari, Jim Van Peursem, Jyri Huopaniemi, Mark Patel, Aleksi Uotila
Programming Wireless Devices with the Java™ 2 Platform, Micro Edition, Second Edition

Sun Microsystems, Inc.
Java™ Look and Feel Design Guidelines: Advanced Topics

Kathy Walrath, Mary Campione, Alison Huml, Sharon Zakhour
The JFC Swing Tutorial, Second Edition: A Guide to Constructing GUIs

Seth White, Maydene Fisher, Rick Cattell, Graham Hamilton, Mark Hapner
JDBC™ API Tutorial and Reference, Second Edition: Universal Data Access for the Java™ 2 Platform

Steve Wilson, Jeff Kesselman
Java™ Platform Performance: Strategies and Tactics

The Jini™ Technology Series

Eric Freeman, Susanne Hupfer, Ken Arnold
JavaSpaces™ Principles, Patterns, and Practice

The Java™ Series, Enterprise Edition

Stephanie Bodoff, Dale Green, Kim Haase, Eric Jendrock
The J2EE™ Tutorial, Second Edition

Rick Cattell, Jim Inscore, Enterprise Partners
J2EE™ Technology in Practice: Building Business Applications with the Java™ 2 Platform, Enterprise Edition

Mark Hapner, Rich Burridge, Rahul Sharma, Joseph Fialli, Kim Haase
Java™ Message Service API Tutorial and Reference: Messaging for the J2EE™ Platform

Inderjeet Singh, Beth Stearns, Mark Johnson, Enterprise Team
Designing Enterprise Applications with the Java™ 2 Platform, Enterprise Edition

Vlada Matena, Sanjeev Krishnan, Linda DeMichiel, Beth Stearns
Applying Enterprise JavaBeans™, Second Edition: Component-Based Development for the J2EE™ Platform

Bill Shannon, Mark Hapner, Vlada Matena, James Davidson, Eduardo Pelegri-Llopart, Larry Cable, Enterprise Team
Java™ 2 Platform, Enterprise Edition: Platform and Component Specifications

Rahul Sharma, Beth Stearns, Tony Ng
J2EE™ Connector Architecture and Enterprise Application Integration

The Java™ Language Specification
Third Edition

James Gosling
Bill Joy
Guy Steele
Gilad Bracha

Addison-Wesley

Upper Saddle River, NJ • Boston • Indianapolis • San Francisco
New York • Toronto • Montreal • London • Munich • Paris • Madrid
Capetown • Sydney • Tokyo • Singapore • Mexico City

Duke logo™ designed by Joe Palrang.

Credits and permissions for quoted material appear in a separate section on page 649.

ISBN 0-321-24678-0
Text printed in the United States on recycled paper at Courier in Stoughton, Massachusetts.
First printing, May 2005

"When *I* use a word," Humpty Dumpty said, in rather a scornful tone, "it means just what I choose it to mean—neither more nor less."

"The question is," said Alice, "whether you *can* make words mean so many different things."

"The question is," said Humpty Dumpty, "which is to be master—that's all."

—Lewis Carroll, *Through the Looking Glass*

Table of Contents

Preface

THE Java™ programming language was originally called Oak, and was designed for use in embedded consumer-electronic applications by James Gosling. After several years of experience with the language, and significant contributions by Ed Frank, Patrick Naughton, Jonathan Payne, and Chris Warth it was retargeted to the Internet, renamed, and substantially revised to be the language specified here. The final form of the language was defined by James Gosling, Bill Joy, Guy Steele, Richard Tuck, Frank Yellin, and Arthur van Hoff, with help from Graham Hamilton, Tim Lindholm, and many other friends and colleagues.

The Java programming language is a general-purpose concurrent class-based object-oriented programming language, specifically designed to have as few implementation dependencies as possible. It allows application developers to write a program once and then be able to run it everywhere on the Internet.

This book attempts a complete specification of the syntax and semantics of the language. We intend that the behavior of every language construct is specified here, so that all implementations will accept the same programs. Except for timing dependencies or other non-determinisms and given sufficient time and sufficient memory space, a program written in the Java programming language should compute the same result on all machines and in all implementations.

We believe that the Java programming language is a mature language, ready for widespread use. Nevertheless, we expect some evolution of the language in the years to come. We intend to manage this evolution in a way that is completely compatible with existing applications. To do this, we intend to make relatively few new versions of the language. Compilers and systems will be able to support the several versions simultaneously, with complete compatibility.

Much research and experimentation with the Java platform is already underway. We encourage this work, and will continue to cooperate with external groups to explore improvements to the language and platform. For example, we have already received several interesting proposals for parameterized types. In technically difficult areas, near the state of the art, this kind of research collaboration is essential.

We acknowledge and thank the many people who have contributed to this book through their excellent feedback, assistance and encouragement:

Particularly thorough, careful, and thoughtful reviews of drafts were provided by Tom Cargill, Peter Deutsch, Paul Hilfinger, Masayuki Ida, David Moon, Steven Muchnick, Charles L. Perkins, Chris Van Wyk, Steve Vinoski, Philip Wadler, Daniel Weinreb, and Kenneth Zadeck. We are very grateful for their extraordinary volunteer efforts.

We are also grateful for reviews, questions, comments, and suggestions from Stephen Adams, Bowen Alpern, Glenn Ammons, Leonid Arbuzov, Kim Bruce, Edwin Chan, David Chase, Pavel Curtis, Drew Dean, William Dietz, David Dill, Patrick Dussud, Ed Felten, John Giannandrea, John Gilmore, Charles Gust, Warren Harris, Lee Hasiuk, Mike Hendrickson, Mark Hill, Urs Hoelzle, Roger Hoover, Susan Flynn Hummel, Christopher Jang, Mick Jordan, Mukesh Kacker, Peter Kessler, James Larus, Derek Lieber, Bill McKeeman, Steve Naroff, Evi Nemeth, Robert O'Callahan, Dave Papay, Craig Partridge, Scott Pfeffer, Eric Raymond, Jim Roskind, Jim Russell, William Scherlis, Edith Schonberg, Anthony Scian, Matthew Self, Janice Shepherd, Kathy Stark, Barbara Steele, Rob Strom, William Waite, Greg Weeks, and Bob Wilson. (This list was generated semi-automatically from our E-mail records. We apologize if we have omitted anyone.)

The feedback from all these reviewers was invaluable to us in improving the definition of the language as well as the form of the presentation in this book. We thank them for their diligence. Any remaining errors in this book—we hope they are few—are our responsibility and not theirs.

We thank Francesca Freedman and Doug Kramer for assistance with matters of typography and layout. We thank Dan Mills of Adobe Systems Incorporated for assistance in exploring possible choices of typefaces.

Many of our colleagues at Sun Microsystems have helped us in one way or another. Lisa Friendly, our series editor, managed our relationship with Addison-Wesley. Susan Stambaugh managed the distribution of many hundreds of copies of drafts to reviewers. We received valuable assistance and technical advice from Ben Adida, Ole Agesen, Ken Arnold, Rick Cattell, Asmus Freytag, Norm Hardy, Steve Heller, David Hough, Doug Kramer, Nancy Lee, Marianne Mueller, Akira Tanaka, Greg Tarsy, David Ungar, Jim Waldo, Ann Wollrath, Geoff Wyant, and Derek White. We thank Alan Baratz, David Bowen, Mike Clary, John Doerr, Jon Kannegaard, Eric Schmidt, Bob Sproull, Bert Sutherland, and Scott McNealy for leadership and encouragement.

The on-line Bartleby Library of Columbia University, at URL:

`http://www.cc.columbia.edu/acis/bartleby/`

was invaluable to us during the process of researching and verifying many of the quotations that are scattered throughout this book. Here is one example:

They lard their lean books with the fat of others' works.
—Robert Burton (1576–1640)

We are grateful to those who have toiled on Project Bartleby, for saving us a great deal of effort and reawakening our appreciation for the works of Walt Whitman.

We are thankful for the tools and services we had at our disposal in writing this book: telephones, overnight delivery, desktop workstations, laser printers, photocopiers, text formatting and page layout software, fonts, electronic mail, the World Wide Web, and, of course, the Internet. We live in three different states, scattered across a continent, but collaboration with each other and with our reviewers has seemed almost effortless. Kudos to the thousands of people who have worked over the years to make these excellent tools and services work quickly and reliably.

Mike Hendrickson, Katie Duffy, Simone Payment, and Rosa Aimée González of Addison-Wesley were very helpful, encouraging, and patient during the long process of bringing this book to print. We also thank the copy editors.

Rosemary Simpson worked hard, on a very tight schedule, to create the index. We got into the act at the last minute, however; blame us and not her for any jokes you may find hidden therein.

Finally, we are grateful to our families and friends for their love and support during this last, crazy, year.

In their book *The C Programming Language*, Brian Kernighan and Dennis Ritchie said that they felt that the C language "wears well as one's experience with it grows." If you like C, we think you will like the Java programming language. We hope that it, too, wears well for you.

James Gosling
Cupertino, California

Bill Joy
Aspen, Colorado

Guy Steele
Chelmsford, Massachusetts

July, 1996

Preface to the Second Edition

... the pyramid must stand unchanged for a millennium;
the organism must evolve or perish.
— Alan Perlis, Foreword to *Structure and Interpretation of Computer Programs*

OVER the past few years, the Java™ programming language has enjoyed unprecedented success. This success has brought a challenge: along with explosive growth in popularity, there has been explosive growth in the demands made on the language and its libraries. To meet this challenge, the language has grown as well (fortunately, not explosively) and so have the libraries.

This second edition of *The Java™ Language Specification* reflects these developments. It integrates all the changes made to the Java programming language since the publication of the first edition in 1996. The bulk of these changes were made in the 1.1 release of the Java platform in 1997, and revolve around the addition of nested type declarations. Later modifications pertained to floating-point operations. In addition, this edition incorporates important clarifications and amendments involving method lookup and binary compatibility.

This specification defines the language as it exists today. The Java programming language is likely to continue to evolve. At this writing, there are ongoing initiatives through the Java Community Process to extend the language with generic types and assertions, refine the memory model, etc. However, it would be inappropriate to delay the publication of the second edition until these efforts are concluded.

The specifications of the libraries are now far too large to fit into this volume, and they continue to evolve. Consequently, API specifications have been removed from this book. The library specifications can be found on the `java.sun.com` Web site (see below); this specification now concentrates solely on the Java programming language proper.

Readers may send comments on this specification to: `jls@java.sun.com`. To learn the latest about the Java 2 platform, or to download the latest Java 2 SDK release, visit `http://java.sun.com`. Updated information about the Java Series, including errata for *The Java™ Language Specification, Second Edition*, and previews of forthcoming books, may be found at `http://java.sun.com/Series`.

Many people contributed to this book, directly and indirectly. Tim Lindholm brought extraordinary dedication to his role as technical editor. He also made invaluable technical contributions, especially on floating-point issues. The book would likely not see the light of day without him. Lisa Friendly, the Series editor, provided encouragement and advice for which I am very thankful.

David Bowen first suggested that I get involved in the specifications of the Java platform. I am grateful to him for introducing me to this uncommonly rich area.

John Rose, the father of nested types in the Java programming language, has been unfailingly gracious and supportive of my attempts to specify them accurately.

Many people have provided valuable comments on this edition. Special thanks go to Roly Perera at Ergnosis and to Leonid Arbouzov and his colleagues on Sun's Java platform conformance team in Novosibirsk: Konstantin Bobrovsky, Natalia Golovleva, Vladimir Ivanov, Alexei Kaigorodov, Serguei Katkov, Dmitri Khukhro, Eugene Latkin, Ilya Neverov, Pavel Ozhdikhin, Igor Pyankov, Viatcheslav Rybalov, Serguei Samoilidi, Maxim Sokolnikov, and Vitaly Tchaiko. Their thorough reading of earlier drafts has greatly improved the accuracy of this specification.

I am indebted to Martin Odersky and to Andrew Bennett and the members of Sun's `javac` compiler team, past and present: Iris Garcia, Bill Maddox, David Stoutamire, and Todd Turnidge. They all worked hard to make sure the reference implementation conformed to the specification. For many enjoyable technical exchanges, I thank them and my other colleagues at Sun: Lars Bak, Joshua Bloch, Cliff Click, Robert Field, Mohammad Gharahgouzloo, Ben Gomes, Steffen Grarup, Robert Griesemer, Graham Hamilton, Gordon Hirsch, Peter Kessler, Sheng Liang, James McIlree, Philip Milne, Srdjan Mitrovic, Anand Palaniswamy, Mike Paleczny, Mark Reinhold, Kenneth Russell, Rene Schmidt, David Ungar, Chris Vick, and Hong Zhang.

Tricia Jordan, my manager, has been a model of patience, consideration and understanding. Thanks are also due to Larry Abrahams, director of Java 2 Standard Edition, for supporting this work.

The following individuals all provided useful comments that have contributed to this specification: Godmar Bak, Hans Boehm, Philippe Charles, David Chase, Joe Darcy, Jim des Rivieres, Sophia Drossopoulou, Susan Eisenbach, Paul Haahr, Urs Hoelzle, Bart Jacobs, Kent Johnson, Mark Lillibridge, Norbert Lindenberg, Phillipe Mulet, Kelly O'Hair, Bill Pugh, Cameron Purdy, Anthony Scian, Janice Shepherd, David Shields, John Spicer, Lee Worall, and David Wragg.

Suzette Pelouch provided invaluable assistance with the index and, together with Doug Kramer and Atul Dambalkar, assisted with FrameMaker expertise; Mike Hendrickson and Julie Dinicola at Addison-Wesley were gracious, helpful and ultimately made this book a reality.

On a personal note, I thank my wife Weihong for her love and support.

Finally, I'd like to thank my coauthors, James Gosling, Bill Joy, and Guy Steele for inviting me to participate in this work. It has been a pleasure and a privilege.

Gilad Bracha
Los Altos, California

April, 2000

This is the FEMALE EDITION of the Dictionary.

The MALE edition is almost identical. But NOT quite.
Be warned that ONE PARAGRAPH is crucially different.

The choice is yours.

— Milorad Pavic, *Dictionary of the Khazars,* Female Edition

Preface to the Third Edition

This edition of the Java™ Programming Language Specification represents the largest set of changes in the language's history. Generics, annotations, asserts, autoboxing and unboxing, enum types, foreach loops, variable arity methods and static imports have all been added to the language recently. All but asserts are new to the 5.0 release of autumn 2004.

This third edition of *The Java™ Language Specification* reflects these developments. It integrates all the changes made to the Java programming language since the publication of the second edition in 2000.

The language has grown a great deal in these past four years. Unfortunately, it is unrealistic to shrink a commercially successful programming language - only to grow it more and more. The challenge of managing this growth under the constraints of compatibility and the conflicting demands of a wide variety of uses and users is non-trivial. I can only hope that we have met this challenge successfully with this specification; time will tell.

Readers may send comments on this specification to: `jls@java.sun.com`. To learn the latest about the Java platform, or to download the latest J2SE release, visit `http://java.sun.com`. Updated information about the Java Series, including errata for *The Java™ Language Specification, Third Edition*, and previews of forthcoming books, may be found at `http://java.sun.com/Series`.

This specification builds on the efforts of many people, both at Sun Microsystems and outside it.

The most crucial contribution is that of the people who actually turn the specification into real software. Chief among these are the maintainers of `javac`, the reference compiler for the Java programming language.

Neal Gafter was "Mr. javac" during the crucial period in which the large changes described here were integrated and productized. Neal's dedication and productivity can honestly be described as heroic. We literally could not have completed the task without him. In addition, his insight and skill made a huge contribution to the design of the new language features across the board. No one deserves more credit for this version of the language than he - but any blame for its deficiencies should be directed at myself and the members of the many JSR expert groups!

Neal has gone on in search of new challenges, and has been succeeded by Peter von der Ahé, who continues to improve and stengthen the implementation. Before Neal's involvement, Bill Maddox was in charge of javac when the previous edition was completed, and he nursed features such as generics and asserts through their early days.

Another individual who deserves to be singled out is Joshua Bloch. Josh participated in endless language design discussions, chaired several expert groups and was a key contributor to the Java platform. It is fair to say that Josh and Neal care more about this book than I do myself!

Many parts of the specification were developed by various expert groups in the framework of the Java community process.

The most pervasive set of language changes is the result of JSR-014: *Adding Generics to the Java Programming Language*. The members of the JSR-014 expert group were: Norman Cohen, Christian Kemper, Martin Odersky, Kresten Krab Thorup, Philip Wadler and myself. In the early stages, Sven-Eric Panitz and Steve Marx were members as well. All deserve thanks for their participation.

JSR-014 represents an unprecedented effort to fundamentally extend the type system of a widely used programming language under very stringent compatibility requirements. A prolonged and arduous process of design and implementation led us to the current language extension. Long before the JSR for generics was initiated, Martin Odersky and Philip Wadler had created an experimental language called Pizza to explore the ideas involved. In the spring of 1998, David Stoutamire and myself began a collaboration with Martin and Phil based on those ideas, that resulted in GJ. When the JSR-014 expert group was convened, GJ was chosen as the basis for extending the Java programming language. Martin Odersky implemented the GJ compiler, and his implementation became the basis for javac (starting with JDK 1.3, even though generics were disabled until 1.5).

The theoretical basis for the core of the generic type system owes a great debt to the expertise of Martin Odersky and Phil Wadler. Later, the system was extended with wildcards. These were based on the work of Atsushi Igarashi and Mirko Viroli, which itself built on earlier work by Kresten Thorup and Mads Torgersen. Wildcards were initially designed and implemented as part of a collaboration between Sun and Aarhus University. Neal Gafter and myself participated on Sun's behalf, and Erik Ernst and Mads Torgersen, together with Peter von der Ahé and Christian Plesner-Hansen, represented Aarhus. Thanks to Ole Lehrmann-Madsen for enabling and supporting that work.

Joe Darcy and Ken Russell implemented much of the specific support for reflection of generics. Neal Gafter, Josh Bloch and Mark Reinhold did a huge amount of work generifying the JDK libraries.

Honorable mention must go to individuals whose comments on the generics design made a significant difference. Alan Jeffrey made crucial contributions to JSR-14 by pointing out subtle flaws in the original type system. Bob Deen suggested the "? super T" syntax for lower bounded wildcards

JSR-201 included a series of changes: autoboxing, enums, foreach loops, variable arity methods and static import. The members of the JSR-201 expert group were: Cédric Beust, David Biesack, Joshua Bloch (co-chair), Corky Cartwright, Jim des Rivieres, David Flanagan, Christian Kemper, Doug Lea, Changshin Lee, Tim Peierls, Michel Trudeau and myself (co-chair). Enums and the foreach loop were primarily designed by Josh Bloch and Neal Gafter. Variable arity methods would never have made it into the language without Neal's special efforts designing them (not to mention the small matter of implementing them).

Josh Bloch bravely took upon himself the responsibility for JSR-175, which added annotations to the language. The members of JSR-175 expert group were Cédric Beust, Joshua Bloch (chair), Ted Farrell, Mike French, Gregor Kiczales, Doug Lea, Deeptendu Majunder, Simon Nash, Ted Neward, Roly Perera, Manfred Schneider, Blake Stone and Josh Street. Neal Gafter, as usual, was a major contributer on this front as well.

Another change in this edition is a complete revision of the Java memory model, undertaken by JSR-133. The members of the JSR-133 expert group were Hans Boehm, Doug Lea, Tim Lindholm (co-chair), Bill Pugh (co-chair), Martin Trotter and Jerry Schwarz. The primary technical authors of the memory model are Sarita Adve, Jeremy Manson and Bill Pugh. The Java memory model chapter in this book is in fact almost entirely their work, with only editorial revisions. Joseph Bowbeer, David Holmes, Victor Luchangco and Jan-Willem Maessen made significant contributions as well. Key sections dealing with finalization in chapter 12 owe much to this work as well, and especially to Doug Lea.

Many people have provided valuable comments on this edition.

I'd like to express my gratitude to Archibald Putt, who provided insight and encouragement. His writings are always an inspiration. Thanks once again to Joe Darcy for introducing us, as well as for many useful comments, and his specific contributions on numerical issues and the design of hexadecimal literals.

Many colleagues at Sun (past or present) have provided useful feedback and discussion, and helped produce this work in myriad ways: Andrew Bennett, Martin Buchholz, Jerry Driscoll, Robert Field, Jonathan Gibbons, Graham Hamilton, Mimi Hills, Jim Holmlund, Janet Koenig, Jeff Norton, Scott Seligman, Wei Tao and David Ungar.

Special thanks to Laurie Tolson, my manager, for her support throughout the long process of deriving these specifications.

The following individuals all provided many valuable comments that have contributed to this specification: Scott Annanian, Martin Bravenboer, Bruce Chapman, Laurence Gonsalves, Tim Hanson, David Holmes, Angelika Langer, Pat Lavarre, Phillipe Mulet and Cal Varnson.

Ann Sellers, Greg Doench and John Fuller at Addison-Wesley were exceedingly patient and ensured that the book materialized, despite the many missed deadlines for this text.

As always, I thank my wife Weihong and my son Teva for their support and cooperation.

Gilad Bracha
Los Altos, California

January, 2005

CHAPTER 1

Introduction

If I have seen further it is by standing upon the shoulders of Giants.
—Sir Isaac Newton

The Java™ programming language is a general-purpose, concurrent, class-based, object-oriented language. It is designed to be simple enough that many programmers can achieve fluency in the language. The Java programming language is related to C and C++ but is organized rather differently, with a number of aspects of C and C++ omitted and a few ideas from other languages included. It is intended to be a production language, not a research language, and so, as C. A. R. Hoare suggested in his classic paper on language design, the design has avoided including new and untested features.

The Java programming language is strongly typed. This specification clearly distinguishes between the *compile-time errors* that can and must be detected at compile time, and those that occur at run time. Compile time normally consists of translating programs into a machine-independent byte code representation. Run-time activities include loading and linking of the classes needed to execute a program, optional machine code generation and dynamic optimization of the program, and actual program execution.

The Java programming language is a relatively high-level language, in that details of the machine representation are not available through the language. It includes automatic storage management, typically using a garbage collector, to avoid the safety problems of explicit deallocation (as in C's `free` or C++'s `delete`). High-performance garbage-collected implementations can have bounded pauses to support systems programming and real-time applications. The language does not include any unsafe constructs, such as array accesses without index checking, since such unsafe constructs would cause a program to behave in an unspecified way.

The Java programming language is normally compiled to the bytecoded instruction set and binary format defined in *The Java™ Virtual Machine Specification, Second Edition* (Addison-Wesley, 1999).

This specification is organized as follows:

Chapter 2 describes grammars and the notation used to present the lexical and syntactic grammars for the language.

Chapter 3 describes the lexical structure of the Java programming language, which is based on C and C++. The language is written in the Unicode character set. It supports the writing of Unicode characters on systems that support only ASCII.

Chapter 4 describes types, values, and variables. Types are subdivided into primitive types and reference types.

The primitive types are defined to be the same on all machines and in all implementations, and are various sizes of two's-complement integers, single- and double-precision IEEE 754 standard floating-point numbers, a `boolean` type, and a Unicode character `char` type. Values of the primitive types do not share state.

Reference types are the class types, the interface types, and the array types. The reference types are implemented by dynamically created objects that are either instances of classes or arrays. Many references to each object can exist. All objects (including arrays) support the methods of the class `Object`, which is the (single) root of the class hierarchy. A predefined `String` class supports Unicode character strings. Classes exist for wrapping primitive values inside of objects. In many cases, wrapping and unwrapping is performed automatically by the compiler (in which case, wrapping is called boxing, and unwrapping is called unboxing). Class and interface declarations may be generic, that is, they may be parameterized by other reference types. Such declarations may then be invoked with specific type arguments.

Variables are typed storage locations. A variable of a primitive type holds a value of that exact primitive type. A variable of a class type can hold a null reference or a reference to an object whose type is that class type or any subclass of that class type. A variable of an interface type can hold a null reference or a reference to an instance of any class that implements the interface. A variable of an array type can hold a null reference or a reference to an array. A variable of class type `Object` can hold a null reference or a reference to any object, whether class instance or array.

Chapter 5 describes conversions and numeric promotions. Conversions change the compile-time type and, sometimes, the value of an expression. These conversions include the boxing and unboxing conversions between primitive types and reference types. Numeric promotions are used to convert the operands of a numeric operator to a common type where an operation can be performed. There are no loopholes in the language; casts on reference types are checked at run time to ensure type safety.

Chapter 6 describes declarations and names, and how to determine what names mean (denote). The language does not require types or their members to be declared before they are used. Declaration order is significant only for local variables, local classes, and the order of initializers of fields in a class or interface.

The Java programming language provides control over the scope of names and supports limitations on external access to members of packages, classes, and interfaces. This helps in writing large programs by distinguishing the implementation of a type from its users and those who extend it. Recommended naming conventions that make for more readable programs are described here.

Chapter 7 describes the structure of a program, which is organized into packages similar to the modules of Modula. The members of a package are classes, interfaces, and subpackages. Packages are divided into compilation units. Compilation units contain type declarations and can import types from other packages to give them short names. Packages have names in a hierarchical name space, and the Internet domain name system can usually be used to form unique package names.

Chapter 8 describes classes. The members of classes are classes, interfaces, fields (variables) and methods. Class variables exist once per class. Class methods operate without reference to a specific object. Instance variables are dynamically created in objects that are instances of classes. Instance methods are invoked on instances of classes; such instances become the current object `this` during their execution, supporting the object-oriented programming style.

Classes support single implementation inheritance, in which the implementation of each class is derived from that of a single superclass, and ultimately from the class `Object`. Variables of a class type can reference an instance of that class or of any subclass of that class, allowing new types to be used with existing methods, polymorphically.

Classes support concurrent programming with `synchronized` methods. Methods declare the checked exceptions that can arise from their execution, which allows compile-time checking to ensure that exceptional conditions are handled. Objects can declare a `finalize` method that will be invoked before the objects are discarded by the garbage collector, allowing the objects to clean up their state.

For simplicity, the language has neither declaration "headers" separate from the implementation of a class nor separate type and class hierarchies.

A special form of classes, enums, support the definition of small sets of values and their manipulation in a type safe manner. Unlike enumerations in other languages, enums are objects and may have their own methods.

Chapter 9 describes interface types, which declare a set of abstract methods, member types, and constants. Classes that are otherwise unrelated can implement the same interface type. A variable of an interface type can contain a reference to any object that implements the interface. Multiple interface inheritance is supported.

Annotation types are specialized interfaces used to annotate declarations. Such annotations are not permitted to affect the semantics of programs in the Java programming language in any way. However, they provide useful input to various tools.

Chapter 10 describes arrays. Array accesses include bounds checking. Arrays are dynamically created objects and may be assigned to variables of type `Object`. The language supports arrays of arrays, rather than multidimensional arrays.

Chapter 11 describes exceptions, which are nonresuming and fully integrated with the language semantics and concurrency mechanisms. There are three kinds of exceptions: checked exceptions, run-time exceptions, and errors. The compiler ensures that checked exceptions are properly handled by requiring that a method or constructor can result in a checked exception only if the method or constructor declares it. This provides compile-time checking that exception handlers exist, and aids programming in the large. Most user-defined exceptions should be checked exceptions. Invalid operations in the program detected by the Java virtual machine result in run-time exceptions, such as `NullPointerException`. Errors result from failures detected by the virtual machine, such as `OutOfMemoryError`. Most simple programs do not try to handle errors.

Chapter 12 describes activities that occur during execution of a program. A program is normally stored as binary files representing compiled classes and interfaces. These binary files can be loaded into a Java virtual machine, linked to other classes and interfaces, and initialized.

After initialization, class methods and class variables may be used. Some classes may be instantiated to create new objects of the class type. Objects that are class instances also contain an instance of each superclass of the class, and object creation involves recursive creation of these superclass instances.

When an object is no longer referenced, it may be reclaimed by the garbage collector. If an object declares a finalizer, the finalizer is executed before the object is reclaimed to give the object a last chance to clean up resources that would not otherwise be released. When a class is no longer needed, it may be unloaded.

Chapter 13 describes binary compatibility, specifying the impact of changes to types on other types that use the changed types but have not been recompiled. These considerations are of interest to developers of types that are to be widely distributed, in a continuing series of versions, often through the Internet. Good program development environments automatically recompile dependent code whenever a type is changed, so most programmers need not be concerned about these details.

Chapter 14 describes blocks and statements, which are based on C and C++. The language has no `goto` statement, but includes labeled `break` and `continue` statements. Unlike C, the Java programming language requires `boolean` (or

Boolean) expressions in control-flow statements, and does not convert types to boolean implicitly (except through unboxing), in the hope of catching more errors at compile time. A synchronized statement provides basic object-level monitor locking. A try statement can include catch and finally clauses to protect against non-local control transfers.

Chapter 15 describes expressions. This document fully specifies the (apparent) order of evaluation of expressions, for increased determinism and portability. Overloaded methods and constructors are resolved at compile time by picking the most specific method or constructor from those which are applicable.

Chapter 16 describes the precise way in which the language ensures that local variables are definitely set before use. While all other variables are automatically initialized to a default value, the Java programming language does not automatically initialize local variables in order to avoid masking programming errors.

Chapter 17 describes the semantics of threads and locks, which are based on the monitor-based concurrency originally introduced with the Mesa programming language. The Java programming language specifies a memory model for shared-memory multiprocessors that supports high-performance implementations.

Chapter 18 presents a syntactic grammar for the language.

The book concludes with an index, credits for quotations used in the book, and a colophon describing how the book was created.

1.1 Example Programs

Most of the example programs given in the text are ready to be executed and are similar in form to:

```
class Test {
    public static void main(String[] args) {
        for (int i = 0; i < args.length; i++)
            System.out.print(i == 0 ? args[i] : " " + args[i]);
        System.out.println();
    }
}
```

On a Sun workstation using Sun's Java 2 Platform Standard Edition Develpment Kit software, this class, stored in the file Test.java, can be compiled and executed by giving the commands:

```
javac Test.java
java Test Hello, world.
```

producing the output:

```
Hello, world.
```

1.2 Notation

Throughout this book we refer to classes and interfaces drawn from the Java and Java 2 platforms. Whenever we refer to a class or interface which is not defined in an example in this book using a single identifier *N*, the intended reference is to the class or interface named *N* in the package `java.lang`. We use the canonical name (§6.7) for classes or interfaces from packages other than `java.lang`.

Whenever we refer to the *The Java™ Virtual Machine Specification* in this book, we mean the second edition, as amended by JSR 924.

1.3 Relationship to Predefined Classes and Interfaces

As noted above, this specification often refers to classes of the Java and Java 2 platforms. In particular, some classes have a special relationship with the Java programming language. Examples include classes such as `Object`, `Class`, `ClassLoader`, `String`, `Thread`, and the classes and interfaces in package `java.lang.reflect`, among others. The language definition constrains the behavior of these classes and interfaces, but this document does not provide a complete specification for them. The reader is referred to other parts of the Java platform specification for such detailed API specifications.

Thus this document does not describe reflection in any detail. Many linguistic constructs have analogues in the reflection API, but these are generally not discussed here. So, for example, when we list the ways in which an object can be created, we generally do not include the ways in which the reflective API can accomplish this. Readers should be aware of these additional mechanisms even though they are not mentioned in this text.

1.4 References

Apple Computer. *Dylan™ Reference Manual.* Apple Computer Inc., Cupertino, California. September 29, 1995. See also `http://www.cambridge.apple.com`.

Bobrow, Daniel G., Linda G. DeMichiel, Richard P. Gabriel, Sonya E. Keene, Gregor Kiczales, and David A. Moon. *Common Lisp Object System Specification*, X3J13 Document 88-002R, June 1988; appears as Chapter 28 of Steele, Guy. *Common Lisp: The Language*, 2nd ed. Digital Press, 1990, ISBN 1-55558-041-6, 770–864.

Ellis, Margaret A., and Bjarne Stroustrup. *The Annotated C++ Reference Manual.* Addison-Wesley, Reading, Massachusetts, 1990, reprinted with corrections October 1992, ISBN 0-201-51459-1.

Goldberg, Adele and Robson, David. *Smalltalk-80: The Language*. Addison-Wesley, Reading, Massachusetts, 1989, ISBN 0-201-13688-0.

Harbison, Samuel. *Modula-3*. Prentice Hall, Englewood Cliffs, New Jersey, 1992, ISBN 0-13-596396.

Hoare, C. A. R. *Hints on Programming Language Design*. Stanford University Computer Science Department Technical Report No. CS-73-403, December 1973. Reprinted in SIGACT/SIGPLAN Symposium on Principles of Programming Languages. Association for Computing Machinery, New York, October 1973.

IEEE Standard for Binary Floating-Point Arithmetic. ANSI/IEEE Std. 754-1985. Available from Global Engineering Documents, 15 Inverness Way East, Englewood, Colorado 80112-5704 USA; 800-854-7179.

Kernighan, Brian W., and Dennis M. Ritchie. *The C Programming Language,* 2nd ed. Prentice Hall, Englewood Cliffs, New Jersey, 1988, ISBN 0-13-110362-8.

Madsen, Ole Lehrmann, Birger Møller-Pedersen, and Kristen Nygaard. *Object-Oriented Programming in the Beta Programming Language*. Addison-Wesley, Reading, Massachusetts, 1993, ISBN 0-201-62430-3.

Mitchell, James G., William Maybury, and Richard Sweet. *The Mesa Programming Language*, Version 5.0. Xerox PARC, Palo Alto, California, CSL 79-3, April 1979.

Stroustrup, Bjarne. *The C++ Progamming Language,* 2nd ed. Addison-Wesley, Reading, Massachusetts, 1991, reprinted with corrections January 1994, ISBN 0-201-53992-6.

Unicode Consortium, The. *The Unicode Standard: Worldwide Character Encoding*, Version 1.0, Volume 1, ISBN 0-201-56788-1, and Volume 2, ISBN 0-201-60845-6. Updates and additions necessary to bring the Unicode Standard up to version 1.1 may be found at `http://www.unicode.org`.

Unicode Consortium, The. *The Unicode Standard, Version 2.0*, ISBN 0-201-48345-9. Updates and additions necessary to bring the Unicode Standard up to version 2.1 may be found at `http://www.unicode.org`.

Unicode Consortium, The. *The Unicode Standard, Version 4.0*, ISBN 0-321-18578-1. Updates and additions may be found at `http://www.unicode.org`.

CHAPTER 2

Grammars

Grammar, which knows how to control even kings . . .
—Molière, *Les Femmes Savantes* (1672), Act II, scene vi

THIS chapter describes the context-free grammars used in this specification to define the lexical and syntactic structure of a program.

2.1 Context-Free Grammars

A *context-free grammar* consists of a number of *productions*. Each production has an abstract symbol called a *nonterminal* as its *left-hand side*, and a sequence of one or more nonterminal and *terminal* symbols as its *right-hand side*. For each grammar, the terminal symbols are drawn from a specified *alphabet*.

Starting from a sentence consisting of a single distinguished nonterminal, called the *goal symbol*, a given context-free grammar specifies a *language*, namely, the set of possible sequences of terminal symbols that can result from repeatedly replacing any nonterminal in the sequence with a right-hand side of a production for which the nonterminal is the left-hand side.

2.2 The Lexical Grammar

A *lexical grammar* for the Java programming language is given in (§3). This grammar has as its terminal symbols the characters of the Unicode character set. It defines a set of productions, starting from the goal symbol *Input* (§3.5), that describe how sequences of Unicode characters (§3.1) are translated into a sequence of input elements (§3.5).

These input elements, with white space (§3.6) and comments (§3.7) discarded, form the terminal symbols for the syntactic grammar for the Java programming language and are called *tokens* (§3.5). These tokens are the identifiers

(§3.8), keywords (§3.9), literals (§3.10), separators (§3.11), and operators (§3.12) of the Java programming language.

2.3 The Syntactic Grammar

The *syntactic grammar* for the Java programming language is given in Chapters 4, 6–10, 14, and 15. This grammar has tokens defined by the lexical grammar as its terminal symbols. It defines a set of productions, starting from the goal symbol *CompilationUnit* (§7.3), that describe how sequences of tokens can form syntactically correct programs.

2.4 Grammar Notation

Terminal symbols are shown in `fixed width` font in the productions of the lexical and syntactic grammars, and throughout this specification whenever the text is directly referring to such a terminal symbol. These are to appear in a program exactly as written.

Nonterminal symbols are shown in *italic* type. The definition of a nonterminal is introduced by the name of the nonterminal being defined followed by a colon. One or more alternative right-hand sides for the nonterminal then follow on succeeding lines. For example, the syntactic definition:

IfThenStatement:
  `if ( ` *Expression* ` )` *Statement*

states that the nonterminal *IfThenStatement* represents the token `if`, followed by a left parenthesis token, followed by an *Expression*, followed by a right parenthesis token, followed by a *Statement*.

As another example, the syntactic definition:

ArgumentList:
  Argument
  ArgumentList `,` *Argument*

states that an *ArgumentList* may represent either a single *Argument* or an *ArgumentList*, followed by a comma, followed by an *Argument*. This definition of *ArgumentList* is *recursive*, that is to say, it is defined in terms of itself. The result is that an *ArgumentList* may contain any positive number of arguments. Such recursive definitions of nonterminals are common.

The subscripted suffix "*opt*", which may appear after a terminal or nonterminal, indicates an *optional symbol*. The alternative containing the optional symbol actually specifies two right-hand sides, one that omits the optional element and one that includes it.

This means that:

BreakStatement:
  `break` *Identifier*$_{opt}$ `;`

is a convenient abbreviation for:

BreakStatement:
  `break ;`
  `break` *Identifier* `;`

and that:

BasicForStatement:
  `for (` *ForInit*$_{opt}$ `;` *Expression*$_{opt}$ `;` *ForUpdate*$_{opt}$ `)` *Statement*

is a convenient abbreviation for:

BasicForStatement:
  `for ( ;` *Expression*$_{opt}$ `;` *ForUpdate*$_{opt}$ `)` *Statement*
  `for (` *ForInit* `;` *Expression*$_{opt}$ `;` *ForUpdate*$_{opt}$ `)` *Statement*

which in turn is an abbreviation for:

BasicForStatement:
  `for ( ; ;` *ForUpdate*$_{opt}$ `)` *Statement*
  `for ( ;` *Expression* `;` *ForUpdate*$_{opt}$ `)` *Statement*
  `for (` *ForInit* `; ;` *ForUpdate*$_{opt}$ `)` *Statement*
  `for (` *ForInit* `;` *Expression* `;` *ForUpdate*$_{opt}$ `)` *Statement*

which in turn is an abbreviation for:

BasicForStatement:
  `for ( ; ; )` *Statement*
  `for ( ; ;` *ForUpdate* `)` *Statement*
  `for ( ;` *Expression* `; )` *Statement*
  `for ( ;` *Expression* `;` *ForUpdate* `)` *Statement*
  `for (` *ForInit* `; ; )` *Statement*
  `for (` *ForInit* `; ;` *ForUpdate* `)` *Statement*
  `for (` *ForInit* `;` *Expression* `; )` *Statement*
  `for (` *ForInit* `;` *Expression* `;` *ForUpdate* `)` *Statement*

so the nonterminal *BasicForStatement* actually has eight alternative right-hand sides.

A very long right-hand side may be continued on a second line by substantially indenting this second line, as in:

ConstructorDeclaration:
    ConstructorModifiers$_{opt}$ *ConstructorDeclarator*
        Throws$_{opt}$ *ConstructorBody*

which defines one right-hand side for the nonterminal *ConstructorDeclaration*.

When the words “one of” follow the colon in a grammar definition, they signify that each of the terminal symbols on the following line or lines is an alternative definition. For example, the lexical grammar contains the production:

ZeroToThree: one of
    `0 1 2 3`

which is merely a convenient abbreviation for:

ZeroToThree:
    `0`
    `1`
    `2`
    `3`

When an alternative in a lexical production appears to be a token, it represents the sequence of characters that would make up such a token. Thus, the definition:

BooleanLiteral: one of
    `true  false`

in a lexical grammar production is shorthand for:

BooleanLiteral:
    `t r u e`
    `f a l s e`

The right-hand side of a lexical production may specify that certain expansions are not permitted by using the phrase “but not” and then indicating the expansions to be excluded, as in the productions for *InputCharacter* (§3.4) and *Identifier* (§3.8):

InputCharacter:
    UnicodeInputCharacter but not CR or LF

Identifier:
    IdentifierName but not a *Keyword* or *BooleanLiteral* or *NullLiteral*

Finally, a few nonterminal symbols are described by a descriptive phrase in roman type in cases where it would be impractical to list all the alternatives:

RawInputCharacter:
    any Unicode character

CHAPTER 3

Lexical Structure

Lexicographer: A writer of dictionaries, a harmless drudge.
—Samuel Johnson, *Dictionary* (1755)

THIS chapter specifies the lexical structure of the Java programming language.

Programs are written in Unicode (§3.1), but lexical translations are provided (§3.2) so that Unicode escapes (§3.3) can be used to include any Unicode character using only ASCII characters. Line terminators are defined (§3.4) to support the different conventions of existing host systems while maintaining consistent line numbers.

The Unicode characters resulting from the lexical translations are reduced to a sequence of input elements (§3.5), which are white space (§3.6), comments (§3.7), and tokens. The tokens are the identifiers (§3.8), keywords (§3.9), literals (§3.10), separators (§3.11), and operators (§3.12) of the syntactic grammar.

3.1 Unicode

Programs are written using the Unicode character set. Information about this character set and its associated character encodings may be found at:

```
http://www.unicode.org
```

The Java platform tracks the Unicode specification as it evolves. The precise version of Unicode used by a given release is specified in the documentation of the class `Character`.

Versions of the Java programming language prior to 1.1 used Unicode version 1.1.5. Upgrades to newer versions of the Unicode Standard occurred in JDK 1.1 (to Unicode 2.0), JDK 1.1.7 (to Unicode 2.1), J2SE 1.4 (to Unicode 3.0), and J2SE 5.0 (to Unicode 4.0).

The Unicode standard was originally designed as a fixed-width 16-bit character encoding. It has since been changed to allow for characters whose representation requires more than 16 bits. The range of legal code points is now U+0000 to U+10FFFF, using the hexadecimal *U+n notation*. Characters whose code points are greater than U+FFFF are called supplementary characters. To represent the complete range of characters using only 16-bit units, the Unicode standard defines an encoding called UTF-16. In this encoding, supplementary characters are represented as pairs of 16-bit code units, the first from the high-surrogates range, (U+D800 to U+DBFF), the second from the low-surrogates range (U+DC00 to U+DFFF). For characters in the range U+0000 to U+FFFF, the values of code points and UTF-16 code units are the same.

The Java programming language represents text in sequences of 16-bit code units, using the UTF-16 encoding. A few APIs, primarily in the `Character` class, use 32-bit integers to represent code points as individual entities. The Java platform provides methods to convert between the two representations.

This book uses the terms *code point* and *UTF-16 code unit* where the representation is relevant, and the generic term *character* where the representation is irrelevant to the discussion.

Except for comments (§3.7), identifiers, and the contents of character and string literals (§3.10.4, §3.10.5), all input elements (§3.5) in a program are formed only from ASCII characters (or Unicode escapes (§3.3) which result in ASCII characters). ASCII (ANSI X3.4) is the American Standard Code for Information Interchange. The first 128 characters of the Unicode character encoding are the ASCII characters.

3.2 Lexical Translations

A raw Unicode character stream is translated into a sequence of tokens, using the following three lexical translation steps, which are applied in turn:

1. A translation of Unicode escapes (§3.3) in the raw stream of Unicode characters to the corresponding Unicode character. A Unicode escape of the form `\u`*`xxxx`*, where *`xxxx`* is a hexadecimal value, represents the UTF-16 code unit whose encoding is *`xxxx`*. This translation step allows any program to be expressed using only ASCII characters.

2. A translation of the Unicode stream resulting from step 1 into a stream of input characters and line terminators (§3.4).

3. A translation of the stream of input characters and line terminators resulting from step 2 into a sequence of input elements (§3.5) which, after white space (§3.6) and comments (§3.7) are discarded, comprise the tokens (§3.5) that are the terminal symbols of the syntactic grammar (§2.3).

The longest possible translation is used at each step, even if the result does not ultimately make a correct program while another lexical translation would. Thus the input characters `a--b` are tokenized (§3.5) as `a`, `--`, `b`, which is not part of any grammatically correct program, even though the tokenization `a`, `-`, `-`, `b` could be part of a grammatically correct program.

3.3 Unicode Escapes

Implementations first recognize *Unicode escapes* in their input, translating the ASCII characters `\u` followed by four hexadecimal digits to the UTF-16 code unit (§3.1) with the indicated hexadecimal value, and passing all other characters unchanged. Representing supplementary characters requires two consecutive Unicode escapes. This translation step results in a sequence of Unicode input characters:

UnicodeInputCharacter:
    UnicodeEscape
    RawInputCharacter

UnicodeEscape:
    `\` *UnicodeMarker HexDigit HexDigit HexDigit HexDigit*

UnicodeMarker:
    `u`
    UnicodeMarker `u`

RawInputCharacter:
    any Unicode character

HexDigit: one of
    `0 1 2 3 4 5 6 7 8 9 a b c d e f A B C D E F`

The `\`, `u`, and hexadecimal digits here are all ASCII characters.

In addition to the processing implied by the grammar, for each raw input character that is a backslash `\`, input processing must consider how many other `\` characters contiguously precede it, separating it from a non-`\` character or the start of the input stream. If this number is even, then the `\` is eligible to begin a Unicode escape; if the number is odd, then the `\` is not eligible to begin a Unicode escape. For example, the raw input `"\\u2297=\u2297"` results in the eleven characters `" \ \ u 2 2 9 7 = ⊗ "` (`\u2297` is the Unicode encoding of the character "⊗").

If an eligible `\` is not followed by `u`, then it is treated as a *RawInputCharacter* and remains part of the escaped Unicode stream. If an eligible `\` is followed by `u`, or more than one u, and the last u is not followed by four hexadecimal digits, then a compile-time error occurs.

The character produced by a Unicode escape does not participate in further Unicode escapes. For example, the raw input \u005cu005a results in the six characters \ u 0 0 5 a, because 005c is the Unicode value for \. It does not result in the character Z, which is Unicode character 005a, because the \ that resulted from the \u005c is not interpreted as the start of a further Unicode escape.

The Java programming language specifies a standard way of transforming a program written in Unicode into ASCII that changes a program into a form that can be processed by ASCII-based tools. The transformation involves converting any Unicode escapes in the source text of the program to ASCII by adding an extra u—for example, \u*xxxx* becomes \uu*xxxx*—while simultaneously converting non-ASCII characters in the source text to Unicode escapes containing a single u each.

This transformed version is equally acceptable to a compiler for the Java programming language ("Java compiler") and represents the exact same program. The exact Unicode source can later be restored from this ASCII form by converting each escape sequence where multiple u's are present to a sequence of Unicode characters with one fewer u, while simultaneously converting each escape sequence with a single u to the corresponding single Unicode character.

Implementations should use the \u*xxxx* notation as an output format to display Unicode characters when a suitable font is not available.

3.4 Line Terminators

Implementations next divide the sequence of Unicode input characters into lines by recognizing *line terminators*. This definition of lines determines the line numbers produced by a Java compiler or other system component. It also specifies the termination of the // form of a comment (§3.7).

LineTerminator:
  the ASCII LF character, also known as "newline"
  the ASCII CR character, also known as "return"
  the ASCII CR character followed by the ASCII LF character

InputCharacter:
  UnicodeInputCharacter but not CR or LF

Lines are terminated by the ASCII characters CR, or LF, or CR LF. The two characters CR immediately followed by LF are counted as one line terminator, not two.

The result is a sequence of line terminators and input characters, which are the terminal symbols for the third step in the tokenization process.

3.5 Input Elements and Tokens

The input characters and line terminators that result from escape processing (§3.3) and then input line recognition (§3.4) are reduced to a sequence of *input elements*. Those input elements that are not white space (§3.6) or comments (§3.7) are *tokens*. The tokens are the terminal symbols of the syntactic grammar (§2.3).

This process is specified by the following productions:

Input:
    $InputElements_{opt}$ Sub_{opt}

InputElements:
    InputElement
    InputElements InputElement

InputElement:
    WhiteSpace
    Comment
    Token

Token:
    Identifier
    Keyword
    Literal
    Separator
    Operator

Sub:
    the ASCII SUB character, also known as "control-Z"

White space (§3.6) and comments (§3.7) can serve to separate tokens that, if adjacent, might be tokenized in another manner. For example, the ASCII characters `-` and `=` in the input can form the operator token `-=` (§3.12) only if there is no intervening white space or comment.

As a special concession for compatibility with certain operating systems, the ASCII SUB character (`\u001a`, or control-Z) is ignored if it is the last character in the escaped input stream.

Consider two tokens `x` and `y` in the resulting input stream. If `x` precedes `y`, then we say that `x` is *to the left of* `y` and that `y` is *to the right of* `x`.

For example, in this simple piece of code:

```
class Empty {
}
```

we say that the } token is to the right of the { token, even though it appears, in this two-dimensional representation on paper, downward and to the left of the { token. This convention about the use of the words left and right allows us to speak, for example, of the right-hand operand of a binary operator or of the left-hand side of an assignment.

3.6 White Space

White space is defined as the ASCII space, horizontal tab, and form feed characters, as well as line terminators (§3.4).

WhiteSpace:
  the ASCII SP character, also known as "space"
  the ASCII HT character, also known as "horizontal tab"
  the ASCII FF character, also known as "form feed"
  LineTerminator

3.7 Comments

There are two kinds of *comments*:

/* *text* */	A *traditional comment*: all the text from the ASCII characters /* to the ASCII characters */ is ignored (as in C and C++).
// *text*	A *end-of-line comment*: all the text from the ASCII characters // to the end of the line is ignored (as in C++).

These comments are formally specified by the following productions:

Comment:
  TraditionalComment
  EndOfLineComment

TraditionalComment:
  / * *CommentTail*

EndOfLineComment:
  / / *CharactersInLine*$_{opt}$

CommentTail:
  * *CommentTailStar*
  NotStar CommentTail

CommentTailStar:
  /
  * *CommentTailStar*
  NotStarNotSlash CommentTail

NotStar:
  InputCharacter but not *
  LineTerminator

NotStarNotSlash:
  InputCharacter but not * or /
  LineTerminator

CharactersInLine:
  InputCharacter
  CharactersInLine InputCharacter

These productions imply all of the following properties:

- Comments do not nest.
- /* and */ have no special meaning in comments that begin with //.
- // has no special meaning in comments that begin with /* or /**.

As a result, the text:

```
/* this comment /* // /** ends here: */
```

is a single complete comment.

The lexical grammar implies that comments do not occur within character literals (§3.10.4) or string literals (§3.10.5).

3.8 Identifiers

An *identifier* is an unlimited-length sequence of *Java letters* and *Java digits*, the first of which must be a Java letter. An identifier cannot have the same spelling (Unicode character sequence) as a keyword (§3.9), boolean literal (§3.10.3), or the null literal (§3.10.7).

Identifier:
IdentifierChars but not a *Keyword* or *BooleanLiteral* or *NullLiteral*

IdentifierChars:
JavaLetter
IdentifierChars JavaLetterOrDigit

JavaLetter:
any Unicode character that is a Java letter (see below)

JavaLetterOrDigit:
any Unicode character that is a Java letter-or-digit (see below)

Letters and digits may be drawn from the entire Unicode character set, which supports most writing scripts in use in the world today, including the large sets for Chinese, Japanese, and Korean. This allows programmers to use identifiers in their programs that are written in their native languages.

A "Java letter" is a character for which the method `Character.isJavaIdentifierStart(int)` returns `true`. A "Java letter-or-digit" is a character for which the method `Character.isJavaIdentifierPart(int)` returns `true`.

The Java letters include uppercase and lowercase ASCII Latin letters `A–Z` (`\u0041–\u005a`), and `a–z` (`\u0061–\u007a`), and, for historical reasons, the ASCII underscore (`_`, or `\u005f`) and dollar sign (`$`, or `\u0024`). The `$` character should be used only in mechanically generated source code or, rarely, to access preexisting names on legacy systems.

The "Java digits" include the ASCII digits `0-9` (`\u0030–\u0039`).

Two identifiers are the same only if they are identical, that is, have the same Unicode character for each letter or digit.

Identifiers that have the same external appearance may yet be different. For example, the identifiers consisting of the single letters LATIN CAPITAL LETTER A (`A`, `\u0041`), LATIN SMALL LETTER A (`a`, `\u0061`), GREEK CAPITAL LETTER ALPHA (`A`, `\u0391`), CYRILLIC SMALL LETTER A (`a`, `\u0430`) and MATHEMATICAL BOLD ITALIC SMALL A (`a`, `\ud835\udc82`) are all different.

Unicode composite characters are different from the decomposed characters. For example, a LATIN CAPITAL LETTER A ACUTE (`Á`, `\u00c1`) could be considered to be the same as a LATIN CAPITAL LETTER A (`A`, `\u0041`) immediately followed by a NON-SPACING ACUTE (`´`, `\u0301`) when sorting, but these are different in identifiers. See *The Unicode Standard*, Volume 1, pages 412ff for details about decomposition, and see pages 626–627 of that work for details about sorting. Examples of identifiers are:

```
String    i3    αρετη    MAX_VALUE    isLetterOrDigit
```

3.9 Keywords

The following character sequences, formed from ASCII letters, are reserved for use as *keywords* and cannot be used as identifiers (§3.8):

Keyword: one of

```
abstract    continue    for           new        switch
assert      default     if            package synchronized
boolean     do          goto          private    this
break       double      implements    protected  throw
byte        else        import        public     throws
case        enum        instanceof    return     transient
catch       extends     int           short      try
char        final       interface     static     void
class       finally     long          strictfp   volatile
const       float       native        super      while
```

The keywords `const` and `goto` are reserved, even though they are not currently used. This may allow a Java compiler to produce better error messages if these C++ keywords incorrectly appear in programs.

While `true` and `false` might appear to be keywords, they are technically Boolean literals (§3.10.3). Similarly, while `null` might appear to be a keyword, it is technically the null literal (§3.10.7).

3.10 Literals

A *literal* is the source code representation of a value of a primitive type (§4.2), the `String` type (§4.3.3), or the null type (§4.1):

Literal:
IntegerLiteral
FloatingPointLiteral
BooleanLiteral
CharacterLiteral
StringLiteral
NullLiteral

3.10.1 Integer Literals

See §4.2.1 for a general discussion of the integer types and values.

An *integer literal* may be expressed in decimal (base 10), hexadecimal (base 16), or octal (base 8):

IntegerLiteral:
  DecimalIntegerLiteral
  HexIntegerLiteral
  OctalIntegerLiteral

DecimalIntegerLiteral:
  DecimalNumeral IntegerTypeSuffix$_{opt}$

HexIntegerLiteral:
  HexNumeral IntegerTypeSuffix$_{opt}$

OctalIntegerLiteral:
  OctalNumeral IntegerTypeSuffix$_{opt}$

IntegerTypeSuffix: one of
  `l L`

An integer literal is of type `long` if it is suffixed with an ASCII letter `L` or `l` (ell); otherwise it is of type `int` (§4.2.1). The suffix `L` is preferred, because the letter `l` (ell) is often hard to distinguish from the digit `1` (one).

A decimal numeral is either the single ASCII character `0`, representing the integer zero, or consists of an ASCII digit from `1` to `9`, optionally followed by one or more ASCII digits from `0` to `9`, representing a positive integer:

DecimalNumeral:
  `0`
  NonZeroDigit Digits$_{opt}$

Digits:
  Digit
  Digits Digit

Digit:
  `0`
  NonZeroDigit

NonZeroDigit: one of
  `1 2 3 4 5 6 7 8 9`

A hexadecimal numeral consists of the leading ASCII characters `0x` or `0X` followed by one or more ASCII hexadecimal digits and can represent a positive, zero, or negative integer. Hexadecimal digits with values 10 through 15 are represented by the ASCII letters `a` through `f` or `A` through `F`, respectively; each letter used as a hexadecimal digit may be uppercase or lowercase.

HexNumeral:
  `0 x` *HexDigits*
  `0 X` *HexDigits*

HexDigits:
  HexDigit
  HexDigit HexDigits

The following production from §3.3 is repeated here for clarity:

HexDigit: one of
  `0 1 2 3 4 5 6 7 8 9 a b c d e f A B C D E F`

An octal numeral consists of an ASCII digit `0` followed by one or more of the ASCII digits `0` through `7` and can represent a positive, zero, or negative integer.

OctalNumeral:
  `0` *OctalDigits*

OctalDigits:
  OctalDigit
  OctalDigit OctalDigits

OctalDigit: one of
  `0 1 2 3 4 5 6 7`

Note that octal numerals always consist of two or more digits; `0` is always considered to be a decimal numeral—not that it matters much in practice, for the numerals `0`, `00`, and `0x0` all represent exactly the same integer value.

The largest decimal literal of type `int` is `2147483648` (2^{31}). All decimal literals from `0` to `2147483647` may appear anywhere an `int` literal may appear, but the literal `2147483648` may appear only as the operand of the unary negation operator `-`.

The largest positive hexadecimal and octal literals of type `int` are `0x7fffffff` and `017777777777`, respectively, which equal `2147483647` ($2^{31} - 1$). The most negative hexadecimal and octal literals of type `int` are `0x80000000` and `020000000000`, respectively, each of which represents the decimal value `-2147483648` (-2^{31}). The hexadecimal and octal literals `0xffffffff` and `037777777777`, respectively, represent the decimal value `-1`.

A compile-time error occurs if a decimal literal of type `int` is larger than `2147483648` (2^{31}), or if the literal `2147483648` appears anywhere other than as the operand of the unary `-` operator, or if a hexadecimal or octal `int` literal does not fit in 32 bits.

Examples of `int` literals:

```
0 2 0372 0xDadaCafe 1996 0x00FF00FF
```

The largest decimal literal of type `long` is `9223372036854775808L` (2^{63}). All decimal literals from `0L` to `9223372036854775807L` may appear anywhere a `long` literal may appear, but the literal `9223372036854775808L` may appear only as the operand of the unary negation operator `-`.

The largest positive hexadecimal and octal literals of type `long` are `0x7fffffffffffffffL` and `0777777777777777777777L`, respectively, which equal `9223372036854775807L` ($2^{63}-1$). The literals `0x8000000000000000L` and `01000000000000000000000L` are the most negative `long` hexadecimal and octal literals, respectively. Each has the decimal value `-9223372036854775808L` (-2^{63}). The hexadecimal and octal literals `0xffffffffffffffffL` and `01777777777777777777777L`, respectively, represent the decimal value `-1L`.

A compile-time error occurs if a decimal literal of type `long` is larger than `9223372036854775808L` (2^{63}), or if the literal `9223372036854775808L` appears anywhere other than as the operand of the unary `-` operator, or if a hexadecimal or octal `long` literal does not fit in 64 bits.

Examples of `long` literals:

```
0l 0777L 0x100000000L 2147483648L  0xC0B0L
```

3.10.2 Floating-Point Literals

See §4.2.3 for a general discussion of the floating-point types and values.

A *floating-point literal* has the following parts: a whole-number part, a decimal or hexadecimal point (represented by an ASCII period character), a fractional part, an exponent, and a type suffix. A floating point number may be written either as a decimal value or as a hexadecimal value. For decimal literals, the exponent, if present, is indicated by the ASCII letter `e` or `E` followed by an optionally signed integer. For hexadecimal literals, the exponent is always required and is indicated by the ASCII letter `p` or `P` followed by an optionally signed integer.

For decimal floating-point literals, at least one digit, in either the whole number or the fraction part, and either a decimal point, an exponent, or a float type suffix are required. All other parts are optional. For hexadecimal floating-point literals, at least one digit is required in either the whole number or fraction part, the exponent is mandatory, and the float type suffix is optional.

A floating-point literal is of type `float` if it is suffixed with an ASCII letter `F` or `f`; otherwise its type is `double` and it can optionally be suffixed with an ASCII letter `D` or `d`.

FloatingPointLiteral:
  DecimalFloatingPointLiteral
  HexadecimalFloatingPointLiteral

DecimalFloatingPointLiteral:
  Digits `.` $Digits_{opt}$ $ExponentPart_{opt}$ $FloatTypeSuffix_{opt}$
  `.` *Digits* $ExponentPart_{opt}$ $FloatTypeSuffix_{opt}$
  Digits ExponentPart $FloatTypeSuffix_{opt}$
  Digits $ExponentPart_{opt}$ *FloatTypeSuffix*

ExponentPart:
  ExponentIndicator SignedInteger

ExponentIndicator: one of
  `e E`

SignedInteger:
  $Sign_{opt}$ *Digits*

Sign: one of
  `+ -`

FloatTypeSuffix: one of
  `f F d D`

HexadecimalFloatingPointLiteral:
  HexSignificand BinaryExponent $FloatTypeSuffix_{opt}$

HexSignificand:
  HexNumeral
  HexNumeral .
  0x $HexDigits_{opt}$ *. HexDigits*
  0X $HexDigits_{opt}$ *. HexDigits*

BinaryExponent:
  BinaryExponentIndicator SignedInteger

BinaryExponentIndicator:one of
  `p P`

The elements of the types `float` and `double` are those values that can be represented using the IEEE 754 32-bit single-precision and 64-bit double-precision binary floating-point formats, respectively.

The details of proper input conversion from a Unicode string representation of a floating-point number to the internal IEEE 754 binary floating-point representation are described for the methods `valueOf` of class `Float` and class `Double` of the package `java.lang`.

The largest positive finite `float` literal is `3.4028235e38f`. The smallest positive finite nonzero literal of type `float` is `1.40e-45f`. The largest positive finite `double` literal is `1.7976931348623157e308`. The smallest positive finite nonzero literal of type `double` is `4.9e-324`.

A compile-time error occurs if a nonzero floating-point literal is too large, so that on rounded conversion to its internal representation it becomes an IEEE 754 infinity. A program can represent infinities without producing a compile-time error by using constant expressions such as `1f/0f` or `-1d/0d` or by using the predefined constants `POSITIVE_INFINITY` and `NEGATIVE_INFINITY` of the classes `Float` and `Double`.

A compile-time error occurs if a nonzero floating-point literal is too small, so that, on rounded conversion to its internal representation, it becomes a zero. A compile-time error does not occur if a nonzero floating-point literal has a small value that, on rounded conversion to its internal representation, becomes a nonzero denormalized number.

Predefined constants representing Not-a-Number values are defined in the classes `Float` and `Double` as `Float.NaN` and `Double.NaN`.

Examples of `float` literals:

```
1e1f2.f.3f0f3.14f6.022137e+23f
```

Examples of `double` literals:

```
1e12..30.03.141e-9d1e137
```

Besides expressing floating-point values in decimal and hexadecimal, the method `intBitsToFloat` of class `Float` and method `longBitsToDouble` of class `Double` provide a way to express floating-point values in terms of hexadecimal or octal integer literals.For example, the value of:

```
Double.longBitsToDouble(0x400921FB54442D18L)
```

is equal to the value of `Math.PI`.

3.10.3 Boolean Literals

The `boolean` type has two values, represented by the literals `true` and `false`, formed from ASCII letters.

A *boolean literal* is always of type `boolean`.

BooleanLiteral: one of

```
true false
```

3.10.4 Character Literals

A *character literal* is expressed as a character or an escape sequence, enclosed in ASCII single quotes. (The single-quote, or apostrophe, character is `\u0027`.)

Character literals can only represent UTF-16 code units (§3.1), i.e., they are limited to values from `\u0000` to `\uffff`. Supplementary characters must be represented either as a surrogate pair within a char sequence, or as an integer, depending on the API they are used with.

A character literal is always of type `char`.

CharacterLiteral:
    `'` *SingleCharacter* `'`
    `'` *EscapeSequence* `'`

SingleCharacter:
    InputCharacter but not `'` or `\`

The escape sequences are described in §3.10.6.

As specified in §3.4, the characters CR and LF are never an *InputCharacter*; they are recognized as constituting a *LineTerminator.*

It is a compile-time error for the character following the *SingleCharacter* or *EscapeSequence* to be other than a `'`.

It is a compile-time error for a line terminator to appear after the opening `'` and before the closing `'`.

The following are examples of `char` literals:

```
'a'
'%'
'\t'
'\\'
'\''
'\u03a9'
'\uFFFF'
'\177'
'Ω'
'⊗'
```

Because Unicode escapes are processed very early, it is not correct to write `'\u000a'` for a character literal whose value is linefeed (LF); the Unicode escape `\u000a` is transformed into an actual linefeed in translation step 1 (§3.3) and the linefeed becomes a *LineTerminator* in step 2 (§3.4), and so the character literal is not valid in step 3. Instead, one should use the escape sequence `'\n'` (§3.10.6). Similarly, it is not correct to write `'\u000d'` for a character literal whose value is carriage return (CR). Instead, use `'\r'`.

In C and C++, a character literal may contain representations of more than one character, but the value of such a character literal is implementation-defined. In the Java programming language, a character literal always represents exactly one character.

3.10.5 String Literals

A *string literal* consists of zero or more characters enclosed in double quotes. Characters may be represented by escape sequences - one escape sequence for characters in the range U+0000 to U+FFFF, two escape sequences for the UTF-16 surrogate code units of characters in the range U+010000 to U+10FFFF.

A string literal is always of type `String` (§4.3.3). A string literal always refers to the same instance (§4.3.1) of class `String`.

StringLiteral:
  " *StringCharacters*$_{opt}$ "

StringCharacters:
  StringCharacter
  StringCharacters StringCharacter

StringCharacter:
  InputCharacter but not " or \
  EscapeSequence

The escape sequences are described in §3.10.6.

As specified in §3.4, neither of the characters CR and LF is ever considered to be an *InputCharacter*; each is recognized as constituting a *LineTerminator*.

It is a compile-time error for a line terminator to appear after the opening " and before the closing matching ". A long string literal can always be broken up into shorter pieces and written as a (possibly parenthesized) expression using the string concatenation operator + (§15.18.1).

The following are examples of string literals:

```
""                    // the empty string
"\""                  // a string containing " alone
"This is a string"    // a string containing 16 characters
"This is a " +        // actually a string-valued constant expression,
    "two-line string" //     formed from two string literals
```

Because Unicode escapes are processed very early, it is not correct to write "`\u000a`" for a string literal containing a single linefeed (LF); the Unicode escape `\u000a` is transformed into an actual linefeed in translation step 1 (§3.3) and the linefeed becomes a *LineTerminator* in step 2 (§3.4), and so the string literal is not valid in step 3. Instead, one should write "`\n`" (§3.10.6). Similarly, it is not correct to write "`\u000d`" for a string literal containing a single carriage return (CR). Instead use "`\r`".

Each string literal is a reference (§4.3) to an instance (§4.3.1, §12.5) of class `String` (§4.3.3). `String` objects have a constant value. String literals—or, more generally, strings that are the values of constant expressions (§15.28)—are "interned" so as to share unique instances, using the method `String.intern`.

Thus, the test program consisting of the compilation unit (§7.3):

```
package testPackage;

class Test {
    public static void main(String[] args) {
        String hello = "Hello", lo = "lo";
        System.out.print((hello == "Hello") + " ");
        System.out.print((Other.hello == hello) + " ");
        System.out.print((other.Other.hello == hello) + " ");
        System.out.print((hello == ("Hel"+"lo")) + " ");
        System.out.print((hello == ("Hel"+lo)) + " ");
        System.out.println(hello == ("Hel"+lo).intern());
    }
}

class Other { static String hello = "Hello"; }
```

and the compilation unit:

```
package other;

public class Other { static String hello = "Hello"; }
```

produces the output:

```
true true true true false true
```

This example illustrates six points:

- Literal strings within the same class (§8) in the same package (§7) represent references to the same `String` object (§4.3.1).
- Literal strings within different classes in the same package represent references to the same `String` object.
- Literal strings within different classes in different packages likewise represent references to the same `String` object.
- Strings computed by constant expressions (§15.28) are computed at compile time and then treated as if they were literals.
- Strings computed by concatenation at run time are newly created and therefore distinct.

The result of explicitly interning a computed string is the same string as any pre-existing literal string with the same contents.

3.10.6 Escape Sequences for Character and String Literals

The character and string *escape sequences* allow for the representation of some nongraphic characters as well as the single quote, double quote, and backslash characters in character literals (§3.10.4) and string literals (§3.10.5).

```
EscapeSequence:
    \ b            /* \u0008: backspace BS */
    \ t            /* \u0009: horizontal tab HT */
    \ n            /* \u000a: linefeed LF */
    \ f            /* \u000c: form feed FF */
    \ r            /* \u000d: carriage return CR */
    \ "            /* \u0022: double quote " */
    \ '            /* \u0027: single quote ' */
    \ \            /* \u005c: backslash \ */
    OctalEscape    /* \u0000 to \u00ff: from octal value */

OctalEscape:
    \ OctalDigit
    \ OctalDigit OctalDigit
    \ ZeroToThree OctalDigit OctalDigit

OctalDigit: one of
    0 1 2 3 4 5 6 7

ZeroToThree: one of
    0 1 2 3
```

It is a compile-time error if the character following a backslash in an escape is not an ASCII b, t, n, f, r, ", ', \, 0, 1, 2, 3, 4, 5, 6, or 7. The Unicode escape \u is processed earlier (§3.3). (Octal escapes are provided for compatibility with C, but can express only Unicode values \u0000 through \u00FF, so Unicode escapes are usually preferred.)

3.10.7 The Null Literal

The null type has one value, the null reference, represented by the literal null, which is formed from ASCII characters. A *null literal* is always of the null type.

```
NullLiteral:
    null
```

3.11 Separators

The following nine ASCII characters are the *separators* (punctuators):

Separator: one of

```
(    )    {    }    [    ]    ;    ,    .
```

3.12 Operators

The following 37 tokens are the *operators*, formed from ASCII characters:

Operator: one of

```
=    >    <    !    ~    ?    :
==   <=   >=   !=   &&   ||   ++   --
+    -    *    /    &    |    ^    %    <<   >>   >>>
+=   -=   *=   /=   &=   |=   ^=   %=   <<=  >>=  >>>=
```

Give her no token but stones; for she's as hard as steel.
—William Shakespeare, *Two Gentlemen of Verona*, Act I, scene i

These lords are visited; you are not free;
For the Lord's tokens on you do I see.
—William Shakespeare, *Love's Labour's Lost*, Act V, scene ii

Thou, thou, Lysander, thou hast given her rhymes,
And interchanged love-tokens with my child.
—William Shakespeare, *A Midsummer Night's Dream*, Act I, scene i

Here is a letter from Queen Hecuba,
A token from her daughter . . .
—William Shakespeare, *Troilus and Cressida*, Act V, scene i

Are there no other tokens . . . ?
—William Shakespeare, *Measure for Measure*, Act IV, scene i

Hush, my darling, don't fear, my darling, the lion sleeps tonight.
—Luigi Creatore, George David Weiss, and Hugo E. Peretti

CHAPTER 4

Types, Values, and Variables

I send no agent or medium,
offer no representative of value,
but offer the value itself.
—Walt Whitman, *Carol of Occupations* (1855),
in *Leaves of Grass*

THE Java programming language is a *strongly typed* language, which means that every variable and every expression has a type that is known at compile time. Types limit the values that a variable (§4.12) can hold or that an expression can produce, limit the operations supported on those values, and determine the meaning of the operations. Strong typing helps detect errors at compile time.

The types of the Java programming language are divided into two categories: primitive types and reference types. The primitive types (§4.2) are the `boolean` type and the numeric types. The numeric types are the integral types `byte`, `short`, `int`, `long`, and `char`, and the floating-point types `float` and `double`. The reference types (§4.3) are class types, interface types, and array types. There is also a special null type. An object (§4.3.1) is a dynamically created instance of a class type or a dynamically created array. The values of a reference type are references to objects. All objects, including arrays, support the methods of class `Object` (§4.3.2). String literals are represented by `String` objects (§4.3.3).

Types exist at compile-time. Some types correspond to classes and interfaces, which exist at run-time. The correspondence between types and classes or interfaces is incomplete for two reasons:

1. At run-time, classes and interfaces are loaded by the Java virtual machine using class loaders. Each class loader defines its own set of classes and interfaces. As a result, it is possible for two loaders to load an identical class or interface definition but produce distinct classes or interfaces at run-time.

2. Type arguments and type variables (§4.4) are not reified at run-time. As a result, different parameterized types (§4.5) are implemented by the same class or interface at run time. Indeed, all invocations of a given generic type declaration (§8.1.2, §9.1.2)share a single run-time implementation.

A consequence of (1) is that code that compiled correctly may fail at link time if the class loaders that load it are inconsistent. See the paper *Dynamic Class Loading in the Java™ Virtual Machine*, by Sheng Liang and Gilad Bracha, in *Proceedings of OOPSLA '98*, published as *ACM SIGPLAN Notices*, Volume 33, Number 10, October 1998, pages 36-44, and *The Java™ Virtual Machine Specification, Second Edition* for more details.

A consequence of (2) is the possibility of *heap pollution* (§4.12.2.1). Under certain conditions, it is possible that a variable of a parameterized type refers to an object that is not of that parameterized type. The variable will always refer to an object that is an instance of a class that implements the parameterized type. See (§4.12.2) for further discussion.

4.1 The Kinds of Types and Values

There are two kinds of *types* in the Java programming language: primitive types (§4.2) and reference types (§4.3). There are, correspondingly, two kinds of data values that can be stored in variables, passed as arguments, returned by methods, and operated on: primitive values (§4.2) and reference values (§4.3).

Type:
  PrimitiveType
  ReferenceType

There is also a special *null type*, the type of the expression `null`, which has no name. Because the null type has no name, it is impossible to declare a variable of the null type or to cast to the null type. The null reference is the only possible value of an expression of null type. The null reference can always be cast to any reference type. In practice, the programmer can ignore the null type and just pretend that `null` is merely a special literal that can be of any reference type.

4.2 Primitive Types and Values

A *primitive type* is predefined by the Java programming language and named by its reserved keyword (§3.9):

PrimitiveType:
  NumericType
  `boolean`

NumericType:
  IntegralType
  FloatingPointType

IntegralType: one of
  `byte short int long char`

FloatingPointType: one of
  `float double`

Primitive values do not share state with other primitive values. A variable whose type is a primitive type always holds a primitive value of that same type. The value of a variable of primitive type can be changed only by assignment operations on that variable (including increment (§15.14.2, §15.15.1) and decrement (§15.14.3, §15.15.2) operators).

The *numeric types* are the integral types and the floating-point types.

The *integral types* are `byte`, `short`, `int`, and `long`, whose values are 8-bit, 16-bit, 32-bit and 64-bit signed two's-complement integers, respectively, and `char`, whose values are 16-bit unsigned integers representing UTF-16 code units (§3.1).

The *floating-point types* are `float`, whose values include the 32-bit IEEE 754 floating-point numbers, and `double`, whose values include the 64-bit IEEE 754 floating-point numbers.

The `boolean` type has exactly two values: `true` and `false`.

4.2.1 Integral Types and Values

The values of the integral types are integers in the following ranges:

- For `byte`, from –128 to 127, inclusive
- For `short`, from –32768 to 32767, inclusive
- For `int`, from –2147483648 to 2147483647, inclusive
- For `long`, from –9223372036854775808 to 9223372036854775807, inclusive
- For `char`, from `'\u0000'` to `'\uffff'` inclusive, that is, from 0 to 65535

4.2.2 Integer Operations

The Java programming language provides a number of operators that act on integral values:

- The comparison operators, which result in a value of type `boolean`:
  - The numerical comparison operators <, <=, >, and >= (§15.20.1)
  - The numerical equality operators == and != (§15.21.1)
- The numerical operators, which result in a value of type `int` or `long`:
  - The unary plus and minus operators + and - (§15.15.3, §15.15.4)
  - The multiplicative operators *, /, and % (§15.17)
  - The additive operators + and - (§15.18)
  - The increment operator ++, both prefix (§15.15.1) and postfix (§15.14.2)
  - The decrement operator --, both prefix (§15.15.2) and postfix (§15.14.3)
  - The signed and unsigned shift operators <<, >>, and >>> (§15.19)
  - The bitwise complement operator ~ (§15.15.5)
  - The integer bitwise operators &, |, and ^ (§15.22.1)
- The conditional operator ? : (§15.25)
- The cast operator, which can convert from an integral value to a value of any specified numeric type (§5.5, §15.16)
- The string concatenation operator + (§15.18.1), which, when given a `String` operand and an integral operand, will convert the integral operand to a `String` representing its value in decimal form, and then produce a newly created `String` that is the concatenation of the two strings

Other useful constructors, methods, and constants are predefined in the classes `Byte`, `Short`, `Integer`, `Long`, and `Character`.

If an integer operator other than a shift operator has at least one operand of type `long`, then the operation is carried out using 64-bit precision, and the result of the numerical operator is of type `long`. If the other operand is not `long`, it is first widened (§5.1.5) to type `long` by numeric promotion (§5.6). Otherwise, the operation is carried out using 32-bit precision, and the result of the numerical operator is of type `int`. If either operand is not an `int`, it is first widened to type `int` by numeric promotion.

The built-in integer operators do not indicate overflow or underflow in any way. Integer operators can throw a `NullPointerException` if unboxing conversion (§5.1.8) of a null reference is required. Other than that, the only integer operators that can throw an exception (§11) are the integer divide operator `/` (§15.17.2) and the integer remainder operator `%` (§15.17.3), which throw an `ArithmeticException` if the right-hand operand is zero, and the increment and decrement operators `++`(§15.15.1, §15.15.2) and `--`(§15.14.3, §15.14.2), which can throw an `OutOfMemoryError` if boxing conversion (§5.1.7) is required and there is not sufficient memory available to perform the conversion.

The example:

```
class Test {
    public static void main(String[] args) {
        int i = 1000000;
        System.out.println(i * i);
        long l = i;
        System.out.println(l * l);
        System.out.println(20296 / (l - i));
    }
}
```

produces the output:

```
-727379968
1000000000000
```

and then encounters an `ArithmeticException` in the division by `l - i`, because `l - i` is zero. The first multiplication is performed in 32-bit precision, whereas the second multiplication is a `long` multiplication. The value `-727379968` is the decimal value of the low 32 bits of the mathematical result, `1000000000000`, which is a value too large for type `int`.

Any value of any integral type may be cast to or from any numeric type. There are no casts between integral types and the type `boolean`.

4.2.3 Floating-Point Types, Formats, and Values

The floating-point types are `float` and `double`, which are conceptually associated with the single-precision 32-bit and double-precision 64-bit format IEEE 754 values and operations as specified in *IEEE Standard for Binary Floating-Point Arithmetic*, ANSI/IEEE Standard 754-1985 (IEEE, New York).

The IEEE 754 standard includes not only positive and negative numbers that consist of a sign and magnitude, but also positive and negative zeros, positive and negative *infinities*, and special *Not-a-Number* values (hereafter abbreviated NaN). A NaN value is used to represent the result of certain invalid operations such as dividing zero by zero. NaN constants of both `float` and `double` type are predefined as `Float.NaN` and `Double.NaN`.

Every implementation of the Java programming language is required to support two standard sets of floating-point values, called the *float value set* and the *double value set*. In addition, an implementation of the Java programming language may support either or both of two extended-exponent floating-point value sets, called the *float-extended-exponent value set* and the *double-extended-exponent value set*. These extended-exponent value sets may, under certain circumstances, be used instead of the standard value sets to represent the values of expressions of type `float` or `double` (§5.1.13, §15.4).

The finite nonzero values of any floating-point value set can all be expressed in the form $s \cdot m \cdot 2^{(e-N+1)}$, where s is +1 or –1, m is a positive integer less than 2^N, and e is an integer between $E_{min} = -(2^{K-1}-2)$ and $E_{max} = 2^{K-1}-1$, inclusive, and where N and K are parameters that depend on the value set. Some values can be represented in this form in more than one way; for example, supposing that a value v in a value set might be represented in this form using certain values for s, m, and e, then if it happened that m were even and e were less than 2^{K-1}, one could halve m and increase e by 1 to produce a second representation for the same value v. A representation in this form is called *normalized* if $m \geq 2^{(N-1)}$; otherwise the representation is said to be *denormalized*. If a value in a value set cannot be represented in such a way that $m \geq 2^{(N-1)}$, then the value is said to be a *denormalized value*, because it has no normalized representation.

The constraints on the parameters N and K (and on the derived parameters E_{min} and E_{max}) for the two required and two optional floating-point value sets are summarized in Table 4.1.

Parameter	**float**	**float-extended-exponent**	double	double-extended-exponent
N	24	24	53	53
K	8	≥ 11	11	≥ 15
E_{max}	+127	≥ +1023	+1023	≥ +16383
E_{min}	−126	≤ −1022	−1022	≤ −16382

Table 4.1 Floating-point value set parameters

Where one or both extended-exponent value sets are supported by an implementation, then for each supported extended-exponent value set there is a specific implementation-dependent constant K, whose value is constrained by Table 4.1; this value K in turn dictates the values for E_{min} and E_{max}.

Each of the four value sets includes not only the finite nonzero values that are ascribed to it above, but also NaN values and the four values positive zero, negative zero, positive infinity, and negative infinity.

Note that the constraints in Table 4.1 are designed so that every element of the float value set is necessarily also an element of the float-extended-exponent value set, the double value set, and the double-extended-exponent value set. Likewise, each element of the double value set is necessarily also an element of the double-extended-exponent value set. Each extended-exponent value set has a larger range of exponent values than the corresponding standard value set, but does not have more precision.

The elements of the float value set are exactly the values that can be represented using the single floating-point format defined in the IEEE 754 standard. The elements of the double value set are exactly the values that can be represented using the double floating-point format defined in the IEEE 754 standard. Note, however, that the elements of the float-extended-exponent and double-extended-exponent value sets defined here do *not* correspond to the values that can be represented using IEEE 754 single extended and double extended formats, respectively.

The float, float-extended-exponent, double, and double-extended-exponent value sets are not types. It is always correct for an implementation of the Java programming language to use an element of the float value set to represent a value of type `float`; however, it may be permissible in certain regions of code for an implementation to use an element of the float-extended-exponent value set instead. Similarly, it is always correct for an implementation to use an element of the double value set to represent a value of type `double`; however, it may be permissible in certain regions of code for an implementation to use an element of the double-extended-exponent value set instead.

Except for NaN, floating-point values are *ordered*; arranged from smallest to largest, they are negative infinity, negative finite nonzero values, positive and negative zero, positive finite nonzero values, and positive infinity.

IEEE 754 allows multiple distinct NaN values for each of its single and double floating-point formats. While each hardware architecture returns a particular bit pattern for NaN when a new NaN is generated, a programmer can also create NaNs with different bit patterns to encode, for example, retrospective diagnostic information.

For the most part, the Java platform treats NaN values of a given type as though collapsed into a single canonical value (and hence this specification normally refers to an arbitrary NaN as though to a canonical value). However, version 1.3 the Java platform introduced methods enabling the programmer to distinguish between NaN values: the `Float.floatToRawIntBits` and `Double.doubleToRawLongBits` methods. The interested reader is referred to the specifications for the `Float` and `Double` classes for more information.

Positive zero and negative zero compare equal; thus the result of the expression `0.0==-0.0` is `true` and the result of `0.0>-0.0` is `false`. But other operations can distinguish positive and negative zero; for example, 1.0/0.0 has the value positive infinity, while the value of 1.0/-0.0 is negative infinity.

NaN is *unordered*, so the numerical comparison operators <, <=, >, and >= return false if either or both operands are NaN (§15.20.1). The equality operator == returns false if either operand is NaN, and the inequality operator != returns true if either operand is NaN (§15.21.1). In particular, x!=x is true if and only if x is NaN, and (x<y) == !(x>=y) will be false if x or y is NaN.

Any value of a floating-point type may be cast to or from any numeric type. There are no casts between floating-point types and the type boolean.

4.2.4 Floating-Point Operations

The Java programming language provides a number of operators that act on floating-point values:

- The comparison operators, which result in a value of type boolean:
  - The numerical comparison operators <, <=, >, and >= (§15.20.1)
  - The numerical equality operators == and != (§15.21.1)
- The numerical operators, which result in a value of type float or double:
  - The unary plus and minus operators + and - (§15.15.3, §15.15.4)
  - The multiplicative operators *, /, and % (§15.17)
  - The additive operators + and - (§15.18.2)
  - The increment operator ++, both prefix (§15.15.1) and postfix (§15.14.2)
  - The decrement operator --, both prefix (§15.15.2) and postfix (§15.14.3)
- The conditional operator ? : (§15.25)
- The cast operator, which can convert from a floating-point value to a value of any specified numeric type (§5.5, §15.16)
- The string concatenation operator + (§15.18.1), which, when given a String operand and a floating-point operand, will convert the floating-point operand to a String representing its value in decimal form (without information loss), and then produce a newly created String by concatenating the two strings

Other useful constructors, methods, and constants are predefined in the classes Float, Double, and Math.

If at least one of the operands to a binary operator is of floating-point type, then the operation is a floating-point operation, even if the other is integral.

If at least one of the operands to a numerical operator is of type `double`, then the operation is carried out using 64-bit floating-point arithmetic, and the result of the numerical operator is a value of type `double`. (If the other operand is not a `double`, it is first widened to type `double` by numeric promotion (§5.6).) Otherwise, the operation is carried out using 32-bit floating-point arithmetic, and the result of the numerical operator is a value of type `float`. If the other operand is not a `float`, it is first widened to type `float` by numeric promotion.

Operators on floating-point numbers behave as specified by IEEE 754 (with the exception of the remainder operator (§15.17.3)). In particular, the Java programming language requires support of IEEE 754 *denormalized* floating-point numbers and *gradual underflow*, which make it easier to prove desirable properties of particular numerical algorithms. Floating-point operations do not "flush to zero" if the calculated result is a denormalized number.

The Java programming language requires that floating-point arithmetic behave as if every floating-point operator rounded its floating-point result to the result precision. *Inexact* results must be rounded to the representable value nearest to the infinitely precise result; if the two nearest representable values are equally near, the one with its least significant bit zero is chosen. This is the IEEE 754 standard's default rounding mode known as *round to nearest*.

The language uses *round toward zero* when converting a floating value to an integer (§5.1.3), which acts, in this case, as though the number were truncated, discarding the mantissa bits. Rounding toward zero chooses at its result the format's value closest to and no greater in magnitude than the infinitely precise result.

Floating-point operators can throw a `NullPointerException` if unboxing conversion (§5.1.8) of a null reference is required. Other than that, the only floating-point operators that can throw an exception (§11) are the increment and decrement operators ++(§15.15.1, §15.15.2) and --(§15.14.3, §15.14.2), which can throw an `OutOfMemoryError` if boxing conversion (§5.1.7) is required and there is not sufficient memory available to perform the conversion.

An operation that overflows produces a signed infinity, an operation that underflows produces a denormalized value or a signed zero, and an operation that has no mathematically definite result produces NaN. All numeric operations with NaN as an operand produce NaN as a result. As has already been described, NaN is unordered, so a numeric comparison operation involving one or two NaNs returns `false` and any `!=` comparison involving NaN returns `true`, including `x!=x` when `x` is NaN.

The example program:

```
class Test {
    public static void main(String[] args) {
        // An example of overflow:
```

```
            double d = 1e308;
            System.out.print("overflow produces infinity: ");
            System.out.println(d + "*10==" + d*10);
            // An example of gradual underflow:
            d = 1e-305 * Math.PI;
            System.out.print("gradual underflow: " + d + "\n   ");
            for (int i = 0; i < 4; i++)
                System.out.print(" " + (d /= 100000));
            System.out.println();
            // An example of NaN:
            System.out.print("0.0/0.0 is Not-a-Number: ");
            d = 0.0/0.0;
            System.out.println(d);
            // An example of inexact results and rounding:
            System.out.print("inexact results with float:");
            for (int i = 0; i < 100; i++) {
                float z = 1.0f / i;
                if (z * i != 1.0f)
                    System.out.print(" " + i);
            }
            System.out.println();
            // Another example of inexact results and rounding:
            System.out.print("inexact results with double:");
            for (int i = 0; i < 100; i++) {
                double z = 1.0 / i;
                if (z * i != 1.0)
                    System.out.print(" " + i);
            }
            System.out.println();
            // An example of cast to integer rounding:
            System.out.print("cast to int rounds toward 0: ");
            d = 12345.6;
            System.out.println((int)d + " " + (int)(-d));
        }
    }
```

produces the output:

```
overflow produces infinity: 1.0e+308*10==Infinity
gradual underflow: 3.141592653589793E-305
   3.1415926535898E-310 3.141592653E-315 3.142E-320 0.0
0.0/0.0 is Not-a-Number: NaN
inexact results with float: 0 41 47 55 61 82 83 94 97
inexact results with double: 0 49 98
cast to int rounds toward 0: 12345 -12345
```

This example demonstrates, among other things, that gradual underflow can result in a gradual loss of precision.

The results when `i` is `0` involve division by zero, so that `z` becomes positive infinity, and `z * 0` is NaN, which is not equal to `1.0`.

4.2.5 The boolean Type and boolean Values

The `boolean` type represents a logical quantity with two possible values, indicated by the literals `true` and `false` (§3.10.3). The boolean operators are:

- The relational operators `==` and `!=` (§15.21.2)
- The logical-complement operator `!` (§15.15.6)
- The logical operators `&`, `^`, and `|` (§15.22.2)
- The conditional-and and conditional-or operators `&&` (§15.23) and `||` (§15.24)
- The conditional operator `? :` (§15.25)
- The string concatenation operator `+` (§15.18.1), which, when given a `String` operand and a boolean operand, will convert the boolean operand to a `String` (either `"true"` or `"false"`), and then produce a newly created `String` that is the concatenation of the two strings

Boolean expressions determine the control flow in several kinds of statements:

- The `if` statement (§14.9)
- The `while` statement (§14.12)
- The `do` statement (§14.13)
- The `for` statement (§14.14)

A `boolean` expression also determines which subexpression is evaluated in the conditional `? :` operator (§15.25).

Only `boolean` or `Boolean` expressions can be used in control flow statements and as the first operand of the conditional operator `? :`. An integer `x` can be converted to a `boolean`, following the C language convention that any nonzero value is `true`, by the expression `x!=0`. An object reference `obj` can be converted to a `boolean`, following the C language convention that any reference other than `null` is `true`, by the expression `obj!=null`.

A cast of a `boolean` value to type `boolean` or `Boolean` is allowed (§5.1.1); no other casts on type `boolean` are allowed. A `boolean` can be converted to a string by string conversion (§5.4).

4.3 Reference Types and Values

There are three kinds of *reference types*: class types (§8), interface types (§9), and array types (§10). Reference types may be parameterized (§4.5) with type arguments (§4.4).

ReferenceType:
    ClassOrInterfaceType
    TypeVariable
    ArrayType

ClassOrInterfaceType:
    ClassType
    InterfaceType

ClassType:
    TypeDeclSpecifier TypeArguments$_{opt}$

InterfaceType:
    TypeDeclSpecifier TypeArguments$_{opt}$

TypeDeclSpecifier:
    TypeName
    ClassOrInterfaceType . Identifier

TypeName:
    Identifier
    TypeName . Identifier

TypeVariable:
    Identifier

ArrayType:
    Type `[ ]`

A class or interface type consists of a *type declaration specifier,* optionally followed by type arguments (in which case it is a parameterized type). Type arguments are described in (§4.5.1).

A type declaration specifier may be either a type name (§6.5.5), or a class or interface type followed by "." and an identifier. In the latter case, the specifier has the form `T.id`, where `id` must be the simple name of an accessible (§6.6) member type (§8.5, §9.5) of `T`, or a compile-time error occurs. The specifier denotes that member type.

The sample code:

```
class Point { int[] metrics; }
interface Move { void move(int deltax, int deltay); }
```

declares a class type `Point`, an interface type `Move`, and uses an array type `int[]` (an array of `int`) to declare the field `metrics` of the class `Point`.

4.3.1 Objects

An *object* is a *class instance* or an array.

The reference values (often just *references*) are *pointers* to these objects, and a special null reference, which refers to no object.

A class instance is explicitly created by a class instance creation expression (§15.9). An array is explicitly created by an array creation expression (§15.10).

A new class instance is implicitly created when the string concatenation operator + (§15.18.1) is used in a non-constant (§15.28) expression, resulting in a new object of type `String` (§4.3.3). A new array object is implicitly created when an array initializer expression (§10.6) is evaluated; this can occur when a class or interface is initialized (§12.4), when a new instance of a class is created (§15.9), or when a local variable declaration statement is executed (§14.4). New objects of the types Boolean, Byte, Short, Character, Integer, Long, Float and Double may be implicitly created by boxing conversion (§5.1.7).

Many of these cases are illustrated in the following example:

```
class Point {
    int x, y;
    Point() { System.out.println("default"); }
    Point(int x, int y) { this.x = x; this.y = y; }
    // A Point instance is explicitly created at class initialization time:
    static Point origin = new Point(0,0);
    // A String can be implicitly created by a + operator:
    public String toString() {
        return "(" + x + "," + y + ")";
    }
}

class Test {
    public static void main(String[] args) {
        // A Point is explicitly created using newInstance:
        Point p = null;
        try {
            p = (Point)Class.forName("Point").newInstance();
        } catch (Exception e) {
            System.out.println(e);
        }
```

```
        // An array is implicitly created by an array constructor:
        Point a[] = { new Point(0,0), new Point(1,1) };
        // Strings are implicitly created by + operators:
        System.out.println("p: " + p);
        System.out.println("a: { " + a[0] + ", "
                                   + a[1] + " }");
        // An array is explicitly created by an array creation expression:
        String sa[] = new String[2];
        sa[0] = "he"; sa[1] = "llo";
        System.out.println(sa[0] + sa[1]);
    }
}
```

which produces the output:

```
default
p: (0,0)
a: { (0,0), (1,1) }
hello
```

The operators on references to objects are:

- Field access, using either a qualified name (§6.6) or a field access expression (§15.11)
- Method invocation (§15.12)
- The cast operator (§5.5, §15.16)
- The string concatenation operator + (§15.18.1), which, when given a `String` operand and a reference, will convert the reference to a `String` by invoking the `toString` method of the referenced object (using `"null"` if either the reference or the result of `toString` is a null reference), and then will produce a newly created `String` that is the concatenation of the two strings
- The `instanceof` operator (§15.20.2)
- The reference equality operators `==` and `!=` (§15.21.3)
- The conditional operator `? :` (§15.25).

There may be many references to the same object. Most objects have state, stored in the fields of objects that are instances of classes or in the variables that are the components of an array object. If two variables contain references to the same object, the state of the object can be modified using one variable's reference to the object, and then the altered state can be observed through the reference in the other variable.

The example program:

```
class Value { int val; }
class Test {
    public static void main(String[] args) {
        int i1 = 3;
        int i2 = i1;
        i2 = 4;
        System.out.print("i1==" + i1);
        System.out.println(" but i2==" + i2);
        Value v1 = new Value();
        v1.val = 5;
        Value v2 = v1;
        v2.val = 6;
        System.out.print("v1.val==" + v1.val);
        System.out.println(" and v2.val==" + v2.val);
    }
}
```

produces the output:

```
i1==3 but i2==4
v1.val==6 and v2.val==6
```

because `v1.val` and `v2.val` reference the same instance variable (§4.12.3) in the one `Value` object created by the only `new` expression, while `i1` and `i2` are different variables.

See §10 and §15.10 for examples of the creation and use of arrays.

Each object has an associated lock (§17.1), which is used by `synchronized` methods (§8.4.3) and the `synchronized` statement (§14.19) to provide control over concurrent access to state by multiple threads (§17).

4.3.2 The Class `Object`

The class `Object` is a superclass (§8.1) of all other classes. A variable of type `Object` can hold a reference to the null reference or to any object, whether it is an instance of a class or an array (§10). All class and array types inherit the methods of class `Object`, which are summarized here:

```
package java.lang;

public class Object {
    public final Class<?> getClass() { ... }
    public String toString() { ... }
    public boolean equals(Object obj) { ... }
    public int hashCode() { ... }
    protected Object clone()
        throws CloneNotSupportedException { ... }
```

```
    public final void wait()
        throws IllegalMonitorStateException,
            InterruptedException { ... }
    public final void wait(long millis)
        throws IllegalMonitorStateException,
            InterruptedException { ... }
    public final void wait(long millis, int nanos) { ... }
        throws IllegalMonitorStateException,
            InterruptedException { ... }
    public final void notify() { ... }
        throws IllegalMonitorStateException
    public final void notifyAll() { ... }
        throws IllegalMonitorStateException
    protected void finalize()
        throws Throwable { ... }
}
```

The members of `Object` are as follows:

- The method `getClass` returns the `Class` object that represents the class of the object. A `Class` object exists for each reference type. It can be used, for example, to discover the fully qualified name of a class, its members, its immediate superclass, and any interfaces that it implements. A class method that is declared `synchronized` (§8.4.3.6) synchronizes on the lock associated with the `Class` object of the class. The method `Object.getClass()` must be treated specially by a Java compiler. The type of a method invocation `e.getClass()`, where the expression `e` has the static type `T`, is `Class<? extends |T|>`.
- The method `toString` returns a `String` representation of the object.
- The methods `equals` and `hashCode` are very useful in hashtables such as `java.util.Hashtable`. The method `equals` defines a notion of object equality, which is based on value, not reference, comparison.
- The method `clone` is used to make a duplicate of an object.
- The methods `wait`, `notify`, and `notifyAll` are used in concurrent programming using threads, as described in §17.
- The method `finalize` is run just before an object is destroyed and is described in §12.6.

4.3.3 The Class `String`

Instances of class `String` represent sequences of Unicode characters. A `String` object has a constant (unchanging) value. String literals (§3.10.5) are references to instances of class `String`.

The string concatenation operator `+` (§15.18.1) implicitly creates a new `String` object when the result is not a compile-time constant (§15.28).

4.3.4 When Reference Types Are the Same

Two reference types are the *same compile-time type* if they have the same binary name (§13.1) and their type parameters, if any, are the same, applying this definition recursively. When two reference types are the same, they are sometimes said to be the *same class* or the *same interface*.

At run time, several reference types with the same binary name may be loaded simultaneously by different class loaders. These types may or may not represent the same type declaration. Even if two such types do represent the same type declaration, they are considered distinct.

Two reference types are the *same run-time type* if:

- They are both class or both interface types, are defined by the same class loader, and have the same binary name (§13.1), in which case they are sometimes said to be the *same run-time class* or the *same run-time interface*.
- They are both array types, and their component types are the same run-time type(§10).

4.4 Type Variables

A type variable (§4.4) is an unqualified identifier. Type variables are introduced by generic class declarations (§8.1.2) generic interface declarations (§9.1.2) generic method declarations (§8.4.4) and by generic constructor declarations (§8.8.4).

TypeParameter:
  TypeVariable TypeBound$_{opt}$

TypeBound:
  `extends` *ClassOrInterfaceType AdditionalBoundList*$_{opt}$

AdditionalBoundList:
  AdditionalBound AdditionalBoundList
  AdditionalBound

AdditionalBound:
  & InterfaceType

Type variables have an optional *bound*, T & I_1 ... I_n. The bound consists of either a type variable, or a class or interface type T possibly followed by further interface types I_1 , ..., I_n. If no bound is given for a type variable, `Object` is assumed. It is a compile-time error if any of the types I_1 ... I_n is a class type or type variable. The erasures (§4.6) of all constituent types of a bound must be pairwise different, or a compile-time error occurs. The order of types in a bound is only significant in that the erasure of a type variable is determined by the first type in its bound, and that a class type or type variable may only appear in the first position.

A type variable may not at the same time be a subtype of two interface types which are different parameterizations of the same generic interface.

See section §6.3 for the rules defining the scope of type variables.

The members of a type variable *X* with bound T & I_1 ... I_n are the members of the intersection type (§4.9) T & I_1 ... I_n appearing at the point where the type variable is declared.

DISCUSSION

The following example illustrates what members a type variable has.

```
package TypeVarMembers;

    class C {
        void mCDefault() {}
        public void mCPublic() {}
        private void mCPrivate() {}
        protected void mCProtected() {}
    }
    class CT extends C implements I {}
    interface I {
        void mI(); }
        <T extends C & I> void test(T t) {
            t.mI(); // OK
            t.mCDefault(); // OK
            t.mCPublic(); // OK
            t.mCPrivate(); // compile-time error
            t.mCProtected(); // OK
        }
    }
```

The type variable T has the same members as the intersection type `C & I`, which in turn has the same members as the empty class CT, defined in the same scope with equivalent supertypes. The members of an interface are always public, and therefore always inherited (unless overridden). Hence mI is a member of CT and of T. Among the members of C, all but `mCPrivate` are inherited by CT, and are therefore members of both CT and T.

If C had been declared in a different package than T, then the call to mCDefault would give rise to a compile-time error, as that member would not be accessible at the point where T is declared.

4.5 Parameterized Types

A *parameterized type* consists of a class or interface name C and an actual type argument list <T_1 , ... , T_n>. It is a compile time error if C is not the name of a generic class or interface, or if the number of type arguments in the actual type argument list differs from the number of declared type parameters of C. In the following, whenever we speak of a class or interface type, we include the generic version as well, unless explicitly excluded. Throughout this section, let A_1 , ... , A_n be the formal type parameters of C, and let be B_i be the declared bound of A_i. The notation [A_i := T_i] denotes substitution of the type variable A_i with the type T_i, for $1 \leq i \leq n$, and is used throughout this specification.

Let P = G<T_1, ..., T_n> be a parameterized type. It must be the case that, after P is subjected to capture conversion (§5.1.10) resulting in the type G<X1, ..., Xn>, for each actual type argument X_i, $1 \leq i \leq n$, X_i <: B_i[A_1 := X_1, ..., A_n := X_n] (§4.10), or a compile time error occurs.

DISCUSSION

Example: Parameterized types.

```
Vector<String>
Seq<Seq<A>>
Seq<String>.Zipper<Integer>
Collection<Integer>
Pair<String,String>

// Vector<int> -- illegal, primitive types cannot be arguments
// Pair<String> -- illegal, not enough arguments
// Pair<String,String,String> -- illegal, too many arguments
```

Two parameterized types are provably distinct if either of the following conditions hold:

- They are invocations of distinct generic type declarations.
- Any of their type arguments are provably distinct.

4.5.1 Type Arguments and Wildcards

Type arguments may be either reference types or *wildcards*.

TypeArguments:
    < *ActualTypeArgumentList* >

ActualTypeArgumentList:
    ActualTypeArgument
    ActualTypeArgumentList , *ActualTypeArgument*

ActualTypeArgument:
    ReferenceType
    Wildcard

Wildcard:
? WildcardBounds$_{Opt}$

WildcardBounds:
    extends ReferenceType
    super ReferenceType

DISCUSSION

Examples

```
void printCollection(Collection<?> c) {  // a wildcard collection
  for (Object o : c) {
    System.out.println(o);
  }
}
```

Note that using Collection<Object> as the type of the incoming parameter, c, would not be nearly as useful; the method could only be used with an actual parameter that had type Collection<Object>, which would be quite rare. In contrast, the use of an unbounded wildcard allows any kind of collection to be used as a parameter.

Wildcards are useful in situations where only partial knowledge about the type parameter is required.

DISCUSSION

Example - Wildcard parameterized types as component types of array types.

```
public Method getMethod(Class<?>[] parameterTypes) { ... }
```

Wildcards may be given explicit bounds, just like regular type variable declarations. An upper bound is signified by the syntax:

```
? extends B
```

, where *B* is the bound.

DISCUSSION

Example: Bounded wildcards.

```
boolean addAll(Collection<? extends E> c)
```

Here, the method is declared within the interface Collection<E>, and is designed to add all the elements of its incoming argument to the collection upon which it is invoked. A natural tendency would be to use Collection<E> as the type of c, but this is unnecessarily restrictive. An alternative would be to declare the method itself to be generic:

```
<T> boolean addAll(Collection<T> c)
```

This version is sufficiently flexible, but note that the type parameter is used only once in the signature. This reflects the fact that the type parameter is not being used to express any kind of interdependency between the type(s) of the argument(s), the return type and/or throws type. In the absence of such interdependency, generic methods are considered bad style, and wildcards are preferred.

Unlike ordinary type variables declared in a method signature, no type inference is required when using a wildcard. Consequently, it is permissible to declare lower bounds on a wildcard, using the syntax:

```
? super B
```

, where *B* is a lower bound.

DISCUSSION

Example: Lower bounds on wildcards.

```
Reference(T referent, ReferenceQueue<? super T> queue);
```

Here, the referent can be inserted into any queue whose element type is a super type of the type T of the referent.

Two type arguments are provably distinct if neither of the arguments is a type variable or wildcard, and the two arguments are not the same type.

DISCUSSION

The relationship of wildcards to established type theory is an interesting one, which we briefly allude to here.

Wildcards are a restricted form of existential types. Given a generic type declaration `G<T extends B>`, `G<?>` is roughly analogous to `Some X <: B. G<X>`.

Readers interested in a more comprehensive discussion should refer to *On Variance-Based Subtyping for Parametric Types* by Atsushi Igarashi and Mirko Viroli, in the proceedings of the 16th European Conference on Object Oriented Programming (ECOOP 2002).

Wildcards differ in certain details from the constructs described in the aforementioned paper, in particular in the use of capture conversion (§5.1.10) ratther than the `close` operation described by Igarashi and Viroli. For a formal account of wildcards, see *Wild FJ* by Mads Torgersen, Erik Ernst and Christian Plesner Hansen, in the 12th workshop on Foundations of Object Oriented Programming (FOOL 2005).

DISCUSSION

Historically, wildcards are a direct descendant of the work by Atsushi Igarashi and Mirko Viroli. This work itself builds upon earlier work by Kresten Thorup and Mads Torgersen ("Unifying Genericity", ECOOP 99), as well as a long tradition of work on declaration based variance that goes back to Pierre America's work on POOL (OOPSLA 89)

4.5.1.1 *Type Argument Containment and Equivalence*

A type argument TA_1 is said to *contain* another type argument TA_2, written $TA_2 <= TA_1$, if the set of types denoted by TA_2 is provably a subset of the set of types denoted by TA_1 under the following rules (where <: denotes subtyping (§4.10)):

- `? extends T` <= `? extends S` if $T <: S$
- `? super T` <= `? super S` if $S <: T$
- `T` <= `T`
- `T` <= `? extends T`
- `T` <= `? super T`

4.5.2 Members and Constructors of Parameterized Types

Let C be a class or interface declaration with formal type parameters $A_1,...,A_n$, and let $C<T_1, ..., T_n>$ be an invocation of C, where, for $1 \le i \le n$, T_i are types (rather than wildcards). Then:

- Let m be a member or constructor declaration in C, whose type as declared is T. Then the type of m (§8.2, §8.8.6) in the type $C<T_1, ..., T_n>$, is $T[A_1 := T_1, ..., A_n := T_n]$.
- Let m be a member or constructor declaration in D, where D is a class extended by C or an interface implemented by C. Let $D<U_1, ..., U_k>$ be the supertype of $C<T_1, ..., T_n>$ that corresponds to D. Then the type of m in $C<T_1, ..., T_n>$ is the type of m in $D<U_1, ..., U_k>$.

If any of the type arguments to a parameterized type are wildcards, the type of its members and constructors is undefined.

DISCUSSION

This is of no consequence, as it is impossible to access a member of a parameterized type without performing capture conversion (§5.1.10), and it is impossible to use a wildcard type after the keyword new in a class instance creation expression

4.6 Type Erasure

Type erasure is a mapping from types (possibly including parameterized types and type variables) to types (that are never parameterized types or type variables). We write |*T*| for the erasure of type *T*. The erasure mapping is defined as follows.

- The erasure of a parameterized type (§4.5) $G<T_1, \ldots, T_n>$ is |*G*|.
- The erasure of a nested type `T.C` is |*T*|`.C`.
- The erasure of an array type `T[]` is |*T*|`[]`.
- The erasure of a type variable (§4.4) is the erasure of its leftmost bound.
- The erasure of every other type is the type itself.

The erasure of a method signature `s` is a signature consisting of the same name as `s`, and the erasures of all the formal parameter types given in `s`.

4.7 Reifiable Types

Because some type information is erased during compilation, not all types are available at run time. Types that are completely available at run time are known as *reifiable types*. A type is *reifiable* if and only if one of the following holds:

- It refers to a non-generic type declaration.
- It is a parameterized type in which all type arguments are unbounded wildcards (§4.5.1).
- It is a raw type (§4.8).
- It is a primitive type (§4.2).
- It is an array type (§10.1) whose component type is reifiable.

DISCUSSION

The decision not to make all generic types reifiable is one of the most crucial, and controversial design decisions involving the language's type system.

Ultimately, the most important motivation for this decision is compatibility with existing code.

Naively, the addition of new constructs such as genericity has no implications for pre-existing code. The programming language per se, is compatible with earlier versions as long as every program written in the previous versions retains its meaning in the new version. However, this notion, which may be termed *language compatibility*, is of purely theoretical interest. Real programs (even trivial ones, such as "Hello World") are composed of several compilation units, some of which are provided by the Java platform (such as elements of `java.lang` or `java.util`).

In practice then, the minimum requirement is *platform compatibillity* - that any program written for the prior version of the platform continues to function unchanged in the new platform.

One way to provide platform compatibillity is to leave existing platform functionality unchanged, only adding new functionality. For example, rather than modify the existing Collections hierarchy in `java.util`, one might introduce a new library utilizing genericity.

The disadvantages of such a scheme is that it is extremely difficult for pre-existing clients of the Collection library to migrate to the new library. Collections are used to exchange data between independently developed modules; if a vendor decides to switch to the new, generic, library, that vendor must also distribute two versions of their code, to be compatible with their clients. Libraries that are dependent on other vendors code cannot be modified to use genericity until the supplier's library is updated. If two modules are mutually dependent, the changes must be made simultaneously.

Clearly, platform compatibility, as outlined above, does not provide a realistic path for adoption of a pervasive new feature such as genericity. Therefore, the design of the generic type system seeks to support *migration compatibility*. Migration compatibiliy allows the evolution of existing code to take advantage of generics without imposing dependencies between independently developed software modules.

The price of migration compatibility is that a full and sound reification of the generic type system is not possible, at least while the migration is taking place.

4.8 Raw Types

To facilitate interfacing with non-generic legacy code, it is also possible to use as a type the erasure (§4.6) of a parameterized type (§4.5). Such a type is called a *raw type*.

More precisely, a raw type is define to be either:

- The name of a generic type declaration used without any accompanying actual type parameters.
- Any non-static type member of a raw type *R* that is not inherited from a superclass or superinterface of *R*.

DISCUSSION

The latter point may not be immediately self evident. Presenting for your consideration, then, the following example:

```
class Outer<T>{
    T t;
    class Inner {
        T setOuterT(T t1) {t = t1;return t;}
    }
}
```

The type of the member(s) of `Inner` depends on the type parameter of `Outer`. If `Outer` is raw, `Inner` must be treated as raw as well, as their is no valid binding for T.

This rule applies only to type members that are not inherited. Inherited type members that depend on type variables will be inherited as raw types as a consequence of the rule that the supertypes of a raw type are erased, described later in this section.

DISCUSSION

Another implication of the rules above is that a generic inner class of a raw type can itself only be used as a raw type:

```
class Outer<T>{
    class Inner<S> {
        S s;
    }
}
```

it is not possible to access `Inner` as partially raw type (a "rare" type)

```
Outer.Inner<Double> x = null; // illegal
Double d = x.s;
```

because `Outer` itself is raw, so are all its inner classes, including `Inner`, and so it is not possible to pass any type parameters to it.

The use of raw types is allowed only as a concession to compatibility of legacy code. The use of raw types in code written after the introduction of genericity into the Java programming language is strongly discouraged. ***It is possible that future versions of the Java programming language will disallow the use of raw types***.

It is a compile-time error to attempt to use a type member of a parameterized type as a raw type.

DISCUSSION

This means that the ban on "rare" types extends to the case where the qualifying type is parameterized, but we attempt to use the inner class as a raw type:

```
Outer<Integer>.Inner x = null; // illegal
```

This is the opposite of the case we discussed above. There is no practical justification for this half baked type. In legacy code, no type parameters are used. In non-legacy code, we should use the generic types correctly and pass all the required actual type parameters.

DISCUSSION

Variables of a raw type can be assigned from values of any of the type's parametric instances.

For instance, it is possible to assign a `Vector<String>` to a `Vector`, based on the subtyping rules (§4.10.2).

The reverse assignment from `Vector` to `Vector<String>` is unsafe (since the raw vector might have had a different element type), but is still permitted using unchecked conversion (§5.1.9) in order to enable interfacing with legacy code. In this case, a compiler will issue an unchecked warning.

The superclasses (respectively, superinterfaces) of a raw type are the erasures of the superclasses (superinterfaces) of any of its parameterized invocations.

The type of a constructor (§8.8), instance method (§8.8, §9.4), or non-static field (§8.3) `M` of a raw type `C` that is not inherited from its superclasses or superinterfaces is the erasure of its type in the generic declaration corresponding to `C`. The type of a static member of a raw type `C` is the same as its type in the generic declaration corresponding to `C`.

It is a compile-time error to pass actual type parameters to a non-static type member of a raw type that is not inherited from its superclasses or superinterfaces.

To make sure that potential violations of the typing rules are always flagged, some accesses to members of a raw type will result in warning messages. The rules for generating warnings when accessing members or constructors of raw types are as follows:

- An invocation of a method or constructor of a raw type generates an unchecked warning if erasure changes any of the types of any of the arguments to the method or constructor.
- An assignment to a field of a raw type generates an unchecked warning (§5.1.9) if erasure changes the field's type.

No unchecked warning is required for a method call when the argument types do not change (even if the result type and/or throws clause changes), for reading from a field, or for a class instance creation of a raw type.

The supertype of a class may be a raw type. Member accesses for the class are treated as normal, and member accesses for the supertype are treated as for raw types. In the constructor of the class, calls to super are treated as method calls on a raw type.

DISCUSSION

Example: Raw types.

```
class Cell<E>
  E value;
  Cell (E v) { value=v; }
  A get() { return value; }
  void set(E v) { value=v; }
}

Cell x = new Cell<String>("abc");
x.value;          // OK, has type Object
x.get();          // OK, has type Object
x.set("def");     // unchecked warning
```

DISCUSSION

For example,

```
import java.util.*;

class NonGeneric {

    Collection<Number> myNumbers(){return null;}
}

abstract class RawMembers<T> extends NonGeneric implements Collec-
tion<String> {
    static Collection<NonGeneric> cng =
                                    new ArrayList<NonGeneric>();

    public static void main(String[] args) {
        RawMembers rw = null;
        Collection<Number> cn = rw.myNumbers(); // ok
        Iterator<String> is = rw.iterator(); // unchecked warning
        Collection<NonGeneric> cnn = rw.cng; // ok - static member
    }
}
```

`RawMembers<T>` inherits the method

`Iterator<String> iterator()`

from the `Collection<String>` superinterface. However, the type `RawMembers` inherits `iterator()` from the erasure of its superinterface, which means that the return type of the member `iterator()` is the erasure of `Iterator<<String>`, `Iterator`. As a result, the attempt to assign to `rw.iterator()` requires an unchecked conversion (§5.1.9) from `Iterator` to `Iterator<String>`, causing an unchecked warning to be issued.

In contrast, the static member `cng` retains its full parameterized type even when accessed through a object of raw type (note that access to a static member through an instance is considered bad style and is to be discouraged). The member `myNumbers` is inherited from the `NonGeneric` (whose erasure is also `NonGeneric`) and so retains its full parameterized type.

DISCUSSION

Raw types are closly related to wildcards. Both are based on existential types. Raw types can be thought of as wildcards whose type rules are deliberately unsound, to accommodate interaction with legacy code.

Historically, raw types preceded wildcards; they were first introduced in GJ, and described in the paper *Making the future safe for the past: Adding Genericity to the Java Programming Language* by Gilad Bracha, Martin Odersky, David Stoutamire, and Philip

Wadler, in Proc. of the ACM Conf. on Object-Oriented Programming, Systems, Languages and Applications, (OOPSLA 98) October 1998.

4.9 Intersection Types

An intersection type takes the form T_1 & ... & T_n, $n > 0$, where T_i, $1 \le i \le n$, are type expressions. Intersection types arise in the processes of capture conversion (§5.1.10) and type inference (§15.12.2.7). It is not possible to write an intersection type directly as part of a program; no syntax supports this. The values of an intersection type are those objects that are values of all of the types T_i, for $1 \le i \le n$.

The members of an intersection type T_1 & ... & T_n are determined as follows:

- For each T_i, $1 \le i \le n$, let C_i be the most specific class or array type such that T_i <: C_i Then there must be some T_k <: C_k such that C_k <: C_i for any i, $1 \le i \le n$, or a compile-time error occurs.
- For $1 \le j \le n$, if T_j is a type variable, then let IT_j be an interface whose members are the same as the public members of T_j; otherwise, if T_j is an interface, then let IT_j be T_j.
- Then the intersection type has the same members as a class type (§8) with an empty body, direct superclass C_k and direct superinterfaces IT_1 , ..., IT_n, declared in the same package in which the intersection type appears.

DISCUSSION

It is worth dwelling upon the distinction between intersection types and the bounds of type variables. Every type variable bound induces an intersection type. This intersection type is often trivial (i.e., consists of a single type).

The form of a bound is restricted (only the first element may be a class or type variable, and only one type variable may appear in the bound) to preclude certain awkward situations coming into existence. However, capture conversion can lead to the creation of type variables whose bounds are more general (e.g., array types).

4.10 Subtyping

The subtype and supertype relations are binary relations on types. The *supertypes* of a type are obtained by reflexive and transitive closure over the direct supertype relation, written $S >_1 T$, which is defined by rules given later in this section. We write $S :> T$ to indicate that the supertype relation holds between S and T. S is a *proper supertype* of T, written $S > T$, if $S :> T$ and $S \neq T$.

The *subtypes* of a type T are all types U such that T is a supertype of U, and the null type. We write $T <: S$ to indicate that that the subtype relation holds between types T and S. T is a *proper subtype* of S, written $T < S$, if $T <: S$ and $S \neq T$. T is a *direct subtype* of S, written $T <_1 S$, if $S >_1 T$.
Subtyping does not extend through generic types: $T <: U$ does not imply that $C<T> <: C<U>$.

4.10.1 Subtyping among Primitive Types

The following rules define the direct supertype relation among the primitive types:

double $>_1$ float
float $>_1$ long
long $>_1$ int
int $>_1$ char
int $>_1$ short
short $>_1$ byte

4.10.2 Subtyping among Class and Interface Types

Let C be a type declaration (§4.12.6, §8.1, §9.1) with zero or more type parameters (§4.4) $F_1, ..., F_n$ which have corresponding bounds $B_1, ..., B_n$. That type declaration defines a set of parameterized types (§4.5) $C_1<T_1, ..., T_n>$, where each argument type T_i ranges over all types that are subtypes of all types listed in the corresponding bound. That is, for each bound type S_i in B_i, T_i is a subtype of $S_i[F_1 := T_1, ..., F_n := T_n]$.
Given a type declaration for $C<F_1, ..., Fn>$, the *direct supertypes* of the parameterized type (§4.5) $C<F_1, ..., F_n>$ are all of the following:

- the direct superclasses of C.
- the direct superinterfaces of C.

- The type `Object`, if *C* is an interface type with no direct superinterfaces.
- The raw type *C*.

The direct supertypes of the type $C<T_1, ..., T_n>$, where T_i, $1 \le i \le n$, is a type, are $D<U_1$ *theta*$, ..., U_k$ *theta*$>$, where

- $D<U_1, ..., U_k>$ is a direct supertype of $C<F_1, ..., F_n>$, and *theta* is the substitution $[F_1 := T_1, ..., F_n := T_n]$.
- $C<S_1, ..., S_n>$ where S_i contains (§4.5.1.1) T_i for $1 \le i \le n$.

The direct supertypes of the type $C<R_1, ..., R_n>$, where at least one of the R_i, $1 \le i \le n$, is a wildcard type argument, are the direct supertypes of $C<X_1, ..., X_n>$, where

$C<X_1, ..., X_n>$ is the result of applying capture conversion (§5.1.10) to $C<R_1, ..., R_n>$.

The direct supertypes of an intersection type (§4.9) T_1 & ... & T_n, are T_i, $1 \le i \le n$.

The direct supertypes of a type variable (§4.4) are the types listed in its bound.

The direct supertypes of the null type are all reference types other than the null type itself.

In addition to the above rules, a type variable is a direct supertype of its lower bound.

4.10.3 Subtyping among Array Types

The following rules define the direct subtype relation among array types:

- If *S* and *T* are both reference types, then $S[] >_1 T[]$ iff $S >_1 T$.
- `Object` $>_1$ `Object[]`
- `Cloneable` $>_1$ `Object[]`
- `java.io.Serializable` $>_1$ `Object[]`
- If *p* is a primitive type, then:
  - `Object` $>_1$ *p[]*
  - `Cloneable` $>_1$ *p[]*
  - `java.io.Serializable` $>_1$ *p[]*

4.11 Where Types Are Used

Types are used when they appear in declarations or in certain expressions.

The following code fragment contains one or more instances of most kinds of usage of a type:

```
import java.util.Random;
class MiscMath<T extends Number>{

    int divisor;
    MiscMath(int divisor) {
        this.divisor = divisor;
    }
    float ratio(long l) {
        try {
            l /= divisor;
        } catch (Exception e) {
            if (e instanceof ArithmeticException)
              l = Long.MAX_VALUE;
            else
              l = 0;
        }
        return (float)l;
    }
    double gausser() {
        Random r = new Random();
        double[] val = new double[2];
        val[0] = r.nextGaussian();
        val[1] = r.nextGaussian();
        return (val[0] + val[1]) / 2;
    }
    Collection<Number> fromArray(Number[] na) {
        Collection<Number> cn = new ArrayList<Number>();
        for (Number n : na) {
            cn.add(n)
        }
        return cn;
    }
    void <S> loop(S s){ this.<S>loop(s);}


}
```

In this example, types are used in declarations of the following:

- Imported types (§7.5); here the type `Random`, imported from the type `java.util.Random` of the package `java.util`, is declared
- Fields, which are the class variables and instance variables of classes (§8.3), and constants of interfaces (§9.3); here the field `divisor` in the class `MiscMath` is declared to be of type `int`
- Method parameters (§8.4.1); here the parameter `l` of the method `ratio` is declared to be of type `long`
- Method results (§8.4); here the result of the method `ratio` is declared to be of type `float`, and the result of the method `gausser` is declared to be of type `double`
- Constructor parameters (§8.8.1); here the parameter of the constructor for `MiscMath` is declared to be of type `int`
- Local variables (§14.4, §14.14); the local variables `r` and `val` of the method `gausser` are declared to be of types `Random` and `double[]` (array of `double`)
- Exception handler parameters (§14.20); here the exception handler parameter `e` of the `catch` clause is declared to be of type `Exception`
- Type variables (§4.4); here the type variable `T` has `Number` as its declared bound.

and in expressions of the following kinds:

- Class instance creations (§15.9); here a local variable `r` of method `gausser` is initialized by a class instance creation expression that uses the type `Random`
- Generic class (§8.1.2) instance creations (§15.9); here `Number` is used as a type argument in the expression `new ArrayList<Number>()`
- Array creations (§15.10); here the local variable `val` of method `gausser` is initialized by an array creation expression that creates an array of `double` with size 2
- Generic method (§8.4.4) or constructor (§8.8.4) invocations (§15.12); here the method `loop` calls itself with an explicit type argument `S`
- Casts (§15.16); here the `return` statement of the method `ratio` uses the `float` type in a cast
- The `instanceof` operator (§15.20.2); here the `instanceof` operator tests whether `e` is assignment compatible with the type `ArithmeticException`

. Types are also used as arguments to parameterized types; here the type `Number` is used as an argument in the parameterized type `Collection<Number>`.

4.12 Variables

A variable is a storage location and has an associated type, sometimes called its *compile-time type*, that is either a primitive type (§4.2) or a reference type (§4.3). A variable's value is changed by an assignment (§15.26) or by a prefix or postfix `++` (increment) or `--` (decrement) operator (§15.14.2, §15.14.3, §15.15.1, §15.15.2).

Compatibility of the value of a variable with its type is guaranteed by the design of the Java programming language, as long as a program does not give rise to unchecked warnings (§4.12.2.1). Default values are compatible (§4.12.5) and all assignments to a variable are checked for assignment compatibility (§5.2), usually at compile time, but, in a single case involving arrays, a run-time check is made (§10.10).

4.12.1 Variables of Primitive Type

A variable of a primitive type always holds a value of that exact primitive type.

4.12.2 Variables of Reference Type

A variable of a class type *T* can hold a null reference or a reference to an instance of class *T* or of any class that is a subclass of *T*. A variable of an interface type can hold a null reference or a reference to any instance of any class that implements the interface.

DISCUSSION

Note that a variable is not guaranteed to always refer to a subtype of its declared type, but only to subclasses or subinterfaces of the declared type. This is due to the possibility of heap pollution discussed below.

If *T* is a primitive type, then a variable of type "array of *T*" can hold a null reference or a reference to any array of type "array of *T*"; if *T* is a reference type, then a variable of type "array of *T*" can hold a null reference or a reference to any array of type "array of *S*" such that type *S* is a subclass or subinterface of type *T*. In addition, a variable of type `Object[]` can hold an array of any reference type.

A variable of type `Object` can hold a null reference or a reference to any object, whether class instance or array.

4.12.2.1 *Heap Pollution*

It is possible that a variable of a parameterized type refers to an object that is not of that parameterized type. This situation is known as *heap pollution*. This situation can only occur if the program performed some operation that would give rise to an unchecked warning at compile-time.

DISCUSSION

For example, the code:

```
List l = new ArrayList<Number>();
List<String> ls = l; // unchecked warning
```

gives rise to an unchecked warning, because it is not possible to ascertain, either at compile-time (within the limits of the compile-time type checking rules) or at run-time, whether the variable l does indeed refer to a `List<String>`.

If the code above is executed, heap pollution arises, as the variable ls, declared to be a `List<String>`, refers to a value that is not in fact a `List<String>`.

The problem cannot be identified at run-time because type variables are not reified, and thus instances do not carry any information at run-time regarding the actual type parameters used to create them.

In a simple example as given above, it may appear that it should be straightforward to identify the situation at compile-time and give a compilation error. However, in the general (and typical) case, the value of the variable l may be the result of an invocation of a separately compiled method, or its value may depend upon arbitrary control flow.

The code above is therefore very atypical, and indeed very bad style.

Assignment from a value of a raw type to a variable of a parameterized type should only be used when combining legacy code which does not make use of parameterized types with more modern code that does.

If no operation that requires an unchecked warning to be issued takes place, heap pollution cannot occur. Note that this does not imply that heap pollution only occurs if an unchecked warning actually occurred. It is possible to run a program where some of the binaries were compiled by a compiler for an older version of the Java programming language, or by a compiler that allows the unchecked warnings to suppressed. This practice is unhealthy at best.

Conversely, it is possible that despite executing code that could (and perhaps did) give rise to an unchecked warning, no heap pollution takes place. Indeed, good programming practice requires that the programmer satisfy herself that despite any unchecked warning, the code is correct and heap pollution will not occur.

The variable will always refer to an object that is an instance of a class that implements the parameterized type.

DISCUSSION

For instance, the value of `l` in the example above is always a `List`.

4.12.3 Kinds of Variables

There are seven kinds of variables:

1. A *class variable* is a field declared using the keyword `static` within a class declaration (§8.3.1.1), or with or without the keyword `static` within an interface declaration (§9.3). A class variable is created when its class or interface is prepared (§12.3.2) and is initialized to a default value (§4.12.5). The class variable effectively ceases to exist when its class or interface is unloaded (§12.7).
2. An *instance variable* is a field declared within a class declaration without using the keyword `static` (§8.3.1.1). If a class *T* has a field *a* that is an instance variable, then a new instance variable *a* is created and initialized to a default value (§4.12.5) as part of each newly created object of class *T* or of any class that is a subclass of *T* (§8.1.4). The instance variable effectively ceases to exist when the object of which it is a field is no longer referenced, after any necessary finalization of the object (§12.6) has been completed.
3. *Array components* are unnamed variables that are created and initialized to default values (§4.12.5) whenever a new object that is an array is created (§15.10). The array components effectively cease to exist when the array is no longer referenced. See §10 for a description of arrays.
4. *Method parameters* (§8.4.1) name argument values passed to a method. For every parameter declared in a method declaration, a new parameter variable is created each time that method is invoked (§15.12). The new variable is initialized with the corresponding argument value from the method invocation. The method parameter effectively ceases to exist when the execution of the body of the method is complete.
5. *Constructor parameters* (§8.8.1) name argument values passed to a constructor. For every parameter declared in a constructor declaration, a new parameter variable is created each time a class instance creation expression (§15.9) or

explicit constructor invocation (§8.8.7) invokes that constructor. The new variable is initialized with the corresponding argument value from the creation expression or constructor invocation. The constructor parameter effectively ceases to exist when the execution of the body of the constructor is complete.

6. An *exception-handler parameter* is created each time an exception is caught by a `catch` clause of a `try` statement (§14.20). The new variable is initialized with the actual object associated with the exception (§11.3, §14.18). The exception-handler parameter effectively ceases to exist when execution of the block associated with the `catch` clause is complete.

7. *Local variables* are declared by local variable declaration statements (§14.4). Whenever the flow of control enters a block (§14.2) or `for` statement (§14.14), a new variable is created for each local variable declared in a local variable declaration statement immediately contained within that block or `for` statement. A local variable declaration statement may contain an expression which initializes the variable. The local variable with an initializing expression is not initialized, however, until the local variable declaration statement that declares it is executed. (The rules of definite assignment (§16) prevent the value of a local variable from being used before it has been initialized or otherwise assigned a value.) The local variable effectively ceases to exist when the execution of the block or `for` statement is complete.

   Were it not for one exceptional situation, a local variable could always be regarded as being created when its local variable declaration statement is executed. The exceptional situation involves the `switch` statement (§14.11), where it is possible for control to enter a block but bypass execution of a local variable declaration statement. Because of the restrictions imposed by the rules of definite assignment (§16), however, the local variable declared by such a bypassed local variable declaration statement cannot be used before it has been definitely assigned a value by an assignment expression (§15.26).

The following example contains several different kinds of variables:

```
class Point {
    static int numPoints;  // numPoints is a class variable
    int x, y;              // x and y are instance variables
    int[] w = new int[10]; // w[0] is an array component
    int setX(int x) {      // x is a method parameter
        int oldx = this.x; // oldx is a local variable
        this.x = x;
        return oldx;
    }
}
```

4.12.4 `final` Variables

A variable can be declared `final`. A final variable may only be assigned to once. It is a compile time error if a final variable is assigned to unless it is definitely unassigned (§16) immediately prior to the assignment.

A *blank final* is a final variable whose declaration lacks an initializer.

Once a `final` variable has been assigned, it always contains the same value. If a `final` variable holds a reference to an object, then the state of the object may be changed by operations on the object, but the variable will always refer to the same object. This applies also to arrays, because arrays are objects; if a `final` variable holds a reference to an array, then the components of the array may be changed by operations on the array, but the variable will always refer to the same array.

Declaring a variable `final` can serve as useful documentation that its value will not change and can help avoid programming errors.

In the example:

```
class Point {
    int x, y;
    int useCount;
    Point(int x, int y) { this.x = x; this.y = y; }
    final static Point origin = new Point(0, 0);
}
```

the class `Point` declares a final class variable `origin`. The `origin` variable holds a reference to an object that is an instance of class `Point` whose coordinates are (0, 0). The value of the variable `Point.origin` can never change, so it always refers to the same `Point` object, the one created by its initializer. However, an operation on this `Point` object might change its state—for example, modifying its `useCount` or even, misleadingly, its `x` or `y` coordinate.

We call a variable, of primitive type or type `String`, that is `final` and initialized with a compile-time constant expression (§15.28) a *constant variable*. Whether a variable is a constant variable or not may have implications with respect to class initialization (§12.4.1), binary compatibility (§13.1, §13.4.9) and definite assignment (§16).

4.12.5 Initial Values of Variables

Every variable in a program must have a value before its value is used:

- Each class variable, instance variable, or array component is initialized with a *default value* when it is created (§15.9, §15.10):
  - For type `byte`, the default value is zero, that is, the value of `(byte)0`.

- For type `short`, the default value is zero, that is, the value of `(short)0`.
- For type `int`, the default value is zero, that is, `0`.
- For type `long`, the default value is zero, that is, `0L`.
- For type `float`, the default value is positive zero, that is, `0.0f`.
- For type `double`, the default value is positive zero, that is, `0.0d`.
- For type `char`, the default value is the null character, that is, `'\u0000'`.
- For type `boolean`, the default value is `false`.
- For all reference types (§4.3), the default value is `null`.

- Each method parameter (§8.4.1) is initialized to the corresponding argument value provided by the invoker of the method (§15.12).
- Each constructor parameter (§8.8.1) is initialized to the corresponding argument value provided by a class instance creation expression (§15.9) or explicit constructor invocation (§8.8.7).
- An exception-handler parameter (§14.20) is initialized to the thrown object representing the exception (§11.3, §14.18).
- A local variable (§14.4, §14.14) must be explicitly given a value before it is used, by either initialization (§14.4) or assignment (§15.26), in a way that can be verified by the compiler using the rules for definite assignment (§16).

The example program:

```
class Point {
    static int npoints;
    int x, y;
    Point root;
}

class Test {
    public static void main(String[] args) {
        System.out.println("npoints=" + Point.npoints);
        Point p = new Point();
        System.out.println("p.x=" + p.x + ", p.y=" + p.y);
        System.out.println("p.root=" + p.root);
    }
}
```

prints:

```
npoints=0
p.x=0, p.y=0
p.root=null
```

illustrating the default initialization of `npoints`, which occurs when the class `Point` is prepared (§12.3.2), and the default initialization of `x`, `y`, and `root`, which occurs when a new `Point` is instantiated. See §12 for a full description of all aspects of loading, linking, and initialization of classes and interfaces, plus a description of the instantiation of classes to make new class instances.

4.12.6 Types, Classes, and Interfaces

In the Java programming language, every variable and every expression has a type that can be determined at compile time. The type may be a primitive type or a reference type. Reference types include class types and interface types. Reference types are introduced by *type declarations*, which include class declarations (§8.1) and interface declarations (§9.1). We often use the term *type* to refer to either a class or an interface.

Every object belongs to some particular class: the class that was mentioned in the creation expression that produced the object, the class whose `Class` object was used to invoke a reflective method to produce the object, or the `String` class for objects implicitly created by the string concatenation operator + (§15.18.1). This class is called the *class of the object*. (Arrays also have a class, as described at the end of this section.) An object is said to be an instance of its class and of all superclasses of its class.

Sometimes a variable or expression is said to have a "run-time type". This refers to the class of the object referred to by the value of the variable or expression at run time, assuming that the value is not `null`.

The compile time type of a variable is always declared, and the compile time type of an expression can be deduced at compile time. The compile time type limits the possible values that the variable can hold or the expression can produce at run time. If a run-time value is a reference that is not `null`, it refers to an object or array that has a class, and that class will necessarily be compatible with the compile-time type.

Even though a variable or expression may have a compile-time type that is an interface type, there are no instances of interfaces. A variable or expression whose type is an interface type can reference any object whose class implements (§8.1.5) that interface.

Here is an example of creating new objects and of the distinction between the type of a variable and the class of an object:

```
public interface Colorable {
    void setColor(byte r, byte g, byte b);
}
class Point { int x, y; }
class ColoredPoint extends Point implements Colorable {
```

```
    byte r, g, b;
    public void setColor(byte rv, byte gv, byte bv) {
        r = rv; g = gv; b = bv;
    }
}
class Test {
    public static void main(String[] args) {
        Point p = new Point();
        ColoredPoint cp = new ColoredPoint();
        p = cp;
        Colorable c = cp;
    }
}
```

In this example:

- The local variable `p` of the method `main` of class `Test` has type `Point` and is initially assigned a reference to a new instance of class `Point`.
- The local variable `cp` similarly has as its type `ColoredPoint`, and is initially assigned a reference to a new instance of class `ColoredPoint`.
- The assignment of the value of `cp` to the variable `p` causes `p` to hold a reference to a `ColoredPoint` object. This is permitted because `ColoredPoint` is a subclass of `Point`, so the class `ColoredPoint` is assignment compatible (§5.2) with the type `Point`. A `ColoredPoint` object includes support for all the methods of a `Point`. In addition to its particular fields `r`, `g`, and `b`, it has the fields of class `Point`, namely `x` and `y`.
- The local variable `c` has as its type the interface type `Colorable`, so it can hold a reference to any object whose class implements `Colorable`; specifically, it can hold a reference to a `ColoredPoint`.

DISCUSSION

Note that an expression such as `new Colorable()` is not valid because it is not possible to create an instance of an interface, only of a class.

Every array also has a class; the method `getClass`, when invoked for an array object, will return a class object (of class `Class`) that represents the class of the array.

The classes for arrays have strange names that are not valid identifiers; for example, the class for an array of `int` components has the name "`[I`" and so the value of the expression:

```
new int[10].getClass().getName()
```

is the string `"[I"`; see the specification of `Class.getName` for details.

Oft on the dappled turf at ease
I sit, and play with similes,
Loose types of things through all degrees.
—William Wordsworth, *To the Same Flower*

CHAPTER 5

Conversions and Promotions

Thou art not for the fashion of these times,
Where none will sweat but for promotion.
—William Shakespeare, *As You Like It*, Act II, scene iii

EVERY expression written in the Java programming language has a type that can be deduced from the structure of the expression and the types of the literals, variables, and methods mentioned in the expression. It is possible, however, to write an expression in a context where the type of the expression is not appropriate. In some cases, this leads to an error at compile time. In other cases, the context may be able to accept a type that is related to the type of the expression; as a convenience, rather than requiring the programmer to indicate a type conversion explicitly, the language performs an implicit *conversion* from the type of the expression to a type acceptable for its surrounding context.

A specific conversion from type *S* to type *T* allows an expression of type *S* to be treated at compile time as if it had type *T* instead. In some cases this will require a corresponding action at run time to check the validity of the conversion or to translate the run-time value of the expression into a form appropriate for the new type *T*. For example:

- A conversion from type `Object` to type `Thread` requires a run-time check to make sure that the run-time value is actually an instance of class `Thread` or one of its subclasses; if it is not, an exception is thrown.
- A conversion from type `Thread` to type `Object` requires no run-time action; `Thread` is a subclass of `Object`, so any reference produced by an expression of type `Thread` is a valid reference value of type `Object`.
- A conversion from type `int` to type `long` requires run-time sign-extension of a 32-bit integer value to the 64-bit `long` representation. No information is lost.

A conversion from type `double` to type `long` requires a nontrivial translation from a 64-bit floating-point value to the 64-bit integer representation. Depending on the actual run-time value, information may be lost.

In every conversion context, only certain specific conversions are permitted. For convenience of description, the specific conversions that are possible in the Java programming language are grouped into several broad categories:

- Identity conversions
- Widening primitive conversions
- Narrowing primitive conversions
- Widening reference conversions
- Narrowing reference conversions
- Boxing conversions
- Unboxing conversions
- Unchecked conversions
- Capture conversions
- String conversions
- Value set conversions

There are five *conversion contexts* in which conversion of expressions may occur. Each context allows conversions in some of the categories named above but not others. The term "conversion" is also used to describe the process of choosing a specific conversion for such a context. For example, we say that an expression that is an actual argument in a method invocation is subject to "method invocation conversion," meaning that a specific conversion will be implicitly chosen for that expression according to the rules for the method invocation argument context.

One conversion context is the operand of a numeric operator such as + or *. The conversion process for such operands is called *numeric promotion*. Promotion is special in that, in the case of binary operators, the conversion chosen for one operand may depend in part on the type of the other operand expression.

This chapter first describes the eleven categories of conversions (§5.1), including the special conversions to `String` allowed for the string concatenation operator +. Then the five conversion contexts are described:

- Assignment conversion (§5.2, §15.26) converts the type of an expression to the type of a specified variable. Assignment conversion may cause a `Out-OfMemoryError` (as a result of boxing conversion (§5.1.7)), a `NullPointer-`

`Exception` (as a result of unboxing conversion (§5.1.8)), or a `ClassCastException` (as a result of an unchecked conversion (§5.1.9)) to be thrown at run time.

- Method invocation conversion (§5.3, §15.9, §15.12) is applied to each argument in a method or constructor invocation and, except in one case, performs the same conversions that assignment conversion does. Method invocation conversion may cause a `OutOfMemoryError` (as a result of boxing conversion (§5.1.7)), a `NullPointerException` (as a result of unboxing conversion (§5.1.8)), or a `ClassCastException` (as a result of an unchecked conversion (§5.1.9)) to be thrown at run time.
- Casting conversion (§5.5) converts the type of an expression to a type explicitly specified by a cast operator (§15.16). It is more inclusive than assignment or method invocation conversion, allowing any specific conversion other than a string conversion, but certain casts to a reference type may cause an exception at run time.
- String conversion (§5.4, §15.18.1) allows any type to be converted to type `String`.
- Numeric promotion (§5.6) brings the operands of a numeric operator to a common type so that an operation can be performed.

Here are some examples of the various contexts for conversion:

```
class Test {
    public static void main(String[] args) {
        // Casting conversion (§5.4) of a float literal to
        // type int. Without the cast operator, this would
        // be a compile-time error, because this is a
        // narrowing conversion (§5.1.3):
        int i = (int)12.5f;

        // String conversion (§5.4) of i’s int value:
        System.out.println("(int)12.5f==" + i);

        // Assignment conversion (§5.2) of i’s value to type
        // float. This is a widening conversion (§5.1.2):
        float f = i;

        // String conversion of f's float value:
        System.out.println("after float widening: " + f);

        // Numeric promotion (§5.6) of i’s value to type
        // float. This is a binary numeric promotion.
        // After promotion, the operation is float*float:
```

```
            System.out.print(f);
            f = f * i;
            // Two string conversions of i and f:
            System.out.println("*" + i + "==" + f);
            // Method invocation conversion (§5.3) of f's value
            // to type double, needed because the method Math.sin
            // accepts only a double argument:
            double d = Math.sin(f);
            // Two string conversions of f and d:
            System.out.println("Math.sin(" + f + ")==" + d);
        }
    }
```

which produces the output:

```
(int)12.5f==12
after float widening: 12.0
12.0*12==144.0
Math.sin(144.0)==-0.49102159389846934
```

5.1 Kinds of Conversion

Specific type conversions in the Java programming language are divided into the following categories.

5.1.1 Identity Conversions

A conversion from a type to that same type is permitted for any type.

This may seem trivial, but it has two practical consequences. First, it is always permitted for an expression to have the desired type to begin with, thus allowing the simply stated rule that every expression is subject to conversion, if only a trivial identity conversion. Second, it implies that it is permitted for a program to include redundant cast operators for the sake of clarity.

5.1.2 Widening Primitive Conversion

The following 19 specific conversions on primitive types are called the *widening primitive conversions*:

- `byte` to `short`, `int`, `long`, `float`, or `double`
- `short` to `int`, `long`, `float`, or `double`
- `char` to `int`, `long`, `float`, or `double`
- `int` to `long`, `float`, or `double`
- `long` to `float` or `double`
- `float` to `double`

Widening primitive conversions do not lose information about the overall magnitude of a numeric value. Indeed, conversions widening from an integral type to another integral type do not lose any information at all; the numeric value is preserved exactly. Conversions widening from `float` to `double` in `strictfp` expressions also preserve the numeric value exactly; however, such conversions that are not `strictfp` may lose information about the overall magnitude of the converted value.

Conversion of an `int` or a `long` value to `float`, or of a `long` value to `double`, may result in *loss of precision*—that is, the result may lose some of the least significant bits of the value. In this case, the resulting floating-point value will be a correctly rounded version of the integer value, using IEEE 754 round-to-nearest mode (§4.2.4).

A widening conversion of a signed integer value to an integral type *T* simply sign-extends the two's-complement representation of the integer value to fill the wider format. A widening conversion of a `char` to an integral type *T* zero-extends the representation of the `char` value to fill the wider format.

Despite the fact that loss of precision may occur, widening conversions among primitive types never result in a run-time exception (§11).

Here is an example of a widening conversion that loses precision:

```
class Test {
    public static void main(String[] args) {
        int big = 1234567890;
        float approx = big;
        System.out.println(big - (int)approx);
    }
}
```

which prints:

```
-46
```

thus indicating that information was lost during the conversion from type `int` to type `float` because values of type `float` are not precise to nine significant digits.

5.1.3 Narrowing Primitive Conversions

The following 22 specific conversions on primitive types are called the *narrowing primitive conversions*:

- `short` to `byte` or `char`
- `char` to `byte` or `short`
- `int` to `byte`, `short`, or `char`
- `long` to `byte`, `short`, `char`, or `int`
- `float` to `byte`, `short`, `char`, `int`, or `long`
- `double` to `byte`, `short`, `char`, `int`, `long`, or `float`

Narrowing conversions may lose information about the overall magnitude of a numeric value and may also lose precision.

A narrowing conversion of a signed integer to an integral type *T* simply discards all but the *n* lowest order bits, where *n* is the number of bits used to represent type *T*. In addition to a possible loss of information about the magnitude of the numeric value, this may cause the sign of the resulting value to differ from the sign of the input value.

A narrowing conversion of a `char` to an integral type *T* likewise simply discards all but the *n* lowest order bits, where *n* is the number of bits used to represent type *T*. In addition to a possible loss of information about the magnitude of the numeric value, this may cause the resulting value to be a negative number, even though `char`s represent 16-bit unsigned integer values.

A narrowing conversion of a floating-point number to an integral type *T* takes two steps:

1. In the first step, the floating-point number is converted either to a `long`, if *T* is `long`, or to an `int`, if *T* is `byte`, `short`, `char`, or `int`, as follows:
   - If the floating-point number is NaN (§4.2.3), the result of the first step of the conversion is an `int` or `long` `0`.
   - Otherwise, if the floating-point number is not an infinity, the floating-point value is rounded to an integer value *V*, rounding toward zero using IEEE 754 round-toward-zero mode (§4.2.3). Then there are two cases:
     - If *T* is `long`, and this integer value can be represented as a `long`, then the result of the first step is the `long` value *V*.
     - Otherwise, if this integer value can be represented as an `int`, then the result of the first step is the `int` value *V*.
   - Otherwise, one of the following two cases must be true:

  - The value must be too small (a negative value of large magnitude or negative infinity), and the result of the first step is the smallest representable value of type `int` or `long`.
  - The value must be too large (a positive value of large magnitude or positive infinity), and the result of the first step is the largest representable value of type `int` or `long`.

2. In the second step:
   - If *T* is `int` or `long`,the result of the conversion is the result of the first step.
   - If *T* is `byte`, `char`, or `short`, the result of the conversion is the result of a narrowing conversion to type *T* (§5.1.3) of the result of the first step.

The example:

```
class Test {
    public static void main(String[] args) {
        float fmin = Float.NEGATIVE_INFINITY;
        float fmax = Float.POSITIVE_INFINITY;
        System.out.println("long: " + (long)fmin +
                        ".." + (long)fmax);
        System.out.println("int: " + (int)fmin +
                        ".." + (int)fmax);
        System.out.println("short: " + (short)fmin +
                        ".." + (short)fmax);
        System.out.println("char: " + (int)(char)fmin +
                        ".." + (int)(char)fmax);
        System.out.println("byte: " + (byte)fmin +
                        ".." + (byte)fmax);
    }
}
```

produces the output:

```
long: -9223372036854775808..9223372036854775807
int: -2147483648..2147483647
short: 0..-1
char: 0..65535
byte: 0..-1
```

The results for `char`, `int`, and `long` are unsurprising, producing the minimum and maximum representable values of the type.

The results for `byte` and `short` lose information about the sign and magnitude of the numeric values and also lose precision. The results can be understood by examining the low order bits of the minimum and maximum `int`. The minimum `int` is, in hexadecimal, `0x80000000`, and the maximum `int` is `0x7fffffff`. This explains the `short` results, which are the low 16 bits of these values, namely,

0x0000 and 0xffff; it explains the char results, which also are the low 16 bits of these values, namely, '\u0000' and '\uffff'; and it explains the byte results, which are the low 8 bits of these values, namely, 0x00 and 0xff.

Despite the fact that overflow, underflow, or other loss of information may occur, narrowing conversions among primitive types never result in a run-time exception (§11).

Here is a small test program that demonstrates a number of narrowing conversions that lose information:

```
class Test {
    public static void main(String[] args) {
        // A narrowing of int to short loses high bits:
        System.out.println("(short)0x12345678==0x" +
                Integer.toHexString((short)0x12345678));
        // A int value not fitting in byte changes sign and magnitude:
        System.out.println("(byte)255==" + (byte)255);
        // A float value too big to fit gives largest int value:
        System.out.println("(int)1e20f==" + (int)1e20f);
        // A NaN converted to int yields zero:
        System.out.println("(int)NaN==" + (int)Float.NaN);
        // A double value too large for float yields infinity:
        System.out.println("(float)-1e100==" + (float)-1e100);
        // A double value too small for float underflows to zero:
        System.out.println("(float)1e-50==" + (float)1e-50);
    }
}
```

This test program produces the following output:

```
(short)0x12345678==0x5678
(byte)255==-1
(int)1e20f==2147483647
(int)NaN==0
(float)-1e100==-Infinity
(float)1e-50==0.0
```

5.1.4 Widening and Narrowing Primitive Conversions

The following conversion combines both widening and narrowing primitive convesions:

- `byte` to `char`

First, the `byte` is converted to an `int` via widening primitive conversion, and then the resulting `int` is converted to a `char` by narrowing primitive conversion.

5.1.5 Widening Reference Conversions

A *widening reference* conversion exists from any type *S* to any type *T*, provided *S* is a subtype (§4.10) of *T*.

Widening reference conversions never require a special action at run time and therefore never throw an exception at run time. They consist simply in regarding a reference as having some other type in a manner that can be proved correct at compile time.

See §8 for the detailed specifications for classes, §9 for interfaces, and §10 for arrays.

5.1.6 Narrowing Reference Conversions

The following conversions are called the *narrowing reference conversions* :

- From any reference type *S* to any reference type *T*, provided that *S* is a proper supertype (§4.10) of *T*. (An important special case is that there is a narrowing conversion from the class type `Object` to any other reference type.)
- From any class type *C* to any non-parameterized interface type *K*, provided that *C* is not final and does not implement *K*.
- From any interface type *J* to any non-parameterized class type *C* that is not `final`.
- From the interface types `Cloneable` and `java.io.Serializable` to any array type *T*[].
- From any interface type *J* to any non-parameterized interface type *K*, provided that *J* is not a subinterface of *K*.
- From any array type *SC*`[]` to any array type *TC*`[]`, provided that *SC* and *TC* are reference types and there is a narrowing conversion from *SC* to *TC*.

Such conversions require a test at run time to find out whether the actual reference value is a legitimate value of the new type. If not, then a `ClassCastException` is thrown.

5.1.7 Boxing Conversion

Boxing conversion converts values of primitive type to corresponding values of reference type. Specifically, the following 8 conversion are called the *boxing conversions*:

- From type `boolean` to type `Boolean`
- From type `byte` to type `Byte`
- From type `char` to type `Character`
- From type `short` to type `Short`
- From type `int` to type `Integer`
- From type `long` to type `Long`
- From type `float` to type `Float`
- From type `double` to type `Double`

At run time, boxing conversion proceeds as follows:

- If *p* is a value of type `boolean`, then boxing conversion converts *p* into a reference *r* of class and type `Boolean`, such that *r*`.booleanValue() ==` *p*
- If *p* is a value of type `byte`, then boxing conversion converts *p* into a reference *r* of class and type `Byte`, such that *r*`.byteValue() ==` *p*
- If *p* is a value of type `char`, then boxing conversion converts *p* into a reference *r* of class and type `Character`, such that *r*`.charValue() ==` *p*
- If *p* is a value of type `short`, then boxing conversion converts *p* into a reference *r* of class and type `Short`, such that *r*`.shortValue() ==` *p*
- If *p* is a value of type `int`, then boxing conversion converts *p* into a reference *r* of class and type `Integer`, such that *r*`.intValue() ==` *p*
- If *p* is a value of type `long`, then boxing conversion converts *p* into a reference *r* of class and type `Long`, such that *r*`.longValue() ==` *p*
- If *p* is a value of type `float` then:
    - If *p* is not NaN, then boxing conversion converts *p* into a reference *r* of class and type `Float`, such that *r*`.floatValue()` evaluates to *p*
    - Otherwise, boxing conversion converts *p* into a reference *r* of class and type `Float` such that *r*`.isNaN()` evaluates to true.
- If *p* is a value of type `double`, then

- If *p* is not NaN, boxing conversion converts *p* into a reference *r* of class and type `Double`, such that `r.doubleValue()` evaluates to *p*
- Otherwise, boxing conversion converts *p* into a reference *r* of class and type `Double` such that `r.isNaN()` evaluates to true.

- If *p* is a value of any other type, boxing conversion is equivalent to an identity conversion (5.1.1).

If the value *p* being boxed is `true`, `false`, a `byte`, a `char` in the range \u0000 to \u007f, or an `int` or `short` number between -128 and 127, then let *r1* and *r2* be the results of any two boxing conversions of *p*. It is always the case that `r1 == r2`.

DISCUSSION

Ideally, boxing a given primitive value p, would always yield an identical reference. In practice, this may not be feasible using existing implementation techniques. The rules above are a pragmatic compromise. The final clause above requires that certain common values always be boxed into indistinguishable objects. The implementation may cache these, lazily or eagerly.

For other values, this formulation disallows any assumptions about the identity of the boxed values on the programmer's part. This would allow (but not require) sharing of some or all of these references.

This ensures that in most common cases, the behavior will be the desired one, without imposing an undue performance penalty, especially on small devices. Less memory-limited implementations might, for example, cache all characters and shorts, as well as integers and longs in the range of -32K - +32K.

A boxing conversion may result in an `OutOfMemoryError` if a new instance of one of the wrapper classes (`Boolean`, `Byte`, `Character`, `Short`, `Integer`, `Long`, `Float`, or `Double`) needs to be allocated and insufficient storage is available.

5.1.8 Unboxing Conversion

Unboxing conversion converts values of reference type to corresponding values of primitive type. Specifically, the following 8 conversion are called the *unboxing conversions*:

- From type `Boolean` to type `boolean`
- From type `Byte` to type `byte`
- From type `Character` to type `char`
- From type `Short` to type `short`
- From type `Integer` to type `int`
- From type `Long` to type `long`
- From type `Float` to type `float`
- From type `Double` to type `double`

At run time, unboxing conversion proceeds as follows:

- If *r* is a reference of type `Boolean`, then unboxing conversion converts *r* into *r*`.booleanValue()`
- If *r* is a reference of type `Byte`, then unboxing conversion converts *r* into *r*`.byteValue()`
- If *r* is a reference of type `Character`, then unboxing conversion converts *r* into *r*`.charValue()`
- If *r* is a reference of type `Short`, then unboxing conversion converts *r* into *r*`.shortValue()`
- If *r* is a reference of type `Integer`, then unboxing conversion converts *r* into *r*`.intValue()`
- If *r* is a reference of type `Long`, then unboxing conversion converts *r* into *r*`.longValue()`
- If *r* is a reference of type `Float`, unboxing conversion converts *r* into *r*`.floatValue()`
- If *r* is a reference of type `Double`, then unboxing conversion converts *r* into *r*`.doubleValue()`
- If *r* is `null`, unboxing conversion throws a `NullPointerException`

A type is said to be *convertible to a numeric type* if it is a numeric type, or it is a reference type that may be converted to a numeric type by unboxing conversion. A type is said to be *convertible to an integral type* if it is an integral type, or it is a reference type that may be converted to an integral type by unboxing conversion.

5.1.9 Unchecked Conversion

Let `G` name a generic type declaration with *n* formal type parameters. There is an *unchecked conversion* from the raw type (§4.8) *G* to any parameterized type of the form $G<T_1 \ldots T_n>$. Use of an unchecked conversion generates a mandatory compile-time warning (which can only be suppressed using the `SuppressWarnings` annotation (§9.6.1.5)) unless the parameterized type `G` is a parameterized type in which all type arguments are unbounded wildcards (§4.5.1).

DISCUSSION

Unchecked conversion is used to enable a smooth interoperation of legacy code, written before the introduction of generic types, with libraries that have undergone a conversion to use genericity (a process we call *generification*).

In such circumstances (most notably, clients of the collections framework in `java.util`), legacy code uses raw types (e.g., `Collection` instead of `Collection<String>`). Expressions of raw types are passed as arguments to library methods that use parameterized versions of those same types as the types of their corresponding formal parameters.

Such calls cannot be shown to be statically safe under the type system using generics. Rejecting such calls would invalidate large bodies of existing code, and prevent them from using newer versions of the libraries. This in turn, would discourage library vendors from taking advantage of genericity.

To prevent such an unwelcome turn of events, a raw type may be converted to an arbitrary invocation of the generic type declaration the raw type refers to. While the conversion is unsound, it is tolerated as a concession to practicality. A warning (known as an *unchecked warning*) is issued in such cases.

5.1.10 Capture Conversion

Let `G` name a generic type declaration with *n* formal type parameters $A_1 \ldots A_n$ with corresponding bounds $U_1 \ldots U_n$. There exists a *capture conversion* from $G<T_1 \ldots T_n>$ to $G<S_1 \ldots S_n>$, where, for $1 \leq i \leq n$:

- If T_i is a wildcard type argument (§4.5.1) of the form ? then S_i is a fresh type variable whose upper bound is $U_i[A_1 := S_1, ..., A_n := S_n]$ and whose lower bound is the null type.
- If T_i is a wildcard type argument of the form ? `extends` B_i, then S_i is a fresh type variable whose upper bound is $glb(B_i, U_i[A_1 := S_1, ..., A_n := S_n])$ and whose lower bound is the null type, where $glb(V_1, ..., V_m)$ is V_1 & ... & V_m. It is a compile-time error if for any two classes (not interfaces) V_i and V_j, V_i is not a subclass of V_j or vice versa.
- If T_i is a wildcard type argument of the form ? `super` B_i, then S_i is a fresh type variable whose upper bound is $U_i[A_1 := S_1, ..., A_n := S_n]$ and whose lower bound is B_i.
- Otherwise, $S_i = T_i$.

Capture conversion on any type other than a parameterized type (§4.5) acts as an identity conversion (§5.1.1). Capture conversions never require a special action at run time and therefore never throw an exception at run time.

Capture conversion is not applied recursively.

DISCUSSION

Capture conversion is designed to make wildcards more useful. To understand the motivation, let's begin by looking at the method `java.util.Collections.reverse()`:

```
public static void reverse(List<?> list);
```

The method reverses the list provided as a parameter. It works for any type of list, and so the use of the wildcard type `List<?>` as the type of the formal parameter is entirely appropriate.

Now consider how one would implement `reverse()`.

```
public static void reverse(List<?> list) { rev(list);}
private static <T> void rev(List<T> list) {
    List<T> tmp = new ArrayList<T>(list);
    for (int i = 0; i < list.size(); i++) {
    list.set(i, tmp.get(list.size() - i - 1));
    }
}
```

The implementation needs to copy the list, extract elements from the copy , and insert them into the original. To do this in a type safe manner, we need to give a name, `T`, to the element type of the incoming list. We do this in the private service method `rev()`.

This requires us to pass the incoming argument list, of type `List<?>`, as an argument to `rev()`. Note that in general, `List<?>` is a list of unknown type. It is not a subtype of `List<T>`, for any type `T`. Allowing such a subtype relation would be unsound. Given the method:

```
public static <T> void fill(List<T> l, T obj)
```

a call

```
List<String> ls = new ArrayList<String>();
List<?> l = ls;
Collections.fill(l, new Object()); // not really legal - but assume
                                   // it was
String s = ls.get(0); // ClassCastException - ls contains Objects,
                      //not Strings.
```

would undermine the type system.

So, without some special dispensation, we can see that the call from `reverse()` to `rev()` would be disallowed. If this were the case, the author of `reverse()` would be forced to write its signature as:

```
public static <T> void reverse(List<T> list)
```

This is undesirable, as it exposes implementation information to the caller. Worse, the designer of an API might reason that the signature using a wildcard is what the callers of the API require, and only later realize that a type safe implementation was precluded.

The call from `reverse()` to `rev()` is in fact harmless, but it cannot be justified on the basis of a general subtyping relation between `List<?>` and `List<T>`. The call is harmless, because the incoming argument is doubtless a list of some type (albeit an unknown one). If we can capture this unknown type in a type variable `X`, we can infer T to be `X`. That is the essence of capture conversion. The specification of course must cope with complications, like non-trivial (and possibly recursively defined) upper or lower bounds, the presence of multiple arguments etc.

DISCUSSION

Mathematically sophisticated readers will want to relate capture conversion to established type theory. Readers unfamiliar with type theory can skip this discussion - or else study a suitable text, such as *Types and Programming Languages* by Benjamin Pierce, and then revisit this section.

Here then is a brief summary of the relationship of capture conversion to established type theoretical notions.

Wildcard types are a restricted form of existential types. Capture conversion corresponds loosely to an opening of a value of existential type. A capture conversion of an expression *e*, can be thought of as an open of *e* in a scope that comprises the top-level expression that encloses *e*.

The classical open operation on existentials requires that the captured type variable must not escape the opened expression. The open that corresponds to capture conversion is always on a scope sufficiently large that the captured type variable can never be visible outside that scope.

The advantage of this scheme is that there is no need for a `close` operation, as defined in the paper *On Variance-Based Subtyping for Parametric Types* by Atsushi Igarashi and Mirko Viroli, in the proceedings of the 16th European Conference on Object Oriented Programming (ECOOP 2002).

For a formal account of wildcards, see *Wild FJ* by Mads Torgersen, Erik Ernst and Christian Plesner Hansen, in the 12th workshop on Foundations of Object Oriented Programming (FOOL 2005).

5.1.11 String Conversions

There is a string conversion to type `String` from every other type, including the null type. See (§5.4) for details of the string conversion context.

5.1.12 Forbidden Conversions

Any conversion that is not explicitly allowed is forbidden.

5.1.13 Value Set Conversion

Value set conversion is the process of mapping a floating-point value from one value set to another without changing its type.

Within an expression that is not FP-strict (§15.4), value set conversion provides choices to an implementation of the Java programming language:

- If the value is an element of the float-extended-exponent value set, then the implementation may, at its option, map the value to the nearest element of the float value set. This conversion may result in overflow (in which case the value is replaced by an infinity of the same sign) or underflow (in which case the value may lose precision because it is replaced by a denormalized number or zero of the same sign).
- If the value is an element of the double-extended-exponent value set, then the implementation may, at its option, map the value to the nearest element of the double value set. This conversion may result in overflow (in which case the value is replaced by an infinity of the same sign) or underflow (in which case the value may lose precision because it is replaced by a denormalized number or zero of the same sign).

Within an FP-strict expression (§15.4), value set conversion does not provide any choices; every implementation must behave in the same way:

- If the value is of type `float` and is not an element of the float value set, then the implementation must map the value to the nearest element of the float value set. This conversion may result in overflow or underflow.
- If the value is of type `double` and is not an element of the double value set, then the implementation must map the value to the nearest element of the double value set. This conversion may result in overflow or underflow.

Within an FP-strict expression, mapping values from the float-extended-exponent value set or double-extended-exponent value set is necessary only when a method is invoked whose declaration is not FP-strict and the implementation has chosen to represent the result of the method invocation as an element of an extended-exponent value set.

Whether in FP-strict code or code that is not FP-strict, value set conversion always leaves unchanged any value whose type is neither `float` nor `double`.

5.2 Assignment Conversion

Assignment conversion occurs when the value of an expression is assigned (§15.26) to a variable: the type of the expression must be converted to the type of the variable. Assignment contexts allow the use of one of the following:

- an identity conversion (§5.1.1)
- a widening primitive conversion (§5.1.2)
- a widening reference conversion (§5.1.5)
- a boxing conversion (§5.1.7) optionally followed by a widening reference conversion
- an unboxing conversion (§5.1.8) optionally followed by a widening primitive conversion.

If, after the conversions listed above have been applied, the resulting type is a raw type (§4.8), unchecked conversion (§5.1.9) may then be applied. It is a compile time error if the chain of conversions contains two parameterized types that are not not in the subtype relation.

DISCUSSION

An example of such an illegal chain would be:

`Integer, Comparable<Integer>, Comparable, Comparable<String>`

The first three elements of the chain are related by widening reference conversion, while the last entry is derived from its predecessor by unchecked conversion. However, this dis not a valid assignment conversion, because the chain contains two parameterized types, `Comparable<Integer>` and `Comparable<String>`, that are not subtypes.

In addition, if the expression is a constant expression (§15.28) of type `byte`, `short`, `char` or `int` :

- A narrowing primitive conversion may be used if the type of the variable is `byte`, `short`, or `char`, and the value of the constant expression is representable in the type of the variable.
- A narrowing primitive conversion followed by a boxing conversion may be used if the type of the variable is :
  - `Byte` and the value of the constant expression is representable in the type `byte`.
  - `Short` and the value of the constant expression is representable in the type `short`.
  - `Character` and the value of the constant expression is representable in the type `char`.

If the type of the expression cannot be converted to the type of the variable by a conversion permitted in an assignment context, then a compile-time error occurs.

If the type of the variable is `float` or `double`, then value set conversion is applied to the value *v* that is the results of the type conversion:

- If *v* is of type `float` and is an element of the float-extended-exponent value set, then the implementation must map *v* to the nearest element of the float value set. This conversion may result in overflow or underflow.
- If *v* is of type `double` and is an element of the double-extended-exponent value set, then the implementation must map *v* to the nearest element of the double value set. This conversion may result in overflow or underflow.

If the type of an expression can be converted to the type of a variable by assignment conversion, we say the expression (or its value) is *assignable to* the variable or, equivalently, that the type of the expression is *assignment compatible with* the type of the variable.

If, after the type conversions above have been applied, the resulting value is an object which is not an instance of a subclass or subinterface of the erasure of the type of the variable, then a `ClassCastException` is thrown.

DISCUSSION

This circumstance can only arise as a result of heap pollution (§4.12.2.1).

In practice, implementations need only perfom casts when accessing a field or method of an object of parametized type, when the erased type of the field, or the erased result type of the method differ from their unerased type.

The only exceptions that an assignment conversion may cause are:

- An `OutOfMemoryError` as a result of a boxing conversion.
- A `ClassCastException` in the special circumstances indicated above.
- A `NullPointerException` as a result of an unboxing conversion on a null reference.

(Note, however, that an assignment may result in an exception in special cases involving array elements or field access —see §10.10 and §15.26.1.)

The compile-time narrowing of constants means that code such as:

```
byte theAnswer = 42;
```

is allowed. Without the narrowing, the fact that the integer literal `42` has type `int` would mean that a cast to `byte` would be required:

```
byte theAnswer = (byte)42;// cast is permitted but not required
```

The following test program contains examples of assignment conversion of primitive values:

```
class Test {
    public static void main(String[] args) {
        short s = 12;           // narrow 12 to short
        float f = s;            // widen short to float
        System.out.println("f=" + f);
        char c = '\u0123';
        long l = c;             // widen char to long
```

```
        System.out.println("l=0x" + Long.toString(l,16));
        f = 1.23f;
        double d = f;           // widen float to double
        System.out.println("d=" + d);
    }
}
```

It produces the following output:

```
f=12.0
l=0x123
d=1.2300000190734863
```

The following test, however, produces compile-time errors:

```
class Test {
    public static void main(String[] args) {
        short s = 123;
        char c = s;             // error: would require cast
        s = c;                  // error: would require cast
    }
}
```

because not all `short` values are `char` values, and neither are all `char` values `short` values.

A value of the null type (the null reference is the only such value) may be assigned to any reference type, resulting in a null reference of that type.

Here is a sample program illustrating assignments of references:

```
public class Point { int x, y; }

public class Point3D extends Point { int z; }

public interface Colorable {
    void setColor(int color);
}

public class ColoredPoint extends Point implements Colorable
{
    int color;
    public void setColor(int color) { this.color = color; }
}

class Test {
    public static void main(String[] args) {
        // Assignments to variables of class type:
        Point p = new Point();
        p = new Point3D();  // ok: because Point3D is a
                            // subclass of Point
```

```
        Point3D p3d = p;       // error: will require a cast because a
                               // Point might not be a Point3D
                               // (even though it is, dynamically,
                               // in this example.)
        // Assignments to variables of type Object:
        Object o = p;          // ok: any object to Object
        int[] a = new int[3];
        Object o2 = a;            // ok: an array to Object
        // Assignments to variables of interface type:
        ColoredPoint cp = new ColoredPoint();
        Colorable c = cp;      // ok: ColoredPoint implements
                                  // Colorable
        // Assignments to variables of array type:
        byte[] b = new byte[4];
        a = b;                 // error: these are not arrays
                               // of the same primitive type
        Point3D[] p3da = new Point3D[3];
        Point[] pa = p3da;     // ok: since we can assign a
                               // Point3D to a Point
        p3da = pa;             // error: (cast needed) since a Point
                                  // can't be assigned to a Point3D
    }
}
```

The following test program illustrates assignment conversions on reference values, but fails to compile, as described in its comments. This example should be compared to the preceding one.

```
public class Point { int x, y; }
public interface Colorable { void setColor(int color); }
public class ColoredPoint extends Point implements Colorable
{
    int color;
    public void setColor(int color) { this.color = color; }
}
class Test {
    public static void main(String[] args) {
        Point p = new Point();
        ColoredPoint cp = new ColoredPoint();
        // Okay because ColoredPoint is a subclass of Point:
        p = cp;
        // Okay because ColoredPoint implements Colorable:
        Colorable c = cp;
```

```
        // The following cause compile-time errors because
        // we cannot be sure they will succeed, depending on
        // the run-time type of p; a run-time check will be
        // necessary for the needed narrowing conversion and
        // must be indicated by including a cast:
        cp = p;     // p might be neither a ColoredPoint
                    // nor a subclass of ColoredPoint
        c = p;      // p might not implement Colorable
    }
}
```

Here is another example involving assignment of array objects:

```
class Point { int x, y; }

class ColoredPoint extends Point { int color; }

class Test {
    public static void main(String[] args) {
        long[] veclong = new long[100];
        Object o = veclong;          // okay
        Long l = veclong;            // compile-time error
        short[] vecshort = veclong;// compile-time error
        Point[] pvec = new Point[100];
        ColoredPoint[] cpvec = new ColoredPoint[100];
        pvec = cpvec;                // okay
        pvec[0] = new Point();       // okay at compile time,
                                     // but would throw an
                                     // exception at run time
        cpvec = pvec;                // compile-time error
    }
}
```

In this example:

- The value of `veclong` cannot be assigned to a `Long` variable, because `Long` is a class type other than `Object`. An array can be assigned only to a variable of a compatible array type, or to a variable of type `Object`, `Cloneable` or `java.io.Serializable`.
- The value of `veclong` cannot be assigned to `vecshort`, because they are arrays of primitive type, and `short` and `long` are not the same primitive type.
- The value of `cpvec` can be assigned to `pvec`, because any reference that could be the value of an expression of type `ColoredPoint` can be the value of a variable of type `Point`. The subsequent assignment of the new `Point` to a component of `pvec` then would throw an `ArrayStoreException` (if the program were otherwise corrected so that it could be compiled), because a

`ColoredPoint` array can't have an instance of `Point` as the value of a component.

- The value of `pvec` cannot be assigned to `cpvec`, because not every reference that could be the value of an expression of type `ColoredPoint` can correctly be the value of a variable of type `Point`. If the value of `pvec` at run time were a reference to an instance of `Point[]`, and the assignment to `cpvec` were allowed, a simple reference to a component of `cpvec`, say, `cpvec[0]`, could return a `Point`, and a `Point` is not a `ColoredPoint`. Thus to allow such an assignment would allow a violation of the type system. A cast may be used (§5.5, §15.16) to ensure that `pvec` references a `ColoredPoint[]`:

```
cpvec = (ColoredPoint[])pvec;// okay, but may throw an
                             // exception at run time
```

5.3 Method Invocation Conversion

Method invocation conversion is applied to each argument value in a method or constructor invocation (§8.8.7.1, §15.9, §15.12): the type of the argument expression must be converted to the type of the corresponding parameter. Method invocation contexts allow the use of one of the following:

- an identity conversion (§5.1.1)
- a widening primitive conversion (§5.1.2)
- a widening reference conversion (§5.1.5)
- a boxing conversion (§5.1.7) optionally followed by widening reference conversion
- an unboxing conversion (§5.1.8) optionally followed by a widening primitive conversion.

If, after the conversions listed above have been applied, the resulting type is a raw type (§4.8), an unchecked conversion (§5.1.9) may then be applied. It is a compile time error if the chain of conversions contains two parameterized types that are not not in the subtype relation.

If the type of an argument expression is either `float` or `double`, then value set conversion (§5.1.13) is applied after the type conversion:

- If an argument value of type `float` is an element of the float-extended-exponent value set, then the implementation must map the value to the nearest element of the float value set. This conversion may result in overflow or underflow.

- If an argument value of type `double` is an element of the double-extended-exponent value set, then the implementation must map the value to the nearest element of the double value set. This conversion may result in overflow or underflow.

If, after the type conversions above have been applied, the resulting value is an object which is not an instance of a subclass or subinterface of the erasure of the corresponding formal parameter type, then a `ClassCastException` is thrown.

DISCUSSION

This circumstance can only arise as a result of heap pollution (§4.12.2.1).

Method invocation conversions specifically do not include the implicit narrowing of integer constants which is part of assignment conversion (§5.2). The designers of the Java programming language felt that including these implicit narrowing conversions would add additional complexity to the overloaded method matching resolution process (§15.12.2).

Thus, the example:

```
class Test {

    static int m(byte a, int b) { return a+b; }

    static int m(short a, short b) { return a-b; }

    public static void main(String[] args) {
        System.out.println(m(12, 2));// compile-time error
    }

}
```

causes a compile-time error because the integer literals `12` and `2` have type `int`, so neither method `m` matches under the rules of (§15.12.2). A language that included implicit narrowing of integer constants would need additional rules to resolve cases like this example.

5.4 String Conversion

String conversion applies only to the operands of the binary + operator when one of the arguments is a `String`. In this single special case, the other argument to the + is converted to a `String`, and a new `String` which is the concatenation of the two strings is the result of the +. String conversion is specified in detail within the description of the string concatenation + operator (§15.18.1).

5.5 Casting Conversion

Sing away sorrow, cast away care.
—Miguel de Cervantes (1547–1616),
Don Quixote (Lockhart's translation), Chapter viii

Casting conversion is applied to the operand of a cast operator (§15.16): the type of the operand expression must be converted to the type explicitly named by the cast operator. Casting contexts allow the use of:

- an identity conversion (§5.1.1)
- a widening primitive conversion (§5.1.2)
- a narrowing primitive conversion (§5.1.3)
- a widening reference conversion (§5.1.5) optionally followed by an unchecked conversion (§5.1.9)
- a narrowing reference conversion (§5.1.6) optionally followed by an unchecked conversion
- a boxing conversion (§5.1.7)
- an unboxing conversion (§5.1.8).

Thus casting conversions are more inclusive than assignment or method invocation conversions: a cast can do any permitted conversion other than a string conversion or a capture conversion (§5.1.10).

Value set conversion (§5.1.13) is applied after the type conversion.

Some casts can be proven incorrect at compile time; such casts result in a compile-time error.

A value of a primitive type can be cast to another primitive type by identity conversion, if the types are the same, or by a widening primitive conversion or a narrowing primitive conversion.

A value of a primitive type can be cast to a reference type by boxing conversion (§5.1.7).

A value of a reference type can be cast to a primitive type by unboxing conversion (§5.1.8).

The remaining cases involve conversion of a compile-time reference type *S* (source) to a compile-time reference type *T* (target).

A cast from a type *S* to a type *T* is *statically known to be correct* if and only if *S* <: *T* (§4.10).

A cast from a type *S* to a parameterized type (§4.5) *T* is *unchecked* unless at least one of the following conditions hold:

- *S* <: *T*.
- All of the type arguments (§4.5.1) of *T* are unbounded wildcards.
- *T* <: *S* and *S* has no subtype $X \neq T$, such that the erasures (§4.6) of *X* and *T* are the same.

A cast to a type variable (§4.4) is always unchecked.

An unchecked cast from *S* to *T* is *completely unchecked* if the cast from |*S*| to |*T*| is statically known to be correct. Otherwise it is *partially unchecked*. An unchecked cast causes an unchecked warning to occur (unless it is suppressed using the `SuppressWarnings` annotation (§9.6.1.5)).

A cast is a *checked cast* if it is not statically known to be correct and it is not unchecked.

The detailed rules for compile-time legality of a casting conversion of a value of compile-time reference type *S* to a compile-time reference type *T* are as follows:

- If *S* is a class type:
  - If *T* is a class type, then either |*S*| <: |*T*|, or |*T*| <: |*S*|; otherwise a compile-time error occurs. Furthermore, if there exists a supertype *X* of *T*, and a supertype *Y* of *S*, such that both *X* and *Y* are provably distinct parameterized types (§4.5), and that the erasures of *X* and *Y* are the same, a compile-time error occurs.
  - If *T* is an interface type:
    - If *S* is not a `final` class (§8.1.1), then, if there exists a supertype *X* of *T*, and a supertype *Y* of *S*, such that both *X* and *Y* are provably distinct parameterized types, and that the erasures of *X* and *Y* are the same, a compile-time error occurs. Otherwise, the cast is always legal at compile time (because even if *S* does not implement *T*, a subclass of *S* might).

    - If *S* is a `final` class (§8.1.1), then *S* must implement *T*, or a compile-time error occurs.
  - If *T* is a type variable, then this algorithm is applied recursively, using the upper bound of *T* in place of *T*.
  - If *T* is an array type, then *S* must be the class `Object`, or a compile-time error occurs.
- If *S* is an interface type:
  - If *T* is an array type, then *T* must implement *S*, or a compile-time error occurs.
  - If *T* is a type that is not `final` (§8.1.1), then if there exists a supertype *X* of *T*, and a supertype *Y* of *S*, such that both *X* and *Y* are provably distinct parameterized types, and that the erasures of *X* and *Y* are the same, a compile-time error occurs. Otherwise, the cast is always legal at compile time (because even if *T* does not implement *S*, a subclass of *T* might).
  - If *T* is a type that is `final`, then:
    - If *S* is not a parameterized type or a raw type, then *T* must implement *S*, and the cast is statically known to be correct, or a compile-time error occurs.
    - Otherwise, *S* is either a parameterized type that is an invocation of some generic type declaration *G*, or a raw type corresponding to a generic type declaration *G*. Then there must exist a supertype *X* of *T*, such that *X* is an invocation of *G*, or a compile-time error occurs. Furthermore, if *S* and *X* are provably distinct parameterized types then a compile-time error occurs.
- If *S* is a type variable, then this algorithm is applied recursively, using the upper bound of *S* in place of *S*.
- If *S* is an array type *SC*`[]`, that is, an array of components of type *SC*:
  - If *T* is a class type, then if *T* is not `Object`, then a compile-time error occurs (because `Object` is the only class type to which arrays can be assigned).
  - If *T* is an interface type, then a compile-time error occurs unless *T* is the type `java.io.Serializable` or the type `Cloneable`, the only interfaces implemented by arrays.
  - If *T* is a type variable, then:

  - If the upper bound of *T* is `Object` or the type `java.io.Serializable` or the type `Cloneable`, or a type variable that *S* could legally be cast to by recursively applying these rules, then the cast is legal (though unchecked).
  - If the upper bound of *T* is an array type *TC[]*, then a compile-time error occurs unless the type *SC[]* can be cast to *TC[]* by a recursive application of these compile-time rules for casting.
  - Otherwise, a compile-time error occurs.

- If *T* is an array type *TC*`[]`, that is, an array of components of type *TC*, then a compile-time error occurs unless one of the following is true:
  - *TC* and *SC* are the same primitive type.
  - *TC* and *SC* are reference types and type *SC* can be cast to *TC* by a recursive application of these compile-time rules for casting.

See §8 for the specification of classes, §9 for interfaces, and §10 for arrays.

If a cast to a reference type is not a compile-time error, there are several cases:

- The cast is statically known to be correct. No run time action is performed for such a cast.
- The cast is a completely unchecked cast. No run time action is performed for such a cast.
- The cast is a partially unchecked cast. Such a cast requires a run-time validity check. The check is performed as if the cast had been a checked cast between |*S*| and |*T*|, as described below.
- The cast is a checked cast. Such a cast requires a run-time validity check. If the value at run time is `null`, then the cast is allowed. Otherwise, let *R* be the class of the object referred to by the run-time reference value, and let *T* be the erasure of the type named in the cast operator. A cast conversion must check, at run time, that the class *R* is assignment compatible with the type *T*. (Note that *R* cannot be an interface when these rules are first applied for any given cast, but *R* may be an interface if the rules are applied recursively because the run-time reference value may refer to an array whose element type is an interface type.) The algorithm for performing the check is shown here:
  - If *R* is an ordinary class (not an array class):
    - If *T* is a class type, then *R* must be either the same class (§4.3.4) as *T* or a subclass of *T*, or a run-time exception is thrown.

- If *T* is an interface type, then *R* must implement (§8.1.5) interface *T*, or a run-time exception is thrown.
- If *T* is an array type, then a run-time exception is thrown.

- If *R* is an interface:
  - If *T* is a class type, then *T* must be `Object` (§4.3.2), or a run-time exception is thrown.
  - If *T* is an interface type, then *R* must be either the same interface as *T* or a subinterface of *T*, or a run-time exception is thrown.
  - If *T* is an array type, then a run-time exception is thrown.
- If *R* is a class representing an array type *RC*`[]`—that is, an array of components of type *RC:*
  - If *T* is a class type, then *T* must be `Object` (§4.3.2), or a run-time exception is thrown.
  - If *T* is an interface type, then a run-time exception is thrown unless *T* is the type `java.io.Serializable` or the type `Cloneable`, the only interfaces implemented by arrays (this case could slip past the compile-time checking if, for example, a reference to an array were stored in a variable of type `Object`).
  - If *T* is an array type *TC*`[]`, that is, an array of components of type *TC,* then a run-time exception is thrown unless one of the following is true:
    - *TC* and *RC* are the same primitive type.
    - *TC* and *RC* are reference types and type *RC* can be cast to *TC* by a recursive application of these run-time rules for casting.

If a run-time exception is thrown, it is a `ClassCastException`.

Here are some examples of casting conversions of reference types, similar to the example in §5.2:

```
public class Point { int x, y; }

public interface Colorable { void setColor(int color); }

public class ColoredPoint extends Point implements Colorable
{
    int color;
    public void setColor(int color) { this.color = color; }
}

final class EndPoint extends Point { }
```

```
class Test {
    public static void main(String[] args) {
        Point p = new Point();
        ColoredPoint cp = new ColoredPoint();
        Colorable c;
        // The following may cause errors at run time because
        // we cannot be sure they will succeed; this possibility
        // is suggested by the casts:
        cp = (ColoredPoint)p;// p might not reference an
                             // object which is a ColoredPoint
                             // or a subclass of ColoredPoint
        c = (Colorable)p;    // p might not be Colorable
        // The following are incorrect at compile time because
        // they can never succeed as explained in the text:
        Long l = (Long)p;    // compile-time error #1
        EndPoint e = new EndPoint();
        c = (Colorable)e;    // compile-time error #2
    }
}
```

Here the first compile-time error occurs because the class types `Long` and `Point` are unrelated (that is, they are not the same, and neither is a subclass of the other), so a cast between them will always fail.

The second compile-time error occurs because a variable of type `EndPoint` can never reference a value that implements the interface `Colorable`. This is because `EndPoint` is a `final` type, and a variable of a `final` type always holds a value of the same run-time type as its compile-time type. Therefore, the run-time type of variable `e` must be exactly the type `EndPoint`, and type `EndPoint` does not implement `Colorable`.

Here is an example involving arrays (§10):

```
class Point {
    int x, y;
    Point(int x, int y) { this.x = x; this.y = y; }
    public String toString() { return "("+x+","+y+")"; }
}
public interface Colorable { void setColor(int color); }
public class ColoredPoint extends Point implements Colorable
{
    int color;
```

```
    ColoredPoint(int x, int y, int color) {
        super(x, y); setColor(color);
    }
    public void setColor(int color) { this.color = color; }
    public String toString() {
        return super.toString() + "@" + color;
    }
}
class Test {
    public static void main(String[] args) {
        Point[] pa = new ColoredPoint[4];
        pa[0] = new ColoredPoint(2, 2, 12);
        pa[1] = new ColoredPoint(4, 5, 24);
        ColoredPoint[] cpa = (ColoredPoint[])pa;
        System.out.print("cpa: {");
        for (int i = 0; i < cpa.length; i++)
            System.out.print((i == 0 ? " " : ", ") + cpa[i]);
        System.out.println(" }");
    }
}
```

This example compiles without errors and produces the output:

```
cpa: { (2,2)@12, (4,5)@24, null, null }
```

The following example uses casts to compile, but it throws exceptions at run time, because the types are incompatible:

```
public class Point { int x, y; }
public interface Colorable { void setColor(int color); }
public class ColoredPoint extends Point implements Colorable
{
    int color;
    public void setColor(int color) { this.color = color; }
}
class Test {
    public static void main(String[] args) {
        Point[] pa = new Point[100];
        // The following line will throw a ClassCastException:
        ColoredPoint[] cpa = (ColoredPoint[])pa;
        System.out.println(cpa[0]);
```

```
        int[] shortvec = new int[2];
        Object o = shortvec;
        // The following line will throw a ClassCastException:
        Colorable c = (Colorable)o;
        c.setColor(0);
    }
}
```

5.6 Numeric Promotions

Numeric promotion is applied to the operands of an arithmetic operator. Numeric promotion contexts allow the use of an identity conversion (§5.1.1) a widening primitive conversion (§5.1.2), or an unboxing conversion (§5.1.8).

Numeric promotions are used to convert the operands of a numeric operator to a common type so that an operation can be performed. The two kinds of numeric promotion are unary numeric promotion (§5.6.1) and binary numeric promotion (§5.6.2).

5.6.1 Unary Numeric Promotion

Some operators apply *unary numeric promotion* to a single operand, which must produce a value of a numeric type:

- If the operand is of compile-time type `Byte`, `Short`, `Character`, or `Integer` it is subjected to unboxing conversion. The result is then promoted to a value of type `int` by a widening conversion (§5.1.2) or an identity conversion.
- Otherwise, if the operand is of compile-time type `Long`, `Float`, or `Double` it is subjected to unboxing conversion.
- Otherwise, if the operand is of compile-time type `byte`, `short`, or `char`, unary numeric promotion promotes it to a value of type `int` by a widening conversion (§5.1.2).
- Otherwise, a unary numeric operand remains as is and is not converted.

In any case, value set conversion (§5.1.13) is then applied.

Unary numeric promotion is performed on expressions in the following situations:

- Each dimension expression in an array creation expression (§15.10)
- The index expression in an array access expression (§15.13)
- The operand of a unary plus operator + (§15.15.3)
- The operand of a unary minus operator - (§15.15.4)
- The operand of a bitwise complement operator ~ (§15.15.5)
- Each operand, separately, of a shift operator >>, >>>, or << (§15.19); therefore a `long` shift distance (right operand) does not promote the value being shifted (left operand) to `long`

Here is a test program that includes examples of unary numeric promotion:

```
class Test {
    public static void main(String[] args) {
        byte b = 2;
        int a[] = new int[b]; // dimension expression promotion
        char c = '\u0001';
        a[c] = 1;           // index expression promotion
        a[0] = -c;          // unary - promotion
        System.out.println("a: " + a[0] + "," + a[1]);
        b = -1;
        int i = ~b;         // bitwise complement promotion
        System.out.println("~0x" + Integer.toHexString(b)
                    + "==0x" + Integer.toHexString(i));
        i = b << 4L;        // shift promotion (left operand)
        System.out.println("0x" + Integer.toHexString(b)
                  + "<<4L==0x" + Integer.toHexString(i));
    }
}
```

This test program produces the output:

```
a: -1,1
~0xffffffff==0x0
0xffffffff<<4L==0xfffffff0
```

5.6.2 Binary Numeric Promotion

When an operator applies *binary numeric promotion* to a pair of operands, each of which must denote a value that is convertible to a numeric type, the following rules apply, in order, using widening conversion (§5.1.2) to convert operands as necessary:

- If any of the operands is of a reference type, unboxing conversion (§5.1.8) is performed. Then:
- If either operand is of type `double`, the other is converted to `double`.
- Otherwise, if either operand is of type `float`, the other is converted to `float`.
- Otherwise, if either operand is of type `long`, the other is converted to `long`.
- Otherwise, both operands are converted to type `int`.

After the type conversion, if any, value set conversion (§5.1.13) is applied to each operand.

Binary numeric promotion is performed on the operands of certain operators:

- The multiplicative operators `*`, `/` and `%` (§15.17)
- The addition and subtraction operators for numeric types `+` and `-` (§15.18.2)
- The numerical comparison operators `<`, `<=`, `>`, and `>=` (§15.20.1)
- The numerical equality operators `==` and `!=` (§15.21.1)
- The integer bitwise operators `&`, `^`, and `|` (§15.22.1)
- In certain cases, the conditional operator `? :` (§15.25)

An example of binary numeric promotion appears above in §5.1. Here is another:

```
class Test {
    public static void main(String[] args) {
        int i = 0;
        float f = 1.0f;
        double d = 2.0;

        // First int*float is promoted to float*float, then
        // float==double is promoted to double==double:
        if (i * f == d)
            System.out.println("oops");
```

```
    // A char&byte is promoted to int&int:
            byte b = 0x1f;
            char c = 'G';
            int control = c & b;
            System.out.println(Integer.toHexString(control));

    // Here int:float is promoted to float:float:
            f = (b==0) ? i : 4.0f;
            System.out.println(1.0/f);
        }
}
```

which produces the output:

```
7
0.25
```

The example converts the ASCII character `G` to the ASCII control-G (BEL), by masking off all but the low 5 bits of the character. The `7` is the numeric value of this control character.

O suns! O grass of graves! O perpetual transfers and promotions!
—Walt Whitman, *Walt Whitman* (1855),
in *Leaves of Grass*

CHAPTER 6

Names

The Tao that can be told is not the eternal Tao;
The name that can be named is not the eternal name.
The Nameless is the origin of Heaven and Earth;
The Named is the mother of all things.
—Lao-Tsu (c. 6th century BC)

NAMES are used to refer to entities declared in a program. A declared entity (§6.1) is a package, class type (normal or enum), interface type (normal or annotation type), member (class, interface, field, or method) of a reference type, type parameter (of a class, interface, method or constructor) (§4.4), parameter (to a method, constructor, or exception handler), or local variable.

Names in programs are either simple, consisting of a single identifier, or qualified, consisting of a sequence of identifiers separated by "`.`" tokens (§6.2).

Every declaration that introduces a name has a *scope* (§6.3), which is the part of the program text within which the declared entity can be referred to by a simple name.

Packages and reference types (that is, class types, interface types, and array types) have members (§6.4). A member can be referred to using a qualified name `N.x`, where `N` is a simple or qualified name and `x` is an identifier. If `N` names a package, then `x` is a member of that package, which is either a class or interface type or a subpackage. If `N` names a reference type or a variable of a reference type, then `x` names a member of that type, which is either a class, an interface, a field, or a method.

In determining the meaning of a name (§6.5), the context of the occurrence is used to disambiguate among packages, types, variables, and methods with the same name.

Access control (§6.6) can be specified in a class, interface, method, or field declaration to control when *access* to a member is allowed. Access is a different concept from scope; access specifies the part of the program text within which the declared entity can be referred to by a qualified name, a field access expression

(§15.11), or a method invocation expression (§15.12) in which the method is not specified by a simple name. The default access is that a member can be accessed anywhere within the package that contains its declaration; other possibilities are `public`, `protected`, and `private`.

Fully qualified and canonical names (§6.7) and naming conventions (§6.8) are also discussed in this chapter.

The name of a field, parameter, or local variable may be used as an expression (§15.14.2). The name of a method may appear in an expression only as part of a method invocation expression (§15.12). The name of a class or interface type may appear in an expression only as part of a class literal (§15.8.2), a qualified `this` expression (§15.8.4), a class instance creation expression (§15.9), an array creation expression (§15.10), a cast expression (§15.16), an `instanceof` expression (§15.20.2), an enum constant (§8.9), or as part of a qualified name for a field or method. The name of a package may appear in an expression only as part of a qualified name for a class or interface type.

6.1 Declarations

A *declaration* introduces an entity into a program and includes an identifier (§3.8) that can be used in a name to refer to this entity. A declared entity is one of the following:

- A package, declared in a `package` declaration (§7.4)
- An imported type, declared in a single-type-import declaration (§7.5.1) or a type-import-on-demand declaration (§7.5.2)
- A class, declared in a class type declaration (§8.1)
- An interface, declared in an interface type declaration (§9.1)
- A type variable (§4.4), declared as a formal type parameter of a generic class (§8.1.2), interface (§9.1.2), method (§8.4.4) or constructor (§8.8.1).
- A member of a reference type (§8.2, §9.2, §10.7), one of the following:
  - A member class (§8.5, §9.5).
  - A member interface (§8.5, §9.5).
  - an enum constant (§8.9).
  - A field, one of the following:
    - A field declared in a class type (§8.3)

    - A constant field declared in an interface type (§9.3)
    - The field `length`, which is implicitly a member of every array type (§10.7)
  - A method, one of the following:
    - A method (`abstract` or otherwise) declared in a class type (§8.4)
    - A method (always `abstract`) declared in an interface type (§9.4)
- A parameter, one of the following:
  - A parameter of a method or constructor of a class (§8.4.1, §8.8.1)
  - A parameter of an `abstract` method of an interface (§9.4)
  - A parameter of an exception handler declared in a `catch` clause of a `try` statement (§14.20)
- A local variable, one of the following:
  - A local variable declared in a block (§14.4)
  - A local variable declared in a `for` statement (§14.14)

Constructors (§8.8) are also introduced by declarations, but use the name of the class in which they are declared rather than introducing a new name.

6.2 Names and Identifiers

A *name* is used to refer to an entity declared in a program.

There are two forms of names: simple names and qualified names. A *simple name* is a single identifier. A *qualified name* consists of a name, a "`.`" token, and an identifier.

In determining the meaning of a name (§6.5), the context in which the name appears is taken into account. The rules of §6.5 distinguish among contexts where a name must denote (refer to) a package (§6.5.3), a type (§6.5.5), a variable or value in an expression (§6.5.6), or a method (§6.5.7).

Not all identifiers in programs are a part of a name. Identifiers are also used in the following situations:

- In declarations (§6.1), where an identifier may occur to specify the name by which the declared entity will be known
- In field access expressions (§15.11), where an identifier occurs after a "." token to indicate a member of an object that is the value of an expression or the keyword super that appears before the "." token
- In some method invocation expressions (§15.12), where an identifier may occur after a "." token and before a "(" token to indicate a method to be invoked for an object that is the value of an expression or the keyword super that appears before the "." token
- In qualified class instance creation expressions (§15.9), where an identifier occurs immediately to the right of the leftmost new token to indicate a type that must be a member of the compile-time type of the primary expression preceding the "." preceding the leftmost new token.
- As labels in labeled statements (§14.7) and in break (§14.15) and continue (§14.16) statements that refer to statement labels.

In the example:

```
class Test {
    public static void main(String[] args) {
        Class c = System.out.getClass();
        System.out.println(c.toString().length() +
                    args[0].length() + args.length);
    }
}
```

the identifiers Test, main, and the first occurrences of args and c are not names; rather, they are used in declarations to specify the names of the declared entities. The names String, Class, System.out.getClass, System.out.println, c.toString, args, and args.length appear in the example. The first occurrence of length is not a name, but rather an identifier appearing in a method invocation expression (§15.12). The second occurrence of length is not a name, but rather an identifier appearing in a method invocation expression (§15.12).

The identifiers used in labeled statements and their associated break and continue statements are completely separate from those used in declarations. Thus, the following code is valid:

```
class TestString {
    char[] value;
    int offset, count;
    int indexOf(TestString str, int fromIndex) {
        char[] v1 = value, v2 = str.value;
        int max = offset + (count - str.count);
```

```
        int start = offset + ((fromIndex < 0) ? 0 : fromIndex);
    i:
        for (int i = start; i <= max; i++)
        {
            int n = str.count, j = i, k = str.offset;
            while (n-- != 0) {
              if (v1[j++] != v2[k++])
                continue i;
            }
            return i - offset;
        }
        return -1;
    }
}
```

This code was taken from a version of the class `String` and its method `indexOf`, where the label was originally called `test`. Changing the label to have the same name as the local variable `i` does not obscure (§6.3.2) the label in the scope of the declaration of `i`. The identifier `max` could also have been used as the statement label; the label would not obscure the local variable `max` within the labeled statement.

6.3 Scope of a Declaration

The *scope* of a declaration is the region of the program within which the entity declared by the declaration can be referred to using a simple name (provided it is visible (§6.3.1)). A declaration is said to be *in scope* at a particular point in a program if and only if the declaration's scope includes that point.

The scoping rules for various constructs are given in the sections that describe those constructs. For convenience, the rules are repeated here:

The scope of the declaration of an observable (§7.4.3) top level package is all observable compilation units (§7.3). The declaration of a package that is not observable is never in scope. Subpackage declarations are never in scope.

The scope of a type imported by a single-type-import declaration (§7.5.1) or a type-import-on-demand declaration (§7.5.2) is all the class and interface type declarations (§7.6) in the compilation unit in which the import declaration appears.

The scope of a member imported by a single-static-import declaration (§7.5.3) or a static-import-on-demand declaration (§7.5.4) is all the class and interface type declarations (§7.6) in the compilation unit in which the import declaration appears.

The scope of a top level type is all type declarations in the package in which the top level type is declared.

The scope of a declaration of a member `m` declared in or inherited by a class type `C` is the entire body of `C`, including any nested type declarations.

The scope of the declaration of a member `m` declared in or inherited by an interface type *I* is the entire body of *I*, including any nested type declarations.

The scope of a parameter of a method (§8.4.1) or constructor (§8.8.1) is the entire body of the method or constructor.

The scope of an interface's type parameter is the entire declaration of the interface including the type parameter section itself. Therefore, type parameters can appear as parts of their own bounds, or as bounds of other type parameters declared in the same section.

The scope of a method's type parameter is the entire declaration of the method, including the type parameter section itself. Therefore, type parameters can appear as parts of their own bounds, or as bounds of other type parameters declared in the same section.

The scope of a constructor's type parameter is the entire declaration of the constructor, including the type parameter section itself. Therefore, type parameters can appear as parts of their own bounds, or as bounds of other type parameters declared in the same section.

The scope of a local variable declaration in a block (§14.4.2) is the rest of the block in which the declaration appears, starting with its own initializer (§14.4) and including any further declarators to the right in the local variable declaration statement.

The scope of a local class immediately enclosed by a block (§14.2) is the rest of the immediately enclosing block, including its own class declaration. The scope of a local class immediately enclosed by in a switch block statement group (§14.11)is the rest of the immediately enclosing switch block statement group, including its own class declaration.

The scope of a local variable declared in the *ForInit* part of a basic `for` statement (§14.14) includes all of the following:

- Its own initializer
- Any further declarators to the right in the *ForInit* part of the `for` statement
- The *Expression* and *ForUpdate* parts of the `for` statement
- The contained *Statement*

The scope of a local variable declared in the *FormalParameter* part of an enhanced `for` statement (§14.14) is the contained *Statement*

The scope of a parameter of an exception handler that is declared in a `catch` clause of a `try` statement (§14.20) is the entire block associated with the `catch`.

These rules imply that declarations of class and interface types need not appear before uses of the types.

In the example:

```
package points;
class Point {
    int x, y;
    PointList list;
    Point next;
}
class PointList {
    Point first;
}
```

the use of `PointList` in class `Point` is correct, because the scope of the class declaration `PointList` includes both class `Point` and class `PointList`, as well as any other type declarations in other compilation units of package `points`.

6.3.1 Shadowing Declarations

Some declarations may be *shadowed* in part of their scope by another declaration of the same name, in which case a simple name cannot be used to refer to the declared entity.

A declaration *d* of a type named *n* shadows the declarations of any other types named *n* that are in scope at the point where *d* occurs throughout the scope of *d*.

A declaration *d* of a field, local variable, method parameter, constructor parameter or exception handler parameter named *n* shadows the declarations of any other fields, local variables, method parameters, constructor parameters or exception handler parameters named *n* that are in scope at the point where *d* occurs throughout the scope of *d*.

A declaration *d* of a method named *n* shadows the declarations of any other methods named *n* that are in an enclosing scope at the point where *d* occurs throughout the scope of *d*.

A package declaration never shadows any other declaration.

A single-type-import declaration *d* in a compilation unit *c* of package *p* that imports a type named *n* shadows the declarations of:

- any top level type named *n* declared in another compilation unit of *p*.
- any type named *n* imported by a type-import-on-demand declaration in `c`.
- any type named *n* imported by a static-import-on-demand declaration in *c*.

throughout `c`.

A single-static-import declaration *d* in a compilation unit *c* of package *p* that imports a field named *n* shadows the declaration of any static field named *n* imported by a static-import-on-demand declaration in *c*, throughout *c*.

A single-static-import declaration *d* in a compilation unit *c* of package *p* that imports a method named *n* with signature *s* shadows the declaration of any static method named *n* with signature *s* imported by a static-import-on-demand declaration in *c*, throughout *c*.

A single-static-import declaration *d* in a compilation unit *c* of package *p* that imports a type named *n* shadows the declarations of:

- any static type named *n* imported by a static-import-on-demand declaration in *c*.
- any top level type (§7.6) named *n* declared in another compilation unit (§7.3) of *p*.
- any type named *n* imported by a type-import-on-demand declaration (§7.5.2) in *c*.

throughout *c*.

A type-import-on-demand declaration never causes any other declaration to be shadowed.

A static-import-on-demand declaration never causes any other declaration to be shadowed.

A declaration *d* is said to be *visible at point p in a program* if the scope of *d* includes *p*, and *d* is not shadowed by any other declaration at *p*. When the program point we are discussing is clear from context, we will often simply say that a declaration is *visible*.

Note that shadowing is distinct from hiding (§8.3, §8.4.8.2, §8.5, §9.3, §9.5). Hiding, in the technical sense defined in this specification, applies only to members which would otherwise be inherited but are not because of a declaration in a subclass. Shadowing is also distinct from obscuring (§6.3.2).

Here is an example of shadowing of a field declaration by a local variable declaration:

```
class Test {
    static int x = 1;
    public static void main(String[] args) {
        int x = 0;
        System.out.print("x=" + x);
        System.out.println(", Test.x=" + Test.x);
    }
}
```

produces the output:

```
x=0, Test.x=1
```

This example declares:

- a class `Test`
- a class (`static`) variable `x` that is a member of the class `Test`
- a class method `main` that is a member of the class `Test`
- a parameter `args` of the `main` method.
- a local variable `x` of the `main` method

Since the scope of a class variable includes the entire body of the class (§8.2) the class variable `x` would normally be available throughout the entire body of the method `main`. In this example, however, the class variable `x` is shadowed within the body of the method `main` by the declaration of the local variable `x`.

A local variable has as its scope the rest of the block in which it is declared (§14.4.2); in this case this is the rest of the body of the `main` method, namely its initializer "`0`" and the invocations of `print` and `println`.

This means that:

- The expression "x" in the invocation of `print` refers to (denotes) the value of the local variable `x`.
- The invocation of `println` uses a qualified name (§6.6) `Test.x`, which uses the class type name `Test` to access the class variable `x`, because the declaration of `Test.x` is shadowed at this point and cannot be referred to by its simple name.

The following example illustrates the shadowing of one type declaration by another:

```
import java.util.*;
class Vector {
    int val[] = { 1 , 2 };
}
class Test {
    public static void main(String[] args) {
        Vector v = new Vector();
        System.out.println(v.val[0]);
    }
}
```

compiles and prints:

```
1
```

using the class `Vector` declared here in preference to the generic (§8.1.2) class `java.util.Vector` that might be imported on demand.

6.3.2 Obscured Declarations

A simple name may occur in contexts where it may potentially be interpreted as the name of a variable, a type or a package. In these situations, the rules of §6.5 specify that a variable will be chosen in preference to a type, and that a type will be chosen in preference to a package. Thus, it is may sometimes be impossible to refer to a visible type or package declaration via its simple name. We say that such a declaration is *obscured*.

Obscuring is distinct from shadowing (§6.3.1) and hiding (§8.3, §8.4.8.2, §8.5, §9.3, §9.5). The naming conventions of §6.8 help reduce obscuring.

6.4 Members and Inheritance

Packages and reference types have *members*.

This section provides an overview of the members of packages and reference types here, as background for the discussion of qualified names and the determination of the meaning of names. For a complete description of membership, see §4.4, §4.5.2, §4.8, §4.9, §7.1, §8.2, §9.2, and §10.7.

6.4.1 The Members of Type Variables, Parameterized Types, Raw Types and Intersection Types

The members of a type variable were specified in §4.4, the members of a parameterized type in §4.5.2, those of a raw type in §4.8, and the members of an intersection type were specified in §4.9.

6.4.2 The Members of a Package

The members of a package (§7) are specified in §7.1. For convenience, we repeat that specification here:

The members of a package are its subpackages and all the top level (§7.6) class types (§8) and top level interface types (§9) declared in all the compilation units (§7.3) of the package.

In general, the subpackages of a package are determined by the host system (§7.2). However, the package `java` always includes the subpackages `lang` and `io` and may include other subpackages. No two distinct members of the same package may have the same simple name (§7.1), but members of different packages may have the same simple name.

For example, it is possible to declare a package:

```
package vector;
public class Vector { Object[] vec; }
```

that has as a member a `public` class named `Vector`, even though the package `java.util` also declares a class named `Vector`. These two class types are different, reflected by the fact that they have different fully qualified names (§6.7). The fully qualified name of this example `Vector` is `vector.Vector`, whereas `java.util.Vector` is the fully qualified name of the `Vector` class usually included in the Java platform. Because the package `vector` contains a class named `Vector`, it cannot also have a subpackage named `Vector`.

6.4.3 The Members of a Class Type

The members of a class type (§8.2) are classes (§8.5, §9.5), interfaces (§8.5, §9.5), fields (§8.3, §9.3, §10.7), and methods (§8.4, §9.4). Members are either declared in the type, or *inherited* because they are accessible members of a superclass or superinterface which are neither private nor hidden nor overridden (§8.4.8).

The members of a class type are all of the following:

- Members inherited from its direct superclass (§8.1.4), if it has one (the class `Object` has no direct superclass)
- Members inherited from any direct superinterfaces (§8.1.5)

Members declared in the body of the class (§8.1.6)

Constructors (§8.8) and type variables (§4.4) are not members.

There is no restriction against a field and a method of a class type having the same simple name. Likewise, there is no restriction against a member class or member interface of a class type having the same simple name as a field or method of that class type.

A class may have two or more fields with the same simple name if they are declared in different interfaces and inherited. An attempt to refer to any of the fields by its simple name results in a compile-time error (§6.5.7.2, §8.2).

In the example:

```
interface Colors {
    int WHITE = 0, BLACK = 1;
}

interface Separates {
    int CYAN = 0, MAGENTA = 1, YELLOW = 2, BLACK = 3;
}
```

```
class Test implements Colors, Separates {
    public static void main(String[] args) {
        System.out.println(BLACK); // compile-time error: ambiguous
    }
}
```

the name BLACK in the method main is ambiguous, because class Test has two members named BLACK, one inherited from Colors and one from Separates.

A class type may have two or more methods with the same simple name if the methods have signatures that are not override-equivalent (§8.4.2). Such a method member name is said to be *overloaded*.

A class type may contain a declaration for a method with the same name and the same signature as a method that would otherwise be inherited from a superclass or superinterface. In this case, the method of the superclass or superinterface is not inherited. If the method not inherited is abstract, then the new declaration is said to *implement* it; if the method not inherited is not abstract, then the new declaration is said to *override* it.

In the example:

```
class Point {
    float x, y;
    void move(int dx, int dy) { x += dx; y += dy; }
    void move(float dx, float dy) { x += dx; y += dy; }
    public String toString() { return "("+x+","+y+")"; }
}
```

the class Point has two members that are methods with the same name, move. The overloaded move method of class Point chosen for any particular method invocation is determined at compile time by the overloading resolution procedure given in §15.12.

In this example, the members of the class Point are the float instance variables x and y declared in Point, the two declared move methods, the declared toString method, and the members that Point inherits from its implicit direct superclass Object (§4.3.2), such as the method hashCode. Note that Point does not inherit the toString method of class Object because that method is overridden by the declaration of the toString method in class Point.

6.4.4 The Members of an Interface Type

The members of an interface type (§9.2) may be classes (§8.5, §9.5), interfaces (§8.5, §9.5), fields (§8.3, §9.3, §10.7), and methods (§8.4, §9.4). The members of an interface are:

- Those members declared in the interface.
- Those members inherited from direct superinterfaces.

- If an interface has no direct superinterfaces, then the interface implicitly declares a public abstract member method *m* with signature `s`, return type `r`, and `throws` clause `t` corresponding to each public instance method *m* with signature `s`, return type `r`, and `throws` clause `t` declared in `Object`, unless a method with the same signature, same return type, and a compatible `throws` clause is explicitly declared by the interface. It is a compile-time error if the interface explicitly declares such a method *m* in the case where *m* is declared to be `final` in `Object`.

Type variables (§4.4) are not members.

An interface may have two or more fields with the same simple name if they are declared in different interfaces and inherited. An attempt to refer to any such field by its simple name results in a compile-time error (§6.5.6.1, §9.2).

In the example:

```
interface Colors {
    int WHITE = 0, BLACK = 1;
}
interface Separates {
    int CYAN = 0, MAGENTA = 1, YELLOW = 2, BLACK = 3;
}
interface ColorsAndSeparates extends Colors, Separates {
            int DEFAULT = BLACK; // compile-time error: ambiguous
}
```

the members of the interface `ColorsAndSeparates` include those members inherited from `Colors` and those inherited from `Separates`, namely `WHITE`, `BLACK` (first of two), `CYAN`, `MAGENTA`, `YELLOW`, and `BLACK` (second of two). The member name `BLACK` is ambiguous in the interface `ColorsAndSeparates`.

6.4.5 The Members of an Array Type

The members of an array type are specified in §10.7. For convenience, we repeat that specification here.

The members of an array type are all of the following:

- The `public final` field `length`, which contains the number of components of the array (`length` may be positive or zero).
- The `public` method `clone`, which overrides the method of the same name in class `Object` and throws no checked exceptions. The return type of the clone method of an array type `T[]` is `T[]`.
- All the members inherited from class `Object`; the only method of `Object` that is not inherited is its `clone` method.

The example:

```
class Test {
    public static void main(String[] args) {
        int[] ia = new int[3];
        int[] ib = new int[6];
        System.out.println(ia.getClass() == ib.getClass());
        System.out.println("ia has length=" + ia.length);
    }
}
```

produces the output:

```
true
ia has length=3
```

This example uses the method `getClass` inherited from class `Object` and the field `length`. The result of the comparison of the `Class` objects in the first `println` demonstrates that all arrays whose components are of type `int` are instances of the same array type, which is `int[]`.

6.5 Determining the Meaning of a Name

The meaning of a name depends on the context in which it is used. The determination of the meaning of a name requires three steps. First, context causes a name syntactically to fall into one of six categories: *PackageName*, *TypeName*, *ExpressionName*, *MethodName*, *PackageOrTypeName,* or *AmbiguousName*. Second, a name that is initially classified by its context as an *AmbiguousName* or as a *PackageOrTypeName* is then reclassified to be a *PackageName*, *TypeName*, or *ExpressionName*. Third, the resulting category then dictates the final determination of the meaning of the name (or a compilation error if the name has no meaning).

PackageName:
  Identifier
  PackageName . *Identifier*

TypeName:
  Identifier
  PackageOrTypeName . *Identifier*

ExpressionName:
  Identifier
  AmbiguousName . *Identifier*

MethodName:
Identifier
AmbiguousName . *Identifier*

PackageOrTypeName:
Identifier
PackageOrTypeName . *Identifier*

AmbiguousName:
Identifier
AmbiguousName . *Identifier*

The use of context helps to minimize name conflicts between entities of different kinds. Such conflicts will be rare if the naming conventions described in §6.8 are followed. Nevertheless, conflicts may arise unintentionally as types developed by different programmers or different organizations evolve. For example, types, methods, and fields may have the same name. It is always possible to distinguish between a method and a field with the same name, since the context of a use always tells whether a method is intended.

6.5.1 Syntactic Classification of a Name According to Context

A name is syntactically classified as a *PackageName* in these contexts:

- In a package declaration (§7.4)
- To the left of the "`.`" in a qualified *PackageName*

A name is syntactically classified as a *TypeName* in these contexts:

- In a single-type-import declaration (§7.5.1)
- To the left of the "." in a single static import (§7.5.3) declaration
- To the left of the "." in a static import-on-demand (§7.5.4) declaration
- To the left of the "<" in a parameterized type (§4.5)
- In an actual type argument list of a parameterized type
- In an explicit actual type argument list in a generic method (§8.4.4) or constructor (§8.8.4) invocation
- In an `extends` clause in a type variable declaration (§8.1.2)
- In an `extends` clause of a wildcard type argument (§4.5.1)
- In a `super` clause of a wildcard type argument (§4.5.1)

- In an `extends` clause in a class declaration (§8.1.4)
- In an `implements` clause in a class declaration (§8.1.5)
- In an `extends` clause in an interface declaration (§9.1.3)
- After the "@" sign in an annotation (§9.7)
- As a *Type* (or the part of a *Type* that remains after all brackets are deleted) in any of the following contexts:
  - In a field declaration (§8.3, §9.3)
  - As the result type of a method (§8.4, §9.4)
  - As the type of a formal parameter of a method or constructor (§8.4.1, §8.8.1, §9.4)
  - As the type of an exception that can be thrown by a method or constructor (§8.4.6, §8.8.5, §9.4)
  - As the type of a local variable (§14.4)
  - As the type of an exception parameter in a `catch` clause of a `try` statement (§14.20)
  - As the type in a class literal (§15.8.2)
  - As the qualifying type of a qualified `this` expression (§15.8.4).
  - As the class type which is to be instantiated in an unqualified class instance creation expression (§15.9)
  - As the direct superclass or direct superinterface of an anonymous class (§15.9.5) which is to be instantiated in an unqualified class instance creation expression (§15.9)
  - As the element type of an array to be created in an array creation expression (§15.10)
  - As the qualifying type of field access using the keyword `super` (§15.11.2)
  - As the qualifying type of a method invocation using the keyword `super` (§15.12)
  - As the type mentioned in the cast operator of a cast expression (§15.16)
  - As the type that follows the `instanceof` relational operator (§15.20.2)

A name is syntactically classified as an *ExpressionName* in these contexts:

- As the qualifying expression in a qualified superclass constructor invocation (§8.8.7.1)
- As the qualifying expression in a qualified class instance creation expression (§15.9)
- As the array reference expression in an array access expression (§15.13)
- As a *PostfixExpression* (§15.14)
- As the left-hand operand of an assignment operator (§15.26)

A name is syntactically classified as a *MethodName* in these contexts:

- Before the "(" in a method invocation expression (§15.12)
- To the left of the "=" sign in an annotation's element value pair (§9.7)

A name is syntactically classified as a *PackageOrTypeName* in these contexts:

- To the left of the "." in a qualified *TypeName*
- In a type-import-on-demand declaration (§7.5.2)

A name is syntactically classified as an *AmbiguousName* in these contexts:

- To the left of the "." in a qualified *ExpressionName*
- To the left of the "." in a qualified *MethodName*
- To the left of the "." in a qualified *AmbiguousName*
- In the default value clause of an annotation type element declaration (§9.6)
- To the right of an "=" in an an element value pair (§9.7)

6.5.2 Reclassification of Contextually Ambiguous Names

An *AmbiguousName* is then reclassified as follows:

- If the *AmbiguousName* is a simple name, consisting of a single *Identifier*:
  - If the *Identifier* appears within the scope (§6.3) of a local variable declaration (§14.4) or parameter declaration (§8.4.1, §8.8.1, §14.20) or field declaration (§8.3) with that name, then the *AmbiguousName* is reclassified as an *ExpressionName*.

  - Otherwise, if a field of that name is declared in the compilation unit (§7.3) containing the *Identifier* by a single-static-import declaration (§7.5.3), or by a static-import-on-demand declaration (§7.5.4) then the *AmbiguousName* is reclassified as an *ExpressionName*.
  - Otherwise, if the *Identifier* appears within the scope (§6.3) of a top level class (§8) or interface type declaration (§9), a local class declaration (§14.3) or member type declaration (§8.5, §9.5) with that name, then the *AmbiguousName* is reclassified as a *TypeName*.
  - Otherwise, if a type of that name is declared in the compilation unit (§7.3) containing the *Identifier*, either by a single-type-import declaration (§7.5.1), or by a type-import-on-demand declaration (§7.5.2), or by a single-static-import declaration (§7.5.3), or by a static-import-on-demand declaration (§7.5.4), then the *AmbiguousName* is reclassified as a *TypeName*.
  - Otherwise, the *AmbiguousName* is reclassified as a *PackageName*. A later step determines whether or not a package of that name actually exists.
- If the *AmbiguousName* is a qualified name, consisting of a name, a "`.`", and an *Identifier*, then the name to the left of the "`.`" is first reclassified, for it is itself an *AmbiguousName*. There is then a choice:
  - If the name to the left of the "`.`" is reclassified as a *PackageName*, then if there is a package whose name is the name to the left of the "`.`" and that package contains a declaration of a type whose name is the same as the *Identifier*, then this *AmbiguousName* is reclassified as a *TypeName*. Otherwise, this *AmbiguousName* is reclassified as a *PackageName*. A later step determines whether or not a package of that name actually exists.
  - If the name to the left of the "`.`" is reclassified as a *TypeName*, then if the *Identifier* is the name of a method or field of the type denoted by *TypeName*, this *AmbiguousName* is reclassified as an *ExpressionName*. Otherwise, if the *Identifier* is the name of a member type of the type denoted by *TypeName*, this *AmbiguousName* is reclassified as a *TypeName*. Otherwise, a compile-time error results.
  - If the name to the left of the "`.`" is reclassified as an *ExpressionName*, then let *T* be the type of the expression denoted by *ExpressionName*. If the *Identifier* is the name of a method or field of the type denoted by *T*, this *AmbiguousName* is reclassified as an *ExpressionName*. Otherwise, if the *Identifier* is the name of a member type (§8.5, §9.5) of the type denoted by *T*, then this *AmbiguousName* is reclassified as a *TypeName*. Otherwise, a compile-time error results.

As an example, consider the following contrived "library code":

```
package org.rpgpoet;
import java.util.Random;
interface Music { Random[] wizards = new Random[4]; }
```

and then consider this example code in another package:

```
package bazola;
class Gabriel {
    static int n = org.rpgpoet.Music.wizards.length;
}
```

First of all, the name `org.rpgpoet.Music.wizards.length` is classified as an *ExpressionName* because it functions as a *PostfixExpression*. Therefore, each of the names:

```
org.rpgpoet.Music.wizards
org.rpgpoet.Music
org.rpgpoet
org
```

is initially classified as an *AmbiguousName*. These are then reclassified:

- The simple name `org` is reclassified as a *PackageName* (since there is no variable or type named `org` in scope).
- Next, assuming that there is no class or interface named `rpgpoet` in any compilation unit of package `org` (and we know that there is no such class or interface because package `org` has a subpackage named `rpgpoet`), the qualified name `org.rpgpoet` is reclassified as a *PackageName*.
- Next, because package `org.rpgpoet` has an interface type named `Music`, the qualified name `org.rpgpoet.Music` is reclassified as a *TypeName*.
- Finally, because the name `org.rpgpoet.Music` is a *TypeName*, the qualified name `org.rpgpoet.Music.wizards` is reclassified as an *ExpressionName*.

6.5.3 Meaning of Package Names

The meaning of a name classified as a *PackageName* is determined as follows.

6.5.3.1 *Simple Package Names*

If a package name consists of a single *Identifier*, then this identifier denotes a top level package named by that identifier. If no top level package of that name is in scope (§7.4.4), then a compile-time error occurs.

6.5.3.2 *Qualified Package Names*

If a package name is of the form `Q.Id`, then `Q` must also be a package name. The package name `Q.Id` names a package that is the member named `Id` within the package named by `Q`. If `Q` does not name an observable package (§7.4.3), or `Id` is not the simple name an observable subpackage of that package, then a compile-time error occurs.

6.5.4 Meaning of *PackageOrTypeNames*

6.5.4.1 *Simple PackageOrTypeNames*

If the *PackageOrTypeName*, `Q`, occurs in the scope of a type named `Q`, then the *PackageOrTypeName* is reclassified as a *TypeName*.

Otherwise, the *PackageOrTypeName* is reclassified as a *PackageName*. The meaning of the *PackageOrTypeName* is the meaning of the reclassified name.

6.5.4.2 *Qualified PackageOrTypeNames*

Given a qualified *PackageOrTypeName* of the form `Q.Id`, if the type or package denoted by `Q` has a member type named `Id`, then the qualified *PackageOrTypeName* name is reclassified as a *TypeName*.

Otherwise, it is reclassified as a *PackageName*. The meaning of the qualified *PackageOrTypeName* is the meaning of the reclassified name.

6.5.5 Meaning of Type Names

The meaning of a name classified as a *TypeName* is determined as follows.

6.5.5.1 *Simple Type Names*

If a type name consists of a single *Identifier*, then the identifier must occur in the scope of exactly one visible declaration of a type with this name, or a compile-time error occurs. The meaning of the type name is that type.

6.5.5.2 *Qualified Type Names*

If a type name is of the form `Q.Id`, then `Q` must be either a type name or a package name. If `Id` names exactly one type that is a member of the type or package denoted by `Q`, then the qualified type name denotes that type. If `Id` does not name a member type (§8.5, §9.5) within `Q`, or the member type named `Id` within `Q` is not accessible (§6.6), or *Id* names more than one member type within *Q*, then a compile-time error occurs.

The example:

```
package wnj.test;
class Test {
    public static void main(String[] args) {
        java.util.Date date =
            new java.util.Date(System.currentTimeMillis());
        System.out.println(date.toLocaleString());
    }
}
```

produced the following output the first time it was run:

```
Sun Jan 21 22:56:29 1996
```

In this example the name `java.util.Date` must denote a type, so we first use the procedure recursively to determine if `java.util` is an accessible type or a package, which it is, and then look to see if the type `Date` is accessible in this package.

DISCUSSION

Type names are distinct from type declaration specifiers (§4.3). A type name is always qualified by meas of another type name. In some cases, it is necessary to access an inner class that is a member of a parameterized type:

```
class GenericOuter<T extends Number> {
    public class Inner<S extends Comparable<S>> {
            T getT() { return null;}
            S getS() { return null;}
    }
};

GenericOuter<Integer>.Inner<Double> x1 = null;
Integer i = x1.getT();
Double d = x1.getS();
```

If we accessed `Inner` by qualifying it with a type name, as in:

```
GenericOuter.Inner x2 = null;
```

we would force its use as a raw type, losing type information.

6.5.6 Meaning of Expression Names

The meaning of a name classified as an *ExpressionName* is determined as follows.

6.5.6.1 *Simple Expression Names*

If an expression name consists of a single *Identifier*, then there must be exactly one visible declaration denoting either a local variable, parameter or field in scope at the point at which the the *Identifier* occurs. Otherwise, a compile-time error occurs.

If the declaration declares a final field, the meaning of the name is the value of that field. Otherwise, the meaning of the expression name is the variable declared by the declaration.

If the field is an instance variable (§8.3), the expression name must appear within the declaration of an instance method (§8.4), constructor (§8.8), instance initializer (§8.6), or instance variable initializer (§8.3.2.2). If it appears within a `static` method (§8.4.3.2), static initializer (§8.7), or initializer for a `static` variable (§8.3.2.1, §12.4.2), then a compile-time error occurs.

The type of the expression name is the declared type of the field, local variable or parameter after capture conversion (§5.1.10).

In the example:

```
class Test {
    static int v;
    static final int f = 3;
    public static void main(String[] args) {
        int i;
        i = 1;
        v = 2;
        f = 33;                         // compile-time error
        System.out.println(i + " " + v + " " + f);
    }
}
```

the names used as the left-hand-sides in the assignments to `i`, `v`, and `f` denote the local variable `i`, the field `v`, and the value of `f` (not the variable `f`, because `f` is a `final` variable). The example therefore produces an error at compile time because the last assignment does not have a variable as its left-hand side. If the erroneous assignment is removed, the modified code can be compiled and it will produce the output:

```
1 2 3
```

6.5.6.2 *Qualified Expression Names*

If an expression name is of the form `Q.Id`, then `Q` has already been classified as a package name, a type name, or an expression name:

- If `Q` is a package name, then a compile-time error occurs.
- If `Q` is a type name that names a class type (§8), then:
  - If there is not exactly one accessible (§6.6) member of the class type that is a field named `Id`, then a compile-time error occurs.
  - Otherwise, if the single accessible member field is not a class variable (that is, it is not declared `static`), then a compile-time error occurs.
  - Otherwise, if the class variable is declared `final`, then `Q.Id` denotes the value of the class variable. The type of the expression `Q.Id` is the declared type of the class variable after capture conversion (§5.1.10). If `Q.Id` appears in a context that requires a variable and not a value, then a compile-time error occurs.
  - Otherwise, `Q.Id` denotes the class variable. The type of the expression `Q.Id` is the declared type of the class variable after capture conversion (§5.1.10). Note that this clause covers the use of enum constants (§8.9), since these always have a corresponding `final` class variable.
- If `Q` is a type name that names an interface type (§9), then:
  - If there is not exactly one accessible (§6.6) member of the interface type that is a field named `Id`, then a compile-time error occurs.
  - Otherwise, `Q.Id` denotes the value of the field. The type of the expression `Q.Id` is the declared type of the field after capture conversion (§5.1.10). If `Q.Id` appears in a context that requires a variable and not a value, then a compile-time error occurs.
- If `Q` is an expression name, let `T` be the type of the expression `Q`:
  - If `T` is not a reference type, a compile-time error occurs.
  - If there is not exactly one accessible (§6.6) member of the type `T` that is a field named `Id`, then a compile-time error occurs.
  - Otherwise, if this field is any of the following:
    - A field of an interface type
    - A `final` field of a class type (which may be either a class variable or an instance variable)

  * The `final` field `length` of an array type

then `Q.Id` denotes the value of the field. The type of the expression `Q.Id` is the declared type of the field after capture conversion (§5.1.10). If `Q.Id` appears in a context that requires a variable and not a value, then a compile-time error occurs.

- Otherwise, `Q.Id` denotes a variable, the field `Id` of class `T`, which may be either a class variable or an instance variable. The type of the expression `Q.Id` is the type of the field member after capture conversion (§5.1.10).

The example:

```
class Point {
    int x, y;
    static int nPoints;
}
class Test {
    public static void main(String[] args) {
        int i = 0;
        i.x++;                  // compile-time error
        Point p = new Point();
        p.nPoints();            // compile-time error
    }
}
```

encounters two compile-time errors, because the `int` variable `i` has no members, and because `nPoints` is not a method of class `Point`.

DISCUSSION

Note that expression names may be qualified by type names, but not by types in general. A consequence is that it is not possible to access a class variable through a parameterized type

```
class Foo<T> {
    public static int classVar = 42;
}
Foo<String>.classVar = 91; // illegal
```

Instead, one writes

```
Foo.classVar = 91;
```

This does not restrict the language in any meaningful way. Type parameters may not be used in the types of static variables, and so the actual parameters of a parameterized type can never influence the type of a static variable. Therefore, no expressive power is lost. Technically, the type name Foo above is a raw type, but this use of raw types is harmless, and does not give rise to warnings

---

6.5.7 Meaning of Method Names

A *MethodName* can appear only in a method invocation expression (§15.12) or as an element name in an element-value pair (§9.7). The meaning of a name classified as a *MethodName* is determined as follows.

6.5.7.1 *Simple Method Names*

A simple method name may appear as the element name in an element-value pair. The *Identifier* in an *ElementValuePair* must be the simple name of one of the elements of the annotation type identified by *TypeName* in the containing annotation. Otherwise, a compile-time error occurs. (In other words, the identifier in an element-value pair must also be a method name in the interface identified by *TypeName*.)

Otherwise, a simple method name necessarily appears in the context of a method invocation expression. In that case, if a method name consists of a single *Identifier*, then *Identifier* is the method name to be used for method invocation. The *Identifier* must name at least one visible (§6.3.1) method that is in scope at the point where the *Identifier* appear or a method imported by a single-static-import declaration (§7.5.3) or static-import-on-demand declaration (§7.5.4) within the compilation unit within which the *Identifier* appears.

See §15.12 for further discussion of the interpretation of simple method names in method invocation expressions.

6.5.7.2 *Qualified Method Names*

A qualified method name can only appear in the context of a method invocation expression. If a method name is of the form `Q.Id`, then `Q` has already been classified as a package name, a type name, or an expression name. If `Q` is a package name, then a compile-time error occurs. Otherwise, `Id` is the method name to be used for method invocation. If `Q` is a type name, then `Id` must name at least one `static` method of the type `Q`. If `Q` is an expression name, then let `T` be the type of the expression `Q`; `Id` must name at least one method of the type `T`. See §15.12 for further discussion of the interpretation of qualified method names in method invocation expressions.

DISCUSSION

Like expression names, method names may be qualified by type names, but not by types in general. The implications are similar to those for expression names as discussed in §6.5.6.2.

6.6 Access Control

The Java programming language provides mechanisms for *access control*, to prevent the users of a package or class from depending on unnecessary details of the implementation of that package or class. If access is permitted, then the accessed entity is said to be *accessible*.

Note that accessibility is a static property that can be determined at compile time; it depends only on types and declaration modifiers. Qualified names are a means of access to members of packages and reference types; related means of access include field access expressions (§15.11) and method invocation expressions (§15.12). All three are syntactically similar in that a "`.`" token appears, preceded by some indication of a package, type, or expression having a type and followed by an *Identifier* that names a member of the package or type. These are collectively known as constructs for *qualified access*.

Access control applies to qualified access and to the invocation of constructors by class instance creation expressions (§15.9) and explicit constructor invocations (§8.8.7.1). Accessibility also effects inheritance of class members (§8.2), including hiding and method overriding (§8.4.8.1).

6.6.1 Determining Accessibility

- A package is always accessible.
- If a class or interface type is declared `public`, then it may be accessed by any code, provided that the compilation unit (§7.3) in which it is declared is observable. If a top level class or interface type is not declared `public`, then it may be accessed only from within the package in which it is declared.
- An array type is accessible if and only if its element type is accessible.

- A member (class, interface, field, or method) of a reference (class, interface, or array) type or a constructor of a class type is accessible only if the type is accessible and the member or constructor is declared to permit access:
  - If the member or constructor is declared `public`, then access is permitted. All members of interfaces are implicitly `public`.
  - Otherwise, if the member or constructor is declared `protected`, then access is permitted only when one of the following is true:
    - Access to the member or constructor occurs from within the package containing the class in which the `protected` member or constructor is declared.
    - Access is correct as described in §6.6.2.
  - Otherwise, if the member or constructor is declared `private`, then access is permitted if and only if it occurs within the body of the top level class (§7.6) that encloses the declaration of the member or constructor.
  - Otherwise, we say there is default access, which is permitted only when the access occurs from within the package in which the type is declared.

6.6.2 Details on `protected` Access

A `protected` member or constructor of an object may be accessed from outside the package in which it is declared only by code that is responsible for the implementation of that object.

6.6.2.1 *Access to a* `protected` *Member*

Let `C` be the class in which a `protected` member m is declared. Access is permitted only within the body of a subclass `S` of `C`. In addition, if *`Id`* denotes an instance field or instance method, then:

- If the access is by a qualified name `Q.`*`Id`*, where `Q` is an *ExpressionName*, then the access is permitted if and only if the type of the expression `Q` is `S` or a subclass of `S`.
- If the access is by a field access expression `E.`*`Id`*, where `E` is a *Primary* expression, or by a method invocation expression `E.`*`Id`*`(. . .)`, where `E` is a *Primary* expression, then the access is permitted if and only if the type of `E` is `S` or a subclass of `S`.

6.6.2.2 *Qualified Access to a* `protected` *Constructor*

Let `C` be the class in which a `protected` constructor is declared and let `S` be the innermost class in whose declaration the use of the `protected` constructor occurs. Then:

- If the access is by a superclass constructor invocation `super(...)` or by a qualified superclass constructor invocation of the form `E.super(...)`, where `E` is a *Primary* expression, then the access is permitted.
- If the access is by an anonymous class instance creation expression of the form `new C(...){...}` or by a qualified class instance creation expression of the form `E.new C(...){...}`, where `E` is a *Primary* expression, then the access is permitted.
- Otherwise, if the access is by a simple class instance creation expression of the form `new C(...)` or by a qualified class instance creation expression of the form `E.new C(...)`, where `E` is a *Primary* expression, then the access is not permitted. A `protected` constructor can be accessed by a class instance creation expression (that does not declare an anonymous class) only from within the package in which it is defined.

6.6.3 An Example of Access Control

For examples of access control, consider the two compilation units:

```
package points;
class PointVec { Point[] vec; }
```

and:

```
package points;
public class Point {
    protected int x, y;
    public void move(int dx, int dy) { x += dx; y += dy; }
    public int getX() { return x; }
    public int getY() { return y; }
}
```

which declare two class types in the package `points`:

- The class type `PointVec` is not `public` and not part of the `public` interface of the package `points`, but rather can be used only by other classes in the package.
- The class type `Point` is declared `public` and is available to other packages. It is part of the `public` interface of the package `points`.

- The methods `move`, `getX`, and `getY` of the class `Point` are declared `public` and so are available to any code that uses an object of type `Point`.
- The fields `x` and `y` are declared `protected` and are accessible outside the package `points` only in subclasses of class `Point`, and only when they are fields of objects that are being implemented by the code that is accessing them.

See §6.6.7 for an example of how the `protected` access modifier limits access.

6.6.4 Example: Access to `public` and Non-`public` Classes

If a class lacks the `public` modifier, access to the class declaration is limited to the package in which it is declared (§6.6). In the example:

```
package points;
public class Point {
    public int x, y;
    public void move(int dx, int dy) { x += dx; y += dy; }
}
class PointList {
    Point next, prev;
}
```

two classes are declared in the compilation unit. The class `Point` is available outside the package `points`, while the class `PointList` is available for access only within the package.

Thus a compilation unit in another package can access `points.Point`, either by using its fully qualified name:

```
package pointsUser;
class Test {
    public static void main(String[] args) {
        points.Point p = new points.Point();
        System.out.println(p.x + " " + p.y);
    }
}
```

or by using a single-type-import declaration (§7.5.1) that mentions the fully qualified name, so that the simple name may be used thereafter:

```
package pointsUser;
import points.Point;
class Test {
    public static void main(String[] args) {
        Point p = new Point();
        System.out.println(p.x + " " + p.y);
    }}
```

However, this compilation unit cannot use or import `points.PointList`, which is not declared `public` and is therefore inaccessible outside package `points`.

6.6.5 Example: Default-Access Fields, Methods, and Constructors

If none of the access modifiers `public`, `protected`, or `private` are specified, a class member or constructor is accessible throughout the package that contains the declaration of the class in which the class member is declared, but the class member or constructor is not accessible in any other package.

If a `public` class has a method or constructor with default access, then this method or constructor is not accessible to or inherited by a subclass declared outside this package.

For example, if we have:

```
package points;
public class Point {
    public int x, y;
    void move(int dx, int dy) { x += dx; y += dy; }
    public void moveAlso(int dx, int dy) { move(dx, dy); }
}
```

then a subclass in another package may declare an unrelated `move` method, with the same signature (§8.4.2) and return type. Because the original `move` method is not accessible from package `morepoints`, `super` may not be used:

```
package morepoints;
public class PlusPoint extends points.Point {
    public void move(int dx, int dy) {
        super.move(dx, dy);     // compile-time error
        moveAlso(dx, dy);
    }
}
```

Because move of `Point` is not overridden by `move` in `PlusPoint`, the method `moveAlso` in `Point` never calls the method move in `PlusPoint`.

Thus if you delete the `super.move` call from `PlusPoint` and execute the test program:

```
import points.Point;
import morepoints.PlusPoint;
class Test {
    public static void main(String[] args) {
        PlusPoint pp = new PlusPoint();
        pp.move(1, 1);
    }
}
```

it terminates normally. If move of `Point` were overridden by `move` in `PlusPoint`, then this program would recurse infinitely, until a `StackoverflowError` occurred.

6.6.6 Example: public Fields, Methods, and Constructors

A `public` class member or constructor is accessible throughout the package where it is declared and from any other package, provided the package in which it is declared is observable (§7.4.3). For example, in the compilation unit:

```
package points;
public class Point {
    int x, y;
    public void move(int dx, int dy) {
        x += dx; y += dy;
        moves++;
    }
    public static int moves = 0;
}
```

the `public` class `Point` has as `public` members the `move` method and the `moves` field. These `public` members are accessible to any other package that has access to package `points`. The fields `x` and `y` are not `public` and therefore are accessible only from within the package `points`.

6.6.7 Example: protected Fields, Methods, and Constructors

Consider this example, where the `points` package declares:

```
package points;
public class Point {
    protected int x, y;
    void warp(threePoint.Point3d a) {
        if (a.z > 0)        // compile-time error: cannot access a.z
            a.delta(this);
    }
}
```

and the `threePoint` package declares:

```
package threePoint;
import points.Point;
public class Point3d extends Point {
    protected int z;
    public void delta(Point p) {
        p.x += this.x;    // compile-time error: cannot access p.x
```

```
            p.y += this.y;   // compile-time error: cannot access p.y
                }
        public void delta3d(Point3d q) {
            q.x += this.x;
            q.y += this.y;
            q.z += this.z;
        }
    }
```

which defines a class `Point3d`. A compile-time error occurs in the method `delta` here: it cannot access the protected members `x` and `y` of its parameter `p`, because while `Point3d` (the class in which the references to fields `x` and `y` occur) is a subclass of `Point` (the class in which `x` and `y` are declared), it is not involved in the implementation of a `Point` (the type of the parameter `p`). The method `delta3d` can access the protected members of its parameter `q`, because the class `Point3d` is a subclass of `Point` and is involved in the implementation of a `Point3d`.

The method `delta` could try to cast (§5.5, §15.16) its parameter to be a `Point3d`, but this cast would fail, causing an exception, if the class of `p` at run time were not `Point3d`.

A compile-time error also occurs in the method warp: it cannot access the protected member `z` of its parameter `a`, because while the class `Point` (the class in which the reference to field `z` occurs) is involved in the implementation of a `Point3d` (the type of the parameter `a`), it is not a subclass of `Point3d` (the class in which `z` is declared).

6.6.8 Example: `private` Fields, Methods, and Constructors

A `private` class member or constructor is accessible only within the body of the top level class (§7.6) that encloses the declaration of the member or constructor. It is not inherited by subclasses. In the example:

```
    class Point {
        Point() { setMasterID(); }
        int x, y;
        private int ID;
        private static int masterID = 0;
        private void setMasterID() { ID = masterID++; }
    }
```

the `private` members `ID`, `masterID`, and `setMasterID` may be used only within the body of class `Point`. They may not be accessed by qualified names, field access expressions, or method invocation expressions outside the body of the declaration of `Point`.

See §8.8.8 for an example that uses a `private` constructor.

6.7 Fully Qualified Names and Canonical Names

Every package, top level class, top level interface, and primitive type has a *fully qualified name*. An array type has a fully qualified name if and only if its element type has a fully qualified name.

- The fully qualified name of a primitive type is the keyword for that primitive type, namely `boolean`, `char`, `byte`, `short`, `int`, `long`, `float`, or `double`.
- The fully qualified name of a named package that is not a subpackage of a named package is its simple name.
- The fully qualified name of a named package that is a subpackage of another named package consists of the fully qualified name of the containing package, followed by "`.`", followed by the simple (member) name of the subpackage.
- The fully qualified name of a top level class or top level interface that is declared in an unnamed package is the simple name of the class or interface.
- The fully qualified name of a top level class or top level interface that is declared in a named package consists of the fully qualified name of the package, followed by "`.`", followed by the simple name of the class or interface.
- A member class or member interface *M* of another class *C* has a fully qualified name if and only if *C* has a fully qualified name. In that case, the fully qualified name of *M* consists of the fully qualified name of *C*, followed by "`.`", followed by the simple name of *M*.
- The fully qualified name of an array type consists of the fully qualified name of the component type of the array type followed by "`[]`".

Examples:

- The fully qualified name of the type `long` is "`long`".
- The fully qualified name of the package `java.lang` is "`java.lang`" because it is subpackage `lang` of package `java`.
- The fully qualified name of the class `Object`, which is defined in the package `java.lang`, is "`java.lang.Object`".
- The fully qualified name of the interface `Enumeration`, which is defined in the package `java.util`, is "`java.util.Enumeration`".
- The fully qualified name of the type "array of `double`" is "`double[]`".
- The fully qualified name of the type "array of array of array of array of `String`" is "`java.lang.String[][][][]`".

In the example:

```
package points;
class Point { int x, y; }
class PointVec {
   Point[] vec;
}
```

the fully qualified name of the type `Point` is "`points.Point`"; the fully qualified name of the type `PointVec` is "`points.PointVec`"; and the fully qualified name of the type of the field `vec` of class `PointVec` is "`points.Point[]`".

Every package, top level class, top level interface, and primitive type has a *canonical name*. An array type has a canonical name if and only if its element type has a canonical name. A member class or member interface *M* declared in another class *C* has a canonical name if and only if *C* has a canonical name. In that case, the canonical name of *M* consists of the canonical name of *C*, followed by "`.`", followed by the simple name of *M*. For every package, top level class, top level interface and primitive type, the canonical name is the same as the fully qualified name. The canonical name of an array type is defined only when the component type of the array has a canonical name. In that case, the canonical name of the array type consists of the canonical name of the component type of the array type followed by "`[]`".

The difference between a fully qualified name and a canonical name can be seen in examples such as:

```
package p;
class O1 { class I{}}
class O2 extends O1{};
```

In this example both `p.O1.I` and `p.O2.I` are fully qualified names that denote the same class, but only `p.O1.I` is its canonical name.

6.8 Naming Conventions

The class libraries of the Java platform attempt to use, whenever possible, names chosen according to the conventions presented here. These conventions help to make code more readable and avoid certain kinds of name conflicts.

We recommend these conventions for use in all programs written in the Java programming language. However, these conventions should not be followed slavishly if long-held conventional usage dictates otherwise. So, for example, the `sin` and `cos` methods of the class `java.lang.Math` have mathematically conventional names, even though these method names flout the convention suggested here because they are short and are not verbs.

6.8.1 Package Names

Names of packages that are to be made widely available should be formed as described in §7.7. Such names are always qualified names whose first identifier consists of two or three lowercase letters that name an Internet domain, such as `com`, `edu`, `gov`, `mil`, `net`, `org`, or a two-letter ISO country code such as `uk` or `jp`. Here are examples of hypothetical unique names that might be formed under this convention:

```
com.JavaSoft.jag.Oak
org.npr.pledge.driver
uk.ac.city.rugby.game
```

Names of packages intended only for local use should have a first identifier that begins with a lowercase letter, but that first identifier specifically should not be the identifier `java`; package names that start with the identifier `java` are reserved by Sun for naming Java platform packages.

When package names occur in expressions:

- If a package name is obscured by a field declaration, then `import` declarations (§7.5) can usually be used to make available the type names declared in that package.
- If a package name is obscured by a declaration of a parameter or local variable, then the name of the parameter or local variable can be changed without affecting other code.

The first component of a package name is normally not easily mistaken for a type name, as a type name normally begins with a single uppercase letter. (The Java programming language does not actually rely on case distinctions to determine whether a name is a package name or a type name.)

6.8.2 Class and Interface Type Names

Names of class types should be descriptive nouns or noun phrases, not overly long, in mixed case with the first letter of each word capitalized. For example:

```
ClassLoader
SecurityManager
Thread
Dictionary
BufferedInputStream
```

Likewise, names of interface types should be short and descriptive, not overly long, in mixed case with the first letter of each word capitalized. The name may be a descriptive noun or noun phrase, which is appropriate when an interface is used as if it were an abstract superclass, such as interfaces `java.io.DataInput` and `java.io.DataOutput`; or it may be an adjective describing a behavior, as for the interfaces `Runnable` and `Cloneable`.

Obscuring involving class and interface type names is rare. Names of fields, parameters, and local variables normally do not obscure type names because they conventionally begin with a lowercase letter whereas type names conventionally begin with an uppercase letter.

6.8.3 Type Variable Names

Type variable names should be pithy (single character if possible) yet evocative, and should not include lower case letters.

DISCUSSION

This makes it easy to distinguish formal type parameters from ordinary classes and interfaces.

Ccontainer types should use the name `E` for their element type. Maps should use `K` for the type of their keys and `V` for the type of their values. The name `X` should be used for arbitrary exception types. We use `T` for type, whenever there isn't anything more specific about the type to distinguish it.

DISCUSSION

This is often the case in generic methods.

If there are multiple type parameters that denote arbitrary types, one should use letters that neighbor `T` in the alphabet, such as `S`. Alternately, it is acceptable to use numeric subscripts (e.g., `T1, T2`) to distinguish among the different type variables. In such cases, all the variables with the same prefix should be subscripted.

DISCUSSION

If a generic method appears inside a generic class, it's a good idea to avoid using the same names for the type parameters of the method and class, to avoid confusion. The same applies to nested generic classes.

DISCUSSION

These conventions are illustrated in the code snippets below:

```
public class HashSet<E> extends AbstractSet<E> { ... }
public class HashMap<K,V> extends AbstractMap<K,V> { ... }
public class ThreadLocal<T> { ... }
public interface Functor<T, X extends Throwable> {
    T eval() throws X;
}
```

When type parameters do not fall conveniently into one of the categories mentioned, names should be chosen to be as meaningful as possible within the confines of a single letter. The names mentioned above (`E`, `K`, `T`, `V`, `X`) should not be used for type parameters that do not fall into the designated categories.

6.8.4 Method Names

Method names should be verbs or verb phrases, in mixed case, with the first letter lowercase and the first letter of any subsequent words capitalized. Here are some additional specific conventions for method names:

- Methods to `get` and `set` an attribute that might be thought of as a variable *V* should be named `get`*V* and `set`*V*. An example is the methods `getPriority` and `setPriority` of class `Thread`.
- A method that returns the length of something should be named `length`, as in class `String`.
- A method that tests a `boolean` condition *V* about an object should be named `is`*V*. An example is the method `isInterrupted` of class `Thread`.

- A method that converts its object to a particular format *F* should be named `to`*F*. Examples are the method `toString` of class `Object` and the methods `toLocaleString` and `toGMTString` of class `java.util.Date`.

Whenever possible and appropriate, basing the names of methods in a new class on names in an existing class that is similar, especially a class from the Java Application Programming Interface classes, will make it easier to use.

Method names cannot obscure or be obscured by other names (§6.5.7).

6.8.5 Field Names

Names of fields that are not `final` should be in mixed case with a lowercase first letter and the first letters of subsequent words capitalized. Note that well-designed classes have very few `public` or `protected` fields, except for fields that are constants (`final static` fields) (§6.8.6).

Fields should have names that are nouns, noun phrases, or abbreviations for nouns. Examples of this convention are the fields `buf`, `pos`, and `count` of the class `java.io.ByteArrayInputStream` and the field `bytesTransferred` of the class `java.io.InterruptedIOException`.

Obscuring involving field names is rare.

- If a field name obscures a package name, then an `import` declaration (§7.5) can usually be used to make available the type names declared in that package.
- If a field name obscures a type name, then a fully qualified name for the type can be used unless the type name denotes a local class (§14.3).
- Field names cannot obscure method names.
- If a field name is shadowed by a declaration of a parameter or local variable, then the name of the parameter or local variable can be changed without affecting other code.

6.8.6 Constant Names

The names of constants in interface types should be, and `final` variables of class types may conventionally be, a sequence of one or more words, acronyms, or abbreviations, all uppercase, with components separated by underscore "_" characters. Constant names should be descriptive and not unnecessarily abbreviated. Conventionally they may be any appropriate part of speech. Examples of names for constants include `MIN_VALUE`, `MAX_VALUE`, `MIN_RADIX`, and `MAX_RADIX` of the class `Character`.

A group of constants that represent alternative values of a set, or, less frequently, masking bits in an integer value, are sometimes usefully specified with a common acronym as a name prefix, as in:

```
interface ProcessStates {
    int PS_RUNNING = 0;
    int PS_SUSPENDED = 1;
}
```

Obscuring involving constant names is rare:

- Constant names normally have no lowercase letters, so they will not normally obscure names of packages or types, nor will they normally shadow fields, whose names typically contain at least one lowercase letter.
- Constant names cannot obscure method names, because they are distinguished syntactically.

6.8.7 Local Variable and Parameter Names

Local variable and parameter names should be short, yet meaningful. They are often short sequences of lowercase letters that are not words. For example:

- Acronyms, that is the first letter of a series of words, as in `cp` for a variable holding a reference to a `ColoredPoint`
- Abbreviations, as in `buf` holding a pointer to a `buffer` of some kind
- Mnemonic terms, organized in some way to aid memory and understanding, typically by using a set of local variables with conventional names patterned after the names of parameters to widely used classes. For example:
    - `in` and `out`, whenever some kind of input and output are involved, patterned after the fields of `System`
    - `off` and `len`, whenever an offset and length are involved, patterned after the parameters to the `read` and `write` methods of the interfaces `DataInput` and `DataOutput` of `java.io`

One-character local variable or parameter names should be avoided, except for temporary and looping variables, or where a variable holds an undistinguished value of a type. Conventional one-character names are:

- `b` for a `byte`
- `c` for a `char`
- `d` for a `double`
- `e` for an `Exception`
- `f` for a `float`

- `i`, `j`, and `k` for integers
- `l` for a `long`
- `o` for an `Object`
- `s` for a `String`
- `v` for an arbitrary value of some type

Local variable or parameter names that consist of only two or three lowercase letters should not conflict with the initial country codes and domain names that are the first component of unique package names (§7.7).

What's in a name? That which we call a rose
By any other name would smell as sweet.
—William Shakespeare, *Romeo and Juliet* (c. 1594), Act II, scene ii

Rose is a rose is a rose is a rose.
—Gertrude Stein, *Sacred Emily* (1913), in *Geographies and Plays*

. . . stat rosa pristina nomine, nomina nuda tenemus.
—Bernard of Morlay, *De contemptu mundi* (12th century),
quoted in Umberto Eco, *The Name of the Rose* (1980)

Rose, Rose, bo-Bose,
Banana-fana fo-Fose,
Fee, fie, mo-Mose—
—Rose!
—Lincoln Chase and Shirley Elliston, *The Name Game*
(#3 pop single in the U.S., January 1965),
as applied to the name "Rose"

CHAPTER 7

Packages

Good things come in small packages.
—Traditional proverb

PROGRAMS are organized as sets of packages. Each package has its own set of names for types, which helps to prevent name conflicts. A top level type is accessible (§6.6) outside the package that declares it only if the type is declared `public`.

The naming structure for packages is hierarchical (§7.1). The members of a package are class and interface types (§7.6), which are declared in compilation units of the package, and subpackages, which may contain compilation units and subpackages of their own.

A package can be stored in a file system (§7.2.1) or in a database (§7.2.2). Packages that are stored in a file system may have certain constraints on the organization of their compilation units to allow a simple implementation to find classes easily.

A package consists of a number of compilation units (§7.3). A compilation unit automatically has access to all types declared in its package and also automatically imports all of the public types declared in the predefined package `java.lang`.

For small programs and casual development, a package can be unnamed (§7.4.2) or have a simple name, but if code is to be widely distributed, unique package names should be chosen (§7.7). This can prevent the conflicts that would otherwise occur if two development groups happened to pick the same package name and these packages were later to be used in a single program.

7.1 Package Members

The members of a package are its subpackages and all the top level (§7.6) class types (§8) and top level interface types (§9) declared in all the compilation units (§7.3) of the package.

For example, in the Java Application Programming Interface:

- The package `java` has subpackages `awt`, `applet`, `io`, `lang`, `net`, and `util`, but no compilation units.
- The package `java.awt` has a subpackage named `image`, as well as a number of compilation units containing declarations of class and interface types.

If the fully qualified name (§6.7) of a package is *P*, and *Q* is a subpackage of *P*, then *P*`.`*Q* is the fully qualified name of the subpackage.

A package may not contain two members of the same name, or a compile-time error results.

Here are some examples:

- Because the package `java.awt` has a subpackage `image`, it cannot (and does not) contain a declaration of a class or interface type named `image`.
- If there is a package named `mouse` and a member type `Button` in that package (which then might be referred to as `mouse.Button`), then there cannot be any package with the fully qualified name `mouse.Button` or `mouse.Button.Click`.
- If `com.sun.java.jag` is the fully qualified name of a type, then there cannot be any package whose fully qualified name is either `com.sun.java.jag` or `com.sun.java.jag.scrabble`.

The hierarchical naming structure for packages is intended to be convenient for organizing related packages in a conventional manner, but has no significance in itself other than the prohibition against a package having a subpackage with the same simple name as a top level type (§7.6) declared in that package. There is no special access relationship between a package named `oliver` and another package named `oliver.twist`, or between packages named `evelyn.wood` and `evelyn.waugh`. For example, the code in a package named `oliver.twist` has no better access to the types declared within package `oliver` than code in any other package.

7.2 Host Support for Packages

Each host determines how packages, compilation units, and subpackages are created and stored, and which compilation units are observable (§7.3) in a particular compilation.

The observability of compilation units in turn determines which packages are observable, and which packages are in scope.

The packages may be stored in a local file system in simple implementations of the Java platform. Other implementations may use a distributed file system or some form of database to store source and/or binary code.

7.2.1 Storing Packages in a File System

As an extremely simple example, all the packages and source and binary code on a system might be stored in a single directory and its subdirectories. Each immediate subdirectory of this directory would represent a top level package, that is, one whose fully qualified name consists of a single simple name. The directory might contain the following immediate subdirectories:

```
com
gls
jag
java
wnj
```

where directory `java` would contain the Java Application Programming Interface packages; the directories `jag`, `gls`, and `wnj` might contain packages that three of the authors of this specification created for their personal use and to share with each other within this small group; and the directory `com` would contain packages procured from companies that used the conventions described in §7.7 to generate unique names for their packages.

Continuing the example, the directory `java` would contain, among others, the following subdirectories:

```
applet
awt
io
lang
net
util
```

corresponding to the packages `java.applet`, `java.awt`, `java.io`, `java.lang`, `java.net`, and `java.util` that are defined as part of the Java Application Programming Interface.

Still continuing the example, if we were to look inside the directory `util`, we might see the following files:

```
BitSet.java                 Observable.java
BitSet.class                Observable.class
Date.java                   Observer.java
Date.class                  Observer.class
...
```

where each of the `.java` files contains the source for a compilation unit (§7.3) that contains the definition of a class or interface whose binary compiled form is contained in the corresponding `.class` file.

Under this simple organization of packages, an implementation of the Java platform would transform a package name into a pathname by concatenating the components of the package name, placing a file name separator (directory indicator) between adjacent components.

For example, if this simple organization were used on a UNIX system, where the file name separator is `/`, the package name:

```
jag.scrabble.board
```

would be transformed into the directory name:

```
jag/scrabble/board
```

and:

```
com.sun.sunsoft.DOE
```

would be transformed to the directory name:

```
com/sun/sunsoft/DOE
```

A package name component or class name might contain a character that cannot correctly appear in a host file system's ordinary directory name, such as a Unicode character on a system that allows only ASCII characters in file names. As a convention, the character can be escaped by using, say, the `@` character followed by four hexadecimal digits giving the numeric value of the character, as in the `\u`*`xxxx`* escape (§3.3), so that the package name:

```
children.activities.crafts.papierM\u00e2ch\u00e9
```

which can also be written using full Unicode as:

```
children.activities.crafts.papierMâché
```

might be mapped to the directory name:

```
children/activities/crafts/papierM@00e2ch@00e9
```

If the `@` character is not a valid character in a file name for some given host file system, then some other character that is not valid in a identifier could be used instead.

7.2.2 Storing Packages in a Database

A host system may store packages and their compilation units and subpackages in a database.

Such a database must not impose the optional restrictions (§7.6) on compilation units in file-based implementations. For example, a system that uses a database to store packages may not enforce a maximum of one `public` class or interface per compilation unit.

Systems that use a database must, however, provide an option to convert a program to a form that obeys the restrictions, for purposes of export to file-based implementations.

7.3 Compilation Units

CompilationUnit is the goal symbol (§2.1) for the syntactic grammar (§2.3) of Java programs. It is defined by the following productions:

CompilationUnit:
    PackageDeclaration$_{opt}$ *ImportDeclarations*$_{opt}$ *TypeDeclarations*$_{opt}$

ImportDeclarations:
    ImportDeclaration
    ImportDeclarations ImportDeclaration

TypeDeclarations:
    TypeDeclaration
    TypeDeclarations TypeDeclaration

Types declared in different compilation units can depend on each other, circularly. A Java compiler must arrange to compile all such types at the same time.

A *compilation unit* consists of three parts, each of which is optional:

- A `package` declaration (§7.4), giving the fully qualified name (§6.7) of the package to which the compilation unit belongs. A compilation unit that has no package declaration is part of an unnamed package (§7.4.2).
- `import` declarations (§7.5) that allow types from other packages and static members of types to be referred to using their simple names
- Top level type declarations (§7.6) of class and interface types

Which compilation units are *observable* is determined by the host system. However, all the compilation units of the package `java` and its subpackages `lang` and `io` must always be observable. The observability of a compilation unit influences the observability of its package (§7.4.3).

Every compilation unit automatically and implicitly imports every `public` type name declared by the predefined package `java.lang`, so that the names of all those types are available as simple names, as described in §7.5.5.

7.4 Package Declarations

A package declaration appears within a compilation unit to indicate the package to which the compilation unit belongs.

7.4.1 Named Packages

A *package declaration* in a compilation unit specifies the name (§6.2) of the package to which the compilation unit belongs.

PackageDeclaration:
    Annotations$_{opt}$ `package` *PackageName* `;`

The keyword `package` may optionally be preceded by annotation modifiers (§9.7). If an annotation *a* on a package declaration corresponds to an annotation type *T*, and *T* has a (meta-)annotation *m* that corresponds to `annotation.Target`, then *m* must have an element whose value is `annotation.ElementType.PACKAGE`, or a compile-time error occurs.

The package name mentioned in a package declaration must be the fully qualified name (§6.7) of the package.

7.4.1.1 *Package Annotations*

Annotations may be used on package declarations, with the restriction that at most one annotated package declaration is permitted for a given package.

DISCUSSION

The manner in which this restriction is enforced must, of necessity, vary from implementation to implementation. The following scheme is strongly recommended for file-system-based implementations: The sole annotated package declaration, if it exists, is placed in a source file called `package-info.java` in the directory containing the source files for the package. This file does not contain the source for a class called package-info.java; indeed it would be illegal for it to do so, as package-info is not a legal identifier. Typically `package-info.java` contains only a package declaration, preceded immediately by the annotations on the package. While the file could technically contain the source code for one or more package-private classes, it would be very bad form.

It is recommended that `package-info.java`, if it is present, take the place of `package.html` for javadoc and other similar documentation generation systems. If this file is present, the documentation generation tool should look for the package documentation comment immediately preceding the (possibly annotated) package declaration in `package-info.java`. In this way, package-info.java becomes the sole repository for package level annotations and documentation. If, in future, it becomes desirable to add any other package-level information, this file should prove a convenient home for this information.

7.4.2 Unnamed Packages

A compilation unit that has no package declaration is part of an unnamed package.

Note that an unnamed package cannot have subpackages, since the syntax of a package declaration always includes a reference to a named top level package.

As an example, the compilation unit:

```
class FirstCall {
    public static void main(String[] args) {
        System.out.println("Mr. Watson, come here. "
                           + "I want you.");
    }
}
```

defines a very simple compilation unit as part of an unnamed package.

An implementation of the Java platform must support at least one unnamed package; it may support more than one unnamed package but is not required to do so. Which compilation units are in each unnamed package is determined by the host system.

In implementations of the Java platform that use a hierarchical file system for storing packages, one typical strategy is to associate an unnamed package with each directory; only one unnamed package is observable at a time, namely the one that is associated with the "current working directory." The precise meaning of "current working directory" depends on the host system.

Unnamed packages are provided by the Java platform principally for convenience when developing small or temporary applications or when just beginning development.

7.4.3 Observability of a Package

A package is *observable* if and only if either:

- A compilation unit containing a declaration of the package is observable.
- A subpackage of the package is observable.

One can conclude from the rule above and from the requirements on observable compilation units, that the packages `java`, `java.lang`, and `java.io` are always observable.

7.4.4 Scope of a Package Declaration

The scope of the declaration of an observable (§7.4.3) top level package is all observable compilation units (§7.3). The declaration of a package that is not observable is never in scope. Subpackage declarations are never in scope.

It follows that the package `java` is always in scope (§6.3).

Package declarations never shadow other declarations.

7.5 Import Declarations

An *import declaration* allows a static member or a named type to be referred to by a simple name (§6.2) that consists of a single identifier. Without the use of an appropriate `import` declaration, the only way to refer to a type declared in another package, or a static member of another type, is to use a fully qualified name (§6.7).

ImportDeclaration:
SingleTypeImportDeclaration
TypeImportOnDemandDeclaration
SingleStaticImportDeclaration
StaticImportOnDemandDeclaration

A single-type-import declaration (§7.5.1) imports a single named type, by mentioning its canonical name (§6.7).

A type-import-on-demand declaration (§7.5.2) imports all the accessible (§6.6) types of a named type or package as needed. It is a compile time error to import a type from the unnamed package.

A single static import declaration (§7.5.3) imports all accessible static members with a given name from a type, by giving its canonical name.

A static-import-on-demand declaration (§7.5.4) imports all accessible static members of a named type as needed.

The scope of a type imported by a single-type-import declaration (§7.5.1) or a type-import-on-demand declaration (§7.5.2) is all the class and interface type declarations (§7.6) in the compilation unit in which the import declaration appears.

The scope of a member imported by a single-static-import declaration (§7.5.3) or a static-import-on-demand declaration (§7.5.4) is all the class and interface type declarations (§7.6) in the compilation unit in which the import declaration appears.

An `import` declaration makes types available by their simple names only within the compilation unit that actually contains the `import` declaration. The scope of the entities(s) it introduces specifically does not include the `package` statement, other `import` declarations in the current compilation unit, or other compilation units in the same package. See §7.5.6 for an illustrative example.

7.5.1 Single-Type-Import Declaration

A *single-type-import declaration* imports a single type by giving its canonical name, making it available under a simple name in the class and interface declarations of the compilation unit in which the single-type import declaration appears.

SingleTypeImportDeclaration:
  `import` *TypeName* `;`

The *TypeName* must be the canonical name of a class or interface type; a compile-time error occurs if the named type does not exist. The named type must be accessible (§6.6) or a compile-time error occurs.

A single-type-import declaration *d* in a compilation unit *c* of package *p* that imports a type named *n* shadows the declarations of:

- any top level type named *n* declared in another compilation unit of *p*.
- any type named *n* imported by a type-import-on-demand declaration in `c`.
- any type named *n* imported by a static-import-on-demand declaration in *c*.

throughout `c`.

The example:

```
import java.util.Vector;
```

causes the simple name `Vector` to be available within the class and interface declarations in a compilation unit. Thus, the simple name `Vector` refers to the type declaration `Vector` in the package `java.util` in all places where it is not shadowed (§6.3.1) or obscured (§6.3.2) by a declaration of a field, parameter, local variable, or nested type declaration with the same name.

DISCUSSION

Note that `Vector` is declared as a generic type. Once imported, the name `Vector` can be used without qualification in a parameterized type such as `Vector<String>`, or as the raw type `Vector`.

This highlights a limitation of the `import` declaration. A type nested inside a generic type declaration can be imported, but its outer type is always erased.

If two single-type-import declarations in the same compilation unit attempt to import types with the same simple name, then a compile-time error occurs, unless the two types are the same type, in which case the duplicate declaration is ignored. If the type imported by the the single-type-import declaration is declared in the compilation unit that contains the import declaration, the import declaration is ignored. If a compilation unit contains both a single-static-import (§7.5.3) declaration that imports a type whose simple name is *n*, and a single-type-import declaration (§7.5.1) that imports a type whose simple name is *n*, a compile-time error occurs.

If another top level type with the same simple name is otherwise declared in the current compilation unit except by a type-import-on-demand declaration (§7.5.2) or a static-import-on-demand declaration (§7.5.4), then a compile-time error occurs.

So the sample program:

```
import java.util.Vector;
class Vector { Object[] vec; }
```

causes a compile-time error because of the duplicate declaration of `Vector`, as does:

```
import java.util.Vector;
import myVector.Vector;
```

where `myVector` is a package containing the compilation unit:

```
package myVector;
public class Vector { Object[] vec; }
```

The compiler keeps track of types by their binary names (§13.1).

Note that an import statement cannot import a subpackage, only a type. For example, it does not work to try to import `java.util` and then use the name `util.Random` to refer to the type `java.util.Random`:

```
import java.util;                    // incorrect: compile-time error
class Test { util.Random generator; }
```

7.5.2 Type-Import-on-Demand Declaration

A *type-import-on-demand declaration* allows all accessible (§6.6) types declared in the type or package named by a canonical name to be imported as needed.

TypeImportOnDemandDeclaration:
  `import` *PackageOrTypeName* `. * ;`

It is a compile-time error for a type-import-on-demand declaration to name a type or package that is not accessible. Two or more type-import-on-demand declarations in the same compilation unit may name the same type or package. All but one of these declarations are considered *redundant*; the effect is as if that type was imported only once.

If a compilation unit contains both a static-import-on-demand declaration and a type-import-on-demand (§7.5.2) declaration that name the same type, the effect is as if the static member types of that type were imported only once.

It is not a compile-time error to name the current package or `java.lang` in a type-import-on-demand declaration. The type-import-on-demand declaration is ignored in such cases.

A type-import-on-demand declaration never causes any other declaration to be shadowed.

The example:

```
import java.util.*;
```

causes the simple names of all `public` types declared in the package `java.util` to be available within the class and interface declarations of the compilation unit. Thus, the simple name `Vector` refers to the type `Vector` in the package `java.util` in all places in the compilation unit where that type declaration is not shadowed (§6.3.1) or obscured (§6.3.2). The declaration might be shadowed by a single-type-import declaration of a type whose simple name is `Vector`; by a type named `Vector` and declared in the package to which the compilation unit belongs; or any nested classes or interfaces. The declaration might be obscured by a declaration of a field, parameter, or local variable named `Vector` (It would be unusual for any of these conditions to occur.)

7.5.3 Single Static Import Declaration

A *single-static-import declaration* imports all accessible (§6.6) static members with a given simple name from a type. This makes these static members available under their simple name in the class and interface declarations of the compilation unit in which the single-static import declaration appears.

SingleStaticImportDeclaration:
    `import static` *TypeName* . *Identifier*;

The *TypeName* must be the canonical name of a class or interface type; a compile-time error occurs if the named type does not exist. The named type must be accessible (§6.6) or a compile-time error occurs. The *Identifier* must name at least one static member of the named type; a compile-time error occurs if there is no member of that name or if all of the named members are not accessible.

A single-static-import declaration `d` in a compilation unit `c` of package `p` that imports a field named `n` shadows the declaration of any static field named `n` imported by a static-import-on-demand declaration in `c`, throughout `c`.

A single-static-import declaration `d` in a compilation unit `c` of package `p` that imports a method named `n` with signature *s* shadows the declaration of any static method named `n` with signature `s` imported by a static-import-on-demand declaration in `c`, throughout `c`.

A single-static-import declaration `d` in a compilation unit `c` of package `p` that imports a type named `n` shadows the declarations of:

- any static type named `n` imported by a static-import-on-demand declaration in `c`.
- any top level type (§7.6) named `n` declared in another compilation unit (§7.3) of `p`.
- any type named `n` imported by a type-import-on-demand declaration (§7.5.2) in `c`.

throughout `c`.

Note that it is permissable for one single-static-import declaration to import several fields or types with the same name, or several methods with the same name and signature.

If a compilation unit contains both a single-static-import (§7.5.3) declaration that imports a type whose simple name is `n`, and a single-type-import declaration (§7.5.1) that imports a type whose simple name is `n`, a compile-time error occurs.

If a single-static-import declaration imports a type whose simple name is `n`, and the compilation unit also declares a top level type (§7.6) whose simple name is `n`, a compile-time error occurs.

7.5.4 Static-Import-on-Demand Declaration

A *static-import-on-demand declaration* allows all accessible (§6.6) static members declared in the type named by a canonical name to be imported as needed.

StaticImportOnDemandDeclaration:
`import static` *TypeName* `. * ;`

It is a compile-time error for a static-import-on-demand declaration to name a type that does not exist or a type that is not accessible. Two or more static-import-on-demand declarations in the same compilation unit may name the same type or package; the effect is as if there was exactly one such declaration. Two or more static-import-on-demand declarations in the same compilation unit may name the same member; the effect is as if the member was imported exactly once.

Note that it is permissable for one static-import-on-demand declaration to import several fields or types with the same name, or several methods with the same name and signature.

If a compilation unit contains both a static-import-on-demand declaration and a type-import-on-demand (§7.5.2) declaration that name the same type, the effect is as if the static member types of that type were imported only once.

A static-import-on-demand declaration never causes any other declaration to be shadowed.

7.5.5 Automatic Imports

Each compilation unit automatically imports all of the `public` type names declared in the predefined package `java.lang`, as if the declaration:

```
import java.lang.*;
```

appeared at the beginning of each compilation unit, immediately following any `package` statement.

7.5.6 A Strange Example

Package names and type names are usually different under the naming conventions described in §6.8. Nevertheless, in a contrived example where there is an unconventionally-named package `Vector`, which declares a `public` class whose name is Mosquito:

```
package Vector;
public class Mosquito { int capacity; }
```

and then the compilation unit:

```
package strange.example;
import java.util.Vector;
import Vector.Mosquito;
class Test {
    public static void main(String[] args) {
        System.out.println(new Vector().getClass());
        System.out.println(new Mosquito().getClass());
    }
}
```

the single-type-import declaration (§7.5.1) importing class `Vector` from package `java.util` does not prevent the package name `Vector` from appearing and being correctly recognized in subsequent `import` declarations. The example compiles and produces the output:

```
class java.util.Vector
class Vector.Mosquito
```

7.6 Top Level Type Declarations

A *top level type declaration* declares a top level class type (§8) or a top level interface type (§9):

TypeDeclaration:
  ClassDeclaration
  InterfaceDeclaration
  ;

By default, the top level types declared in a package are accessible only within the compilation units of that package, but a type may be declared to be `public` to grant access to the type from code in other packages (§6.6, §8.1.1, §9.1.1).

The scope of a top level type is all type declarations in the package in which the top level type is declared.

If a top level type named *T* is declared in a compilation unit of a package whose fully qualified name is *P*, then the fully qualified name of the type is *P*.*T*. If the type is declared in an unnamed package (§7.4.2), then the type has the fully qualified name *T*.

Thus in the example:

```
package wnj.points;
class Point { int x, y; }
```

the fully qualified name of class `Point` is `wnj.points.Point`.

An implementation of the Java platform must keep track of types within packages by their binary names (§13.1). Multiple ways of naming a type must be expanded to binary names to make sure that such names are understood as referring to the same type.

For example, if a compilation unit contains the single-type-import declaration (§7.5.1):

```
import java.util.Vector;
```

then within that compilation unit the simple name `Vector` and the fully qualified name `java.util.Vector` refer to the same type.

When packages are stored in a file system (§7.2.1), the host system may choose to enforce the restriction that it is a compile-time error if a type is not found in a file under a name composed of the type name plus an extension (such as `.java` or `.jav`) if either of the following is true:

- The type is referred to by code in other compilation units of the package in which the type is declared.
- The type is declared `public` (and therefore is potentially accessible from code in other packages).

This restriction implies that there must be at most one such type per compilation unit. This restriction makes it easy for a compiler for the Java programming language or an implementation of the Java virtual machine to find a named class within a package; for example, the source code for a `public` type `wet.sprocket.Toad` would be found in a file `Toad.java` in the directory `wet/sprocket`, and the corresponding object code would be found in the file `Toad.class` in the same directory.

When packages are stored in a database (§7.2.2), the host system must not impose such restrictions. In practice, many programmers choose to put each class or interface type in its own compilation unit, whether or not it is public or is referred to by code in other compilation units.

A compile-time error occurs if the name of a top level type appears as the name of any other top level class or interface type declared in the same package (§7.6).

A compile-time error occurs if the name of a top level type is also declared as a type by a single-type-import declaration (§7.5.1) in the compilation unit (§7.3) containing the type declaration.

In the example:

```
class Point { int x, y; }
```

the class `Point` is declared in a compilation unit with no `package` statement, and thus `Point` is its fully qualified name, whereas in the example:

```
package vista;
class Point { int x, y; }
```

the fully qualified name of the class `Point` is `vista.Point`. (The package name `vista` is suitable for local or personal use; if the package were intended to be widely distributed, it would be better to give it a unique package name (§7.7).)

In the example:

```
package test;

import java.util.Vector;

class Point {
    int x, y;
}

interface Point {                    // compile-time error #1
    int getR();
    int getTheta();
}

class Vector { Point[] pts; }// compile-time error #2
```

the first compile-time error is caused by the duplicate declaration of the name `Point` as both a `class` and an `interface` in the same package. A second error detected at compile time is the attempt to declare the name `Vector` both by a class type declaration and by a single-type-import declaration.

Note, however, that it is not an error for the name of a class to also to name a type that otherwise might be imported by a type-import-on-demand declaration (§7.5.2) in the compilation unit (§7.3) containing the class declaration. In the example:

```
package test;

import java.util.*;

class Vector { Point[] pts; }// not a compile-time error
```

the declaration of the class `Vector` *is permitted even though there is also a class* `java.util.Vector`. Within this compilation unit, the simple name `Vector` refers to the class `test.Vector`, not to `java.util.Vector` (which can still be referred to by code within the compilation unit, but only by its fully qualified name).

As another example, the compilation unit:

```
package points;

class Point {
    int x, y;                          // coordinates
    PointColor color;                  // color of this point
    Point next;                        // next point with this color
    static int nPoints;
}

class PointColor {
    Point first;                       // first point with this color
    PointColor(int color) {
        this.color = color;
    }
    private int color;                 // color components
}
```

defines two classes that use each other in the declarations of their class members. Because the class types `Point` and `PointColor` have all the type declarations in package `points`, including all those in the current compilation unit, as their scope, this example compiles correctly—that is, forward reference is not a problem.

It is a compile-time error if a top level type declaration contains any one of the following access modifiers: `protected`, `private` or `static`.

7.7 Unique Package Names

Did I ever tell you that Mrs. McCave
Had twenty-three sons and she named them all "Dave"?
Well, she did. And that wasn't a smart thing to do. . . .
—Dr. Seuss (Theodore Geisel), *Too Many Daves* (1961)

Developers should take steps to avoid the possibility of two published packages having the same name by choosing *unique package names* for packages that are widely distributed. This allows packages to be easily and automatically installed and catalogued. This section specifies a suggested convention for generating such unique package names. Implementations of the Java platform are encouraged to provide automatic support for converting a set of packages from local and casual package names to the unique name format described here.

If unique package names are not used, then package name conflicts may arise far from the point of creation of either of the conflicting packages. This may create a situation that is difficult or impossible for the user or programmer to resolve. The class `ClassLoader` can be used to isolate packages with the same name from each other in those cases where the packages will have constrained interactions, but not in a way that is transparent to a naïve program.

You form a unique package name by first having (or belonging to an organization that has) an Internet domain name, such as `sun.com`. You then reverse this name, component by component, to obtain, in this example, `com.sun`, and use this as a prefix for your package names, using a convention developed within your organization to further administer package names.

In some cases, the internet domain name may not be a valid package name. Here are some suggested conventions for dealing with these situations:

- If the domain name contains a hyphen, or any other special character not allowed in an identifier (§3.8), convert it into an underscore.
- If any of the resulting package name components are keywords (§3.9) then append underscore to them.
- If any of the resulting package name components start with a digit, or any other character that is not allowed as an initial character of an identifier, have an underscore prefixed to the component.

Such a convention might specify that certain directory name components be division, department, project, machine, or login names. Some possible examples:

```
com.sun.sunsoft.DOE
com.sun.java.jag.scrabble
com.apple.quicktime.v2
edu.cmu.cs.bovik.cheese
gov.whitehouse.socks.mousefinder
```

The first component of a unique package name is always written in all-lowercase ASCII letters and should be one of the top level domain names, currently `com`, `edu`, `gov`, `mil`, `net`, `org`, or one of the English two-letter codes identifying countries as specified in ISO Standard 3166, 1981. For more information, refer to the documents stored at `ftp://rs.internic.net/rfc`, for example, `rfc920.txt` and `rfc1032.txt`.

The name of a package is not meant to imply where the package is stored within the Internet; for example, a package named `edu.cmu.cs.bovik.cheese` is not necessarily obtainable from Internet address `cmu.edu` or from `cs.cmu.edu` or from `bovik.cs.cmu.edu`. The suggested convention for generating unique package names is merely a way to piggyback a package naming convention on top of an existing, widely known unique name registry instead of having to create a separate registry for package names.

Brown paper packages tied up with strings,
These are a few of my favorite things.
—Oscar Hammerstein II, *My Favorite Things* (1959)

CHAPTER 8

Classes

class 1. The noun *class* derives from
Medieval French and French *classe* from Latin *classis*,
probably originally a summons,
hence a summoned collection of persons,
a group liable to be summoned:
perhaps for *callassis* from *calare*,
to call, hence to summon.
—Eric Partridge
Origins: A Short Etymological Dictionary of Modern English

CLASS declarations define new reference types and describe how they are implemented (§8.1).

A *nested class* is any class whose declaration occurs within the body of another class or interface. A *top level class* is a class that is not a nested class.

This chapter discusses the common semantics of all classes—top level (§7.6) and nested (including member classes (§8.5, §9.5), local classes (§14.3) and anonymous classes (§15.9.5)). Details that are specific to particular kinds of classes are discussed in the sections dedicated to these constructs.

A named class may be declared `abstract` (§8.1.1.1) and must be declared `abstract` if it is incompletely implemented; such a class cannot be instantiated, but can be extended by subclasses. A class may be declared `final` (§8.1.1.2), in which case it cannot have subclasses. If a class is declared `public`, then it can be referred to from other packages. Each class except `Object` is an extension of (that is, a subclass of) a single existing class (§8.1.4) and may implement interfaces (§8.1.5). Classes may be *generic*, that is, they may declare type variables (§4.4) whose bindings may differ among different instances of the class.

Classes may be decorated with annotations (§9.7) just like any other kind of declaration.

The body of a class declares members (fields and methods and nested classes and interfaces), instance and static initializers, and constructors (§8.1.6). The scope (§6.3) of a member (§8.2) is the entire body of the declaration of the class to which the member belongs. Field, method, member class, member interface, and constructor declarations may include the access modifiers (§6.6) `public`, `protected`, or `private`. The members of a class include both declared and inherited members (§8.2). Newly declared fields can hide fields declared in a superclass or superinterface. Newly declared class members and interface members can hide class or interface members declared in a superclass or superinterface. Newly declared methods can hide, implement, or override methods declared in a superclass or superinterface.

Field declarations (§8.3) describe class variables, which are incarnated once, and instance variables, which are freshly incarnated for each instance of the class. A field may be declared `final` (§8.3.1.2), in which case it can be assigned to only once. Any field declaration may include an initializer.

Member class declarations (§8.5) describe nested classes that are members of the surrounding class. Member classes may be `static`, in which case they have no access to the instance variables of the surrounding class; or they may be inner classes (§8.1.3).

Member interface declarations (§8.5) describe nested interfaces that are members of the surrounding class.

Method declarations (§8.4) describe code that may be invoked by method invocation expressions (§15.12). A class method is invoked relative to the class type; an instance method is invoked with respect to some particular object that is an instance of a class type. A method whose declaration does not indicate how it is implemented must be declared `abstract`. A method may be declared `final` (§8.4.3.3), in which case it cannot be hidden or overridden. A method may be implemented by platform-dependent `native` code (§8.4.3.4). A `synchronized` method (§8.4.3.6) automatically locks an object before executing its body and automatically unlocks the object on return, as if by use of a `synchronized` statement (§14.19), thus allowing its activities to be synchronized with those of other threads (§17).

Method names may be overloaded (§8.4.9).

Instance initializers (§8.6) are blocks of executable code that may be used to help initialize an instance when it is created (§15.9).

Static initializers (§8.7) are blocks of executable code that may be used to help initialize a class.

Constructors (§8.8) are similar to methods, but cannot be invoked directly by a method call; they are used to initialize new class instances. Like methods, they may be overloaded (§8.8.8).

8.1 Class Declaration

A *class declaration* specifies a new named reference type. There are two kinds of class declarations - *normal class declarations* and *enum declarations*:

ClassDeclaration:
NormalClassDeclaration
EnumDeclaration

NormalClassDeclaration:
ClassModifiers$_{opt}$ `class` *Identifier TypeParameters*$_{opt}$ *Super*$_{opt}$ *Interfaces*$_{opt}$ *ClassBody*

The rules in this section apply to all class declarations unless this specification explicitly states otherwise. In many cases, special restrictions apply to enum declarations. Enum declarations are described in detail in §8.9.

The *Identifier* in a class declaration specifies the name of the class. A compile-time error occurs if a class has the same simple name as any of its enclosing classes or interfaces.

8.1.1 Class Modifiers

A class declaration may include *class modifiers*.

ClassModifiers:
ClassModifier
ClassModifiers ClassModifier

ClassModifier: one of
Annotation `public protected private`
`abstract static final strictfp`

Not all modifiers are applicable to all kinds of class declarations. The access modifier `public` pertains only to top level classes (§7.6) and to member classes (§8.5, §9.5), and is discussed in §6.6, §8.5 and §9.5. The access modifiers `protected` and `private` pertain only to member classes within a directly enclosing class declaration (§8.5) and are discussed in §8.5.1. The access modifier `static` pertains only to member classes (§8.5, §9.5). A compile-time error occurs if the same modifier appears more than once in a class declaration.

If an annotation *a* on a class declaration corresponds to an annotation type *T*, and *T* has a (meta-)annotation *m* that corresponds to `annotation.Target`, then *m* must have an element whose value is `annotation.ElementType.TYPE`, or a compile-time error occurs. Annotation modifiers are described further in §9.7.

If two or more class modifiers appear in a class declaration, then it is customary, though not required, that they appear in the order consistent with that shown above in the production for *ClassModifier*.

8.1.1.1 `abstract` *Classes*

An `abstract` class is a class that is incomplete, or to be considered incomplete. Normal classes may have `abstract` methods (§8.4.3.1, §9.4), that is methods that are declared but not yet implemented, only if they are `abstract` classes. If a normal class that is not `abstract` contains an `abstract` method, then a compile-time error occurs.

Enum types (§8.9) must not be declared `abstract`; doing so will result in a compile-time error. It is a compile-time error for an enum type `E` to have an abstract method `m` as a member unless `E` has one or more enum constants, and all of `E`'s enum constants have class bodies that provide concrete implementations of `m`. It is a compile-time error for the class body of an enum constant to declare an abstract method.

A class *C* has `abstract` methods if any of the following is true:

- *C* explicitly contains a declaration of an `abstract` method (§8.4.3).
- Any of *C*'s superclasses has an `abstract` method and *C* neither declares nor inherits a method that implements (§8.4.8.1) it.
- A direct superinterface (§8.1.5) of *C* declares or inherits a method (which is therefore necessarily `abstract`) and *C* neither declares nor inherits a method that implements it.

In the example:

```
abstract class Point {
    int x = 1, y = 1;
    void move(int dx, int dy) {
        x += dx;
        y += dy;
        alert();
    }
    abstract void alert();
}
abstract class ColoredPoint extends Point {
    int color;
}
```

```
class SimplePoint extends Point {
    void alert() { }
}
```

a class Point is declared that must be declared abstract, because it contains a declaration of an abstract method named alert. The subclass of Point named ColoredPoint inherits the abstract method alert, so it must also be declared abstract. On the other hand, the subclass of Point named SimplePoint provides an implementation of alert, so it need not be abstract.

A compile-time error occurs if an attempt is made to create an instance of an abstract class using a class instance creation expression (§15.9).

Thus, continuing the example just shown, the statement:

```
Point p = new Point();
```

would result in a compile-time error; the class Point cannot be instantiated because it is abstract. However, a Point variable could correctly be initialized with a reference to any subclass of Point, and the class SimplePoint is not abstract, so the statement:

```
Point p = new SimplePoint();
```

would be correct.

A subclass of an abstract class that is not itself abstract may be instantiated, resulting in the execution of a constructor for the abstract class and, therefore, the execution of the field initializers for instance variables of that class. Thus, in the example just given, instantiation of a SimplePoint causes the default constructor and field initializers for x and y of Point to be executed.

It is a compile-time error to declare an abstract class type such that it is not possible to create a subclass that implements all of its abstract methods. This situation can occur if the class would have as members two abstract methods that have the same method signature (§8.4.2) but incompatible return types.

As an example, the declarations:

```
interface Colorable { void setColor(int color); }
abstract class Colored implements Colorable {
    abstract int setColor(int color);
}
```

result in a compile-time error: it would be impossible for any subclass of class Colored to provide an implementation of a method named setColor, taking one argument of type int, that can satisfy both abstract method specifications, because the one in interface Colorable requires the same method to return no value, while the one in class Colored requires the same method to return a value of type int (§8.4).

A class type should be declared abstract only if the intent is that subclasses can be created to complete the implementation. If the intent is simply to prevent instantiation of a class, the proper way to express this is to declare a constructor (§8.8.10) of no arguments, make it `private`, never invoke it, and declare no other constructors. A class of this form usually contains class methods and variables. The class `Math` is an example of a class that cannot be instantiated; its declaration looks like this:

```
public final class Math {
    private Math() { }        // never instantiate this class
            . . . declarations of class variables and methods . . .
}
```

8.1.1.2 `final` *Classes*

A class can be declared `final` if its definition is complete and no subclasses are desired or required. A compile-time error occurs if the name of a `final` class appears in the `extends` clause (§8.1.4) of another `class` declaration; this implies that a `final` class cannot have any subclasses. A compile-time error occurs if a class is declared both `final` and `abstract`, because the implementation of such a class could never be completed (§8.1.1.1).

Because a `final` class never has any subclasses, the methods of a `final` class are never overridden (§8.4.8.1).

8.1.1.3 `strictfp` *Classes*

The effect of the `strictfp` modifier is to make all `float` or `double` expressions within the class declaration be explicitly FP-strict (§15.4). This implies that all methods declared in the class, and all nested types declared in the class, are implicitly `strictfp`.

Note also that all `float` or `double` expressions within all variable initializers, instance initializers, static initializers and constructors of the class will also be explicitly FP-strict.

8.1.2 Generic Classes and Type Parameters

A class is *generic* if it declares one or more type variables (§4.4). These type variables are known as the *type parameters* of the class. The type parameter section follows the class name and is delimited by angle brackets. It defines one or more type variables that act as parameters. A generic class declaration defines a set of parameterized types, one for each possible invocation of the type parameter section. All of these parameterized types share the same class at runtime.

DISCUSSION

For instance, executing the code

```
Vector<String> x = new Vector<String>();
Vector<Integer> y = new Vector<Integer>();
boolean b = x.getClass() == y.getClass();
```

will result in the variable b holding the value `true`.

TypeParameters ::= < TypeParameterList >

TypeParameterList ::= TypeParameterList , TypeParameter
 | *TypeParameter*

It is a compile-time error if a generic class is a direct or indirect subclass of `Throwable`.

DISCUSSION

This restriction is needed since the catch mechanism of the Java virtual machine works only with non-generic classes.

The scope of a class' type parameter is the entire declaration of the class including the type parameter section itself. Therefore, type parameters can appear as parts of their own bounds, or as bounds of other type parameters declared in the same section.

It is a compile-time error to refer to a type parameter of a class *C* anywhere in the declaration of a static member of *C* or the declaration of a static member of any type declaration nested within *C*. It is a compile-time error to refer to a type parameter of a class C within a static initializer of *C* or any class nested within *C*.

DISCUSSION

Example: Mutually recursive type variable bounds.

```
interface ConvertibleTo<T> {
```

```
    T convert();
}
class ReprChange<T implements ConvertibleTo<S>,
                 S implements ConvertibleTo<T>> {
    T t;
    void set(S s) { t = s.convert(); }
    S get() { return t.convert(); }
}
```

Parameterized class declarations can be nested inside other declarations.

Discussion

This is illustrated in the following example:

```
class Seq<T> {
    T head;
    Seq<T> tail;
    Seq() { this(null, null); }
    boolean isEmpty() { return tail == null; }
    Seq(T head, Seq<T> tail) { this.head = head; this.tail = tail; }
    class Zipper<S> {
        Seq<Pair<T,S>> zip(Seq<S> that) {
            if (this.isEmpty() || that.isEmpty())
              return new Seq<Pair<T,S>>();
            else
              return new Seq<Pair<T,S>>(
                new Pair<T,S>(this.head, that.head),
                this.tail.zip(that.tail));
        }
    }
}
class Pair<T, S> {
    T fst; S Snd;
    Pair(T f, S s) {fst = f; snd = s;}
}
class Client {
    {
        Seq<String> strs =
        new Seq<String>("a", new Seq<String>("b",
                              new Seq<String>()));
        Seq<Number> nums =
            new Seq<Number>(new Integer(1),
                              new Seq<Number>(new Double(1.5),
```

```
                                        new Seq<Number>()));
        Seq<String>.Zipper<Number> zipper =
                    strs.new Zipper<Number>();
        Seq<Pair<String,Number>> combined = zipper.zip(nums);
    }
}
```

8.1.3 Inner Classes and Enclosing Instances

An *inner class* is a nested class that is not explicitly or implicitly declared `static`. Inner classes may not declare static initializers (§8.7) or member interfaces. Inner classes may not declare static members, unless they are compile-time constant fields (§15.28).

To illustrate these rules, consider the example below:

```
class HasStatic{
    static int j = 100;
}
class Outer{
    class Inner extends HasStatic{
        static final int x = 3;// ok - compile-time constant
        static int y = 4; // compile-time error, an inner class
    }
    static class NestedButNotInner{
        static int z = 5; // ok, not an inner class
    }
    interface NeverInner{}// interfaces are never inner
}
```

Inner classes may inherit static members that are not compile-time constants even though they may not declare them. Nested classes that are not inner classes may declare static members freely, in accordance with the usual rules of the Java programming language. Member interfaces (§8.5) are always implicitly static so they are never considered to be inner classes.

A statement or expression *occurs in a static context* if and only if the innermost method, constructor, instance initializer, static initializer, field initializer, or explicit constructor invocation statement enclosing the statement or expression is a static method, a static initializer, the variable initializer of a static variable, or an explicit constructor invocation statement (§8.8.7).

An inner class `C` is a *direct inner class of a class* `O` if `O` is the immediately lexically enclosing class of `C` and the declaration of `C` does not occur in a static context. A class C is an *inner class of class O* if it is either a direct inner class of O or an inner class of an inner class of O.

A class O is the *zeroth lexically enclosing class of itself*. A class O is the *nth lexically enclosing class of a class C* if it is the immediately enclosing class of the $n-1$ st lexically enclosing class of C.

An instance i of a direct inner class C of a class O is associated with an instance of O, known as the *immediately enclosing instance* of i. The immediately enclosing instance of an object, if any, is determined when the object is created (§15.9.2).

An object o is the *zeroth lexically enclosing instance of itself*. An object o is the *nth lexically enclosing instance of an instance* i if it is the immediately enclosing instance of the $n-1$ st lexically enclosing instance of i.

When an inner class refers to an instance variable that is a member of a lexically enclosing class, the variable of the corresponding lexically enclosing instance is used. A blank final (§4.12.4) field of a lexically enclosing class may not be assigned within an inner class.

An instance of an inner class I whose declaration occurs in a static context has no lexically enclosing instances. However, if I is immediately declared within a static method or static initializer then I does have an *enclosing block*, which is the innermost block statement lexically enclosing the declaration of I.

Furthermore, for every superclass S of C which is itself a direct inner class of a class SO, there is an instance of SO associated with i, known as *the immediately enclosing instance of i with respect to S*. The immediately enclosing instance of an object with respect to its class' direct superclass, if any, is determined when the superclass constructor is invoked via an explicit constructor invocation statement.

Any local variable, formal method parameter or exception handler parameter used but not declared in an inner class must be declared `final`. Any local variable, used but not declared in an inner class must be definitely assigned (§16) before the body of the inner class.

Inner classes include local (§14.3), anonymous (§15.9.5) and non-static member classes (§8.5). Here are some examples:

```
class Outer {
    int i = 100;
    static void classMethod() {
        final int l = 200;
        class LocalInStaticContext{
            int k = i; // compile-time error
            int m = l; // ok
        }
    }
```

```
    void foo() {
        class Local { // a local class
            int j = i;
        }
    }
}
```

The declaration of class `LocalInStaticContext` occurs in a static context—within the static method `classMethod`. Instance variables of class `Outer` are not available within the body of a static method. In particular, instance variables of `Outer` are not available inside the body of `LocalInStaticContext`. However, local variables from the surrounding method may be referred to without error (provided they are marked `final`).

Inner classes whose declarations do not occur in a static context may freely refer to the instance variables of their enclosing class. An instance variable is always defined with respect to an instance. In the case of instance variables of an enclosing class, the instance variable must be defined with respect to an enclosing instance of that class. So, for example, the class `Local` above has an enclosing instance of class `Outer`. As a further example:

```
class WithDeepNesting{
    boolean toBe;
    WithDeepNesting(boolean b) { toBe = b;}
    class Nested {
        boolean theQuestion;
        class DeeplyNested {
            DeeplyNested(){
              theQuestion = toBe || !toBe;
            }
        }
    }
}
```

Here, every instance of `WithDeepNesting.Nested.DeeplyNested` has an enclosing instance of class `WithDeepNesting.Nested` (its immediately enclosing instance) and an enclosing instance of class `WithDeepNesting` (its 2nd lexically enclosing instance).

8.1.4 Superclasses and Subclasses

The optional `extends` clause in a normal class declaration specifies the *direct superclass* of the current class.

Super:
  `extends` *ClassType*

The following is repeated from §4.3 to make the presentation here clearer:

ClassType:
  TypeDeclSpecifier TypeArguments$_{opt}$

A class is said to be a *direct subclass* of its direct superclass. The direct superclass is the class from whose implementation the implementation of the current class is derived. The direct superclass of an enum type `E` is `Enum<E>`. The `extends` clause must not appear in the definition of the class `Object`, because it is the primordial class and has no direct superclass.

Given a (possibly generic) class declaration for $C<F_1, ..., F_n>$, $n \geq 0$, $C \neq Object$, the *direct superclass* of the class type (§4.5) $C<F_1, ..., F_n>$ is the type given in the extends clause of the declaration of C if an extends clause is present, or `Object` otherwise.

Let $C<F_1, ..., F_n>$, $n > 0$, be a generic class declaration. The direct superclass of the parameterized class type $C<T_1, ..., T_n>$, where T_i, $1 \leq i \leq n$, is a type, is $D<U_1$ *theta* , ..., U_k *theta*$>$, where $D<U_1, ..., U_k>$ is the direct superclass of $C<F_1, ..., F_n>$, and *theta* is the substitution $[F_1 := T_1, ..., F_n := T_n]$.

The *ClassType* must name an accessible (§6.6) class type, or a compile-time error occurs. If the specified *ClassType* names a class that is `final` (§8.1.1.2), then a compile-time error occurs; `final` classes are not allowed to have subclasses. It is a compile-time error if the *ClassType* names the class `Enum` or any invocation of it. If the *TypeName* is followed by any type arguments, it must be a correct invocation of the type declaration denoted by *TypeName*, and none of the type arguments may be wildcard type arguments, or a compile-time error occurs.

In the example:

```
class Point { int x, y; }
final class ColoredPoint extends Point { int color; }
class Colored3DPoint extends ColoredPoint { int z; } // error
```

the relationships are as follows:

- The class `Point` is a direct subclass of `Object`.
- The class `Object` is the direct superclass of the class `Point`.
- The class `ColoredPoint` is a direct subclass of class `Point`.

- The class `Point` is the direct superclass of class `ColoredPoint`.

The declaration of class `Colored3dPoint` causes a compile-time error because it attempts to extend the `final` class `ColoredPoint`.

The *subclass* relationship is the transitive closure of the direct subclass relationship. A class *A* is a subclass of class *C* if either of the following is true:

- *A* is the direct subclass of *C*.
- There exists a class *B* such that *A* is a subclass of *B*, and *B* is a subclass of *C*, applying this definition recursively.

Class *C* is said to be a *superclass* of class *A* whenever *A* is a subclass of *C*.

In the example:

```
class Point { int x, y; }
class ColoredPoint extends Point { int color; }
final class Colored3dPoint extends ColoredPoint { int z; }
```

the relationships are as follows:

- The class `Point` is a superclass of class `ColoredPoint`.
- The class `Point` is a superclass of class `Colored3dPoint`.
- The class `ColoredPoint` is a subclass of class `Point`.
- The class `ColoredPoint` is a superclass of class `Colored3dPoint`.
- The class `Colored3dPoint` is a subclass of class `ColoredPoint`.
- The class `Colored3dPoint` is a subclass of class `Point`.

A class *C directly depends* on a type *T* if *T* is mentioned in the `extends` or `implements` clause of *C* either as a superclass or superinterface, or as a qualifier of a superclass or superinterface name. A class *C depends* on a reference type *T* if any of the following conditions hold:

- *C* directly depends on *T*.
- *C* directly depends on an interface *I* that depends (§9.1.3) on *T*.
- *C* directly depends on a class *D* that depends on *T* (using this definition recursively).

It is a compile-time error if a class depends on itself.

For example:

```
class Point extends ColoredPoint { int x, y; }
class ColoredPoint extends Point { int color; }
```

causes a compile-time error.

If circularly declared classes are detected at run time, as classes are loaded (§12.2), then a `ClassCircularityError` is thrown.

8.1.5 Superinterfaces

The optional `implements` clause in a class declaration lists the names of interfaces that are *direct superinterfaces* of the class being declared:

Interfaces:
  `implements` *InterfaceTypeList*

InterfaceTypeList:
  InterfaceType
  InterfaceTypeList `,` *InterfaceType*

The following is repeated from §4.3 to make the presentation here clearer:

InterfaceType:
  TypeDeclSpecifier TypeArguments$_{opt}$

Given a (possibly generic) class declaration for $C<F_1, \ldots, F_n>$, $n \geq 0$, $C \neq Object$, the *direct superinterfaces* of the class type (§4.5) $C<F_1, \ldots, F_n>$ are the types given in the implements clause of the declaration of C if an implements clause is present.

Let $C<F_1, \ldots, F_n>$, $n > 0$, be a generic class declaration. The direct superinterfaces of the parameterized class type $C<T_1, \ldots, T_n>$, where T_i, $1 \leq i \leq n$, is a type, are all types $I<U_1\ theta, \ldots, U_k\ theta>$, where $I<U_1, \ldots, U_k>$ is a direct superinterface of $C<F_1, \ldots, F_n>$, and *theta* is the substitution $[F_1 := T_1, \ldots, F_n := T_n]$.

Each *InterfaceType* must name an accessible (§6.6) interface type, or a compile-time error occurs. If the *TypeName* is followed by any type arguments, it must be a correct invocation of the type declaration denoted by *TypeName*, and none of the type arguments may be wildcard type arguments, or a compile-time error occurs.

A compile-time error occurs if the same interface is mentioned as a direct superinterface two or more times in a single `implements` clause names.

This is true even if the interface is named in different ways; for example, the code:

```
class Redundant implements java.lang.Cloneable, Cloneable {
    int x;
}
```

results in a compile-time error because the names `java.lang.Cloneable` and `Cloneable` refer to the same interface.

An interface type *I* is a *superinterface* of class type *C* if any of the following is true:

- *I* is a direct superinterface of *C*.
- *C* has some direct superinterface *J* for which *I* is a superinterface, using the definition of "superinterface of an interface" given in §9.1.3.
- *I* is a superinterface of the direct superclass of *C*.

A class is said to *implement* all its superinterfaces.

In the example:

```
public interface Colorable {
    void setColor(int color);
    int getColor();
}
public enum Finish {MATTE, GLOSSY}
public interface Paintable extends Colorable {
    void setFinish(Finish finish);
    Finish getFinish();
}
class Point { int x, y; }
class ColoredPoint extends Point implements Colorable {
    int color;
    public void setColor(int color) { this.color = color; }
    public int getColor() { return color; }
}
class PaintedPoint extends ColoredPoint implements Paintable
{
    Finish finish;
    public void setFinish(Finish finish) {
        this.finish = finish;
    }
    public Finish getFinish() { return finish; }
}
```

the relationships are as follows:

- The interface `Paintable` is a superinterface of class `PaintedPoint`.
- The interface `Colorable` is a superinterface of class `ColoredPoint` and of class `PaintedPoint`.

- The interface `Paintable` is a subinterface of the interface `Colorable`, and `Colorable` is a superinterface of `Paintable`, as defined in §9.1.3.

A class can have a superinterface in more than one way. In this example, the class `PaintedPoint` has `Colorable` as a superinterface both because it is a superinterface of `ColoredPoint` and because it is a superinterface of `Paintable`. Unless the class being declared is `abstract`, the declarations of all the method members of each direct superinterface must be implemented either by a declaration in this class or by an existing method declaration inherited from the direct superclass, because a class that is not `abstract` is not permitted to have `abstract` methods (§8.1.1.1).

Thus, the example:

```
interface Colorable {
    void setColor(int color);
    int getColor();
}
class Point { int x, y; };
class ColoredPoint extends Point implements Colorable {
    int color;
}
```

causes a compile-time error, because `ColoredPoint` is not an `abstract` class but it fails to provide an implementation of methods `setColor` and `getColor` of the interface `Colorable`.

It is permitted for a single method declaration in a class to implement methods of more than one superinterface. For example, in the code:

```
interface Fish { int getNumberOfScales(); }
interface Piano { int getNumberOfScales(); }
class Tuna implements Fish, Piano {
    // You can tune a piano, but can you tuna fish?
    int getNumberOfScales() { return 91; }
}
```

the method `getNumberOfScales` in class `Tuna` has a name, signature, and return type that matches the method declared in interface `Fish` and also matches the method declared in interface `Piano`; it is considered to implement both.

On the other hand, in a situation such as this:

```
interface Fish { int getNumberOfScales(); }
interface StringBass { double getNumberOfScales(); }
class Bass implements Fish, StringBass {
    // This declaration cannot be correct, no matter what type is used.
```

```
    public ??? getNumberOfScales() { return 91; }
}
```

It is impossible to declare a method named `getNumberOfScales` whose signature and return type are compatible with those of both the methods declared in interface `Fish` and in interface `StringBass`, because a class cannot have multiple methods with the same signature and different primitive return types (§8.4). Therefore, it is impossible for a single class to implement both interface `Fish` and interface `StringBass` (§8.4.8).

A class may not at the same time be a subtype of two interface types which are different invocations of the same generic interface (§9.1.2), or an invocation of a generic interface and a raw type naming that same generic interface.

DISCUSSION

Here is an example of an illegal multiple inheritance of an interface:

```
class B implements I<Integer>
class C extends B implements I<String>
```

This requirement was introduced in order to support translation by type erasure (§4.6).

8.1.6 Class Body and Member Declarations

A *class body* may contain declarations of members of the class, that is, fields (§8.3), classes (§8.5), interfaces (§8.5) and methods (§8.4). A class body may also contain instance initializers (§8.6), static initializers (§8.7), and declarations of constructors (§8.8) for the class.

ClassBody:
    { *ClassBodyDeclarations*$_{opt}$ }

ClassBodyDeclarations:
    ClassBodyDeclaration
    ClassBodyDeclarations ClassBodyDeclaration

ClassBodyDeclaration:
    ClassMemberDeclaration
    InstanceInitializer
    StaticInitializer
    ConstructorDeclaration

ClassMemberDeclaration:
  FieldDeclaration
  MethodDeclaration
  ClassDeclaration
  InterfaceDeclaration
  ;

The scope of a declaration of a member `m` declared in or inherited by a class type `C` is the entire body of `C`, including any nested type declarations.

If `C` itself is a nested class, there may be definitions of the same kind (variable, method, or type) and name as `m` in enclosing scopes. (The scopes may be blocks, classes, or packages.) In all such cases, the member `m` declared or inherited in C shadows (§6.3.1) the other definitions of the same kind and name.

8.2 Class Members

I wouldn't want to belong to any club that would accept me as a member.
—Groucho Marx

The members of a class type are all of the following:

- Members inherited from its direct superclass (§8.1.4), except in class `Object`, which has no direct superclass
- Members inherited from any direct superinterfaces (§8.1.5)
- Members declared in the body of the class (§8.1.6)

Members of a class that are declared `private` are not inherited by subclasses of that class. Only members of a class that are declared `protected` or `public` are inherited by subclasses declared in a package other than the one in which the class is declared.

We use the phrase *the type of a member* to denote:

- For a field, its type.
- For a method, an ordered 3-tuple consisting of:
  - **argument types:** a list of the types of the arguments to the method member.
  - **return type:** the return type of the method member and the
  - **throws clause:** exception types declared in the throws clause of the method member.

Constructors, static initializers, and instance initializers are not members and therefore are not inherited.

The example:

```
class Point {
   int x, y;
   private Point() { reset(); }
   Point(int x, int y) { this.x = x; this.y = y; }
   private void reset() { this.x = 0; this.y = 0; }
}
class ColoredPoint extends Point {
   int color;
   void clear() { reset(); }                        // error
}
class Test {
   public static void main(String[] args) {
      ColoredPoint c = new ColoredPoint(0, 0);// error
      c.reset();                                    // error
   }
}
```

causes four compile-time errors:

- An error occurs because `ColoredPoint` has no constructor declared with two integer parameters, as requested by the use in `main`. This illustrates the fact that `ColoredPoint` does not inherit the constructors of its superclass `Point`.
- Another error occurs because `ColoredPoint` declares no constructors, and therefore a default constructor for it is automatically created (§8.8.9), and this default constructor is equivalent to:

  ```
  ColoredPoint() { super(); }
  ```

  which invokes the constructor, with no arguments, for the direct superclass of the class `ColoredPoint`. The error is that the constructor for `Point` that takes no arguments is `private`, and therefore is not accessible outside the class `Point`, even through a superclass constructor invocation (§8.8.7).

Two more errors occur because the method `reset` of class `Point` is `private`, and therefore is not inherited by class `ColoredPoint`. The method invocations in method `clear` of class `ColoredPoint` and in method `main` of class `Test` are therefore not correct.

8.2.1 Examples of Inheritance

This section illustrates inheritance of class members through several examples.

8.2.1.1 *Example: Inheritance with Default Access*

Consider the example where the `points` package declares two compilation units:

```
package points;
public class Point {
    int x, y;
    public void move(int dx, int dy) { x += dx; y += dy; }
}
```

and:

```
package points;
public class Point3d extends Point {
    int z;
    public void move(int dx, int dy, int dz) {
        x += dx; y += dy; z += dz;
    }
}
```

and a third compilation unit, in another package, is:

```
import points.Point3d;
class Point4d extends Point3d {
    int w;
    public void move(int dx, int dy, int dz, int dw) {
        x += dx; y += dy; z += dz; w += dw; // compile-time errors
    }
}
```

Here both classes in the `points` package compile. The class `Point3d` inherits the fields `x` and `y` of class `Point`, because it is in the same package as `Point`. The class `Point4d`, which is in a different package, does not inherit the fields `x` and `y` of class `Point` or the field `z` of class `Point3d`, and so fails to compile.

A better way to write the third compilation unit would be:

```
import points.Point3d;
class Point4d extends Point3d {
    int w;
    public void move(int dx, int dy, int dz, int dw) {
        super.move(dx, dy, dz); w += dw;
    }
}
```

using the `move` method of the superclass `Point3d` to process `dx`, `dy`, and `dz`. If `Point4d` is written in this way it will compile without errors.

8.2.1.2 *Inheritance with* `public` *and* `protected`

Given the class `Point`:

```
package points;
public class Point {
    public int x, y;
    protected int useCount = 0;
    static protected int totalUseCount = 0;
    public void move(int dx, int dy) {
        x += dx; y += dy; useCount++; totalUseCount++;
    }
}
```

the `public` and `protected` fields `x`, `y`, `useCount` and `totalUseCount` are inherited in all subclasses of `Point`.

Therefore, this test program, in another package, can be compiled successfully:

```
class Test extends points.Point {
    public void moveBack(int dx, int dy) {
        x -= dx; y -= dy; useCount++; totalUseCount++;
    }
}
```

8.2.1.3 *Inheritance with* `private`

In the example:

```
class Point {
    int x, y;
    void move(int dx, int dy) {
        x += dx; y += dy; totalMoves++;
    }
    private static int totalMoves;
    void printMoves() { System.out.println(totalMoves); }
}
```

```
class Point3d extends Point {
    int z;
    void move(int dx, int dy, int dz) {
        super.move(dx, dy); z += dz; totalMoves++;
    }
}
```

the class variable `totalMoves` can be used only within the class `Point`; it is not inherited by the subclass `Point3d`. A compile-time error occurs because method `move` of class `Point3d` tries to increment `totalMoves`.

8.2.1.4 *Accessing Members of Inaccessible Classes*

Even though a class might not be declared `public`, instances of the class might be available at run time to code outside the package in which it is declared by means a `public` superclass or superinterface. An instance of the class can be assigned to a variable of such a `public` type. An invocation of a `public` method of the object referred to by such a variable may invoke a method of the class if it implements or overrides a method of the `public` superclass or superinterface. (In this situation, the method is necessarily declared `public`, even though it is declared in a class that is not `public`.)

Consider the compilation unit:

```
package points;
public class Point {
    public int x, y;
    public void move(int dx, int dy) {
        x += dx; y += dy;
    }
}
```

and another compilation unit of another package:

```
package morePoints;
class Point3d extends points.Point {
    public int z;
    public void move(int dx, int dy, int dz) {
        super.move(dx, dy); z += dz;
    }
    public void move(int dx, int dy) {
        move(dx, dy, 0);
    }
}
```

```
public class OnePoint {
    public static points.Point getOne() {
        return new Point3d();
    }
}
```

An invocation morePoints.OnePoint.getOne() in yet a third package would return a Point3d that can be used as a Point, even though the type Point3d is not available outside the package morePoints. The two argument version of method move could then be invoked for that object, which is permissible because method move of Point3d is public (as it must be, for any method that overrides a public method must itself be public, precisely so that situations such as this will work out correctly). The fields x and y of that object could also be accessed from such a third package.

While the field z of class Point3d is public, it is not possible to access this field from code outside the package morePoints, given only a reference to an instance of class Point3d in a variable p of type Point. This is because the expression p.z is not correct, as p has type Point and class Point has no field named z; also, the expression ((Point3d)p).z is not correct, because the class type Point3d cannot be referred to outside package morePoints.

The declaration of the field z as public is not useless, however. If there were to be, in package morePoints, a public subclass Point4d of the class Point3d:

```
package morePoints;
public class Point4d extends Point3d {
    public int w;
    public void move(int dx, int dy, int dz, int dw) {
        super.move(dx, dy, dz); w += dw;
    }
}
```

then class Point4d would inherit the field z, which, being public, could then be accessed by code in packages other than morePoints, through variables and expressions of the public type Point4d.

8.3 Field Declarations

Poetic fields encompass me around,
And still I seem to tread on classic ground.
—Joseph Addison (1672–1719), *A Letter from Italy*

The variables of a class type are introduced by *field declarations*:

FieldDeclaration:
  FieldModifiers$_{opt}$ *Type VariableDeclarators* ;

VariableDeclarators:
  VariableDeclarator
  VariableDeclarators , *VariableDeclarator*

VariableDeclarator:
  VariableDeclaratorId
  VariableDeclaratorId = *VariableInitializer*

VariableDeclaratorId:
  Identifier
  VariableDeclaratorId [ ]

VariableInitializer:
  Expression
  ArrayInitializer

The *FieldModifiers* are described in §8.3.1. The *Identifier* in a *FieldDeclarator* may be used in a name to refer to the field. Fields are members; the scope (§6.3) of a field declaration is specified in §8.1.6. More than one field may be declared in a single field declaration by using more than one declarator; the *FieldModifiers* and *Type* apply to all the declarators in the declaration. Variable declarations involving array types are discussed in §10.2.

It is a compile-time error for the body of a class declaration to declare two fields with the same name. Methods, types, and fields may have the same name, since they are used in different contexts and are disambiguated by different lookup procedures (§6.5).

If the class declares a field with a certain name, then the declaration of that field is said to *hide* any and all accessible declarations of fields with the same name in superclasses, and superinterfaces of the class. The field declaration also shadows (§6.3.1) declarations of any accessible fields in enclosing classes or interfaces, and any local variables, formal method parameters, and exception handler parameters with the same name in any enclosing blocks.

If a field declaration hides the declaration of another field, the two fields need not have the same type.

A class inherits from its direct superclass and direct superinterfaces all the non-private fields of the superclass and superinterfaces that are both accessible to code in the class and not hidden by a declaration in the class.

Note that a private field of a superclass might be accessible to a subclass (for example, if both classes are members of the same class). Nevertheless, a private field is never inherited by a subclass.

It is possible for a class to inherit more than one field with the same name (§8.3.3.3). Such a situation does not in itself cause a compile-time error. However, any attempt within the body of the class to refer to any such field by its simple name will result in a compile-time error, because such a reference is ambiguous.

There might be several paths by which the same field declaration might be inherited from an interface. In such a situation, the field is considered to be inherited only once, and it may be referred to by its simple name without ambiguity.

A hidden field can be accessed by using a qualified name (if it is `static`) or by using a field access expression (§15.11) that contains the keyword `super` or a cast to a superclass type. See §15.11.2 for discussion and an example.

A value stored in a field of type `float` is always an element of the float value set (§4.2.3); similarly, a value stored in a field of type `double` is always an element of the double value set. It is not permitted for a field of type `float` to contain an element of the float-extended-exponent value set that is not also an element of the float value set, nor for a field of type `double` to contain an element of the double-extended-exponent value set that is not also an element of the double value set.

8.3.1 Field Modifiers

FieldModifiers:
    FieldModifier
    FieldModifiers FieldModifier

FieldModifier: one of
    Annotation `public protected private`
    `static final transient volatile`

The access modifiers `public`, `protected`, and `private` are discussed in §6.6. A compile-time error occurs if the same modifier appears more than once in a field declaration, or if a field declaration has more than one of the access modifiers `public`, `protected`, and `private`.

If an annotation *a* on a field declaration corresponds to an annotation type *T*, and *T* has a (meta-)annotation *m* that corresponds to `annotation.Target`, then *m* must have an element whose value is `annotation.ElementType.FIELD`, or a compile-time error occurs. Annotation modifiers are described further in §9.7.

If two or more (distinct) field modifiers appear in a field declaration, it is customary, though not required, that they appear in the order consistent with that shown above in the production for *FieldModifier*.

8.3.1.1 `static` *Fields*

If a field is declared `static`, there exists exactly one incarnation of the field, no matter how many instances (possibly zero) of the class may eventually be created. A `static` field, sometimes called a *class variable*, is incarnated when the class is initialized (§12.4).

A field that is not declared `static` (sometimes called a non-`static` field) is called an *instance variable*. Whenever a new instance of a class is created, a new variable associated with that instance is created for every instance variable declared in that class or any of its superclasses. The example program:

```
class Point {
    int x, y, useCount;
    Point(int x, int y) { this.x = x; this.y = y; }
    final static Point origin = new Point(0, 0);
}

class Test {
    public static void main(String[] args) {
        Point p = new Point(1,1);
        Point q = new Point(2,2);
        p.x = 3; p.y = 3; p.useCount++; p.origin.useCount++;
        System.out.println("(" + q.x + "," + q.y + ")");
        System.out.println(q.useCount);
        System.out.println(q.origin == Point.origin);
        System.out.println(q.origin.useCount);
    }
}
```

prints:

```
(2,2)
0
true
1
```

showing that changing the fields `x`, `y`, and `useCount` of `p` does not affect the fields of `q`, because these fields are instance variables in distinct objects. In this example, the class variable `origin` of the class `Point` is referenced both using the class name as a qualifier, in `Point.origin`, and using variables of the class type in field access expressions (§15.11), as in `p.origin` and `q.origin`. These two ways of accessing the `origin` class variable access the same object, evidenced by the fact that the value of the reference equality expression (§15.21.3):

```
q.origin==Point.origin
```

is `true`. Further evidence is that the incrementation:

```
p.origin.useCount++;
```

causes the value of `q.origin.useCount` to be `1`; this is so because `p.origin` and `q.origin` refer to the same variable.

8.3.1.2 `final` *Fields*

A field can be declared `final` (§4.12.4). Both class and instance variables (`static` and non-`static` fields) may be declared `final`.

It is a compile-time error if a blank `final` (§4.12.4) class variable is not definitely assigned (§16.8) by a static initializer (§8.7) of the class in which it is declared.

A blank `final` instance variable must be definitely assigned (§16.9) at the end of every constructor (§8.8) of the class in which it is declared; otherwise a compile-time error occurs.

8.3.1.3 `transient` *Fields*

Variables may be marked `transient` to indicate that they are not part of the persistent state of an object.

If an instance of the class `Point`:

```
class Point {
    int x, y;
    transient float rho, theta;
}
```

were saved to persistent storage by a system service, then only the fields `x` and `y` would be saved. This specification does not specify details of such services; see the specification of `java.io.Serializable` for an example of such a service.

8.3.1.4 `volatile` *Fields*

As described in §17, the Java programming language allows threads to access shared variables. As a rule, to ensure that shared variables are consistently and reliably updated, a thread should ensure that it has exclusive use of such variables by obtaining a lock that, conventionally, enforces mutual exclusion for those shared variables.

The Java programming language provides a second mechanism, volatile fields, that is more convenient than locking for some purposes.

A field may be declared `volatile`, in which case the Java memory model (§17) ensures that all threads see a consistent value for the variable.

If, in the following example, one thread repeatedly calls the method `one` (but no more than `Integer.MAX_VALUE` times in all), and another thread repeatedly calls the method `two`:

```
class Test {

    static int i = 0, j = 0;

    static void one() { i++; j++; }
    static void two() {
        System.out.println("i=" + i + " j=" + j);
    }

}
```

then method `two` could occasionally print a value for `j` that is greater than the value of `i`, because the example includes no synchronization and, under the rules explained in §17, the shared values of `i` and `j` might be updated out of order.

One way to prevent this out-or-order behavior would be to declare methods `one` and `two` to be `synchronized` (§8.4.3.6):

```
class Test {

    static int i = 0, j = 0;

    static synchronized void one() { i++; j++; }
    static synchronized void two() {
        System.out.println("i=" + i + " j=" + j);
    }

}
```

This prevents method `one` and method `two` from being executed concurrently, and furthermore guarantees that the shared values of `i` and `j` are both updated before method `one` returns. Therefore method `two` never observes a value for `j` greater than that for `i`; indeed, it always observes the same value for `i` and `j`.

Another approach would be to declare `i` and `j` to be `volatile`:

```
class Test {

    static volatile int i = 0, j = 0;

    static void one() { i++; j++; }
    static void two() {
        System.out.println("i=" + i + " j=" + j);
    }

}
```

This allows method `one` and method `two` to be executed concurrently, but guarantees that accesses to the shared values for `i` and `j` occur exactly as many times, and in exactly the same order, as they appear to occur during execution of the program text by each thread. Therefore, the shared value for `j` is never greater than that for `i`, because each update to `i` must be reflected in the shared value for `i` before the update to `j` occurs. It is possible, however, that any given invocation of method `two` might observe a value for `j` that is much greater than the value observed for `i`, because method `one` might be executed many times between the moment when method `two` fetches the value of `i` and the moment when method `two` fetches the value of `j`.

See §17 for more discussion and examples.

A compile-time error occurs if a `final` variable is also declared `volatile`.

8.3.2 Initialization of Fields

If a field declarator contains a *variable initializer*, then it has the semantics of an assignment (§15.26) to the declared variable, and:

- If the declarator is for a class variable (that is, a `static` field), then the variable initializer is evaluated and the assignment performed exactly once, when the class is initialized (§12.4).
- If the declarator is for an instance variable (that is, a field that is not `static`), then the variable initializer is evaluated and the assignment performed each time an instance of the class is created (§12.5).

The example:

```
class Point {
    int x = 1, y = 5;
}
class Test {
    public static void main(String[] args) {
        Point p = new Point();
        System.out.println(p.x + ", " + p.y);
    }
}
```

produces the output:

```
1, 5
```

because the assignments to `x` and `y` occur whenever a new `Point` is created.

Variable initializers are also used in local variable declaration statements (§14.4), where the initializer is evaluated and the assignment performed each time the local variable declaration statement is executed.

It is a compile-time error if the evaluation of a variable initializer for a `static` field of a named class (or of an interface) can complete abruptly with a checked exception (§11.2).

It is compile-time error if an instance variable initializer of a named class can throw a checked exception unless that exception or one of its supertypes is explicitly declared in the `throws` clause of each constructor of its class and the class has at least one explicitly declared constructor. An instance variable initializer in an anonymous class (§15.9.5) can throw any exceptions.

8.3.2.1 *Initializers for Class Variables*

If a reference by simple name to any instance variable occurs in an initialization expression for a class variable, then a compile-time error occurs.

If the keyword `this` (§15.8.3) or the keyword `super` (§15.11.2, §15.12) occurs in an initialization expression for a class variable, then a compile-time error occurs.

One subtlety here is that, at run time, `static` variables that are `final` and that are initialized with compile-time constant values are initialized first. This also applies to such fields in interfaces (§9.3.1). These variables are "constants" that will never be observed to have their default initial values (§4.12.5), even by devious programs. See §12.4.2 and §13.4.9 for more discussion.

Use of class variables whose declarations appear textually after the use is sometimes restricted, even though these class variables are in scope. See §8.3.2.3 for the precise rules governing forward reference to class variables.

8.3.2.2 *Initializers for Instance Variables*

Initialization expressions for instance variables may use the simple name of any `static` variable declared in or inherited by the class, even one whose declaration occurs textually later.

Thus the example:

```
class Test {
    float f = j;
    static int j = 1;
}
```

compiles without error; it initializes `j` to `1` when class `Test` is initialized, and initializes `f` to the current value of `j` every time an instance of class `Test` is created.

Initialization expressions for instance variables are permitted to refer to the current object `this` (§15.8.3) and to use the keyword `super` (§15.11.2, §15.12).

Use of instance variables whose declarations appear textually after the use is sometimes restricted, even though these instance variables are in scope. See §8.3.2.3 for the precise rules governing forward reference to instance variables.

8.3.2.3 *Restrictions on the use of Fields during Initialization*

The declaration of a member needs to appear textually before it is used only if the member is an instance (respectively `static`) field of a class or interface *C* and all of the following conditions hold:

- The usage occurs in an instance (respectively `static`) variable initializer of *C* or in an instance (respectively `static`) initializer of *C*.
- The usage is not on the left hand side of an assignment.
- The usage is via a simple name.
- *C* is the innermost class or interface enclosing the usage.

A compile-time error occurs if any of the four requirements above are not met.

This means that a compile-time error results from the test program:

```
class Test {
    int i = j;// compile-time error: incorrect forward reference
    int j = 1;
}
```

whereas the following example compiles without error:

```
class Test {
    Test() { k = 2; }
    int j = 1;
    int i = j;
    int k;
}
```

even though the constructor (§8.8) for `Test` refers to the field `k` that is declared three lines later.

These restrictions are designed to catch, at compile time, circular or otherwise malformed initializations. Thus, both:

```
class Z {
    static int i = j + 2;
    static int j = 4;
}
```

and:

```
class Z {
    static { i = j + 2; }
```

```
    static int i, j;
    static { j = 4; }
}
```

result in compile-time errors. Accesses by methods are not checked in this way, so:

```
class Z {
    static int peek() { return j; }
    static int i = peek();
    static int j = 1;
}
class Test {
    public static void main(String[] args) {
        System.out.println(Z.i);
    }
}
```

produces the output:

```
0
```

because the variable initializer for `i` uses the class method `peek` to access the value of the variable `j` before `j` has been initialized by its variable initializer, at which point it still has its default value (§4.12.5).

A more elaborate example is:

```
class UseBeforeDeclaration {
    static {
        x = 100; // ok - assignment
        int y = x + 1; // error - read before declaration
        int v = x = 3; // ok - x at left hand side of assignment
        int z = UseBeforeDeclaration.x * 2;
    // ok - not accessed via simple name
        Object o = new Object(){
            void foo(){x++;} // ok - occurs in a different class
            {x++;} // ok - occurs in a different class
        };
    }

    {
        j = 200; // ok - assignment
        j = j + 1; // error - right hand side reads before declaration
        int k = j = j + 1;
        int n = j = 300; // ok - j at left hand side of assignment
        int h = j++; // error - read before declaration
        int l = this.j * 3; // ok - not accessed via simple name
        Object o = new Object(){
            void foo(){j++;} // ok - occurs in a different class
            { j = j + 1;} // ok - occurs in a different class
```

```
        };
    }
    int w = x = 3; // ok - x at left hand side of assignment
    int p = x; // ok - instance initializers may access static fields
    static int u = (new Object(){int bar(){return x;}}).bar();
    // ok - occurs in a different class
    static int x;
    int m = j = 4; // ok - j at left hand side of assignment
    int o = (new Object(){int bar(){return j;}}).bar();
    // ok - occurs in a different class
    int j;
}
```

8.3.3 Examples of Field Declarations

The following examples illustrate some (possibly subtle) points about field declarations.

8.3.3.1 *Example: Hiding of Class Variables*

The example:

```
class Point {
    static int x = 2;
}
class Test extends Point {
    static double x = 4.7;
    public static void main(String[] args) {
        new Test().printX();
    }
    void printX() {
        System.out.println(x + " " + super.x);
    }
}
```

produces the output:

```
4.7 2
```

because the declaration of `x` in class `Test` hides the definition of `x` in class `Point`, so class `Test` does not inherit the field `x` from its superclass `Point`. Within the declaration of class `Test`, the simple name `x` refers to the field declared within class `Test`. Code in class `Test` may refer to the field `x` of class `Point` as `super.x` (or, because `x` is `static`, as `Point.x`). If the declaration of `Test.x` is deleted:

```
class Point {
    static int x = 2;
}
```

```
class Test extends Point {
    public static void main(String[] args) {
        new Test().printX();
    }
    void printX() {
        System.out.println(x + " " + super.x);
    }
}
```

then the field x of class Point is no longer hidden within class Test; instead, the simple name x now refers to the field Point.x. Code in class Test may still refer to that same field as super.x. Therefore, the output from this variant program is:

```
2 2
```

8.3.3.2 *Example: Hiding of Instance Variables*

This example is similar to that in the previous section, but uses instance variables rather than static variables. The code:

```
class Point {
    int x = 2;
}

class Test extends Point {
    double x = 4.7;
    void printBoth() {
        System.out.println(x + " " + super.x);
    }
    public static void main(String[] args) {
        Test sample = new Test();
        sample.printBoth();
        System.out.println(sample.x + " " +
                                        ((Point)sample).x);
    }
}
```

produces the output:

```
4.7 2
4.7 2
```

because the declaration of x in class Test hides the definition of x in class Point, so class Test does not inherit the field x from its superclass Point. It must be noted, however, that while the field x of class Point is not *inherited* by class Test, it is nevertheless *implemented* by instances of class Test. In other words, every instance of class Test contains two fields, one of type int and one of type double. Both fields bear the name x, but within the declaration of class Test, the simple name x always refers to the field declared within class Test. Code in instance methods of class `Test` may refer to the instance variable `x` of class `Point` as `super.x`.

Code that uses a field access expression to access field `x` will access the field named `x` in the class indicated by the type of reference expression. Thus, the expression `sample.x` accesses a `double` value, the instance variable declared in class `Test`, because the type of the variable sample is `Test`, but the expression `((Point)sample).x` accesses an `int` value, the instance variable declared in class `Point`, because of the cast to type `Point`.

If the declaration of `x` is deleted from class `Test`, as in the program:

```
class Point {
    static int x = 2;
}
class Test extends Point {
    void printBoth() {
        System.out.println(x + " " + super.x);
    }
    public static void main(String[] args) {
        Test sample = new Test();
        sample.printBoth();
        System.out.println(sample.x + " " +
                                    ((Point)sample).x);
    }
}
```

then the field `x` of class `Point` is no longer hidden within class `Test`. Within instance methods in the declaration of class `Test`, the simple name `x` now refers to the field declared within class `Point`. Code in class `Test` may still refer to that same field as `super.x`. The expression `sample.x` still refers to the field `x` within type `Test`, but that field is now an inherited field, and so refers to the field `x` declared in class `Point`. The output from this variant program is:

```
2 2
2 2
```

8.3.3.3 *Example: Multiply Inherited Fields*

A class may inherit two or more fields with the same name, either from two interfaces or from its superclass and an interface. A compile-time error occurs on any attempt to refer to any ambiguously inherited field by its simple name. A qualified name or a field access expression that contains the keyword `super` (§15.11.2) may be used to access such fields unambiguously. In the example:

```
interface Frob { float v = 2.0f; }
class SuperTest { int v = 3; }
```

```
class Test extends SuperTest implements Frob {
    public static void main(String[] args) {
        new Test().printV();
    }
    void printV() { System.out.println(v); }
}
```

the class Test inherits two fields named v, one from its superclass SuperTest and one from its superinterface Frob. This in itself is permitted, but a compile-time error occurs because of the use of the simple name v in method printV: it cannot be determined which v is intended.

The following variation uses the field access expression super.v to refer to the field named v declared in class SuperTest and uses the qualified name Frob.v to refer to the field named v declared in interface Frob:

```
interface Frob { float v = 2.0f; }
class SuperTest { int v = 3; }
class Test extends SuperTest implements Frob {
    public static void main(String[] args) {
        new Test().printV();
    }
    void printV() {
        System.out.println((super.v + Frob.v)/2);
    }
}
```

It compiles and prints:

```
2.5
```

Even if two distinct inherited fields have the same type, the same value, and are both final, any reference to either field by simple name is considered ambiguous and results in a compile-time error. In the example:

```
interface Color { int RED=0, GREEN=1, BLUE=2; }
interface TrafficLight { int RED=0, YELLOW=1, GREEN=2; }
class Test implements Color, TrafficLight {
    public static void main(String[] args) {
        System.out.println(GREEN);    // compile-time error
        System.out.println(RED);      // compile-time error
    }
}
```

it is not astonishing that the reference to GREEN should be considered ambiguous, because class Test inherits two different declarations for GREEN with different values. The point of this example is that the reference to RED is also considered ambiguous, because two distinct declarations are inherited. The fact that the two fields named RED happen to have the same type and the same unchanging value does not affect this judgment.

8.3.3.4 *Example: Re-inheritance of Fields*

If the same field declaration is inherited from an interface by multiple paths, the field is considered to be inherited only once. It may be referred to by its simple name without ambiguity. For example, in the code:

```
public interface Colorable {
    int RED = 0xff0000, GREEN = 0x00ff00, BLUE = 0x0000ff;
}
public interface Paintable extends Colorable {
    int MATTE = 0, GLOSSY = 1;
}
class Point { int x, y; }
class ColoredPoint extends Point implements Colorable {
    ...
}
class PaintedPoint extends ColoredPoint implements Paintable
{
    ... RED ...
}
```

the fields RED, GREEN, and BLUE are inherited by the class PaintedPoint both through its direct superclass ColoredPoint and through its direct superinterface Paintable. The simple names RED, GREEN, and BLUE may nevertheless be used without ambiguity within the class PaintedPoint to refer to the fields declared in interface Colorable.

8.4 Method Declarations

The diversity of physical arguments and opinions embraces all sorts of methods.
—Michael de Montaigne (1533–1592), *Of Experience*

A *method* declares executable code that can be invoked, passing a fixed number of values as arguments.

MethodDeclaration:
MethodHeader MethodBody

MethodHeader:
MethodModifiers$_{opt}$ *TypeParameters*$_{opt}$ *ResultType MethodDeclarator Throws*$_{opt}$

ResultType:
Type
`void`

MethodDeclarator:
Identifier `(` *FormalParameterList*$_{opt}$ `)`

The *MethodModifiers* are described in §8.4.3, the *TypeParameters* clause of a method in §8.4.4, the *Throws* clause in §8.4.6, and the *MethodBody* in §8.4.7. A method declaration either specifies the type of value that the method returns or uses the keyword `void` to indicate that the method does not return a value.

The *Identifier* in a *MethodDeclarator* may be used in a name to refer to the method. A class can declare a method with the same name as the class or a field, member class or member interface of the class, but this is discouraged as a matter of syle.

For compatibility with older versions of the Java platform, a declaration form for a method that returns an array is allowed to place (some or all of) the empty bracket pairs that form the declaration of the array type after the parameter list. This is supported by the obsolescent production:

MethodDeclarator:
MethodDeclarator `[ ]`

but should not be used in new code.

It is a compile-time error for the body of a class to declare as members two methods with override-equivalent signatures (§8.4.2) (name, number of parameters, and types of any parameters). Methods and fields may have the same name, since they are used in different contexts and are disambiguated by different lookup procedures (§6.5).

8.4.1 Formal Parameters

The *formal parameters* of a method or constructor, if any, are specified by a list of comma-separated parameter specifiers. Each parameter specifier consists of a type (optionally preceded by the `final` modifier and/or one or more annotations (§9.7)) and an identifier (optionally followed by brackets) that specifies the name of the parameter. The last formal parameter in a list is special; it may be a *variable arity parameter,* indicated by an elipsis following the type:

FormalParameterList:
  LastFormalParameter
  FormalParameters , *LastFormalParameter*

FormalParameters:
  FormalParameter
  FormalParameters , *FormalParameter*

FormalParameter:
  VariableModifiers Type VariableDeclaratorId

VariableModifiers:
  VariableModifier
  VariableModifiers VariableModifier

VariableModifier: one of
  `final` *Annotation*

LastFormalParameter:
  VariableModifiers Type `...`$_{opt}$ *VariableDeclaratorId*
  FormalParameter

The following is repeated from §8.3 to make the presentation here clearer:

VariableDeclaratorId:
  Identifier
  VariableDeclaratorId `[ ]`

If a method or constructor has no parameters, only an empty pair of parentheses appears in the declaration of the method or constructor.

If two formal parameters of the same method or constructor are declared to have the same name (that is, their declarations mention the same *Identifier*), then a compile-time error occurs.

If an annotation *a* on a formal parameter corresponds to an annotation type *T*, and *T* has a (meta-)annotation *m* that corresponds to `annotation.Target`, then *m* must have an element whose value is `annotation.ElementType.PARAMETER`, or a compile-time error occurs. Annotation modifiers are described further in §9.7.

It is a compile-time error if a method or constructor parameter that is declared `final` is assigned to within the body of the method or constructor.

When the method or constructor is invoked (§15.12), the values of the actual argument expressions initialize newly created parameter variables, each of the declared *Type,* before execution of the body of the method or constructor. The

Identifier that appears in the *DeclaratorId* may be used as a simple name in the body of the method or constructor to refer to the formal parameter.

If the last formal parameter is a variable arity parameter of type *T*, it is considered to define a formal parameter of type *T[]*. The method is then a *variable arity method*. Otherwise, it is a *fixed arity method*. Invocations of a variable arity method may contain more actual argument expressions than formal parameters. All the actual argument expressions that do not correspond to the formal parameters preceding the variable arity parameter will be evaluated and the results stored into an array that will be passed to the method invocation (§15.12.4.2).

The scope of a parameter of a method (§8.4.1) or constructor (§8.8.1) is the entire body of the method or constructor.

These parameter names may not be redeclared as local variables of the method, or as exception parameters of catch clauses in a try statement of the method or constructor. However, a parameter of a method or constructor may be shadowed anywhere inside a class declaration nested within that method or constructor. Such a nested class declaration could declare either a local class (§14.3) or an anonymous class (§15.9).

Formal parameters are referred to only using simple names, never by using qualified names (§6.6).

A method or constructor parameter of type `float` always contains an element of the float value set (§4.2.3); similarly, a method or constructor parameter of type `double` always contains an element of the double value set. It is not permitted for a method or constructor parameter of type `float` to contain an element of the float-extended-exponent value set that is not also an element of the float value set, nor for a method parameter of type `double` to contain an element of the double-extended-exponent value set that is not also an element of the double value set.

Where an actual argument expression corresponding to a parameter variable is not FP-strict (§15.4), evaluation of that actual argument expression is permitted to use intermediate values drawn from the appropriate extended-exponent value sets. Prior to being stored in the parameter variable the result of such an expression is mapped to the nearest value in the corresponding standard value set by method invocation conversion (§5.3).

8.4.2 Method Signature

It is a compile-time error to declare two methods with override-equivalent signatures (defined below) in a class.

Two methods have the *same signature* if they have the same name and argument types.

Two method or constructor declarations `M` and `N` have *the same argument types* if all of the following conditions hold:

- They have the same number of formal parameters (possibly zero)
- They have the same number of type parameters (possibly zero)
- Let $<A_1, \ldots, A_n>$ be the formal type parameters of `M` and let $<B_1, \ldots, B_n>$ be the formal type parameters of `N`. After renaming each occurrence of a B_i in `N`'s type to A_i the bounds of corresponding type variables and the argument types of `M` and `N` are the same.

The signature of a method `m1` is a *subsignature* of the signature of a method `m2` if either

- `m2` has the same signature as `m1`, or
- the signature of `m1` is the same as the erasure of the signature of `m2`.

DISCUSSION

The notion of subsignature defined here is designed to express a relationship between two methods whose signatures are not identical, but in which one may override the other.

Specifically, it allows a method whose signature does not use generic types to override any generified version of that method. This is important so that library designers may freely generify methods independently of clients that define subclasses or subinterfaces of the library.

Consider the example:

```
class CollectionConverter {
    List toList(Collection c) {...}
}
class Overrider extends CollectionConverter{
    List toList(Collection c) {...}
}
```

Now, assume this code was written before the introduction of genericity, and now the author of class `CollectionConverter` decides to generify the code, thus:

```
class CollectionConverter {
    <T> List<T> toList(Collection<T> c) {...}
}
```

Without special dispensation, `Overrider.toList()` would no longer override `CollectionConverter`.toList(). Instead, the code would be illegal. This would significantly inhibit the use of genericity, since library writers would hesitate to migrate existing code.

Two method signatures `m1` and `m2` are *override-equivalent* iff either `m1` is a subsignature of `m2` or `m2` is a subsignature of `m1`.

The example:

```
class Point implements Move {
    int x, y;
    abstract void move(int dx, int dy);
    void move(int dx, int dy) { x += dx; y += dy; }
}
```

causes a compile-time error because it declares two `move` methods with the same (and hence, override-equivalent) signature. This is an error even though one of the declarations is `abstract`.

8.4.3 Method Modifiers

MethodModifiers:
  MethodModifier
  MethodModifiers MethodModifier

MethodModifier: one of
  Annotation `public` `protected` `private` `abstract` `static`
  `final` `synchronized` `native` `strictfp`

The access modifiers `public`, `protected`, and `private` are discussed in §6.6. A compile-time error occurs if the same modifier appears more than once in a method declaration, or if a method declaration has more than one of the access modifiers `public`, `protected`, and `private`. A compile-time error occurs if a method declaration that contains the keyword `abstract` also contains any one of the keywords `private`, `static`, `final`, `native`, `strictfp`, or `synchronized`. A compile-time error occurs if a method declaration that contains the keyword `native` also contains `strictfp`.

If an annotation *a* on a method declaration corresponds to an annotation type *T*, and *T* has a (meta-)annotation *m* that corresponds to `annotation.Target`, then *m* must have an element whose value is `annotation.ElementType.METHOD`, or a compile-time error occurs. Annotations are discussed further in §9.7.

If two or more method modifiers appear in a method declaration, it is customary, though not required, that they appear in the order consistent with that shown above in the production for *MethodModifier*.

8.4.3.1 `abstract` *Methods*

An `abstract` method declaration introduces the method as a member, providing its signature (§8.4.2), return type, and `throws` clause (if any), but does not provide an implementation. The declaration of an `abstract` method *m* must appear directly within an `abstract` class (call it *A*) unless it occurs within an enum (§8.9); otherwise a compile-time error results. Every subclass of *A* that is not `abstract` must provide an implementation for *m*, or a compile-time error occurs as specified in §8.1.1.1.

It is a compile-time error for a `private` method to be declared `abstract`.

It would be impossible for a subclass to implement a `private abstract` method, because `private` methods are not inherited by subclasses; therefore such a method could never be used.

It is a compile-time error for a `static` method to be declared `abstract`.

It is a compile-time error for a `final` method to be declared `abstract`.

An `abstract` class can override an `abstract` method by providing another `abstract` method declaration.

This can provide a place to put a documentation comment, to refine the return type, or to declare that the set of checked exceptions (§11.2) that can be thrown by that method, when it is implemented by its subclasses, is to be more limited. For example, consider this code:

```
class BufferEmpty extends Exception {
    BufferEmpty() { super(); }
    BufferEmpty(String s) { super(s); }
}
class BufferError extends Exception {
    BufferError() { super(); }
    BufferError(String s) { super(s); }
}
public interface Buffer {
    char get() throws BufferEmpty, BufferError;
}
public abstract class InfiniteBuffer implements Buffer {
    public abstract char get() throws BufferError;
}
```

The overriding declaration of method `get` in class `InfiniteBuffer` states that method `get` in any subclass of `InfiniteBuffer` never throws a `BufferEmpty` exception, putatively because it generates the data in the buffer, and thus can never run out of data.

An instance method that is not `abstract` can be overridden by an `abstract` method.

For example, we can declare an abstract class Point that requires its subclasses to implement toString if they are to be complete, instantiable classes:

```
abstract class Point {
    int x, y;
    public abstract String toString();
}
```

This abstract declaration of toString overrides the non-abstract toString method of class Object. (Class Object is the implicit direct superclass of class Point.) Adding the code:

```
class ColoredPoint extends Point {
    int color;
    public String toString() {
        return super.toString() + ": color " + color; // error
    }
}
```

results in a compile-time error because the invocation super.toString() refers to method toString in class Point, which is abstract and therefore cannot be invoked. Method toString of class Object can be made available to class ColoredPoint only if class Point explicitly makes it available through some other method, as in:

```
abstract class Point {
    int x, y;
    public abstract String toString();
    protected String objString() { return super.toString(); }
}

class ColoredPoint extends Point {
    int color;
    public String toString() {
        return objString() + ": color " + color;  // correct
    }
}
```

8.4.3.2 static *Methods*

A method that is declared static is called a *class method*. A class method is always invoked without reference to a particular object. An attempt to reference the current object using the keyword this or the keyword super or to reference the type parameters of any surrounding declaration in the body of a class method results in a compile-time error. It is a compile-time error for a static method to be declared abstract.

A method that is not declared static is called an *instance method,* and sometimes called a non-static method. An instance method is always invoked with respect to an object, which becomes the current object to which the keywords `this` and `super` refer during execution of the method body.

8.4.3.3 `final` *Methods*

A method can be declared `final` to prevent subclasses from overriding or hiding it. It is a compile-time error to attempt to override or hide a `final` method.

A `private` method and all methods declared immediately within a `final` class (§8.1.1.2) behave as if they are `final`, since it is impossible to override them.

It is a compile-time error for a `final` method to be declared `abstract`.

At run time, a machine-code generator or optimizer can "inline" the body of a `final` method, replacing an invocation of the method with the code in its body. The inlining process must preserve the semantics of the method invocation. In particular, if the target of an instance method invocation is `null`, then a `NullPointerException` must be thrown even if the method is inlined. The compiler must ensure that the exception will be thrown at the correct point, so that the actual arguments to the method will be seen to have been evaluated in the correct order prior to the method invocation.

Consider the example:

```
final class Point {
    int x, y;
    void move(int dx, int dy) { x += dx; y += dy; }
}
class Test {
    public static void main(String[] args) {
        Point[] p = new Point[100];
        for (int i = 0; i < p.length; i++) {
            p[i] = new Point();
            p[i].move(i, p.length-1-i);
        }
    }
}
```

Here, inlining the method move of class `Point` in method `main` would transform the `for` loop to the form:

```
        for (int i = 0; i < p.length; i++) {
            p[i] = new Point();
            Point pi = p[i];
            int j = p.length-1-i;
            pi.x += i;
            pi.y += j;
        }
```

The loop might then be subject to further optimizations.

Such inlining cannot be done at compile time unless it can be guaranteed that `Test` and `Point` will always be recompiled together, so that whenever `Point`—and specifically its `move` method—changes, the code for `Test.main` will also be updated.

8.4.3.4 `native` *Methods*

A method that is `native` is implemented in platform-dependent code, typically written in another programming language such as C, C++, FORTRAN,or assembly language. The body of a `native` method is given as a semicolon only, indicating that the implementation is omitted, instead of a block.

A compile-time error occurs if a `native` method is declared `abstract`.

For example, the class `RandomAccessFile` of the package `java.io` might declare the following `native` methods:

```
package java.io;

public class RandomAccessFile
    implements DataOutput, DataInput
{   . . .
    public native void open(String name, boolean writeable)
        throws IOException;
    public native int readBytes(byte[] b, int off, int len)
        throws IOException;
    public native void writeBytes(byte[] b, int off, int len)
        throws IOException;
    public native long getFilePointer() throws IOException;
    public native void seek(long pos) throws IOException;
    public native long length() throws IOException;
    public native void close() throws IOException;
}
```

8.4.3.5 `strictfp` *Methods*

The effect of the `strictfp` modifier is to make all `float` or `double` expressions within the method body be explicitly FP-strict (§15.4).

8.4.3.6 `synchronized` *Methods*

A `synchronized` method acquires a monitor (§17.1) before it executes. For a class (`static`) method, the monitor associated with the `Class` object for the method's class is used. For an instance method, the monitor associated with `this` (the object for which the method was invoked) is used.

These are the same locks that can be used by the `synchronized` statement (§14.19); thus, the code:

```
class Test {
    int count;
    synchronized void bump() { count++; }
    static int classCount;
    static synchronized void classBump() {
        classCount++;
    }
}
```

has exactly the same effect as:

```
class BumpTest {
    int count;
    void bump() {
        synchronized (this) {
            count++;
        }
    }
    static int classCount;
    static void classBump() {
        try {
            synchronized (Class.forName("BumpTest")) {
              classCount++;
            }
        } catch (ClassNotFoundException e) {
              ...
        }
    }
}
```

The more elaborate example:

```
public class Box {

    private Object boxContents;

    public synchronized Object get() {
        Object contents = boxContents;
        boxContents = null;
        return contents;
    }

    public synchronized boolean put(Object contents) {
        if (boxContents != null)
            return false;
        boxContents = contents;
        return true;
    }
}
```

defines a class which is designed for concurrent use. Each instance of the class `Box` has an instance variable `boxContents` that can hold a reference to any object. You can put an object in a `Box` by invoking `put`, which returns `false` if the box is already full. You can get something out of a `Box` by invoking `get`, which returns a null reference if the box is empty.

If `put` and `get` were not `synchronized`, and two threads were executing methods for the same instance of `Box` at the same time, then the code could misbehave. It might, for example, lose track of an object because two invocations to `put` occurred at the same time.

See §17 for more discussion of threads and locks.

8.4.4 Generic Methods

A method is *generic* if it declares one or more type variables (§4.4). These type variables are known as the *formal type parameters* of the method. The form of the formal type parameter list is identical to a type parameter list of a class or interface, as described in §8.1.2.

The scope of a method's type parameter is the entire declaration of the method, including the type parameter section itself. Therefore, type parameters can appear as parts of their own bounds, or as bounds of other type parameters declared in the same section.

Type parameters of generic methods need not be provided explicitly when a generic method is invoked. Instead, they are almost always inferred as specified in §15.12.2.7

8.4.5 Method Return Type

The return type of a method declares the type of value a method returns, if it returns a value, or states that the method is `void`.

A method declaration d_1 with return type R_1 is *return-type-substitutable* for another method d_2 with return type R_2, if and only if the following conditions hold:

- If R_1 is a primitive type, then R_2 is identical to R_1.
- If R_1 is a reference type then:
  - R_1 is either a subtype of R_2 or R_1 can be converted to a subtype of R_2 by unchecked conversion (§5.1.9), or
  - $R_1 = | R_2 |$.

- If R_1 is `void` then R_2 is `void`.

DISCUSSION

The notion of return-type substitutability summarizes the ways in which return types may vary among methods that override each other.

Note that this definition supports *covariant returns* - that is, the specialization of the return type to a subtype (but only for reference types).

Also note that unchecked conversions are allowed as well. This is unsound, and requires an unchecked warning whenever it is used; it is a special allowance is made to allow smooth migration from non-generic to generic code.

8.4.6 Method Throws

A *throws clause* is used to declare any checked exceptions (§11.2) that can result from the execution of a method or constructor:

Throws:
  `throws` *ExceptionTypeList*

ExceptionTypeList:
  ExceptionType
  ExceptionTypeList , *ExceptionType*

ExceptionType:
  ClassType
  TypeVariable

A compile-time error occurs if any *ExceptionType* mentioned in a `throws` clause is not a subtype (§4.10) of `Throwable`. It is permitted but not required to mention other (unchecked) exceptions in a `throws` clause.

For each checked exception that can result from execution of the body of a method or constructor, a compile-time error occurs unless that exception type or a supertype of that exception type is mentioned in a `throws` clause in the declaration of the method or constructor.

The requirement to declare checked exceptions allows the compiler to ensure that code for handling such error conditions has been included. Methods or constructors that fail to handle exceptional conditions thrown as checked exceptions will normally result in a compile-time error because of the lack of a proper exception type in a `throws` clause. The Java programming language thus encourages a programming style where rare and otherwise truly exceptional conditions are documented in this way.

The predefined exceptions that are not checked in this way are those for which declaring every possible occurrence would be unimaginably inconvenient:

- Exceptions that are represented by the subclasses of class `Error`, for example `OutOfMemoryError`, are thrown due to a failure in or of the virtual machine. Many of these are the result of linkage failures and can occur at unpredictable points in the execution of a program. Sophisticated programs may yet wish to catch and attempt to recover from some of these conditions.
- The exceptions that are represented by the subclasses of the class `RuntimeException`, for example `NullPointerException`, result from runtime integrity checks and are thrown either directly from the program or in library routines. It is beyond the scope of the Java programming language, and perhaps beyond the state of the art, to include sufficient information in the program to reduce to a manageable number the places where these can be proven not to occur.

A method that overrides or hides another method (§8.4.8), including methods that implement `abstract` methods defined in interfaces, may not be declared to throw more checked exceptions than the overridden or hidden method.

More precisely, suppose that *B* is a class or interface, and *A* is a superclass or superinterface of *B*, and a method declaration *n* in *B* overrides or hides a method declaration *m* in *A*. If *n* has a `throws` clause that mentions any checked exception types, then *m* must have a `throws` clause, and for every checked exception type listed in the `throws` clause of *n*, that same exception class or one of its supertypes must occur in the erasure of the `throws` clause of *m*; otherwise, a compile-time error occurs.

If the unerased `throws` clause of *m* does not contain a supertype of each exception type in the `throws` clause of *n*, an unchecked warning must be issued.

DISCUSSION

See §11 for more information about exceptions and a large example.

Type variables are allowed in throws lists even though they are not allowed in catch clauses.

```
interface PrivilegedExceptionAction<E extends Exception> {
  void run() throws E;
}
class AccessController {
  public static <E extends Exception>
```

```
  Object doPrivileged(PrivilegedExceptionAction<E> action) throws E
  { ... }
}
class Test {
  public static void main(String[] args) {
    try {
      AccessController.doPrivileged(
        new PrivilegedExceptionAction<FileNotFoundException>() {
          public void run() throws FileNotFoundException
          {... delete a file  ...}
        });
    } catch (FileNotFoundException f) {...} // do something
  }
}
```

8.4.7 Method Body

A *method body* is either a block of code that implements the method or simply a semicolon, indicating the lack of an implementation. The body of a method must be a semicolon if and only if the method is either `abstract` (§8.4.3.1) or `native` (§8.4.3.4).

MethodBody:
  Block
  ;

A compile-time error occurs if a method declaration is either `abstract` or `native` and has a block for its body. A compile-time error occurs if a method declaration is neither `abstract` nor `native` and has a semicolon for its body.

If an implementation is to be provided for a method declared `void`, but the implementation requires no executable code, the method body should be written as a block that contains no statements: "`{ }`".

If a method is declared `void`, then its body must not contain any `return` statement (§14.17) that has an *Expression*.

If a method is declared to have a return type, then every `return` statement (§14.17) in its body must have an *Expression*. A compile-time error occurs if the body of the method can complete normally (§14.1).

In other words, a method with a return type must return only by using a return statement that provides a value return; it is not allowed to "drop off the end of its body."

Note that it is possible for a method to have a declared return type and yet contain no return statements. Here is one example:

```
class DizzyDean {
    int pitch() { throw new RuntimeException("90 mph?!"); }
}
```

8.4.8 Inheritance, Overriding, and Hiding

A class `C` *inherits* from its direct superclass and direct superinterfaces all non-private methods (whether `abstract` or not) of the superclass and superinterfaces that are public, protected or declared with default access in the same package as `C` and are neither overridden (§8.4.8.1) nor hidden (§8.4.8.2) by a declaration in the class.

8.4.8.1 *Overriding (by Instance Methods)*

An instance method `m1` declared in a class `C` *overrides* another instance method, `m2`, declared in class `A` iff all of the following are true:

1. C is a subclass of `A`.
2. The signature of `m1` is a subsignature (§8.4.2) of the signature of `m2`.
3. Either
   - `m2` is public, protected or declared with default access in the same package as `C`, or
   - `m1` overrides a method `m3`, `m3` distinct from `m1`, `m3` distinct from `m2`, such that `m3` overrides `m2`.

Moreover, if `m1` is not `abstract`, then `m1` is said to *implement* any and all declarations of `abstract` methods that it overrides.

DISCUSSION

The signature of an overriding method may differ from the overridden one if a formal parameter in one of the methods has raw type, while the corresponding parameter in the other has a parameterized type.

The rules allow the signature of the overriding method to differ from the overridden one, to accommodate migration of pre-existing code to take advantage of genericity. See section §8.4.2 for further analysis.

A compile-time error occurs if an instance method overrides a `static` method.

In this respect, overriding of methods differs from hiding of fields (§8.3), for it is permissible for an instance variable to hide a `static` variable.

An overridden method can be accessed by using a method invocation expression (§15.12) that contains the keyword `super`. Note that a qualified name or a cast to a superclass type is not effective in attempting to access an overridden method; in this respect, overriding of methods differs from hiding of fields. See §15.12.4.9 for discussion and examples of this point.

The presence or absence of the `strictfp` modifier has absolutely no effect on the rules for overriding methods and implementing abstract methods. For example, it is permitted for a method that is not FP-strict to override an FP-strict method and it is permitted for an FP-strict method to override a method that is not FP-strict.

8.4.8.2 *Hiding (by Class Methods)*

If a class declares a `static` method *m*, then the declaration *m* is said to *hide* any method *m'*, where the signature of *m* is a subsignature (§8.4.2) of the signature of *m'*, in the superclasses and superinterfaces of the class that would otherwise be accessible to code in the class. A compile-time error occurs if a `static` method hides an instance method.

In this respect, hiding of methods differs from hiding of fields (§8.3), for it is permissible for a `static` variable to hide an instance variable. Hiding is also distinct from shadowing (§6.3.1) and obscuring (§6.3.2).

A hidden method can be accessed by using a qualified name or by using a method invocation expression (§15.12) that contains the keyword `super` or a cast to a superclass type. In this respect, hiding of methods is similar to hiding of fields.

8.4.8.3 *Requirements in Overriding and Hiding*

If a method declaration d_1 with return type R_1 overrides or hides the declaration of another method d_2 with return type R_2, then d_1 must be return-type substitutable for d_2, or a compile-time error occurs. Furthermore, if R_1 is not a subtype of R_2, an unchecked warning must be issued (unless suppressed (§9.6.1.5)).

A method declaration must not have a `throws` clause that conflicts (§8.4.6) with that of any method that it overrides or hides; otherwise, a compile-time error occurs.

DISCUSSION

The rules above allow for *covariant return types* - refining the return type of a method when overriding it.

For example, the following declarations are legal although they were illegal in prior versions of the Java programming language:

```
class C implements Cloneable {
   C copy() { return (C)clone(); }
}
class D extends C implements Cloneable {
   D copy() { return (D)clone(); }
}
```

The relaxed rule for overriding also allows one to relax the conditions on abstract classes implementing interfaces.

DISCUSSION

Consider

```
class StringSorter {
// takes a collection of strings and converts it to a sortedlist
    List toList(Collection c) {...}
}
```

and assume that someone subclasses `StringCollector`

```
class Overrider extends StringSorter{
    List toList(Collection c) {...}
}
```

Now, at some point the author of `StringSorter` decides to generify the code

```
class StringSorter {
// takes a collection of strings and converts it to a list
    List<String> toList(Collection<String> c) {...}
}
```

An unchecked warning would be given when compiling `Overrider` against the new definition of `StringSorter` because the return type of `Overrider.toList()` is `List`, which is not a subtype of the return type of the overridden method, `List<String`.

In these respects, overriding of methods differs from hiding of fields (§8.3), for it is permissible for a field to hide a field of another type.

It is a compile time error if a type declaration *T* has a member method m_1 and there exists a method m_2 declared in *T* or a supertype of *T* such that all of the following conditions hold:

- m_1 and m_2 have the same name.
- m_2 is accessible from *T*.
- The signature of m_1 is not a subsignature (§8.4.2) of the signature of m_2.
- m_1 or some method m_1 overrides (directly or indirectly) has the same erasure as m_2 or some method m_2 overrides (directly or indirectly).

DISCUSSION

These restrictions are necessary because generics are implemented via erasure. The rule above implies that methods declared in the same class with the same name must have different erasures. It also implies that a type declaration cannot implement or extend two distinct invocations of the same generic interface. Here are some further examples.

A class cannot have two member methods with the same name and type erasure.

```
class C<T> { T id (T x) {...} }
class D extends C<String> {
    Object id(Object x) {...}
}
```

This is illegal since `D.id(Object)` is a member of `D`, `C<String>.id(String)` is declared in a supertype of `D` and:

- The two methods have the same name, `id`
- `C<String>.id(String)` is accessible to `D`
- The signature of `D.id(Object)` is not a subsignature of that of `C<String>.id(String)`
- The two methods have the same erasure

DISCUSSION

Two different methods of a class may not override methods with the same erasure.

```
class C<T> { T id (T x) {...} }
interface I<T> { Tid(T x); }
class D extends C<String> implements I<Integer> {
```

```
    String id(String x) {...}
    Integer id(Integer x) {...}
}
```

This is also illegal, since `D.id(String)` is a member of `D`, `D.id(Integer)` is declared in `D` and:

- the two methods have the same name, `id`
- the two methods have different signatures.
- `D.id(Integer)` is accessible to `D`
- `D.id(String)` overrides `C<String>.id(String)` and `D.id(Integer)` overrides `I.id(Integer)` yet the two overridden methods have the same erasure

---

The access modifier (§6.6) of an overriding or hiding method must provide at least as much access as the overridden or hidden method, or a compile-time error occurs. In more detail:

- If the overridden or hidden method is `public`, then the overriding or hiding method must be `public`; otherwise, a compile-time error occurs.
- If the overridden or hidden method is `protected`, then the overriding or hiding method must be `protected` or `public`; otherwise, a compile-time error occurs.
- If the overridden or hidden method has default (package) access, then the overriding or hiding method must not be `private`; otherwise, a compile-time error occurs.

Note that a `private` method cannot be hidden or overridden in the technical sense of those terms. This means that a subclass can declare a method with the same signature as a `private` method in one of its superclasses, and there is no requirement that the return type or `throws` clause of such a method bear any relationship to those of the `private` method in the superclass.

8.4.8.4 *Inheriting Methods with Override-Equivalent Signatures*

It is possible for a class to inherit multiple methods with override-equivalent (§8.4.2) signatures.

It is a compile time error if a class *C* inherits a concrete method whose signatures is a subsignature of another concrete method inherited by *C*.

DISCUSSION

This can happen, if a superclass is parametric, and it has two methods that were distinct in the generic declaration, but have the same signature in the particular invocation used.

Otherwise, there are two possible cases:

- If one of the inherited methods is not `abstract`, then there are two subcases:
  - If the method that is not `abstract` is `static`, a compile-time error occurs.
  - Otherwise, the method that is not `abstract` is considered to override, and therefore to implement, all the other methods on behalf of the class that inherits it. If the signature of the non-abstract method is not a subsignature of each of the other inherited methods an unchecked warning must be issued (unless suppressed (§9.6.1.5)). A compile-time error also occurs if the return type of the non-abstract method is not return type substitutable (§8.4.5) for each of the other inherited methods. If the return type of the non-abstract method is not a subtype of the return type of any of the other inherited methods, an unchecked warning must be issued. Moreover, a compile-time error occurs if the inherited method that is not `abstract` has a `throws` clause that conflicts (§8.4.6) with that of any other of the inherited methods.
- If all the inherited methods are `abstract`, then the class is necessarily an `abstract` class and is considered to inherit all the `abstract` methods. A compile-time error occurs if, for any two such inherited methods, one of the methods is not return type substitutable for the other (The `throws` clauses do not cause errors in this case.)

There might be several paths by which the same method declaration might be inherited from an interface. This fact causes no difficulty and never, of itself, results in a compile-time error.

8.4.9 Overloading

If two methods of a class (whether both declared in the same class, or both inherited by a class, or one declared and one inherited) have the same name but signatures that are not override-equivalent, then the method name is said to be *overloaded*. This fact causes no difficulty and never of itself results in a compile-time error. There is no required relationship between the return types or between the `throws` clauses of two methods with the same name, unless their signatures are override-equivalent.

Methods are overridden on a signature-by-signature basis.

If, for example, a class declares two `public` methods with the same name, and a subclass overrides one of them, the subclass still inherits the other method.

When a method is invoked (§15.12), the number of actual arguments (and any explicit type arguments) and the compile-time types of the arguments are used, at compile time, to determine the signature of the method that will be invoked (§15.12.2). If the method that is to be invoked is an instance method, the actual method to be invoked will be determined at run time, using dynamic method lookup (§15.12.4).

8.4.10 Examples of Method Declarations

The following examples illustrate some (possibly subtle) points about method declarations.

8.4.10.1 *Example: Overriding*

In the example:

```
class Point {
    int x = 0, y = 0;
    void move(int dx, int dy) { x += dx; y += dy; }
}
class SlowPoint extends Point {
    int xLimit, yLimit;
    void move(int dx, int dy) {
        super.move(limit(dx, xLimit), limit(dy, yLimit));
    }
    static int limit(int d, int limit) {
        return d > limit ? limit : d < -limit ? -limit : d;
    }
}
```

the class `SlowPoint` overrides the declarations of method `move` of class `Point` with its own `move` method, which limits the distance that the point can move on each invocation of the method. When the `move` method is invoked for an instance of class `SlowPoint`, the overriding definition in class `SlowPoint` will always be called, even if the reference to the SlowPoint object is taken from a variable whose type is Point.

8.4.10.2 *Example: Overloading, Overriding, and Hiding*

In the example:

```
class Point {
    int x = 0, y = 0;
    void move(int dx, int dy) { x += dx; y += dy; }
    int color;
}
class RealPoint extends Point {
    float x = 0.0f, y = 0.0f;
    void move(int dx, int dy) { move((float)dx, (float)dy); }
    void move(float dx, float dy) { x += dx; y += dy; }
}
```

the class RealPoint hides the declarations of the int instance variables x and y of class Point with its own float instance variables x and y, and overrides the method move of class Point with its own move method. It also overloads the name move with another method with a different signature (§8.4.2).

In this example, the members of the class RealPoint include the instance variable color inherited from the class Point, the float instance variables x and y declared in RealPoint, and the two move methods declared in RealPoint.

Which of these overloaded move methods of class RealPoint will be chosen for any particular method invocation will be determined at compile time by the overloading resolution procedure described in §15.12.

8.4.10.3 *Example: Incorrect Overriding*

This example is an extended variation of that in the preceding section:

```
class Point {
    int x = 0, y = 0, color;
    void move(int dx, int dy) { x += dx; y += dy; }
    int getX() { return x; }
    int getY() { return y; }
}
```

```
class RealPoint extends Point {
    float x = 0.0f, y = 0.0f;
    void move(int dx, int dy) { move((float)dx, (float)dy); }
    void move(float dx, float dy) { x += dx; y += dy; }
    float getX() { return x; }
    float getY() { return y; }
}
```

Here the class `Point` provides methods `getX` and `getY` that return the values of its fields `x` and `y`; the class `RealPoint` then overrides these methods by declaring methods with the same signature. The result is two errors at compile time, one for each method, because the return types do not match; the methods in class `Point` return values of type `int`, but the wanna-be overriding methods in class `RealPoint` return values of type `float`.

8.4.10.4 *Example: Overriding versus Hiding*

This example corrects the errors of the example in the preceding section:

```
class Point {
    int x = 0, y = 0;
    void move(int dx, int dy) { x += dx; y += dy; }
    int getX() { return x; }
    int getY() { return y; }
    int color;
}
class RealPoint extends Point {
    float x = 0.0f, y = 0.0f;
    void move(int dx, int dy) { move((float)dx, (float)dy); }
    void move(float dx, float dy) { x += dx; y += dy; }
    int getX() { return (int)Math.floor(x); }
    int getY() { return (int)Math.floor(y); }
}
```

Here the overriding methods `getX` and `getY` in class `RealPoint` have the same return types as the methods of class `Point` that they override, so this code can be successfully compiled.

Consider, then, this test program:

```
class Test {
    public static void main(String[] args) {
        RealPoint rp = new RealPoint();
        Point p = rp;
        rp.move(1.71828f, 4.14159f);
        p.move(1, -1);
        show(p.x, p.y);
        show(rp.x, rp.y);
        show(p.getX(), p.getY());
        show(rp.getX(), rp.getY());
    }
    static void show(int x, int y) {
        System.out.println("(" + x + ", " + y + ")");
    }
    static void show(float x, float y) {
        System.out.println("(" + x + ", " + y + ")");
    }
}
```

The output from this program is:

```
(0, 0)
(2.7182798, 3.14159)
(2, 3)
(2, 3)
```

The first line of output illustrates the fact that an instance of `RealPoint` actually contains the two integer fields declared in class `Point`; it is just that their names are hidden from code that occurs within the declaration of class `RealPoint` (and those of any subclasses it might have). When a reference to an instance of class `RealPoint` in a variable of type `Point` is used to access the field `x`, the integer field `x` declared in class `Point` is accessed. The fact that its value is zero indicates that the method invocation `p.move(1, -1)` did not invoke the method `move` of class `Point`; instead, it invoked the overriding method `move` of class `RealPoint`.

The second line of output shows that the field access `rp.x` refers to the field `x` declared in class `RealPoint`. This field is of type `float`, and this second line of output accordingly displays floating-point values. Incidentally, this also illustrates the fact that the method name `show` is overloaded; the types of the arguments in the method invocation dictate which of the two definitions will be invoked.

The last two lines of output show that the method invocations `p.getX()` and `rp.getX()` each invoke the `getX` method declared in class `RealPoint`. Indeed, there is no way to invoke the `getX` method of class `Point` for an instance of class

RealPoint from outside the body of RealPoint, no matter what the type of the variable we may use to hold the reference to the object. Thus, we see that fields and methods behave differently: hiding is different from overriding.

8.4.10.5 *Example: Invocation of Hidden Class Methods*

A hidden class (static) method can be invoked by using a reference whose type is the class that actually contains the declaration of the method. In this respect, hiding of static methods is different from overriding of instance methods. The example:

```
class Super {
    static String greeting() { return "Goodnight"; }
    String name() { return "Richard"; }
}
class Sub extends Super {
    static String greeting() { return "Hello"; }
    String name() { return "Dick"; }
}
class Test {
    public static void main(String[] args) {
        Super s = new Sub();
        System.out.println(s.greeting() + ", " + s.name());
    }
}
```

produces the output:

```
Goodnight, Dick
```

because the invocation of greeting uses the type of s, namely Super, to figure out, at compile time, which class method to invoke, whereas the invocation of name uses the class of s, namely Sub, to figure out, at run time, which instance method to invoke.

8.4.10.6 *Large Example of Overriding*

Overriding makes it easy for subclasses to extend the behavior of an existing class, as shown in this example:

```
import java.io.OutputStream;
import java.io.IOException;
class BufferOutput {
    private OutputStream o;
    BufferOutput(OutputStream o) { this.o = o; }
```

```
    protected byte[] buf = new byte[512];

    protected int pos = 0;

    public void putchar(char c) throws IOException {
        if (pos == buf.length)
            flush();
        buf[pos++] = (byte)c;
    }

    public void putstr(String s) throws IOException {
        for (int i = 0; i < s.length(); i++)
            putchar(s.charAt(i));
    }

    public void flush() throws IOException {
        o.write(buf, 0, pos);
        pos = 0;
    }
}

class LineBufferOutput extends BufferOutput {

    LineBufferOutput(OutputStream o) { super(o); }

    public void putchar(char c) throws IOException {
        super.putchar(c);
        if (c == '\n')
            flush();
    }
}

class Test {
    public static void main(String[] args)
        throws IOException
    {
        LineBufferOutput lbo =
            new LineBufferOutput(System.out);
        lbo.putstr("lbo\nlbo");
        System.out.print("print\n");
        lbo.putstr("\n");
    }
}
```

This example produces the output:

```
lbo
print
lbo
```

The class `BufferOutput` implements a very simple buffered version of an `OutputStream`, flushing the output when the buffer is full or `flush` is invoked.

The subclass `LineBufferOutput` declares only a constructor and a single method `putchar`, which overrides the method `putchar` of `BufferOutput`. It inherits the methods `putstr` and `flush` from class `BufferOutput`.

In the `putchar` method of a `LineBufferOutput` object, if the character argument is a newline, then it invokes the `flush` method. The critical point about overriding in this example is that the method `putstr`, which is declared in class `BufferOutput`, invokes the `putchar` method defined by the current object `this`, which is not necessarily the `putchar` method declared in class `BufferOutput`.

Thus, when `putstr` is invoked in `main` using the `LineBufferOutput` object `lbo`, the invocation of `putchar` in the body of the `putstr` method is an invocation of the `putchar` of the object `lbo`, the overriding declaration of `putchar` that checks for a newline. This allows a subclass of `BufferOutput` to change the behavior of the `putstr` method without redefining it.

Documentation for a class such as `BufferOutput`, which is designed to be extended, should clearly indicate what is the contract between the class and its subclasses, and should clearly indicate that subclasses may override the `putchar` method in this way. The implementor of the `BufferOutput` class would not, therefore, want to change the implementation of `putstr` in a future implementation of `BufferOutput` not to use the method `putchar`, because this would break the preexisting contract with subclasses. See the further discussion of binary compatibility in §13, especially §13.2.

8.4.10.7 *Example: Incorrect Overriding because of Throws*

This example uses the usual and conventional form for declaring a new exception type, in its declaration of the class `BadPointException`:

```
class BadPointException extends Exception {
    BadPointException() { super(); }
    BadPointException(String s) { super(s); }
}

class Point {
    int x, y;
    void move(int dx, int dy) { x += dx; y += dy; }
}

class CheckedPoint extends Point {
    void move(int dx, int dy) throws BadPointException {
        if ((x + dx) < 0 || (y + dy) < 0)
            throw new BadPointException();
        x += dx; y += dy;
    }
}
```

This example results in a compile-time error, because the override of method `move` in class `CheckedPoint` declares that it will throw a checked exception that the `move` in class `Point` has not declared. If this were not considered an error, an invoker of the method `move` on a reference of type `Point` could find the contract between it and `Point` broken if this exception were thrown.

Removing the `throws` clause does not help:

```
class CheckedPoint extends Point {
    void move(int dx, int dy) {
        if ((x + dx) < 0 || (y + dy) < 0)
            throw new BadPointException();
        x += dx; y += dy;
    }
}
```

A different compile-time error now occurs, because the body of the method `move` cannot throw a checked exception, namely `BadPointException`, that does not appear in the `throws` clause for `move`.

8.5 Member Type Declarations

A *member class* is a class whose declaration is directly enclosed in another class or interface declaration. Similarly, a *member interface* is an interface whose declaration is directly enclosed in another class or interface declaration. The scope (§6.3) of a member class or interface is specified in §8.1.6.

If the class declares a member type with a certain name, then the declaration of that type is said to *hide* any and all accessible declarations of member types with the same name in superclasses and superinterfaces of the class.

Within a class *C*, a declaration *d* of a member type named *n* shadows the declarations of any other types named *n* that are in scope at the point where *d* occurs.

If a member class or interface declared with simple name *C* is directly enclosed within the declaration of a class with fully qualified name *N*, then the member class or interface has the fully qualified name *N.C*. A class inherits from its direct superclass and direct superinterfaces all the non-private member types of the superclass and superinterfaces that are both accessible to code in the class and not hidden by a declaration in the class.

A class may inherit two or more type declarations with the same name, either from two interfaces or from its superclass and an interface. A compile-time error occurs on any attempt to refer to any ambiguously inherited class or interface by its simple name

If the same type declaration is inherited from an interface by multiple paths, the class or interface is considered to be inherited only once. It may be referred to by its simple name without ambiguity.

8.5.1 Modifiers

The access modifiers `public`, `protected`, and `private` are discussed in §6.6. A compile-time error occurs if a member type declaration has more than one of the access modifiers `public`, `protected`, and `private`.

Member type declarations may have annotation modifers just like any type or member declaration.

8.5.2 Static Member Type Declarations

The `static` keyword may modify the declaration of a member type *C* within the body of a non-inner class *T*. Its effect is to declare that *C* is not an inner class. Just as a static method of *T* has no current instance of *T* in its body, *C* also has no current instance of *T*, nor does it have any lexically enclosing instances.

It is a compile-time error if a `static` class contains a usage of a non-`static` member of an enclosing class.

Member interfaces are always implicitly `static`. It is permitted but not required for the declaration of a member interface to explicitly list the `static` modifier.

8.6 Instance Initializers

An *instance initializer* declared in a class is executed when an instance of the class is created (§15.9), as specified in §8.8.7.1.

InstanceInitializer:
  Block

It is compile-time error if an instance initializer of a named class can throw a checked exception unless that exception or one of its supertypes is explicitly declared in the `throws` clause of each constructor of its class and the class has at least one explicitly declared constructor. An instance initializer in an anonymous class (§15.9.5) can throw any exceptions.

The rules above distinguish between instance initializers in named and anonymous classes. This distinction is deliberate. A given anonymous class is only instantiated at a single point in a program. It is therefore possible to directly propagate information about what exceptions might be raised by an anonymous class' instance initializer to the surrounding expression. Named classes, on the other hand, can be instantiated in many places. Therefore the only way to propagate information about what exceptions might be raised by an instance initializer of a named class is through the `throws` clauses of its constructors. It follows that a more liberal rule can be used in the case of anonymous classes. Similar comments apply to instance variable initializers.

It is a compile-time error if an instance initializer cannot complete normally (§14.21). If a `return` statement (§14.17) appears anywhere within an instance initializer, then a compile-time error occurs.

Use of instance variables whose declarations appear textually after the use is sometimes restricted, even though these instance variables are in scope. See §8.3.2.3 for the precise rules governing forward reference to instance variables.

Instance initializers are permitted to refer to the current object `this` (§15.8.3), to any type variables (§4.4) in scope and to use the keyword `super` (§15.11.2, §15.12).

8.7 Static Initializers

Any *static initializers* declared in a class are executed when the class is initialized and, together with any field initializers (§8.3.2) for class variables, may be used to initialize the class variables of the class (§12.4).

StaticInitializer:
    `static` *Block*

It is a compile-time error for a static initializer to be able to complete abruptly (§14.1, §15.6) with a checked exception (§11.2). It is a compile-time error if a static initializer cannot complete normally (§14.21).

The static initializers and class variable initializers are executed in textual order.

Use of class variables whose declarations appear textually after the use is sometimes restricted, even though these class variables are in scope. See §8.3.2.3 for the precise rules governing forward reference to class variables.

If a `return` statement (§14.17) appears anywhere within a static initializer, then a compile-time error occurs.

If the keyword `this` (§15.8.3) or any type variable (§4.4) defined outside the initializer or the keyword `super` (§15.11, §15.12) appears anywhere within a static initializer, then a compile-time error occurs.

8.8 Constructor Declarations

The constructor of wharves, bridges, piers, bulk-heads,
floats, stays against the sea . . .
—Walt Whitman, *Song of the Broad-Axe* (1856)

A *constructor* is used in the creation of an object that is an instance of a class:

ConstructorDeclaration:
  ConstructorModifiers$_{opt}$ *ConstructorDeclarator*
    Throws$_{opt}$ *ConstructorBody*

ConstructorDeclarator:
  TypeParameters$_{opt}$ *SimpleTypeName* (*FormalParameterList*$_{opt}$)

The *SimpleTypeName* in the *ConstructorDeclarator* must be the simple name of the class that contains the constructor declaration; otherwise a compile-time error occurs. In all other respects, the constructor declaration looks just like a method declaration that has no result type.

Here is a simple example:

```
class Point {
    int x, y;
    Point(int x, int y) { this.x = x; this.y = y; }
}
```

Constructors are invoked by class instance creation expressions (§15.9), by the conversions and concatenations caused by the string concatenation operator + (§15.18.1), and by explicit constructor invocations from other constructors (§8.8.7). Constructors are never invoked by method invocation expressions (§15.12).

Access to constructors is governed by access modifiers (§6.6).

This is useful, for example, in preventing instantiation by declaring an inaccessible constructor (§8.8.10).

Constructor declarations are not members. They are never inherited and therefore are not subject to hiding or overriding.

8.8.1 Formal Parameters and Formal Type Parameter

The formal parameters and formal type parameters of a constructor are identical in structure and behavior to the formal parameters of a method (§8.4.1).

8.8.2 Constructor Signature

It is a compile-time error to declare two constructors with override-equivalent (§8.4.2) *signatures* in a class. It is a compile-time error to declare two constructors whose signature has the same erasure (§4.6) in a class.

8.8.3 Constructor Modifiers

ConstructorModifiers:
    ConstructorModifier
    ConstructorModifiers ConstructorModifier

ConstructorModifier: one of
    Annotation `public protected private`

The access modifiers `public`, `protected`, and `private` are discussed in §6.6. A compile-time error occurs if the same modifier appears more than once in a constructor declaration, or if a constructor declaration has more than one of the access modifiers `public`, `protected`, and `private`.

If no access modifier is specified for the constructor of a normal class, the constructor has default access. If no access modifier is specified for the constructor of an enum type, the constructor is `private`. It is a compile-time error if the constructor of an enum type (§8.9) is declared `public` or `protected`.

If an annotation *a* on a constructor corresponds to an annotation type *T*, and *T* has a (meta-)annotation *m* that corresponds to `annotation.Target`, then *m* must have an element whose value is `annotation.ElementType.CONSTRUCTOR`, or a compile-time error occurs. Annotations are further discussed in §9.7.

Unlike methods, a constructor cannot be `abstract`, `static`, `final`, `native`, `strictfp`, or `synchronized`. A constructor is not inherited, so there is no need to declare it `final` and an `abstract` constructor could never be implemented. A constructor is always invoked with respect to an object, so it makes no sense for a constructor to be `static`. There is no practical need for a constructor to be `synchronized`, because it would lock the object under construction, which is normally not made available to other threads until all constructors for the object have completed their work. The lack of `native` constructors is an arbitrary language design choice that makes it easy for an implementation of the Java virtual machine to verify that superclass constructors are always properly invoked during object creation.

Note that a *ConstructorModifier* cannot be declared `strictfp`. This difference in the definitions for *ConstructorModifier* and *MethodModifier* (§8.4.3) is an intentional language design choice; it effectively ensures that a constructor is FP-strict (§15.4) if and only if its class is FP-strict.

8.8.4 Generic Constructors

It is possible for a constructor to be declared generic, independently of whether the class the constructor is declared in is itself generic. A constructor is *generic* if it declares one or more type variables (§4.4). These type variables are known as the *formal type parameters* of the constructor. The form of the formal type parameter list is identical to a type parameter list of a generic class or interface, as described in §8.1.2.

The scope of a constructor's type parameter is the entire declaration of the constructor, including the type parameter section itself. Therefore, type parameters can appear as parts of their own bounds, or as bounds of other type parameters declared in the same section.

Type parameters of generic constructor need not be provided explicitly when a generic constructor is invoked. When they are not provided, they are inferred as specified in §15.12.2.7.

8.8.5 Constructor Throws

The `throws` clause for a constructor is identical in structure and behavior to the `throws` clause for a method (§8.4.6).

8.8.6 The Type of a Constructor

The type of a constructor consists of its signature and the exception types given its throws clause.

8.8.7 Constructor Body

The first statement of a constructor body may be an explicit invocation of another constructor of the same class or of the direct superclass (§8.8.7.1).

ConstructorBody:
    { *ExplicitConstructorInvocation*$_{opt}$ *BlockStatements*$_{opt}$ }

It is a compile-time error for a constructor to directly or indirectly invoke itself through a series of one or more explicit constructor invocations involving `this`. If the constructor is a constructor for an enum type (§8.9), it is a compile-time error for it to invoke the superclass constructor explicitly.

If a constructor body does not begin with an explicit constructor invocation and the constructor being declared is not part of the primordial class `Object`, then the constructor body is implicitly assumed by the compiler to begin with a superclass constructor invocation "`super();`", an invocation of the constructor of its direct superclass that takes no arguments.

Except for the possibility of explicit constructor invocations, the body of a constructor is like the body of a method (§8.4.7). A `return` statement (§14.17) may be used in the body of a constructor if it does not include an expression.

In the example:

```
class Point {
    int x, y;
    Point(int x, int y) { this.x = x; this.y = y; }
}
class ColoredPoint extends Point {
    static final int WHITE = 0, BLACK = 1;
    int color;
    ColoredPoint(int x, int y) {
        this(x, y, WHITE);
    }
    ColoredPoint(int x, int y, int color) {
        super(x, y);
        this.color = color;
    }
}
```

the first constructor of `ColoredPoint` invokes the second, providing an additional argument; the second constructor of `ColoredPoint` invokes the constructor of its superclass `Point`, passing along the coordinates.

§12.5 and §15.9 describe the creation and initialization of new class instances.

8.8.7.1 *Explicit Constructor Invocations*

ExplicitConstructorInvocation:
  NonWildTypeArguments$_{opt}$ `this` (*ArgumentList$_{opt}$*) ;
  NonWildTypeArguments$_{opt}$ `super` (*ArgumentList$_{opt}$*) ;
  Primary. NonWildTypeArguments$_{opt}$ `super` (*ArgumentList$_{opt}$*) ;

NonWildTypeArguments:
  < *ReferenceTypeList* >

ReferenceTypeList:
  ReferenceType
  ReferenceTypeList , *ReferenceType*

Explicit constructor invocation statements can be divided into two kinds:

- *Alternate constructor invocations* begin with the keyword `this` (possibly prefaced with explicit type arguments). They are used to invoke an alternate constructor of the same class.
- *Superclass constructor invocations* begin with either the keyword `super` (possibly prefaced with explicit type arguments) or a *Primary* expression. They are used to invoke a constructor of the direct superclass. Superclass constructor invocations may be further subdivided:
  - *Unqualified superclass constructor invocations* begin with the keyword `super` (possibly prefaced with explicit type arguments).
  - *Qualified superclass constructor invocations* begin with a *Primary* expression . They allow a subclass constructor to explicitly specify the newly created object's immediately enclosing instance with respect to the direct superclass (§8.1.3). This may be necessary when the superclass is an inner class.

Here is an example of a qualified superclass constructor invocation:

```
class Outer {
    class Inner{}
}
class ChildOfInner extends Outer.Inner {
    ChildOfInner(){(new Outer()).super();}
}
```

An explicit constructor invocation statement in a constructor body may not refer to any instance variables or instance methods declared in this class or any superclass, or use `this` or `super` in any expression; otherwise, a compile-time error occurs.

For example, if the first constructor of `ColoredPoint` in the example above were changed to:

```
ColoredPoint(int x, int y) {
    this(x, y, color);
}
```

then a compile-time error would occur, because an instance variable cannot be used within a superclass constructor invocation.

An explicit constructor invocation statement can throw an exception type *E* iff either:

- Some subexpression of the constructor invocation's parameter list can throw *E*; or

- *E* is declared in the throws clause of the constructor that is invoked.

If an anonymous class instance creation expression appears within an explicit constructor invocation statement, then the anonymous class may not refer to any of the enclosing instances of the class whose constructor is being invoked.

For example:

```
class Top {
    int x;
    class Dummy {
        Dummy(Object o) {}
    }
    class Inside extends Dummy {
        Inside() {
            super(new Object() { int r = x; }); // error
        }
        Inside(final int y) {
            super(new Object() { int r = y; }); // correct
        }
    }
}
```

Let `C` be the class being instantiated, let `S` be the direct superclass of `C`, and let `i` be the instance being created. The evaluation of an explicit constructor invocation proceeds as follows:

- First, if the constructor invocation statement is a superclass constructor invocation, then the immediately enclosing instance of `i` with respect to `S` (if any) must be determined. Whether or not `i` has an immediately enclosing instance with respect to `S` is determined by the superclass constructor invocation as follows:
    - If `S` is not an inner class, or if the declaration of `S` occurs in a static context, no immediately enclosing instance of `i` with respect to `S` exists. A compile-time error occurs if the superclass constructor invocation is a qualified superclass constructor invocation.
    - Otherwise:
        - If the superclass constructor invocation is qualified, then the *Primary* expression `p` immediately preceding "`.super`" is evaluated. If the primary expression evaluates to `null`, a `NullPointerException` is raised, and the superclass constructor invocation completes abruptly. Otherwise, the result of this evaluation is the immediately enclosing instance of `i` with

respect to *S*. Let *O* be the immediately lexically enclosing class of *S*; it is a compile-time error if the type of *p* is not *O* or a subclass of *O*.

- Otherwise:
  - If *S* is a local class (§14.3), then let *O* be the innermost lexically enclosing class of *S*. Let *n* be an integer such that *O* is the *n*th lexically enclosing class of *C*. The immediately enclosing instance of *i* with respect to *S* is the *n*th lexically enclosing instance of `this`.
  - Otherwise, *S* is an inner member class (§8.5). It is a compile-time error if *S* is not a member of a lexically enclosing class, or of a superclass or superinterface thereof. Let *O* be the innermost lexically enclosing class of which *S* is a member, and let *n* be an integer such that *O* is the *n*th lexically enclosing class of *C*. The immediately enclosing instance of *i* with respect to *S* is the *n*th lexically enclosing instance of `this`.

- Second, the arguments to the constructor are evaluated, left-to-right, as in an ordinary method invocation.
- Next, the constructor is invoked.
- Finally, if the constructor invocation statement is a superclass constructor invocation and the constructor invocation statement completes normally, then all instance variable initializers of *C* and all instance initializers of *C* are executed. If an instance initializer or instance variable initializer *I* textually precedes another instance initializer or instance variable initializer *J*, then *I* is executed before *J*. This action is performed regardless of whether the superclass constructor invocation actually appears as an explicit constructor invocation statement or is provided automatically. An alternate constructor invocation does not perform this additional implicit action.

8.8.8 Constructor Overloading

Overloading of constructors is identical in behavior to overloading of methods. The overloading is resolved at compile time by each class instance creation expression (§15.9).

8.8.9 Default Constructor

If a class contains no constructor declarations, then a *default constructor* that takes no parameters is automatically provided:

- If the class being declared is the primordial class `Object`, then the default constructor has an empty body.
- Otherwise, the default constructor takes no parameters and simply invokes the superclass constructor with no arguments.

A compile-time error occurs if a default constructor is provided by the compiler but the superclass does not have an accessible constructor that takes no arguments.

A default constructor has no `throws` clause.

It follows that if the nullary constructor of the superclass has a `throws` clause, then a compile-time error will occur.

In an enum type (§8.9), the default constructor is implicitly `private`. Otherwise, if the class is declared `public`, then the default constructor is implicitly given the access modifier `public` (§6.6); if the class is declared `protected`, then the default constructor is implicitly given the access modifier `protected` (§6.6); if the class is declared `private`, then the default constructor is implicitly given the access modifier `private` (§6.6); otherwise, the default constructor has the default access implied by no access modifier.

Thus, the example:

```
public class Point {
    int x, y;
}
```

is equivalent to the declaration:

```
public class Point {
    int x, y;
    public Point() { super(); }
}
```

where the default constructor is `public` because the class `Point` is `public`.

The rule that the default constructor of a class has the same access modifier as the class itself is simple and intuitive. Note, however, that this does not imply that the constructor is accessible whenever the class is accessible. Consider

```
package p1;
public class Outer {
    protected class Inner{}
}
```

```
package p2;
class SonOfOuter extends p1.Outer {
    void foo() {
        new Inner(); // compile-time access error
    }
}
```

The constructor for `Inner` is protected. However, the constructor is protected relative to `Inner`, while `Inner` is protected relative to `Outer`. So, `Inner` is accessible in `SonOfOuter`, since it is a subclass of `Outer`. `Inner`'s constructor is not accessible in `SonOfOuter`, because the class `SonOfOuter` is not a subclass of `Inner`! Hence, even though `Inner` is accessible, its default constructor is not.

8.8.10 Preventing Instantiation of a Class

A class can be designed to prevent code outside the class declaration from creating instances of the class by declaring at least one constructor, to prevent the creation of an implicit constructor, and declaring all constructors to be `private`. A `public` class can likewise prevent the creation of instances outside its package by declaring at least one constructor, to prevent creation of a default constructor with `public` access, and declaring no constructor that is `public`.

Thus, in the example:

```
class ClassOnly {
    private ClassOnly() { }
    static String just = "only the lonely";
}
```

the class `ClassOnly` cannot be instantiated, while in the example:

```
package just;
public class PackageOnly {
    PackageOnly() { }
    String[] justDesserts = { "cheesecake", "ice cream" };
}
```

the class `PackageOnly` can be instantiated only within the package `just`, in which it is declared.

8.9 Enums

An enum declaration has the form:

EnumDeclaration:
  ClassModifiers$_{opt}$ `enum` *Identifier Interfaces*$_{opt}$ *EnumBody*

EnumBody:
  { EnumConstants$_{opt}$ *,*$_{opt}$ *EnumBodyDeclarations*$_{opt}$ *}*

The body of an enum type may contain *enum constants*. An enum constant defines an instance of the enum type. An enum type has no instances other than those defined by its enum constants.

DISCUSSION

It is a compile-time error to attempt to explicitly instantiate an enum type (§15.9.1). The final `clone` method in `Enum` ensures that enum constants can never be cloned, and the special treatment by the serialization mechanism ensures that duplicate instances are never created as a result of deserialization. Reflective instantiation of enum types is prohibited. Together, these four things ensure that no instances of an enum type exist beyond those defined by the enum constants.

Because there is only one instance of each enum constant, it is permissible to use the == operator in place of the `equals` method when comparing two object references if it is known that at least one of them refers to an enum constant. (The `equals` method in `Enum` is a final method that merely invokes `super.equals` on its argument and returns the result, thus performing an identity comparison.)

EnumConstants:
  EnumConstant
  EnumConstants , EnumConstant

EnumConstant:
  Annotations Identifier Arguments$_{opt}$ *ClassBody*$_{opt}$

Arguments:
  (ArgumentList$_{opt}$ *)*

EnumBodyDeclarations:
  ; ClassBodyDeclarations$_{opt}$

An enum constant may be preceded by annotation (§9.7) modifiers. If an annotation *a* on an enum constant corresponds to an annotation type *T*, and *T* has a (meta-)annotation *m* that corresponds to `annotation.Target`, then *m* must have an element whose value is `annotation.ElementType.FIELD`, or a compile-time error occurs.

An enum constant may be followed by arguments, which are passed to the constructor of the enum type when the constant is created during class initialization as described later in this section. The constructor to be invoked is chosen using the normal overloading rules (§15.12.2). If the arguments are omitted, an empty argument list is assumed. If the enum type has no constructor declarations, a parameterless default constructor is provided (which matches the implicit empty argument list). This default constructor is `private`.

The optional class body of an enum constant implicitly defines an anonymous class declaration (§15.9.5) that extends the immediately enclosing enum type. The class body is governed by the usual rules of anonymous classes; in particular it cannot contain any constructors.

DISCUSSION

Instance methods declared in these class bodies are may be invoked outside the enclosing enum type only if they override accessible methods in the enclosing enum type.

Enum types (§8.9) must not be declared `abstract`; doing so will result in a compile-time error. It is a compile-time error for an enum type *E* to have an abstract method *m* as a member unless *E* has one or more enum constants, and all of *E*'s enum constants have class bodies that provide concrete implementations of *m*. It is a compile-time error for the class body of an enum constant to declare an abstract method.

An enum type is implicitly `final` unless it contains at least one enum constant that has a class body. In any case, it is a compile-time error to explicitly declare an enum type to be `final`.

Nested enum types are implicitly `static`. It is permissable to explicitly declare a nested enum type to be `static`.

DISCUSSION

This implies that it is impossible to define a local (§14.3) enum, or to define an enum in an inner class (§8.1.3).

Any constructor or member declarations within an enum declaration apply to the enum type exactly as if they had been present in the class body of a normal class declaration unless explicitly stated otherwise.

The direct superclass of an enum type named *E* is `Enum<E>`. In addition to the members it inherits from `Enum<E>`, for each declared enum constant with the name *n* the enum type has an implicitly declared public `static final` field named *n* of type `E`. These fields are considered to be declared in the same order as the corresponding enum constants, before any static fields explicitly declared in the enum type. Each such field is initialized to the enum constant that corresponds to it. Each such field is also considered to be annotated by the same annotations as the corresponding enum constant. The enum constant is said to be *created* when the corresponding field is initialized.

It is a compile-time error for an enum to declare a finalizer. An instance of an enum may never be finalized.

In addition, if *E* is the name of an enum type, then that type has the following implicitly declared static methods:

```
/**
* Returns an array containing the constants of this enum
* type, in the order they're declared.  This method may be
* used to iterate over the constants as follows:
*
*    for(E c : E.values())
*        System.out.println(c);
*
* @return an array containing the constants of this enum
* type, in the order they're declared
*/
public static E[] values();

/**
* Returns the enum constant of this type with the specified
* name.
* The string must match exactly an identifier used to declare
* an enum constant in this type.  (Extraneous whitespace
* characters are not permitted.)
*
* @return the enum constant with the specified name
```

```
* @throws IllegalArgumentException if this enum type has no
* constant with the specified name
*/
public static E valueOf(String name);
```

DISCUSSION

It follows that enum type declarations cannot contain fields that conflict with the enum constants, and cannot contain methods that conflict with the automatically generated methods (`values()` and `valueOf(String)`) or methods that override the final methods in `Enum`: (`equals(Object)`, `hashCode()`, `clone()`, `compareTo(Object)`, `name()`, `ordinal()`, and `getDeclaringClass()`).

It is a compile-time error to reference a static field of an enum type that is not a compile-time constant (§15.28) from constructors, instance initializer blocks, or instance variable initializer expressions of that type. It is a compile-time error for the constructors, instance initializer blocks, or instance variable initializer expressions of an enum constant `e` to refer to itself or to an enum constant of the same type that is declared to the right of `e`.

DISCUSSION

Without this rule, apparently reasonable code would fail at run time due to the initialization circularity inherent in enum types. (A circularity exists in any class with a "self-typed" static field.) Here is an example of the sort of code that would fail:

```
enum Color {
        RED, GREEN, BLUE;
        static final Map<String,Color> colorMap =
                                    new HashMap<String,Color>();
        Color() {
            colorMap.put(toString(), this);
        }
    }
```

Static initialization of this enum type would throw a `NullPointerException` because the static variable `colorMap` is uninitialized when the constructors for the enum constants run. The restriction above ensures that such code won't compile.

Note that the example can easily be refactored to work properly:

```
enum Color {
        RED, GREEN, BLUE;
        static final Map<String,Color> colorMap =
                                       new HashMap<String,Color>();
        static {
            for (Color c : Color.values())
                colorMap.put(c.toString(), c);
        }
    }
```

The refactored version is clearly correct, as static initialization occurs top to bottom.

DISCUSSION

Here is program with a nested enum declaration that uses an enhanced for loop to iterate over the constants in the enum:

```
public class Example1 {
    public enum Season { WINTER, SPRING, SUMMER, FALL }

    public static void main(String[] args) {
        for (Season s : Season.values())
            System.out.println(s);
    }
}
```

Running this program produces the following output:

```
WINTER
SPRING
SUMMER
FALL
```

Here is a program illustrating the use of `EnumSet` to work with subranges:

```
import java.util.*;

public class Example2 {
    enum Day { MONDAY, TUESDAY, WEDNESDAY, THURSDAY, FRIDAY, SATUR-
DAY, SUNDAY }

    public static void main(String[] args) {
        System.out.print("Weekdays: ");
        for (Day d : EnumSet.range(Day.MONDAY, Day.FRIDAY))
            System.out.print(d + " ");
        System.out.println();
    }
}
```

Running this program produces the following output:

```
Weekdays: MONDAY TUESDAY WEDNESDAY THURSDAY FRIDAY
```

EnumSet contains a rich family of static factories, so this technique can be generalized to work non-contiguous subsets as well as subranges. At first glance, it might appear wasteful to generate an EnumSet for a single iteration, but they are so cheap that this is the recommended idiom for iteration over a subrange. Internally, an EnumSet is represented with a single long assuming the enum type has 64 or fewer elements.

Here is a slightly more complex enum declaration for an enum type with an explicit instance field and an accessor for this field. Each member has a different value in the field, and the values are passed in via a constructor. In this example, the field represents the value, in cents, of an American coin. Note, however, that their are no restrictions on the type or number of parameters that may be passed to an enum constructor.

```
public enum Coin {
    PENNY(1), NICKEL(5), DIME(10), QUARTER(25);

    Coin(int value) { this.value = value; }

    private final int value;

    public int value() { return value; }
}
```

Switch statements are useful for simulating the addition of a method to an enum type from outside the type. This example "adds" a color method to the Coin type, and prints a table of coins, their values, and their colors.

```
public class CoinTest {
    public static void main(String[] args) {
        for (Coin c : Coin.values())
            System.out.println(c + ":   "+ c.value() +"¢ "        +
color(c));
    }
    private enum CoinColor { COPPER, NICKEL, SILVER }
    private static CoinColor color(Coin c) {
        switch(c) {
          case PENNY:
            return CoinColor.COPPER;
          case NICKEL:
            return CoinColor.NICKEL;
          case DIME: case QUARTER:
            return CoinColor.SILVER;
          default:
            throw new AssertionError("Unknown coin: " + c);
        }
    }
}
```

Running the program prints:

```
PENNY:          1¢      COPPER
NICKEL:         5¢      NICKEL
```

```
DIME:            10¢      SILVER
QUARTER:         25¢      SILVER
```

In the following example, a playing card class is built atop two simple enum types. Note that each enum type would be as long as the entire example in the absence of the enum facility:

```
import java.util.*;
public class Card implements Comparable<Card>, java.io.Serializable
{
    public enum Rank { DEUCE, THREE, FOUR, FIVE, SIX, SEVEN, EIGHT,
NINE, TEN,JACK, QUEEN, KING, ACE }
    public enum Suit { CLUBS, DIAMONDS, HEARTS, SPADES }
    private final Rank rank;
    private final Suit suit;

    private Card(Rank rank, Suit suit) {
        if (rank == null || suit == null)
            throw new NullPointerException(rank + ", " + suit);
        this.rank = rank;
        this.suit = suit;
    }

    public Rank rank() { return rank; }
    public Suit suit() { return suit; }
    public String toString() { return rank + " of " + suit; }

    // Primary sort on suit, secondary sort on rank
    public int compareTo(Card c) {
        int suitCompare = suit.compareTo(c.suit);
            return (suitCompare != 0 ? suitCompare : rank.comp-
areTo(c.rank));
    }

    private static final List<Card> prototypeDeck = new ArrayL-
ist<Card>(52);

    static {
        for (Suit suit : Suit.values())
            for (Rank rank : Rank.values())
                prototypeDeck.add(new Card(rank, suit));
    }

    // Returns a new deck
    public static List<Card> newDeck() {
        return new ArrayList<Card>(prototypeDeck);
    }
}
```

Here's a little program that exercises the Card class. It takes two integer parameters on the command line, representing the number of hands to deal and the number of cards in each hand:

```
import java.util.*;
class Deal {
    public static void main(String args[]) {
```

```
        int numHands     = Integer.parseInt(args[0]);
        int cardsPerHand = Integer.parseInt(args[1]);
        List<Card> deck  = Card.newDeck();
        Collections.shuffle(deck);
        for (int i=0; i < numHands; i++)
            System.out.println(dealHand(deck, cardsPerHand));
    }

    /**
     * Returns a new ArrayList consisting of the last n elements of
     * deck, which are removed from deck.  The returned list is
     * sorted using the elements' natural ordering.
     */
    public static <E extends Comparable<E>> ArrayList<E>
            dealHand(List<E> deck, int n) {
        int deckSize = deck.size();
        List<E> handView = deck.subList(deckSize - n, deckSize);
        ArrayList<E> hand = new ArrayList<E>(handView);
        handView.clear();
        Collections.sort(hand);
        return hand;
    }
}
```

Running the program produces results like this:

```
java Deal 4 5
[FOUR of SPADES, NINE of CLUBS, NINE of SPADES, QUEEN of SPADES,
KING of SPADES]
[THREE of DIAMONDS, FIVE of HEARTS, SIX of SPADES, SEVEN of DIA-
MONDS, KING of DIAMONDS]
[FOUR of DIAMONDS, FIVE of SPADES, JACK of CLUBS, ACE of DIAMONDS,
ACE of HEARTS]
[THREE of HEARTS, FIVE of DIAMONDS, TEN of HEARTS, JACK of HEARTS,
QUEEN of HEARTS]
```

The next example demonstrates the use of constant-specific class bodies to attach behaviors to the constants. (It is anticipated that the need for this will be rare.):

```
import java.util.*;

public enum Operation {
    PLUS {
        double eval(double x, double y) { return x + y; }
    },
    MINUS {
        double eval(double x, double y) { return x - y; }
    },
    TIMES {
        double eval(double x, double y) { return x * y; }
    },
    DIVIDED_BY {
        double eval(double x, double y) { return x / y; }
    };

    // Perform the arithmetic operation represented by this constant
   // abstract double eval(double x, double y);
```

```
    public static void main(String args[]) {
        double x = Double.parseDouble(args[0]);
        double y = Double.parseDouble(args[1]);

        for (Operation op : Operation.values())
            System.out.println(x + " " + op + " " + y + " = " +
op.eval(x, y));
    }
}
```

Running this program produces the following output:

```
java Operation 2.0 4.0
2.0 PLUS 4.0 = 6.0
2.0 MINUS 4.0 = -2.0
2.0 TIMES 4.0 = 8.0
2.0 DIVIDED_BY 4.0 = 0.5
```

The above pattern is suitable for moderately sophisticated programmers. It is admittedly a bit tricky, but it is much safer than using a case statement in the base type (Operation), as the pattern precludes the possibility of forgetting to add a behavior for a new constant (you'd get a compile-time error).

Bow, bow, ye lower middle classes!
Bow, bow, ye tradesmen, bow, ye masses!
Blow the trumpets, bang the brasses!
Tantantara! Tzing! Boom!

—W. S. Gilbert, *Iolanthe*

CHAPTER 9

Interfaces

My apple trees will never get across
And eat the cones under his pines, I tell him.
He only says "Good Fences Make Good Neighbors."
—Robert Frost, *Mending Wall* (1914)

AN interface declaration introduces a new reference type whose members are classes, interfaces, constants and abstract methods. This type has no implementation, but otherwise unrelated classes can implement it by providing implementations for its abstract methods.

A *nested interface* is any interface whose declaration occurs within the body of another class or interface. A *top-level interface* is an interface that is not a nested interface.

We distinguish between two kinds of interfaces - normal interfaces and annotation types.

This chapter discusses the common semantics of all interfaces—normal interfaces and annotation types (§9.6), top-level (§7.6) and nested (§8.5, §9.5). Details that are specific to particular kinds of interfaces are discussed in the sections dedicated to these constructs.

Programs can use interfaces to make it unnecessary for related classes to share a common abstract superclass or to add methods to `Object`.

An interface may be declared to be a *direct extension* of one or more other interfaces, meaning that it implicitly specifies all the member types, abstract methods and constants of the interfaces it extends, except for any member types and constants that it may hide.

A class may be declared to *directly implement* one or more interfaces, meaning that any instance of the class implements all the abstract methods specified by the interface or interfaces. A class necessarily implements all the interfaces that its direct superclasses and direct superinterfaces do. This (multiple) interface inheritance allows objects to support (multiple) common behaviors without sharing any implementation.

A variable whose declared type is an interface type may have as its value a reference to any instance of a class which implements the specified interface. It is not sufficient that the class happen to implement all the abstract methods of the interface; the class or one of its superclasses must actually be declared to implement the interface, or else the class is not considered to implement the interface.

9.1 Interface Declarations

An *interface declaration* specifies a new named reference type. There are two kinds of interface declarations - *normal interface declarations* and *annotation type declarations*:

InterfaceDeclaration:
NormalInterfaceDeclaration
AnnotationTypeDeclaration

Annotation types are described further in §9.6.

NormalInterfaceDeclaration:
InterfaceModifiers$_{opt}$ `interface` *Identifier TypeParameters$_{opt}$ ExtendsInterfaces$_{opt}$ InterfaceBody*

The *Identifier* in an interface declaration specifies the name of the interface. A compile-time error occurs if an interface has the same simple name as any of its enclosing classes or interfaces.

9.1.1 Interface Modifiers

An interface declaration may include *interface modifiers*:

InterfaceModifiers:
InterfaceModifier
InterfaceModifiers InterfaceModifier

InterfaceModifier: one of
Annotation `public protected private`
`abstract static strictfp`

The access modifier `public` is discussed in §6.6. Not all modifiers are applicable to all kinds of interface declarations. The access modifiers `protected` and `private` pertain only to member interfaces within a directly enclosing class declaration (§8.5) and are discussed in §8.5.1. The access modifier `static` pertains only to member interfaces (§8.5, §9.5). A compile-time error occurs if the same modifier appears more than once in an interface declaration. If an annotation `a` on an interface declaration corresponds to an annotation type `T`, and `T` has a (meta-)annotation `m` that corresponds to `annotation.Target`, then `m` must have an element whose value is `annotation.ElementType.TYPE`, or a compile-time error occurs. Annotation modifiers are described further in §9.7.

9.1.1.1 `abstract` *Interfaces*

Every interface is implicitly `abstract`. This modifier is obsolete and should not be used in new programs.

9.1.1.2 `strictfp` *Interfaces*

The effect of the `strictfp` modifier is to make all `float` or `double` expressions within the interface declaration be explicitly FP-strict (§15.4).

This implies that all nested types declared in the interface are implicitly `strictfp`.

9.1.2 Generic Interfaces and Type Parameters

An interface is *generic* if it declares one or more type variables (§4.4). These type variables are known as the *type parameters* of the interface. The type parameter section follows the interface name and is delimited by angle brackets. It defines one or more type variables that act as parameters. A generic interface declaration defines a set of types, one for each possible invocation of the type parameter section. All parameterized types share the same interface at runtime.

The scope of an interface's type parameter is the entire declaration of the interface including the type parameter section itself. Therefore, type parameters can appear as parts of their own bounds, or as bounds of other type parameters declared in the same section.

It is a compile-time error to refer to a type parameter of an interface *I* anywhere in the declaration of a field or type member of *I*.

9.1.3 Superinterfaces and Subinterfaces

If an `extends` clause is provided, then the interface being declared extends each of the other named interfaces and therefore inherits the member types, methods, and constants of each of the other named interfaces. These other named interfaces are the *direct superinterfaces* of the interface being declared. Any class that `implements` the declared interface is also considered to implement all the interfaces that this interface `extends`.

ExtendsInterfaces:
  `extends` *InterfaceType*
  ExtendsInterfaces , *InterfaceType*

The following is repeated from §4.3 to make the presentation here clearer:

InterfaceType:
  TypeDeclSpecifier TypeArguments$_{opt}$

Given a (possibly generic) interface declaration for $I<F_1, \ldots, F_n>$, $n \geq 0$, the *direct superinterfaces* of the interface type (§4.5) $I<F_1, \ldots, F_n>$ are the types given in the extends clause of the declaration of I if an extends clause is present.

Let $I<F_1, \ldots, F_n>$, $n > 0$, be a generic interface declaration. The direct superinterfaces of the parameterized interface type $I<T_1, \ldots, T_n>$, where T_i, $1 \leq i \leq n$, is a type, are all types $J<U_1\ theta, \ldots, U_k\ theta>$, where $J<U_1, \ldots, U_k>$ is a direct superinterface of $I<F_1, \ldots, F_n>$, and *theta* is the substitution $[F_1 := T_1, \ldots, F_n := T_n]$.

Each *InterfaceType* in the `extends` clause of an interface declaration must name an accessible interface type; otherwise a compile-time error occurs.

An interface I *directly depends* on a type T if T is mentioned in the `extends` clause of I either as a superinterface or as a qualifier within a superinterface name. An interface I *depends* on a reference type T if any of the following conditions hold:

- I directly depends on T.
- I directly depends on a class C that depends (§8.1.5) on T.
- I directly depends on an interface J that depends on T (using this definition recursively).

A compile-time error occurs if an interface depends on itself.

While every class is an extension of class `Object`, there is no single interface of which all interfaces are extensions.

The *superinterface* relationship is the transitive closure of the direct superinterface relationship. An interface K is a superinterface of interface I if either of the following is true:

- K is a direct superinterface of I.
- There exists an interface J such that K is a superinterface of J, and J is a superinterface of I, applying this definition recursively.

Interface I is said to be a *subinterface* of interface K whenever K is a superinterface of I.

9.1.4 Interface Body and Member Declarations

The body of an interface may declare members of the interface:

InterfaceBody:
 { *InterfaceMemberDeclarations*$_{opt}$ }

InterfaceMemberDeclarations:
 InterfaceMemberDeclaration
 InterfaceMemberDeclarations InterfaceMemberDeclaration

InterfaceMemberDeclaration:
 ConstantDeclaration
 AbstractMethodDeclaration
 ClassDeclaration
 InterfaceDeclaration
 ;

The scope of the declaration of a member `m` declared in or inherited by an interface type `I` is the entire body of `I`, including any nested type declarations.

9.1.5 Access to Interface Member Names

All interface members are implicitly `public`. They are accessible outside the package where the interface is declared if the interface is also declared `public` or `protected`, in accordance with the rules of §6.6.

9.2 Interface Members

The members of an interface are:

- Those members declared in the interface.
- Those members inherited from direct superinterfaces.
- If an interface has no direct superinterfaces, then the interface implicitly declares a public abstract member method `m` with signature `s`, return type `r`, and `throws` clause `t` corresponding to each public instance method `m` with signature `s`, return type `r`, and `throws` clause `t` declared in `Object`, unless a method with the same signature, same return type, and a compatible `throws` clause is explicitly declared by the interface. It is a compile-time error if the interface explicitly declares such a method `m` in the case where `m` is declared to be `final` in `Object`.

It follows that is a compile-time error if the interface declares a method with a signature that is override-equivalent (§8.4.2) to a public method of `Object`, but has a different return type or incompatible `throws` clause.

The interface inherits, from the interfaces it extends, all members of those interfaces, except for fields, classes, and interfaces that it hides and methods that it overrides.

9.3 Field (Constant) Declarations

The materials of action are variable,
but the use we make of them should be constant.
—Epictetus (circa 60 A.D.),
translated by Thomas Wentworth Higginson

ConstantDeclaration:
  ConstantModifiers$_{opt}$ Type VariableDeclarators ;

ConstantModifiers:
  ConstantModifier
  ConstantModifier ConstantModifers

ConstantModifier: one of
  Annotation `public static final`

Every field declaration in the body of an interface is implicitly `public`, `static`, and `final`. It is permitted to redundantly specify any or all of these modifiers for such fields.

If an annotation *a* on a field declaration corresponds to an annotation type *T*, and *T* has a (meta-)annotation *m* that corresponds to `annotation.Target`, then *m* must have an element whose value is `annotation.ElementType.FIELD`, or a compile-time error occurs. Annotation modifiers are described further in §9.7.

If the interface declares a field with a certain name, then the declaration of that field is said to *hide* any and all accessible declarations of fields with the same name in superinterfaces of the interface.

It is a compile-time error for the body of an interface declaration to declare two fields with the same name.

It is possible for an interface to inherit more than one field with the same name (§8.3.3.3). Such a situation does not in itself cause a compile-time error. However, any attempt within the body of the interface to refer to either field by its simple name will result in a compile-time error, because such a reference is ambiguous.

There might be several paths by which the same field declaration might be inherited from an interface. In such a situation, the field is considered to be inherited only once, and it may be referred to by its simple name without ambiguity.

9.3.1 Initialization of Fields in Interfaces

Every field in the body of an interface must have an initialization expression, which need not be a constant expression. The variable initializer is evaluated and the assignment performed exactly once, when the interface is initialized (§12.4).

A compile-time error occurs if an initialization expression for an interface field contains a reference by simple name to the same field or to another field whose declaration occurs textually later in the same interface.

Thus:

```
interface Test {
    float f = j;
    int j = 1;
    int k = k+1;
}
```

causes two compile-time errors, because `j` is referred to in the initialization of `f` before `j` is declared and because the initialization of `k` refers to `k` itself.

One subtlety here is that, at run time, fields that are initialized with compile-time constant values are initialized first. This applies also to `static final` fields in classes (§8.3.2.1). This means, in particular, that these fields will never be observed to have their default initial values (§4.12.5), even by devious programs. See §12.4.2 and §13.4.9 for more discussion.

If the keyword `this` (§15.8.3) or the keyword `super` (15.11.2, 15.12) occurs in an initialization expression for a field of an interface, then unless the occurrence is within the body of an anonymous class (§15.9.5), a compile-time error occurs.

9.3.2 Examples of Field Declarations

The following example illustrates some (possibly subtle) points about field declarations.

9.3.2.1 *Ambiguous Inherited Fields*

If two fields with the same name are inherited by an interface because, for example, two of its direct superinterfaces declare fields with that name, then a single *ambiguous member* results. Any use of this ambiguous member will result in a compile-time error.

Thus in the example:

```
interface BaseColors {
    int RED = 1, GREEN = 2, BLUE = 4;
}

interface RainbowColors extends BaseColors {
    int YELLOW = 3, ORANGE = 5, INDIGO = 6, VIOLET = 7;
}

interface PrintColors extends BaseColors {
    int YELLOW = 8, CYAN = 16, MAGENTA = 32;
}

interface LotsOfColors extends RainbowColors, PrintColors {
    int FUCHSIA = 17, VERMILION = 43, CHARTREUSE = RED+90;
}
```

the interface `LotsOfColors` inherits two fields named `YELLOW`. This is all right as long as the interface does not contain any reference by simple name to the field `YELLOW`. (Such a reference could occur within a variable initializer for a field.)

Even if interface `PrintColors` were to give the value `3` to `YELLOW` rather than the value `8`, a reference to field `YELLOW` within interface `LotsOfColors` would still be considered ambiguous.

9.3.2.2 *Multiply Inherited Fields*

If a single field is inherited multiple times from the same interface because, for example, both this interface and one of this interface's direct superinterfaces extend the interface that declares the field, then only a single member results. This situation does not in itself cause a compile-time error.

In the example in the previous section, the fields `RED`, `GREEN`, and `BLUE` are inherited by interface `LotsOfColors` in more than one way, through interface `RainbowColors` and also through interface `PrintColors`, but the reference to field `RED` in interface `LotsOfColors` is not considered ambiguous because only one actual declaration of the field `RED` is involved.

9.4 Abstract Method Declarations

AbstractMethodDeclaration:
    AbstractMethodModifiers$_{opt}$ TypeParameters$_{opt}$ ResultType MethodDeclarator Throws$_{opt}$;

AbstractMethodModifiers:
    AbstractMethodModifier
    AbstractMethodModifiers AbstractMethodModifier

AbstractMethodModifier: one of
    Annotation `public` `abstract`

The access modifier `public` is discussed in §6.6. A compile-time error occurs if the same modifier appears more than once in an abstract method declaration.

Every method declaration in the body of an interface is implicitly `abstract`, so its body is always represented by a semicolon, not a block.

Every method declaration in the body of an interface is implicitly `public`.

For compatibility with older versions of the Java platform, it is permitted but discouraged, as a matter of style, to redundantly specify the `abstract` modifier for methods declared in interfaces.

It is permitted, but strongly discouraged as a matter of style, to redundantly specify the `public` modifier for interface methods.

Note that a method declared in an interface must not be declared `static`, or a compile-time error occurs, because `static` methods cannot be `abstract`.

Note that a method declared in an interface must not be declared `strictfp` or `native` or `synchronized`, or a compile-time error occurs, because those keywords describe implementation properties rather than interface properties. However, a method declared in an interface may be implemented by a method that is declared `strictfp` or `native` or `synchronized` in a class that implements the interface.

If an annotation *a* on a method declaration corresponds to an annotation type *T*, and *T* has a (meta-)annotation *m* that corresponds to `annotation.Target`, then *m* must have an element whose value is `annotation.ElementType.METHOD`, or a compile-time error occurs. Annotation modifiers are described further in §9.7.

It is a compile-time error for the body of an interface to declare, explicitly or implicitly, two methods with override-equivalent signatures (§8.4.2). However, an interface may inherit several methods with such signatures (§9.4.1).

Note that a method declared in an interface must not be declared `final` or a compile-time error occurs. However, a method declared in an interface may be implemented by a method that is declared `final` in a class that implements the interface.

A method in an interface may be generic. The rules for formal type parameters of a generic method in an interface are the same as for a generic method in a class (§8.4.4).

9.4.1 Inheritance and Overriding

An instance method m_1 declared in an interface *I overrides* another instance method, m_2, declared in interface *J* iff both of the following are true:

1. *I* is a subinterface of *J*.

2. The signature of m_1 is a subsignature (§8.4.2) of the signature of m_2.

If a method declaration d_1 with return type R_1 overrides or hides the declaration of another method d_2 with return type R_2, then d_1 must be return-type-substitutable (§8.4.5) for d_2, or a compile-time error occurs. Furthermore, if R_1 is not a subtype of R_2, an unchecked warning must be issued.

Moreover, a method declaration must not have a `throws` clause that conflicts (§8.4.6) with that of any method that it overrides; otherwise, a compile-time error occurs.

It is a compile time error if a type declaration T has a member method m_1 and there exists a method m_2 declared in T or a supertype of T such that all of the following conditions hold:

- m_1 and m_2 have the same name.
- m_2 is accessible from T.
- The signature of m_1 is not a subsignature (§8.4.2) of the signature of m_2.
- m_1 or some method m_1 overrides (directly or indirectly) has the same erasure as m_2 or some method m_2 overrides (directly or indirectly).

Methods are overridden on a signature-by-signature basis. If, for example, an interface declares two `public` methods with the same name, and a subinterface overrides one of them, the subinterface still inherits the other method.

An interface inherits from its direct superinterfaces all methods of the superinterfaces that are not overridden by a declaration in the interface.

It is possible for an interface to inherit several methods with override-equivalent signatures (§8.4.2). Such a situation does not in itself cause a compile-time error. The interface is considered to inherit all the methods. However, one of the inherited methods must must be return type substitutable for any other inherited method; otherwise, a compile-time error occurs (The `throws` clauses do not cause errors in this case.)

There might be several paths by which the same method declaration is inherited from an interface. This fact causes no difficulty and never of itself results in a compile-time error.

9.4.2 Overloading

If two methods of an interface (whether both declared in the same interface, or both inherited by an interface, or one declared and one inherited) have the same name but different signatures that are not override-equivalent (§8.4.2), then the method name is said to be *overloaded*. This fact causes no difficulty and never of itself results in a compile-time error. There is no required relationship between the return types or between the `throws` clauses of two methods with the same name but different signatures that are not override-equivalent.

9.4.3 Examples of Abstract Method Declarations

The following examples illustrate some (possibly subtle) points about abstract method declarations.

9.4.3.1 *Example: Overriding*

Methods declared in interfaces are `abstract` and thus contain no implementation. About all that can be accomplished by an overriding method declaration, other than to affirm a method signature, is to refine the return type or to restrict the exceptions that might be thrown by an implementation of the method. Here is a variation of the example shown in (§8.4.3.1):

```
class BufferEmpty extends Exception {
    BufferEmpty() { super(); }
    BufferEmpty(String s) { super(s); }
}
class BufferException extends Exception {
    BufferException() { super(); }
    BufferException(String s) { super(s); }
}
public interface Buffer {
    char get() throws BufferEmpty, BufferException;
}
public interface InfiniteBuffer extends Buffer {
     char get() throws BufferException;// override
}
```

9.4.3.2 *Example: Overloading*

In the example code:

```
interface PointInterface {
    void move(int dx, int dy);
}
interface RealPointInterface extends PointInterface {
    void move(float dx, float dy);
    void move(double dx, double dy);
}
```

the method name `move` is overloaded in interface `RealPointInterface` with three different signatures, two of them declared and one inherited. Any non-`abstract` class that implements interface `RealPointInterface` must provide implementations of all three method signatures.

9.5 Member Type Declarations

Interfaces may contain member type declarations (§8.5). A member type declaration in an interface is implicitly `static` and `public`.

If a member type declared with simple name *C* is directly enclosed within the declaration of an interface with fully qualified name *N*, then the member type has the fully qualified name *N.C*.

If the interface declares a member type with a certain name, then the declaration of that field is said to *hide* any and all accessible declarations of member types with the same name in superinterfaces of the interface.

An interface inherits from its direct superinterfaces all the non-private member types of the superinterfaces that are both accessible to code in the interface and not hidden by a declaration in the interface.

An interface may inherit two or more type declarations with the same name. A compile-time error occurs on any attempt to refer to any ambiguously inherited class or interface by its simple name. If the same type declaration is inherited from an interface by multiple paths, the class or interface is considered to be inherited only once; it may be referred to by its simple name without ambiguity.

9.6 Annotation Types

An *annotation type* declaration is a special kind of interface declaration. To distinguish an annotation type declaration from an ordinary interface declaration, the keyword `interface` is preceded by an at sign (`@`).

DISCUSSION

Note that the at sign (`@`) and the keyword `interface` are two distinct tokens; technically it is possible to separate them with whitespace, but this is strongly discouraged as a matter of style.

AnnotationTypeDeclaration:
  InterfaceModifiers$_{opt}$ @ interface Identifier AnnotationTypeBody

AnnotationTypeBody:
  { AnnotationTypeElementDeclarations$_{opt}$ }

AnnotationTypeElementDeclarations:
  AnnotationTypeElementDeclaration
  AnnotationTypeElementDeclarations AnnotationTypeElementDeclaration

AnnotationTypeElementDeclaration:
  AbstractMethodModifiers$_{opt}$ Type Identifier ( ) DefaultValue$_{opt}$;
  ConstantDeclaration
  ClassDeclaration
  InterfaceDeclaration
  EnumDeclaration
  AnnotationTypeDeclaration
  ;

DefaultValue:
  default ElementValue

DISCUSSION

The following restrictions are imposed on annotation type declarations by virtue of their context free syntax:

- Annotation type declarations cannot be generic.
- No extends clause is permitted. (Annotation types implicitly extend `annotation.Annotation`.)
- Methods cannot have any parameters
- Methods cannot have any type parameters

• Method declarations cannot have a `throws` clause

Unless explicitly modified herein, all of the rules that apply to ordinary interface declarations apply to annotation type declarations.

DISCUSSION

For example, annotation types share the same namespace as ordinary class and interface types.

Annotation type declarations are legal wherever interface declarations are legal, and have the same scope and accessibility.

The *Identifier* in an annotation type declaration specifies the name of the annotation type. A compile-time error occurs if an annotation type has the same simple name as any of its enclosing classes or interfaces.

If an annotation *a* on an annotation type declaration corresponds to an annotation type *T*, and *T* has a (meta-)annotation *m* that corresponds to `annotation.Target`, then *m* must have either an element whose value is `annotation.ElementType.ANNOTATION_TYPE`, or an element whose value is `annotation.ElementType.TYPE`, or a compile-time error occurs.

DISCUSSION

By convention, no *AbstractMethodModifiers* should be present except for annotations.

The direct superinterface of an annotation type is always `annotation.Annotation`.

DISCUSSION

A consequence of the fact that an annotation type cannot explicitly declare a superclass or superinterface is that a subclass or subinterface of an annotation type is never itself an annotation type. Similarly, `annotation.Annotation` is not itself an annotation type.

It is a compile-time error if the return type of a method declared in an annotation type is any type other than one of the following: one of the primitive types, `String`, `Class` and any invocation of `Class`, an enum type (§8.9), an annotation type, or an array (§10) of one of the preceding types. It is also a compile-time error if any method declared in an annotation type has a signature that is override-equivalent to that of any `public` or `protected` method declared in class `Object` or in the interface `annotation.Annotation`.

DISCUSSION

Note that this does not conflict with the prohibition on generic methods, as wildcards eliminate the need for an explicit type parameter.

Each method declaration in an annotation type declaration defines an *element* of the annotation type. Annotation types can have zero or more elements. An annotation type has no elements other than those defined by the methods it explicitly declares.

DISCUSSION

Thus, an annotation type declaration inherits several members from `annotation.Annotation`, including the implicitly declared methods corresponding to the instance methods in `Object`, yet these methods do not define elements of the annotation type and it is illegal to use them in annotations.

Without this rule, we could not ensure that the elements were of the types representable in annotations, or that access methods for them would be available.

It is a compile-time error if an annotation type *T* contains an element of type *T*, either directly or indirectly.

DISCUSSION

For example, this is illegal:

```
// Illegal self-reference!!
@interface SelfRef {
    SelfRef value();
}
```

and so is this:

```
// Illegal circularity!!
@interface Ping {
    Pong value();
}

@interface Pong {
    Ping value();
}
```

Note also that this specification precludes elements whose types are nested arrays. For example, this annotation type declaration is illegal:

```
// Illegal nested array!!
@interface Verboten {
    String[][] value();
}
```

An annotation type element may have a default value specified for it. This is done by following its (empty) parameter list with the keyword `default` and the default value of the element.

Defaults are applied dynamically at the time annotations are read; default values are not compiled into annotations. Thus, changing a default value affects annotations even in classes that were compiled before the change was made (presuming these annotations lack an explicit value for the defaulted element).

An *ElementValue* is used to specify a default value. It is a compile-time error if the type of the element is not commensurate (§9.7) with the default value specified. An *ElementValue* is always FP-strict (§15.4).

DISCUSSION

The following annotation type declaration defines an annotation type with several elements:

```
// Normal annotation type declaration with several elements

/**
    * Describes the "request-for-enhancement" (RFE)
    * that led to the presence of
    * the annotated API element.
  */
public @interface RequestForEnhancement {
    int    id();          // Unique ID number associated with RFE
    String synopsis();    // Synopsis of RFE
    String engineer();    // Name of engineer who implemented RFE
    String date();        // Date RFE was implemented
}
```

The following annotation type declaration defines an annotation type with no elements, termed a marker annotation type:

```
// Marker annotation type declaration

/**
  * Annotation with this type indicates that the specification of
the
  * annotated API element is preliminary and subject to change.
  */
public @interface Preliminary { }
```

By convention, the name of the sole element in a single-element annotation type is `value`.

DISCUSSION

Linguistic support for this convention is provided by the single element annotation construct (§9.7); one must obey the convention in order to take advantage of the construct.

DISCUSSION

The convention is illustrated in the following annotation type declaration:

```
// Single-element annotation type declaration

/**
 * Associates a copyright notice with the annotated API element.
 */
public @interface Copyright {
    String value();
}
```

The following annotation type declaration defines a single-element annotation type whose sole element has an array type:

```
// Single-element annotation type declaration with array-typed
// element

/**
 * Associates a list of endorsers with the annotated class.
 */
public @interface Endorsers {
    String[] value();
}
```

Here is an example of complex annotation types, annotation types that contain one or more elements whose types are also annotation types.

```
// Complex Annotation Type

/**
 * A person's name.  This annotation type is not designed to be used
 * directly to annotate program elements, but to define elements
 * of other annotation types.
 */
public @interface Name {
    String first();
    String last();
}

/**
 * Indicates the author of the annotated program element.
 */
public @interface Author {
    Name value();
}

/**
 * Indicates the reviewer of the annotated program element.
 */
public @interface Reviewer {
    Name value();
}
```

The following annotation type declaration provides default values for two of its four elements:

```
// Annotation type declaration with defaults on some elements
public @interface RequestForEnhancement {
    int    id();       // No default - must be specified in
                       // each annotation
    String synopsis(); // No default - must be specified in
                       // each annotation
    String engineer()  default "[unassigned]";
    String date()      default "[unimplemented]";
}
```

The following annotation type declaration shows a `Class` annotation whose value is restricted by a bounded wildcard.

```
// Annotation type declaration with bounded wildcard to
//  restrict Class annotation
// The annotation type declaration below presumes the existence
// of this interface, which describes a formatter for Java
// programming language source code
public interface Formatter { ... }

// Designates a formatter to pretty-print the annotated class.
public @interface PrettyPrinter {
    Class<? extends Formatter> value();
}
```

Note that the grammar for annotation type declarations permits other element declarations besides method declarations. For example, one might choose to declare a nested enum for use in conjunction with an annotation type:

```
// Annotation type declaration with nested enum type declaration
public @interface Quality {
    enum Level { BAD, INDIFFERENT, GOOD }

    Level value();
}
```

9.6.1 Predefined Annotation Types

Several annotation types are predefined in the libraries of the Java platform. Some of these predefined annotation types have special semantics. These semantics are specified in this section. This section does not provide a complete specification for the predefined annotations contained here in; that is the role of the appropriate API specifications. Only those semantics that require special behavior on the part of the Java compiler or virtual machine are specified here.

9.6.1.1 *Target*

The annotation type `annotation.Target` is intended to be used in meta-annotations that indicate the kind of program element that an annotation type is applicable to. `Target` has one element, of type `annotation.ElementType[]`. It is a compile-time error if a given enum constant appears more than once in an annotation whose corresponding type is `annotation.Target`. See sections §7.4.1, §8.1.1, §8.3.1, §8.4.1, §8.4.3, §8.8.3, §8.9, §9.1.1, §9.3, §9.4, §9.6 and §14.4 for the other effects of `@annotation.Target` annotations.

9.6.1.2 *Retention*

Annotations may be present only in the source code, or they may be present in the binary form of a class or interface. An annotation that is present in the binary may or may not be available at run-time via the reflective libraries of the Java platform.

The annotation type `annotation.Retention` is used to choose among the above possibilities. If an annotation *a* corresponds to a type *T*, and *T* has a (meta-)annotation *m* that corresponds to `annotation.Retention`, then:

- If *m* has an element whose value is `annotation.RetentionPolicy.SOURCE`, then a Java compiler must ensure that *a* is not present in the binary representation of the class or interface in which *a* appears.
- If *m* has an element whose value is `annotation.RetentionPolicy.CLASS`, or `annotation.RetentionPolicy.RUNTIME` a Java compiler must ensure that *a* is represented in the binary representation of the class or interface in which *a* appears, unless *m* annotates a local variable declaration. An annotation on a local variable declaration is never retained in the binary representation.

If *T* does not have a (meta-)annotation *m* that corresponds to `annotation.Retention`, then a Java compiler must treat *T* as if it does have such a meta-annotation *m* with an element whose value is `annotation.RetentionPolicy.CLASS`.

DISCUSSION

If *m* has an element whose value is `annotation.RetentionPolicy.RUNTIME`, the reflective libraries of the Java platform will make *a* available at run-time as well.

9.6.1.3 *Inherited*

The annotation type `annotation.Inherited` is used to indicate that annotations on a class *C* corresponding to a given annotation type are inherited by subclasses of *C*.

9.6.1.4 *Override*

Programmers occasionally overload a method declaration when they mean to override it.

DISCUSSION

The classic example concerns the equals method. Programmers write the following:

```
public boolean equals(Foo that) { ... }
```

when they mean to write:

```
public boolean equals(Object that) { ... }
```

This is perfectly legal, but class Foo inherits the `equals` implementation from `Object`, which can cause some very subtle bugs.

The annotation type `Override` supports early detection of such problems. If a method declaration is annotated with the annotation `@Override`, but the method does not in fact override any method declared in a superclass, a compile-time error will occur.

DISCUSSION

Note that if a method overrides a method from a superinterface but not from a superclass, using `@Override` will cause a compile-time error.

The rationale for this is that a concrete class that implements an interface will necessarily override all the interface's methods irrespective of the `@Override` annotation, and so it would be confusing to have the semantics of this annotation interact with the rules for implementing interfaces.

A by product of this rule is that it is never possible to use the `@Override` annotation in an interface declaration.

9.6.1.5 *SuppressWarnings*

The annotation type `SuppressWarnings` supports programmer control over warnings otherwise issued by the Java compiler. It contains a single element that is an array of `String`. If a program declaration is annotated with the annotation `@SuppressWarnings(value = {`S_1`, ... ,` S_k`})`, then a Java compiler must not report any warning identified by one of S_1, ... , S_k if that warning would have been generated as a result of the annotated declaration or any of its parts.

Unchecked warnings are identified by the string `"unchecked"`.

DISCUSSION

Recent Java compilers issue more warnings than previous ones did, and these "lint-like" warnings are very useful. It is likely that more such warnings will be added over time. To encourage their use, there should be some way to disable a warning in a particular part of the program when the programmer knows that the warning is inappropriate.

DISCUSSION

Compiler vendors should document the warning names they support in conjunction with this annotation type. They are encouraged to cooperate to ensure that the same names work across multiple compilers.

9.6.1.6 *Deprecated*

A program element annotated `@Deprecated` is one that programmers are discouraged from using, typically because it is dangerous, or because a better alternative exists. A Java compiler must produce a warning when a deprecated type, method, field, or constructor is used (overridden, invoked, or referenced by name) unless:

- The use is within an entity that itself is is annotated with the annotation `@Deprecated`; or
- The declaration and use are both within the same outermost class; or

- The use site is within an entity that is annotated to suppress the warning with the annotation `@SuppressWarnings("deprecation")`

Use of the annotation `@Deprecated` on a local variable declaration or on a parameter declaration has no effect.

9.7 Annotations

An *annotation* is a modifier consisting of the name of an annotation type (§9.6) and zero or more element-value pairs, each of which associates a value with a different element of the annotation type. The purpose of an annotation is simply to associate information with the annotated program element.

Annotations must contain an element-value pair for every element of the corresponding annotation type, except for those elements with default values, or a compile-time error occurs. Annotations may, but are not required to, contain element-value pairs for elements with default values.

Annotations may be used as modifiers in any declaration, whether package (§7.4), class (§8), interface, field (§8.3, §9.3), method (§8.4, §9.4), parameter, constructor (§8.8), or local variable (§14.4).

DISCUSSION

Note that classes include enums (§8.9), and interfaces include annotation types (§9.6)

Annotations may also be used on enum constants. Such annotations are placed immediately before the enum constant they annotate.

It is a compile-time error if a declaration is annotated with more than one annotation for a given annotation type.

DISCUSSION

Annotations are conventionally placed before all other modifiers, but this is not a requirement; they may be freely intermixed with other modifiers.

There are three kinds of annotations. The first (normal annotation) is fully general. The others (marker annotation and single-element annotation) are merely shorthands.

Annotations:
  Annotation
  Annotations Annotation

Annotation:
  NormalAnnotation
  MarkerAnnotation
  SingleElementAnnotation

A normal annotation is used to annotate a program element:

NormalAnnotation:
  @ *TypeName* (*ElementValuePairs*$_{opt}$)

ElementValuePairs:
  ElementValuePair
  ElementValuePairs , *ElementValuePair*

ElementValuePair:
  Identifier = *ElementValue*

ElementValue:
  ConditionalExpression
  Annotation
  ElementValueArrayInitializer

ElementValueArrayInitializer:
  { *ElementValues*$_{opt}$,$_{opt}$ }

ElementValues:
  ElementValue
  ElementValues , *ElementValue*

DISCUSSION

Note that the at-sign (@) is a token unto itself. Technically it is possible to put whitespace in between the at-sign and the *TypeName*, but this is discouraged.

TypeName names the annotation type corresponding to the annotation. It is a compile-time error if *TypeName* does not name an annotation type. The annotation type named by an annotation must be accessible (§6.6) at the point where the annotation is used, or a compile-time error occurs.

The *Identifier* in an *ElementValuePair* must be the simple name of one of the elements of the annotation type identified by *TypeName* in the containing annotation. Otherwise, a compile-time error occurs. (In other words, the identifier in an element-value pair must also be a method name in the interface identified by *TypeName*.)

The return type of this method defines the element type of the element-value pair. An *ElementValueArrayInitializer* is similar to a normal array initializer (§10.6), except that annotations are permitted in place of expressions.

An element type `T` is *commensurate* with an element value `V` if and only if one of the following conditions is true:

- `T` is an array type `E[]` and either:
  - `V` is an *ElementValueArrayInitializer* and each *ElementValueInitializer* (analogous to a variable initializer in an array initializer) in `V` is commensurate with `E`. Or
  - `V` is an *ElementValue* that is commensurate with `T`.
- The type of `V` is assignment compatible (§5.2) with `T` and, furthermore:
  - If `T` is a primitive type or `String`, `V` is a constant expression (§15.28).
  - `V` is not null.
  - if `T` is `Class`, or an invocation of `Class`, and `V` is a class literal (§15.8.2).
  - If `T` is an enum type, and `V` is an enum constant.

It is a compile-time error if the element type is not commensurate with the *ElementValue*.

If the element type is not an annotation type or an array type, *ElementValue* must be a *ConditionalExpression* (§15.25).

DISCUSSION

Note that `null` is not a legal element value for any element type.

If the element type is an array type and the corresponding *ElementValue* is not an *ElementValueArrayInitializer*, an array value whose sole element is the value represented by the *ElementValue* is associated with the element. Otherwise, the value represented by *ElementValue* is associated with the element.

DISCUSSION

In other words, it is permissible to omit the curly braces when a single-element array is to be associated with an array-valued annotation type element.

Note that the array's element type cannot be an array type, that is, nested array types are not permitted as element types. (While the annotation syntax would permit this, the annotation type declaration syntax would not.)

An annotation on an annotation type declaration is known as a *meta-annotation*. An annotation type may be used to annotate its own declaration. More generally, circularities in the transitive closure of the "annotates" relation are permitted. For example, it is legal to annotate an annotation type declaration with another annotation type, and to annotate the latter type's declaration with the former type. (The pre-defined meta-annotation types contain several such circularities.)

DISCUSSION

Here is an example of a normal annotation:

```
// Normal annotation
@RequestForEnhancement(
    id        = 2868724,
    synopsis  = "Provide time-travel functionality",
    engineer  = "Mr. Peabody",
    date      = "4/1/2004"
)
public static void travelThroughTime(Date destination) { ... }
```

Note that the types of the annotations in the examples in this section are the annotation types defined in the examples in §9.6. Note also that the elements are in the above annotation are in the same order as in the corresponding annotation type declaration. This is not required, but unless specific circumstances dictate otherwise, it is a reasonable convention to follow.

The second form of annotation, marker annotation, is a shorthand designed for use with marker annotation types:

MarkerAnnotation:
  @ *TypeName*

It is simply a shorthand for the normal annotation:

```
@TypeName()
```

DISCUSSION

Example:

```
// Marker annotation
@Preliminary public class TimeTravel { ... }
```

Note that it is legal to use marker annotations for annotation types with elements, so long as all the elements have default values.

The third form of annotation, single-element annotation, is a shorthand designed for use with single-element annotation types:

SingleElementAnnotation:
  @ *TypeName* (*ElementValue*)

It is shorthand for the normal annotation:

```
@TypeName ( value = ElementValue )
```

DISCUSSION

Example:

```
// Single-element annotation
@Copyright("2002 Yoyodyne Propulsion Systems, Inc., All rights
reserved.")
public class OscillationOverthruster { ... }
```

Example with array-valued single-element annotation:

```
// Array-valued single-element annotation
@Endorsers({"Children", "Unscrupulous dentists"})
public class Lollipop { ... }
```

Example with single-element array-valued single-element annotation (note that the curly braces are omitted):

```
// Single-element array-valued single-element annotation
@Endorsers("Epicurus")
public class Pleasure { ... }
```

Example with complex annotation:

```
// Single-element complex annotation
@Author(@Name(first = "Joe", last = "Hacker"))
public class BitTwiddle { ... }
```

Note that it is legal to use single-element annotations for annotation types with multiple elements, so long as one element is named value, and all other elements have default values.

Here is an example of an annotation that takes advantage of default values:

```
// Normal annotation with default values
@RequestForEnhancement(
    id       = 4561414,
    synopsis = "Balance the federal budget"
)
public static void balanceFederalBudget() {
    throw new UnsupportedOperationException("Not implemented");
}
```

Here is an example of an annotation with a Class element whose value is restricted by the use of a bounded wildcard.

```
// Single-element annotation with Class element restricted by
bounded wildcard
// The annotation presumes the existence of this class.
class GorgeousFormatter implements Formatter { ... }
@PrettyPrinter(GorgeousFormatter.class) public class Petunia {...}
// This annotation is illegal, as String is not a subtype of Format-
ter!!
@PrettyPrinter(String.class) public class Begonia { ... }
```

Here is an example of an annotation using an enum type defined inside the annotation type:

```
// Annotation using enum type declared inside the annotation type
@Quality(Quality.Level.GOOD)
public class Karma {
    ...
}
```

Death, life, and sleep, reality and thought,
Assist me, God, their boundaries to know . . .
—William Wordsworth, *Maternal Grief*

CHAPTER 10

Arrays

Even Solomon in all his glory was not arrayed like one of these.
—Matthew 6:29

IN the Java programming language *arrays* are objects (§4.3.1), are dynamically created, and may be assigned to variables of type `Object` (§4.3.2). All methods of class `Object` may be invoked on an array.

An array object contains a number of variables. The number of variables may be zero, in which case the array is said to be *empty*. The variables contained in an array have no names; instead they are referenced by array access expressions that use nonnegative integer index values. These variables are called the *components* of the array. If an array has n components, we say n is the *length* of the array; the components of the array are referenced using integer indices from 0 to $n-1$, inclusive.

All the components of an array have the same type, called the *component type* of the array. If the component type of an array is *T*, then the type of the array itself is written *T*`[]`.

The value of an array component of type `float` is always an element of the float value set (§4.2.3); similarly, the value of an array component of type `double` is always an element of the double value set. It is not permitted for the value of an array component of type `float` to be an element of the float-extended-exponent value set that is not also an element of the float value set, nor for the value of an array component of type `double` to be an element of the double-extended-exponent value set that is not also an element of the double value set.

The component type of an array may itself be an array type. The components of such an array may contain references to subarrays. If, starting from any array type, one considers its component type, and then (if that is also an array type) the component type of that type, and so on, eventually one must reach a component type that is not an array type; this is called the *element type* of the original array, and the components at this level of the data structure are called the *elements* of the original array.

There are some situations in which an element of an array can be an array: if the element type is `Object` or `Cloneable` or `java.io.Serializable`, then some or all of the elements may be arrays, because any array object can be assigned to any variable of these types.

10.1 Array Types

An array type is written as the name of an element type followed by some number of empty pairs of square brackets `[]`. The number of bracket pairs indicates the depth of array nesting. An array's length is not part of its type.

The element type of an array may be any type, whether primitive or reference. In particular:

- Arrays with an interface type as the component type are allowed. The elements of such an array may have as their value a null reference or instances of any type that implements the interface.
- Arrays with an `abstract` class type as the component type are allowed. The elements of such an array may have as their value a null reference or instances of any subclass of the `abstract` class that is not itself `abstract`.

Array types are used in declarations and in cast expressions (§15.16).

10.2 Array Variables

A variable of array type holds a reference to an object. Declaring a variable of array type does not create an array object or allocate any space for array components. It creates only the variable itself, which can contain a reference to an array. However, the initializer part of a declarator (§8.3) may create an array, a reference to which then becomes the initial value of the variable.

Because an array's length is not part of its type, a single variable of array type may contain references to arrays of different lengths.

Here are examples of declarations of array variables that do not create arrays:

```
int[] ai;               // array of int
short[][] as;           // array of array of short
Object[]  ao,           // array of Object
          otherAo;      // array of Object
Collection<?>[] ca;     // array of Collection of unknown type
short s,                // scalar short
      aas[][];          // array of array of short
```

Here are some examples of declarations of array variables that create array objects:

```
Exception ae[] = new Exception[3];
Object aao[][] = new Exception[2][3];
int[] factorial = { 1, 1, 2, 6, 24, 120, 720, 5040 };
char ac[] = { 'n', 'o', 't', ' ', 'a', ' ',
              'S', 't', 'r', 'i', 'n', 'g' };
String[] aas = { "array", "of", "String", };
```

The `[]` may appear as part of the type at the beginning of the declaration, or as part of the declarator for a particular variable, or both, as in this example:

```
byte[] rowvector, colvector, matrix[];
```

This declaration is equivalent to:

```
byte rowvector[], colvector[], matrix[][];
```

Once an array object is created, its length never changes. To make an array variable refer to an array of different length, a reference to a different array must be assigned to the variable.

If an array variable `v` has type `A[]`, where `A` is a reference type, then `v` can hold a reference to an instance of any array type `B[]`, provided `B` can be assigned to `A`. This may result in a run-time exception on a later assignment; see §10.10 for a discussion.

10.3 Array Creation

An array is created by an array creation expression (§15.10) or an array initializer (§10.6).

An array creation expression specifies the element type, the number of levels of nested arrays, and the length of the array for at least one of the levels of nesting. The array's length is available as a final instance variable `length`. It is a compile-time error if the element type is not a reifiable type (§4.7)

An array initializer creates an array and provides initial values for all its components.

10.4 Array Access

A component of an array is accessed by an array access expression (§15.13) that consists of an expression whose value is an array reference followed by an indexing expression enclosed by `[` and `]`, as in `A[i]`. All arrays are `0`-origin. An array with length *n* can be indexed by the integers `0` to *n*`-1`.

Arrays must be indexed by `int` values; `short`, `byte`, or `char` values may also be used as index values because they are subjected to unary numeric promotion (§) and become `int` values. An attempt to access an array component with a `long` index value results in a compile-time error.

All array accesses are checked at run time; an attempt to use an index that is less than zero or greater than or equal to the length of the array causes an `ArrayIndexOutOfBoundsException` to be thrown.

10.5 Arrays: A Simple Example

The example:

```
class Gauss {
    public static void main(String[] args) {
        int[] ia = new int[101];
        for (int i = 0; i < ia.length; i++)
            ia[i] = i;
        int sum = 0;
        for (int e : ia)
            sum += e;
        System.out.println(sum);
    }
}
```

that produces the output:

```
5050
```

declares a variable `ia` that has type array of `int`, that is, `int[]`. The variable `ia` is initialized to reference a newly created array object, created by an array creation expression (§15.10). The array creation expression specifies that the array should have `101` components. The length of the array is available using the field `length`, as shown.

The example program fills the array with the integers from `0` to `100`, sums these integers, and prints the result.

10.6 Array Initializers

An *array initializer* may be specified in a declaration, or as part of an array creation expression (§15.10), creating an array and providing some initial values:

ArrayInitializer:
  { *VariableInitializers*$_{opt}$,$_{opt}$ }

VariableInitializers:
  VariableInitializer
  VariableInitializers , *VariableInitializer*

The following is repeated from §8.3 to make the presentation here clearer:

VariableInitializer:
  Expression
  ArrayInitializer

An array initializer is written as a comma-separated list of expressions, enclosed by braces "{" and "}".

The length of the constructed array will equal the number of expressions.

The expressions in an array initializer are executed from left to right in the textual order they occur in the source code. The *n*th variable initializer specifies the value of the *n-1*st array component. Each expression must be assignment-compatible (§5.2) with the array's component type, or a compile-time error results. It is a compile-time error if the component type of the array being initialized is not reifiable (§4.7).

If the component type is itself an array type, then the expression specifying a component may itself be an array initializer; that is, array initializers may be nested.

A trailing comma may appear after the last expression in an array initializer and is ignored.

As an example:

```
class Test {
    public static void main(String[] args) {
        int ia[][] = { {1, 2}, null };
        for (int[] ea : ia)
            for (int e: ea)
              System.out.println(e);
    }
}
```

prints:

```
1
2
```

before causing a `NullPointerException` in trying to index the second component of the array `ia`, which is a null reference.

10.7 Array Members

The members of an array type are all of the following:

- The `public` `final` field `length`, which contains the number of components of the array (`length` may be positive or zero).
- The `public` method `clone`, which overrides the method of the same name in class `Object` and throws no checked exceptions. The return type of the clone method of an array type *T[]* is *T[]*.
- All the members inherited from class `Object`; the only method of `Object` that is not inherited is its `clone` method.

An array thus has the same public fields and methods as the following class:

```
class A<T> implements Cloneable, java.io.Serializable {
    public final int length = X;
    public T[] clone() {
        try {
            return (T[])super.clone(); // unchecked warning
        } catch (CloneNotSupportedException e) {
            throw new InternalError(e.getMessage());
        }
    }
}
```

Note that the cast in the example above would generate an unchecked warning (§5.1.9) if arrays were really implemented this way.

Every array implements the interfaces `Cloneable` and `java.io.Serializable`.

That arrays are cloneable is shown by the test program:

```
class Test {
    public static void main(String[] args) {
        int ia1[] = { 1, 2 };
        int ia2[] = ia1.clone();
        System.out.print((ia1 == ia2) + " ");
        ia1[1]++;
        System.out.println(ia2[1]);
    }
}
```

which prints:

```
false 2
```

showing that the components of the arrays referenced by `ia1` and `ia2` are different variables. (In some early implementations of the Java programming language this example failed to compile because the compiler incorrectly believed that the clone method for an array could throw a `CloneNotSupportedException`.)

A `clone` of a multidimensional array is shallow, which is to say that it creates only a single new array. Subarrays are shared.

This is shown by the example program:

```
class Test {
    public static void main(String[] args) throws Throwable {
        int ia[][] = { { 1 , 2}, null };
        int ja[][] = ia.clone();
        System.out.print((ia == ja) + " ");
        System.out.println(ia[0] == ja[0] && ia[1] == ja[1]);
    }
}
```

which prints:

```
false true
```

showing that the `int[]` array that is `ia[0]` and the `int[]` array that is `ja[0]` are the same array.

10.8 Class Objects for Arrays

Every array has an associated `Class` object, shared with all other arrays with the same component type. The direct superclass of an array type is `Object`. Every array type implements the interfaces `Cloneable` and `java.io.Serializable`.

This is shown by the following example code:

```
class Test {
    public static void main(String[] args) {
        int[] ia = new int[3];
        System.out.println(ia.getClass());
        System.out.println(ia.getClass().getSuperclass());
    }
}
```

which prints:

```
class [I
class java.lang.Object
```

where the string "`[I`" is the run-time type signature for the class object "array with component type `int`".

10.9 An Array of Characters is Not a `String`

In the Java programming language, unlike C, an array of `char` is not a `String`, and neither a `String` nor an array of `char` is terminated by `'\u0000'` (the NUL character).

A `String` object is immutable, that is, its contents never change, while an array of `char` has mutable elements. The method `toCharArray` in class `String` returns an array of characters containing the same character sequence as a `String`. The class `StringBuffer` implements useful methods on mutable arrays of characters.

10.10 Array Store Exception

If an array variable *v* has type *A*`[]`, where *A* is a reference type, then *v* can hold a reference to an instance of any array type *B*`[]`, provided *B* can be assigned to *A*.

Thus, the example:

```
class Point { int x, y; }

class ColoredPoint extends Point { int color; }

class Test {
    public static void main(String[] args) {
        ColoredPoint[] cpa = new ColoredPoint[10];
        Point[] pa = cpa;
        System.out.println(pa[1] == null);
        try {
            pa[0] = new Point();
        } catch (ArrayStoreException e) {
            System.out.println(e);
        }
    }
}
```

produces the output:

```
true
java.lang.ArrayStoreException
```

Here the variable `pa` has type `Point[]` and the variable `cpa` has as its value a reference to an object of type `ColoredPoint[]`. A `ColoredPoint` can be assigned to a `Point`; therefore, the value of `cpa` can be assigned to `pa`.

A reference to this array `pa`, for example, testing whether `pa[1]` is `null`, will not result in a run-time type error. This is because the element of the array of type `ColoredPoint[]` is a `ColoredPoint`, and every `ColoredPoint` can stand in for a `Point`, since `Point` is the superclass of `ColoredPoint`.

On the other hand, an assignment to the array `pa` can result in a run-time error. At compile time, an assignment to an element of `pa` is checked to make sure that the value assigned is a `Point`. But since `pa` holds a reference to an array of `ColoredPoint`, the assignment is valid only if the type of the value assigned at run-time is, more specifically, a `ColoredPoint`.

The Java virtual machine checks for such a situation at run-time to ensure that the assignment is valid; if not, an `ArrayStoreException` is thrown. More formally: an assignment to an element of an array whose type is *A*`[]`, where *A* is a reference type, is checked at run-time to ensure that the value assigned can be assigned to the actual element type of the array, where the actual element type may be any reference type that is assignable to *A*.

DISCUSSION

If the element type of an array were not reifiable (§4.7), the virtual machine could not perform the store check described in the preceding paragraph. This is why creation of arrays of non-reifiable types is forbidden. One may declare variables of array types whose element type is not reifiable, but any attempt to assign them a value will give rise to an unchecked warning (§5.1.9).

At length burst in the argent revelry,
With plume, tiara, and all rich array . . .
—John Keats, *The Eve of St. Agnes* (1819)

CHAPTER 11

Exceptions

If anything can go wrong, it will.
—Finagle's Law
(often incorrectly attributed to Murphy, whose law is rather different—which only goes to show that Finagle was right)

WHEN a program violates the semantic constraints of the Java programming language, the Java virtual machine signals this error to the program as an *exception*. An example of such a violation is an attempt to index outside the bounds of an array. Some programming languages and their implementations react to such errors by peremptorily terminating the program; other programming languages allow an implementation to react in an arbitrary or unpredictable way. Neither of these approaches is compatible with the design goals of the Java platform: to provide portability and robustness. Instead, the Java programming language specifies that an exception will be thrown when semantic constraints are violated and will cause a non-local transfer of control from the point where the exception occurred to a point that can be specified by the programmer. An exception is said to be *thrown* from the point where it occurred and is said to be *caught* at the point to which control is transferred.

Programs can also throw exceptions explicitly, using `throw` statements (§14.18).

Explicit use of `throw` statements provides an alternative to the old-fashioned style of handling error conditions by returning funny values, such as the integer value `-1` where a negative value would not normally be expected. Experience shows that too often such funny values are ignored or not checked for by callers, leading to programs that are not robust, exhibit undesirable behavior, or both.

Every exception is represented by an instance of the class `Throwable` or one of its subclasses; such an object can be used to carry information from the point at which an exception occurs to the handler that catches it. Handlers are established by `catch` clauses of `try` statements (§14.20). During the process of throwing an exception, the Java virtual machine abruptly completes, one by one, any expressions, statements, method and constructor invocations, initializers, and field initialization expressions that have begun but not completed execution in the current thread. This process continues until a handler is found that indicates that it handles that particular exception by naming the class of the exception or a superclass of the class of the exception. If no such handler is found, then the method `uncaughtException` is invoked for the `ThreadGroup` that is the parent of the current thread—thus every effort is made to avoid letting an exception go unhandled.

The exception mechanism of the Java platform is integrated with its synchronization model (§17), so that locks are released as `synchronized` statements (§14.19) and invocations of `synchronized` methods (§8.4.3.6, §15.12) complete abruptly.

This chapter describes the different causes of exceptions (§11.1). It details how exceptions are checked at compile time (§11.2) and processed at run time (§11.3). A detailed example (§11.4) is then followed by an explanation of the exception hierarchy (§11.5).

11.1 The Causes of Exceptions

If we do not succeed, then we run the risk of failure.
—J. Danforth Quayle (1990)

An exception is thrown for one of three *reasons*:

- An abnormal execution condition was synchronously detected by the Java virtual machine. Such conditions arise because:
  - evaluation of an expression violates the normal semantics of the language, such as an integer divide by zero, as summarized in §15.6
  - an error occurs in loading or linking part of the program (§12.2, §12.3)
  - some limitation on a resource is exceeded, such as using too much memory

  These exceptions are not thrown at an arbitrary point in the program, but rather at a point where they are specified as a possible result of an expression evaluation or statement execution.
- A `throw` statement (§14.18) was executed.
- An asynchronous exception occurred either because:
  - the (deprecated) method `stop` of class `Thread` was invoked
  - an internal error has occurred in the virtual machine (§11.5.2)

Exceptions are represented by instances of the class `Throwable` and instances of its subclasses. These classes are, collectively, the *exception classes*.

11.2 Compile-Time Checking of Exceptions

A compiler for the Java programming language checks, at compile time, that a program contains handlers for *checked exceptions*, by analyzing which checked exceptions can result from execution of a method or constructor. For each checked exception which is a possible result, the `throws` clause for the method (§8.4.6) or constructor (§8.8.5) must mention the class of that exception or one of the superclasses of the class of that exception. This compile-time checking for the presence of exception handlers is designed to reduce the number of exceptions which are not properly handled.

The *unchecked exceptions classes* are the class `RuntimeException` and its subclasses, and the class `Error` and its subclasses. All other exception classes are *checked exception classes*. The Java API defines a number of exception classes, both checked and unchecked. Additional exception classes, both checked and unchecked, may be declared by programmers. See §11.5 for a description of the exception class hierarchy and *some of* the exception classes defined by the Java API and Java virtual machine.

The checked exception classes named in the `throws` clause are part of the contract between the implementor and user of the method or constructor. The `throws` clause of an overriding method may not specify that this method will result in throwing any checked exception which the overridden method is not permitted, by its `throws` clause, to throw. When interfaces are involved, more than one method declaration may be overridden by a single overriding declaration. In this case, the overriding declaration must have a `throws` clause that is compatible with *all* the overridden declarations (§9.4).

We say that a statement or expression can throw a checked exception type `E` if, according to the rules given below, the execution of the statement or expression can result in an exception of type `E` being thrown.

11.2.1 Exception Analysis of Expressions

A method invocation expression can throw an exception type `E` iff either:

- The method to be invoked is of the form *Primary.Identifier* and the *Primary* expression can throw `E;` or
- Some expression of the argument list can throw `E;` or
- `E` is listed in the throws clause of the type of method that is invoked.

A class instance creation expression can throw an exception type `E` iff either:

- The expression is a qualified class instance creation expression and the qualifying expression can throw `E;` or
- Some expression of the argument list can throw `E;` or
- `E` is listed in the throws clause of the type of the constructor that is invoked; or
- The class instance creation expression includes a *ClassBody*, and some instnance initializer block or instance variable initializer expression in the *ClassBody* can throw `E`.

For every other kind of expression, the expression can throw type *E* iff one of its immediate subexpressions can throw *E*.

11.2.2 Exception Analysis of Statements

A throw statement can throw an exception type `E` iff the static type of the throw expression is `E` or a subtype of `E,` or the thrown expression can throw `E`.

An explicit constructor invocation statement can throw an exception type *E* iff either:

- Some subexpression of the constructor invocation's parameter list can throw *E*; or
- *E* is declared in the throws clause of the constructor that is invoked.

A `try` statement can throw an exception type `E` iff either:

- The `try` block can throw `E` and `E` is not assignable to any `catch` parameter of the `try` statement and either no `finally` block is present or the `finally` block can complete normally; or
- Some `catch` block of the `try` statement can throw `E` and either no `finally` block is present or the `finally` block can complete normally; or
- A `finally` block is present and can throw `E`.

Any other statement *S* can throw an exception type `E` iff an expression or statement immediately contained in *S* can throw `E`.

11.2.3 Exception Checking

It is a compile-time error if a method or constructor body can throw some exception type `E` when both of the following hold:

- `E` is a checked exception type
- `E` is not a subtype of some type declared in the throws clause of the method or constructor.

It is a compile-time error if a static initializer (§8.7) or class variable initializer within a named class or interface §8.3.2, can throw a checked exception type.

It is compile-time error if an instance variable initializer of a named class can throw a checked exception unless that exception or one of its supertypes is explicitly declared in the `throws` clause of each constructor of its class and the class has at least one explicitly declared constructor. An instance variable initializer in an anonymous class (§15.9.5) can throw any exceptions.

It is a compile-time error if a `catch` clause catches checked exception type `E1` but there exists no checked exception type `E2` such that all of the following hold:

- `E2 <: E1`
- The `try` block corresponding to the `catch` clause can throw `E2`
- No preceding `catch` block of the immediately enclosing `try` statement catches `E2` or a supertype of `E2`.

unless `E1` is the class `Exception`.

11.2.4 Why Errors are Not Checked

Those unchecked exception classes which are the *error classes* (`Error` and its subclasses) are exempted from compile-time checking because they can occur at many points in the program and recovery from them is difficult or impossible. A program declaring such exceptions would be cluttered, pointlessly.

11.2.5 Why Runtime Exceptions are Not Checked

The *runtime exception classes* (`RuntimeException` and its subclasses) are exempted from compile-time checking because, in the judgment of the designers of the Java programming language, having to declare such exceptions would not aid significantly in establishing the correctness of programs. Many of the operations and constructs of the Java programming language can result in runtime exceptions. The information available to a compiler, and the level of analysis the compiler performs, are usually not sufficient to establish that such run-time exceptions cannot occur, even though this may be obvious to the programmer. Requiring such exception classes to be declared would simply be an irritation to programmers.

For example, certain code might implement a circular data structure that, by construction, can never involve `null` references; the programmer can then be certain that a `NullPointerException` cannot occur, but it would be difficult for a compiler to prove it. The theorem-proving technology that is needed to establish such global properties of data structures is beyond the scope of this specification.

11.3 Handling of an Exception

When an exception is thrown, control is transferred from the code that caused the exception to the nearest dynamically-enclosing `catch` clause of a `try` statement (§14.20) that handles the exception.

A statement or expression is *dynamically enclosed* by a `catch` clause if it appears within the `try` block of the `try` statement of which the `catch` clause is a part, or if the caller of the statement or expression is dynamically enclosed by the `catch` clause.

The *caller* of a statement or expression depends on where it occurs:

- If within a method, then the caller is the method invocation expression (§15.12) that was executed to cause the method to be invoked.
- If within a constructor or an instance initializer or the initializer for an instance variable, then the caller is the class instance creation expression (§15.9) or the method invocation of `newInstance` that was executed to cause an object to be created.
- If within a static initializer or an initializer for a `static` variable, then the caller is the expression that used the class or interface so as to cause it to be initialized.

Whether a particular `catch` clause *handles* an exception is determined by comparing the class of the object that was thrown to the declared type of the parameter of the `catch` clause. The `catch` clause handles the exception if the type of its parameter is the class of the exception or a superclass of the class of the exception. Equivalently, a `catch` clause will catch any exception object that is an `instanceof` (§15.20.2) the declared parameter type.

The control transfer that occurs when an exception is thrown causes abrupt completion of expressions (§15.6) and statements (§14.1) until a `catch` clause is encountered that can handle the exception; execution then continues by executing the block of that `catch` clause. The code that caused the exception is never resumed.

If no `catch` clause handling an exception can be found, then the current thread (the thread that encountered the exception) is terminated, but only after all `finally` clauses have been executed and the method `uncaughtException` has been invoked for the `ThreadGroup` that is the parent of the current thread.

In situations where it is desirable to ensure that one block of code is always executed after another, even if that other block of code completes abruptly, a `try` statement with a `finally` clause (§14.20.2) may be used.

If a `try` or `catch` block in a `try`–`finally` or `try`–`catch`–`finally` statement completes abruptly, then the `finally` clause is executed during propagation of the exception, even if no matching `catch` clause is ultimately found. If a `finally` clause is executed because of abrupt completion of a `try` block and the `finally` clause itself completes abruptly, then the reason for the abrupt completion of the `try` block is discarded and the new reason for abrupt completion is propagated from there.

The exact rules for abrupt completion and for the catching of exceptions are specified in detail with the specification of each statement in §14 and for expressions in §15 (especially §15.6).

11.3.1 Exceptions are Precise

Exceptions are *precise*: when the transfer of control takes place, all effects of the statements executed and expressions evaluated before the point from which the exception is thrown must appear to have taken place. No expressions, statements, or parts thereof that occur after the point from which the exception is thrown may appear to have been evaluated. If optimized code has speculatively executed some of the expressions or statements which follow the point at which the exception occurs, such code must be prepared to hide this speculative execution from the user-visible state of the program.

11.3.2 Handling Asynchronous Exceptions

Most exceptions occur synchronously as a result of an action by the thread in which they occur, and at a point in the program that is specified to possibly result in such an exception. An asynchronous exception is, by contrast, an exception that can potentially occur at any point in the execution of a program.

Proper understanding of the semantics of asynchronous exceptions is necessary if high-quality machine code is to be generated.

Asynchronous exceptions are rare. They occur only as a result of:

- An invocation of the `stop` methods of class `Thread` or `ThreadGroup`
- An internal error (§11.5.2) in the Java virtual machine

The `stop` methods may be invoked by one thread to affect another thread or all the threads in a specified thread group. They are asynchronous because they may occur at any point in the execution of the other thread or threads. An `InternalError` is considered asynchronous.

The Java platform permits a small but bounded amount of execution to occur before an asynchronous exception is thrown. This delay is permitted to allow optimized code to detect and throw these exceptions at points where it is practical to handle them while obeying the semantics of the Java programming language.

A simple implementation might poll for asynchronous exceptions at the point of each control transfer instruction. Since a program has a finite size, this provides a bound on the total delay in detecting an asynchronous exception. Since no asynchronous exception will occur between control transfers, the code generator has some flexibility to reorder computation between control transfers for greater performance.

The paper *Polling Efficiently on Stock Hardware* by Marc Feeley, *Proc. 1993 Conference on Functional Programming and Computer Architecture*, Copenhagen, Denmark, pp. 179–187, is recommended as further reading.

Like all exceptions, asynchronous exceptions are precise (§11.3.1).

11.4 An Example of Exceptions

Consider the following example:

```
class TestException extends Exception {

    TestException() { super(); }

    TestException(String s) { super(s); }

}

class Test {
    public static void main(String[] args) {
        for (String arg :args) {
            try {
              thrower(arg);
              System.out.println("Test \"" + arg +
```

```
                "\" didn't throw an exception");
            } catch (Exception e) {
              System.out.println("Test \"" + arg +
                "\" threw a " + e.getClass() +
                "\n    with message: " + e.getMessage());
            }
        }
    }
    static int thrower(String s) throws TestException {
        try {
            if (s.equals("divide")) {
              int i = 0;
              return i/i;
            }
            if (s.equals("null")) {
              s = null;
              return s.length();
            }
            if (s.equals("test"))
              throw new TestException("Test message");
            return 0;
        } finally {
            System.out.println("[thrower(\"" + s +
               "\") done]");
        }
    }
}
```

If we execute the test program, passing it the arguments:

```
divide null not test
```

it produces the output:

```
[thrower("divide") done]
Test "divide" threw a class java.lang.ArithmeticException
    with message: / by zero
[thrower("null") done]
Test "null" threw a class java.lang.NullPointerException
    with message: null
[thrower("not") done]
Test "not" didn't throw an exception
[thrower("test") done]
Test "test" threw a class TestException
    with message: Test message
```

This example declares an exception class `TestException`. The `main` method of class `Test` invokes the `thrower` method four times, causing exceptions to be thrown three of the four times. The `try` statement in method `main` catches each exception that the thrower throws. Whether the invocation of thrower completes normally or abruptly, a message is printed describing what happened.

The declaration of the method thrower must have a throws clause because it can throw instances of TestException, which is a checked exception class (§11.2). A compile-time error would occur if the throws clause were omitted.

Notice that the finally clause is executed on every invocation of thrower, whether or not an exception occurs, as shown by the "[thrower(...) done]" output that occurs for each invocation.

11.5 The Exception Hierarchy

The possible exceptions in a program are organized in a hierarchy of classes, rooted at class Throwable (§11.5), a direct subclass of Object. The classes Exception and Error are direct subclasses of Throwable. The class RuntimeException is a direct subclass of Exception.

Programs can use the pre-existing exception classes in throw statements, or define additional exception classes, as subclasses of Throwable or of any of its subclasses, as appropriate. To take advantage of the Java platform's compile-time checking for exception handlers, it is typical to define most new exception classes as checked exception classes, specifically as subclasses of Exception that are not subclasses of RuntimeException.

The class Exception is the superclass of all the exceptions that ordinary programs may wish to recover from. The class RuntimeException is a subclass of class Exception. The subclasses of RuntimeException are unchecked exception classes. The subclasses of Exception other than RuntimeException and its subclasses are all checked exception classes.

The class Error and its subclasses are exceptions from which ordinary programs are not ordinarily expected to recover. See the Java API specification for a detailed description of the exception hierarchy.

The class Error is a separate subclass of Throwable, distinct from Exception in the class hierarchy, to allow programs to use the idiom:

```
} catch (Exception e) {
```

to catch all exceptions from which recovery may be possible without catching errors from which recovery is typically not possible.

11.5.1 Loading and Linkage Errors

The Java virtual machine throws an object that is an instance of a subclass of `LinkageError` when a loading, linkage, preparation, verification or initialization error occurs:

- The loading process is described in §12.2.
- The linking process is described in §12.3.
- The class verification process is described in §12.3.1.
- The class preparation process is described in §12.3.2.
- The class initialization process is described in §12.4.

11.5.2 Virtual Machine Errors

The Java virtual machine throws an object that is an instance of a subclass of the class `VirtualMachineError` when an internal error or resource limitation prevents it from implementing the semantics of the Java programming language. See *The Java™ Virtual Machine Specification Second Edition* for the definitive discussion of these errors.

I never forget a face—but in your case I'll be glad to make an exception.
—Groucho Marx

CHAPTER 12

Execution

We must all hang together, or assuredly we shall all hang separately.
—Benjamin Franklin (July 4, 1776)

THIS chapter specifies activities that occur during execution of a program. It is organized around the life cycle of a Java virtual machine and of the classes, interfaces, and objects that form a program.

A Java virtual machine starts up by loading a specified class and then invoking the method `main` in this specified class. Section §12.1 outlines the loading, linking, and initialization steps involved in executing `main`, as an introduction to the concepts in this chapter. Further sections specify the details of loading (§12.2), linking (§12.3), and initialization (§12.4).

The chapter continues with a specification of the procedures for creation of new class instances (§12.5); and finalization of class instances (§12.6). It concludes by describing the unloading of classes (§12.7) and the procedure followed when a program exits (§12.8).

12.1 Virtual Machine Start-Up

A Java virtual machine starts execution by invoking the method `main` of some specified class, passing it a single argument, which is an array of strings. In the examples in this specification, this first class is typically called `Test`.

The precise semantics of virtual machine start-up are given in chapter 5 of *The Java™ Virtual Machine Specification, Second Edition*. Here we present an overview of the process from the viewpoint of the Java programming language.

The manner in which the initial class is specified to the Java virtual machine is beyond the scope of this specification, but it is typical, in host environments that use command lines, for the fully-qualified name of the class to be specified as a command-line argument and for following command-line arguments to be used as strings to be provided as the argument to the method `main`. For example, in a UNIX implementation, the command line:

```
java Test reboot Bob Dot Enzo
```

will typically start a Java virtual machine by invoking method `main` of class `Test` (a class in an unnamed package), passing it an array containing the four strings `"reboot"`, `"Bob"`, `"Dot"`, and `"Enzo"`.

We now outline the steps the virtual machine may take to execute `Test`, as an example of the loading, linking, and initialization processes that are described further in later sections.

12.1.1 Load the Class `Test`

The initial attempt to execute the method `main` of class `Test` discovers that the class `Test` is not loaded—that is, that the virtual machine does not currently contain a binary representation for this class. The virtual machine then uses a class loader to attempt to find such a binary representation. If this process fails, then an error is thrown. This loading process is described further in §12.2.

12.1.2 Link `Test`: Verify, Prepare, (Optionally) Resolve

After `Test` is loaded, it must be initialized before `main` can be invoked. And `Test`, like all (class or interface) types, must be linked before it is initialized. Linking involves verification, preparation and (optionally) resolution. Linking is described further in §12.3.

Verification checks that the loaded representation of `Test` is well-formed, with a proper symbol table. Verification also checks that the code that implements `Test` obeys the semantic requirements of the Java programming language and the Java virtual machine. If a problem is detected during verification, then an error is thrown. Verification is described further in §12.3.1.

Preparation involves allocation of static storage and any data structures that are used internally by the virtual machine, such as method tables. Preparation is described further in §12.3.2.

Resolution is the process of checking symbolic references from `Test` to other classes and interfaces, by loading the other classes and interfaces that are mentioned and checking that the references are correct.

The resolution step is optional at the time of initial linkage. An implementation may resolve symbolic references from a class or interface that is being linked very early, even to the point of resolving all symbolic references from the classes and interfaces that are further referenced, recursively. (This resolution may result in errors from these further loading and linking steps.) This implementation choice represents one extreme and is similar to the kind of "static" linkage that has been done for many years in simple implementations of the C language. (In these implementations, a compiled program is typically represented as an "`a.out`" file that contains a fully-linked version of the program, including completely resolved links to library routines used by the program. Copies of these library routines are included in the "`a.out`" file.)

An implementation may instead choose to resolve a symbolic reference only when it is actively used; consistent use of this strategy for all symbolic references would represent the "laziest" form of resolution.

In this case, if `Test` had several symbolic references to another class, then the references might be resolved one at a time, as they are used, or perhaps not at all, if these references were never used during execution of the program.

The only requirement on when resolution is performed is that any errors detected during resolution must be thrown at a point in the program where some action is taken by the program that might, directly or indirectly, require linkage to the class or interface involved in the error. Using the "static" example implementation choice described above, loading and linkage errors could occur before the program is executed if they involved a class or interface mentioned in the class `Test` or any of the further, recursively referenced, classes and interfaces. In a system that implemented the "laziest" resolution, these errors would be thrown only when an incorrect symbolic reference is actively used.

The resolution process is described further in §12.3.3.

12.1.3 Initialize `Test`: Execute Initializers

In our continuing example, the virtual machine is still trying to execute the method `main` of class `Test`. This is permitted only if the class has been initialized (§12.4.1).

Initialization consists of execution of any class variable initializers and static initializers of the class `Test`, in textual order. But before `Test` can be initialized, its direct superclass must be initialized, as well as the direct superclass of its direct superclass, and so on, recursively. In the simplest case, `Test` has `Object` as its implicit direct superclass; if class `Object` has not yet been initialized, then it must be initialized before `Test` is initialized. Class `Object` has no superclass, so the recursion terminates here.

If class `Test` has another class `Super` as its superclass, then `Super` must be initialized before `Test`. This requires loading, verifying, and preparing `Super` if this has not already been done and, depending on the implementation, may also involve resolving the symbolic references from `Super` and so on, recursively.

Initialization may thus cause loading, linking, and initialization errors, including such errors involving other types.

The initialization process is described further in §12.4.

12.1.4 Invoke `Test.main`

Finally, after completion of the initialization for class `Test` (during which other consequential loading, linking, and initializing may have occurred), the method `main` of `Test` is invoked.

The method `main` must be declared `public`, `static`, and `void`. It must accept a single argument that is an array of strings. This method can be declared as either

```
public static void main(String[] args)
```

or

```
public static void main(String... args)
```

12.2 Loading of Classes and Interfaces

Loading refers to the process of finding the binary form of a class or interface type with a particular name, perhaps by computing it on the fly, but more typically by retrieving a binary representation previously computed from source code by a compiler, and constructing, from that binary form, a `Class` object to represent the class or interface.

The precise semantics of loading are given in chapter 5 of *The Java™ Virtual Machine Specification* (whenever we refer to the Java virtual machine specification in this book, we mean the second edition, as amended by JSR 924). Here we present an overview of the process from the viewpoint of the Java programming language.

The binary format of a class or interface is normally the `class` file format described in *The Java™ Virtual Machine Specification* cited above, but other formats are possible, provided they meet the requirements specified in §13.1. The method `defineClass` of class `ClassLoader` may be used to construct `Class` objects from binary representations in the `class` file format.

Well-behaved class loaders maintain these properties:

- Given the same name, a good class loader should always return the same class object.
- If a class loader *L1* delegates loading of a class *C* to another loader *L2*, then for any type *T* that occurs as the direct superclass or a direct superinterface of *C*, or as the type of a field in *C*, or as the type of a formal parameter of a method or constructor in *C*, or as a return type of a method in *C*, *L1* and *L2* should return the same class object.

A malicious class loader could violate these properties. However, it could not undermine the security of the type system, because the Java virtual machine guards against this.

For further discussion of these issues, see *The Java™ Virtual Machine Specification* and the paper *Dynamic Class Loading in the Java™ Virtual Machine*, by Sheng Liang and Gilad Bracha, in *Proceedings of OOPSLA '98*, published as *ACM SIGPLAN Notices*, Volume 33, Number 10, October 1998, pages 36-44. A basic principle of the design of the Java programming language is that the run-time type system cannot be subverted by code written in the language, not even by implementations of such otherwise sensitive system classes as `ClassLoader` and `SecurityManager`.

12.2.1 The Loading Process

The loading process is implemented by the class `ClassLoader` and its subclasses. Different subclasses of `ClassLoader` may implement different loading policies. In particular, a class loader may cache binary representations of classes and interfaces, prefetch them based on expected usage, or load a group of related classes together. These activities may not be completely transparent to a running application if, for example, a newly compiled version of a class is not found because an older version is cached by a class loader. It is the responsibility of a class loader, however, to reflect loading errors only at points in the program they could have arisen without prefetching or group loading.

If an error occurs during class loading, then an instance of one of the following subclasses of class `LinkageError` will be thrown at any point in the program that (directly or indirectly) uses the type:

- `ClassCircularityError`: A class or interface could not be loaded because it would be its own superclass or superinterface (§13.4.4).
- `ClassFormatError`: The binary data that purports to specify a requested compiled class or interface is malformed.
- `NoClassDefFoundError`: No definition for a requested class or interface could be found by the relevant class loader.

Because loading involves the allocation of new data structures, it may fail with an `OutOfMemoryError`.

12.3 Linking of Classes and Interfaces

Linking is the process of taking a binary form of a class or interface type and combining it into the runtime state of the Java virtual machine, so that it can be executed. A class or interface type is always loaded before it is linked.

Three different activities are involved in linking: verification, preparation, and resolution of symbolic references.The precise semantics of linking are given in chapter 5 of *The Java™ Virtual Machine Specification, Second Edition*. Here we present an overview of the process from the viewpoint of the Java programming language.

This specification allows an implementation flexibility as to when linking activities (and, because of recursion, loading) take place, provided that the semantics of the language are respected, that a class or interface is completely verified and prepared before it is initialized, and that errors detected during linkage are thrown at a point in the program where some action is taken by the program that might require linkage to the class or interface involved in the error.

For example, an implementation may choose to resolve each symbolic reference in a class or interface individually, only when it is used (lazy or late resolution), or to resolve them all at once while the class is being verified (static resolution). This means that the resolution process may continue, in some implementations, after a class or interface has been initialized.

Because linking involves the allocation of new data structures, it may fail with an `OutOfMemoryError`.

12.3.1 Verification of the Binary Representation

Verification ensures that the binary representation of a class or interface is structurally correct. For example, it checks that every instruction has a valid operation code; that every branch instruction branches to the start of some other instruction, rather than into the middle of an instruction; that every method is provided with a structurally correct signature; and that every instruction obeys the type discipline of the Java virtual machine language.

For the specification of the verification process, see the separate volume of this series, *The Java™ Virtual Machine Specification*. and the specification of the J2ME Connected Limited Device Configuration, version 1.1.

If an error occurs during verification, then an instance of the following subclass of class `LinkageError` will be thrown at the point in the program that caused the class to be verified:

- `VerifyError`: The binary definition for a class or interface failed to pass a set of required checks to verify that it obeys the semantics of the Java virtual machine language and that it cannot violate the integrity of the Java virtual machine. (See §13.4.2, §13.4.4, §13.4.9, and §13.4.17 for some examples.)

12.3.2 Preparation of a Class or Interface Type

Preparation involves creating the `static` fields (class variables and constants) for a class or interface and initializing such fields to the default values (§4.12.5). This does not require the execution of any source code; explicit initializers for `static` fields are executed as part of initialization (§12.4), not preparation.

Implementations of the Java virtual machine may precompute additional data structures at preparation time in order to make later operations on a class or interface more efficient. One particularly useful data structure is a "method table" or other data structure that allows any method to be invoked on instances of a class without requiring a search of superclasses at invocation time.

12.3.3 Resolution of Symbolic References

The binary representation of a class or interface references other classes and interfaces and their fields, methods, and constructors symbolically, using the binary names (§13.1) of the other classes and interfaces (§13.1). For fields and methods, these symbolic references include the name of the class or interface type of which the field or method is a member, as well as the name of the field or method itself, together with appropriate type information.

Before a symbolic reference can be used it must undergo *resolution*, wherein a symbolic reference is checked to be correct and, typically, replaced with a direct reference that can be more efficiently processed if the reference is used repeatedly.

If an error occurs during resolution, then an error will be thrown. Most typically, this will be an instance of one of the following subclasses of the class `IncompatibleClassChangeError`, but it may also be an instance of some other subclass of `IncompatibleClassChangeError` or even an instance of the class `IncompatibleClassChangeError` itself. This error may be thrown at any point in the program that uses a symbolic reference to the type, directly or indirectly:

- `IllegalAccessError`: A symbolic reference has been encountered that specifies a use or assignment of a field, or invocation of a method, or creation of an instance of a class, to which the code containing the reference does not have access because the field or method was declared `private`, `protected`, or default access (not `public`), or because the class was not declared `public`.

  This can occur, for example, if a field that is originally declared `public` is changed to be `private` after another class that refers to the field has been compiled (§13.4.7).

- `InstantiationError`: A symbolic reference has been encountered that is used in class instance creation expression, but an instance cannot be created because the reference turns out to refer to an interface or to an `abstract` class.

  This can occur, for example, if a class that is originally not `abstract` is changed to be `abstract` after another class that refers to the class in question has been compiled (§13.4.1).

- `NoSuchFieldError`: A symbolic reference has been encountered that refers to a specific field of a specific class or interface, but the class or interface does not contain a field of that name.

  This can occur, for example, if a field declaration was deleted from a class after another class that refers to the field was compiled (§13.4.8).

- `NoSuchMethodError`: A symbolic reference has been encountered that refers to a specific method of a specific class or interface, but the class or interface does not contain a method of that signature.

  This can occur, for example, if a method declaration was deleted from a class after another class that refers to the method was compiled (§13.4.12).

Additionally, an `UnsatisfiedLinkError` (a subclass of `LinkageError`) may be thrown if a class declares a `native` method for which no implementation can be found. The error will occur if the method is used, or earlier, depending on what kind of resolution strategy is being used by the virtual machine (§12.3).

12.4 Initialization of Classes and Interfaces

Initialization of a class consists of executing its static initializers and the initializers for `static` fields (class variables) declared in the class. Initialization of an interface consists of executing the initializers for fields (constants) declared there.

Before a class is initialized, its superclass must be initialized, but interfaces implemented by the class are not initialized. Similarly, the superinterfaces of an interface are not initialized before the interface is initialized.

12.4.1 When Initialization Occurs

Initialization of a class consists of executing its static initializers and the initializers for static fields declared in the class. *Initialization* of an interface consists of executing the initializers for fields declared in the interface.

Before a class is initialized, its direct superclass must be initialized, but interfaces implemented by the class need not be initialized. Similarly, the superinterfaces of an interface need not be initialized before the interface is initialized.

A class or interface type *T* will be initialized immediately before the first occurrence of any one of the following:

- *T* is a class and an instance of *T* is created.
- *T* is a class and a static method declared by *T* is invoked.
- A static field declared by *T* is assigned.
- A static field declared by *T* is used and the field is not a constant variable (§4.12.4).
- *T* is a top-level class, and an `assert` statement (§14.10) lexically nested within *T* is executed.

Invocation of certain reflective methods in class `Class` and in package `java.lang.reflect` also causes class or interface initialization. A class or interface will not be initialized under any other circumstance.

The intent here is that a class or interface type has a set of initializers that put it in a consistent state, and that this state is the first state that is observed by other classes. The static initializers and class variable initializers are executed in textual order, and may not refer to class variables declared in the class whose declarations appear textually after the use, even though these class variables are in scope (§8.3.2.3). This restriction is designed to detect, at compile time, most circular or otherwise malformed initializations.

As shown in an example in §8.3.2.3, the fact that initialization code is unrestricted allows examples to be constructed where the value of a class variable can be observed when it still has its initial default value, before its initializing expression is evaluated, but such examples are rare in practice. (Such examples can be also constructed for instance variable initialization; see the example at the end of §12.5). The full power of the language is available in these initializers; programmers must exercise some care. This power places an extra burden on code generators, but this burden would arise in any case because the language is concurrent (§12.4.3).

Before a class is initialized, its superclasses are initialized, if they have not previously been initialized.

Thus, the test program:

```
class Super {
    static { System.out.print("Super "); }
}
```

```
class One {
   static { System.out.print("One "); }
}

class Two extends Super {
   static { System.out.print("Two "); }
}

class Test {
   public static void main(String[] args) {
      One o = null;
      Two t = new Two();
      System.out.println((Object)o == (Object)t);
   }
}
```

prints:

```
Super Two false
```

The class `One` is never initialized, because it not used actively and therefore is never linked to. The class `Two` is initialized only after its superclass `Super` has been initialized.

A reference to a class field causes initialization of only the class or interface that actually declares it, even though it might be referred to through the name of a subclass, a subinterface, or a class that implements an interface.

The test program:

```
class Super { static int taxi = 1729; }
class Sub extends Super {
   static { System.out.print("Sub "); }
}

class Test {
   public static void main(String[] args) {
      System.out.println(Sub.taxi);
   }
}
```

prints only:

```
1729
```

because the class `Sub` is never initialized; the reference to `Sub.taxi` is a reference to a field actually declared in class `Super` and does not trigger initialization of the class `Sub`.

Initialization of an interface does not, of itself, cause initialization of any of its superinterfaces.

Thus, the test program:

```
interface I {
   int i = 1, ii = Test.out("ii", 2);
}
interface J extends I {
   int j = Test.out("j", 3), jj = Test.out("jj", 4);
}
interface K extends J {
   int k = Test.out("k", 5);
}
class Test {
   public static void main(String[] args) {
      System.out.println(J.i);
      System.out.println(K.j);
   }
   static int out(String s, int i) {
      System.out.println(s + "=" + i);
      return i;
   }
}
```

produces the output:

```
1
j=3
jj=4
3
```

The reference to `J.i` is to a field that is a compile-time constant; therefore, it does not cause `I` to be initialized. The reference to `K.j` is a reference to a field actually declared in interface `J` that is not a compile-time constant; this causes initialization of the fields of interface `J`, but not those of its superinterface `I`, nor those of interface `K`. Despite the fact that the name `K` is used to refer to field `j` of interface `J`, interface `K` is not initialized.

12.4.2 Detailed Initialization Procedure

Because the Java programming language is multithreaded, initialization of a class or interface requires careful synchronization, since some other thread may be trying to initialize the same class or interface at the same time. There is also the possibility that initialization of a class or interface may be requested recursively as part of the initialization of that class or interface; for example, a variable initializer in class *A* might invoke a method of an unrelated class *B*, which might in turn invoke a method of class `A`. The implementation of the Java virtual machine is responsible for taking care of synchronization and recursive initialization by using the following procedure. It assumes that the `Class` object has already been verified and prepared, and that the `Class` object contains state that indicates one of four situations:

- This `Class` object is verified and prepared but not initialized.
- This `Class` object is being initialized by some particular thread `T`.
- This `Class` object is fully initialized and ready for use.
- This `Class` object is in an erroneous state, perhaps because initialization was attempted and failed.

The procedure for initializing a class or interface is then as follows:

1. Synchronize (§14.19) on the `Class` object that represents the class or interface to be initialized. This involves waiting until the current thread can obtain the lock for that object (§17.1).
2. If initialization is in progress for the class or interface by some other thread, then `wait` on this `Class` object (which temporarily releases the lock). When the current thread awakens from the `wait`, repeat this step.
3. If initialization is in progress for the class or interface by the current thread, then this must be a recursive request for initialization. Release the lock on the `Class` object and complete normally.
4. If the class or interface has already been initialized, then no further action is required. Release the lock on the `Class` object and complete normally.
5. If the `Class` object is in an erroneous state, then initialization is not possible. Release the lock on the `Class` object and throw a `NoClassDefFoundError`.
6. Otherwise, record the fact that initialization of the `Class` object is now in progress by the current thread and release the lock on the `Class` object.
7. Next, if the `Class` object represents a class rather than an interface, and the superclass of this class has not yet been initialized, then recursively perform this entire procedure for the superclass. If necessary, verify and prepare the superclass first. If the initialization of the superclass completes abruptly because of a thrown exception, then lock this `Class` object, label it erroneous, notify all waiting threads, release the lock, and complete abruptly, throwing the same exception that resulted from initializing the superclass.

8. Next, determine whether assertions are enabled (§14.10) for this class by querying its defining class loader.

9. Next, execute either the class variable initializers and static initializers of the class, or the field initializers of the interface, in textual order, as though they were a single block, except that `final` class variables and fields of interfaces whose values are compile-time constants are initialized first (§8.3.2.1, §9.3.1, §13.4.9).

10. If the execution of the initializers completes normally, then lock this `Class` object, label it fully initialized, notify all waiting threads, release the lock, and complete this procedure normally.

11. Otherwise, the initializers must have completed abruptly by throwing some exception *E*. If the class of *E* is not `Error` or one of its subclasses, then create a new instance of the class `ExceptionInInitializerError`, with *E* as the argument, and use this object in place of *E* in the following step. But if a new instance of `ExceptionInInitializerError` cannot be created because an `OutOfMemoryError` occurs, then instead use an `OutOfMemoryError` object in place of *E* in the following step.

12. Lock the `Class` object, label it erroneous, notify all waiting threads, release the lock, and complete this procedure abruptly with reason *E* or its replacement as determined in the previous step.

(Due to a flaw in some early implementations, a exception during class initialization was ignored, rather than causing an `ExceptionInInitializerError` as described here.)

12.4.3 Initialization: Implications for Code Generation

Code generators need to preserve the points of possible initialization of a class or interface, inserting an invocation of the initialization procedure just described. If this initialization procedure completes normally and the `Class` object is fully initialized and ready for use, then the invocation of the initialization procedure is no longer necessary and it may be eliminated from the code—for example, by patching it out or otherwise regenerating the code.

Compile-time analysis may, in some cases, be able to eliminate many of the checks that a type has been initialized from the generated code, if an initialization order for a group of related types can be determined. Such analysis must, however, fully account for concurrency and for the fact that initialization code is unrestricted.

12.5 Creation of New Class Instances

A new class instance is explicitly created when evaluation of a class instance creation expression (§15.9) causes a class to be instantiated.

A new class instance may be implicitly created in the following situations:

- Loading of a class or interface that contains a `String` literal (§3.10.5) may create a new `String` object to represent that literal. (This might not occur if the same `String` has previously been interned (§3.10.5).)
- Execution of an operation that causes boxing conversion (§5.1.7). Boxing conversion may create a new object of a wrapper class associated with one of the primitive types.
- Execution of a string concatenation operator (§15.18.1) that is not part of a constant expression sometimes creates a new `String` object to represent the result. String concatenation operators may also create temporary wrapper objects for a value of a primitive type.

Each of these situations identifies a particular constructor to be called with specified arguments (possibly none) as part of the class instance creation process.

Whenever a new class instance is created, memory space is allocated for it with room for all the instance variables declared in the class type and all the instance variables declared in each superclass of the class type, including all the instance variables that may be hidden (§8.3). If there is not sufficient space available to allocate memory for the object, then creation of the class instance completes abruptly with an `OutOfMemoryError`. Otherwise, all the instance variables in the new object, including those declared in superclasses, are initialized to their default values (§4.12.5).

Just before a reference to the newly created object is returned as the result, the indicated constructor is processed to initialize the new object using the following procedure:

1. Assign the arguments for the constructor to newly created parameter variables for this constructor invocation.
2. If this constructor begins with an explicit constructor invocation of another constructor in the same class (using `this`), then evaluate the arguments and process that constructor invocation recursively using these same five steps. If that constructor invocation completes abruptly, then this procedure completes abruptly for the same reason; otherwise, continue with step 5.
3. This constructor does not begin with an explicit constructor invocation of another constructor in the same class (using `this`). If this constructor is for a

class other than `Object`, then this constructor will begin with an explicit or implicit invocation of a superclass constructor (using `super`). Evaluate the arguments and process that superclass constructor invocation recursively using these same five steps. If that constructor invocation completes abruptly, then this procedure completes abruptly for the same reason. Otherwise, continue with step 4.

4. Execute the instance initializers and instance variable initializers for this class, assigning the values of instance variable initializers to the corresponding instance variables, in the left-to-right order in which they appear textually in the source code for the class. If execution of any of these initializers results in an exception, then no further initializers are processed and this procedure completes abruptly with that same exception. Otherwise, continue with step 5. (In some early implementations, the compiler incorrectly omitted the code to initialize a field if the field initializer expression was a constant expression whose value was equal to the default initialization value for its type.)
5. Execute the rest of the body of this constructor. If that execution completes abruptly, then this procedure completes abruptly for the same reason. Otherwise, this procedure completes normally.

In the example:

```
class Point {
    int x, y;
    Point() { x = 1; y = 1; }
}

class ColoredPoint extends Point {
    int color = 0xFF00FF;
}

class Test {
    public static void main(String[] args) {
        ColoredPoint cp = new ColoredPoint();
        System.out.println(cp.color);
    }
}
```

a new instance of `ColoredPoint` is created. First, space is allocated for the new `ColoredPoint`, to hold the fields `x`, `y`, and `color`. All these fields are then initialized to their default values (in this case, `0` for each field). Next, the `ColoredPoint` constructor with no arguments is first invoked. Since `ColoredPoint` declares no constructors, a default constructor of the form:

```
ColoredPoint() { super(); }
```

is provided for it automatically by the Java compiler.

This constructor then invokes the `Point` constructor with no arguments. The `Point` constructor does not begin with an invocation of a constructor, so the compiler provides an implicit invocation of its superclass constructor of no arguments, as though it had been written:

```
Point() { super(); x = 1; y = 1; }
```

Therefore, the constructor for `Object` which takes no arguments is invoked.

The class `Object` has no superclass, so the recursion terminates here. Next, any instance initializers, instance variable initializers of `Object` are invoked. Next, the body of the constructor of `Object` that takes no arguments is executed. No such constructor is declared in `Object`, so the compiler supplies a default one, which in this special case is:

```
Object() { }
```

This constructor executes without effect and returns.

Next, all initializers for the instance variables of class `Point` are executed. As it happens, the declarations of `x` and `y` do not provide any initialization expressions, so no action is required for this step of the example. Then the body of the `Point` constructor is executed, setting `x` to `1` and `y` to `1`.

Next, the initializers for the instance variables of class `ColoredPoint` are executed. This step assigns the value `0xFF00FF` to `color`. Finally, the rest of the body of the `ColoredPoint` constructor is executed (the part after the invocation of `super`); there happen to be no statements in the rest of the body, so no further action is required and initialization is complete.

Unlike C++, the Java programming language does not specify altered rules for method dispatch during the creation of a new class instance. If methods are invoked that are overridden in subclasses in the object being initialized, then these overriding methods are used, even before the new object is completely initialized. Thus, compiling and running the example:

```
class Super {
    Super() { printThree(); }
    void printThree() { System.out.println("three"); }
}

class Test extends Super {
    int three = (int)Math.PI;                // That is, 3
    public static void main(String[] args) {
        Test t = new Test();
        t.printThree();
    }

    void printThree() { System.out.println(three); }
}
```

produces the output:

```
0
3
```

This shows that the invocation of `printThree` in the constructor for class `Super` does not invoke the definition of `printThree` in class `Super`, but rather invokes the overriding definition of `printThree` in class `Test`. This method therefore runs before the field initializers of `Test` have been executed, which is why the first value output is `0`, the default value to which the field `three` of `Test` is initialized. The later invocation of `printThree` in method `main` invokes the same definition of `printThree`, but by that point the initializer for instance variable `three` has been executed, and so the value `3` is printed.

See §8.8 for more details on constructor declarations.

12.6 Finalization of Class Instances

The class `Object` has a `protected` method called `finalize`; this method can be overridden by other classes. The particular definition of `finalize` that can be invoked for an object is called the *finalizer* of that object. Before the storage for an object is reclaimed by the garbage collector, the Java virtual machine will invoke the finalizer of that object.

Finalizers provide a chance to free up resources that cannot be freed automatically by an automatic storage manager. In such situations, simply reclaiming the memory used by an object would not guarantee that the resources it held would be reclaimed.

The Java programming language does not specify how soon a finalizer will be invoked, except to say that it will happen before the storage for the object is reused. Also, the language does not specify which thread will invoke the finalizer for any given object. It is guaranteed, however, that the thread that invokes the finalizer will not be holding any user-visible synchronization locks when the finalizer is invoked. If an uncaught exception is thrown during the finalization, the exception is ignored and finalization of that object terminates.

The completion of an object's constructor happens-before (§17.4.5) the execution of its `finalize` method (in the formal sense of happens-before).

DISCUSSION

It is important to note that many finalizer threads may be active (this is sometimes needed on large shared memory multiprocessors), and that if a large connected data structure becomes garbage, all of the finalize methods for every object in that data structure could be invoked at the same time, each finalizer invocation running in a different thread.

The `finalize` method declared in class `Object` takes no action. The fact that class `Object` declares a `finalize` method means that the `finalize` method for any class can always invoke the `finalize` method for its superclass. This should always be done, unless it is the programmer's intent to nullify the actions of the finalizer in the superclass. (Unlike constructors, finalizers do not automatically invoke the finalizer for the superclass; such an invocation must be coded explicitly.)

For efficiency, an implementation may keep track of classes that do not override the `finalize` method of class `Object`, or override it in a trivial way, such as:

```
protected void finalize() throws Throwable {
    super.finalize();
}
```

We encourage implementations to treat such objects as having a finalizer that is not overridden, and to finalize them more efficiently, as described in §12.6.1.

A finalizer may be invoked explicitly, just like any other method.

The package `java.lang.ref` describes weak references, which interact with garbage collection and finalization. As with any API that has special interactions with the language, implementors must be cognizant of any requirements imposed by the `java.lang.ref` API. This specification does not discuss weak references in any way. Readers are referred to the API documentation for details.

12.6.1 Implementing Finalization

Every object can be characterized by two attributes: it may be *reachable*, *finalizer-reachable*, or *unreachable*, and it may also be *unfinalized*, *finalizable*, or *finalized*.

A *reachable* object is any object that can be accessed in any potential continuing computation from any live thread. Optimizing transformations of a program can be designed that reduce the number of objects that are reachable to be less than those which would naively be considered reachable. For example, a compiler or code generator may choose to set a variable or parameter that will no longer be used to `null` to cause the storage for such an object to be potentially reclaimable sooner.

DISCUSSION

Another example of this occurs if the values in an object's fields are stored in registers. The program may then access the registers instead of the object, and never access the object again. This would imply that the object is garbage.

Note that this sort of optimization is only allowed if references are on the stack, not stored in the heap.

For example, consider the *Finalizer Guardian* pattern:

```
class Foo {
    private final Object finalizerGuardian = new Object() {
      protected void finalize() throws Throwable {
        /* finalize outer Foo object */
      }
    }
  }
```

The finalizer guardian forces `super.finalize` to be called if a subclass overrides finalize and does not explicitly call `super.finalize`.

If these optimizations are allowed for references that are stored on the heap, then the compiler can detect that the `finalizerGuardian` field is never read, null it out, collect the object immediately, and call the finalizer early. This runs counter to the intent: the programmer probably wanted to call the `Foo` finalizer when the `Foo` instance became unreachable. This sort of transformation is therefore not legal: the inner class object should be reachable for as long as the outer class object is reachable.

Transformations of this sort may result in invocations of the `finalize` method occurring earlier than might be otherwise expected. In order to allow the user to prevent this, we enforce the notion that synchronization may keep the object alive. *If an object's finalizer can result in synchronization on that object, then that object must be alive and considered reachable whenever a lock is held on it.*

Note that this does not prevent synchronization elimination: synchronization only keeps an object alive if a finalizer might synchronize on it. Since the finalizer occurs in another thread, in many cases the synchronization could not be removed anyway.

A *finalizer-reachable* object can be reached from some finalizable object through some chain of references, but not from any live thread. An *unreachable* object cannot be reached by either means.

An *unfinalized* object has never had its finalizer automatically invoked; a *finalized* object has had its finalizer automatically invoked. A *finalizable* object has never had its finalizer automatically invoked, but the Java virtual machine may eventually automatically invoke its finalizer.

An object *o* is not finalizable until its constructor has invoked the constructor for `Object` on *o* and that invocation has completed successfully (that is, without throwing an exception). Every pre-finalization write to a field of an object must be visible to the finalization of that object. Furthermore, none of the pre-finalization reads of fields of that object may see writes that occur after finalization of that object is initiated.

12.6.1.1 *Interaction with the Memory Model*

It must be possible for the memory model (§17) to decide when it can commit actions that take place in a finalizer. This section describes the interaction of finalization with the memory model.

Each execution has a number of *reachability decision points*, labeled *di*. Each action either *comes-before di* or *comes-after di*. Other than as explicitly mentioned, the comes-before ordering described in this section is unrelated to all other orderings in the memory model.

If *r* is a read that sees a write *w* and *r* comes-before *di*, then *w* must come-before *di*. If *x* and *y* are synchronization actions on the same variable or monitor such that *so(x, y)* (§17.4.4) and *y* comes-before *di*, then *x* must come-before *di*.

At each reachability decision point, some set of objects are marked as unreachable, and some subset of those objects are marked as finalizable. These reachability decision points are also the points at which references are checked, enqueued and cleared according to the rules provided in the API documentation for the package `java.lang.ref`.

The only objects that are considered definitely reachable at a point *di* are those that can be shown to be reachable by the application of these rules:

- An object *B* is definitely reachable at *di* from static fields if there exists a write *w1* to a static field *v* of a class *C* such that the value written by *w1* is a reference to *B*, the class *C* is loaded by a reachable classloader and there does not exist a write *w2* to *v* such that *hb(w2, w1)* is not true and both *w1* and *w2* come-before *di*.
- An object *B* is definitely reachable from *A* at *di* if there is a write *w1* to an element *v* of *A* such that the value written by *w1* is a reference to *B* and there does not exist a write *w2* to *v* such that *hb(w2, w1)* is not true and both *w1* and *w2* come-before *di*.
- If an object *C* is definitely reachable from an object *B*, and object *B* is definitely reachable from an object *A*, then *C* is definitely reachable from *A*.

An action *a* is an active use of *X* if and only if at least one of the following conditions holds:

- *a* reads or writes an element of *X*
- *a* locks or unlocks *X* and there is a lock action on *X* that happens-after the invocation of the finalizer for *X*.
- *a* writes a reference to *X*
- *a* is an active use of an object *Y*, and *X* is definitely reachable from *Y*

If an object *X* is marked as unreachable at *di*,

- *X* must not be definitely reachable at *di* from static fields,
- All active uses of *X* in thread t that come-after *di* must occur in the finalizer invocation for *X* or as a result of thread t performing a read that comes-after *di* of a reference to *X*.
- All reads that come-after *di* that see a reference to *X* must see writes to elements of objects that were unreachable at *di*, or see writes that came after *di*.

If an object *X* is marked as finalizable at *di*, then

- *X* must be marked as unreachable at *di*,
- *di* must be the only place where *X* is marked as finalizable,
- actions that happen-after the finalizer invocation must come-after *di*

12.6.2 Finalizer Invocations are Not Ordered

The Java programming language imposes no ordering on finalize method calls. Finalizers may be called in any order, or even concurrently.

As an example, if a circularly linked group of unfinalized objects becomes unreachable (or finalizer-reachable), then all the objects may become finalizable together. Eventually, the finalizers for these objects may be invoked, in any order, or even concurrently using multiple threads. If the automatic storage manager later finds that the objects are unreachable, then their storage can be reclaimed.

It is straightforward to implement a class that will cause a set of finalizer-like methods to be invoked in a specified order for a set of objects when all the objects become unreachable. Defining such a class is left as an exercise for the reader.

12.7 Unloading of Classes and Interfaces

An implementation of the Java programming language may *unload* classes. A class or interface may be unloaded if and only if its defining class loader may be reclaimed by the garbage collector as discussed in §12.6. Classes and interfaces loaded by the bootstrap loader may not be unloaded.

Here is the rationale for the rule given in the previous paragraph:

Class unloading is an optimization that helps reduce memory use. Obviously, the semantics of a program should not depend on whether and how a system chooses to implement an optimization such as class unloading. To do otherwise would compromise the portability of programs. Consequently, whether a class or interface has been unloaded or not should be transparent to a program.

However, if a class or interface `C` was unloaded while its defining loader was potentially reachable, then `C` might be reloaded. One could never ensure that this would not happen. Even if the class was not referenced by any other currently loaded class, it might be referenced by some class or interface, `D`, that had not yet been loaded. When `D` is loaded by `C`'s defining loader, its execution might cause reloading of `C`.

Reloading may not be transparent if, for example, the class has:

- Static variables (whose state would be lost).
- Static initializers (which may have side effects).

Native methods (which may retain static state).

Furthermore the hash value of the `Class` object is dependent on its identity. Therefore it is, in general, impossible to reload a class or interface in a completely transparent manner.

Since we can never guarantee that unloading a class or interface whose loader is potentially reachable will not cause reloading, and reloading is never transparent, but unloading must be transparent, it follows that one must not unload a class or interface while its loader is potentially reachable. A similar line of reasoning can be used to deduce that classes and interfaces loaded by the bootstrap loader can never be unloaded.

One must also argue why it is safe to unload a class `C` if its defining class loader can be reclaimed. If the defining loader can be reclaimed, then there can never be any live references to it (this includes references that are not live, but might be resurrected by finalizers). This, in turn, can only be true if there are can never be any live references to any of the classes defined by that loader, including `C`, either from their instances or from code.

Class unloading is an optimization that is only significant for applications that load large numbers of classes and that stop using most of those classes after some time. A prime example of such an application is a web browser, but there are others. A characteristic of such applications is that they manage classes through explicit use of class loaders. As a result, the policy outlined above works well for them.

Strictly speaking, it is not essential that the issue of class unloading be discussed by this specification, as class unloading is merely an optimization. However, the issue is very subtle, and so it is mentioned here by way of clarification.

12.8 Program Exit

A program terminates all its activity and *exits* when one of two things happens:

- All the threads that are not daemon threads terminate.
- Some thread invokes the `exit` method of class `Runtime` or class `System` and the exit operation is not forbidden by the security manager.

. . . Farewell!
The day frowns more and more. Thou'rt like to have
A lullaby too rough: I never saw
The heavens so dim by day: A savage clamour!
Well may I get aboard! This is the chase.
I am gone for ever!
[Exit, pursued by a bear]
—William Shakespeare, *The Winter's Tale*, Act III, scene iii

CHAPTER 13

Binary Compatibility

Despite all of its promise, software reuse in object-oriented programming has yet to reach its full potential. A major impediment to reuse is the inability to evolve a compiled class library without abandoning the support for already compiled applications. . . . [A]n object-oriented model must be carefully designed so that class-library transformations that should not break already compiled applications, indeed, do not break such applications.

—Ira Forman, Michael Conner, Scott Danforth, and Larry Raper, Release-to-Release Binary Compatibility in SOM (1995)

Development tools for the Java programming language should support automatic recompilation as necessary whenever source code is available. Particular implementations may also store the source and binary of types in a versioning database and implement a `ClassLoader` that uses integrity mechanisms of the database to prevent linkage errors by providing binary-compatible versions of types to clients.

Developers of packages and classes that are to be widely distributed face a different set of problems. In the Internet, which is our favorite example of a widely distributed system, it is often impractical or impossible to automatically recompile the pre-existing binaries that directly or indirectly depend on a type that is to be changed. Instead, this specification defines a set of changes that developers are permitted to make to a package or to a class or interface type while preserving (not breaking) compatibility with existing binaries.

The paper quoted above appears in *Proceedings of OOPSLA '95*, published as *ACM SIGPLAN Notices*, Volume 30, Number 10, October 1995, pages 426–438. Within the framework of that paper, Java programming language binaries are binary compatible under all relevant transformations that the authors identify (with some caveats with respect to the addition of instance variables). Using their scheme, here is a list of some important binary compatible changes that the Java programming language supports:

- Reimplementing existing methods, constructors, and initializers to improve performance.
- Changing methods or constructors to return values on inputs for which they previously either threw exceptions that normally should not occur or failed by going into an infinite loop or causing a deadlock.
- Adding new fields, methods, or constructors to an existing class or interface.
- Deleting `private` fields, methods, or constructors of a class.
- When an entire package is updated, deleting default (package-only) access fields, methods, or constructors of classes and interfaces in the package.
- Reordering the fields, methods, or constructors in an existing type declaration.
- Moving a method upward in the class hierarchy.
- Reordering the list of direct superinterfaces of a class or interface.
- Inserting new class or interface types in the type hierarchy.

This chapter specifies minimum standards for binary compatibility guaranteed by all implementations. The Java programming language guarantees compatibility when binaries of classes and interfaces are mixed that are not known to be from compatible sources, but whose sources have been modified in the compatible ways described here. Note that we are discussing compatibility between releases of an application. A discussion of compatibility among releases of the Java platform is beyond the scope of this chapter.

We encourage development systems to provide facilities that alert developers to the impact of changes on pre-existing binaries that cannot be recompiled.

This chapter first specifies some properties that any binary format for the Java programming language must have (§13.1). It next defines binary compatibility, explaining what it is and what it is not (§13.2). It finally enumerates a large set of possible changes to packages (§13.3), classes (§13.4) and interfaces (§13.5), specifying which of these changes are guaranteed to preserve binary compatibility and which are not.

13.1 The Form of a Binary

Programs must be compiled either into the `class` file format specified by the *The Java™ Virtual Machine Specification,* or into a representation that can be mapped into that format by a class loader written in the Java programming language. Furthermore, the resulting `class` file must have certain properties. A number of these properties are specifically chosen to support source code transformations that preserve binary compatibility.

The required properties are:

- The class or interface must be named by its *binary name*, which must meet the following constraints:
  - The binary name of a top-level type is its canonical name (§6.7).
  - The binary name of a member type consists of the binary name of its immediately enclosing type, followed by $, followed by the simple name of the member.
  - The binary name of a local class (§14.3) consists of the binary name of its immediately enclosing type, followed by $, followed by a non-empty sequence of digits, followed by the simple name of the local class.
  - The binary name of an anonymous class (§15.9.5) consists of the binary name of its immediately enclosing type, followed by $, followed by a non-empty sequence of digits.
  - The binary name of a type variable declared by a generic class or interface is the binary name of its immediately enclosing type, followed by $, followed by the simple name of the type variable.
  - The binary name of a type variable declared by a generic method is the binary name of the type declaring the method, followed by $, followed by the descriptor of the method as defined in the *Java™ Virtual Machine Specification*, followed by $, followed by the simple name of the type variable.
  - The binary name of a type variable declared by a generic constructor is the binary name of the type declaring the constructor, followed by $, followed by the descriptor of the constructor as defined in the *Java™ Virtual Machine Specification*, followed by $, followed by the simple name of the type variable.
- A reference to another class or interface type must be symbolic, using the binary name of the type.

- Given a legal expression denoting a field access in a class `C`, referencing a non-constant (§13.4.9) field named `f` declared in a (possibly distinct) class or interface `D`, we define the *qualifying type of the field reference* as follows:
  - If the expression is of the form *Primary.f* then:
    - If the compile-time type of *Primary* is an intersection type (§4.9) *V1* & ... & *Vn*, then the qualifying type of the reference is *V1*.
    - Otherwise, the compile-time type of *Primary* is the qualifying type of the reference.
  - If the expression is of the form `super.f` then the superclass of `C` is the qualifying type of the reference.
  - If the expression is of the form `X.super.f` then the superclass of `X` is the qualifying type of the reference.
  - If the reference is of the form `X.f`, where `X` denotes a class or interface, then the class or interface denoted by `X` is the qualifying type of the reference
  - If the expression is referenced by a simple name, then if `f` is a member of the current class or interface, `C`, then let `T` be `C`. Otherwise, let `T` be the innermost lexically enclosing class of which `f` is a member. `T` is the qualifying type of the reference.

  The reference to `f` must be compiled into a symbolic reference to the erasure (§4.6) of the qualifying type of the reference, plus the simple name of the field, `f`. The reference must also include a symbolic reference to the erasure of the declared type of the field so that the verifier can check that the type is as expected.

- References to fields that are constant variables (§4.12.4) are resolved at compile time to the constant value that is denoted. No reference to such a constant field should be present in the code in a binary file (except in the class or interface containing the constant field, which will have code to initialize it), and such constant fields must always appear to have been initialized; the default initial value for the type of such a field must never be observed. See §13.4.8 for a discussion.

- Given a method invocation expression in a class or interface `C` referencing a method named `m` declared in a (possibly distinct) class or interface `D`, we define the *qualifying type of the method invocation* as follows:

  If `D` is `Object` then the qualifying type of the expression is `Object`. Otherwise:

- If the expression is of the form *Primary.m* then:
  - If the compile-time type of *Primary* is an intersection type (§4.9) *V1* & ... & *Vn*, then the qualifying type of the method invocation is *V1*.
  - Otherwise, the compile-time type of *Primary* is the qualifying type of the method invocation.
- If the expression is of the form `super.`*m* then the superclass of *C* is the qualifying type of the method invocation.
- If the expression is of the form *X*`.super.`*m* then the superclass of *X* is the qualifying type of the method invocation.
- If the reference is of the form *X.m*, where *X* denotes a class or interface, then the class or interface denoted by *X* is the qualifying type of the method invocation
- If the method is referenced by a simple name, then if *m* is a member of the current class or interface, *C*, let *T* be *C*. Otherwise, let *T* be the innermost lexically enclosing class of which *m* is a member. *T* is the qualifying type of the method invocation.

A reference to a method must be resolved at compile time to a symbolic reference to the erasure (§4.6) of the qualifying type of the invocation, plus the erasure of the signature of the method (§8.4.2). A reference to a method must also include either a symbolic reference to the erasure of the return type of the denoted method or an indication that the denoted method is declared `void` and does not return a value. The signature of a method must include all of the following:

- The simple name of the method
- The number of parameters to the method
- A symbolic reference to the type of each parameter

• Given a class instance creation expression (§15.9) or a constructor invocation statement (§8.8.7.1) in a class or interface *C* referencing a constructor *m* declared in a (possibly distinct) class or interface *D*, we define the *qualifying type of the constructor invocation* as follows:
  - If the expression is of the form `new` *D*(...) or *X*.`new` *D*(...), then the qualifying type of the invocation is *D*.
  - If the expression is of the form `new` *D*(..){...} or *X*.`new` *D*(...){...}, then the qualifying type of the expression is the compile-time type of the expression.

  - If the expression is of the form `super(...)` or *Primary*.`super(...)` then the qualifying type of the expression is the direct superclass of *C*.
  - If the expression is of the form `this(...)`, then the qualifying type of the expression is *C*.

  A reference to a constructor must be resolved at compile time to a symbolic reference to the erasure (§4.6) of the qualifying type of the invocation, plus the signature of the constructor (§8.8.2). The signature of a constructor must include both:

  - The number of parameters to the constructor
  - A symbolic reference to the type of each parameter

  In addition the constructor of a non-private inner member class must be compiled such that it has as its first parameter, an additional implicit parameter representing the immediately enclosing instance (§8.1.3).

- Any constructs introduced by the compiler that do not have a corresponding construct in the source code must be marked as synthetic, except for default constructors and the class initialization method.

A binary representation for a class or interface must also contain all of the following:

- If it is a class and is not class `Object`, then a symbolic reference to the erasure of the direct superclass of this class
- A symbolic reference to the erasure of each direct superinterface, if any
- A specification of each field declared in the class or interface, given as the simple name of the field and a symbolic reference to the erasure of the type of the field
- If it is a class, then the erased signature of each constructor, as described above
- For each method declared in the class or interface, its erased signature and return type, as described above
- The code needed to implement the class or interface:
  - For an interface, code for the field initializers
  - For a class, code for the field initializers, the instance and static initializers, and the implementation of each method or constructor

- Every type must contain sufficient information to recover its canonical name (§6.7).
- Every member type must have sufficient information to recover its source level access modifier.
- Every nested class must have a symbolic reference to its immediately enclosing class.
- Every class that contains a nested class must contain symbolic references to all of its member classes, and to all local and anonymous classes that appear in its methods, constructors and static or instance initializers.

The following sections discuss changes that may be made to class and interface type declarations without breaking compatibility with pre-existing binaries. Under the translation requirements given above, the Java virtual machine and its `class` file format support these changes. Any other valid binary format, such as a compressed or encrypted representation that is mapped back into class files by a class loader under the above requirements will necessarily support these changes as well.

13.2 What Binary Compatibility Is and Is Not

A change to a type is *binary compatible with* (equivalently, does not *break binary compatibility* with) preexisting binaries if preexisting binaries that previously linked without error will continue to link without error.

Binaries are compiled to rely on the accessible members and constructors of other classes and interfaces. To preserve binary compatibility, a class or interface should treat its accessible members and constructors, their existence and behavior, as a *contract* with its users.

The Java programming language is designed to prevent additions to contracts and accidental name collisions from breaking binary compatibility; specifically:

- Addition of more methods overloading a particular method name does not break compatibility with preexisting binaries. The method signature that the preexisting binary will use for method lookup is chosen by the method overload resolution algorithm at compile time (§15.12.2). (If the language had been designed so that the particular method to be executed was chosen at run time, then such an ambiguity might be detected at run time. Such a rule would imply that adding an additional overloaded method so as to make ambiguity possible at a call site could break compatibility with an unknown number of preexisting binaries. See §13.4.23 for more discussion.)

Binary compatibility is not the same as source compatibility. In particular, the example in §13.4.6 shows that a set of compatible binaries can be produced from sources that will not compile all together. This example is typical: a new declaration is added, changing the meaning of a name in an unchanged part of the source code, while the preexisting binary for that unchanged part of the source code retains the fully-qualified, previous meaning of the name. Producing a consistent set of source code requires providing a qualified name or field access expression corresponding to the previous meaning.

13.3 Evolution of Packages

A new top-level class or interface type may be added to a package without breaking compatibility with pre-existing binaries, provided the new type does not reuse a name previously given to an unrelated type. If a new type reuses a name previously given to an unrelated type, then a conflict may result, since binaries for both types could not be loaded by the same class loader.

Changes in top-level class and interface types that are not `public` and that are not a superclass or superinterface, respectively, of a `public` type, affect only types within the package in which they are declared. Such types may be deleted or otherwise changed, even if incompatibilities are otherwise described here, provided that the affected binaries of that package are updated together.

13.4 Evolution of Classes

This section describes the effects of changes to the declaration of a class and its members and constructors on pre-existing binaries.

13.4.1 `abstract` Classes

If a class that was not `abstract` is changed to be declared `abstract`, then pre-existing binaries that attempt to create new instances of that class will throw either an `InstantiationError` at link time, or (if a reflective method is used) an `InstantiationException` at run time; such a change is therefore not recommended for widely distributed classes.

Changing a class that was declared `abstract` to no longer be declared `abstract` does not break compatibility with pre-existing binaries.

13.4.2 `final` Classes

If a class that was not declared `final` is changed to be declared `final`, then a `VerifyError` is thrown if a binary of a pre-existing subclass of this class is loaded, because `final` classes can have no subclasses; such a change is not recommended for widely distributed classes.

Changing a class that was declared `final` to no longer be declared `final` does not break compatibility with pre-existing binaries.

13.4.3 `public` Classes

Changing a class that was not declared `public` to be declared `public` does not break compatibility with pre-existing binaries.

If a class that was declared `public` is changed to not be declared `public`, then an `IllegalAccessError` is thrown if a pre-existing binary is linked that needs but no longer has access to the class type; such a change is not recommended for widely distributed classes.

13.4.4 Superclasses and Superinterfaces

A `ClassCircularityError` is thrown at load time if a class would be a superclass of itself. Changes to the class hierarchy that could result in such a circularity when newly compiled binaries are loaded with pre-existing binaries are not recommended for widely distributed classes.

Changing the direct superclass or the set of direct superinterfaces of a class type will not break compatibility with pre-existing binaries, provided that the total set of superclasses or superinterfaces, respectively, of the class type loses no members.

If a change to the direct superclass or the set of direct superinterfaces results in any class or interface no longer being a superclass or superinterface, respectively, then link-time errors may result if pre-existing binaries are loaded with the binary of the modified class. Such changes are not recommended for widely distributed classes.

For example, suppose that the following test program:

```
class Hyper { char h = 'h'; }
class Super extends Hyper { char s = 's'; }
class Test extends Super {
    public static void printH(Hyper h) {
        System.out.println(h.h);
    }
```

```
        public static void main(String[] args) {
            printH(new Super());
        }
    }
```

is compiled and executed, producing the output:

```
h
```

Suppose that a new version of class `Super` is then compiled:

```
class Super { char s = 's'; }
```

This version of class `Super` is not a subclass of `Hyper`. If we then run the existing binaries of `Hyper` and `Test` with the new version of `Super`, then a `VerifyError` is thrown at link time. The verifier objects because the result of `new Super()` cannot be passed as an argument in place of a formal parameter of type `Hyper`, because `Super` is not a subclass of `Hyper`.

It is instructive to consider what might happen without the verification step: the program might run and print:

```
s
```

This demonstrates that without the verifier the type system could be defeated by linking inconsistent binary files, even though each was produced by a correct Java compiler.

The lesson is that an implementation that lacks a verifier or fails to use it will not maintain type safety and is, therefore, not a valid implementation.

13.4.5 Class Formal Type Parameters

Renaming a type variable (§4.4) declared as a formal type parameter of a class has no effect with respect to pre-existing binaries. Adding or removing a type parameter does not, in itself, have any implications for binary compatibility.

DISCUSSION

Note that if such type variables are used in the type of a field or method, that may have the normal implications of changing the aforementioned type.

Changing the first bound of a type parameter will change the erasure (§4.6) of any member that uses that type variable in its own type, and this may effect binary compatibility. Changing any other bound has no effect on binary compatibility.

13.4.6 Class Body and Member Declarations

No incompatibility with pre-existing binaries is caused by adding an instance (respectively `static`) member that has the same name, accessibility, (for fields) or same name, accessibility, signature, and return type (for methods) as an instance (respectively `static`) member of a superclass or subclass. No error occurs even if the set of classes being linked would encounter a compile-time error.

Deleting a class member or constructor that is not declared `private` may cause a linkage error if the member or constructor is used by a pre-existing binary.

If the program:

```
class Hyper {
    void hello() { System.out.println("hello from Hyper"); }
}
class Super extends Hyper {
    void hello() { System.out.println("hello from Super"); }
}
class Test {
    public static void main(String[] args) {
        new Super().hello();
    }
}
```

is compiled and executed, it produces the output:

```
hello from Super
```

Suppose that a new version of class `Super` is produced:

```
class Super extends Hyper { }
```

then recompiling `Super` and executing this new binary with the original binaries for `Test` and `Hyper` produces the output:

```
hello from Hyper
```

as expected.

The `super` keyword can be used to access a method declared in a superclass, bypassing any methods declared in the current class. The expression:

`super.`*Identifier*

is resolved, at compile time, to a method *M* in the superclass *S*. If the method *M* is an instance method, then the method *MR* invoked at run time is the method with the same signature as *M* that is a member of the direct superclass of the class containing the expression involving `super`. Thus, if the program:

```
class Hyper {
    void hello() { System.out.println("hello from Hyper"); }
}
```

```
class Super extends Hyper { }
class Test extends Super {
   public static void main(String[] args) {
      new Test().hello();
   }
   void hello() {
      super.hello();
   }
}
```

is compiled and executed, it produces the output:

```
hello from Hyper
```

Suppose that a new version of class `Super` is produced:

```
class Super extends Hyper {
   void hello() { System.out.println("hello from Super"); }
}
```

If `Super` and `Hyper` are recompiled but not `Test`, then running the new binaries with the existing binary of `Test` produces the output:

```
hello from Super
```

as you might expect. (A flaw in some early implementations caused them to print:

```
hello from Hyper
```

incorrectly.)

13.4.7 Access to Members and Constructors

Changing the declared access of a member or constructor to permit less access may break compatibility with pre-existing binaries, causing a linkage error to be thrown when these binaries are resolved. Less access is permitted if the access modifier is changed from default access to `private` access; from `protected` access to default or `private` access; or from `public` access to `protected`, default, or `private` access. Changing a member or constructor to permit less access is therefore not recommended for widely distributed classes.

Perhaps surprisingly, the binary format is defined so that changing a member or constructor to be more accessible does not cause a linkage error when a subclass (already) defines a method to have less access.

So, for example, if the package `points` defines the class `Point`:

```
package points;
public class Point {
   public int x, y;
```

```
    protected void print() {
        System.out.println("(" + x + "," + y + ")");
    }
}
```

used by the Test program:

```
class Test extends points.Point {
    protected void print() {
        System.out.println("Test");
    }
    public static void main(String[] args) {
        Test t = new Test();
        t.print();
    }
}
```

then these classes compile and Test executes to produce the output:

```
Test
```

If the method print in class Point is changed to be public, and then only the Point class is recompiled, and then executed with the previously existing binary for Test then no linkage error occurs, even though it is improper, at compile time, for a public method to be overridden by a protected method (as shown by the fact that the class Test could not be recompiled using this new Point class unless print were changed to be public.)

Allowing superclasses to change protected methods to be public without breaking binaries of preexisting subclasses helps make binaries less fragile. The alternative, where such a change would cause a linkage error, would create additional binary incompatibilities.

13.4.8 Field Declarations

Widely distributed programs should not expose any fields to their clients. Apart from the binary compatibility issues discussed below, this is generally good software engineering practice. Adding a field to a class may break compatibility with pre-existing binaries that are not recompiled.

Assume a reference to a field *f* with qualifying type *T*. Assume further that *f* is in fact an instance (respectively static) field declared in a superclass of *T*, *S*, and that the type of *f* is *X*. If a new field of type *X* with the same name as *f* is added to a subclass of *S* that is a superclass of *T* or *T* itself, then a linkage error may occur. Such a linkage error will occur only if, in addition to the above, either one of the following conditions hold:

- The new field is less accessible than the old one.
- The new field is a `static` (respectively instance) field.

In particular, no linkage error will occur in the case where a class could no longer be recompiled because a field access previously referenced a field of a superclass with an incompatible type. The previously compiled class with such a reference will continue to reference the field declared in a superclass.

Thus compiling and executing the code:

```
class Hyper { String h = "hyper"; }
class Super extends Hyper { String s = "super"; }
class Test {
    public static void main(String[] args) {
        System.out.println(new Super().h);
    }
}
```

produces the output:

```
hyper
```

Changing `Super` to be defined as:

```
class Super extends Hyper {
    String s = "super";
    int h = 0;
}
```

recompiling `Hyper` and `Super`, and executing the resulting new binaries with the old binary of `Test` produces the output:

```
hyper
```

The field `h` of `Hyper` is output by the original binary of `main`. While this may seem surprising at first, it serves to reduce the number of incompatibilities that occur at run time. (In an ideal world, all source files that needed recompilation would be recompiled whenever any one of them changed, eliminating such surprises. But such a mass recompilation is often impractical or impossible, especially in the Internet. And, as was previously noted, such recompilation would sometimes require further changes to the source code.)

As an example, if the program:

```
class Hyper { String h = "Hyper"; }
class Super extends Hyper { }
class Test extends Super {
    public static void main(String[] args) {
        String s = new Test().h;
```

```
        System.out.println(s);
    }
}
```

is compiled and executed, it produces the output:

```
Hyper
```

Suppose that a new version of class `Super` is then compiled:

```
class Super extends Hyper { char h = 'h'; }
```

If the resulting binary is used with the existing binaries for `Hyper` and `Test`, then the output is still:

```
Hyper
```

even though compiling the source for these binaries:

```
class Hyper { String h = "Hyper"; }
class Super extends Hyper { char h = 'h'; }
class Test extends Super {
    public static void main(String[] args) {
        String s = new Test().h;
        System.out.println(s);
    }
}
```

would result in a compile-time error, because the `h` in the source code for `main` would now be construed as referring to the `char` field declared in `Super`, and a `char` value can't be assigned to a `String`.

Deleting a field from a class will break compatibility with any pre-existing binaries that reference this field, and a `NoSuchFieldError` will be thrown when such a reference from a pre-existing binary is linked. Only `private` fields may be safely deleted from a widely distributed class.

For purposes of binary compatibility, adding or removing a field *f* whose type involves type variables (§4.4) or parameterized types (§4.5) is equivalent to the addition (respectively, removal) of a field of the same name whose type is the erasure (§4.6) of the type of *f*.

13.4.9 `final` Fields and Constants

If a field that was not `final` is changed to be `final`, then it can break compatibility with pre-existing binaries that attempt to assign new values to the field.

For example, if the program:

```
class Super { static char s; }
class Test extends Super {
    public static void main(String[] args) {
        s = 'a';
```

```
            System.out.println(s);
        }
    }
```

is compiled and executed, it produces the output:

```
    a
```

Suppose that a new version of class `Super` is produced:

```
    class Super { final static char s = 'b'; }
```

If `Super` is recompiled but not `Test`, then running the new binary with the existing binary of `Test` results in a `IllegalAccessError`.

Deleting the keyword `final` or changing the value to which a field is initialized does not break compatibility with existing binaries.

If a field is a constant variable (§4.12.4), then deleting the keyword `final` or changing its value will not break compatibility with pre-existing binaries by causing them not to run, but they will not see any new value for the usage of the field unless they are recompiled. This is true even if the usage itself is not a compile-time constant expression (§15.28)

If the example:

```
    class Flags { final static boolean debug = true; }
    class Test {
        public static void main(String[] args) {
            if (Flags.debug)
                System.out.println("debug is true");
        }
    }
```

is compiled and executed, it produces the output:

```
    debug is true
```

Suppose that a new version of class `Flags` is produced:

```
    class Flags { final static boolean debug = false; }
```

If `Flags` is recompiled but not `Test`, then running the new binary with the existing binary of `Test` produces the output:

```
    debug is true
```

because the value of `debug` was a compile-time constant, and could have been used in compiling `Test` without making a reference to the class `Flags`.

This result is a side-effect of the decision to support conditional compilation, as discussed at the end of §14.21.

This behavior would not change if `Flags` were changed to be an interface, as in the modified example:

```
    interface Flags { boolean debug = true; }
    class Test {
        public static void main(String[] args) {
```

```
        if (Flags.debug)
            System.out.println("debug is true");
    }
}
```

(One reason for requiring inlining of constants is that `switch` statements require constants on each `case`, and no two such constant values may be the same. The compiler checks for duplicate constant values in a `switch` statement at compile time; the `class` file format does not do symbolic linkage of `case` values.)

The best way to avoid problems with "inconstant constants" in widely-distributed code is to declare as compile time constants only values which truly are unlikely ever to change. Other than for true mathematical constants, we recommend that source code make very sparing use of class variables that are declared `static` and `final`. If the read-only nature of `final` is required, a better choice is to declare a `private static` variable and a suitable accessor method to get its value. Thus we recommend:

```
private static int N;
public static int getN() { return N; }
```

rather than:

```
public static final int N = ...;
```

There is no problem with:

```
public static int N = ...;
```

if `N` need not be read-only. We also recommend, as a general rule, that only truly constant values be declared in interfaces. We note, but do not recommend, that if a field of primitive type of an interface may change, its value may be expressed idiomatically as in:

```
interface Flags {
    boolean debug = new Boolean(true).booleanValue();
}
```

insuring that this value is not a constant. Similar idioms exist for the other primitive types.

One other thing to note is that `static final` fields that have constant values (whether of primitive or `String` type) must never appear to have the default initial value for their type (§4.12.5). This means that all such fields appear to be initialized first during class initialization (§8.3.2.1, §9.3.1, §12.4.2).

13.4.10 `static` Fields

If a field that is not declared `private` was not declared `static` and is changed to be declared `static`, or vice versa, then a linkage time error, specifically an `IncompatibleClassChangeError`, will result if the field is used by a preexisting binary which expected a field of the other kind. Such changes are not recommended in code that has been widely distributed.

13.4.11 `transient` Fields

Adding or deleting a `transient` modifier of a field does not break compatibility with pre-existing binaries.

13.4.12 Method and Constructor Declarations

Adding a method or constructor declaration to a class will not break compatibility with any pre-existing binaries, in the case where a type could no longer be recompiled because an invocation previously referenced a method or constructor of a superclass with an incompatible type. The previously compiled class with such a reference will continue to reference the method or constructor declared in a superclass.

Assume a reference to a method *m* with qualifying type *T*. Assume further that *m* is in fact an instance (respectively `static`) method declared in a superclass of *T*, *S*. If a new method of type *X* with the same signature and return type as *m* is added to a subclass of *S* that is a superclass of *T* or *T* itself, then a linkage error may occur. Such a linkage error will occur only if, in addition to the above, either one of the following conditions hold:

- The new method is less accessible than the old one.
- The new method is a `static` (respectively instance) method.

Deleting a method or constructor from a class may break compatibility with any pre-existing binary that referenced this method or constructor; a `NoSuchMethodError` may be thrown when such a reference from a pre-existing binary is linked. Such an error will occur only if no method with a matching signature and return type is declared in a superclass.

If the source code for a class contains no declared constructors, the Java compiler automatically supplies a constructor with no parameters. Adding one or more constructor declarations to the source code of such a class will prevent this default constructor from being supplied automatically, effectively deleting a constructor, unless one of the new constructors also has no parameters, thus replacing the default constructor. The automatically supplied constructor with no parameters is given the same access modifier as the class of its declaration, so any replacement should have as much or more access if compatibility with pre-existing binaries is to be preserved.

13.4.13 Method and Constructor Formal Type Parameters

Renaming a type variable (§4.4) declared as a formal type parameter of a method or constructor has no effect with respect to pre-existing binaries. Adding or removing a type parameter does not, in itself, have any implications for binary compatibility.

DISCUSSION

Note that if such type variables are used in the type of the method or constructor, that may have the normal implications of changing the aforementioned type.

Changing the first bound of a type parameter may change the erasure (§4.6) of any member that uses that type variable in its own type, and this may effect binary compatibility. Specifically:

- If the type parameter is used as the type of a field, the effect is as if the field was removed and a field with the same name, whose type is the new erasure of the type variable, was added.
- If the type variable is used as the type of any formal parameter of a method, but not as the return type, the effect is as if that method were removed, and replaced with a new method that is identical except for the types of the aforementioned formal parameters, which now have the new erasure of the type variable as their type.
- If the type variable is used as a return type of a method, but not as the type of any formal parameter of the method, the effect is as if that method were removed, and replaced with a new method that is identical except for the return type, which is now the new erasure of the type variable.
- If the type variable is used as a return type of a method and as the type of some formal paramters of the method, the effect is as if that method were removed, and replaced with a new method that is identical except for the return type, which is now the new erasure of the type variable, and except for the types of the aforementioned formal parameters, which now have the new erasure of the type variable as their type.

Changing any other bound has no effect on binary compatibility.

13.4.14 Method and Constructor Parameters

Changing the name of a formal parameter of a method or constructor does not impact pre-existing binaries. Changing the name of a method, the type of a formal parameter to a method or constructor, or adding a parameter to or deleting a parameter from a method or constructor declaration creates a method or constructor with a new signature, and has the combined effect of deleting the method or constructor with the old signature and adding a method or constructor with the new signature (see §13.4.12).

For purposes of binary compatibility, adding or removing a method or constructor *m* whose signature involves type variables (§4.4) or parameterized types (§4.5) is equivalent to the addition (respectively, removal) of an otherwise equivalent method whose signature is the erasure (§4.6) of the signature of *m*.

13.4.15 Method Result Type

Changing the result type of a method, replacing a result type with `void`, or replacing `void` with a result type has the combined effect of deleting the old method and adding a new method with the new result type or newly `void` result (see §13.4.12).

For purposes of binary compatibility, adding or removing a method or constructor *m* whose return type involves type variables (§4.4) or parameterized types (§4.5) is equivalent to the addition (respectively, removal) of the an otherwise equivalent method whose return type is the erasure (§4.6) of the return type of *m*.

13.4.16 `abstract` Methods

Changing a method that is declared `abstract` to no longer be declared `abstract` does not break compatibility with pre-existing binaries.

Changing a method that is not declared `abstract` to be declared `abstract` will break compatibility with pre-existing binaries that previously invoked the method, causing an `AbstractMethodError`.

If the example program:

```
class Super { void out() { System.out.println("Out"); } }
```

```
class Test extends Super {
    public static void main(String[] args) {
        Test t = new Test();
        System.out.println("Way ");
        t.out();
    }
}
```

is compiled and executed, it produces the output:

```
Way
Out
```

Suppose that a new version of class `Super` is produced:

```
abstract class Super {
    abstract void out();
}
```

If `Super` is recompiled but not `Test`, then running the new binary with the existing binary of `Test` results in a `AbstractMethodError`, because class `Test` has no implementation of the method `out`, and is therefore is (or should be) abstract.

13.4.17 `final` Methods

Changing an instance method that is not `final` to be `final` may break compatibility with existing binaries that depend on the ability to override the method.

If the test program:

```
class Super { void out() { System.out.println("out"); } }
class Test extends Super {
    public static void main(String[] args) {
        Test t = new Test();
        t.out();
    }
    void out() { super.out(); }
}
```

is compiled and executed, it produces the output:

```
out
```

Suppose that a new version of class `Super` is produced:

```
class Super { final void out() { System.out.println("!"); } }
```

If `Super` is recompiled but not `Test`, then running the new binary with the existing binary of `Test` results in a `VerifyError` because the class `Test` improperly tries to override the instance method `out`.

Changing a class (`static`) method that is not `final` to be `final` does not break compatibility with existing binaries, because the method could not have been overridden.

Removing the `final` modifier from a method does not break compatibility with pre-existing binaries.

13.4.18 `native` Methods

Adding or deleting a `native` modifier of a method does not break compatibility with pre-existing binaries.

The impact of changes to types on preexisting `native` methods that are not recompiled is beyond the scope of this specification and should be provided with the description of an implementation. Implementations are encouraged, but not required, to implement `native` methods in a way that limits such impact.

13.4.19 `static` Methods

If a method that is not declared `private` was declared `static` (that is, a class method) and is changed to not be declared `static` (that is, to an instance method), or vice versa, then compatibility with pre-existing binaries may be broken, resulting in a linkage time error, namely an `IncompatibleClassChangeError`, if these methods are used by the pre-existing binaries. Such changes are not recommended in code that has been widely distributed.

13.4.20 `synchronized` Methods

Adding or deleting a `synchronized` modifier of a method does not break compatibility with existing binaries.

13.4.21 Method and Constructor Throws

Changes to the `throws` clause of methods or constructors do not break compatibility with existing binaries; these clauses are checked only at compile time.

13.4.22 Method and Constructor Body

Changes to the body of a method or constructor do not break compatibility with pre-existing binaries.

We note that a compiler cannot expand a method inline at compile time.
The keyword `final` on a method does not mean that the method can be safely inlined; it means only that the method cannot be overridden. It is still possible that a new version of that method will be provided at link time. Furthermore, the structure of the original program must be preserved for purposes of reflection.

In general we suggest that implementations use late-bound (run-time) code generation and optimization.

13.4.23 Method and Constructor Overloading

Adding new methods or constructors that overload existing methods or constructors does not break compatibility with pre-existing binaries. The signature to be used for each invocation was determined when these existing binaries were compiled; therefore newly added methods or constructors will not be used, even if their signatures are both applicable and more specific than the signature originally chosen.

While adding a new overloaded method or constructor may cause a compile-time error the next time a class or interface is compiled because there is no method or constructor that is most specific (§15.12.2.5), no such error occurs when a program is executed, because no overload resolution is done at execution time.

If the example program:

```
class Super {
    static void out(float f) { System.out.println("float"); }
}
class Test {
    public static void main(String[] args) {
        Super.out(2);
    }
}
```

is compiled and executed, it produces the output:

```
float
```

Suppose that a new version of class `Super` is produced:

```
class Super {
    static void out(float f) { System.out.println("float"); }
    static void out(int i) { System.out.println("int"); }
}
```

If `Super` is recompiled but not `Test`, then running the new binary with the existing binary of `Test` still produces the output:

```
float
```

However, if `Test` is then recompiled, using this new `Super`, the output is then:

```
int
```

as might have been naively expected in the previous case.

13.4.24 Method Overriding

If an instance method is added to a subclass and it overrides a method in a superclass, then the subclass method will be found by method invocations in pre-existing binaries, and these binaries are not impacted. If a class method is added to a class, then this method will not be found unless the qualifying type of the reference is the subclass type.

13.4.25 Static Initializers

Adding, deleting, or changing a static initializer (§8.7) of a class does not impact pre-existing binaries.

13.4.26 Evolution of Enums

Adding or reordering constants from an enum type will not break compatibility with pre-existing binaries.

If a precompiled binary attempts to access an enum constant that no longer exists, the client will fail at runtime with a `NoSuchFieldError`. Therefore such a change is not recommended for widely distributed enums.

In all other respects, the binary compatibility rules for enums are identical to those for classes.

13.5 Evolution of Interfaces

This section describes the impact of changes to the declaration of an interface and its members on pre-existing binaries.

13.5.1 `public` Interfaces

Changing an interface that is not declared `public` to be declared `public` does not break compatibility with pre-existing binaries.

If an interface that is declared `public` is changed to not be declared `public`, then an `IllegalAccessError` is thrown if a pre-existing binary is linked that needs but no longer has access to the interface type, so such a change is not recommended for widely distributed interfaces.

13.5.2 Superinterfaces

Changes to the interface hierarchy cause errors in the same way that changes to the class hierarchy do, as described in §13.4.4. In particular, changes that result in any previous superinterface of a class no longer being a superinterface can break compatibility with pre-existing binaries, resulting in a `VerifyError`.

13.5.3 The Interface Members

Adding a method to an interface does not break compatibility with pre-existing binaries. A field added to a superinterface of *C* may hide a field inherited from a superclass of *C*. If the original reference was to an instance field, an `IncompatibleClassChangeError` will result. If the original reference was an assignment, an `IllegalAccessError` will result.

Deleting a member from an interface may cause linkage errors in pre-existing binaries.

If the example program:

```
interface I { void hello(); }
class Test implements I {
    public static void main(String[] args) {
        I anI = new Test();
        anI.hello();
    }
    public void hello() { System.out.println("hello"); }
}
```

is compiled and executed, it produces the output:

```
hello
```

Suppose that a new version of interface `I` is compiled:

```
interface I { }
```

If `I` is recompiled but not `Test`, then running the new binary with the existing binary for `Test` will result in a `NoSuchMethodError`. (In some early implementations this program still executed; the fact that the method `hello` no longer exists in interface `I` was not correctly detected.)

13.5.4 Interface Formal Type Parameters

The effects of changes to the formal type parameters of an interface are the same as those of analogous changes to the formal type parameters of a class.

13.5.5 Field Declarations

The considerations for changing field declarations in interfaces are the same as those for `static final` fields in classes, as described in §13.4.8 and §13.4.9.

13.5.6 Abstract Method Declarations

The considerations for changing abstract method declarations in interfaces are the same as those for `abstract` methods in classes, as described in §13.4.14, §13.4.15, §13.4.21, and §13.4.23.

13.5.7 Evolution of Annotation Types

Annotation types behave exactly like any other interface. Adding or removing an element from an annotation type is analogous to adding or removing a method. There are important considerations governing other changes to annotation types, but these have no effect on the linkage of binaries by the Java virtual machine. Rather, such changes effect the behavior of reflective APIs that manipulate annotations. The documentation of these APIs specifes their behavior when various changes are made to the underlying annotation types.

Adding or removing annotations has no effect on the correct linkage of the binary representations of programs in the Java programming language.

Lo! keen-eyed, towering Science! . . .
Yet again, lo! the Soul—above all science . . .
For it, the partial to the permanent flowing,
For it, the Real to the Ideal tends.
For it, the mystic evolution . . .

—Walt Whitman, *Song of the Universal* (1874)

CHAPTER 14

Blocks and Statements

He was not merely a chip of the old block, but the old block itself.
—Edmund Burke, *On Pitt's First Speech*

THE sequence of execution of a program is controlled by *statements*, which are executed for their effect and do not have values.

Some statements *contain* other statements as part of their structure; such other statements are substatements of the statement. We say that statement `S` *immediately contains* statement `U` if there is no statement `T` different from `S` and `U` such that `S` contains `T` and `T` contains `U`. In the same manner, some statements contain expressions (§15) as part of their structure.

The first section of this chapter discusses the distinction between normal and abrupt completion of statements (§14.1). Most of the remaining sections explain the various kinds of statements, describing in detail both their normal behavior and any special treatment of abrupt completion.

Blocks are explained first (§14.2), followed by local class declarations (§14.3) and local variable declaration statements (§14.4).

Next a grammatical maneuver that sidesteps the familiar "dangling `else`" problem (§14.5) is explained.

The last section (§14.21) of this chapter addresses the requirement that every statement be *reachable* in a certain technical sense.

14.1 Normal and Abrupt Completion of Statements

Poirot's abrupt departure had intrigued us all greatly.
—Agatha Christie, *The Mysterious Affair at Styles* (1920), Chapter 12

Every statement has a normal mode of execution in which certain computational steps are carried out. The following sections describe the normal mode of execution for each kind of statement.

If all the steps are carried out as described, with no indication of abrupt completion, the statement is said to *complete normally*. However, certain events may prevent a statement from completing normally:

- The `break` (§14.15), `continue` (§14.16), and `return` (§14.17) statements cause a transfer of control that may prevent normal completion of statements that contain them.
- Evaluation of certain expressions may throw exceptions from the Java virtual machine; these expressions are summarized in §15.6. An explicit `throw` (§14.18) statement also results in an exception. An exception causes a transfer of control that may prevent normal completion of statements.

If such an event occurs, then execution of one or more statements may be terminated before all steps of their normal mode of execution have completed; such statements are said to *complete abruptly*.

An abrupt completion always has an associated *reason*, which is one of the following:

- A `break` with no label
- A `break` with a given label
- A `continue` with no label
- A `continue` with a given label
- A `return` with no value
- A `return` with a given value
- A `throw` with a given value, including exceptions thrown by the Java virtual machine

The terms "complete normally" and "complete abruptly" also apply to the evaluation of expressions (§15.6). The only reason an expression can complete abruptly is that an exception is thrown, because of either a `throw` with a given value (§14.18) or a run-time exception or error (§11, §15.6).

If a statement evaluates an expression, abrupt completion of the expression always causes the immediate abrupt completion of the statement, with the same reason. All succeeding steps in the normal mode of execution are not performed.

Unless otherwise specified in this chapter, abrupt completion of a substatement causes the immediate abrupt completion of the statement itself, with the same reason, and all succeeding steps in the normal mode of execution of the statement are not performed.

Unless otherwise specified, a statement completes normally if all expressions it evaluates and all substatements it executes complete normally.

14.2 Blocks

He wears his faith but as the fashion of his hat;
it ever changes with the next block.
—William Shakespeare, *Much Ado about Nothing* (1623), Act I, scene i

A *block* is a sequence of statements, local class declarations and local variable declaration statements within braces.

Block:
  { *BlockStatements*$_{opt}$ }

BlockStatements:
  BlockStatement
  BlockStatements BlockStatement

BlockStatement:
  LocalVariableDeclarationStatement
  ClassDeclaration
  Statement

A block is executed by executing each of the local variable declaration statements and other statements in order from first to last (left to right). If all of these block statements complete normally, then the block completes normally. If any of these block statements complete abruptly for any reason, then the block completes abruptly for the same reason.

14.3 Local Class Declarations

A *local class* is a nested class (§8) that is not a member of any class and that has a name. All local classes are inner classes (§8.1.3). Every local class declaration statement is immediately contained by a block. Local class declaration statements may be intermixed freely with other kinds of statements in the block.

The scope of a local class immediately enclosed by a block (§14.2) is the rest of the immediately enclosing block, including its own class declaration. The scope of a local class immediately enclosed by in a switch block statement group (§14.11)is the rest of the immediately enclosing switch block statement group, including its own class declaration.

The name of a local class *C* may not be redeclared as a local class of the directly enclosing method, constructor, or initializer block within the scope of *C*, or a compile-time error occurs. However, a local class declaration may be shadowed (§6.3.1) anywhere inside a class declaration nested within the local class declaration's scope. A local class does not have a canonical name, nor does it have a fully qualified name.

It is a compile-time error if a local class declaration contains any one of the following access modifiers: `public`, `protected`, `private`, or `static`.

Here is an example that illustrates several aspects of the rules given above:

```
class Global {
    class Cyclic {}
    void foo() {
        new Cyclic(); // create a Global.Cyclic
        class Cyclic extends Cyclic{}; // circular definition
        {
            class Local{};
            {
              class Local{}; // compile-time error
            }
            class Local{}; // compile-time error
            class AnotherLocal {
              void bar() {
                class Local {}; // ok
              }
            }
        }
        class Local{}; // ok, not in scope of prior Local
}
```

The first statement of method `foo` creates an instance of the member class `Global.Cyclic` rather than an instance of the local class `Cyclic`, because the local class declaration is not yet in scope.

The fact that the scope of a local class encompasses its own declaration (not only its body) means that the definition of the local class `Cyclic` is indeed cyclic because it extends itself rather than `Global.Cyclic`. Consequently, the declaration of the local class `Cyclic` will be rejected at compile time.

Since local class names cannot be redeclared within the same method (or constructor or initializer, as the case may be), the second and third declarations of `Local` result in compile-time errors. However, `Local` can be redeclared in the context of another, more deeply nested, class such as `AnotherLocal`.

The fourth and last declaration of `Local` is legal, since it occurs outside the scope of any prior declaration of `Local`.

14.4 Local Variable Declaration Statements

A *local variable declaration statement* declares one or more local variable names.

LocalVariableDeclarationStatement:
  LocalVariableDeclaration `;`

LocalVariableDeclaration:
  VariableModifiers Type VariableDeclarators

The following are repeated from §8.3 to make the presentation here clearer:

VariableDeclarators:
  VariableDeclarator
  VariableDeclarators `,` *VariableDeclarator*

VariableDeclarator:
  VariableDeclaratorId
  VariableDeclaratorId `=` *VariableInitializer*

VariableDeclaratorId:
  Identifier
  VariableDeclaratorId `[ ]`

VariableInitializer:
  Expression
  ArrayInitializer

Every local variable declaration statement is immediately contained by a block. Local variable declaration statements may be intermixed freely with other kinds of statements in the block.

A local variable declaration can also appear in the header of a `for` statement (§14.14). In this case it is executed in the same manner as if it were part of a local variable declaration statement.

14.4.1 Local Variable Declarators and Types

Each *declarator* in a local variable declaration declares one local variable, whose name is the *Identifier* that appears in the declarator.

If the optional keyword `final` appears at the start of the declarator, the variable being declared is a final variable(§4.12.4).

If an annotation *a* on a local variable declaration corresponds to an annotation type *T*, and *T* has a (meta-)annotation *m* that corresponds to `annotation.Target`, then *m* must have an element whose value is `annotation.ElementType.LOCAL_VARIABLE`, or a compile-time error occurs. Annotation modifiers are described further in (§9.7).

The type of the variable is denoted by the *Type* that appears in the local variable declaration, followed by any bracket pairs that follow the *Identifier* in the declarator.

Thus, the local variable declaration:

```
int a, b[], c[][];
```

is equivalent to the series of declarations:

```
int a;
int[] b;
int[][] c;
```

Brackets are allowed in declarators as a nod to the tradition of C and C++. The general rule, however, also means that the local variable declaration:

```
float[][] f[][], g[][][], h[];// Yechh!
```

is equivalent to the series of declarations:

```
float[][][][] f;
float[][][][][] g;
float[][][] h;
```

We do not recommend such "mixed notation" for array declarations.

A local variable of type `float` always contains a value that is an element of the float value set (§4.2.3); similarly, a local variable of type `double` always contains a value that is an element of the double value set. It is not permitted for a local variable of type `float` to contain an element of the float-extended-exponent value set that is not also an element of the float value set, nor for a local variable of type `double` to contain an element of the double-extended-exponent value set that is not also an element of the double value set.

14.4.2 Scope of Local Variable Declarations

The scope of a local variable declaration in a block (§14.4.2) is the rest of the block in which the declaration appears, starting with its own initializer (§14.4) and including any further declarators to the right in the local variable declaration statement.

The name of a local variable `v` may not be redeclared as a local variable of the directly enclosing method, constructor or initializer block within the scope of *v*, or a compile-time error occurs. The name of a local variable `v` may not be redeclared as an exception parameter of a catch clause in a try statement of the directly enclosing method, constructor or initializer block within the scope of `v`, or a compile-time error occurs. However, a local variable of a method or initializer block may be shadowed (§6.3.1) anywhere inside a class declaration nested within the scope of the local variable.

A local variable cannot be referred to using a qualified name (§6.6), only a simple name.

The example:

```
class Test {
    static int x;
    public static void main(String[] args) {
        int x = x;
    }
}
```

causes a compile-time error because the initialization of `x` is within the scope of the declaration of `x` as a local variable, and the local `x` does not yet have a value and cannot be used.

The following program does compile:

```
class Test {
    static int x;
    public static void main(String[] args) {
        int x = (x=2)*2;
        System.out.println(x);
    }
}
```

because the local variable `x` is definitely assigned (§16) before it is used. It prints:

```
4
```

Here is another example:

```
class Test {
    public static void main(String[] args) {
        System.out.print("2+1=");
        int two = 2, three = two + 1;
        System.out.println(three);
    }
}
```

which compiles correctly and produces the output:

```
2+1=3
```

The initializer for `three` can correctly refer to the variable `two` declared in an earlier declarator, and the method invocation in the next line can correctly refer to the variable `three` declared earlier in the block.

The scope of a local variable declared in a `for` statement is the rest of the `for` statement, including its own initializer.

If a declaration of an identifier as a local variable of the same method, constructor, or initializer block appears within the scope of a parameter or local variable of the same name, a compile-time error occurs.

Thus the following example does not compile:

```
class Test {
    public static void main(String[] args) {
        int i;
        for (int i = 0; i < 10; i++)
            System.out.println(i);
    }
}
```

This restriction helps to detect some otherwise very obscure bugs. A similar restriction on shadowing of members by local variables was judged impractical, because the addition of a member in a superclass could cause subclasses to have to rename local variables. Related considerations make restrictions on shadowing of local variables by members of nested classes, or on shadowing of local variables by local variables declared within nested classes unattractive as well. Hence, the following example compiles without error:

```
class Test {
    public static void main(String[] args) {
        int i;
        class Local {
            {
              for (int i = 0; i < 10; i++)
              System.out.println(i);
            }
        }
        new Local();
    }
}
```

On the other hand, local variables with the same name may be declared in two separate blocks or `for` statements neither of which contains the other. Thus:

```
class Test {
    public static void main(String[] args) {
        for (int i = 0; i < 10; i++)
            System.out.print(i + " ");
        for (int i = 10; i > 0; i--)
            System.out.print(i + " ");
```

```
        System.out.println();
    }
}
```

compiles without error and, when executed, produces the output:

```
0 1 2 3 4 5 6 7 8 9 10 9 8 7 6 5 4 3 2 1
```

14.4.3 Shadowing of Names by Local Variables

If a name declared as a local variable is already declared as a field name, then that outer declaration is shadowed (§6.3.1) throughout the scope of the local variable. Similarly, if a name is already declared as a variable or parameter name, then that outer declaration is shadowed throughout the scope of the local variable (provided that the shadowing does not cause a compile-time error under the rules of §14.4.2). The shadowed name can sometimes be accessed using an appropriately qualified name.

For example, the keyword `this` can be used to access a shadowed field `x`, using the form `this.x`. Indeed, this idiom typically appears in constructors (§8.8):

```
class Pair {
    Object first, second;
    public Pair(Object first, Object second) {
        this.first = first;
        this.second = second;
    }
}
```

In this example, the constructor takes parameters having the same names as the fields to be initialized. This is simpler than having to invent different names for the parameters and is not too confusing in this stylized context. In general, however, it is considered poor style to have local variables with the same names as fields.

14.4.4 Execution of Local Variable Declarations

A local variable declaration statement is an executable statement. Every time it is executed, the declarators are processed in order from left to right. If a declarator has an initialization expression, the expression is evaluated and its value is assigned to the variable. If a declarator does not have an initialization expression, then a Java compiler must prove, using exactly the algorithm given in §16, that every reference to the variable is necessarily preceded by execution of an assignment to the variable. If this is not the case, then a compile-time error occurs.

Each initialization (except the first) is executed only if the evaluation of the preceding initialization expression completes normally. Execution of the local variable declaration completes normally only if evaluation of the last initialization expression completes normally; if the local variable declaration contains no initialization expressions, then executing it always completes normally.

14.5 Statements

There are many kinds of statements in the Java programming language. Most correspond to statements in the C and C++ languages, but some are unique.

As in C and C++, the `if` statement of the Java programming language suffers from the so-called "dangling `else` problem," illustrated by this misleadingly formatted example:

```
if (door.isOpen())
    if (resident.isVisible())
        resident.greet("Hello!");
else door.bell.ring();     // A "dangling else"
```

The problem is that both the outer `if` statement and the inner `if` statement might conceivably own the `else` clause. In this example, one might surmise that the programmer intended the `else` clause to belong to the outer `if` statement. The Java programming language, like C and C++ and many programming languages before them, arbitrarily decree that an `else` clause belongs to the innermost `if` to which it might possibly belong. This rule is captured by the following grammar:

Statement:
    StatementWithoutTrailingSubstatement
    LabeledStatement
    IfThenStatement
    IfThenElseStatement
    WhileStatement
    ForStatement

StatementWithoutTrailingSubstatement:
    Block
    EmptyStatement
    ExpressionStatement
    AssertStatement
    SwitchStatement
    DoStatement
    BreakStatement

ContinueStatement
ReturnStatement
SynchronizedStatement
ThrowStatement
TryStatement

StatementNoShortIf:
StatementWithoutTrailingSubstatement
LabeledStatementNoShortIf
IfThenElseStatementNoShortIf
WhileStatementNoShortIf
ForStatementNoShortIf

The following are repeated from §14.9 to make the presentation here clearer:

IfThenStatement:
`if` (*Expression*) *Statement*

IfThenElseStatement:
`if` (*Expression*) *StatementNoShortIf* `else` *Statement*

IfThenElseStatementNoShortIf:
`if` (*Expression*) *StatementNoShortIf* `else` *StatementNoShortIf*

Statements are thus grammatically divided into two categories: those that might end in an `if` statement that has no `else` clause (a "short `if` statement") and those that definitely do not. Only statements that definitely do not end in a short `if` statement may appear as an immediate substatement before the keyword `else` in an `if` statement that does have an `else` clause.

This simple rule prevents the "dangling `else`" problem. The execution behavior of a statement with the "no short `if`" restriction is identical to the execution behavior of the same kind of statement without the "no short `if`" restriction; the distinction is drawn purely to resolve the syntactic difficulty.

14.6 The Empty Statement

I did never know so full a voice issue from so empty a heart:
but the saying is true 'The empty vessel makes the greatest sound.'
—William Shakespeare, *Henry V* (1623), Act IV, scene iv

An *empty statement* does nothing.

EmptyStatement:
    ;

Execution of an empty statement always completes normally.

14.7 Labeled Statements

Inside of five minutes I was mounted, and perfectly satisfied
with my outfit. I had no time to label him "This is a horse,"
and so if the public took him for a sheep I cannot help it.
—Mark Twain, *Roughing It* (1871)

Statements may have *label* prefixes.

LabeledStatement:
    Identifier : *Statement*

LabeledStatementNoShortIf:
    Identifier : *StatementNoShortIf*

The *Identifier* is declared to be the label of the immediately contained *Statement*.

Unlike C and C++, the Java programming language has no `goto` statement; identifier statement labels are used with `break` (§14.15) or `continue` (§14.16) statements appearing anywhere within the labeled statement.

Let *l* be a label, and let *m* be the immediately enclosing method, constructor, instance initializer or static initializer. It is a compile-time error if *l* shadows (§6.3.1) the declaration of another label immediately enclosed in *m*.

There is no restriction against using the same identifier as a label and as the name of a package, class, interface, method, field, parameter, or local variable. Use of an identifier to label a statement does not obscure (§6.3.2) a package, class, interface, method, field, parameter, or local variable with the same name. Use of an identifier as a class, interface, method, field, local variable or as the parameter of an exception handler (§14.20) does not obscure a statement label with the same name.

A labeled statement is executed by executing the immediately contained *Statement*. If the statement is labeled by an *Identifier* and the contained *Statement* completes abruptly because of a `break` with the same *Identifier*, then the labeled statement completes normally. In all other cases of abrupt completion of the *Statement*, the labeled statement completes abruptly for the same reason.

14.8 Expression Statements

Certain kinds of expressions may be used as statements by following them with semicolons:

ExpressionStatement:
    StatementExpression ;

StatementExpression:
    Assignment
    PreIncrementExpression
    PreDecrementExpression
    PostIncrementExpression
    PostDecrementExpression
    MethodInvocation
    ClassInstanceCreationExpression

An *expression statement* is executed by evaluating the expression; if the expression has a value, the value is discarded. Execution of the expression statement completes normally if and only if evaluation of the expression completes normally.

Unlike C and C++, the Java programming language allows only certain forms of expressions to be used as expression statements. Note that the Java programming language does not allow a "cast to `void`"—`void` is not a type—so the traditional C trick of writing an expression statement such as:

```
(void) ... ;// incorrect!
```

does not work. On the other hand, the language allows all the most useful kinds of expressions in expressions statements, and it does not require a method invocation used as an expression statement to invoke a `void` method, so such a trick is almost never needed. If a trick is needed, either an assignment statement (§15.26) or a local variable declaration statement (§14.4) can be used instead.

14.9 The `if` Statement

The `if` statement allows conditional execution of a statement or a conditional choice of two statements, executing one or the other but not both.

IfThenStatement:
  `if ( `*Expression*` ) `*Statement*

IfThenElseStatement:
  `if ( `*Expression*` ) `*StatementNoShortIf* `else` *Statement*

IfThenElseStatementNoShortIf:
  `if ( `*Expression*` ) `*StatementNoShortIf* `else` *StatementNoShortIf*

The *Expression* must have type `boolean` or `Boolean`, or a compile-time error occurs.

14.9.1 The `if–then` Statement

I took an early opportunity of testing that statement . . .
—Agatha Christie, *The Mysterious Affair at Styles* (1920), Chapter 12

An `if–then` statement is executed by first evaluating the *Expression*. If the result is of type `Boolean`, it is subject to unboxing conversion (§5.1.8). If evaluation of the *Expression* or the subsequent unboxing conversion (if any) completes abruptly for some reason, the `if–then` statement completes abruptly for the same reason. Otherwise, execution continues by making a choice based on the resulting value:

- If the value is `true`, then the contained *Statement* is executed; the `if–then` statement completes normally if and only if execution of the *Statement* completes normally.
- If the value is `false`, no further action is taken and the `if–then` statement completes normally.

14.9.2 The `if–then–else` Statement

Did you ever have to finally decide—
To say yes to one, and let the other one ride?
—John Sebastian, *Did You Ever Have to Make Up Your Mind?*

An `if–then–else` statement is executed by first evaluating the *Expression*. If the result is of type `Boolean`, it is subject to unboxing conversion (§5.1.8). If evaluation of the *Expression* or the subsequent unboxing conversion (if any) completes abruptly for some reason, then the `if–then–else` statement completes abruptly for the same reason. Otherwise, execution continues by making a choice based on the resulting value:

- If the value is `true`, then the first contained *Statement* (the one before the `else` keyword) is executed; the `if–then–else` statement completes normally if and only if execution of that statement completes normally.
- If the value is `false`, then the second contained *Statement* (the one after the `else` keyword) is executed; the `if–then–else` statement completes normally if and only if execution of that statement completes normally.

14.10 The `assert` Statement

An *assertion* is a statement containing a boolean expression. An assertion is either *enabled* or *disabled*. If the assertion is enabled, evaluation of the assertion causes evaluation of the boolean expression and an error is reported if the expression evaluates to false. If the assertion is disabled, evaluation of the assertion has no effect whatsoever.

AssertStatement:

`assert` *Expression1 ;*

`assert` *Expression1 : Expression2 ;*

It is a compile-time error if *Expression1* does not have type `boolean` or `Boolean`. In the second form of the `assert` statement, it is a compile-time error if *Expression2* is void (§15.1).

Assertions may be enabled or disabled on a per-class basis. At the time a class is initialized (§12.4.2), prior to the execution of any field initializers for class variables (§8.3.2.1) and static initializers (§8.7), the class's class loader determines whether assertions are enabled or disabled as described below. Once a class has been initialized, its assertion status (enabled or disabled) does not change.

DISCUSSION

There is one case that demands special treatment. Recall that the assertion status of a class is set at the time it is initialized. It is possible, though generally not desirable, to execute methods or constructors prior to initialization. This can happen when a class hierarchy contains a circularity in its static initialization, as in the following example:

```
public class Foo {
    public static void main(String[] args) {
```

```
            Baz.testAsserts();
            // Will execute after Baz is initialized.
        }
    }
    class Bar {
        static {
            Baz.testAsserts();
            // Will execute before Baz is initialized!
        }
    }
    class Baz extends Bar {
        static void testAsserts(){
            boolean enabled = false;
            assert enabled = true;
            System.out.println("Asserts " +
                                (enabled ? "enabled" : "disabled"));
        }
    }
```

Invoking `Baz.testAsserts()` causes `Baz` to get initialized. Before this can happen, `Bar` must get initialized. `Bar`'s static initializer again invokes `Baz.testAsserts()`. Because initialization of `Baz` is already in progress by the current thread, the second invocation executes immediately, though `Baz` is not initialized (JLS 12.4.2).

If an `assert` statement executes before its class is initialized, as in the above example, the execution must behave as if assertions were enabled in the class.

DISCUSSION

In other words, if the program above is executed without enabling assertions, it must print:

```
Asserts enabled
Asserts disabled
```

An `assert` statement is enabled if and only if the top-level class (§8) that lexically contains it enables assertions. Whether or not a top-level class enables assertions is determined by its defining class loader before the class is initialized (§12.4.2), and cannot be changed thereafter.

An `assert` statement causes the enclosing top level class (if it exists) to be initialized, if it has not already been initialized (§12.4.1).

DISCUSSION

Note that an assertion that is enclosed by a top-level interface does not cause initialization.

Usually, the top level class enclosing an assertion will already be initialized. However, if the assertion is located within a static nested class, it may be that the initialization has not taken place.

A disabled `assert` statement does nothing. In particular neither *Expression1* nor *Expression2* (if it is present) are evaluated. Execution of a disabled `assert` statement always completes normally.

An enabled `assert` statement is executed by first evaluating *Expression1*. If the result is of type `Boolean`, it is subject to unboxing conversion (§5.1.8). If evaluation of *Expression1* or the subsequent unboxing conversion (if any) completes abruptly for some reason, the `assert` statement completes abruptly for the same reason. Otherwise, execution continues by making a choice based on the value of *Expression1* :

- If the value is `true`, no further action is taken and the assert statement completes normally.
- If the value is `false`, the execution behavior depends on whether *Expression2* is present:
  - If *Expression2* is present, it is evaluated.
    - If the evaluation completes abruptly for some reason, the `assert` statement completes abruptly for the same reason.
    - If the evaluation completes normally, the resulting value is converted to a `String` using string conversion (§15.18.1.1).
      - If the string conversion completes abruptly for some reason, the `assert` statement completes abruptly for the same reason.
      - If the string conversion completes normally, an `AssertionError` instance whose "detail message" is the result of the string conversion is created.
        - If the instance creation completes abruptly for some reason, the `assert` statement completes abruptly for the same reason.

    - If the instance creation completes normally, the `assert` statement completes abruptly by throwing the newly created `AssertionError` object.
- If *Expression2* is not present, an `AssertionError` instance with no "detail message" is created.
    - If the instance creation completes abruptly for some reason, the `assert` statement completes abruptly for the same reason.
    - If the instance creation completes normally, the `assert` statement completes abruptly by throwing the newly created `AssertionError` object.

DISCUSSION

For example, after unmarshalling all of the arguments from a data buffer, a programmer might assert that the number of bytes of data remaining in the buffer is zero. By verifying that the boolean expression is indeed true, the system corroborates the programmer's knowledge of the program and increases one's confidence that the program is free of bugs.

Typically, assertion-checking is enabled during program development and testing, and disabled for deployment, to improve performance.

Because assertions may be disabled, programs must not assume that the expressions contained in assertions will be evaluated. Thus, these boolean expressions should generally be free of side effects:

Evaluating such a boolean expression should not affect any state that is visible after the evaluation is complete. It is not illegal for a boolean expression contained in an assertion to have a side effect, but it is generally inappropriate, as it could cause program behavior to vary depending on whether assertions were enabled or disabled.

Along similar lines, assertions should not be used for argument-checking in public methods. Argument-checking is typically part of the contract of a method, and this contract must be upheld whether assertions are enabled or disabled.

Another problem with using assertions for argument checking is that erroneous arguments should result in an appropriate runtime exception (such as `IllegalArgumentException`, `IndexOutOfBoundsException` or `NullPointerException`). An assertion failure will not throw an appropriate exception. Again, it is not illegal to use assertions for argument checking on public methods, but it is generally inappropriate. It is intended that `AssertionError` never be caught, but it is possible to do so, thus the rules for `try` statements should treat assertions appearing in a `try` block similarly to the current treatment of throw statements.

14.11 The `switch` Statement

Fetch me a dozen crab-tree staves, and strong ones: these are but switches . . .
—William Shakespeare, *Henry VIII* (1623), Act V, scene iv

The `switch` statement transfers control to one of several statements depending on the value of an expression.

SwitchStatement:
  `switch (` *Expression* `)` *SwitchBlock*

SwitchBlock:
  `{` *SwitchBlockStatementGroups*$_{opt}$ *SwitchLabels*$_{opt}$ `}`

SwitchBlockStatementGroups:
  SwitchBlockStatementGroup
  SwitchBlockStatementGroups SwitchBlockStatementGroup

SwitchBlockStatementGroup:
  SwitchLabels BlockStatements

SwitchLabels:
  SwitchLabel
  SwitchLabels SwitchLabel

SwitchLabel:
  `case` *ConstantExpression* `:`
  `case` *EnumConstantName* `:`
  `default :`

EnumConstantName:
  Identifier

The type of the *Expression* must be `char`, `byte`, `short`, `int`, `Character`, `Byte`, `Short`, `Integer`, or an enum type (§8.9), or a compile-time error occurs.

The body of a `switch` statement is known as a *switch block*. Any statement immediately contained by the switch block may be labeled with one or more `case` or `default` labels. These labels are said to be *associated* with the `switch` statement, as are the values of the constant expressions (§15.28) in the `case` labels.

All of the following must be true, or a compile-time error will result:

- Every `case` constant expression associated with a `switch` statement must be assignable (§5.2) to the type of the `switch` *Expression*.
- No switch label is `null`.

- No two of the `case` constant expressions associated with a `switch` statement may have the same value.
- At most one `default` label may be associated with the same `switch` statement.

DISCUSSION

The prohibition against using null as a switch label prevents one from writing code that can never be executed. If the switch expression is of a reference type, such as a boxed primitive type or an enum, a run-time error will occur if the expression evaluates to null at run-time.

It follows that if the switch expression is of an enum type, the possible values of the switch labels must all be enum constants of that type.

Compilers are encouraged (but not required) to provide a warning if a switch on an enum-valued expression lacks a default case and lacks cases for one or more of the enum type's constants. (Such a statement will silently do nothing if the expression evaluates to one of the missing constants.)

In C and C++ the body of a `switch` statement can be a statement and statements with `case` labels do not have to be immediately contained by that statement. Consider the simple loop:

```
for (i = 0; i < n; ++i) foo();
```

where `n` is known to be positive. A trick known as *Duff's device* can be used in C or C++ to unroll the loop, but this is not valid code in the Java programming language:

```
int q = (n+7)/8;
switch (n%8) {
case 0:   do {foo();          // Great C hack, Tom,
case 7:        foo();          // but it's not valid here.
case 6:        foo();
case 5:        foo();
case 4:        foo();
case 3:        foo();
case 2:        foo();
case 1:        foo();
            } while (--q > 0);
}
```

Fortunately, this trick does not seem to be widely known or used. Moreover, it is less needed nowadays; this sort of code transformation is properly in the province of state-of-the-art optimizing compilers.

When the `switch` statement is executed, first the *Expression* is evaluated. If the *Expression* evaluates to `null`, a `NullPointerException` is thrown and the entire `switch` statement completes abruptly for that reason. Otherwise, if the result is of a reference type, it is subject to unboxing conversion (§5.1.8). If evaluation of the *Expression* or the subsequent unboxing conversion (if any) completes abruptly for some reason, the `switch` statement completes abruptly for the same reason. Otherwise, execution continues by comparing the value of the *Expression* with each `case` constant. Then there is a choice:

- If one of the `case` constants is equal to the value of the expression, then we say that the `case` matches, and all statements after the matching `case` label in the switch block, if any, are executed in sequence. If all these statements complete normally, or if there are no statements after the matching `case` label, then the entire `switch` statement completes normally.
- If no `case` matches but there is a `default` label, then all statements after the matching `default` label in the switch block, if any, are executed in sequence. If all these statements complete normally, or if there are no statements after the `default` label, then the entire `switch` statement completes normally.
- If no `case` matches and there is no `default` label, then no further action is taken and the `switch` statement completes normally.

If any statement immediately contained by the *Block* body of the `switch` statement completes abruptly, it is handled as follows:

- If execution of the *Statement* completes abruptly because of a `break` with no label, no further action is taken and the `switch` statement completes normally.
- If execution of the *Statement* completes abruptly for any other reason, the `switch` statement completes abruptly for the same reason. The case of abrupt completion because of a `break` with a label is handled by the general rule for labeled statements (§14.7).

As in C and C++, execution of statements in a switch block "falls through labels."

For example, the program:

```
class Toomany {
    static void howMany(int k) {
        switch (k) {
        case 1:System.out.print("one ");
        case 2:System.out.print("too ");
        case 3:System.out.println("many");
```

```
        }
    }

    public static void main(String[] args) {
        howMany(3);
        howMany(2);
        howMany(1);
    }
}
```

contains a switch block in which the code for each case falls through into the code for the next case. As a result, the program prints:

```
many
too many
one too many
```

If code is not to fall through case to case in this manner, then `break` statements should be used, as in this example:

```
class Twomany {
    static void howMany(int k) {
        switch (k) {
        case 1:System.out.println("one");
               break;          // exit the switch
        case 2:System.out.println("two");
               break;          // exit the switch
        case 3:System.out.println("many");
               break;          // not needed, but good style
        }
    }

    public static void main(String[] args) {
        howMany(1);
        howMany(2);
        howMany(3);
    }
}
```

This program prints:

```
one
two
many
```

14.12 The `while` Statement

The `while` statement executes an *Expression* and a *Statement* repeatedly until the value of the *Expression* is `false`.

WhileStatement:
    `while ( ` *Expression* ` ) ` *Statement*

WhileStatementNoShortIf:
    `while ( ` *Expression* ` ) ` *StatementNoShortIf*

The *Expression* must have type `boolean` or `Boolean`, or a compile-time error occurs.

A `while` statement is executed by first evaluating the *Expression*. If the result is of type `Boolean`, it is subject to unboxing conversion (§5.1.8). If evaluation of the *Expression* or the subsequent unboxing conversion (if any) completes abruptly for some reason, the `while` statement completes abruptly for the same reason. Otherwise, execution continues by making a choice based on the resulting value:

- If the value is `true`, then the contained *Statement* is executed. Then there is a choice:
    - If execution of the *Statement* completes normally, then the entire `while` statement is executed again, beginning by re-evaluating the *Expression*.
    - If execution of the *Statement* completes abruptly, see §14.12.1 below.
- If the (possibly unboxed) value of the *Expression* is `false`, no further action is taken and the `while` statement completes normally.

If the (possibly unboxed) value of the *Expression* is `false` the first time it is evaluated, then the *Statement* is not executed.

14.12.1 Abrupt Completion

Abrupt completion of the contained *Statement* is handled in the following manner:

- If execution of the *Statement* completes abruptly because of a `break` with no label, no further action is taken and the `while` statement completes normally.
    - If execution of the *Statement* completes abruptly because of a `continue` with no label, then the entire `while` statement is executed again.
    - If execution of the *Statement* completes abruptly because of a `continue` with label `L`, then there is a choice:
        - If the `while` statement has label `L`, then the entire `while` statement is executed again.
        - If the `while` statement does not have label `L`, the `while` statement completes abruptly because of a `continue` with label `L`.

- If execution of the *Statement* completes abruptly for any other reason, the `while` statement completes abruptly for the same reason. Note that the case of abrupt completion because of a `break` with a label is handled by the general rule for labeled statements (§14.7).

14.13 The do Statement

"She would not see it," he said at last, curtly,
feeling at first that this statement must do without explanation.
—George Eliot, *Middlemarch* (1871), Chapter 76

The `do` statement executes a *Statement* and an *Expression* repeatedly until the value of the *Expression* is `false`.

DoStatement:
  `do` *Statement* `while (` *Expression* `) ;`

The *Expression* must have type `boolean` or `Boolean`, or a compile-time error occurs.

A `do` statement is executed by first executing the *Statement*. Then there is a choice:

- If execution of the *Statement* completes normally, then the *Expression* is evaluated. If the result is of type `Boolean`, it is subject to unboxing conversion (§5.1.8). If evaluation of the *Expression* or the subsequent unboxing conversion (if any) completes abruptly for some reason, the `do` statement completes abruptly for the same reason. Otherwise, there is a choice based on the resulting value:
  - If the value is `true`, then the entire `do` statement is executed again.
  - If the value is `false`, no further action is taken and the `do` statement completes normally.
- If execution of the *Statement* completes abruptly, see §14.13.1 below.

Executing a `do` statement always executes the contained *Statement* at least once.

14.13.1 Abrupt Completion

Abrupt completion of the contained *Statement* is handled in the following manner:

- If execution of the *Statement* completes abruptly because of a `break` with no label, then no further action is taken and the `do` statement completes normally.
- If execution of the *Statement* completes abruptly because of a `continue` with no label, then the *Expression* is evaluated. Then there is a choice based on the resulting value:
  - If the value is `true`, then the entire `do` statement is executed again.
  - If the value is `false`, no further action is taken and the `do` statement completes normally.
- If execution of the *Statement* completes abruptly because of a `continue` with label `L`, then there is a choice:
  - If the `do` statement has label `L`, then the *Expression* is evaluated. Then there is a choice:
    - If the value of the *Expression* is `true`, then the entire `do` statement is executed again.
    - If the value of the *Expression* is `false`, no further action is taken and the `do` statement completes normally.
  - If the `do` statement does not have label `L`, the `do` statement completes abruptly because of a `continue` with label `L`.
- If execution of the *Statement* completes abruptly for any other reason, the `do` statement completes abruptly for the same reason. The case of abrupt completion because of a `break` with a label is handled by the general rule (§14.7).

14.13.2 Example of do statement

The following code is one possible implementation of the `toHexString` method of class `Integer`:

```
public static String toHexString(int i) {
    StringBuffer buf = new StringBuffer(8);
    do {
        buf.append(Character.forDigit(i & 0xF, 16));
        i >>>= 4;
    } while (i != 0);
    return buf.reverse().toString();
}
```

Because at least one digit must be generated, the do statement is an appropriate control structure.

14.14 The for Statement

ForStatement:
  BasicForStatement
  EnhancedForStatement

The `for` statement has two forms:

- The basic `for` statement.
- The enhanced `for` statement

14.14.1 The basic for Statement

The basic for statement executes some initialization code, then executes an *Expression*, a *Statement*, and some update code repeatedly until the value of the *Expression* is `false`.

BasicForStatement:
  `for (` $ForInit_{opt}$ `;` $Expression_{opt}$ `;` $ForUpdate_{opt}$ `)` *Statement*

ForStatementNoShortIf:
  `for (` $ForInit_{opt}$ `;` $Expression_{opt}$ `;` $ForUpdate_{opt}$ `)`
   StatementNoShortIf

ForInit:
  StatementExpressionList
  LocalVariableDeclaration

ForUpdate:
  StatementExpressionList

StatementExpressionList:
  StatementExpression
  StatementExpressionList , *StatementExpression*

The *Expression* must have type `boolean` or `Boolean`, or a compile-time error occurs.

14.14.1.1 *Initialization of `for` statement*

A `for` statement is executed by first executing the *ForInit* code:

- If the *ForInit* code is a list of statement expressions (§14.8), the expressions are evaluated in sequence from left to right; their values, if any, are discarded. If evaluation of any expression completes abruptly for some reason, the `for` statement completes abruptly for the same reason; any *ForInit* statement expressions to the right of the one that completed abruptly are not evaluated.

If the *ForInit* code is a local variable declaration, it is executed as if it were a local variable declaration statement (§14.4) appearing in a block. The scope of a local variable declared in the *ForInit* part of a basic `for` statement (§14.14) includes all of the following:

- Its own initializer
- Any further declarators to the right in the *ForInit* part of the `for` statement
- The *Expression* and *ForUpdate* parts of the `for` statement
- The contained *Statement*

If execution of the local variable declaration completes abruptly for any reason, the `for` statement completes abruptly for the same reason.

- If the *ForInit* part is not present, no action is taken.

14.14.1.2 *Iteration of `for` statement*

Next, a `for` iteration step is performed, as follows:

- If the *Expression* is present, it is evaluated. If the result is of type `Boolean`, it is subject to unboxing conversion (§5.1.8). If evaluation of the *Expression* or the subsequent unboxing conversion (if any) completes abruptly, the `for` statement completes abruptly for the same reason. Otherwise, there is then a choice based on the presence or absence of the *Expression* and the resulting value if the *Expression* is present:
  - If the *Expression* is not present, or it is present and the value resulting from its evaluation (including any possible unboxing) is `true`, then the contained *Statement* is executed. Then there is a choice:
    - If execution of the *Statement* completes normally, then the following two steps are performed in sequence:

- First, if the *ForUpdate* part is present, the expressions are evaluated in sequence from left to right; their values, if any, are discarded. If evaluation of any expression completes abruptly for some reason, the `for` statement completes abruptly for the same reason; any *ForUpdate* statement expressions to the right of the one that completed abruptly are not evaluated. If the *ForUpdate* part is not present, no action is taken.
- Second, another `for` iteration step is performed.

- If execution of the *Statement* completes abruptly, see §14.14.1.3 below.

- If the *Expression* is present and the value resulting from its evaluation (including any possible unboxing) is `false`, no further action is taken and the `for` statement completes normally.

If the (possibly unboxed) value of the *Expression* is `false` the first time it is evaluated, then the *Statement* is not executed.

If the *Expression* is not present, then the only way a `for` statement can complete normally is by use of a `break` statement.

14.14.1.3 *Abrupt Completion of* `for` *statement*

Abrupt completion of the contained *Statement* is handled in the following manner:

- If execution of the *Statement* completes abruptly because of a `break` with no label, no further action is taken and the `for` statement completes normally.
- If execution of the *Statement* completes abruptly because of a `continue` with no label, then the following two steps are performed in sequence:
  - First, if the *ForUpdate* part is present, the expressions are evaluated in sequence from left to right; their values, if any, are discarded. If the *ForUpdate* part is not present, no action is taken.
  - Second, another `for` iteration step is performed.
- If execution of the *Statement* completes abruptly because of a `continue` with label `L`, then there is a choice:
  - If the `for` statement has label `L`, then the following two steps are performed in sequence:
    - First, if the *ForUpdate* part is present, the expressions are evaluated in sequence from left to right; their values, if any, are discarded. If the *ForUpdate* is not present, no action is taken.
    - Second, another `for` iteration step is performed.

- If the `for` statement does not have label *L*, the `for` statement completes abruptly because of a `continue` with label *L*.

- If execution of the *Statement* completes abruptly for any other reason, the `for` statement completes abruptly for the same reason. Note that the case of abrupt completion because of a `break` with a label is handled by the general rule for labeled statements (§14.7).

14.14.2 The enhanced for statement

The enhanced `for` statement has the form:

EnhancedForStatement:
    `for (` *VariableModifiers_{opt} Type Identifier*`:` *Expression*`)` *Statement*

The *Expression* must either have type `Iterable` or else it must be of an array type (§10.1), or a compile-time error occurs.

The scope of a local variable declared in the *FormalParameter* part of an enhanced `for` statement (§14.14) is the contained *Statement*

The meaning of the enhanced `for` statement is given by translation into a basic `for` statement.

If the type of *Expression* is a subtype of `Iterable`, then let I be the type of the expression *Expression*.`iterator()`. The enhanced `for` statement is equivalent to a basic `for` statement of the form:

```
for (I #i = Expression.iterator(); #i.hasNext(); ) {
    VariableModifiersopt Type Identifier = #i.next();
    Statement
}
```

Where *#i* is a compiler-generated identifier that is distinct from any other identifiers (compiler-generated or otherwise) that are in scope (§6.3) at the point where the enhanced `for` statement occurs.

Otherwise, the *Expression* necessarily has an array type, *T[]*. Let L_1 ... L_m be the (possibly empty) sequence of labels immediately preceding the enhanced `for` statement. Then the meaning of the enhanced `for` statement is given by the following basic `for` statement:

```
T[] a = Expression;
L1: L2: ... Lm:
for (int i = 0; i < a.length; i++) {
    VariableModifiersopt Type Identifier = a[i];
    Statement
}
```

Where *a* and *i* are compiler-generated identifiers that are distinct from any other identifiers (compiler-generated or otherwise) that are in scope at the point where the enhanced `for` statement occurs.

DISCUSSION

The following example, which calculates the sum of an integer array, shows how enhanced for works for arrays:

```
int sum(int[] a) {
    int sum = 0;
    for (int i : a)
        sum += i;
    return sum;
}
```

Here is an example that combines the enhanced for statement with auto-unboxing to translate a histogram into a frequency table:

```
Map<String, Integer> histogram = ...;
double total = 0;
for (int i : histogram.values())
    total += i;
for (Map.Entry<String, Integer> e : histogram.entrySet())
    System.out.println(e.getKey() + "" + e.getValue() / total);
```

14.15 The break Statement

A break statement transfers control out of an enclosing statement.

BreakStatement:
    `break` *Identifier*$_{opt}$ `;`

A `break` statement with no label attempts to transfer control to the innermost enclosing `switch`, `while`, `do`, or `for` statement of the immediately enclosing method or initializer block; this statement, which is called the *break target*, then immediately completes normally.

To be precise, a `break` statement with no label always completes abruptly, the reason being a `break` with no label. If no `switch`, `while`, `do`, or `for` statement in the immediately enclosing method, constructor or initializer encloses the `break` statement, a compile-time error occurs.

A `break` statement with label *Identifier* attempts to transfer control to the enclosing labeled statement (§14.7) that has the same *Identifier* as its label; this statement, which is called the *break target*, then immediately completes normally. In this case, the `break` target need not be a `while`, `do`, `for`, or `switch` statement. A `break` statement must refer to a label within the immediately enclosing method or initializer block. There are no non-local jumps.

To be precise, a `break` statement with label *Identifier* always completes abruptly, the reason being a `break` with label *Identifier*. If no labeled statement with *Identifier* as its label encloses the `break` statement, a compile-time error occurs.

It can be seen, then, that a `break` statement always completes abruptly.

The preceding descriptions say "attempts to transfer control" rather than just "transfers control" because if there are any `try` statements (§14.20) within the break target whose `try` blocks contain the `break` statement, then any `finally` clauses of those `try` statements are executed, in order, innermost to outermost, before control is transferred to the break target. Abrupt completion of a `finally` clause can disrupt the transfer of control initiated by a `break` statement.

In the following example, a mathematical graph is represented by an array of arrays. A graph consists of a set of nodes and a set of edges; each edge is an arrow that points from some node to some other node, or from a node to itself. In this example it is assumed that there are no redundant edges; that is, for any two nodes `P` and `Q`, where `Q` may be the same as `P`, there is at most one edge from `P` to `Q`. Nodes are represented by integers, and there is an edge from node `i` to node `edges[i][j]` for every `i` and `j` for which the array reference `edges[i][j]` does not throw an `IndexOutOfBoundsException`.

The task of the method `loseEdges`, given integers `i` and `j`, is to construct a new graph by copying a given graph but omitting the edge from node `i` to node `j`, if any, and the edge from node `j` to node `i`, if any:

```
class Graph {
    int edges[][];
            public Graph(int[][] edges) { this.edges = edges;
}
    public Graph loseEdges(int i, int j) {
        int n = edges.length;
        int[][] newedges = new int[n][];
        for (int k = 0; k < n; ++k) {
            edgelist: {
              int z;
              search: {
                if (k == i) {
                    for (z = 0; z < edges[k].length; ++z)
                        if (edges[k][z] == j)
                            break search;
                } else if (k == j) {
```

```
                    for (z = 0; z < edges[k].length; ++z)
                        if (edges[k][z] == i)
                            break search;
                }
                // No edge to be deleted; share this list.
                newedges[k] = edges[k];
                break edgelist;
                } //search
            // Copy the list, omitting the edge at position z.
            int m = edges[k].length - 1;
            int ne[] = new int[m];
            System.arraycopy(edges[k], 0, ne, 0, z);
            System.arraycopy(edges[k], z+1, ne, z, m-z);
            newedges[k] = ne;
          } //edgelist
        }
        return new Graph(newedges);
    }
}
```

Note the use of two statement labels, `edgelist` and `search`, and the use of `break` statements. This allows the code that copies a list, omitting one edge, to be shared between two separate tests, the test for an edge from node `i` to node `j`, and the test for an edge from node `j` to node `i`.

14.16 The `continue` Statement

"Your experience has been a most entertaining one," remarked Holmes as his client paused and refreshed his memory with a huge pinch of snuff. "Pray continue your very interesting statement."
—Sir Arthur Conan Doyle, *The Red-headed League* (1891)

A `continue` statement may occur only in a `while`, do, or `for` statement; statements of these three kinds are called *iteration statements*. Control passes to the loop-continuation point of an iteration statement.

ContinueStatement:
  `continue` $Identifier_{opt}$ `;`

A `continue` statement with no label attempts to transfer control to the innermost enclosing `while`, do, or `for` statement of the immediately enclosing method *or initializer block*; this statement, which is called the *continue target*, then immediately ends the current iteration and begins a new one.

To be precise, such a `continue` statement always completes abruptly, the reason being a `continue` with no label. If no `while`, `do`, or `for` statement of the immediately enclosing method or initializer block encloses the `continue` statement, a compile-time error occurs.

A `continue` statement with label *Identifier* attempts to transfer control to the enclosing labeled statement (§14.7) that has the same *Identifier* as its label; that statement, which is called the *continue target*, then immediately ends the current iteration and begins a new one. The continue target must be a `while`, `do`, or `for` statement or a compile-time error occurs. A `continue` statement must refer to a label within the immediately enclosing method or initializer block. There are no non-local jumps.

More precisely, a `continue` statement with label *Identifier* always completes abruptly, the reason being a `continue` with label *Identifier*. If no labeled statement with *Identifier* as its label contains the `continue` statement, a compile-time error occurs.

It can be seen, then, that a `continue` statement always completes abruptly.

See the descriptions of the `while` statement (§14.12), `do` statement (§14.13), and `for` statement (§14.14) for a discussion of the handling of abrupt termination because of `continue`.

The preceding descriptions say "attempts to transfer control" rather than just "transfers control" because if there are any `try` statements (§14.20) within the continue target whose `try` blocks contain the `continue` statement, then any `finally` clauses of those `try` statements are executed, in order, innermost to outermost, before control is transferred to the continue target. Abrupt completion of a `finally` clause can disrupt the transfer of control initiated by a `continue` statement.

In the `Graph` example in the preceding section, one of the `break` statements is used to finish execution of the entire body of the outermost `for` loop. This `break` can be replaced by a `continue` if the `for` loop itself is labeled:

```
class Graph {
    ...
    public Graph loseEdges(int i, int j) {
        int n = edges.length;
        int[][] newedges = new int[n][];
        edgelists: for (int k = 0; k < n; ++k) {
            int z;
            search: {
              if (k == i) {
                ...
              } else if (k == j) {
```

```
                ...
            }
            newedges[k] = edges[k];
            continue edgelists;
        } // search
        ...
    } // edgelists
    return new Graph(newedges);
  }
}
```

Which to use, if either, is largely a matter of programming style.

14.17 The `return` Statement

"Know you, O judges and people of Helium," he said, "that John Carter, one time Prince of Helium, has returned by his own statement from the Valley Dor . . ."
—Edgar Rice Burroughs, *The Gods of Mars* (1913)

A `return` statement returns control to the invoker of a method (§8.4, §15.12) or constructor (§8.8, §15.9).

ReturnStatement:
`return` *Expression*$_{opt}$ `;`

A `return` statement with no *Expression* must be contained in the body of a method that is declared, using the keyword `void`, not to return any value (§8.4), or in the body of a constructor (§8.8). A compile-time error occurs if a `return` statement appears within an instance initializer or a static initializer (§8.7). A `return` statement with no *Expression* attempts to transfer control to the invoker of the method or constructor that contains it.

To be precise, a `return` statement with no *Expression* always completes abruptly, the reason being a `return` with no value.

A `return` statement with an *Expression* must be contained in a method declaration that is declared to return a value (§8.4) or a compile-time error occurs. The *Expression* must denote a variable or value of some type *T*, or a compile-time error occurs. The type *T* must be assignable (§5.2) to the declared result type of the method, or a compile-time error occurs.

A `return` statement with an *Expression* attempts to transfer control to the invoker of the method that contains it; the value of the *Expression* becomes the value of the method invocation. More precisely, execution of such a `return` statement first evaluates the *Expression*. If the evaluation of the *Expression* completes abruptly for some reason, then the `return` statement completes abruptly for that reason. If evaluation of the *Expression* completes normally, producing a value `V`, then the `return` statement completes abruptly, the reason being a `return` with value `V`. If the expression is of type `float` and is not FP-strict (§15.4), then the value may be an element of either the float value set or the float-extended-exponent value set (§4.2.3). If the expression is of type `double` and is not FP-strict, then the value may be an element of either the double value set or the double-extended-exponent value set.

It can be seen, then, that a `return` statement always completes abruptly.

The preceding descriptions say "attempts to transfer control" rather than just "transfers control" because if there are any `try` statements (§14.20) within the method or constructor whose `try` blocks contain the `return` statement, then any `finally` clauses of those `try` statements will be executed, in order, innermost to outermost, before control is transferred to the invoker of the method or constructor. Abrupt completion of a `finally` clause can disrupt the transfer of control initiated by a `return` statement.

14.18 The `throw` Statement

A `throw` statement causes an exception (§11) to be thrown. The result is an immediate transfer of control (§11.3) that may exit multiple statements and multiple constructor, instance initializer, static initializer and field initializer evaluations, and method invocations until a `try` statement (§14.20) is found that catches the thrown value. If no such `try` statement is found, then execution of the thread (§17) that executed the `throw` is terminated (§11.3) after invocation of the `uncaughtException` method for the thread group to which the thread belongs.

ThrowStatement:
  `throw` *Expression* `;`

A throw statement can throw an exception type `E` iff the static type of the throw expression is `E` or a subtype of `E`, or the thrown expression can throw `E`.

The *Expression* in a throw statement must denote a variable or value of a reference type which is assignable (§5.2) to the type `Throwable`, or a compile-time error occurs. Moreover, at least one of the following three conditions must be true, or a compile-time error occurs:

- The exception is not a checked exception (§11.2)—specifically, one of the following situations is true:
  - The type of the *Expression* is the class `RuntimeException` or a subclass of `RuntimeException`.

    - The type of the *Expression* is the class `Error` or a subclass of `Error`.

- The `throw` statement is contained in the `try` block of a `try` statement (§14.20) and the type of the *Expression* is assignable (§5.2) to the type of the parameter of at least one `catch` clause of the `try` statement. (In this case we say the thrown value is *caught* by the `try` statement.)
- The `throw` statement is contained in a method or constructor declaration and the type of the *Expression* is assignable (§5.2) to at least one type listed in the `throws` clause (§8.4.6, §8.8.5) of the declaration.

A `throw` statement first evaluates the *Expression*. If the evaluation of the *Expression* completes abruptly for some reason, then the `throw` completes abruptly for that reason. If evaluation of the *Expression* completes normally, producing a non-`null` value *V*, then the `throw` statement completes abruptly, the reason being a `throw` with value *V*. If evaluation of the *Expression* completes normally, producing a `null` value, then an instance *V'* of class `NullPointerException` is created and thrown instead of `null`. The `throw` statement then completes abruptly, the reason being a `throw` with value *V'*.

It can be seen, then, that a `throw` statement always completes abruptly.

If there are any enclosing `try` statements (§14.20) whose `try` blocks contain the `throw` statement, then any `finally` clauses of those `try` statements are executed as control is transferred outward, until the thrown value is caught. Note that abrupt completion of a `finally` clause can disrupt the transfer of control initiated by a `throw` statement.

If a `throw` statement is contained in a method declaration, but its value is not caught by some `try` statement that contains it, then the invocation of the method completes abruptly because of the `throw`.

If a `throw` statement is contained in a constructor declaration, but its value is not caught by some `try` statement that contains it, then the class instance creation expression that invoked the constructor will complete abruptly because of the `throw`.

If a `throw` statement is contained in a static initializer (§8.7), then a compile-time check ensures that either its value is always an unchecked exception or its value is always caught by some `try` statement that contains it. If at run-time, despite this check, the value is not caught by some `try` statement that contains the `throw` statement, then the value is rethrown if it is an instance of class `Error` or one of its subclasses; otherwise, it is wrapped in an `ExceptionInInitializerError` object, which is then thrown (§12.4.2).

If a `throw` statement is contained in an instance initializer (§8.6), then a compile-time check ensures that either its value is always an unchecked exception or its value is always caught by some `try` statement that contains it, or the type of the thrown exception (or one of its superclasses) occurs in the `throws` *clause of every* constructor of the class.

By convention, user-declared throwable types should usually be declared to be subclasses of class `Exception`, which is a subclass of class `Throwable` (§11.5).

14.19 The `synchronized` Statement

A `synchronized` statement acquires a mutual-exclusion lock (§17.1) on behalf of the executing thread, executes a block, then releases the lock. While the executing thread owns the lock, no other thread may acquire the lock.

SynchronizedStatement:
    `synchronized (` *Expression* `)` *Block*

The type of *Expression* must be a reference type, or a compile-time error occurs.

A `synchronized` statement is executed by first evaluating the *Expression*.

If evaluation of the *Expression* completes abruptly for some reason, then the `synchronized` statement completes abruptly for the same reason.

Otherwise, if the value of the *Expression* is `null`, a `NullPointerException` is thrown.

Otherwise, let the non-`null` value of the *Expression* be *V*. The executing thread locks the lock associated with *V*. Then the *Block* is executed. If execution of the *Block* completes normally, then the lock is unlocked and the `synchronized` statement completes normally. If execution of the *Block* completes abruptly for any reason, then the lock is unlocked and the `synchronized` statement then completes abruptly for the same reason.

Acquiring the lock associated with an object does not of itself prevent other threads from accessing fields of the object or invoking unsynchronized methods on the object. Other threads can also use `synchronized` methods or the `synchronized` statement in a conventional manner to achieve mutual exclusion.

The locks acquired by `synchronized` statements are the same as the locks that are acquired implicitly by `synchronized` methods; see §8.4.3.6. A single thread may hold a lock more than once.

The example:

```
class Test {
    public static void main(String[] args) {
        Test t = new Test();
```

```
            synchronized(t) {
                synchronized(t) {
                    System.out.println("made it!");
                }
            }
        }
    }
```

prints:

```
    made it!
```

This example would deadlock if a single thread were not permitted to lock a lock more than once.

14.20 The `try` statement

These are the times that try men's souls.
—Thomas Paine, *The American Crisis* (1780)

. . . and they all fell to playing the game of catch as catch can, till the gunpowder ran out at the heels of their boots.
—Samuel Foote

A `try` statement executes a block. If a value is thrown and the `try` statement has one or more `catch` clauses that can catch it, then control will be transferred to the first such `catch` clause. If the `try` statement has a `finally` clause, then another block of code is executed, no matter whether the `try` block completes normally or abruptly, and no matter whether a `catch` clause is first given control.

TryStatement:
  `try` *Block Catches*
  `try` *Block* $Catches_{opt}$ *Finally*

Catches:
  CatchClause
  Catches CatchClause

CatchClause:
  `catch (` *FormalParameter* `)` *Block*

Finally:
  `finally` *Block*

The following is repeated from §8.4.1 to make the presentation here clearer:

FormalParameter:
VariableModifiers Type VariableDeclaratorId

The following is repeated from §8.3 to make the presentation here clearer:

VariableDeclaratorId:
Identifier
VariableDeclaratorId `[ ]`

The *Block* immediately after the keyword `try` is called the `try` block of the `try` statement. The *Block* immediately after the keyword `finally` is called the `finally` block of the `try` statement.

A `try` statement may have `catch` clauses (also called *exception handlers*). A `catch` clause must have exactly one parameter (which is called an *exception parameter*); the declared type of the exception parameter must be the class `Throwable` or a subclass (not just a subtype) of `Throwable`, or a compile-time error occurs.In particular, it is a compile-time error if the declared type of the exception parameter is a type variable (§4.4). The scope of the parameter variable is the *Block* of the `catch` clause.

An exception parameter of a catch clause must not have the same name as a local variable or parameter of the method or initializer block immediately enclosing the catch clause, or a compile-time error occurs.

The scope of a parameter of an exception handler that is declared in a `catch` clause of a `try` statement (§14.20) is the entire block associated with the `catch`. Within the *Block* of the `catch` clause, the name of the parameter may not be redeclared as a local variable of the directly enclosing method or initializer block, nor may it be redeclared as an exception parameter of a catch clause in a try statement of the directly enclosing method or initializer block, or a compile-time error occurs. However, an exception parameter may be shadowed (§6.3.1) anywhere inside a class declaration nested within the *Block* of the `catch` clause.

A `try` statement can throw an exception type `E` iff either:

- The `try` block can throw `E` and `E` is not assignable to any `catch` parameter of the `try` statement and either no `finally` block is present or the `finally` block can complete normally; or
- Some `catch` block of the `try` statement can throw `E` and either no `finally` block is present or the `finally` block can complete normally; or
- A `finally` block is present and can throw `E`.

It is a compile-time error if an exception parameter that is declared `final` is assigned to within the body of the catch clause.

It is a compile-time error if a `catch` clause catches checked exception type *E1* but there exists no checked exception type *E2* such that all of the following hold:

- *E2* <: *E1*
- The `try` block corresponding to the `catch` clause can throw *E2*
- No preceding `catch` block of the immediately enclosing `try` statement catches *E2* or a supertype of *E2*.

unless *E1* is the class `Exception`.

Exception parameters cannot be referred to using qualified names (§6.6), only by simple names.

Exception handlers are considered in left-to-right order: the earliest possible `catch` clause accepts the exception, receiving as its actual argument the thrown exception object.

A `finally` clause ensures that the `finally` block is executed after the `try` block and any `catch` block that might be executed, no matter how control leaves the `try` block or `catch` block.

Handling of the `finally` block is rather complex, so the two cases of a `try` statement with and without a `finally` block are described separately.

14.20.1 Execution of `try–catch`

Our supreme task is the resumption of our onward, normal way.
—Warren G. Harding, Inaugural Address (1921)

A `try` statement without a `finally` block is executed by first executing the `try` block. Then there is a choice:

- If execution of the `try` block completes normally, then no further action is taken and the `try` statement completes normally.
- If execution of the `try` block completes abruptly because of a `throw` of a value *V*, then there is a choice:
  - If the run-time type of *V* is assignable (§5.2) to the *Parameter* of any `catch` clause of the `try` statement, then the first (leftmost) such `catch` clause is selected. The value *V* is assigned to the parameter of the selected `catch` clause, and the *Block* of that `catch` clause is executed. If that block completes normally, then the `try` statement completes normally; if that block

completes abruptly for any reason, then the `try` statement completes abruptly for the same reason.

- If the run-time type of *V* is not assignable to the parameter of any `catch` clause of the `try` statement, then the `try` statement completes abruptly because of a `throw` of the value *V*.

- If execution of the `try` block completes abruptly for any other reason, then the `try` statement completes abruptly for the same reason.

In the example:

```
class BlewIt extends Exception {
            BlewIt() { }
            BlewIt(String s) { super(s); }
}
class Test {
    static void blowUp() throws BlewIt { throw new BlewIt(); }
    public static void main(String[] args) {
        try {
            blowUp();
        } catch (RuntimeException r) {
            System.out.println("RuntimeException:" + r);
        } catch (BlewIt b) {
            System.out.println("BlewIt");
        }
    }
}
```

the exception `BlewIt` is thrown by the method `blowUp`. The `try–catch` statement in the body of `main` has two `catch` clauses. The run-time type of the exception is `BlewIt` which is not assignable to a variable of type `RuntimeException`, but is assignable to a variable of type `BlewIt`, so the output of the example is:

```
BlewIt
```

14.20.2 Execution of `try–catch–finally`

After the great captains and engineers have accomplish'd their work,
After the noble inventors—after the scientists, the chemist,
the geologist, ethnologist,
Finally shall come the Poet . . .
—Walt Whitman, *Passage to India* (1870)

A `try` statement with a `finally` block is executed by first executing the `try` block. Then there is a choice:

- If execution of the `try` block completes normally, then the `finally` block is executed, and then there is a choice:
  - If the `finally` block completes normally, then the `try` statement completes normally.
  - If the `finally` block completes abruptly for reason *S*, then the `try` statement completes abruptly for reason *S*.
- If execution of the `try` block completes abruptly because of a `throw` of a value *V*, then there is a choice:
  - If the run-time type of *V* is assignable to the parameter of any `catch` clause of the `try` statement, then the first (leftmost) such `catch` clause is selected. The value *V* is assigned to the parameter of the selected `catch` clause, and the *Block* of that `catch` clause is executed. Then there is a choice:
    - If the `catch` block completes normally, then the `finally` block is executed. Then there is a choice:
      - If the `finally` block completes normally, then the `try` statement completes normally.
      - If the `finally` block completes abruptly for any reason, then the `try` statement completes abruptly for the same reason.
    - If the `catch` block completes abruptly for reason *R*, then the `finally` block is executed. Then there is a choice:
      - If the `finally` block completes normally, then the `try` statement completes abruptly for reason *R*.
      - If the `finally` block completes abruptly for reason *S*, then the `try` statement completes abruptly for reason *S* (and reason *R* is discarded).
  - If the run-time type of *V* is not assignable to the parameter of any `catch` clause of the `try` statement, then the `finally` block is executed. Then there is a choice:
    - If the `finally` block completes normally, then the `try` statement completes abruptly because of a `throw` of the value *V*.
    - If the `finally` block completes abruptly for reason *S*, then the `try` statement completes abruptly for reason *S* (and the `throw` of value *V* is discarded and forgotten).
- If execution of the `try` block completes abruptly for any other reason *R*, then the `finally` block is executed. Then there is a choice:

- If the `finally` block completes normally, then the `try` statement completes abruptly for reason *R*.
- If the `finally` block completes abruptly for reason *S*, then the `try` statement completes abruptly for reason *S* (and reason *R* is discarded).

The example:

```
class BlewIt extends Exception {
            BlewIt() { }
            BlewIt(String s) { super(s); }
}
class Test {
    static void blowUp() throws BlewIt {
        throw new NullPointerException();
    }
    public static void main(String[] args) {
        try {
            blowUp();
        } catch (BlewIt b) {
            System.out.println("BlewIt");
        } finally {
            System.out.println("Uncaught Exception");
        }
    }
}
```

produces the output:

```
Uncaught Exception
java.lang.NullPointerException
    at Test.blowUp(Test.java:7)
    at Test.main(Test.java:11)
```

The `NullPointerException` (which is a kind of `RuntimeException`) that is thrown by method `blowUp` is not caught by the `try` statement in `main`, because a `NullPointerException` is not assignable to a variable of type `BlewIt`. This causes the `finally` clause to execute, after which the thread executing `main`, which is the only thread of the test program, terminates because of an uncaught exception, which typically results in printing the exception name and a simple backtrace. However, a backtrace is not required by this specification.

DISCUSSION

The problem with mandating a backtrace is that an exception can be created at one point in the program and thrown at a later one. It is prohibitively expensive to store a stack trace in an exception unless it is actually thrown (in which case the trace may be generated while unwinding the stack). Hence we do not mandate a back trace in every exception.

14.21 Unreachable Statements

That looks like a path.
Is that the way to reach the top from here?
—Robert Frost, *The Mountain* (1915)

It is a compile-time error if a statement cannot be executed because it is *unreachable*. Every Java compiler must carry out the conservative flow analysis specified here to make sure all statements are reachable.

This section is devoted to a precise explanation of the word "reachable." The idea is that there must be some possible execution path from the beginning of the constructor, method, instance initializer or static initializer that contains the statement to the statement itself. The analysis takes into account the structure of statements. Except for the special treatment of `while`, `do`, and `for` statements whose condition expression has the constant value `true`, the values of expressions are not taken into account in the flow analysis.

For example, a Java compiler will accept the code:

```
{
    int n = 5;
    while (n > 7) k = 2;
}
```

even though the value of `n` is known at compile time and in principle it can be known at compile time that the assignment to `k` can never be executed.

A Java compiler must operate according to the rules laid out in this section.

The rules in this section define two technical terms:

- whether a statement is *reachable*
- whether a statement *can complete normally*

The definitions here allow a statement to complete normally only if it is reachable.

To shorten the description of the rules, the customary abbreviation "iff" is used to mean "if and only if."

The rules are as follows:

- The block that is the body of a constructor, method, instance initializer or static initializer is reachable.
- An empty block that is not a switch block can complete normally iff it is reachable. A nonempty block that is not a switch block can complete normally iff the last statement in it can complete normally. The first statement in a nonempty block that is not a switch block is reachable iff the block is reachable. Every other statement `S` in a nonempty block that is not a switch block is reachable iff the statement preceding `S` can complete normally.
- A local class declaration statement can complete normally iff it is reachable.
- A local variable declaration statement can complete normally iff it is reachable.
- An empty statement can complete normally iff it is reachable.
- A labeled statement can complete normally if at least one of the following is true:
    - The contained statement can complete normally.
    - There is a reachable `break` statement that exits the labeled statement.

  The contained statement is reachable iff the labeled statement is reachable.
- An expression statement can complete normally iff it is reachable.
- The `if` statement, whether or not it has an `else` part, is handled in an unusual manner. For this reason, it is discussed separately at the end of this section.
- An `assert` statement can complete normally iff it is reachable.
- A `switch` statement can complete normally iff at least one of the following is true:
    - The last statement in the switch block can complete normally.
    - The switch block is empty or contains only switch labels.
    - There is at least one switch label after the last switch block statement group.
    - The switch block does not contain a `default` label.
    - There is a reachable `break` statement that exits the `switch` statement.
- A switch block is reachable iff its `switch` statement is reachable.

- A statement in a switch block is reachable iff its `switch` statement is reachable and at least one of the following is true:
  - It bears a `case` or `default` label.
  - There is a statement preceding it in the `switch` block and that preceding statement can complete normally.
- A `while` statement can complete normally iff at least one of the following is true:
  - The `while` statement is reachable and the condition expression is not a constant expression with value `true`.
  - There is a reachable `break` statement that exits the `while` statement.

  The contained statement is reachable iff the `while` statement is reachable and the condition expression is not a constant expression whose value is `false`.
- A `do` statement can complete normally iff at least one of the following is true:
  - The contained statement can complete normally and the condition expression is not a constant expression with value `true`.
  - The `do` statement contains a reachable `continue` statement with no label, and the `do` statement is the innermost `while`, `do`, or `for` statement that contains that `continue` statement, and the condition expression is not a constant expression with value `true`.
  - The `do` statement contains a reachable `continue` statement with a label *L*, and the `do` statement has label *L*, and the condition expression is not a constant expression with value `true`.
  - There is a reachable `break` statement that exits the `do` statement.

  The contained statement is reachable iff the `do` statement is reachable.
- A basic `for` statement can complete normally iff at least one of the following is true:
  - The `for` statement is reachable, there is a condition expression, and the condition expression is not a constant expression with value `true`.
  - There is a reachable `break` statement that exits the `for` statement.

  The contained statement is reachable iff the `for` statement is reachable and the condition expression is not a constant expression whose value is `false`.
- An enhanced `for` statement can complete normally iff it is reachable.

- A `break`, `continue`, `return`, or `throw` statement cannot complete normally.
- A `synchronized` statement can complete normally iff the contained statement can complete normally. The contained statement is reachable iff the `synchronized` statement is reachable.
- A `try` statement can complete normally iff both of the following are true:
    - The `try` block can complete normally or any `catch` block can complete `normally`.
    - If the `try` statement has a `finally` block, then the `finally` block can complete normally.
- The `try` block is reachable iff the `try` statement is reachable.
- A `catch` block *C* is reachable iff both of the following are true:
    - Some expression or `throw` statement in the `try` block is reachable and can throw an exception whose type is assignable to the parameter of the `catch` clause *C*. (An expression is considered reachable iff the innermost statement containing it is reachable.)
    - There is no earlier `catch` block *A* in the `try` statement such that the type of *C*'s parameter is the same as or a subclass of the type of *A*'s parameter.
- If a `finally` block is present, it is reachable iff the `try` statement is reachable.

One might expect the `if` statement to be handled in the following manner, but these are not the rules that the Java programming language actually uses:

- HYPOTHETICAL: An `if-then` statement can complete normally iff at least one of the following is `true`:
    - The `if-then` statement is reachable and the condition expression is not a constant expression whose value is `true`.
    - The `then`–statement can complete normally.
- The `then`–statement is reachable iff the `if-then` statement is reachable and the condition expression is not a constant expression whose value is `false`.
- HYPOTHETICAL: An `if-then-else` statement can complete normally iff the `then`–statement can complete normally or the `else`–statement can complete normally. The `then`-statement is reachable iff the `if-then-else` statement is reachable and the condition expression is not a constant expression whose value is `false`. The `else` statement is reachable iff the `if-then-else`

statement is reachable and the condition expression is not a constant expression whose value is `true`.

This approach would be consistent with the treatment of other control structures. However, in order to allow the if statement to be used conveniently for "conditional compilation" purposes, the actual rules differ.

The actual rules for the if statement are as follows:

- ACTUAL: An `if–then` statement can complete normally iff it is reachable. The `then`–statement is reachable iff the `if–then` statement is reachable.
- ACTUAL: An `if–then–else` statement can complete normally iff the `then`–statement can complete normally or the `else`–statement can complete normally. The `then`-statement is reachable iff the `if–then–else` statement is reachable. The `else`-statement is reachable iff the `if–then–else` statement is reachable.

As an example, the following statement results in a compile-time error:

```
while (false) { x=3; }
```

because the statement `x=3;` is not reachable; but the superficially similar case:

```
if (false) { x=3; }
```

does not result in a compile-time error. An optimizing compiler may realize that the statement `x=3;` will never be executed and may choose to omit the code for that statement from the generated `class` file, but the statement `x=3;` is not regarded as "unreachable" in the technical sense specified here.

The rationale for this differing treatment is to allow programmers to define "flag variables" such as:

```
static final boolean DEBUG = false;
```

and then write code such as:

```
if (DEBUG) { x=3; }
```

The idea is that it should be possible to change the value of `DEBUG` from `false` to `true` or from `true` to `false` and then compile the code correctly with no other changes to the program text.

This ability to "conditionally compile" has a significant impact on, and relationship to, binary compatibility (§13). If a set of classes that use such a "flag" variable are compiled and conditional code is omitted, it does not suffice later to distribute just a new version of the class or interface that contains the definition of the flag. A change to the value of a flag is, therefore, not binary compatible with preexisting binaries (§13.4.9). (There are other reasons for such incompatibility as well, such as the use of constants in `case` labels in `switch` statements; see §13.4.9.)

One ought not to be thrown into confusion
By a plain statement of relationship . . .
—Robert Frost, *The Generations of Men* (1914)

CHAPTER 15

Expressions

When you can measure what you are speaking about,
and express it in numbers, you know something about it;
but when you cannot measure it, when you cannot express it in numbers,
your knowledge of it is of a meager and unsatisfactory kind:
it may be the beginning of knowledge, but you have scarcely,
in your thoughts, advanced to the stage of science.
—William Thompson, Lord Kelvin

MUCH of the work in a program is done by evaluating *expressions*, either for their side effects, such as assignments to variables, or for their values, which can be used as arguments or operands in larger expressions, or to affect the execution sequence in statements, or both.

This chapter specifies the meanings of expressions and the rules for their evaluation.

15.1 Evaluation, Denotation, and Result

When an expression in a program is *evaluated* (*executed*), the *result* denotes one of three things:

- A variable (§4.12) (in C, this would be called an *lvalue*)
- A value (§4.2, §4.3)
- Nothing (the expression is said to be void)

Evaluation of an expression can also produce side effects, because expressions may contain embedded assignments, increment operators, decrement operators, and method invocations.

An expression denotes nothing if and only if it is a method invocation (§15.12) that invokes a method that does not return a value, that is, a method declared `void` (§8.4). Such an expression can be used only as an expression statement (§14.8), because every other context in which an expression can appear requires the expression to denote something. An expression statement that is a method invocation may also invoke a method that produces a result; in this case the value returned by the method is quietly discarded.

Value set conversion (§5.1.13) is applied to the result of every expression that produces a value.

Each expression occurs in either:

- The declaration of some (class or interface) type that is being declared: in a field initializer, in a static initializer, in an instance initializer, in a constructor declaration, in an annotation, or in the code for a method.
- An annotation of a package or of a top-level type declaration .

15.2 Variables as Values

If an expression denotes a variable, and a value is required for use in further evaluation, then the value of that variable is used. In this context, if the expression denotes a variable or a value, we may speak simply of the *value* of the expression.

If the value of a variable of type `float` or `double` is used in this manner, then value set conversion (§5.1.13) is applied to the value of the variable.

15.3 Type of an Expression

If an expression denotes a variable or a value, then the expression has a type known at compile time. The rules for determining the type of an expression are explained separately below for each kind of expression.

The value of an expression is assignment compatible (§5.2) with the type of the expression, unless heap pollution (§4.12.2.1) occurs. Likewise the value stored in a variable is always compatible with the type of the variable, unless heap pollution occurs. In other words, the value of an expression whose type is *T* is always suitable for assignment to a variable of type *T*.

Note that an expression whose type is a class type *F* that is declared `final` is guaranteed to have a value that is either a null reference or an object whose class is *F* itself, because `final` types have no subclasses.

15.4 FP-strict Expressions

If the type of an expression is `float` or `double`, then there is a question as to what value set (§4.2.3) the value of the expression is drawn from. This is governed by the rules of value set conversion (§5.1.13); these rules in turn depend on whether or not the expression is *FP-strict*.

Every compile-time constant expression (§15.28) is FP-strict. If an expression is not a compile-time constant expression, then consider all the class declarations, interface declarations, and method declarations that contain the expression. If *any* such declaration bears the `strictfp` modifier, then the expression is FP-strict.

If a class, interface, or method, *X*, is declared `strictfp`, then *X* and any class, interface, method, constructor, instance initializer, static initializer or variable initializer within *X* is said to be *FP-strict*. Note that an annotation (§9.7) element value (§9.6) is always FP-strict, because it is always a compile-time constant (§15.28).

It follows that an expression is not FP-strict if and only if it is not a compile-time constant expression *and* it does not appear within any declaration that has the `strictfp` modifier.

Within an FP-strict expression, all intermediate values must be elements of the float value set or the double value set, implying that the results of all FP-strict expressions must be those predicted by IEEE 754 arithmetic on operands represented using single and double formats. Within an expression that is not FP-strict, some leeway is granted for an implementation to use an extended exponent range to represent intermediate results; the net effect, roughly speaking, is that a calculation might produce "the correct answer" in situations where exclusive use of the float value set or double value set might result in overflow or underflow.

15.5 Expressions and Run-Time Checks

If the type of an expression is a primitive type, then the value of the expression is of that same primitive type. But if the type of an expression is a reference type, then the class of the referenced object, or even whether the value is a reference to an object rather than `null`, is not necessarily known at compile time. There are a few places in the Java programming language where the actual class of a referenced object affects program execution in a manner that cannot be deduced from the type of the expression. They are as follows:

- Method invocation (§15.12). The particular method used for an invocation `o.m(...)` is chosen based on the methods that are part of the class or interface that is the type of `o`. For instance methods, the class of the object referenced by the run-time value of `o` participates because a subclass may override a specific method already declared in a parent class so that this overriding method is invoked. (The overriding method may or may not choose to further invoke the original overridden `m` method.)

- The `instanceof` operator (§15.20.2). An expression whose type is a reference type may be tested using `instanceof` to find out whether the class of the object referenced by the run-time value of the expression is assignment compatible (§5.2) with some other reference type.
- Casting (§5.5, §15.16). The class of the object referenced by the run-time value of the operand expression might not be compatible with the type specified by the cast. For reference types, this may require a run-time check that throws an exception if the class of the referenced object, as determined at run time, is not assignment compatible (§5.2) with the target type.
- Assignment to an array component of reference type (§10.10, §15.13, §15.26.1). The type-checking rules allow the array type `S[]` to be treated as a subtype of `T[]` if `S` is a subtype of `T`, but this requires a run-time check for assignment to an array component, similar to the check performed for a cast.
- Exception handling (§14.20). An exception is caught by a `catch` clause only if the class of the thrown exception object is an `instanceof` the type of the formal parameter of the `catch` clause.

Situations where the class of an object is not statically known may lead to run-time type errors.

In addition, there are situations where the statically known type may not be accurate at run-time. Such situations can arise in a program that gives rise to unchecked warnings. Such warnings are given in response to operations that cannot be statically guaranteed to be safe, and cannot immediately be subjected to dynamic checking because they involve non-reifiable (§4.7) types. As a result, dynamic checks later in the course of program execution may detect inconsistencies and result in run-time type errors.

A run-time type error can occur only in these situations:

- In a cast, when the actual class of the object referenced by the value of the operand expression is not compatible with the target type specified by the cast operator (§5.5, §15.16); in this case a `ClassCastException` is thrown.
- In an implicit, compiler-generated cast introduced to ensure the validity of an operation on a non-reifiable type.

- In an assignment to an array component of reference type, when the actual class of the object referenced by the value to be assigned is not compatible with the actual run-time component type of the array (§10.10, §15.13, §15.26.1); in this case an `ArrayStoreException` is thrown.
- When an exception is not caught by any `catch` handler (§11.3); in this case the thread of control that encountered the exception first invokes the method `uncaughtException` for its thread group and then terminates.

15.6 Normal and Abrupt Completion of Evaluation

No more: the end is sudden and abrupt.
—William Wordsworth, *Apology for the Foregoing Poems* (1831)

Every expression has a normal mode of evaluation in which certain computational steps are carried out. The following sections describe the normal mode of evaluation for each kind of expression. If all the steps are carried out without an exception being thrown, the expression is said to *complete normally*.

If, however, evaluation of an expression throws an exception, then the expression is said to *complete abruptly*. An abrupt completion always has an associated *reason*, which is always a `throw` with a given value.

Run-time exceptions are thrown by the predefined operators as follows:

- A class instance creation expression (§15.9), array creation expression (§15.10), or string concatenation operator expression (§15.18.1) throws an `OutOfMemoryError` if there is insufficient memory available.
- An array creation expression throws a `NegativeArraySizeException` if the value of any dimension expression is less than zero (§15.10).
- A field access (§15.11) throws a `NullPointerException` if the value of the object reference expression is `null`.
- A method invocation expression (§15.12) that invokes an instance method throws a `NullPointerException` if the target reference is `null`.
- An array access (§15.13) throws a `NullPointerException` if the value of the array reference expression is `null`.
- An array access (§15.13) throws an `ArrayIndexOutOfBoundsException` if the value of the array index expression is negative or greater than or equal to the `length` of the array.

- A cast (§15.16) throws a `ClassCastException` if a cast is found to be impermissible at run time.
- An integer division (§15.17.2) or integer remainder (§15.17.3) operator throws an `ArithmeticException` if the value of the right-hand operand expression is zero.
- An assignment to an array component of reference type (§15.26.1), a metthod invocation (§15.12), a prefix or postfix increment (§15.14.2, §15.15.1) or decrement operator (§15.14.3, §15.15.2) may all throw an `OutOfMemoryError` as a result of boxing conversion (§5.1.7).
- An assignment to an array component of reference type (§15.26.1) throws an `ArrayStoreException` when the value to be assigned is not compatible with the component type of the array.

A method invocation expression can also result in an exception being thrown if an exception occurs that causes execution of the method body to complete abruptly. A class instance creation expression can also result in an exception being thrown if an exception occurs that causes execution of the constructor to complete abruptly. Various linkage and virtual machine errors may also occur during the evaluation of an expression. By their nature, such errors are difficult to predict and difficult to handle.

If an exception occurs, then evaluation of one or more expressions may be terminated before all steps of their normal mode of evaluation are complete; such expressions are said to complete abruptly. The terms "complete normally" and "complete abruptly" are also applied to the execution of statements (§14.1). A statement may complete abruptly for a variety of reasons, not just because an exception is thrown.

If evaluation of an expression requires evaluation of a subexpression, abrupt completion of the subexpression always causes the immediate abrupt completion of the expression itself, with the same reason, and all succeeding steps in the normal mode of evaluation are not performed.

15.7 Evaluation Order

Let all things be done decently and in order.
—I Corinthians 14:40

The Java programming language guarantees that the operands of operators appear to be evaluated in a specific *evaluation order*, namely, from left to right.

It is recommended that code not rely crucially on this specification. Code is usually clearer when each expression contains at most one side effect, as its outermost operation, and when code does not depend on exactly which exception arises as a consequence of the left-to-right evaluation of expressions.

15.7.1 Evaluate Left-Hand Operand First

The left-hand operand of a binary operator appears to be fully evaluated before any part of the right-hand operand is evaluated. For example, if the left-hand operand contains an assignment to a variable and the right-hand operand contains a reference to that same variable, then the value produced by the reference will reflect the fact that the assignment occurred first.

Thus:

```
class Test {
    public static void main(String[] args) {
        int i = 2;
        int j = (i=3) * i;
        System.out.println(j);
    }
}
```

prints:

```
9
```

It is not permitted for it to print 6 instead of 9.

If the operator is a compound-assignment operator (§15.26.2), then evaluation of the left-hand operand includes both remembering the variable that the left-hand operand denotes and fetching and saving that variable's value for use in the implied combining operation. So, for example, the test program:

```
class Test {
    public static void main(String[] args) {
        int a = 9;
        a += (a = 3);                    // first example
        System.out.println(a);
        int b = 9;
        b = b + (b = 3);                 // second example
        System.out.println(b);
    }
}
```

prints:

```
12
12
```

because the two assignment statements both fetch and remember the value of the left-hand operand, which is 9, before the right-hand operand of the addition is evaluated, thereby setting the variable to 3. It is not permitted for either example to produce the result 6. Note that both of these examples have unspecified behavior in C, according to the ANSI/ISO standard.

If evaluation of the left-hand operand of a binary operator completes abruptly, no part of the right-hand operand appears to have been evaluated.

Thus, the test program:

```
class Test {
    public static void main(String[] args) {
        int j = 1;
        try {
            int i = forgetIt() / (j = 2);
        } catch (Exception e) {
            System.out.println(e);
            System.out.println("Now j = " + j);
        }
    }
    static int forgetIt() throws Exception {
        throw new Exception("I'm outta here!");
    }
}
```

prints:

```
java.lang.Exception: I'm outta here!
Now j = 1
```

That is, the left-hand operand `forgetIt()` of the operator `/` throws an exception before the right-hand operand is evaluated and its embedded assignment of 2 to `j` occurs.

15.7.2 Evaluate Operands before Operation

The Java programming language also guarantees that every operand of an operator (except the conditional operators `&&`, `||`, and `? :`) appears to be fully evaluated before any part of the operation itself is performed.

If the binary operator is an integer division `/` (§15.17.2) or integer remainder `%` (§15.17.3), then its execution may raise an `ArithmeticException`, but this exception is thrown only after both operands of the binary operator have been evaluated and only if these evaluations completed normally.

So, for example, the program:

```
class Test {
    public static void main(String[] args) {
        int divisor = 0;
        try {
```

```
            int i = 1 / (divisor * loseBig());
        } catch (Exception e) {
            System.out.println(e);
        }
    }
    static int loseBig() throws Exception {
        throw new Exception("Shuffle off to Buffalo!");
    }
}
```

always prints:

```
java.lang.Exception: Shuffle off to Buffalo!
```

and not:

```
java.lang.ArithmeticException: / by zero
```

since no part of the division operation, including signaling of a divide-by-zero exception, may appear to occur before the invocation of `loseBig` completes, even though the implementation may be able to detect or infer that the division operation would certainly result in a divide-by-zero exception.

15.7.3 Evaluation Respects Parentheses and Precedence

Java programming language implementations must respect the order of evaluation as indicated explicitly by parentheses and implicitly by operator precedence. An implementation may not take advantage of algebraic identities such as the associative law to rewrite expressions into a more convenient computational order unless it can be proven that the replacement expression is equivalent in value and in its observable side effects, even in the presence of multiple threads of execution (using the thread execution model in §17), for all possible computational values that might be involved.

In the case of floating-point calculations, this rule applies also for infinity and not-a-number (NaN) values. For example, `!(x<y)` may not be rewritten as `x>=y`, because these expressions have different values if either `x` or `y` is NaN or both are NaN.

Specifically, floating-point calculations that appear to be mathematically associative are unlikely to be computationally associative. Such computations must not be naively reordered.

For example, it is not correct for a Java compiler to rewrite `4.0*x*0.5` as `2.0*x`; while roundoff happens not to be an issue here, there are large values of `x` for which the first expression produces infinity (because of overflow) but the second expression produces a finite result.

So, for example, the test program:

```
strictfp class Test {
    public static void main(String[] args) {
        double d = 8e+307;
        System.out.println(4.0 * d * 0.5);
        System.out.println(2.0 * d);
    }
}
```

prints:

```
Infinity
1.6e+308
```

because the first expression overflows and the second does not.

In contrast, integer addition and multiplication *are* provably associative in the Java programming language.

For example a+b+c, where a, b, and c are local variables (this simplifying assumption avoids issues involving multiple threads and volatile variables), will always produce the same answer whether evaluated as (a+b)+c or a+(b+c); if the expression b+c occurs nearby in the code, a smart compiler may be able to use this common subexpression.

15.7.4 Argument Lists are Evaluated Left-to-Right

In a method or constructor invocation or class instance creation expression, argument expressions may appear within the parentheses, separated by commas. Each argument expression appears to be fully evaluated before any part of any argument expression to its right.

Thus:

```
class Test {
    public static void main(String[] args) {
        String s = "going, ";
        print3(s, s, s = "gone");
    }
    static void print3(String a, String b, String c) {
        System.out.println(a + b + c);
    }
}
```

always prints:

```
going, going, gone
```

because the assignment of the string "gone" to s occurs after the first two arguments to print3 have been evaluated.

If evaluation of an argument expression completes abruptly, no part of any argument expression to its right appears to have been evaluated.

Thus, the example:

```
class Test {
            static int id;
    public static void main(String[] args) {
        try {
            test(id = 1, oops(), id = 3);
        } catch (Exception e) {
            System.out.println(e + ", id=" + id);
        }
    }

    static int oops() throws Exception {
        throw new Exception("oops");
    }

    static int test(int a, int b, int c) {
        return a + b + c;
    }

}
```

prints:

```
java.lang.Exception: oops, id=1
```

because the assignment of `3` to `id` is not executed.

15.7.5 Evaluation Order for Other Expressions

The order of evaluation for some expressions is not completely covered by these general rules, because these expressions may raise exceptional conditions at times that must be specified. See, specifically, the detailed explanations of evaluation order for the following kinds of expressions:

- class instance creation expressions (§15.9.4)
- array creation expressions (§15.10.1)
- method invocation expressions (§15.12.4)
- array access expressions (§15.13.1)
- assignments involving array components (§15.26)

15.8 Primary Expressions

Primary expressions include most of the simplest kinds of expressions, from which all others are constructed: literals, class literals, field accesses, method invocations, and array accesses. A parenthesized expression is also treated syntactically as a primary expression.

Primary:
    PrimaryNoNewArray
    ArrayCreationExpression

PrimaryNoNewArray:
    Literal
    Type . *class*
    `void` . *class*
    `this`
    ClassName.`this`
    (*Expression*)
    ClassInstanceCreationExpression
    FieldAccess
    MethodInvocation
    ArrayAccess

15.8.1 Lexical Literals

A literal (§3.10) denotes a fixed, unchanging value.

The following production from §3.10 is repeated here for convenience:

Literal:
    IntegerLiteral
    FloatingPointLiteral
    BooleanLiteral
    CharacterLiteral
    StringLiteral
    NullLiteral

The type of a literal is determined as follows:

- The type of an integer literal that ends with `L` or `l` is `long`; the type of any other integer literal is `int`.
- The type of a floating-point literal that ends with `F` or `f` is `float` and its value must be an element of the float value set (§4.2.3). The type of any other float-

ing-point literal is `double` and its value must be an element of the double value set.

- The type of a boolean literal is `boolean`.
- The type of a character literal is `char`.
- The type of a string literal is `String`.
- The type of the null literal `null` is the null type; its value is the null reference.

Evaluation of a lexical literal always completes normally.

15.8.2 Class Literals

A *class literal* is an expression consisting of the name of a class, interface, array, or primitive type, or the pseudo-type `void`, followed by a '.' and the token `class`. The type of a class literal, `C.Class`, where `C` is the name of a class, interface or array type, is `Class<C>`. If `p` is the name of a primitive type, let `B` be the type of an expression of type `p` after boxing conversion (§5.1.7). Then the type of `p.class` is `Class<B>`. The type of `void.class` is `Class<Void>`.

A class literal evaluates to the `Class` object for the named type (or for void) as defined by the defining class loader of the class of the current instance.

It is a compile time error if any of the following occur:

- The named type is a type variable (§4.4) or a parameterized type (§4.5) or an array whose element type is a type variable or parameterized type.
- The named type does not denote a type that is accessible (§6.6) and in scope (§6.3) at the point where the class literal appears.

15.8.3 `this`

The keyword `this` may be used only in the body of an instance method, instance initializer or constructor, or in the initializer of an instance variable of a class. If it appears anywhere else, a compile-time error occurs.

When used as a primary expression, the keyword `this` denotes a value that is a reference to the object for which the instance method was invoked (§15.12), or to the object being constructed. The type of `this` is the class `C` within which the keyword `this` occurs. At run time, the class of the actual object referred to may be the class `C` or any subclass of `C`.

In the example:

```
class IntVector {
    int[] v;
    boolean equals(IntVector other) {
        if (this == other)
            return true;
        if (v.length != other.v.length)
            return false;
        for (int i = 0; i < v.length; i++)
            if (v[i] != other.v[i])
              return false;
        return true;
    }
}
```

the class `IntVector` implements a method `equals`, which compares two vectors. If the `other` vector is the same vector object as the one for which the `equals` method was invoked, then the check can skip the length and value comparisons. The `equals` method implements this check by comparing the reference to the `other` object to `this`.

The keyword `this` is also used in a special explicit constructor invocation statement, which can appear at the beginning of a constructor body (§8.8.7).

15.8.4 Qualified `this`

Any lexically enclosing instance can be referred to by explicitly qualifying the keyword `this`.

Let *C* be the class denoted by *ClassName*. Let *n* be an integer such that *C* is the *n*th lexically enclosing class of the class in which the qualified `this` expression appears. The value of an expression of the form *ClassName*.`this` is the *n*th lexically enclosing instance of `this` (§8.1.3). The type of the expression is *C*. It is a compile-time error if the current class is not an inner class of class *C* or *C* itself.

15.8.5 Parenthesized Expressions

A parenthesized expression is a primary expression whose type is the type of the contained expression and whose value at run time is the value of the contained expression. If the contained expression denotes a variable then the parenthesized expression also denotes that variable.

The use of parentheses only effects the order of evaluation, with one fascinating exception.

DISCUSSION

Consider the case if the smallest possible negative value of type long. This value, `9223372036854775808L`, is allowed only as an operand of the unary minus operator (§3.10.1). Therefore, enclosing it in parentheses, as in `-(9223372036854775808L)` causes a compile time error.

In particular, the presence or absence of parentheses around an expression does not (except for the case noted above) affect in any way:

- the choice of value set (§4.2.3) for the value of an expression of type `float` or `double`.
- whether a variable is definitely assigned, definitely assigned when true, definitely assigned when false, definitely unassigned, definitely unassigned when true, or definitely unassigned when false (§16).

15.9 Class Instance Creation Expressions

And now a new object took possession of my soul.
—Edgar Allen Poe, *A Tale of the Ragged Mountains* (1844)

A class instance creation expression is used to create new objects that are instances of classes.

ClassInstanceCreationExpression:
  `new` *TypeArguments$_{opt}$ ClassOrInterfaceType* `(` *ArgumentList$_{opt}$* `)` *ClassBody$_{opt}$*
  Primary. `new` *TypeArguments$_{opt}$ Identifier TypeArguments$_{opt}$* `(` *ArgumentList$_{opt}$* `)` *ClassBody$_{opt}$*

ArgumentList:
  Expression
  ArgumentList `,` *Expression*

A class instance creation expression specifies a class to be instantiated, possibly followed by type arguments (if the class being instantiated is generic (§8.1.2)), followed by (a possibly empty) list of actual value arguments to the constructor. It is also possible to pass explicit type arguments to the constructor itself (if it is a generic constructor (§8.8.4)). The type arguments to the constructor immediately follow the keyword `new`. It is a compile-time error if any of the type arguments used in a class instance creation expression are wildcard type arguments (§4.5.1). Class instance creation expressions have two forms:

- *Unqualified class instance creation expressions* begin with the keyword `new`. An unqualified class instance creation expression may be used to create an instance of a class, regardless of whether the class is a top-level (§7.6), member (§8.5, §9.5), local (§14.3) or anonymous class (§15.9.5).
- *Qualified class instance creation expressions* begin with a *Primary*. A qualified class instance creation expression enables the creation of instances of inner member classes and their anonymous subclasses.

A class instance creation expression can throw an exception type `E` iff either:

- The expression is a qualified class instance creation expression and the qualifying expression can throw `E;` or
- Some expression of the argument list can throw `E;` or
- `E` is listed in the throws clause of the type of the constructor that is invoked; or
- The class instance creation expression includes a *ClassBody*, and some instnance initializer block or instance variable initializer expression in the *ClassBody* can throw `E.`

Both unqualified and qualified class instance creation expressions may optionally end with a class body. Such a class instance creation expression declares an *anonymous class* (§15.9.5) and creates an instance of it.

We say that a class is *instantiated* when an instance of the class is created by a class instance creation expression. Class instantiation involves determining what class is to be instantiated, what the enclosing instances (if any) of the newly created instance are, what constructor should be invoked to create the new instance and what arguments should be passed to that constructor.

15.9.1 Determining the Class being Instantiated

If the class instance creation expression ends in a class body, then the class being instantiated is an anonymous class. Then:

- If the class instance creation expression is an unqualified class instance creation expression, then *let* `T` be the *ClassOrInterfaceType* after the *`new`* token. It is a compile-time error if the class or interface named by `T` is not accessible (§6.6) or if `T` is an enum type (§8.9). If `T` denotes a class, then an anonymous direct subclass of the class named by *T* is declared. It is a compile-time error if the class denoted by *T* is a `final` class. If *T* denotes an interface then an anonymous direct subclass of `Object` that implements the interface named by *T* is *declared. In either case, the body of the subclass is the ClassBody* given in the class instance creation expression. The class being instantiated is the anonymous subclass.

- Otherwise, the class instance creation expression is a qualified class instance creation expression. Let *T* be the name of the *Identifier* after the *new* token. It is a compile-time error if *T* is not the simple name (§6.2) of an accessible (§6.6) non-`final` inner class (§8.1.3) that is a member of the compile-time type of the *Primary*. It is also a compile-time error if *T* is ambiguous (§8.5) or if *T* denotes an enum type. An anonymous direct subclass of the class named by *T* is declared. The body of the subclass is the *ClassBody* given in the class instance creation expression. The class being instantiated is the anonymous subclass.

If a class instance creation expression does not declare an anonymous class, then:

- If the class instance creation expression is an unqualified class instance creation expression, then the *ClassOrInterfaceType* must denote a class that is accessible (§6.6) and is not an enum type and not `abstract`, or a compile-time error occurs. In this case, the class being instantiated is the class denoted by *ClassOrInterfaceType*.
- Otherwise, the class instance creation expression is a qualified class instance creation expression. It is a compile-time error if *Identifier* is not the simple name (§6.2) of an accessible (§6.6) non-`abstract` inner class (§8.1.3) *T* that is a member of the compile-time type of the *Primary*. It is also a compile-time error if *Identifier* is ambiguous (§8.5), or if *Identifier* denotes an enum type (§8.9). The class being instantiated is the class denoted by *Identifier*.

The type of the class instance creation expression is the class type being instantiated.

15.9.2 Determining Enclosing Instances

Let *C* be the class being instantiated, and let *i* the instance being created. If *C* is an inner class then *i* may have an immediately enclosing instance. The immediately enclosing instance of *i* (§8.1.3) is determined as follows:

- If `C` is an anonymous class, then:
  - If the class instance creation expression occurs in a static context (§8.1.3), then `i` has no immediately enclosing instance.
  - Otherwise, the immediately enclosing instance of `i` is `this`.
- If `C` is a local class (§14.3), then let `O` be the innermost lexically enclosing class of `C`. Let *n* be an integer such that `O` is the *n*th lexically enclosing class of the class in which the class instance creation expression appears. Then:
  - If `C` occurs in a static context, then `i` has no immediately enclosing instance.
  - Otherwise, if the class instance creation expression occurs in a static context, then a compile-time error occurs.
  - Otherwise, the immediately enclosing instance of `i` is the *n*th lexically enclosing instance of `this` (§8.1.3).
- Otherwise, `C` is an inner member class (§8.5).
  - If the class instance creation expression is an unqualified class instance creation expression, then:
    - If the class instance creation expression occurs in a static context, then a compile-time error occurs.
    - Otherwise, if `C` is a member of an enclosing class then let `O` be the innermost lexically enclosing class of which `C` is a member, and let *n* be an integer such that `O` is the *n*th lexically enclosing class of the class in which the class instance creation expression appears. The immediately enclosing instance of `i` is the *n*th lexically enclosing instance of `this`.
    - Otherwise, a compile-time error occurs.
  - Otherwise, the class instance creation expression is a qualified class instance creation expression. The immediately enclosing instance of `i` is the object that is the value of the *Primary* expression.

In addition, if `C` is an anonymous class, and the direct superclass of `C`, `S`, is an inner class then `i` may have an immediately enclosing instance with respect to `S` which is determined as follows:

- If *S* is a local class (§14.3), then let *O* be the innermost lexically enclosing class of *S*. Let *n* be an integer such that *O* is the *n*th lexically enclosing class of the class in which the class instance creation expression appears. Then:
  - If *S* occurs within a static context, then `i` has no immediately enclosing instance with respect to *S*.
  - Otherwise, if the class instance creation expression occurs in a static context, then a compile-time error occurs.
  - Otherwise, the immediately enclosing instance of `i` with respect to *S* is the *n*th lexically enclosing instance of `this`.
- Otherwise, *S* is an inner member class (§8.5).
  - If the class instance creation expression is an unqualified class instance creation expression, then:
    - If the class instance creation expression occurs in a static context, then a compile-time error occurs.
    - Otherwise, if *S* is a member of an enclosing class then let *O* be the innermost lexically enclosing class of which *S* is a member, and let *n* be an integer such that *O* is the *n*th lexically enclosing class of the class in which the class instance creation expression appears. The immediately enclosing instance of `i` with respect to *S* is the *n*th lexically enclosing instance of `this`.
    - Otherwise, a compile-time error occurs.
  - Otherwise, the class instance creation expression is a qualified class instance creation expression. The immediately enclosing instance of `i` with respect to *S* is the object that is the value of the *Primary* expression.

15.9.3 Choosing the Constructor and its Arguments

Let *C* be the class type being instantiated. To create an instance of *C*, `i`, a constructor of *C* is chosen at compile-time by the following rules:

- First, the actual arguments to the constructor invocation are determined.
  - If *C* is an anonymous class, and the direct superclass of *C*, *S*, is an inner class, then:
    - If the *S* is a local class and *S* occurs in a static context, then the arguments in the argument list, if any, are the arguments to the constructor, in the order they appear in the expression.

- Otherwise, the immediately enclosing instance of *i* with respect to *S* is the first argument to the constructor, followed by the arguments in the argument list of the class instance creation expression, if any, in the order they appear in the expression.
- Otherwise the arguments in the argument list, if any, are the arguments to the constructor, in the order they appear in the expression.

- Once the actual arguments have been determined, they are used to select a constructor of *C*, using the same rules as for method invocations (§15.12). As in method invocations, a compile-time method matching error results if there is no unique most-specific constructor that is both applicable and accessible.

Note that the type of the class instance creation expression may be an anonymous class type, in which case the constructor being invoked is an anonymous constructor.

15.9.4 Run-time Evaluation of Class Instance Creation Expressions

At run time, evaluation of a class instance creation expression is as follows.

First, if the class instance creation expression is a qualified class instance creation expression, the qualifying primary expression is evaluated. If the qualifying expression evaluates to `null`, a `NullPointerException` is raised, and the class instance creation expression completes abruptly. If the qualifying expression completes abruptly, the class instance creation expression completes abruptly for the same reason.

Next, space is allocated for the new class instance. If there is insufficient space to allocate the object, evaluation of the class instance creation expression completes abruptly by throwing an `OutOfMemoryError` (§15.9.6).

The new object contains new instances of all the fields declared in the specified class type and all its superclasses. As each new field instance is created, it is initialized to its default value (§4.12.5).

Next, the actual arguments to the constructor are evaluated, left-to-right. If any of the argument evaluations completes abruptly, any argument expressions to its right are not evaluated, and the class instance creation expression completes abruptly for the same reason.

Next, the selected constructor of the specified class type is invoked. This results in invoking at least one constructor for each superclass of the class type. This process can be directed by explicit constructor invocation statements (§8.8) and is described in detail in §12.5.

The value of a class instance creation expression is a reference to the newly created object of the specified class. Every time the expression is evaluated, a fresh object is created.

15.9.5 Anonymous Class Declarations

An anonymous class declaration is automatically derived from a class instance creation expression by the compiler.

An anonymous class is never `abstract` (§8.1.1.1). An anonymous class is always an inner class (§8.1.3); it is never `static` (§8.1.1, §8.5.2). An anonymous class is always implicitly `final` (§8.1.1.2).

15.9.5.1 *Anonymous Constructors*

An anonymous class cannot have an explicitly declared constructor. Instead, the compiler must automatically provide an *anonymous constructor* for the anonymous class. The form of the anonymous constructor of an anonymous class *C* with direct superclass *S* is as follows:

- If *S* is not an inner class, or if *S* is a local class that occurs in a static context, then the anonymous constructor has one formal parameter for each actual argument to the class instance creation expression in which *C* is declared. The actual arguments to the class instance creation expression are used to determine a constructor *cs* of *S*, using the same rules as for method invocations (§15.12). The type of each formal parameter of the anonymous constructor must be identical to the corresponding formal parameter of *cs*.

  The body of the constructor consists of an explicit constructor invocation (§8.8.7.1) of the form `super(...)`, where the actual arguments are the formal parameters of the constructor, in the order they were declared.

- Otherwise, the first formal parameter of the constructor of *C* represents the value of the immediately enclosing instance of *i* with respect to *S*. The type of this parameter is the class type that immediately encloses the declaration of *S*. The constructor has an additional formal parameter for each actual argument to the class instance creation expression that declared the anonymous class. The *n*th formal parameter *e* corresponds to the $n-1$ st actual argument. The actual arguments to the class instance creation expression are used to determine a constructor *cs* of *S*, using the same rules as for method invocations (§15.12). The type of each formal parameter of the anonymous constructor must be identical to the corresponding formal parameter of *cs*. The body of the constructor consists of an explicit constructor invocation (§8.8.7.1) of the form *o*.`super(...)`, where *o* is the first formal parameter of the constructor, and the actual arguments are the subsequent formal parameters of the constructor, in the order they were declared.

In all cases, the `throws` clause of an anonymous constructor must list all the checked exceptions thrown by the explicit superclass constructor invocation statement contained within the anonymous constructor, and all checked exceptions thrown by any instance initializers or instance variable initializers of the anonymous class.

Note that it is possible for the signature of the anonymous constructor to refer to an inaccessible type (for example, if such a type occurred in the signature of the superclass constructor *cs*). This does not, in itself, cause any errors at either compile time or run time.

15.9.6 Example: Evaluation Order and Out-of-Memory Detection

If evaluation of a class instance creation expression finds there is insufficient memory to perform the creation operation, then an `OutOfMemoryError` is thrown. This check occurs before any argument expressions are evaluated.

So, for example, the test program:

```
class List {
    int value;
    List next;
    static List head = new List(0);
    List(int n) { value = n; next = head; head = this; }
}

class Test {
    public static void main(String[] args) {
        int id = 0, oldid = 0;
        try {
            for (;;) {
              ++id;
              new List(oldid = id);
            }
        } catch (Error e) {
            System.out.println(e + ", " + (oldid==id));
        }
    }
}
```

prints:

```
java.lang.OutOfMemoryError: List, false
```

because the out-of-memory condition is detected before the argument expression `oldid = id` is evaluated.

Compare this to the treatment of array creation expressions (§15.10), for which the out-of-memory condition is detected after evaluation of the dimension expressions (§15.10.3).

15.10 Array Creation Expressions

This was all as it should be, and I went out in my new array . . .
—Charles Dickens, *Great Expectations* (1861)

An array instance creation expression is used to create new arrays (§10).

ArrayCreationExpression:
    `new` *PrimitiveType DimExprs* $Dims_{opt}$
    `new` *ClassOrInterfaceType DimExprs* $Dims_{opt}$
    `new` *PrimitiveType Dims ArrayInitializer*
    `new` *ClassOrInterfaceType Dims ArrayInitializer*

DimExprs:
    DimExpr
    DimExprs DimExpr

DimExpr:
    `[` *Expression* `]`

Dims:
    `[ ]`
    Dims `[ ]`

An array creation expression creates an object that is a new array whose elements are of the type specified by the *PrimitiveType* or *ClassOrInterfaceType*. It is a compile-time error if the *ClassOrInterfaceType* does not denote a reifiable type (§4.7). Otherwise, the *ClassOrInterfaceType* may name any named reference type, even an `abstract` class type (§8.1.1.1) or an interface type (§9).

DISCUSSION

The rules above imply that the element type in an array creation expression cannot be a parameterized type, other than an unbounded wildcard.

The type of the creation expression is an array type that can denoted by a copy of the creation expression from which the new keyword and every *DimExpr* expression and array initializer have been deleted.

For example, the type of the creation expression:

```
new double[3][3][]
```

is:

```
double[][][]
```

The type of each dimension expression within a *DimExpr* must be a type that is convertible (§5.1.8) to an integral type, or a compile-time error occurs. Each expression undergoes unary numeric promotion (§). The promoted type must be int, or a compile-time error occurs; this means, specifically, that the type of a dimension expression must not be long.

If an array initializer is provided, the newly allocated array will be initialized with the values provided by the array initializer as described in §10.6.

15.10.1 Run-time Evaluation of Array Creation Expressions

At run time, evaluation of an array creation expression behaves as follows. If there are no dimension expressions, then there must be an array initializer. The value of the array initializer is the value of the array creation expression. Otherwise:

First, the dimension expressions are evaluated, left-to-right. If any of the expression evaluations completes abruptly, the expressions to the right of it are not evaluated.

Next, the values of the dimension expressions are checked. If the value of any *DimExpr* expression is less than zero, then an NegativeArraySizeException is thrown.

Next, space is allocated for the new array. If there is insufficient space to allocate the array, evaluation of the array creation expression completes abruptly by throwing an OutOfMemoryError.

Then, if a single *DimExpr* appears, a single-dimensional array is created of the specified length, and each component of the array is initialized to its default value (§4.12.5).

If an array creation expression contains N *DimExpr* expressions, then it effectively executes a set of nested loops of depth $N - 1$ to create the implied arrays of arrays.

For example, the declaration:

```
float[][] matrix = new float[3][3];
```

is equivalent in behavior to:

```
float[][] matrix = new float[3][];
for (int d = 0; d < matrix.length; d++)
    matrix[d] = new float[3];
```

and:

```
Age[][][][][] Aquarius = new Age[6][10][8][12][];
```

is equivalent to:

```
Age[][][][][] Aquarius = new Age[6][][][][];
for (int d1 = 0; d1 < Aquarius.length; d1++) {
    Aquarius[d1] = new Age[10][][][];
    for (int d2 = 0; d2 < Aquarius[d1].length; d2++) {
        Aquarius[d1][d2] = new Age[8][][];
        for (int d3 = 0; d3 < Aquarius[d1][d2].length; d3++) {
            Aquarius[d1][d2][d3] = new Age[12][];
        }
    }
}
```

with *d*, *d1*, *d2* and *d3* replaced by names that are not already locally declared. Thus, a single new expression actually creates one array of length 6, 6 arrays of length 10, $6 \times 10 = 60$ arrays of length 8, and $6 \times 10 \times 8 = 480$ arrays of length 12. This example leaves the fifth dimension, which would be arrays containing the actual array elements (references to `Age` objects), initialized only to null references. These arrays can be filled in later by other code, such as:

```
Age[] Hair = { new Age("quartz"), new Age("topaz") };
Aquarius[1][9][6][9] = Hair;
```

A multidimensional array need not have arrays of the same length at each level.

Thus, a triangular matrix may be created by:

```
float triang[][] = new float[100][];
for (int i = 0; i < triang.length; i++)
    triang[i] = new float[i+1];
```

15.10.2 Example: Array Creation Evaluation Order

In an array creation expression (§15.10), there may be one or more dimension expressions, each within brackets. Each dimension expression is fully evaluated before any part of any dimension expression to its right.

Thus:

```
class Test {
    public static void main(String[] args) {
        int i = 4;
        int ia[][] = new int[i][i=3];
        System.out.println(
            "[" + ia.length + "," + ia[0].length + "]");
    }
}
```

prints:

```
[4,3]
```

because the first dimension is calculated as 4 before the second dimension expression sets `i` to 3.

If evaluation of a dimension expression completes abruptly, no part of any dimension expression to its right will appear to have been evaluated. Thus, the example:

```
class Test {
    public static void main(String[] args) {
        int[][] a = { { 00, 01 }, { 10, 11 } };
        int i = 99;
        try {
            a[val()][i = 1]++;
        } catch (Exception e) {
            System.out.println(e + ", i=" + i);
        }
    }

    static int val() throws Exception {
        throw new Exception("unimplemented");
    }
}
```

prints:

```
java.lang.Exception: unimplemented, i=99
```

because the embedded assignment that sets `i` to `1` is never executed.

15.10.3 Example: Array Creation and Out-of-Memory Detection

If evaluation of an array creation expression finds there is insufficient memory to perform the creation operation, then an `OutOfMemoryError` is thrown. This check occurs only after evaluation of all dimension expressions has completed normally.

So, for example, the test program:

```
class Test {
    public static void main(String[] args) {
        int len = 0, oldlen = 0;
        Object[] a = new Object[0];
        try {
            for (;;) {
                ++len;
                Object[] temp = new Object[oldlen = len];
                temp[0] = a;
                a = temp;
            }
        } catch (Error e) {
```

```
                System.out.println(e + ", " + (oldlen==len));
            }
        }
    }
```

prints:

```
    java.lang.OutOfMemoryError, true
```

because the out-of-memory condition is detected after the dimension expression `oldlen = len` is evaluated.

Compare this to class instance creation expressions (§15.9), which detect the out-of-memory condition before evaluating argument expressions (§15.9.6).

15.11 Field Access Expressions

A field access expression may access a field of an object or array, a reference to which is the value of either an expression or the special keyword `super`. (It is also possible to refer to a field of the current instance or current class by using a simple name; see §6.5.6.)

FieldAccess:
    Primary . *Identifier*
    `super` . *Identifier*
    ClassName `.super` . *Identifier*

The meaning of a field access expression is determined using the same rules as for qualified names (§6.6), but limited by the fact that an expression cannot denote a package, class type, or interface type.

15.11.1 Field Access Using a Primary

The type of the *Primary* must be a reference type *T*, or a compile-time error occurs. The meaning of the field access expression is determined as follows:

- If the identifier names several accessible member fields of type *T*, then the field access is ambiguous and a compile-time error occurs.
- If the identifier does not name an accessible member field of type *T*, then the field access is undefined and a compile-time error occurs.
- Otherwise, the identifier names a single accessible member field of type *T* and the type of the field access expression is the type of the member field after

capture conversion (§5.1.10). At run time, the result of the field access expression is computed as follows:

- If the field is `static`:
  - The *Primary* expression is evaluated, and the result is discarded. If evaluation of the *Primary* expression completes abruptly, the field access expression completes abruptly for the same reason.
  - If the field is `final`, then the result is the value of the specified class variable in the class or interface that is the type of the *Primary* expression.
  - If the field is not `final`, then the result is a variable, namely, the specified class variable in the class that is the type of the *Primary* expression.
- If the field is not `static`:
  - The *Primary* expression is evaluated. If evaluation of the *Primary* expression completes abruptly, the field access expression completes abruptly for the same reason.
  - If the value of the *Primary* is `null`, then a `NullPointerException` is thrown.
  - If the field is `final`, then the result is the value of the specified instance variable in the object referenced by the value of the *Primary*.
  - If the field is not `final`, then the result is a variable, namely, the specified instance variable in the object referenced by the value of the *Primary*.

Note, specifically, that only the type of the *Primary* expression, not the class of the actual object referred to at run time, is used in determining which field to use.

Thus, the example:

```
class S { int x = 0; }
class T extends S { int x = 1; }
class Test {
    public static void main(String[] args) {
        T t = new T();
        System.out.println("t.x=" + t.x + when("t", t));
        S s = new S();
        System.out.println("s.x=" + s.x + when("s", s));
        s = t;
        System.out.println("s.x=" + s.x + when("s", s));
    }
```

```
        static String when(String name, Object t) {
            return " when " + name + " holds a "
                + t.getClass() + " at run time.";
        }
    }
```

produces the output:

```
t.x=1 when t holds a class T at run time.
s.x=0 when s holds a class S at run time.
s.x=0 when s holds a class T at run time.
```

The last line shows that, indeed, the field that is accessed does not depend on the run-time class of the referenced object; even if `s` holds a reference to an object of class `T`, the expression `s.x` refers to the `x` field of class `S`, because the type of the expression `s` is `S`. Objects of class `T` contain two fields named `x`, one for class `T` and one for its superclass `S`.

This lack of dynamic lookup for field accesses allows programs to be run efficiently with straightforward implementations. The power of late binding and overriding is available, but only when instance methods are used. Consider the same example using instance methods to access the fields:

```
class S { int x = 0; int z() { return x; } }
class T extends S { int x = 1; int z() { return x; } }
class Test {
    public static void main(String[] args) {
        T t = new T();
        System.out.println("t.z()=" + t.z() + when("t", t));
        S s = new S();
        System.out.println("s.z()=" + s.z() + when("s", s));
        s = t;
        System.out.println("s.z()=" + s.z() + when("s", s));
    }
    static String when(String name, Object t) {
        return " when " + name + " holds a "
            + t.getClass() + " at run time.";
    }
}
```

Now the output is:

```
t.z()=1 when t holds a class T at run time.
s.z()=0 when s holds a class S at run time.
s.z()=1 when s holds a class T at run time.
```

The last line shows that, indeed, the method that is accessed *does* depend on the run-time class of referenced object; when `s` holds a reference to an object of class

T, the expression s.z() refers to the z method of class T, despite the fact that the type of the expression s is S. Method z of class T overrides method z of class S.

The following example demonstrates that a null reference may be used to access a class (static) variable without causing an exception:

```
class Test {
    static String mountain = "Chocorua";
    static Test favorite(){
        System.out.print("Mount ");
        return null;
    }
    public static void main(String[] args) {
        System.out.println(favorite().mountain);
    }
}
```

It compiles, executes, and prints:

```
Mount Chocorua
```

Even though the result of favorite() is null, a NullPointerException is *not* thrown. That "Mount " is printed demonstrates that the *Primary* expression is indeed fully evaluated at run time, despite the fact that only its type, not its value, is used to determine which field to access (because the field mountain is static).

15.11.2 Accessing Superclass Members using super

The special forms using the keyword super are valid only in an instance method, instance initializer or constructor, or in the initializer of an instance variable of a class; these are exactly the same situations in which the keyword this may be used (§15.8.3). The forms involving super may not be used anywhere in the class Object, since Object has no superclass; if super appears in class Object, then a compile-time error results.

Suppose that a field access expression super.*name* appears within class *C*, and the immediate superclass of *C* is class *S*. Then super.*name* is treated exactly as if it had been the expression ((*S*)this).*name*; thus, it refers to the field named *name* of the current object, but with the current object viewed as an instance of the superclass. Thus it can access the field named *name* that is visible in class *S*, even if that field is hidden by a declaration of a field named *name* in class *C*.

The use of super is demonstrated by the following example:

```
interface I { int x = 0; }
class T1 implements I { int x = 1; }
class T2 extends T1 { int x = 2; }
class T3 extends T2 {
```

```
    int x = 3;
    void test() {
        System.out.println("x=\t\t"+x);
        System.out.println("super.x=\t\t"+super.x);
        System.out.println("((T2)this).x=\t"+((T2)this).x);
        System.out.println("((T1)this).x=\t"+((T1)this).x);
        System.out.println("((I)this).x=\t"+((I)this).x);
    }
}

class Test {
    public static void main(String[] args) {
        new T3().test();
    }
}
```

which produces the output:

```
x=            3
super.x=      2
((T2)this).x=2
((T1)this).x=1
((I)this).x= 0
```

Within class `T3`, the expression `super.x` is treated exactly as if it were:

```
((T2)this).x
```

Suppose that a field access expression *T*`.super.`*name* appears within class *C*, and the immediate superclass of the class denoted by *T* is a class whose fully qualified name is *S*. Then *T*`.super.`*name* is treated exactly as if it had been the expression `((`*S*`)`*T*`.this).`*name*.

Thus the expression *T*`.super.`*name* can access the field named *name* that is visible in the class named by *S*, even if that field is hidden by a declaration of a field named *name* in the class named by *T*.

It is a compile-time error if the current class is not an inner class of class *T* or *T* itself.

15.12 Method Invocation Expressions

A method invocation expression is used to invoke a class or instance method.

MethodInvocation:
  MethodName (*ArgumentList*$_{opt}$)
  Primary . *NonWildTypeArguments*$_{opt}$ *Identifier* (*ArgumentList*$_{opt}$)
  `super` . *NonWildTypeArguments*$_{opt}$ *Identifier* (*ArgumentList*$_{opt}$)
  ClassName . `super` . *NonWildTypeArguments*$_{opt}$ *Identifier* (
ArgumentList$_{opt}$)
  TypeName . *NonWildTypeArguments* *Identifier* (*ArgumentList*$_{opt}$)

The definition of *ArgumentList* from §15.9 is repeated here for convenience:

ArgumentList:
  Expression
  ArgumentList , *Expression*

Resolving a method name at compile time is more complicated than resolving a field name because of the possibility of method overloading. Invoking a method at run time is also more complicated than accessing a field because of the possibility of instance method overriding.

Determining the method that will be invoked by a method invocation expression involves several steps. The following three sections describe the compile-time processing of a method invocation; the determination of the type of the method invocation expression is described in §15.12.3.

15.12.1 Compile-Time Step 1: Determine Class or Interface to Search

The first step in processing a method invocation at compile time is to figure out the name of the method to be invoked and which class or interface to check for definitions of methods of that name. There are several cases to consider, depending on the form that precedes the left parenthesis, as follows:

- If the form is *MethodName*, then there are three subcases:
  - If it is a simple name, that is, just an *Identifier*, then the name of the method is the *Identifier*. If the *Identifier* appears within the scope (§6.3) of a visible method declaration with that name, then there must be an enclosing type declaration of which that method is a member. Let *T* be the innermost such type declaration. The class or interface to search is *T*.
  - If it is a qualified name of the form *TypeName* . *Identifier*, then the name of the method is the *Identifier* and the class to search is the one named by the

TypeName. If *TypeName* is the name of an interface rather than a class, then a compile-time error occurs, because this form can invoke only `static` methods and interfaces have no `static` methods.

- In all other cases, the qualified name has the form *FieldName* `.` *Identifier*; then the name of the method is the *Identifier* and the class or interface to search is the declared type *T* of the field named by the *FieldName*, if *T* is a class or interface type, or the upper bound of *T* if *T* is a type variable.

- If the form is *Primary*`.`$NonWildTypeArguments_{opt}$ *Identifier*, then the name of the method is the *Identifier*. Let *T* be the type of the *Primary* expression; then the class or interface to be searched is *T* if *T* is a class or interface type, or the upper bound of *T* if *T* is a type variable.

- If the form is `super.`$NonWildTypeArguments_{opt}$ *Identifier*, then the name of the method is the *Identifier* and the class to be searched is the superclass of the class whose declaration contains the method invocation. Let *T* be the type declaration immediately enclosing the method invocation. It is a compile-time error if any of the following situations occur:
  - *T* is the class `Object`.
  - *T* is an interface.

- If the form is *ClassName*`.super.`$NonWildTypeArguments_{opt}$ *Identifier*, then the name of the method is the *Identifier* and the class to be searched is the superclass of the class *C* denoted by *ClassName*. It is a compile-time error if *C* is not a lexically enclosing class of the current class. It is a compile-time error if *C* is the class `Object`. Let *T* be the type declaration immediately enclosing the method invocation. It is a compile-time error if any of the following situations occur:
  - *T* is the class `Object`.
  - *T* is an interface.

- If the form is *TypeName*`.`*NonWildTypeArguments Identifier*, then the name of the method is the *Identifier* and the class to be searched is the class *C* denoted by *TypeName*. If *TypeName* is the name of an interface rather than a class, then a compile-time error occurs, because this form can invoke only `static` methods and interfaces have no `static` methods.

15.12.2 Compile-Time Step 2: Determine Method Signature

The hand-writing experts were called upon for their opinion of the signature . . .
—Agatha Christie, *The Mysterious Affair at Styles* (1920), Chapter 11

The second step searches the type determined in the previous step for member methods. This step uses the name of the method and the types of the argument expressions to locate methods that are both *accessible* and *applicable*, that is, declarations that can be correctly invoked on the given arguments. There may be more than one such method, in which case the *most specific* one is chosen. The descriptor (signature plus return type) of the most specific method is one used at run time to perform the method dispatch.

A method is *applicable* if it is either applicable by subtyping (§15.12.2.2), applicable by method invocation conversion (§15.12.2.3), or it is an applicable variable arity method (§15.12.2.4).

The process of determining applicability begins by determining the potentially applicable methods (§15.12.2.1). The remainder of the process is split into three phases.

DISCUSSION

The purpose of the division into phases is to ensure compatibility with older versions of the Java programming language.

The first phase (§15.12.2.2) performs overload resolution without permitting boxing or unboxing conversion, or the use of variable arity method invocation. If no applicable method is found during this phase then processing continues to the second phase.

DISCUSSION

This guarantees that any calls that were valid in older versions of the language are not considered ambiguous as a result of the introduction of variable arity methods, implicit boxing and/or unboxing.

The second phase (§15.12.2.3) performs overload resolution while allowing boxing and unboxing, but still precludes the use of variable arity method invocation. If no applicable method is found during this phase then processing continues to the third phase.

DISCUSSION

This ensures that a variable arity method is never invoked if an applicable fixed arity method exists.

The third phase (§15.12.2.4) allows overloading to be combined with variable arity methods, boxing and unboxing.

Deciding whether a method is applicable will, in the case of generic methods (§8.4.4), require that actual type arguments be determined. Actual type arguments may be passed explicitly or implicitly. If they are passed implicitly, they must be inferred (§15.12.2.7) from the types of the argument expressions.

If several applicable methods have been identified during one of the three phases of applicability testing, then the *most specific* one is chosen, as specified in section §15.12.2.5. See the following subsections for details.

15.12.2.1 *Identify Potentially Applicable Methods*

A member method is *potentially applicable* to a method invocation if and only if all of the following are true:

- The name of the member is identical to the name of the method in the method invocation.
- The member is accessible (§6.6) to the class or interface in which the method invocation appears.
- The arity of the member is lesser or equal to the arity of the method invocation.
- If the member is a variable arity method with arity *n*, the arity of the method invocation is greater or equal to *n-1*.
- If the member is a fixed arity method with arity *n*, the arity of the method invocation is equal to *n*.

- If the method invocation includes explicit type parameters, and the member is a generic method, then the number of actual type parameters is equal to the number of formal type parameters.

DISCUSSION

The clause above implies that a non-generic method may be potentially applicable to an invocation that supplies explicit type parameters. Indeed, it may turn out to be applicable. In such a case, the type parameters will simply be ignored.

This rule stems from issues of compatibility and principles of substitutability. Since interfaces or superclasses may be generified independently of their subtypes, we may override a generic method with a non-generic one. However, the overriding (non-generic) method must be applicable to calls to the generic method, including calls that explicitly pass type parameters. Otherwise the subtype would not be substitutable for its generified supertype.

Whether a member method is accessible at a method invocation depends on the access modifier (`public`, none, `protected`, or `private`) in the member's declaration and on where the method invocation appears.

The class or interface determined by compile-time step 1 (§15.12.1) is searched for all member methods that are potentially applicable to this method invocation; members inherited from superclasses and superinterfaces are included in this search.

In addition, if the method invocation has, before the left parenthesis, a *MethodName* of the form *Identifier*, then the search process also examines all methods that are (a) imported by single-static-import declarations (§7.5.3) and static-import-on-demand declarations (§7.5.4) within the compilation unit (§7.3) within which the method invocation occurs, and (b) not shadowed (§6.3.1) at the place where the method invocation appears.

If the search does not yield at least one method that is potentially applicable, then a compile-time error occurs.

15.12.2.2 *Phase 1: Identify Matching Arity Methods Applicable by Subtyping*

Let m be a potentially applicable method (§15.12.2.1), let $e_1, \ldots, e_n$ be the actual argument expressions of the method invocation and let A_i be the type of e_i, $1 \le i \le n$. Then:

- If m is a generic method, then let $F_1 \ldots F_n$ be the types of the formal parameters of m and let $R_1 \ldots R_p$ $p \ge 1$, be the formal type parameters of m, and let B_l be the declared bound of R_l, $1 \le l \le p$. Then:
  - If the method invocation does not provide explicit type arguments then let $U_1 \ldots U_p$ be the actual type arguments inferred (§15.12.2.7) for this invocation of m, using a set of initial constraints consisting of the constraints A_i << F_i for each actual argument expression e_i whose type is a reference type, $1 \le i \le n$.
  - Otherwise let $U_1 \ldots U_p$ be the explicit type arguments given in the method invocation.

  Then let $S_i = F_i[R_1 = U_1, \ldots, R_p = U_p]$ $1 \le i < n$, be the types inferred for of the formal parameters of m.
- Otherwise, let $S_1 \ldots S_n$ be the types of the formal parameters of m.

The method m is *applicable by subtyping* if and only if both of the following conditions hold:

- For $1 \le i \le n$, either:
  - A_i is a subtype (§4.10) of S_i (A_i <: S_i) or
  - A_i is convertible to some type C_i by unchecked conversion (§5.1.9), and C_i <: S_i.
- If m is a generic method as described above then U_l <: $B_l[R_1 = U_1, \ldots, R_p = U_p]$, $1 \le l \le p$.

If no method applicable by subtyping is found, the search for applicable methods continues with phase 2 (§15.12.2.3). Otherwise, the most specific method (§15.12.2.5) is chosen among the methods that are applicable by subtyping.

15.12.2.3 *Phase 2: Identify Matching Arity Methods Applicable by Method Invocation Conversion*

Let m be a potentially applicable method (§15.12.2.1), let $e_1, \ldots, e_n$ be the actual argument expressions of the method invocation and let A_i be the type of e_i, $1 \le i \le n$. Then:

- If m is a generic method, then let $F_1 \ldots F_n$ be the types of the formal parameters of m, and let $R_1 \ldots R_p$ $p \ge 1$, be the formal type parameters of m, and let B_l be the declared bound of R_l, $1 \le l \le p$. Then:
  - If the method invocation does not provide explicit type arguments then let $U_1 \ldots U_p$ be the actual type arguments inferred (§15.12.2.7) for this invocation of m, using a set of initial constraints consisting of the constraints $A_i << F_i$, $1 \le i \le n$.
  - Otherwise let $U_1 \ldots U_p$ be the explicit type arguments given in the method invocation.

  Then let $S_i = F_i[R_1 = U_1, \ldots, R_p = U_p]$ $1 \le i \le n$, be the types inferred for the formal parameters of m.
- Otherwise, let $S_1 \ldots S_n$ be the types of the formal parameters of m.

The method m is *applicable by method invocation conversion* if and only if both of the following conditions hold:

- For $1 \le i \le n$, the type of e_i, A_i, can be converted by method invocation conversion (§5.3) to S_i.
- If m is a generic method as described above then $U_l <: B_l[R_1 = U_1, \ldots, R_p = U_p]$, $1 \le l \le p$.

If no method applicable by method invocation conversion is found, the search for applicable methods continues with phase 3 (§15.12.2.4). Otherwise, the most specific method (§15.12.2.5) is chosen among the methods that are applicable by method invocation conversion.

15.12.2.4 *Phase 3: Identify Applicable Variable Arity Methods*

Let m be a potentially applicable method (§15.12.2.1) with variable arity, let $e_1, \ldots, e_k$ be the actual argument expressions of the method invocation and let A_i be the type of e_i, $1 \le i \le k$. Then:

- If m is a generic method, then let $F_1 \ldots F_n$, where $1 \le n \le k+1$, be the types of the formal parameters of m, where $F_n = T[]$ for some type T, and let R_1

$\ldots$ R_p $p \geq 1$, be the formal type parameters of `m`, and let B_l be the declared bound of R_l, $1 \leq l \leq p$. Then:

- ◆ If the method invocation does not provide explicit type arguments then let U_1 ... U_p be the actual type arguments inferred (§15.12.2.7) for this invocation of `m`, using a set of initial constraints consisting of the constraints A_i << F_i, $1 \leq i < n$ and the constraints A_j << T, $n \leq j \leq k$.
- ◆ Otherwise let U_1 ... U_p be the explicit type arguments given in the method invocation.

Then let $S_i = F_i[R_1 = U_1, \ldots, R_p = U_p]$ $1 \leq i \leq n$, be the types inferred for the formal parameters of `m`.

- Otherwise, let S_1 ... S_n, where $n \leq k+1$, be the types of the formal parameters of `m`.

The method `m` is an *applicable variable-arity method* if and only if all three of the following conditions hold:

- For $1 \leq i < n$, the type of e_i, A_i, can be converted by method invocation conversion to S_i.
- If $k \geq n$, then for $n \leq i \leq k$, the type of e_i, A_i, can be converted by method invocation conversion to the component type of S_n.
- If `m` is a generic method as described above then $U_l <: B_l[R_1 = U_1, \ldots, R_p = U_p]$, $1 \leq l \leq p$.

If no applicable variable arity method is found, a compile-time error occurs. Otherwise, the most specific method (§15.12.2.5) is chosen among the applicable variable-arity methods.

15.12.2.5 *Choosing the Most Specific Method*

If more than one member method is both accessible and applicable to a method invocation, it is necessary to choose one to provide the descriptor for the run-time method dispatch. The Java programming language uses the rule that the *most specific* method is chosen.

The informal intuition is that one method is more specific than another if any invocation handled by the first method could be passed on to the other one without a compile-time type error.

One fixed-arity member method named *m* is *more specific* than another member method of the same name and arity if all of the following conditions hold:

- The declared types of the parameters of the first member method are $T_1, \ldots, T_n$.
- The declared types of the parameters of the other method are $U_1, \ldots, U_n$.
- If the second method is generic then let $R_1 \ldots R_p$ $p \geq 1$, be its formal type parameters, let B_l be the declared bound of R_l, $1 \leq l < p$, let $A_1 \ldots A_p$ be the actual type arguments inferred (§15.12.2.7) for this invocation under the initial constraints $T_i << U_i$, $1 \leq i \leq n$ and let $S_i = U_i[R_1 = A_1, \ldots, R_p = A_p]$ $1 \leq i \leq n$; otherwise let $S_i = U_i$ $1 \leq i \leq n$.
- For all *j* from 1 to n, $T_j <: S_j$.
- If the second method is a generic method as described above then $A_l <: B_l[R_1 = A_1, \ldots, R_p = A_p]$, $1 \leq l \leq p$.

In addition, one variable arity member method named *m* is *more specific* than another variable arity member method of the same name if either:

- One member method has *n* parameters and the other has *k* parameters, where $n \geq k$. The types of the parameters of the first member method are $T_1, \ldots, T_{n-1}, T_n[]$, the types of the parameters of the other method are $U_1, \ldots, U_{k-1}, U_k[]$. If the second method is generic then let $R_1 \ldots R_p$ $p \geq 1$, be its formal type parameters, let B_l be the declared bound of R_l, $1 \leq l \leq p$, let $A_1 \ldots A_p$ be the actual type arguments inferred (§15.12.2.7) for this invocation under the initial constraints $T_i << U_i$, $1 \leq i \leq k-1$, $T_i << U_k$, $k \leq i \leq n$ and let $S_i = U_i[R_1 = A_1, \ldots, R_p = A_p]$ $1 \leq i \leq k$; otherwise let $S_i = U_i$, $1 \leq i \leq k$. Then:
  - for all *j* from 1 to $k-1$, $T_j <: S_j$, and,
  - for all *j* from *k* to n, $T_j <: S_k$, and,
  - If the second method is a generic method as described above then $A_l <: B_l[R_1 = A_1, \ldots, R_p = A_p]$, $1 \leq l < p$.
- One member method has *k* parameters and the other has *n* parameters, where $n \geq k$. The types of the parameters of the first method are $U_1, \ldots, U_{k-1}, U_k[]$, the types of the parameters of the other method are $T_1, \ldots, T_{n-1}, T_n[]$. If the second method is generic then let $R_1 \ldots R_p$ $p \geq 1$, be its formal type parameters, let B_l be the declared bound of R_l, $1 \leq l \leq p$, let $A_1 \ldots A_p$ be the actual type arguments inferred (§15.12.2.7) for this invocation

under the initial constraints U_i << T_i, $1 \le i \le k-1$, U_k << T_i, $k \le i \le n$ and let S_i = T_i[R_1 = A_1, ..., R_p = A_p] $1 \le i \le n$; otherwise let S_i = T_i, $1 \le i \le n$. Then:

- for all j from 1 to $k-1$, U_j <: S_j, and,
- for all j from k to n , U_k <: S_j, and,
- If the second method is a generic method as described above then A_l <: B_l[R_1 = A_1, ..., R_p = A_p], $1 \le l \le p$.

The above conditions are the only circumstances under which one method may be more specific than another.

A method m_1 is *strictly more specific* than another method m_2 if and only if m_1 is more specific than m_2 and m_2 is not more specific than m_1.

A method is said to be *maximally specific* for a method invocation if it is accessible and applicable and there is no other method that is applicable and accessible that is strictly more specific.

If there is exactly one maximally specific method, then that method is in fact *the most specific method*; it is necessarily more specific than any other accessible method that is applicable. It is then subjected to some further compile-time checks as described in §15.12.3.

It is possible that no method is the most specific, because there are two or more methods that are maximally specific. In this case:

- If all the maximally specific methods have override-equivalent (§8.4.2) signatures, then:
  - If exactly one of the maximally specific methods is not declared `abstract`, it is the most specific method.
  - Otherwise, if all the maximally specific methods are declared `abstract`, and the signatures of all of the maximally specific methods have the same erasure (§4.6), then the most specific method is chosen arbitrarily among the subset of the maximally specific methods that have the most specific return type. However, the most specific method is considered to throw a checked exception if and only if that exception or its erasure is declared in the `throws` clauses of each of the maximally specific methods.
- Otherwise, we say that the method invocation is *ambiguous*, and a compile-time error occurs.

15.12.2.6 *Method Result and Throws Types*

- The result type of the chosen method is determined as follows:
  - If the method being invoked is declared with a return type of `void`, then the result is `void`.
  - Otherwise, if unchecked conversion was necessary for the method to be applicable then the result type is the erasure (§4.6) of the method's declared return type.
  - Otherwise, if the method being invoked is generic, then for $1 \le i \le n$, let F_i be the formal type parameters of the method, let A_i be the actual type arguments inferred for the method invocation, and let R be the declared return type of the method being invoked. The result type is obtained by applying capture conversion (§5.1.10) to $R[F_1 := A_1, ..., F_n := A_n]$.
  - Otherwise, the result type is obtained by applying capture conversion (§5.1.10) to the type given in the method declaration.

The exception types of the throws clause of the chosen method are determined as follows:

- If unchecked conversion was necessary for the method to be applicable then the throws clause is composed of the erasure (§4.6) of the types in the method's declared throws clause.
- Otherwise, if the method being invoked is generic, then for $1 \le i \le n$, let F_i be the formal type parameters of the method, let A_i be the actual type arguments inferred for the method invocation, and let E_j, $1 \le j \le m$ be the exception types declared in the throws clause of the method being invoked. The throws clause consists of the types to $E_j[F_1 := A_1, ..., F_n := A_n]$.
- Otherwise, the type of the throws clause is the type given in the method declaration.

A method invocation expression can throw an exception type *E* iff either:

- The method to be invoked is of the form *Primary.Identifier* and the *Primary* expression can throw *E*; or
- Some expression of the argument list can throw *E*; or
- *E* is listed in the throws clause of the type of method that is invoked.

15.12.2.7 *Inferring Type Arguments Based on Actual Arguments*

In this section, we describe the process of inferring type arguments for method and constructor invocations. This process is invoked as a subroutine when testing for method (or constructor) applicability (§15.12.2.2 - §15.12.2.4).

DISCUSSION

The process of type inference is inherently complex. Therefore, it is useful to give an informal overview of the process before delving into the detailed specification.

Inference begins with an initial set of constraints. Generally, the constraints require that the statically known types of the actual arguments are acceptable given the declared formal argument types. We discuss the meaning of "acceptable" below.

Given these initial constraints, one may derive a set of supertype and/or equality constraints on the formal type parameters of the method or constructor.

Next, one must try and find a solution that satisfies the constraints on the type parameters. As a first approximation, if a type parameter is constrained by an equality constraint, then that constraint gives its solution. Bear in mind that the constraint may equate one type parameter with another, and only when the entire set of constraints on all type variables is resolved will we have a solution.

A supertype constraint *T :> X* implies that the solution is one of supertypes of *X*. Given several such constraints on *T*, we can intersect the sets of supertypes implied by each of the constraints, since the type parameter must be a member of all of them. We can then choose the most specific type that is in the intersection.

Computing the intersection is more complicated than one might first realize. Given that a type parameter is constrained to be a supertype of two distinct invocations of a generic type, say `List<Object>` and `List<String>`, the naive intersection operation might yield `Object`. However, a more sophisticated analysis yields a set containing `List<?>`. Similarly, if a type parameter, `T`, is constrained to be a supertype of two unrelated interfaces `I` and `J`, we might infer `T` must be `Object`, or we might obtain a tighter bound of `I & J`. These issues are discussed in more detail later in this section.

We will use the following notational conventions in this section:

- Type expressions are represented using the letters *A, F, U, V* and *W*. The letter *A* is only used to denote the type of an actual parameter, and *F* is only used to denote the type of a formal parameter.
- Type parameters are represented using the letters *S* and *T*
- Arguments to parameterized types are represented using the letters *X, Y*.
- Generic type declarations are represented using the letters *G* and *H*.

Inference begins with a set of *initial constraints* of the form $A << F$, $A = F$, or $A >> F$, where $U << V$ indicates that type U is convertible to type V by method invocation conversion (§5.3), and $U >> V$ indicates that type V is convertible to type U by method invocation conversion.

DISCUSSION

In a simpler world, the constraints could be of the form $A <: F$ - simply requiring that the actual argument types be subtypes of the formal ones. However, reality is more involved. As discussed earlier, method applicability testing consists of up to three phases; this is required for compatibility reasons. Each phase imposes slightly different constraints. If a method is applicable by subtyping (§15.12.2.2), the constraints are indeed subtyping constraints. If a method is applicable by method invocation conversion (§15.12.2.3), the constraints imply that the actual type is convertible to the formal type by method invocation conversion. The situation is similar for the third phase (§15.12.2.4), but the exact form of the constraints differ due to the variable arity.

These constraints are then reduced to a set of simpler constraints of the forms $T :> X$, $T = X$ or $T <: X$, where T is a type parameter of the method. This reduction is achieved by the procedure given below:

DISCUSSION

It may be that the initial constraints are unsatisfiable; we say that inference is *overconstrained*. In that case, we do not necessarily derive unsatisfiable constraints on the type parameters. Instead, we may infer actual type arguments for the invocation, but once we substitute the actual type arguments for the formal type parameters, the applicability test may fail because the actual argument types are not acceptable given the substituted formals.

An alternative strategy would be to have type inference itself fail in such cases. Compilers may choose to do so, provided the effect is equivalent to that specified here.

Given a constraint of the form $A << F$, $A = F$, or $A >> F$:

- If F does not involve a type parameter T_j then no constraint is implied on T_j.
- Otherwise, F involves a type parameter T_j.

- If A is the type of `null`, no constraint is implied on T_j.
- Otherwise, if the constraint has the form $A << F$
  - If A is a primitive type, then A is converted to a reference type U via boxing conversion and this algorithm is applied recursively to the constraint $U << F$.
  - Otherwise, if $F = Tj$, then the constraint $T_j :> A$ is implied.
  - If $F = U[]$, where the type U involves T_j, then if A is an array type $V[]$, or a type variable with an upper bound that is an array type $V[]$, where V is a reference type, this algorithm is applied recursively to the constraint $V << U$.

DISCUSSION

This follows from the covariant subtype relation among array types. The constraint *A << F*, in this case means that *A << U[]*. *A* is therefore necessarily an array type *V[]*, or a type variable whose upper bound is an array type *V[]* - otherwise the relation *A << U[]* could never hold true. It follows that *V[] << U[]*. Since array subtyping is covariant, it must be the case that *V << U*.

  - If F has the form $G<..., Y_{k-1}, U, Y_{k+1}, ...>$, $1 \leq k \leq n$ where U is a type expression that involves T_j, then if A has a supertype of the form $G<..., X_{k-1}, V, X_{k+1}, ...>$ where V is a type expression, this algorithm is applied recursively to the constraint $V = U$.

DISCUSSION

For simplicity, assume that *G* takes a single type argument. If the method invocation being examined is to be applicable, it must be the case that *A* is a subtype of some invocation of *G*. Otherwise, *A << F* would never be true.

In other words, *A << F*, where *F = G<U>*, implies that *A << G<V>* for some *V*. Now, since *U* is a type expression (and therefore, *U* is *not* a wildcard type argument), it must be the case that *U = V*, by the non-variance of ordinary parameterized type invocations.

The formulation above merely generalizes this reasoning to generics with an arbitrary number of type arguments.

- If F has the form $G<..., Y_{k-1}, ?\ extends\ U, Y_{k+1}, ...>$, where U involves T_j, then if A has a supertype that is one of:
  - $G<..., X_{k-1}, V, X_{k+1}, ...>$, where V is a type expression. Then this algorithm is applied recursively to the constraint $V << U$.

DISCUSSION

Again, let's keep things as simple as possible, and consider only the case where *G* has a single type argument.

A <<*F* in this case means *A* << *G<? extends U>*. As above, it must be the case that *A* is a subtype of some invocation of *G*. However, *A* may now be a subtype of either *G<V>*, or *G<? extends V>*, or *G<? super V>*. We examine these cases in turn. The first variation is described (generalized to multiple arguments) by the sub-bullet directly above. We therefore have *A* = *G<V>* << *G<? extends U>*. The rules of subtyping for wildcards imply that *V* << *U*.

  - $G<..., X_{k-1}, ?\ extends\ V, X_{k+1}, ...>$. Then this algorithm is applied recursively to the constraint $V << U$.

DISCUSSION

Extending the analysis above, we have *A* = *G<? extends V>* << *G<? extends U>*. The rules of subtyping for wildcards again imply that *V* << *U*.

  - Otherwise, no constraint is implied on T_j.

DISCUSSION

Here, we have *A* = *G<? super V>* << *G<? extends U>*. In general, we cannot conclude anything in this case. However, it is not necessarily an error. It may be that *U* will eventually be inferred to be `Object`, in which case the call may indeed be valid. Therefore, we simply refrain from placing any constraint on *U*.

- If F has the form G<..., Y_{k-1}, *? super U*, Y_{k+1}, ...>, where U involves T_j, then if A has a supertype that is one of:
  - G<..., X_{k-1}, V, X_{k+1}, ...>. Then this algorithm is applied recursively to the constraint $V >> U$.

DISCUSSION

As usual, we consider only the case where *G* has a single type argument.

A <<*F* in this case means *A* << *G*<*? super U*>. As above, it must be the case that *A* is a subtype of some invocation of *G*. A may now be a subtype of either *G*<*V*>, or *G*<*? extends V*>, or *G*<*? super V*>. We examine these cases in turn. The first variation is described (generalized to multiple arguments) by the sub-bullet directly above. We therefore have *A* = *G*<*V*> << *G*<*? super U*>. The rules of subtyping for wildcards imply that *V* >> *U*.

- G<..., X_{k-1}, *? super V*, X_{k+1}, ...>. Then this algorithm is applied recursively to the constraint $V >> U$.

DISCUSSION

We have *A* = *G*<*? super V*> << *G*<*? super U*>. The rules of subtyping for lower-bounded wildcards again imply that *V* >> *U*.

- Otherwise, no constraint is implied on T_j.

DISCUSSION

Here, we have *A* = *G*<*? extends V*> << *G*<*? super U*>. In general, we cannot conclude anything in this case. However, it is not necessarily an error. It may be that *U* will eventually be inferred to the `null` type, in which case the call may indeed be valid. Therefore, we simply refrain from placing any constraint on *U*.

- Otherwise, no constraint is implied on T_j.

- Otherwise, if the constraint has the form $A = F$

DISCUSSION

Such a constraint is never part of the initial constraints. However, it can arise as the algorithm recurses. We have seen this occur above, when the constraint *A* << *F* relates two parameterized types, as in *G<V>* << *G<U>*.

- If $F = T_j$, then the constraint $T_j = A$ is implied.
- If $F = U[]$ where the type U involves T_j, then if A is an array type $V[]$, or a type variable with an upper bound that is an array type $V[]$, where V is a reference type, this algorithm is applied recursively to the constraint $V = U$.

DISCUSSION

Clearly, if the array types *U[]* and *V[]* are the same, their component types must be the same.

- If F has the form $G<\ldots, Y_{k-1}, U, Y_{k+1}, \ldots>$, $1 \le k \le n$ where U is type expression that involves T_j, then if A is of the form $G<\ldots, X_{k-1}, V, X_{k+1},\ldots>$ where V is a type expression, this algorithm is applied recursively to the constraint $V = U$.
- If F has the form $G<\ldots, Y_{k-1}, ?\ extends\ U, Y_{k+1}, \ldots>$, where U involves T_j, then if A is one of:
  - $G<\ldots, X_{k-1}, ?\ extends\ V, X_{k+1}, \ldots>$. Then this algorithm is applied recursively to the constraint $V = U$.
  - Otherwise, no constraint is implied on T_j.
- If F has the form $G<\ldots, Y_{k-1}, ?\ super\ U, Y_{k+1}, \ldots>$, where U involves T_j, then if A is one of:

    - $G<..., X_{k-1}, ?\ super\ V, X_{k+1}, ...>$. Then this algorithm is applied recursively to the constraint $V = U$.
    - Otherwise, no constraint is implied on T_j.
  - Otherwise, no constraint is implied on T_j.

- Otherwise, if the constraint has the form $A >> F$

DISCUSSION

Such situations arise when the algorithm recurses, due to the contravariant subtyping rules associated with lower-bounded wildcards (those of the form *G<? super X>*).

It might be tempting to consider *A>> F* as being the same as *F << A*, but the problem of inference is not symmetric. We need to remember which participant in the relation includes a type to be inferred.

  - If $F = T_j$, then the constraint $T_j <: A$ is implied.

DISCUSSION

We do not make use of such constraints in the main body of the inference algorithm. However, they are used in section §15.12.2.8.

  - If $F = U[]$, where the type U involves T_j, then if A is an array type $V[]$, or a type variable with an upper bound that is an array type $V[]$, where V is a reference type, this algorithm is applied recursively to the constraint $V >> U$. Otherwise, no constraint is implied on T_j.

DISCUSSION

This follows from the covariant subtype relation among array types. The constraint *A >> F*, in this case means that *A >> U[]*. *A* is therefore necessarily an array type *V[]*, or a type variable whose upper bound is an array type *V[]* - otherwise the relation *A >> U[]* could never hold true. It follows that *V[] >> U[]*. Since array subtyping is covariant, it must be the case that *V >> U*.

- If F has the form $G<..., Y_{k-1}, U, Y_{k+1}, ...>$, where U is a type expression that involves T_j, then:
  - If A is an instance of a non-generic type, then no constraint is implied on T_j.

DISCUSSION

In this case (once again restricting the analysis to the unary case), we have the constraint *A >> F = G<U>*. *A* must be a supertype of the generic type *G*. However, since *A* is not a parameterized type, it cannot depend upon the type argument *U* in any way. It is a supertype of *G<X>* for every *X* that is a valid type argument to *G*. No meaningful constraint on *U* can be derived from *A*.

  - If A is an invocation of a generic type declaration H, where H is either G or superclass or superinterface of G, then:
    - If $H \neq G$, then let $S_1, ..., S_n$ be the formal type parameters of G, and let $H<U_1, ..., U_l>$ be the unique invocation of H that is a supertype of $G<S_1 , ..., S_n>$, and let $V = H<U_1, ..., U_l>[S_k = U]$. Then, if $V :> F$ this algorithm is applied recursively to the constraint $A >> V$.

DISCUSSION

Our goal here is to simplify the relationship between *A* and *F.* We aim to recursively invoke the algorithm on a simpler case, where the actual type argument is known to be an invocation of the same generic type declaration as the formal.

Let's consider the case where both *H* and *G* have only a single type argument. Since we have the constraint *A = H<X> >> F = G<U>*, where *H* is distinct from *G*, it must be the case that *H* is some proper superclass or superinterface of *G*. There must be a (non-wildcard) invocation of *H* that is a supertype of *F = G<U>*. Call this invocation *V*.

If we replace *F* by *V* in the constraint, we will have accomplished the goal of relating two invocations of the same generic (as it happens, *H*).

How do we compute *V?* The declaration of *G* must introduce a formal type parameter S, and there must be some (non-wildcard) invocation of *H, H<U1>*, that is a supertype of

G<S>. Substituting the type expression *U* for *S* will then yield a (non-wildcard) invocation of *H*, *H<U1>[S = U]*, that is a supertype of *G<U>*. For example, in the simplest instance, *U1* might be *S*, in which case we have *G<S> <: H<S>*, and *G<U> <: H<U> = H<S>[S = U] = V*.

It may be the case that *H<U1>* is independent of *S* - that is, *S* does not occur in *U1* at all. However, the substitution described above is still valid - in this situation, *V = H<U1>[S = U] = H<U1>*. Furthermore, in this circumstance, *G<T> <: H<U1>* for any *T*, and in particular *G<U> <: H<U1> = V*.

Regardless of whether *U1* depends on *S*, we have determined the type *V*, the invocation of *H* that is a supertype of G<U>. We can now invoke the algorithm recursively on the constraint *H<X> = A >> V = H<U1>[S = U]*. We will then be able to relate the type arguments of both invocations of *H* and extract the relevant constraints from them.

- Otherwise, if *A* is of the form *G*<..., X_{k-1}, *W*, X_{k+1}, ...>, where *W* is a type expression this algorithm is applied recursively to the constraint *W = U*.

DISCUSSION

We have *A = G<W> >> F = G<U>* for some type expression *W*. Since *W* is a type expression (and *not* a wildcard type argument), it must be the case that *W = U*, by the non-variance of parameterized types.

- Otherwise, if *A* is of the form *G*<..., X_{k-1}, *? extends W*, X_{k+1}, ...>, this algorithm is applied recursively to the constraint *W >> U*.

DISCUSSION

We have *A = G<? extends W> >> F = G<U>* for some type expression *W*. It must be the case that *W >> U*, by the subtyping rules for wildcard types.

- Otherwise, if *A* is of the form *G*<..., X_{k-1}, *? super W*, X_{k+1}, ...>, this algorithm is applied recursively to the constraint *W << U*.

DISCUSSION

We have *A = G<? super W>* >> *F = G<U>* for some type expression *W*. It must be the case that *W* << *U*, by the subtyping rules for wildcard types.

- Otherwise, no constraint is implied on T_j.

- Otherwise, no constraint is implied on T_j.

- If *F* has the form *G<...,* Y_{k-1}*, ? extends U,* Y_{k+1}*, ...>*, where *U* is a type expression that involves T_j, then:

  - If *A* is an instance of a non-generic type, then no constraint is implied on T_j.

DISCUSSION

Once again restricting the analysis to the unary case, we have the constraint *A* >> *F* = *G<? extends U>*. *A* must be a supertype of the generic type *G*. However, since *A* is not a parameterized type, it cannot depend upon *U* in any way. It is a supertype of the type *G<? extends X>* for every *X* such that *? extends X* is a valid type argument to *G*. No meaningful constraint on *U* can be derived from *A*.

  - If *A* is an invocation of a generic type declaration *H*, where *H* is either *G* or superclass or superinterface of *G*, then:

    - If $H \neq G$, then let $S_1, ..., S_n$ be the formal type parameters of *G*, and let *H<*$U_1, ..., U_l$*>* be the unique invocation of *H* that is a supertype of *G<*S_1 , ..., S_n*>*, and let *V = H<? extends* U_1*, ..., ? extends* U_l*>[*S_k *= U]*. Then this algorithm is applied recursively to the constraint *A* >> *V*.

DISCUSSION

Our goal here is once more to simplify the relationship between *A* and *F*, and recursively invoke the algorithm on a simpler case, where the actual type argument is known to be an invocation of the same generic type as the formal.

Assume both *H* and *G* have only a single type argument. Since we have the constraint *A = H<X> >> F = G<? extends U>*, where *H* is distinct from *G*, it must be the case that *H* is some proper superclass or superinterface of *G*. There must be an invocation of *H<Y>* such that *H<X> >> H<Y>* that we can use instead of *F = G<? extends U>*.

How do we compute *H<Y>*? As before, note that the declaration of *G* must introduce a formal type parameter *S*, and there must be some (non-wildcard) invocation of *H*, *H<U1>*, that is a supertype of *G<S>*. However, substituting *? extends U* for *S* is not generally valid. To see this, assume *U1 = T[]*.

Instead, we produce an invocation of *H*, *H<? extends U1>[S = U]*. In the simplest instance, *U1* might be *S*, in which case we have *G<S> <: H<S>*, and *G<? extends U> <: H<? extends U> = H<? extends S>[S = U] = V*.

- Otherwise, if *A* is of the form *G<...,* X_{k-1}*, ? extends W,* X_{k+1}*, ...>*, this algorithm is applied recursively to the constraint *W >>U*.

DISCUSSION

We have *A = G<? extends W> >> F = G<? extends U>* for some type expression *W*. By the subtyping rules for wildcards it must be the case that *W >> U*.

- Otherwise, no constraint is implied on T_j.

- If *F* has the form *G<... ,* Y_{k-1}*, ? super U,* Y_{k+1}*, ...>*, where *U* is a type expression that involves T_j, then *A* is either:
  - If *A* is an instance of a non-generic type, then no constraint is implied on T_j.

DISCUSSION

Restricting the analysis to the unary case, we have the constraint *A >> F = G<? super U>*. *A* must be a supertype of the generic type *G*. However, since *A* is not a parameterized type, it cannot depend upon *U* in any way. It is a supertype of the type *G<? super X>* for every *X* such that *? super X* is a valid type argument to *G*. No meaningful constraint on *U* can be derived from *A*.

- If *A* is an invocation of a generic type declaration *H*, where *H* is either *G* or superclass or superinterface of *G*, then:
  - If $H \neq G$, then let S_1, ..., S_n be the formal type parameters of *G*, and let $H<U_1, ..., U_l>$ be the unique invocation of *H* that is a supertype of $G<S_1, ..., S_n>$, and let $V = H<? \text{ super } U_1, ..., ? \text{ super } U_l>[S_k = U]$. Then this algorithm is applied recursively to the constraint *A >> V*.

DISCUSSION

The treatment here is analogous to the case where *A = G<? extends U>*. Here our example would produce an invocation *H<? super U1>[S = U]*

  - Otherwise, if *A* is of the form $G<..., X_{k-1}, ? \text{ super } W, ..., X_{k+1}, ...>$, this algorithm is applied recursively to the constraint *W << U*.

DISCUSSION

We have *A = G<? super W> >> F = G<? super U>* for some type expression *W*. It must be the case that *W << U*, by the subtyping rules for wildcard types.

  - Otherwise, no constraint is implied on T_j.

DISCUSSION

This concludes the process of determining constraints on the formal type parameters of a method.

Note that this process does not impose any constraints on the type parameters based on their declared bounds. Once the actual type arguments are inferred, they will be tested against the declared bounds of the formal type parameters as part of applicability testing.

Note also that type inference does not affect soundness in any way. If the types inferred are nonsensical, the invocation will yield a type error. The type inference algorithm should be viewed as a heuristic, designed to perfdorm well in practice. If it fails to infer the desired result, explicit type paramneters may be used instead.

Next, for each type variable T_j, $1 \leq j \leq n$, the implied equality constraints are resolved as follows:

For each implied equality constraint $T_j = U$ or $U = T_j$:

- If U is not one of the type parameters of the method, then U is the type inferred for T_j. Then all remaining constraints involving T_j are rewritten such that T_j is replaced with U. There are necessarily no further equality constraints involving T_j, and processing continues with the next type parameter, if any.
- Otherwise, if U is T_j, then this constraint carries no information and may be discarded.
- Otherwise, the constraint is of the form $T_j = T_k$ for $k \neq j$. Then all constraints involving T_j are rewritten such that T_j is replaced with T_k, and processing continues with the next type variable.

Then, for each remaining type variable T_j, the constraints $T_j :> U$ are considered. Given that these constraints are $T_j :> U_1 \ldots T_j :> U_k$, the type of T_j is inferred as $lub(U_1 \ldots U_k)$, computed as follows:

For a type U, we write $ST(U)$ for the set of supertypes of U, and define the erased supertype set of U,

$EST(U) = \{ V \mid W \text{ in } ST(U) \text{ and } V = |W| \}$

where $|W|$ is the erasure (§4.6) of W.

DISCUSSION

The reason for computing the set of erased supertypes is to deal with situations where a type variable is constrained to be a supertype of several distinct invocations of a generic type declaration, For example, if *T :> List<String>* and *T :> List<Object>*, simply intersecting the sets *ST(List<String>) = {List<String>, Collection<String>, Object}* and *ST(List<Object>) = {List<Object>), Collection<Object>, Object}* would yield a set *{Object}*, and we would have lost track of the fact that *T* can safely be assumed to be a *List*.

In contrast, intersecting *EST(List<String>) = {List, Collection, Object}* and *EST(List<Object>) = {List, Collection, Object}* yields *{List, Collection, Object}*, which we will eventually enable us to infer *T = List<?>* as described below.

The erased candidate set for type parameter T_j , *EC*, is the intersection of all the sets *EST(U)* for each *U* in U_1 .. U_k. The minimal erased candidate set for T_j is

$$MEC = \{ V \mid V \text{ in } EC, \text{ and for all } W \neq V \text{ in } EC, \text{ it is not the case that } W <: V\}$$

DISCUSSION

Because we are seeking to infer more precise types, we wish to filter out any candidates that are supertypes of other candidates. This is what computing *MEC* accomplishes.

In our running example, we had *EC = {List, Collection, Object}*, and now *MEC = {List}*.

The next step will be to recover actual type arguments for the inferred types.

For any element *G* of *MEC* that is a generic type declaration, define the relevant invocations of *G*, *Inv(G)* to be:

$$Inv(G) = \{ V \mid 1 \leq i \leq k, V \text{ in } ST(U_i), V = G<...>\}$$

DISCUSSION

In our running example, the only generic element of *MEC* is *List*, and *Inv(List) = {List<String>, List<Object>}*. We now will seek to find a type argument for List that contains (§4.5.1.1) both *String* and *Object*.

This is done by means of the least containing invocation (*lci*) operation defined below. The first line defines *lci()* on a set, such as *Inv(List)*, as an operation on a list of the elements of the set. The next line defines the operation on such lists, as a pairwise reduction on the elements of the list. The third line is the definition of *lci()* on pairs of parameterized types, which in turn relies on the notion of least containing type argument (*lcta*).

lcta() is defined for all six possible cases. Then *CandidateInvocation(G)* defines the most specific invocation of the generic *G* that is contains all the invocations of *G* that are known to be supertypes of T_j. This will be our candidate invocation of *G* in the bound we infer for T_j.

---

and let *CandidateInvocation(G)* = *lci(Inv(G))* where *lci*, the least containing invocation is defined

$lci(S) = lci(e_1, ..., e_n)$ where e_i in S, $1 \le i \le n$

$lci(e_1, ..., e_n) = lci(lci(e_1, e_2), e_3, ..., e_n)$

$lci(G<X_1, ..., X_n>, G<Y_1, ..., Y_n>) = G<lcta(X_1, Y_1),..., lcta(X_n, Y_n)>$

where *lcta()* is the the least containing type argument function defined (assuming U and V are type expressions) as:

lcta(U, V) = *U* if *U* = *V*, *? extends lub(U, V)* otherwise

lcta(U, ? extends V) = *? extends lub(U, V)*

lcta(U, ? super V) = *? super glb(U, V)*

lcta(? extends U, ? extends V) = *? extends lub(U, V)*

lcta(? extends U, ? super V) = *U* if *U* = *V*, *?* otherwise

lcta(? super U, ? super V) = *? super glb(U, V)*

where *glb()* is as defined in (§5.1.10).

DISCUSSION

Finally, we define a bound for T_j based on on all the elements of the minimal erased candidate set of its supertypes. If any of these elements are generic, we use the *CandidateInvocation()* function to recover the type argument information.

Then, define *Candidate(W)* = *CandidateInvocation(W)* if *W* is generic, *W* otherwise.

Then the inferred type for T_j is

$lub(U_1 ... U_k) = Candidate(W_1)$ & ... & $Candidate(W_r)$ where W_i, $1 \le i \le r$, are the elements of *MEC*.

It is possible that the process above yields an infinite type. This is permissible, and Java compilers must recognize such situations and represent them appropriately using cyclic data structures.

DISCUSSION

The possibility of an infinite type stems from the recursive calls to *lub()*.

Readers familiar with recursive types should note that an infinite type is not the same as a recursive type.

15.12.2.8 *Inferring Unresolved Type Arguments*

If any of the method's type arguments were not inferred from the types of the actual arguments, they are now inferred as follows.

- If the method result occurs in a context where it will be subject to assignment conversion (§5.2) to a type S, then let R be the declared result type of the method, and let $R' = R[T_1 = B(T_1) \ldots T_n = B(T_n)]$ where $B(T_i)$ is the type inferred for T_i in the previous section, or T_i if no type was inferred.

  Then, a set of initial constraints consisting of:

- the constraint $S \gg R'$, provided R is not `void`; and
- additional constraints $B_i[T_1 = B(T_1) \ldots T_n = B(T_n)] \gg T_i$, where B_i is the declared bound of T_i,

is created and used to infer constraints on the type arguments using the algorithm of section (§15.12.2.7). Any equality constraints are resolved, and then, for each remaining constraint of the form $T_i <: U_k$, the argument T_i is inferred to be $glb(U_1, \ldots, U_k)$ (§5.1.10).

Any remaining type variables that have not yet been inferred are then inferred to have type `Object`

- Otherwise, the unresolved type arguments are inferred by invoking the procedure described in this section under the assumption that the method result was assigned to a variable of type `Object`.

15.12.2.9 *Examples*

In the example program:

```
public class Doubler {
    static int two() { return two(1); }
    private static int two(int i) { return 2*i; }
}
class Test extends Doubler {
```

```
        public static long two(long j) {return j+j; }
        public static void main(String[] args) {
            System.out.println(two(3));
            System.out.println(Doubler.two(3)); // compile-time error
        }
    }
```

for the method invocation `two(1)` within class `Doubler`, there are two accessible methods named `two`, but only the second one is applicable, and so that is the one invoked at run time. For the method invocation `two(3)` within class `Test`, there are two applicable methods, but only the one in class `Test` is accessible, and so that is the one to be invoked at run time (the argument `3` is converted to type `long`). For the method invocation `Doubler.two(3)`, the class `Doubler`, not class `Test`, is searched for methods named `two`; the only applicable method is not accessible, and so this method invocation causes a compile-time error.

Another example is:

```
class ColoredPoint {
    int x, y;
    byte color;
    void setColor(byte color) { this.color = color; }
}
class Test {
    public static void main(String[] args) {
        ColoredPoint cp = new ColoredPoint();
        byte color = 37;
        cp.setColor(color);
        cp.setColor(37);                    // compile-time error
    }
}
```

Here, a compile-time error occurs for the second invocation of `setColor`, because no applicable method can be found at compile time. The type of the literal `37` is `int`, and `int` cannot be converted to `byte` by method invocation conversion. Assignment conversion, which is used in the initialization of the variable `color`, performs an implicit conversion of the constant from type `int` to `byte`, which is permitted because the value `37` is small enough to be represented in type `byte`; but such a conversion is not allowed for method invocation conversion.

If the method `setColor` had, however, been declared to take an `int` instead of a `byte`, then both method invocations would be correct; the first invocation would be allowed because method invocation conversion does permit a widening conversion from `byte` to `int`. However, a narrowing cast would then be required in the body of `setColor`:

```
void setColor(int color) { this.color = (byte)color; }
```

15.12.2.10 *Example: Overloading Ambiguity*

Consider the example:

```
class Point { int x, y; }
class ColoredPoint extends Point { int color; }

class Test {
	static void test(ColoredPoint p, Point q) {
		System.out.println("(ColoredPoint, Point)");
	}
	static void test(Point p, ColoredPoint q) {
		System.out.println("(Point, ColoredPoint)");
	}
	public static void main(String[] args) {
		ColoredPoint cp = new ColoredPoint();
		test(cp, cp);					// compile-time error
	}
}
```

This example produces an error at compile time. The problem is that there are two declarations of *test* that are applicable and accessible, and neither is more specific than the other. Therefore, the method invocation is ambiguous.

If a third definition of `test` were added:

```
static void test(ColoredPoint p, ColoredPoint q) {
	System.out.println("(ColoredPoint, ColoredPoint)");
}
```

then it would be more specific than the other two, and the method invocation would no longer be ambiguous.

15.12.2.11 *Example: Return Type Not Considered*

As another example, consider:

```
class Point { int x, y; }
class ColoredPoint extends Point { int color; }
class Test {
	static int test(ColoredPoint p) {
		return p.color;
	}
	static String test(Point p) {
		return "Point";
	}
	public static void main(String[] args) {
```

```
        ColoredPoint cp = new ColoredPoint();
        String s = test(cp);               // compile-time error
    }
}
```

Here the most specific declaration of method `test` is the one taking a parameter of type `ColoredPoint`. Because the result type of the method is `int`, a compile-time error occurs because an `int` cannot be converted to a `String` by assignment conversion. This example shows that the result types of methods do not participate in resolving overloaded methods, so that the second `test` method, which returns a `String`, is not chosen, even though it has a result type that would allow the example program to compile without error.

15.12.2.12 *Example: Compile-Time Resolution*

The most applicable method is chosen at compile time; its descriptor determines what method is actually executed at run time. If a new method is added to a class, then source code that was compiled with the old definition of the class might not use the new method, even if a recompilation would cause this method to be chosen.

So, for example, consider two compilation units, one for class `Point`:

```
package points;
public class Point {
    public int x, y;
    public Point(int x, int y) { this.x = x; this.y = y; }
    public String toString() { return toString(""); }
    public String toString(String s) {
        return "(" + x + "," + y + s + ")";
    }
}
```

and one for class `ColoredPoint`:

```
package points;
public class ColoredPoint extends Point {
    public static final int
        RED = 0, GREEN = 1, BLUE = 2;
    public static String[] COLORS =
        { "red", "green", "blue" };
            public byte color;
    public ColoredPoint(int x, int y, int color) {
        super(x, y); this.color = (byte)color;
    }
```

```
        /** Copy all relevant fields of the argument into
            this ColoredPoint object. */
        public void adopt(Point p) { x = p.x; y = p.y; }

        public String toString() {
            String s = "," + COLORS[color];
            return super.toString(s);
        }
    }
```

Now consider a third compilation unit that uses ColoredPoint:

```
import points.*;
class Test {
    public static void main(String[] args) {
        ColoredPoint cp =
            new ColoredPoint(6, 6, ColoredPoint.RED);
        ColoredPoint cp2 =
            new ColoredPoint(3, 3, ColoredPoint.GREEN);
        cp.adopt(cp2);
        System.out.println("cp: " + cp);
    }
}
```

The output is:

```
cp: (3,3,red)
```

The application programmer who coded class Test has expected to see the word green, because the actual argument, a ColoredPoint, has a color field, and color would seem to be a "relevant field" (of course, the documentation for the package Points ought to have been much more precise!).

Notice, by the way, that the most specific method (indeed, the only applicable method) for the method invocation of adopt has a signature that indicates a method of one parameter, and the parameter is of type Point. This signature becomes part of the binary representation of class Test produced by the compiler and is used by the method invocation at run time.

Suppose the programmer reported this software error and the maintainer of the points package decided, after due deliberation, to correct it by adding a method to class ColoredPoint:

```
public void adopt(ColoredPoint p) {
    adopt((Point)p); color = p.color;
}
```

If the application programmer then runs the old binary file for Test with the new binary file for ColoredPoint, the output is still:

```
cp: (3,3,red)
```

because the old binary file for `Test` still has the descriptor "one parameter, whose type is `Point; void`" associated with the method call `cp.adopt(cp2)`. If the source code for `Test` is recompiled, the compiler will then discover that there are now two applicable `adopt` methods, and that the signature for the more specific one is "one parameter, whose type is `ColoredPoint; void`"; running the program will then produce the desired output:

```
cp: (3,3,green)
```

With forethought about such problems, the maintainer of the `points` package could fix the `ColoredPoint` class to work with both newly compiled and old code, by adding defensive code to the old `adopt` method for the sake of old code that still invokes it on `ColoredPoint` arguments:

```
public void adopt(Point p) {
    if (p instanceof ColoredPoint)
        color = ((ColoredPoint)p).color;
    x = p.x; y = p.y;
}
```

Ideally, source code should be recompiled whenever code that it depends on is changed. However, in an environment where different classes are maintained by different organizations, this is not always feasible. Defensive programming with careful attention to the problems of class evolution can make upgraded code much more robust. See §13 for a detailed discussion of binary compatibility and type evolution.

15.12.3 Compile-Time Step 3: Is the Chosen Method Appropriate?

If there is a most specific method declaration for a method invocation, it is called the *compile-time declaration* for the method invocation. Three further checks must be made on the compile-time declaration:

- If the method invocation has, before the left parenthesis, a *MethodName* of the form *Identifier*, and the method is an instance method, then:
  - If the invocation appears within a static context (§8.1.3), then a compile-time error occurs. (The reason is that a method invocation of this form cannot be used to invoke an instance method in places where `this` (§15.8.3) is not defined.)
  - Otherwise, let *C* be the innermost enclosing class of which the method is a member. If the invocation is not directly enclosed by *C* or an inner class of *C*, then a compile-time error occurs
- If the method invocation has, before the left parenthesis, a *MethodName* of the form *TypeName*.*Identifier*, or if the method invocation , before the left

parenthesis, has the form *TypeName*`.`*NonWildTypeArguments Identifier*, then the compile-time declaration should be `static`. If the compile-time declaration for the method invocation is for an instance method, then a compile-time error occurs. (The reason is that a method invocation of this form does not specify a reference to an object that can serve as `this` within the instance method.)

- If the method invocation has, before the left parenthesis, the form `super.`$NonWildTypeArguments_{opt}$ *Identifier*, then:
  - If the method is `abstract`, a compile-time error occurs
  - If the method invocation occurs in a static context, a compile-time error occurs
- If the method invocation has, before the left parenthesis, the form *ClassName*`.super.`$NonWildTypeArguments_{opt}$ *Identifier*, then:
  - If the method is `abstract`, a compile-time error occurs
  - If the method invocation occurs in a static context, a compile-time error occurs
  - Otherwise, let `C` be the class denoted by *ClassName*. If the invocation is not directly enclosed by `C` or an inner class of `C`, then a compile-time error occurs
- If the compile-time declaration for the method invocation is `void`, then the method invocation must be a top-level expression, that is, the *Expression* in an expression statement (§14.8) or in the *ForInit* or *ForUpdate* part of a `for` statement (§14.14), or a compile-time error occurs. (The reason is that such a method invocation produces no value and so must be used only in a situation where a value is not needed.)

The following compile-time information is then associated with the method invocation for use at run time:

- The name of the method.
- The qualifying type of the method invocation (§13.1).
- The number of parameters and the types of the parameters, in order.
- The result type, or `void`.
- The invocation mode, computed as follows:

- If the compile-time declaration has the `static` modifier, then the invocation mode is `static`.
- Otherwise, if the compile-time declaration has the `private` modifier, then the invocation mode is `nonvirtual`.
- Otherwise, if the part of the method invocation before the left parenthesis is of the form `super .` *Identifier* or of the form *ClassName*`.super.`*Identifier* then the invocation mode is `super`.
- Otherwise, if the compile-time declaration is in an interface, then the invocation mode is `interface`.
- Otherwise, the invocation mode is `virtual`.

If the compile-time declaration for the method invocation is not `void`, then the type of the method invocation expression is the result type specified in the compile-time declaration.

15.12.4 Runtime Evaluation of Method Invocation

At run time, method invocation requires five steps. First, a *target reference* may be computed. Second, the argument expressions are evaluated. Third, the accessibility of the method to be invoked is checked. Fourth, the actual code for the method to be executed is located. Fifth, a new activation frame is created, synchronization is performed if necessary, and control is transferred to the method code.

15.12.4.1 *Compute Target Reference (If Necessary)*

There are several cases to consider, depending on which of the five productions for *MethodInvocation* (§15.12) is involved:

- If the first production for *MethodInvocation*, which includes a *MethodName*, is involved, then there are three subcases:
  - If the *MethodName* is a simple name, that is, just an *Identifier*, then there are two subcases:
    - If the invocation mode is `static`, then there is no target reference.
    - Otherwise, let *T* be the enclosing type declaration of which the method is a member, and let *n* be an integer such that *T* is the *n*th lexically enclosing type declaration (§8.1.3) of the class whose declaration immediately contains the method invocation. Then the target reference is the *n*th lexically enclosing instance (§8.1.3) of `this`. It is a compile-time error if the *n*th lexically enclosing instance (§8.1.3) of `this` does not exist.

  - If the *MethodName* is a qualified name of the form *TypeName* . *Identifier*, then there is no target reference.
  - If the *MethodName* is a qualified name of the form *FieldName* . *Identifier*, then there are two subcases:
    - If the invocation mode is `static`, then there is no target reference. The expression *FieldName* is evaluated, but the result is then discarded.
    - Otherwise, the target reference is the value of the expression *FieldName*.
- If the second production for *MethodInvocation*, which includes a *Primary*, is involved, then there are two subcases:
  - If the invocation mode is `static`, then there is no target reference. The expression *Primary* is evaluated, but the result is then discarded.
  - Otherwise, the expression *Primary* is evaluated and the result is used as the target reference.

  In either case, if the evaluation of the *Primary* expression completes abruptly, then no part of any argument expression appears to have been evaluated, and the method invocation completes abruptly for the same reason.
- If the third production for *MethodInvocation*, which includes the keyword `super`, is involved, then the target reference is the value of `this`.
- If the fourth production for *MethodInvocation*, *ClassName*.`super`, is involved, then the target reference is the value of *ClassName*.`this`.
- If the fifth production for *MethodInvocation*, beginning with *TypeName*.*NonWildTypeArguments*, is involved, then there is no target reference.

15.12.4.2 *Evaluate Arguments*

The process of evaluating of the argument list differs, depending on whether the method being invoked is a fixed arity method or a variable arity method (§8.4.1).

If the method being invoked is a variable arity method (§8.4.1) *m*, it necessarily has $n > 0$ formal parameters. The final formal parameter of *m* necessarily has type *T[]* for some *T*, and *m* is necessarily being invoked with $k \geq 0$ actual argument expressions.

If *m* is being invoked with $k \neq n$ actual argument expressions, or, if *m* is being invoked with $k = n$ actual argument expressions and the type of the *k*th argument expression is not assignment compatible with `T[]`, then the argument list $(e_1, \ldots, e_{n-1}, e_n, \ldots e_k)$ is evaluated as if it were written as $(e_1, \ldots, e_{n-1}, new\ T[]\{e_n, \ldots, e_k\})$.

The argument expressions (possibly rewritten as described above) are now evaluated to yield *argument values*. Each argument value corresponds to exactly one of the method's *n* formal parameters.

The argument expressions, if any, are evaluated in order, from left to right. If the evaluation of any argument expression completes abruptly, then no part of any argument expression to its right appears to have been evaluated, and the method invocation completes abruptly for the same reason.The result of evaluating the *j*th argument expression is the *j*th argument value, for $1 \le j \le n$. Evaluation then continues, using the argument values, as described below.

15.12.4.3 *Check Accessibility of Type and Method*

Let `C` be the class containing the method invocation, and let `T` be the qualifying type of the method invocation (§13.1), and `m` be the name of the method, as determined at compile time (§15.12.3). An implementation of the Java programming language must insure, as part of linkage, that the method `m` still exists in the type `T`. If this is not true, then a `NoSuchMethodError` (which is a subclass of `IncompatibleClassChangeError`) occurs. If the invocation mode is `interface`, then the implementation must also check that the target reference type still implements the specified interface. If the target reference type does not still implement the interface, then an `IncompatibleClassChangeError` occurs.

The implementation must also insure, during linkage, that the type `T` and the method `m` are accessible. For the type `T`:

- If `T` is in the same package as `C`, then `T` is accessible.
- If `T` is in a different package than `C`, and `T` is `public`, then `T` is accessible.
- If `T` is in a different package than `C`, and `T` is `protected`, then `T` is accessible if and only if `C` is a subclass of `T`.

For the method `m`:

- If `m` is `public`, then `m` is accessible. (All members of interfaces are `public` (§9.2)).
- If `m` is `protected`, then `m` is accessible if and only if either `T` is in the same package as `C`, or `C` is `T` or a subclass of `T`.
- If `m` has default (package) access, then `m` is accessible if and only if `T` is in the same package as `C`.

- If *m* is `private`, then *m* is accessible if and only if *C* is *T*, or *C* encloses *T*, or *T* encloses *C*, or *T* and *C* are both enclosed by a third class.

If either *T* or *m* is not accessible, then an `IllegalAccessError` occurs (§12.3).

15.12.4.4 *Locate Method to Invoke*

Here inside my paper cup,
Everything is looking up.
—Jim Webb, *Paper Cup* (1967)

The strategy for method lookup depends on the invocation mode.

If the invocation mode is `static`, no target reference is needed and overriding is not allowed. Method *m* of class *T* is the one to be invoked.

Otherwise, an instance method is to be invoked and there is a target reference. If the target reference is `null`, a `NullPointerException` is thrown at this point. Otherwise, the target reference is said to refer to a *target object* and will be used as the value of the keyword `this` in the invoked method. The other four possibilities for the invocation mode are then considered.

If the invocation mode is `nonvirtual`, overriding is not allowed. Method *m* of class *T* is the one to be invoked.

Otherwise, the invocation mode is `interface`, `virtual`, or `super`, and overriding may occur. A *dynamic method lookup* is used. The dynamic lookup process starts from a class *S*, determined as follows:

- If the invocation mode is `interface` or `virtual`, then *S* is initially the actual run-time class *R* of the target object. This is true even if the target object is an array instance. (Note that for invocation mode `interface`, *R* necessarily implements *T*; for invocation mode `virtual`, *R* is necessarily either *T* or a subclass of *T*.)
- If the invocation mode is `super`, then *S* is initially the qualifying type (§13.1) of the method invocation.

The dynamic method lookup uses the following procedure to search class *S*, and then the superclasses of class *S*, as necessary, for method *m*.

Let *X* be the compile-time type of the target reference of the method invocation.

1. If class *S* contains a declaration for a non-abstract method named *m* with the same descriptor (same number of parameters, the same parameter types, and the same return type) required by the method invocation as determined at compile time (§15.12.3), then:

- If the invocation mode is `super` or `interface`, then this is the method to be invoked, and the procedure terminates.
- If the invocation mode is `virtual`, and the declaration in *S* overrides (§8.4.8.1) *X.m*, then the method declared in *S* is the method to be invoked, and the procedure terminates.

2. Otherwise, if *S* has a superclass, this same lookup procedure is performed recursively using the direct superclass of *S* in place of *S*; the method to be invoked is the result of the recursive invocation of this lookup procedure.

The above procedure will always find a non-abstract, accessible method to invoke, provided that all classes and interfaces in the program have been consistently compiled. However, if this is not the case, then various errors may occur. The specification of the behavior of a Java virtual machine under these circumstances is given by *The Java Virtual Machine Specification*.We note that the dynamic lookup process, while described here explicitly, will often be implemented implicitly, for example as a side-effect of the construction and use of per-class method dispatch tables, or the construction of other per-class structures used for efficient dispatch.

15.12.4.5 *Create Frame, Synchronize, Transfer Control*

A method *m* in some class *S* has been identified as the one to be invoked.

Now a new *activation frame* is created, containing the target reference (if any) and the argument values (if any), as well as enough space for the local variables and stack for the method to be invoked and any other bookkeeping information that may be required by the implementation (stack pointer, program counter, reference to previous activation frame, and the like). If there is not sufficient memory available to create such an activation frame, an `StackOverflowError` is thrown.

The newly created activation frame becomes the current activation frame. The effect of this is to assign the argument values to corresponding freshly created parameter variables of the method, and to make the target reference available as `this`, if there is a target reference. Before each argument value is assigned to its corresponding parameter variable, it is subjected to method invocation conversion (§5.3), which includes any required value set conversion (§5.1.13).

If the erasure of the type of the method being invoked differs in its signature from the erasure of the type of the compile-time declaration for the method invocation (§15.12.3), then if any of the argument values is an object which is not an instance of a subclass or subinterface of the erasure of the corresponding formal parameter type in the compile-time declaration for the method invocation, then a `ClassCastException` is thrown.

DISCUSSION

As an example of such a situation, consider the declarations:

```
class C<T> { abstract T id(T x); }
class D extends C<String> { String id(String x) { return x; } }
```

Now, given an invocation

```
C c = new D();
c.id(new Object()); // fails with a ClassCastException
```

The erasure of the actual method being invoked, `D.id()`, differs in its signature from that of the compile-time method declaration, `C.id()`. The former takes an argument of type `String` while the latter takes an argument of type `Object`. The invocation fails with a `ClassCastException` before the body of the method is executed.

Such situations can only arise if the program gives rise to an unchecked warning (§5.1.9).

Implementations can enforce these semantics by creating *bridge methods*. In the above example, the following bridge method would be created in class D:

```
Object id(Object x) { return id((String) x); }
```

This is the method that would actually be invoked by the Java virtual machine in response to the call `c.id(new Object())` shown above, and it will execute the cast and fail, as required.

If the method *m* is a `native` method but the necessary native, implementation-dependent binary code has not been loaded or otherwise cannot be dynamically linked, then an `UnsatisfiedLinkError` is thrown.

If the method *m* is not `synchronized`, control is transferred to the body of the method *m* to be invoked.

If the method *m* is `synchronized`, then an object must be locked before the transfer of control. No further progress can be made until the current thread can obtain the lock. If there is a target reference, then the target must be locked; otherwise the `Class` object for class *S*, the class of the method *m*, must be locked. Control is then transferred to the body of the method *m* to be invoked. The object is automatically unlocked when execution of the body of the method has completed, whether normally or abruptly. The locking and unlocking behavior is exactly as if the body of the method were embedded in a `synchronized` statement (§14.19).

15.12.4.6 *Example: Target Reference and Static Methods*

When a target reference is computed and then discarded because the invocation mode is `static`, the reference is not examined to see whether it is `null`:

```
class Test {
    static void mountain() {
        System.out.println("Monadnock");
    }
    static Test favorite(){
        System.out.print("Mount ");
        return null;
    }

    public static void main(String[] args) {
        favorite().mountain();
    }

}
```

which prints:

```
Mount Monadnock
```

Here `favorite` returns `null`, yet no `NullPointerException` is thrown.

15.12.4.7 *Example: Evaluation Order*

As part of an instance method invocation (§15.12), there is an expression that denotes the object to be invoked. This expression appears to be fully evaluated before any part of any argument expression to the method invocation is evaluated.

So, for example, in:

```
class Test {
    public static void main(String[] args) {
        String s = "one";
        if (s.startsWith(s = "two"))
            System.out.println("oops");
    }
}
```

the occurrence of `s` before "`.startsWith`" is evaluated first, before the argument expression `s="two"`. Therefore, a reference to the string `"one"` is remembered as the target reference before the local variable `s` is changed to refer to the string `"two"`. As a result, the `startsWith` method is invoked for target object `"one"` with argument `"two"`, so the result of the invocation is `false`, as the string `"one"` does not start with `"two"`. It follows that the test program does not print "`oops`".

15.12.4.8 *Example: Overriding*

In the example:

```
class Point {
    final int EDGE = 20;
    int x, y;
    void move(int dx, int dy) {
        x += dx; y += dy;
        if (Math.abs(x) >= EDGE || Math.abs(y) >= EDGE)
            clear();
    }

    void clear() {
        System.out.println("\tPoint clear");
        x = 0; y = 0;
    }
}

class ColoredPoint extends Point {
    int color;
    void clear() {
        System.out.println("\tColoredPoint clear");
        super.clear();
        color = 0;
    }
}
```

the subclass `ColoredPoint` extends the `clear` abstraction defined by its superclass `Point`. It does so by overriding the `clear` method with its own method, which invokes the `clear` method of its superclass, using the form `super.clear`.

This method is then invoked whenever the target object for an invocation of `clear` is a `ColoredPoint`. Even the method `move` in `Point` invokes the `clear` method of class `ColoredPoint` when the class of `this` is `ColoredPoint`, as shown by the output of this test program:

```
class Test {
    public static void main(String[] args) {
        Point p = new Point();
        System.out.println("p.move(20,20):");
        p.move(20, 20);
        ColoredPoint cp = new ColoredPoint();
        System.out.println("cp.move(20,20):");
        cp.move(20, 20);
        p = new ColoredPoint();
        System.out.println("p.move(20,20), p colored:");
        p.move(20, 20);
```

```
    }
}
```

which is:

```
p.move(20,20):
    Point clear
cp.move(20,20):
    ColoredPoint clear
    Point clear
p.move(20,20), p colored:
    ColoredPoint clear
    Point clear
```

Overriding is sometimes called "late-bound self-reference"; in this example it means that the reference to `clear` in the body of `Point.move` (which is really syntactic shorthand for `this.clear`) invokes a method chosen "late" (at run time, based on the run-time class of the object referenced by `this`) rather than a method chosen "early" (at compile time, based only on the type of `this`). This provides the programmer a powerful way of extending abstractions and is a key idea in object-oriented programming.

15.12.4.9 *Example: Method Invocation using* `super`

An overridden instance method of a superclass may be accessed by using the keyword `super` to access the members of the immediate superclass, bypassing any overriding declaration in the class that contains the method invocation.

When accessing an instance variable, `super` means the same as a cast of `this` (§15.11.2), but this equivalence does not hold true for method invocation. This is demonstrated by the example:

```
class T1 {
    String s() { return "1"; }
}
class T2 extends T1 {
    String s() { return "2"; }
}
class T3 extends T2 {
            String s() { return "3"; }
    void test() {
        System.out.println("s()=\t\t"+s());
        System.out.println("super.s()=\t"+super.s());
        System.out.print("((T2)this).s()=\t");
        System.out.println(((T2)this).s());
        System.out.print("((T1)this).s()=\t");
```

```
            System.out.println(((T1)this).s());
        }
    }
    class Test {
        public static void main(String[] args) {
            T3 t3 = new T3();
            t3.test();
        }
    }
```

which produces the output:

```
s()=            3
super.s()=      2
((T2)this).s()= 3
((T1)this).s()= 3
```

The casts to types T1 and T2 do not change the method that is invoked, because the instance method to be invoked is chosen according to the run-time class of the object referred to be this. A cast does not change the class of an object; it only checks that the class is compatible with the specified type.

15.13 Array Access Expressions

An array access expression refers to a variable that is a component of an array.

ArrayAccess:
  ExpressionName [*Expression*]
  PrimaryNoNewArray [*Expression*]

An array access expression contains two subexpressions, the *array reference expression* (before the left bracket) and the *index expression* (within the brackets). Note that the array reference expression may be a name or any primary expression that is not an array creation expression (§15.10).

The type of the array reference expression must be an array type (call it *T*[], an array whose components are of type *T*) or a compile-time error results. Then the type of the array access expression is the result of applying capture conversion (§5.1.10) to *T*.

The index expression undergoes unary numeric promotion (§); the promoted type must be int.

The result of an array reference is a variable of type *T*, namely the variable within the array selected by the value of the index expression. This resulting variable, which is a component of the array, is never considered final, even if the array reference was obtained from a final variable.

15.13.1 Runtime Evaluation of Array Access

An array access expression is evaluated using the following procedure:

- First, the array reference expression is evaluated. If this evaluation completes abruptly, then the array access completes abruptly for the same reason and the index expression is not evaluated.
- Otherwise, the index expression is evaluated. If this evaluation completes abruptly, then the array access completes abruptly for the same reason.
- Otherwise, if the value of the array reference expression is `null`, then a `NullPointerException` is thrown.
- Otherwise, the value of the array reference expression indeed refers to an array. If the value of the index expression is less than zero, or greater than or equal to the array's length, then an `ArrayIndexOutOfBoundsException` is thrown.
- Otherwise, the result of the array access is the variable of type *T*, within the array, selected by the value of the index expression. (Note that this resulting variable, which is a component of the array, is never considered `final`, even if the array reference expression is a `final` variable.)

15.13.2 Examples: Array Access Evaluation Order

In an array access, the expression to the left of the brackets appears to be fully evaluated before any part of the expression within the brackets is evaluated. For example, in the (admittedly monstrous) expression `a[(a=b)[3]]`, the expression `a` is fully evaluated before the expression `(a=b)[3]`; this means that the original value of `a` is fetched and remembered while the expression `(a=b)[3]` is evaluated. This array referenced by the original value of `a` is then subscripted by a value that is element `3` of another array (possibly the same array) that was referenced by `b` and is now also referenced by `a`.

Thus, the example:

```
class Test {
    public static void main(String[] args) {
        int[] a = { 11, 12, 13, 14 };
        int[] b = { 0, 1, 2, 3 };
        System.out.println(a[(a=b)[3]]);
    }
}
```

prints:

```
14
```

because the monstrous expression's value is equivalent to `a[b[3]]` or `a[3]` or `14`.

If evaluation of the expression to the left of the brackets completes abruptly, no part of the expression within the brackets will appear to have been evaluated. Thus, the example:

```
class Test {
    public static void main(String[] args) {
        int index = 1;
        try {
            skedaddle()[index=2]++;
        } catch (Exception e) {
            System.out.println(e + ", index=" + index);
        }
    }
    static int[] skedaddle() throws Exception {
        throw new Exception("Ciao");
    }
}
```

prints:

```
java.lang.Exception: Ciao, index=1
```

because the embedded assignment of 2 to `index` never occurs.

If the array reference expression produces `null` instead of a reference to an array, then a `NullPointerException` is thrown at run time, but only after all parts of the array access expression have been evaluated and only if these evaluations completed normally. Thus, the example:

```
class Test {
    public static void main(String[] args) {
        int index = 1;
        try {
            nada()[index=2]++;
        } catch (Exception e) {
            System.out.println(e + ", index=" + index);
        }
    }

            static int[] nada() { return null; }
}
```

prints:

```
java.lang.NullPointerException, index=2
```

because the embedded assignment of 2 to `index` occurs before the check for a null pointer. As a related example, the program:

```
class Test {
    public static void main(String[] args) {
        int[] a = null;
        try {
```

```
            int i = a[vamoose()];
            System.out.println(i);
        } catch (Exception e) {
            System.out.println(e);
        }
    }
    static int vamoose() throws Exception {
        throw new Exception("Twenty-three skidoo!");
    }
}
```

always prints:

```
java.lang.Exception: Twenty-three skidoo!
```

A `NullPointerException` never occurs, because the index expression must be completely evaluated before any part of the indexing operation occurs, and that includes the check as to whether the value of the left-hand operand is `null`.

15.14 Postfix Expressions

Postfix expressions include uses of the postfix ++ and -- operators. Also, as discussed in §15.8, names are not considered to be primary expressions, but are handled separately in the grammar to avoid certain ambiguities. They become interchangeable only here, at the level of precedence of postfix expressions.

PostfixExpression:
  Primary
  ExpressionName
  PostIncrementExpression
  PostDecrementExpression

15.14.1 Expression Names

The rules for evaluating expression names are given in §6.5.6.

15.14.2 Postfix Increment Operator ++

PostIncrementExpression:
  PostfixExpression ++

A postfix expression followed by a ++ operator is a postfix increment expression. The result of the postfix expression must be a variable of a type that is convertible (§5.1.8) to a numeric type, or a compile-time error occurs. The type of the postfix increment expression is the type of the variable. The result of the postfix increment expression is not a variable, but a value.

At run time, if evaluation of the operand expression completes abruptly, then the postfix increment expression completes abruptly for the same reason and no incrementation occurs. Otherwise, the value `1` is added to the value of the variable and the sum is stored back into the variable. Before the addition, binary numeric promotion (§5.6.2) is performed on the value `1` and the value of the variable. If necessary, the sum is narrowed by a narrowing primitive conversion (§5.1.3) and/or subjected to boxing conversion (§5.1.7) to the type of the variable before it is stored. The value of the postfix increment expression is the value of the variable *before* the new value is stored.

Note that the binary numeric promotion mentioned above may include unboxing conversion (§5.1.8) and value set conversion (§5.1.13). If necessary, value set conversion is applied to the sum prior to its being stored in the variable.

A variable that is declared `final` cannot be incremented (unless it is a definitely unassigned (§16) blank final variable (§4.12.4)), because when an access of such a `final` variable is used as an expression, the result is a value, not a variable. Thus, it cannot be used as the operand of a postfix increment operator.

15.14.3 Postfix Decrement Operator `--`

PostDecrementExpression:
  PostfixExpression `--`

A postfix expression followed by a `--` operator is a postfix decrement expression. The result of the postfix expression must be a variable of a type that is convertible (§5.1.8) to a numeric type, or a compile-time error occurs. The type of the postfix decrement expression is the type of the variable. The result of the postfix decrement expression is not a variable, but a value.

At run time, if evaluation of the operand expression completes abruptly, then the postfix decrement expression completes abruptly for the same reason and no decrementation occurs. Otherwise, the value `1` is subtracted from the value of the variable and the difference is stored back into the variable. Before the subtraction, binary numeric promotion (§5.6.2) is performed on the value `1` and the value of the variable. If necessary, the difference is narrowed by a narrowing primitive conversion (§5.1.3) and/or subjected to boxing conversion (§5.1.7) to the type of the variable before it is stored. The value of the postfix decrement expression is the value of the variable *before* the new value is stored.

Note that the binary numeric promotion mentioned above may include unboxing conversion (§5.1.8) and value set conversion (§5.1.13). If necessary, value set conversion is applied to the difference prior to its being stored in the variable.

A variable that is declared `final` cannot be decremented (unless it is a definitely unassigned (§16) blank final variable (§4.12.4)), because when an access of such a `final` variable is used as an expression, the result is a value, not a variable. Thus, it cannot be used as the operand of a postfix decrement operator.

15.15 Unary Operators

The *unary operators* include `+`, `-`, `++`, `--`, `~`, `!`, and cast operators. Expressions with unary operators group right-to-left, so that `-~x` means the same as `-(~x)`.

UnaryExpression:
  PreIncrementExpression
  PreDecrementExpression
  `+` *UnaryExpression*
  `-` *UnaryExpression*
  UnaryExpressionNotPlusMinus

PreIncrementExpression:
  `++` *UnaryExpression*

PreDecrementExpression:
  `--` *UnaryExpression*

UnaryExpressionNotPlusMinus:
  PostfixExpression
  `~` *UnaryExpression*
  `!` *UnaryExpression*
  CastExpression

The following productions from §15.16 are repeated here for convenience:

CastExpression:
  `(` *PrimitiveType* `)` *UnaryExpression*
  `(` *ReferenceType* `)` *UnaryExpressionNotPlusMinus*

15.15.1 Prefix Increment Operator ++

A unary expression preceded by a `++` operator is a prefix increment expression. The result of the unary expression must be a variable of a type that is convertible (§5.1.8) to a numeric type, or a compile-time error occurs. The type of the prefix increment expression is the type of the variable. The result of the prefix increment expression is not a variable, but a value.

At run time, if evaluation of the operand expression completes abruptly, then the prefix increment expression completes abruptly for the same reason and no incrementation occurs. Otherwise, the value `1` is added to the value of the variable and the sum is stored back into the variable. Before the addition, binary numeric promotion (§5.6.2) is performed on the value `1` and the value of the variable. If necessary, the sum is narrowed by a narrowing primitive conversion (§5.1.3) and/or subjected to boxing conversion (§5.1.7) to the type of the variable before it is stored. The value of the prefix increment expression is the value of the variable *after* the new value is stored.

Note that the binary numeric promotion mentioned above may include unboxing conversion (§5.1.8) and value set conversion (§5.1.13). If necessary, value set conversion is applied to the sum prior to its being stored in the variable.

A variable that is declared `final` cannot be incremented (unless it is a definitely unassigned (§16) blank final variable (§4.12.4)), because when an access of such a `final` variable is used as an expression, the result is a value, not a variable. Thus, it cannot be used as the operand of a prefix increment operator.

15.15.2 Prefix Decrement Operator `--`

He must increase, but I must decrease.
—John 3:30

A unary expression preceded by a `--` operator is a prefix decrement expression. The result of the unary expression must be a variable of a type that is convertible (§5.1.8) to a numeric type, or a compile-time error occurs. The type of the prefix decrement expression is the type of the variable. The result of the prefix decrement expression is not a variable, but a value.

At run time, if evaluation of the operand expression completes abruptly, then the prefix decrement expression completes abruptly for the same reason and no decrementation occurs. Otherwise, the value `1` is subtracted from the value of the variable and the difference is stored back into the variable. Before the subtraction, binary numeric promotion (§5.6.2) is performed on the value `1` and the value of the variable. If necessary, the difference is narrowed by a narrowing primitive conversion (§5.1.3) and/or subjected to boxing conversion (§5.1.7) to the type of the variable before it is stored. The value of the prefix decrement expression is the value of the variable *after* the new value is stored.

Note that the binary numeric promotion mentioned above may include unboxing conversion (§5.1.8) and value set conversion (§5.1.13). If necessary, format conversion is applied to the difference prior to its being stored in the variable.

A variable that is declared `final` cannot be decremented (unless it is a definitely unassigned (§16) blank final variable (§4.12.4)), because when an access of such a `final` variable is used as an expression, the result is a value, not a variable. Thus, it cannot be used as the operand of a prefix decrement operator.

15.15.3 Unary Plus Operator +

The type of the operand expression of the unary + operator must be a type that is convertible (§5.1.8) to a primitive numeric type, or a compile-time error occurs. Unary numeric promotion (§) is performed on the operand. The type of the unary plus expression is the promoted type of the operand. The result of the unary plus expression is not a variable, but a value, even if the result of the operand expression is a variable.

At run time, the value of the unary plus expression is the promoted value of the operand.

15.15.4 Unary Minus Operator -

It is so very agreeable to hear a voice and to see all the signs of that expression.
—Gertrude Stein, *Rooms* (1914), in *Tender Buttons*

The type of the operand expression of the unary - operator must be a type that is convertible (§5.1.8) to a primitive numeric type, or a compile-time error occurs. Unary numeric promotion (§) is performed on the operand. The type of the unary minus expression is the promoted type of the operand.

Note that unary numeric promotion performs value set conversion (§5.1.13). Whatever value set the promoted operand value is drawn from, the unary negation operation is carried out and the result is drawn from that same value set. That result is then subject to further value set conversion.

At run time, the value of the unary minus expression is the arithmetic negation of the promoted value of the operand.

For integer values, negation is the same as subtraction from zero. The Java programming language uses two's-complement representation for integers, and the range of two's-complement values is not symmetric, so negation of the maximum negative `int` or `long` results in that same maximum negative number. Overflow occurs in this case, but no exception is thrown. For all integer values `x`, `-x` equals `(~x)+1`.

For floating-point values, negation is not the same as subtraction from zero, because if `x` is `+0.0`, then `0.0-x` is `+0.0`, but `-x` is `-0.0`. Unary minus merely inverts the sign of a floating-point number. Special cases of interest:

- If the operand is NaN, the result is NaN (recall that NaN has no sign).
- If the operand is an infinity, the result is the infinity of opposite sign.

- If the operand is a zero, the result is the zero of opposite sign.

15.15.5 Bitwise Complement Operator ~

The type of the operand expression of the unary ~ operator must be a type that is convertible (§5.1.8) to a primitive integral type, or a compile-time error occurs. Unary numeric promotion (§) is performed on the operand. The type of the unary bitwise complement expression is the promoted type of the operand.

At run time, the value of the unary bitwise complement expression is the bitwise complement of the promoted value of the operand; note that, in all cases, `~x` equals `(-x)-1`.

15.15.6 Logical Complement Operator !

The type of the operand expression of the unary `!` operator must be `boolean` or `Boolean`, or a compile-time error occurs. The type of the unary logical complement expression is `boolean`.

At run time, the operand is subject to unboxing conversion (§5.1.8) if necessary; the value of the unary logical complement expression is `true` if the (possibly converted) operand value is `false` and `false` if the (possibly converted) operand value is `true`.

15.16 Cast Expressions

My days among the dead are passed;
Around me I behold,
Where'er these casual eyes are cast,
The mighty minds of old . . .

—Robert Southey (1774–1843),
Occasional Pieces, xviii

A cast expression converts, at run time, a value of one numeric type to a similar value of another numeric type; or confirms, at compile time, that the type of an expression is `boolean`; or checks, at run time, that a reference value refers to an object whose class is compatible with a specified reference type.

CastExpression:
(*PrimitiveType* $Dims_{opt}$) *UnaryExpression*
(*ReferenceType*) *UnaryExpressionNotPlusMinus*

See §15.15 for a discussion of the distinction between *UnaryExpression* and *UnaryExpressionNotPlusMinus*.

The type of a cast expression is the result of applying capture conversion (§5.1.10) to the type whose name appears within the parentheses. (The parentheses and the type they contain are sometimes called the *cast operator*.) The result of a cast expression is not a variable, but a value, even if the result of the operand expression is a variable.

A cast operator has no effect on the choice of value set (§4.2.3) for a value of type `float` or type `double`. Consequently, a cast to type `float` within an expression that is not FP-strict (§15.4) does not necessarily cause its value to be converted to an element of the float value set, and a cast to type `double` within an expression that is not FP-strict does not necessarily cause its value to be converted to an element of the double value set.

It is a compile-time error if the compile-time type of the operand may never be cast to the type specified by the cast operator according to the rules of casting conversion (§5.5). Otherwise, at run-time, the operand value is converted (if necessary) by casting conversion to the type specified by the cast operator.

Some casts result in an error at compile time. Some casts can be proven, at compile time, always to be correct at run time. For example, it is always correct to convert a value of a class type to the type of its superclass; such a cast should require no special action at run time. Finally, some casts cannot be proven to be either always correct or always incorrect at compile time. Such casts require a test at run time. See for §5.5 details.

A `ClassCastException` is thrown if a cast is found at run time to be impermissible.

15.17 Multiplicative Operators

The operators `*`, `/`, and `%` are called the *multiplicative operators*. They have the same precedence and are syntactically left-associative (they group left-to-right).

MultiplicativeExpression:
    UnaryExpression
    MultiplicativeExpression `*` *UnaryExpression*
    MultiplicativeExpression `/` *UnaryExpression*
    MultiplicativeExpression `%` *UnaryExpression*

The type of each of the operands of a multiplicative operator must be a type that is convertible (§5.1.8) to a primitive numeric type, or a compile-time error occurs. Binary numeric promotion is performed on the operands (§5.6.2). The type of a multiplicative expression is the promoted type of its operands. If this promoted type is `int` or `long`, then integer arithmetic is performed; if this promoted type is `float` or `double`, then floating-point arithmetic is performed.

Note that binary numeric promotion performs unboxing conversion (§5.1.8) and value set conversion (§5.1.13).

15.17.1 Multiplication Operator *

Entia non sunt multiplicanda praeter necessitatem.
—William of Occam (c. 1320)

The binary `*` operator performs multiplication, producing the product of its operands. Multiplication is a commutative operation if the operand expressions have no side effects. While integer multiplication is associative when the operands are all of the same type, floating-point multiplication is not associative.

If an integer multiplication overflows, then the result is the low-order bits of the mathematical product as represented in some sufficiently large two's-complement format. As a result, if overflow occurs, then the sign of the result may not be the same as the sign of the mathematical product of the two operand values.

The result of a floating-point multiplication is governed by the rules of IEEE 754 arithmetic:

- If either operand is NaN, the result is NaN.
- If the result is not NaN, the sign of the result is positive if both operands have the same sign, and negative if the operands have different signs.
- Multiplication of an infinity by a zero results in NaN.
- Multiplication of an infinity by a finite value results in a signed infinity. The sign is determined by the rule stated above.
- In the remaining cases, where neither an infinity nor NaN is involved, the exact mathematical product is computed. A floating-point value set is then chosen:
  - If the multiplication expression is FP-strict (§15.4):
    - If the type of the multiplication expression is `float`, then the float value set must be chosen.
    - If the type of the multiplication expression is `double`, then the double value set must be chosen.
  - If the multiplication expression is not FP-strict:

- If the type of the multiplication expression is `float`, then either the float value set or the float-extended-exponent value set may be chosen, at the whim of the implementation.
- If the type of the multiplication expression is `double`, then either the double value set or the double-extended-exponent value set may be chosen, at the whim of the implementation.

Next, a value must be chosen from the chosen value set to represent the product. If the magnitude of the product is too large to represent, we say the operation overflows; the result is then an infinity of appropriate sign. Otherwise, the product is rounded to the nearest value in the chosen value set using IEEE 754 round-to-nearest mode. The Java programming language requires support of gradual underflow as defined by IEEE 754 (§4.2.4).

Despite the fact that overflow, underflow, or loss of information may occur, evaluation of a multiplication operator `*` never throws a run-time exception.

15.17.2 Division Operator /

Gallia est omnis divisa in partes tres.
—Julius Caesar, *Commentaries on the Gallic Wars* (58 B.C.)

The binary `/` operator performs division, producing the quotient of its operands. The left-hand operand is the dividend and the right-hand operand is the divisor.

Integer division rounds toward `0`. That is, the quotient produced for operands n and d that are integers after binary numeric promotion (§5.6.2) is an integer value q whose magnitude is as large as possible while satisfying $|d \cdot q| \leq |n|$; moreover, q is positive when $|n| \geq |d|$ and n and d have the same sign, but q is negative when $|n| \geq |d|$ and n and d have opposite signs. There is one special case that does not satisfy this rule: if the dividend is the negative integer of largest possible magnitude for its type, and the divisor is `-1`, then integer overflow occurs and the result is equal to the dividend. Despite the overflow, no exception is thrown in this case. On the other hand, if the value of the divisor in an integer division is `0`, then an `ArithmeticException` is thrown.

The result of a floating-point division is determined by the specification of IEEE arithmetic:

- If either operand is NaN, the result is NaN.
- If the result is not NaN, the sign of the result is positive if both operands have the same sign, negative if the operands have different signs.

- Division of an infinity by an infinity results in NaN.
- Division of an infinity by a finite value results in a signed infinity. The sign is determined by the rule stated above.
- Division of a finite value by an infinity results in a signed zero. The sign is determined by the rule stated above.
- Division of a zero by a zero results in NaN; division of zero by any other finite value results in a signed zero. The sign is determined by the rule stated above.
- Division of a nonzero finite value by a zero results in a signed infinity. The sign is determined by the rule stated above.
- In the remaining cases, where neither an infinity nor NaN is involved, the exact mathematical quotient is computed. A floating-point value set is then chosen:
  - If the division expression is FP-strict (§15.4):
    - If the type of the division expression is `float`, then the float value set must be chosen.
    - If the type of the division expression is `double`, then the double value set must be chosen.
  - If the division expression is not FP-strict:
    - If the type of the division expression is `float`, then either the float value set or the float-extended-exponent value set may be chosen, at the whim of the implementation.
    - If the type of the division expression is `double`, then either the double value set or the double-extended-exponent value set may be chosen, at the whim of the implementation.

  Next, a value must be chosen from the chosen value set to represent the quotient. If the magnitude of the quotient is too large to represent, we say the operation overflows; the result is then an infinity of appropriate sign. Otherwise, the quotient is rounded to the nearest value in the chosen value set using IEEE 754 round-to-nearest mode. The Java programming language requires support of gradual underflow as defined by IEEE 754 (§4.2.4).

Despite the fact that overflow, underflow, division by zero, or loss of information may occur, evaluation of a floating-point division operator `/` never throws a run-time exception

15.17.3 Remainder Operator %

And on the pedestal these words appear:
"My name is Ozymandias, king of kings:
Look on my works, ye Mighty, and despair!"
Nothing beside remains.
—Percy Bysshe Shelley, *Ozymandias* (1817)

The binary % operator is said to yield the remainder of its operands from an implied division; the left-hand operand is the dividend and the right-hand operand is the divisor.

In C and C++, the remainder operator accepts only integral operands, but in the Java programming language, it also accepts floating-point operands.

The remainder operation for operands that are integers after binary numeric promotion (§5.6.2) produces a result value such that `(a/b)*b+(a%b)` is equal to `a`. This identity holds even in the special case that the dividend is the negative integer of largest possible magnitude for its type and the divisor is `-1` (the remainder is `0`). It follows from this rule that the result of the remainder operation can be negative only if the dividend is negative, and can be positive only if the dividend is positive; moreover, the magnitude of the result is always less than the magnitude of the divisor. If the value of the divisor for an integer remainder operator is `0`, then an `ArithmeticException` is thrown.Examples:

`5%3` produces `2` (note that `5/3` produces `1`)
`5%(-3)` produces `2` (note that `5/(-3)` produces `-1`)
`(-5)%3` produces `-2` (note that `(-5)/3` produces `-1`)
`(-5)%(-3)` produces `-2` (note that `(-5)/(-3)` produces `1`)

The result of a floating-point remainder operation as computed by the % operator is *not* the same as that produced by the remainder operation defined by IEEE 754. The IEEE 754 remainder operation computes the remainder from a rounding division, not a truncating division, and so its behavior is *not* analogous to that of the usual integer remainder operator. Instead, the Java programming language defines % on floating-point operations to behave in a manner analogous to that of the integer remainder operator; this may be compared with the C library function `fmod`. The IEEE 754 remainder operation may be computed by the library routine `Math.IEEEremainder`.

The result of a floating-point remainder operation is determined by the rules of IEEE arithmetic:

- If either operand is NaN, the result is NaN.
- If the result is not NaN, the sign of the result equals the sign of the dividend.
- If the dividend is an infinity, or the divisor is a zero, or both, the result is NaN.

- If the dividend is finite and the divisor is an infinity, the result equals the dividend.
- If the dividend is a zero and the divisor is finite, the result equals the dividend.
- In the remaining cases, where neither an infinity, nor a zero, nor NaN is involved, the floating-point remainder *r* from the division of a dividend *n* by a divisor *d* is defined by the mathematical relation $r = n - (d \cdot q)$ where *q* is an integer that is negative only if n/d is negative and positive only if n/d is positive, and whose magnitude is as large as possible without exceeding the magnitude of the true mathematical quotient of *n* and *d*.

Evaluation of a floating-point remainder operator `%` never throws a run-time exception, even if the right-hand operand is zero. Overflow, underflow, or loss of precision cannot occur.

Examples:

`5.0%3.0` produces `2.0`
`5.0%(-3.0)` produces `2.0`
`(-5.0)%3.0` produces `-2.0`
`(-5.0)%(-3.0)` produces `-2.0`

15.18 Additive Operators

The operators `+` and `-` are called the *additive operators*. They have the same precedence and are syntactically left-associative (they group left-to-right).

AdditiveExpression:
  MultiplicativeExpression
  AdditiveExpression `+` *MultiplicativeExpression*
  AdditiveExpression `-` *MultiplicativeExpression*

If the type of either operand of a `+` operator is `String`, then the operation is string concatenation.

Otherwise, the type of each of the operands of the `+` operator must be a type that is convertible (§5.1.8) to a primitive numeric type, or a compile-time error occurs.

In every case, the type of each of the operands of the binary `-` operator must be a type that is convertible (§5.1.8) to a primitive numeric type, or a compile-time error occurs.

15.18.1 String Concatenation Operator +

"The fifth string was added after an unfortunate episode in the Garden of Eden . . ."
—John Philip Sousa, *The Fifth String* (1902), Chapter 6

If only one operand expression is of type `String`, then string conversion is performed on the other operand to produce a string at run time. The result is a reference to a `String` object (newly created, unless the expression is a compile-time constant expression (§15.28))that is the concatenation of the two operand strings. The characters of the left-hand operand precede the characters of the right-hand operand in the newly created string. If an operand of type `String` is `null`, then the string `"null"` is used instead of that operand.

15.18.1.1 *String Conversion*

Any type may be converted to type `String` by *string conversion.*

A value `x` of primitive type `T` is first converted to a reference value as if by giving it as an argument to an appropriate class instance creation expression:

- If `T` is `boolean`, then use `new Boolean(x)`.
- If `T` is `char`, then use `new Character(x)`.
- If `T` is `byte`, `short`, or `int`, then use `new Integer(x)`.
- If `T` is `long`, then use `new Long(x)`.
- If `T` is `float`, then use `new Float(x)`.
- If `T` is `double`, then use `new Double(x)`.

This reference value is then converted to type `String` by string conversion.

Now only reference values need to be considered. If the reference is `null`, it is converted to the string `"null"` (four ASCII characters `n`, `u`, `l`, `l`). Otherwise, the conversion is performed as if by an invocation of the `toString` method of the referenced object with no arguments; but if the result of invoking the `toString` method is `null`, then the string `"null"` is used instead.

The `toString` method is defined by the primordial class `Object`; many classes override it, notably `Boolean`, `Character`, `Integer`, `Long`, `Float`, `Double`, and `String`.

15.18.1.2 *Optimization of String Concatenation*

An implementation may choose to perform conversion and concatenation in one step to avoid creating and then discarding an intermediate `String` object. To increase the performance of repeated string concatenation, a Java compiler may use the `StringBuffer` class or a similar technique to reduce the number of intermediate `String` objects that are created by evaluation of an expression.

For primitive types, an implementation may also optimize away the creation of a wrapper object by converting directly from a primitive type to a string.

15.18.1.3 *Examples of String Concatenation*

The example expression:

```
"The square root of 2 is " + Math.sqrt(2)
```

produces the result:

```
"The square root of 2 is 1.4142135623730952"
```

The + operator is syntactically left-associative, no matter whether it is later determined by type analysis to represent string concatenation or addition. In some cases care is required to get the desired result. For example, the expression:

```
a + b + c
```

is always regarded as meaning:

```
(a + b) + c
```

Therefore the result of the expression:

```
1 + 2 + " fiddlers"
```

is:

```
"3 fiddlers"
```

but the result of:

```
"fiddlers " + 1 + 2
```

is:

```
"fiddlers 12"
```

In this jocular little example:

```
class Bottles {
	static void printSong(Object stuff, int n) {
		String plural = (n == 1) ? "" : "s";
		loop: while (true) {
			System.out.println(n + " bottle" + plural
			  + " of " + stuff + " on the wall,");
			System.out.println(n + " bottle" + plural
			  + " of " + stuff + ";");
			System.out.println("You take one down "
			  + "and pass it around:");
			--n;
			plural = (n == 1) ? "" : "s";
```

```
            if (n == 0)
              break loop;
            System.out.println(n + " bottle" + plural
              + " of " + stuff + " on the wall!");
            System.out.println();
        }
        System.out.println("No bottles of " +
                        stuff + " on the wall!");
    }
}
```

the method printSong will print a version of a children's song. Popular values for stuff include "pop" and "beer"; the most popular value for n is 100. Here is the output that results from Bottles.printSong("slime", 3):

```
3 bottles of slime on the wall,
3 bottles of slime;
You take one down and pass it around:
2 bottles of slime on the wall!

2 bottles of slime on the wall,
2 bottles of slime;
You take one down and pass it around:
1 bottle of slime on the wall!

1 bottle of slime on the wall,
1 bottle of slime;
You take one down and pass it around:
No bottles of slime on the wall!
```

In the code, note the careful conditional generation of the singular "bottle" when appropriate rather than the plural "bottles"; note also how the string concatenation operator was used to break the long constant string:

```
"You take one down and pass it around:"
```

into two pieces to avoid an inconveniently long line in the source code.

15.18.2 Additive Operators (+ and -) for Numeric Types

We discern a grand force in the lover which he lacks whilst a free man; but there is a breadth of vision in the free man which in the lover we vainly seek. Where there is much bias there must be some narrowness, and love, though added emotion, is subtracted capacity.
—Thomas Hardy, *Far from the Madding Crowd* (1874), Act IV, scene i

The binary + operator performs addition when applied to two operands of numeric type, producing the sum of the operands. The binary - operator performs subtraction, producing the difference of two numeric operands.

Binary numeric promotion is performed on the operands (§5.6.2). The type of an additive expression on numeric operands is the promoted type of its operands. If this promoted type is `int` or `long`, then integer arithmetic is performed; if this promoted type is `float` or `double`, then floating-point arithmetic is performed.

Note that binary numeric promotion performs value set conversion (§5.1.13) and unboxing conversion (§5.1.8).

Addition is a commutative operation if the operand expressions have no side effects. Integer addition is associative when the operands are all of the same type, but floating-point addition is not associative.

If an integer addition overflows, then the result is the low-order bits of the mathematical sum as represented in some sufficiently large two's-complement format. If overflow occurs, then the sign of the result is not the same as the sign of the mathematical sum of the two operand values.

The result of a floating-point addition is determined using the following rules of IEEE arithmetic:

- If either operand is NaN, the result is NaN.
- The sum of two infinities of opposite sign is NaN.
- The sum of two infinities of the same sign is the infinity of that sign.
- The sum of an infinity and a finite value is equal to the infinite operand.
- The sum of two zeros of opposite sign is positive zero.
- The sum of two zeros of the same sign is the zero of that sign.
- The sum of a zero and a nonzero finite value is equal to the nonzero operand.
- The sum of two nonzero finite values of the same magnitude and opposite sign is positive zero.
- In the remaining cases, where neither an infinity, nor a zero, nor NaN is involved, and the operands have the same sign or have different magnitudes,

the exact mathematical sum is computed. A floating-point value set is then chosen:

- If the addition expression is FP-strict (§15.4):
  - If the type of the addition expression is `float`, then the float value set must be chosen.
  - If the type of the addition expression is `double`, then the double value set must be chosen.
- If the addition expression is not FP-strict:
  - If the type of the addition expression is `float`, then either the float value set or the float-extended-exponent value set may be chosen, at the whim of the implementation.
  - If the type of the addition expression is `double`, then either the double value set or the double-extended-exponent value set may be chosen, at the whim of the implementation.

Next, a value must be chosen from the chosen value set to represent the sum. If the magnitude of the sum is too large to represent, we say the operation overflows; the result is then an infinity of appropriate sign. Otherwise, the sum is rounded to the nearest value in the chosen value set using IEEE 754 round-to-nearest mode. The Java programming language requires support of gradual underflow as defined by IEEE 754 (§4.2.4).

The binary `-` operator performs subtraction when applied to two operands of numeric type producing the difference of its operands; the left-hand operand is the minuend and the right-hand operand is the subtrahend. For both integer and floating-point subtraction, it is always the case that `a-b` produces the same result as `a+(-b)`.

Note that, for integer values, subtraction from zero is the same as negation. However, for floating-point operands, subtraction from zero is *not* the same as negation, because if `x` is `+0.0`, then `0.0-x` is `+0.0`, but `-x` is `-0.0`.

Despite the fact that overflow, underflow, or loss of information may occur, evaluation of a numeric additive operator never throws a run-time exception.

15.19 Shift Operators

What, I say, is to become of those wretches?
. . . What more can you say to them than "shift for yourselves?"
—Thomas Paine, *The American Crisis* (1780)

The *shift operators* include left shift <<, signed right shift >>, and unsigned right shift >>>; they are syntactically left-associative (they group left-to-right). The left-hand operand of a shift operator is the value to be shifted; the right-hand operand specifies the shift distance.

ShiftExpression:
  AdditiveExpression
  ShiftExpression << *AdditiveExpression*
  ShiftExpression >> *AdditiveExpression*
  ShiftExpression >>> *AdditiveExpression*

The type of each of the operands of a shift operator must be a type that is convertible (§5.1.8) to a primitive integral type, or a compile-time error occurs. Binary numeric promotion (§5.6.2) is *not* performed on the operands; rather, unary numeric promotion (§) is performed on each operand separately. The type of the shift expression is the promoted type of the left-hand operand.

If the promoted type of the left-hand operand is `int`, only the five lowest-order bits of the right-hand operand are used as the shift distance. It is as if the right-hand operand were subjected to a bitwise logical AND operator & (§15.22.1) with the mask value `0x1f`. The shift distance actually used is therefore always in the range 0 to 31, inclusive.

If the promoted type of the left-hand operand is `long`, then only the six lowest-order bits of the right-hand operand are used as the shift distance. It is as if the right-hand operand were subjected to a bitwise logical AND operator & (§15.22.1) with the mask value `0x3f`. The shift distance actually used is therefore always in the range 0 to 63, inclusive.

At run time, shift operations are performed on the two's complement integer representation of the value of the left operand.

The value of `n<<s` is `n` left-shifted `s` bit positions; this is equivalent (even if overflow occurs) to multiplication by two to the power `s`.

The value of `n>>s` is `n` right-shifted `s` bit positions with sign-extension. The resulting value is $\lfloor n/2^s \rfloor$. For nonnegative values of `n`, this is equivalent to truncating integer division, as computed by the integer division operator `/`, by two to the power `s`.

The value of `n>>>s` is `n` right-shifted `s` bit positions with zero-extension. If `n` is positive, then the result is the same as that of `n>>s`; if `n` is negative, the result is equal to that of the expression `(n>>s)+(2<<~s)` if the type of the left-hand operand is `int`, and to the result of the expression `(n>>s)+(2L<<~s)` if the type of the left-hand operand is `long`. The added term `(2<<~s)` or `(2L<<~s)` cancels out the propagated sign bit. (Note that, because of the implicit masking of the right-hand operand of a shift operator, `~s` as a shift distance is equivalent to `31-s` when shifting an `int` value and to `63-s` when shifting a `long` value.)

15.20 Relational Operators

The *relational operators* are syntactically left-associative (they group left-to-right), but this fact is not useful; for example, `a<b<c` parses as `(a<b)<c`, which is always a compile-time error, because the type of `a<b` is always `boolean` and `<` is not an operator on `boolean` values.

RelationalExpression:
    ShiftExpression
    RelationalExpression `<` *ShiftExpression*
    RelationalExpression `>` *ShiftExpression*
    RelationalExpression `<=` *ShiftExpression*
    RelationalExpression `>=` *ShiftExpression*
    RelationalExpression `instanceof` *ReferenceType*

The type of a relational expression is always `boolean`.

15.20.1 Numerical Comparison Operators <, <=, >, and >=

The type of each of the operands of a numerical comparison operator must be a type that is convertible (§5.1.8) to a primitive numeric type, or a compile-time error occurs. Binary numeric promotion is performed on the operands (§5.6.2). If the promoted type of the operands is `int` or `long`, then signed integer comparison is performed; if this promoted type is `float` or `double`, then floating-point comparison is performed.

Note that binary numeric promotion performs value set conversion (§5.1.13) and unboxing conversion (§5.1.8). Comparison is carried out accurately on floating-point values, no matter what value sets their representing values were drawn from.

The result of a floating-point comparison, as determined by the specification of the IEEE 754 standard, is:

- If either operand is NaN, then the result is `false`.
- All values other than NaN are ordered, with negative infinity less than all finite values, and positive infinity greater than all finite values.
- Positive zero and negative zero are considered equal. Therefore, `-0.0<0.0` is `false`, for example, but `-0.0<=0.0` is `true`. (Note, however, that the methods `Math.min` and `Math.max` treat negative zero as being strictly smaller than positive zero.)

Subject to these considerations for floating-point numbers, the following rules then hold for integer operands or for floating-point operands other than NaN:

- The value produced by the < operator is `true` if the value of the left-hand operand is less than the value of the right-hand operand, and otherwise is `false`.
- The value produced by the <= operator is `true` if the value of the left-hand operand is less than or equal to the value of the right-hand operand, and otherwise is `false`.
- The value produced by the > operator is `true` if the value of the left-hand operand is greater than the value of the right-hand operand, and otherwise is `false`.
- The value produced by the >= operator is `true` if the value of the left-hand operand is greater than or equal to the value of the right-hand operand, and otherwise is `false`.

15.20.2 Type Comparison Operator `instanceof`

The type of a *RelationalExpression* operand of the `instanceof` operator must be a reference type or the null type; otherwise, a compile-time error occurs. The *ReferenceType* mentioned after the `instanceof` operator must denote a reference type; otherwise, a compile-time error occurs. It is a compile-time error if the *ReferenceType* mentioned after the `instanceof` operator does not denote a reifiable type (§4.7).

At run time, the result of the `instanceof` operator is `true` if the value of the *RelationalExpression* is not `null` and the reference could be cast (§15.16) to the *ReferenceType* without raising a `ClassCastException`. Otherwise the result is `false`.

If a cast of the *RelationalExpression* to the *ReferenceType* would be rejected as a compile-time error, then the `instanceof` relational expression likewise produces a compile-time error. In such a situation, the result of the `instanceof` expression could never be `true`.

Consider the example program:

```
class Point { int x, y; }
class Element { int atomicNumber; }
class Test {
    public static void main(String[] args) {
        Point p = new Point();
        Element e = new Element();
        if (e instanceof Point) {        // compile-time error
            System.out.println("I get your point!");
            p = (Point)e;                // compile-time error
        }
    }
}
```

This example results in two compile-time errors. The cast `(Point)e` is incorrect because no instance of `Element` or any of its possible subclasses (none are shown here) could possibly be an instance of any subclass of `Point`. The `instanceof` expression is incorrect for exactly the same reason. If, on the other hand, the class `Point` were a subclass of `Element` (an admittedly strange notion in this example):

```
class Point extends Element { int x, y; }
```

then the cast would be possible, though it would require a run-time check, and the `instanceof` expression would then be sensible and valid. The cast `(Point)e` would never raise an exception because it would not be executed if the value of `e` could not correctly be cast to type `Point`.

15.21 Equality Operators

The equality operators are syntactically left-associative (they group left-to-right), but this fact is essentially never useful; for example, `a==b==c` parses as `(a==b)==c`. The result type of `a==b` is always `boolean`, and `c` must therefore be of type `boolean` or a compile-time error occurs. Thus, `a==b==c` does *not* test to see whether `a`, `b`, and `c` are all equal.

EqualityExpression:
  RelationalExpression
  EqualityExpression `==` *RelationalExpression*
  EqualityExpression `!=` *RelationalExpression*

The == (equal to) and the!= (not equal to) operators are analogous to the relational operators except for their lower precedence. Thus, `a<b==c<d` is `true` whenever `a<b` and `c<d` have the same truth value.

The equality operators may be used to compare two operands that are convertible (§5.1.8) to numeric type, or two operands of type `boolean` or `Boolean`, or two operands that are each of either reference type or the null type. All other cases result in a compile-time error. The type of an equality expression is always `boolean`.

In all cases, `a!=b` produces the same result as `!(a==b)`. The equality operators are commutative if the operand expressions have no side effects.

15.21.1 Numerical Equality Operators == and !=

If the operands of an equality operator are both of numeric type, or one is of numeric type and the other is convertible (§5.1.8) to numeric type, binary numeric promotion is performed on the operands (§5.6.2). If the promoted type of the operands is `int` or `long`, then an integer equality test is performed; if the promoted type is `float` or `double`, then a floating-point equality test is performed.

Note that binary numeric promotion performs value set conversion (§5.1.13) and unboxing conversion (§5.1.8). Comparison is carried out accurately on floating-point values, no matter what value sets their representing values were drawn from.

Floating-point equality testing is performed in accordance with the rules of the IEEE 754 standard:

- If either operand is NaN, then the result of == is `false` but the result of `!=` is `true`. Indeed, the test `x!=x` is true if and only if the value of `x` is NaN. (The methods `Float.isNaN` and `Double.isNaN` may also be used to test whether a value is NaN.)

- Positive zero and negative zero are considered equal. Therefore, `-0.0==0.0` is `true`, for example.

- Otherwise, two distinct floating-point values are considered unequal by the equality operators. In particular, there is one value representing positive infinity and one value representing negative infinity; each compares equal only to itself, and each compares unequal to all other values.

Subject to these considerations for floating-point numbers, the following rules then hold for integer operands or for floating-point operands other than NaN:

- The value produced by the == operator is `true` if the value of the left-hand operand is equal to the value of the right-hand operand; otherwise, the result is `false`.
- The value produced by the != operator is `true` if the value of the left-hand operand is not equal to the value of the right-hand operand; otherwise, the result is `false`.

15.21.2 Boolean Equality Operators == and !=

If the operands of an equality operator are both of type `boolean`, or if one operand is of type `boolean` and the other is of type `Boolean`, then the operation is boolean equality. The boolean equality operators are associative.

If one of the operands is of type `Boolean` it is subjected to unboxing conversion (§5.1.8).

The result of == is `true` if the operands (after any required unboxing conversion) are both `true` or both `false`; otherwise, the result is `false`.

The result of != is `false` if the operands are both `true` or both `false`; otherwise, the result is `true`. Thus != behaves the same as ^ (§15.22.2) when applied to boolean operands.

15.21.3 Reference Equality Operators == and !=

Things are more like they are now than they ever were before.
—Dwight D. Eisenhower

If the operands of an equality operator are both of either reference type or the null type, then the operation is object equality.

A compile-time error occurs if it is impossible to convert the type of either operand to the type of the other by a casting conversion (§5.5). The run-time values of the two operands would necessarily be unequal.

At run time, the result of == is `true` if the operand values are both `null` or both refer to the same object or array; otherwise, the result is `false`.

The result of != is `false` if the operand values are both `null` or both refer to the same object or array; otherwise, the result is `true`.

While == may be used to compare references of type `String`, such an equality test determines whether or not the two operands refer to the same `String` object. The result is `false` if the operands are distinct `String` objects, even if they contain the same sequence of characters. The contents of two strings `s` and `t` can be tested for equality by the method invocation `s.equals(t)`. See also §3.10.5.

15.22 Bitwise and Logical Operators

The *bitwise operators* and *logical operators* include the AND operator `&`, exclusive OR operator `^`, and inclusive OR operator `|`. These operators have different precedence, with `&` having the highest precedence and `|` the lowest precedence. Each of these operators is syntactically left-associative (each groups left-to-right). Each operator is commutative if the operand expressions have no side effects. Each operator is associative.

AndExpression:
  EqualityExpression
  AndExpression `&` *EqualityExpression*

ExclusiveOrExpression:
  AndExpression
  ExclusiveOrExpression `^` *AndExpression*

InclusiveOrExpression:
  ExclusiveOrExpression
  InclusiveOrExpression `|` *ExclusiveOrExpression*

The bitwise and logical operators may be used to compare two operands of numeric type or two operands of type `boolean`. All other cases result in a compile-time error.

15.22.1 Integer Bitwise Operators `&`, `^`, and `|`

When both operands of an operator `&`, `^`, or `|` are of a type that is convertible (§5.1.8) to a primitive integral type, binary numeric promotion is first performed on the operands (§5.6.2). The type of the bitwise operator expression is the promoted type of the operands.

For `&`, the result value is the bitwise AND of the operand values.

For `^`, the result value is the bitwise exclusive OR of the operand values.

For `|`, the result value is the bitwise inclusive OR of the operand values.

For example, the result of the expression `0xff00 & 0xf0f0` is `0xf000`. The result of `0xff00 ^ 0xf0f0` is `0x0ff0`.The result of `0xff00 | 0xf0f0` is `0xfff0`.

15.22.2 Boolean Logical Operators `&`, `^`, and `|`

When both operands of a `&`, `^`, or `|` operator are of type `boolean` or `Boolean`, then the type of the bitwise operator expression is `boolean`. In all cases, the operands are subject to unboxing conversion (§5.1.8) as necessary.

For &, the result value is `true` if both operand values are `true`; otherwise, the result is `false`.

For ^, the result value is `true` if the operand values are different; otherwise, the result is `false`.

For |, the result value is `false` if both operand values are `false`; otherwise, the result is `true`.

15.23 Conditional-And Operator &&

The && operator is like & (§15.22.2), but evaluates its right-hand operand only if the value of its left-hand operand is `true`. It is syntactically left-associative (it groups left-to-right). It is fully associative with respect to both side effects and result value; that is, for any expressions *a*, *b*, and *c*, evaluation of the expression `((a)&&(b))&&(c)` produces the same result, with the same side effects occurring in the same order, as evaluation of the expression `(a)&&((b)&&(c))`.

ConditionalAndExpression:
  InclusiveOrExpression
  ConditionalAndExpression && *InclusiveOrExpression*

Each operand of && must be of type `boolean` or `Boolean`, or a compile-time error occurs. The type of a conditional-and expression is always `boolean`.

At run time, the left-hand operand expression is evaluated first; if the result has type `Boolean`, it is subjected to unboxing conversion (§5.1.8); if the resulting value is `false`, the value of the conditional-and expression is `false` and the right-hand operand expression is not evaluated. If the value of the left-hand operand is `true`, then the right-hand expression is evaluated; if the result has type `Boolean`, it is subjected to unboxing conversion (§5.1.8); the resulting value becomes the value of the conditional-and expression. Thus, && computes the same result as & on `boolean` operands. It differs only in that the right-hand operand expression is evaluated conditionally rather than always.

15.24 Conditional-Or Operator ||

The || operator is like | (§15.22.2), but evaluates its right-hand operand only if the value of its left-hand operand is `false`. It is syntactically left-associative (it groups left-to-right). It is fully associative with respect to both side effects and result value; that is, for any expressions *a*, *b*, and *c*, evaluation of the expression `((a)||(b))||(c)` produces the same result, with the same side effects occurring in the same order, as evaluation of the expression `(a)||((b)||(c))`.

ConditionalOrExpression:
  ConditionalAndExpression
  ConditionalOrExpression `||` *ConditionalAndExpression*

Each operand of `||` must be of type `boolean` or `Boolean`, or a compile-time error occurs. The type of a conditional-or expression is always `boolean`.

At run time, the left-hand operand expression is evaluated first; if the result has type `Boolean`, it is subjected to unboxing conversion (§5.1.8); if the resulting value is `true`, the value of the conditional-or expression is `true` and the right-hand operand expression is not evaluated. If the value of the left-hand operand is `false`, then the right-hand expression is evaluated; if the result has type `Boolean`, it is subjected to unboxing conversion (§5.1.8); the resulting value becomes the value of the conditional-or expression.

Thus, `||` computes the same result as `|` on `boolean` or `Boolean` operands. It differs only in that the right-hand operand expression is evaluated conditionally rather than always.

15.25 Conditional Operator ? :

But be it as it may. I here entail
The crown to thee and to thine heirs for ever;
Conditionally . . .
—William Shakespeare, *Henry VI, Part III* (1623), Act I, scene i

The conditional operator `? :` uses the boolean value of one expression to decide which of two other expressions should be evaluated.

The conditional operator is syntactically right-associative (it groups right-to-left), so that `a?b:c?d:e?f:g` means the same as `a?b:(c?d:(e?f:g))`.

ConditionalExpression:
  ConditionalOrExpression
  ConditionalOrExpression `?` *Expression* `:` *ConditionalExpression*

The conditional operator has three operand expressions; `?` appears between the first and second expressions, and `:` appears between the second and third expressions.

The first expression must be of type `boolean` or `Boolean`, or a compile-time error occurs.

Note that it is a compile-time error for either the second or the third operand expression to be an invocation of a `void` method. In fact, it is not permitted for a conditional expression to appear in any context where an invocation of a `void` method could appear (§14.8).

The type of a conditional expression is determined as follows:

- If the second and third operands have the same type (which may be the null type), then that is the type of the conditional expression.
- If one of the second and third operands is of type `boolean` and the type of the other is of type `Boolean`, then the type of the conditional expression is `boolean`.
- If one of the second and third operands is of the null type and the type of the other is a reference type, then the type of the conditional expression is that reference type.
- Otherwise, if the second and third operands have types that are convertible (§5.1.8) to numeric types, then there are several cases:
  - If one of the operands is of type `byte` or `Byte` and the other is of type `short` or `Short`, then the type of the conditional expression is `short`.
  - If one of the operands is of type *T* where *T* is `byte`, `short`, or `char`, and the other operand is a constant expression of type `int` whose value is representable in type *T*, then the type of the conditional expression is *T*.
  - If one of the operands is of type `Byte` and the other operand is a constant expression of type `int` whose value is representable in type `byte`, then the type of the conditional expression is `byte`.
  - If one of the operands is of type `Short` and the other operand is a constant expression of type `int` whose value is representable in type `short`, then the type of the conditional expression is `short`.
  - If one of the operands is of type `Character` and the other operand is a constant expression of type `int` whose value is representable in type `char`, then the type of the conditional expression is `char`.
  - Otherwise, binary numeric promotion (§5.6.2) is applied to the operand types, and the type of the conditional expression is the promoted type of the second and third operands. Note that binary numeric promotion performs unboxing conversion (§5.1.8) and value set conversion (§5.1.13).
- Otherwise, the second and third operands are of types *S1* and *S2* respectively. Let *T1* be the type that results from applying boxing conversion to *S1*, and let *T2* be the type that results from applying boxing conversion to *S2*. The type of the conditional expression is the result of applying capture conversion (§5.1.10) to *lub(T1, T2)* (§15.12.2.7).

At run time, the first operand expression of the conditional expression is evaluated first; if necessary, unboxing conversion is performed on the result; the resulting `boolean` value is then used to choose either the second or the third operand expression:

- If the value of the first operand is `true`, then the second operand expression is chosen.
- If the value of the first operand is `false`, then the third operand expression is chosen.

The chosen operand expression is then evaluated and the resulting value is converted to the type of the conditional expression as determined by the rules stated above. This conversion may include boxing (§5.1.7) or unboxing conversion. The operand expression not chosen is not evaluated for that particular evaluation of the conditional expression.

15.26 Assignment Operators

There are 12 *assignment operators*; all are syntactically right-associative (they group right-to-left). Thus, `a=b=c` means `a=(b=c)`, which assigns the value of `c` to `b` and then assigns the value of `b` to `a`.

AssignmentExpression:
  ConditionalExpression
  Assignment

Assignment:
  LeftHandSide AssignmentOperator AssignmentExpression

LeftHandSide:
  ExpressionName
  FieldAccess
  ArrayAccess

AssignmentOperator: one of
  `=  *=  /=  %=  +=  -=  <<=  >>=  >>>=  &=  ^=  |=`

The result of the first operand of an assignment operator must be a variable, or a compile-time error occurs. This operand may be a named variable, such as a local variable or a field of the current object or class, or it may be a computed variable, as can result from a field access (§15.11) or an array access (§15.13). The type of the assignment expression is the type of the variable after capture conversion (§5.1.10).

At run time, the result of the assignment expression is the value of the variable after the assignment has occurred. The result of an assignment expression is not itself a variable.

A variable that is declared `final` cannot be assigned to (unless it is a definitely unassigned (§16) blank final variable (§4.12.4)), because when an access of such a `final` variable is used as an expression, the result is a value, not a variable, and so it cannot be used as the first operand of an assignment operator.

15.26.1 Simple Assignment Operator =

A compile-time error occurs if the type of the right-hand operand cannot be converted to the type of the variable by assignment conversion (§5.2).

At run time, the expression is evaluated in one of three ways:

- If the left-hand operand expression is a field access expression (§15.11) *e.f*, possibly enclosed in one or more pairs of parentheses, then:
  - First, the expression *e* is evaluated. If evaluation of *e* completes abruptly, the assignment expression completes abruptly for the same reason.
  - Next, the right hand operand is evaluated. If evaluation of the right hand expression completes abruptly, the assignment expression completes abruptly for the same reason.
  - Then, if the field denoted by *e.f* is not `static` and the result of the evaluation of *e* above is `null`, then a `NullPointerException` is thrown.
  - Otherwise, the variable denoted by *e.f* is assigned the value of the right hand operand as computed above.
- If the left-hand operand is an array access expression (§15.13), possibly enclosed in one or more pairs of parentheses, then:
  - First, the array reference subexpression of the left-hand operand array access expression is evaluated. If this evaluation completes abruptly, then the assignment expression completes abruptly for the same reason; the index subexpression (of the left-hand operand array access expression) and the right-hand operand are not evaluated and no assignment occurs.
  - Otherwise, the index subexpression of the left-hand operand array access expression is evaluated. If this evaluation completes abruptly, then the assignment expression completes abruptly for the same reason and the right-hand operand is not evaluated and no assignment occurs.

- Otherwise, the right-hand operand is evaluated. If this evaluation completes abruptly, then the assignment expression completes abruptly for the same reason and no assignment occurs.
- Otherwise, if the value of the array reference subexpression is `null`, then no assignment occurs and a `NullPointerException` is thrown.
- Otherwise, the value of the array reference subexpression indeed refers to an array. If the value of the index subexpression is less than zero, or greater than or equal to the length of the array, then no assignment occurs and an `ArrayIndexOutOfBoundsException` is thrown.
- Otherwise, the value of the index subexpression is used to select a component of the array referred to by the value of the array reference subexpression. This component is a variable; call its type *SC*. Also, let *TC* be the type of the left-hand operand of the assignment operator as determined at compile time.
- If *TC* is a primitive type, then *SC* is necessarily the same as *TC*. The value of the right-hand operand is converted to the type of the selected array component, is subjected to value set conversion (§5.1.13) to the appropriate standard value set (not an extended-exponent value set), and the result of the conversion is stored into the array component.
- If *TC* is a reference type, then *SC* may not be the same as *TC*, but rather a type that extends or implements *TC*. Let *RC* be the class of the object referred to by the value of the right-hand operand at run time.

  The compiler may be able to prove at compile time that the array component will be of type *TC* exactly (for example, *TC* might be `final`). But if the compiler cannot prove at compile time that the array component will be of type *TC* exactly, then a check must be performed at run time to ensure that the class *RC* is assignment compatible (§5.2) with the actual type *SC* of the array component. This check is similar to a narrowing cast (§5.5, §15.16), except that if the check fails, an `ArrayStoreException` is thrown rather than a `ClassCastException`. Therefore:

  - If class *RC* is not assignable to type *SC*, then no assignment occurs and an `ArrayStoreException` is thrown.
- Otherwise, the reference value of the right-hand operand is stored into the selected array component.

• Otherwise, three steps are required:

- First, the left-hand operand is evaluated to produce a variable. If this evaluation completes abruptly, then the assignment expression completes abruptly for the same reason; the right-hand operand is not evaluated and no assignment occurs.
- Otherwise, the right-hand operand is evaluated. If this evaluation completes abruptly, then the assignment expression completes abruptly for the same reason and no assignment occurs.

Otherwise, the value of the right-hand operand is converted to the type of the left-hand variable, is subjected to value set conversion (§5.1.13) to the appropriate standard value set (not an extended-exponent value set), and the result of the conversion is stored into the variable.The rules for assignment to an array component are illustrated by the following example program:

```
class ArrayReferenceThrow extends RuntimeException { }
class IndexThrow extends RuntimeException { }
class RightHandSideThrow extends RuntimeException { }
class IllustrateSimpleArrayAssignment {
    static Object[] objects = { new Object(), new Object() };
    static Thread[] threads = { new Thread(), new Thread() };
    static Object[] arrayThrow() {
        throw new ArrayReferenceThrow();
    }
    static int indexThrow() { throw new IndexThrow(); }
    static Thread rightThrow() {
        throw new RightHandSideThrow();
    }
    static String name(Object q) {
        String sq = q.getClass().getName();
        int k = sq.lastIndexOf('.');
        return (k < 0) ? sq : sq.substring(k+1);
    }
    static void testFour(Object[] x, int j, Object y) {
        String sx = x == null ? "null" : name(x[0]) + "s";
        String sy = name(y);
        System.out.println();
        try {
            System.out.print(sx + "[throw]=throw => ");
            x[indexThrow()] = rightThrow();
            System.out.println("Okay!");
        } catch (Throwable e) { System.out.println(name(e)); }
```

```
        try {
            System.out.print(sx + "[throw]=" + sy + " => ");
            x[indexThrow()] = y;
            System.out.println("Okay!");
        } catch (Throwable e) { System.out.println(name(e)); }
        try {
            System.out.print(sx + "[" + j + "]=throw => ");
            x[j] = rightThrow();
            System.out.println("Okay!");
        } catch (Throwable e) { System.out.println(name(e)); }
        try {
            System.out.print(sx + "[" + j + "]=" + sy + " => ");
            x[j] = y;
            System.out.println("Okay!");
        } catch (Throwable e) { System.out.println(name(e)); }
    }

    public static void main(String[] args) {
        try {
            System.out.print("throw[throw]=throw => ");
            arrayThrow()[indexThrow()] = rightThrow();
            System.out.println("Okay!");
        } catch (Throwable e) { System.out.println(name(e)); }
        try {
            System.out.print("throw[throw]=Thread => ");
            arrayThrow()[indexThrow()] = new Thread();
            System.out.println("Okay!");
        } catch (Throwable e) { System.out.println(name(e)); }
        try {
            System.out.print("throw[1]=throw => ");
            arrayThrow()[1] = rightThrow();
            System.out.println("Okay!");
        } catch (Throwable e) { System.out.println(name(e)); }
        try {
            System.out.print("throw[1]=Thread => ");
            arrayThrow()[1] = new Thread();
            System.out.println("Okay!");
        } catch (Throwable e) { System.out.println(name(e)); }
        testFour(null, 1, new StringBuffer());
        testFour(null, 1, new StringBuffer());
        testFour(null, 9, new Thread());
        testFour(null, 9, new Thread());
        testFour(objects, 1, new StringBuffer());
        testFour(objects, 1, new Thread());
        testFour(objects, 9, new StringBuffer());
        testFour(objects, 9, new Thread());
        testFour(threads, 1, new StringBuffer());
        testFour(threads, 1, new Thread());
```

```
        testFour(threads, 9, new StringBuffer());
        testFour(threads, 9, new Thread());
    }
}
```

This program prints:

```
throw[throw]=throw => ArrayReferenceThrow
throw[throw]=Thread => ArrayReferenceThrow
throw[1]=throw => ArrayReferenceThrow
throw[1]=Thread => ArrayReferenceThrow

null[throw]=throw => IndexThrow
null[throw]=StringBuffer => IndexThrow
null[1]=throw => RightHandSideThrow
null[1]=StringBuffer => NullPointerException

null[throw]=throw => IndexThrow
null[throw]=StringBuffer => IndexThrow
null[1]=throw => RightHandSideThrow
null[1]=StringBuffer => NullPointerException

null[throw]=throw => IndexThrow
null[throw]=Thread => IndexThrow
null[9]=throw => RightHandSideThrow
null[9]=Thread => NullPointerException

null[throw]=throw => IndexThrow
null[throw]=Thread => IndexThrow
null[9]=throw => RightHandSideThrow
null[9]=Thread => NullPointerException

Objects[throw]=throw => IndexThrow
Objects[throw]=StringBuffer => IndexThrow
Objects[1]=throw => RightHandSideThrow
Objects[1]=StringBuffer => Okay!

Objects[throw]=throw => IndexThrow
Objects[throw]=Thread => IndexThrow
Objects[1]=throw => RightHandSideThrow
Objects[1]=Thread => Okay!

Objects[throw]=throw => IndexThrow
Objects[throw]=StringBuffer => IndexThrow
Objects[9]=throw => RightHandSideThrow
Objects[9]=StringBuffer => ArrayIndexOutOfBoundsException

Objects[throw]=throw => IndexThrow
Objects[throw]=Thread => IndexThrow
Objects[9]=throw => RightHandSideThrow
Objects[9]=Thread => ArrayIndexOutOfBoundsException
```

```
Threads[throw]=throw => IndexThrow
Threads[throw]=StringBuffer => IndexThrow
Threads[1]=throw => RightHandSideThrow
Threads[1]=StringBuffer => ArrayStoreException
Threads[throw]=throw => IndexThrow
Threads[throw]=Thread => IndexThrow
Threads[1]=throw => RightHandSideThrow
Threads[1]=Thread => Okay!
Threads[throw]=throw => IndexThrow
Threads[throw]=StringBuffer => IndexThrow
Threads[9]=throw => RightHandSideThrow
Threads[9]=StringBuffer => ArrayIndexOutOfBoundsException
Threads[throw]=throw => IndexThrow
Threads[throw]=Thread => IndexThrow
Threads[9]=throw => RightHandSideThrow
Threads[9]=Thread => ArrayIndexOutOfBoundsException
```

The most interesting case of the lot is the one thirteenth from the end:

```
Threads[1]=StringBuffer => ArrayStoreException
```

which indicates that the attempt to store a reference to a `StringBuffer` into an array whose components are of type `Thread` throws an `ArrayStoreException`. The code is type-correct at compile time: the assignment has a left-hand side of type `Object[]` and a right-hand side of type `Object`. At run time, the first actual argument to method `testFour` is a reference to an instance of "array of `Thread`" and the third actual argument is a reference to an instance of class `StringBuffer`.

15.26.2 Compound Assignment Operators

A compound assignment expression of the form *`E1 op= E2`* is equivalent to *`E1`*` = (`*`T`*`)((`*`E1`*`) `*`op`*` (`*`E2`*`))`, where *`T`* is the type of *`E1`*, except that *`E1`* is evaluated only once.

For example, the following code is correct:

```
short x = 3;
x += 4.6;
```

and results in `x` having the value `7` because it is equivalent to:

```
short x = 3;
x = (short)(x + 4.6);
```

At run time, the expression is evaluated in one of two ways. If the left-hand operand expression is not an array access expression, then four steps are required:

- First, the left-hand operand is evaluated to produce a variable. If this evaluation completes abruptly, then the assignment expression completes abruptly for the same reason; the right-hand operand is not evaluated and no assignment occurs.
- Otherwise, the value of the left-hand operand is saved and then the right-hand operand is evaluated. If this evaluation completes abruptly, then the assignment expression completes abruptly for the same reason and no assignment occurs.
- Otherwise, the saved value of the left-hand variable and the value of the right-hand operand are used to perform the binary operation indicated by the compound assignment operator. If this operation completes abruptly, then the assignment expression completes abruptly for the same reason and no assignment occurs.
- Otherwise, the result of the binary operation is converted to the type of the left-hand variable, subjected to value set conversion (§5.1.13) to the appropriate standard value set (not an extended-exponent value set), and the result of the conversion is stored into the variable.

If the left-hand operand expression is an array access expression (§15.13), then many steps are required:

- First, the array reference subexpression of the left-hand operand array access expression is evaluated. If this evaluation completes abruptly, then the assignment expression completes abruptly for the same reason; the index subexpression (of the left-hand operand array access expression) and the right-hand operand are not evaluated and no assignment occurs.
- Otherwise, the index subexpression of the left-hand operand array access expression is evaluated. If this evaluation completes abruptly, then the assignment expression completes abruptly for the same reason and the right-hand operand is not evaluated and no assignment occurs.
- Otherwise, if the value of the array reference subexpression is `null`, then no assignment occurs and a `NullPointerException` is thrown.
- Otherwise, the value of the array reference subexpression indeed refers to an array. If the value of the index subexpression is less than zero, or greater than or equal to the length of the array, then no assignment occurs and an `ArrayIndexOutOfBoundsException` is thrown.
- Otherwise, the value of the index subexpression is used to select a component of the array referred to by the value of the array reference subexpression. The

value of this component is saved and then the right-hand operand is evaluated. If this evaluation completes abruptly, then the assignment expression completes abruptly for the same reason and no assignment occurs. (For a simple assignment operator, the evaluation of the right-hand operand occurs before the checks of the array reference subexpression and the index subexpression, but for a compound assignment operator, the evaluation of the right-hand operand occurs after these checks.)

- Otherwise, consider the array component selected in the previous step, whose value was saved. This component is a variable; call its type *S*. Also, let *T* be the type of the left-hand operand of the assignment operator as determined at compile time.
  - If *T* is a primitive type, then *S* is necessarily the same as *T*.
    - The saved value of the array component and the value of the right-hand operand are used to perform the binary operation indicated by the compound assignment operator. If this operation completes abruptly (the only possibility is an integer division by zero—see §15.17.2), then the assignment expression completes abruptly for the same reason and no assignment occurs.
    - Otherwise, the result of the binary operation is converted to the type of the selected array component, subjected to value set conversion (§5.1.13) to the appropriate standard value set (not an extended-exponent value set), and the result of the conversion is stored into the array component.
  - If *T* is a reference type, then it must be `String`. Because class `String` is a `final` class, *S* must also be `String`. Therefore the run-time check that is sometimes required for the simple assignment operator is never required for a compound assignment operator.
    - The saved value of the array component and the value of the right-hand operand are used to perform the binary operation (string concatenation) indicated by the compound assignment operator (which is necessarily +=). If this operation completes abruptly, then the assignment expression completes abruptly for the same reason and no assignment occurs.

Otherwise, the `String` result of the binary operation is stored into the array component.

The rules for compound assignment to an array component are illustrated by the following example program:

```
class ArrayReferenceThrow extends RuntimeException { }
class IndexThrow extends RuntimeException { }
```

```
class RightHandSideThrow extends RuntimeException { }
class IllustrateCompoundArrayAssignment {
   static String[] strings = { "Simon", "Garfunkel" };
   static double[] doubles = { Math.E, Math.PI };
   static String[] stringsThrow() {
      throw new ArrayReferenceThrow();
   }
   static double[] doublesThrow() {
      throw new ArrayReferenceThrow();
   }
   static int indexThrow() { throw new IndexThrow(); }
   static String stringThrow() {
      throw new RightHandSideThrow();
   }
   static double doubleThrow() {
      throw new RightHandSideThrow();
   }
   static String name(Object q) {
      String sq = q.getClass().getName();
      int k = sq.lastIndexOf('.');
      return (k < 0) ? sq : sq.substring(k+1);
   }
   static void testEight(String[] x, double[] z, int j) {
      String sx = (x == null) ? "null" : "Strings";
      String sz = (z == null) ? "null" : "doubles";
      System.out.println();
      try {
         System.out.print(sx + "[throw]+=throw => ");
         x[indexThrow()] += stringThrow();
         System.out.println("Okay!");
      } catch (Throwable e) { System.out.println(name(e)); }
      try {
         System.out.print(sz + "[throw]+=throw => ");
         z[indexThrow()] += doubleThrow();
         System.out.println("Okay!");
      } catch (Throwable e) { System.out.println(name(e)); }
      try {
         System.out.print(sx + "[throw]+=\"heh\" => ");
         x[indexThrow()] += "heh";
         System.out.println("Okay!");
      } catch (Throwable e) { System.out.println(name(e)); }
      try {
```

```
            System.out.print(sz + "[throw]+=12345 => ");
            z[indexThrow()] += 12345;
            System.out.println("Okay!");
        } catch (Throwable e) { System.out.println(name(e)); }
        try {
            System.out.print(sx + "[" + j + "]+=throw => ");
            x[j] += stringThrow();
            System.out.println("Okay!");
        } catch (Throwable e) { System.out.println(name(e)); }
        try {
            System.out.print(sz + "[" + j + "]+=throw => ");
            z[j] += doubleThrow();
            System.out.println("Okay!");
        } catch (Throwable e) { System.out.println(name(e)); }
        try {
            System.out.print(sx + "[" + j + "]+=\"heh\" => ");
            x[j] += "heh";
            System.out.println("Okay!");
        } catch (Throwable e) { System.out.println(name(e)); }
        try {
            System.out.print(sz + "[" + j + "]+=12345 => ");
            z[j] += 12345;
            System.out.println("Okay!");
        } catch (Throwable e) { System.out.println(name(e)); }
    }

    public static void main(String[] args) {
        try {
            System.out.print("throw[throw]+=throw => ");
            stringsThrow()[indexThrow()] += stringThrow();
            System.out.println("Okay!");
        } catch (Throwable e) { System.out.println(name(e)); }
        try {
            System.out.print("throw[throw]+=throw => ");
            doublesThrow()[indexThrow()] += doubleThrow();
            System.out.println("Okay!");
        } catch (Throwable e) { System.out.println(name(e)); }
        try {
            System.out.print("throw[throw]+=\"heh\" => ");
            stringsThrow()[indexThrow()] += "heh";
            System.out.println("Okay!");
        } catch (Throwable e) { System.out.println(name(e)); }
        try {
            System.out.print("throw[throw]+=12345 => ");
            doublesThrow()[indexThrow()] += 12345;
            System.out.println("Okay!");
        } catch (Throwable e) { System.out.println(name(e)); }
        try {
```

```
            System.out.print("throw[1]+=throw => ");
            stringsThrow()[1] += stringThrow();
            System.out.println("Okay!");
        } catch (Throwable e) { System.out.println(name(e)); }
        try {
            System.out.print("throw[1]+=throw => ");
            doublesThrow()[1] += doubleThrow();
            System.out.println("Okay!");
        } catch (Throwable e) { System.out.println(name(e)); }
        try {
            System.out.print("throw[1]+=\"heh\" => ");
            stringsThrow()[1] += "heh";
            System.out.println("Okay!");
        } catch (Throwable e) { System.out.println(name(e)); }
        try {
            System.out.print("throw[1]+=12345 => ");
            doublesThrow()[1] += 12345;
            System.out.println("Okay!");
        } catch (Throwable e) { System.out.println(name(e)); }
        testEight(null, null, 1);
        testEight(null, null, 9);
        testEight(strings, doubles, 1);
        testEight(strings, doubles, 9);
    }
}
```

This program prints:

```
throw[throw]+=throw => ArrayReferenceThrow
throw[throw]+=throw => ArrayReferenceThrow
throw[throw]+="heh" => ArrayReferenceThrow
throw[throw]+=12345 => ArrayReferenceThrow
throw[1]+=throw => ArrayReferenceThrow
throw[1]+=throw => ArrayReferenceThrow
throw[1]+="heh" => ArrayReferenceThrow
throw[1]+=12345 => ArrayReferenceThrow
null[throw]+=throw => IndexThrow
null[throw]+=throw => IndexThrow
null[throw]+="heh" => IndexThrow
null[throw]+=12345 => IndexThrow
null[1]+=throw => NullPointerException
null[1]+=throw => NullPointerException
null[1]+="heh" => NullPointerException
null[1]+=12345 => NullPointerException
null[throw]+=throw => IndexThrow
null[throw]+=throw => IndexThrow
null[throw]+="heh" => IndexThrow
```

```
null[throw]+=12345 => IndexThrow
null[9]+=throw => NullPointerException
null[9]+=throw => NullPointerException
null[9]+="heh" => NullPointerException
null[9]+=12345 => NullPointerException
Strings[throw]+=throw => IndexThrow
doubles[throw]+=throw => IndexThrow
Strings[throw]+="heh" => IndexThrow
doubles[throw]+=12345 => IndexThrow
Strings[1]+=throw => RightHandSideThrow
doubles[1]+=throw => RightHandSideThrow
Strings[1]+="heh" => Okay!
doubles[1]+=12345 => Okay!
Strings[throw]+=throw => IndexThrow
doubles[throw]+=throw => IndexThrow
Strings[throw]+="heh" => IndexThrow
doubles[throw]+=12345 => IndexThrow
Strings[9]+=throw => ArrayIndexOutOfBoundsException
doubles[9]+=throw => ArrayIndexOutOfBoundsException
Strings[9]+="heh" => ArrayIndexOutOfBoundsException
doubles[9]+=12345 => ArrayIndexOutOfBoundsException
```

The most interesting cases of the lot are tenth and eleventh from the end:

```
Strings[1]+=throw => RightHandSideThrow
doubles[1]+=throw => RightHandSideThrow
```

They are the cases where a right-hand side that throws an exception actually gets to throw the exception; moreover, they are the only such cases in the lot. This demonstrates that the evaluation of the right-hand operand indeed occurs after the checks for a null array reference value and an out-of-bounds index value.

The following program illustrates the fact that the value of the left-hand side of a compound assignment is saved before the right-hand side is evaluated:

```
class Test {
    public static void main(String[] args) {
        int k = 1;
        int[] a = { 1 };
        k += (k = 4) * (k + 2);
        a[0] += (a[0] = 4) * (a[0] + 2);
        System.out.println("k==" + k + " and a[0]==" + a[0]);
    }
}
```

This program prints:

```
k==25 and a[0]==25
```

The value `1` of `k` is saved by the compound assignment operator `+=` before its right-hand operand `(k = 4) * (k + 2)` is evaluated. Evaluation of this right-hand operand then assigns 4 to k, calculates the value 6 for k + 2, and then multiplies 4 by 6 to get 24. This is added to the saved value 1 to get 25, which is then stored into k by the += operator. An identical analysis applies to the case that uses a[0]. In short, the statements

```
k += (k = 4) * (k + 2);
a[0] += (a[0] = 4) * (a[0] + 2);
```

behave in exactly the same manner as the statements:

```
k = k + (k = 4) * (k + 2);
a[0] = a[0] + (a[0] = 4) * (a[0] + 2);
```

15.27 Expression

An *Expression* is any assignment expression:

Expression:
  AssignmentExpression

Unlike C and C++, the Java programming language has no comma operator.

15.28 Constant Expression

. . . the old and intent expression was a constant, not an occasional, thing . . .
—Charles Dickens, *A Tale of Two Cities* (1859)

ConstantExpression:
  Expression

A compile-time *constant expression* is an expression denoting a value of primitive type or a String that does not complete abruptly and is composed using only the following:

- Literals of primitive type and literals of type String (§3.10.5)
- Casts to primitive types and casts to type String
- The unary operators +, -, ~, and ! (but not ++ or --)
- The multiplicative operators *, /, and %
- The additive operators + and -
- The shift operators <<, >>, and >>>
- The relational operators <, <=, >, and >= (but not instanceof)

- The equality operators == and !=
- The bitwise and logical operators &, ^, and |
- The conditional-and operator && and the conditional-or operator ||
- The ternary conditional operator ? :
- Parenthesized expressions whose contained expression is a constant expression.
- Simple names that refer to constant variables (§4.12.4).
- Qualified names of the form *TypeName* . *Identifier* that refer to constant variables (§4.12.4).

Compile-time constant expressions are used in `case` labels in `switch` statements (§14.11) and have a special significance for assignment conversion (§5.2). Compile-time constants of type `String` are always "interned" so as to share unique instances, using the method `String.intern`.

A compile-time constant expression is always treated as FP-strict (§15.4), even if it occurs in a context where a non-constant expression would not be considered to be FP-strict.

Examples of constant expressions:

```
true
(short)(1*2*3*4*5*6)
Integer.MAX_VALUE / 2
2.0 * Math.PI
"The integer " + Long.MAX_VALUE + " is mighty big."
```

. . . when faces of the throng turned toward him and ambiguous eyes stared into his, he assumed the most romantic of expressions . . .
—F. Scott Fitzgerald, *This Side of Paradise* (1920)

CHAPTER 16

Definite Assignment

All the evolution we know of proceeds from the vague to the definite.
—Charles Peirce

EACH local variable (§14.4) and every blank `final` (§4.12.4) field (§8.3.1.2) must have a *definitely assigned* value when any access of its value occurs. An access to its value consists of the simple name of the variable occurring anywhere in an expression except as the left-hand operand of the simple assignment operator =. A Java compiler must carry out a specific conservative flow analysis to make sure that, for every access of a local variable or blank `final` field `f`, `f` is definitely assigned before the access; otherwise a compile-time error must occur.

Similarly, every blank `final` variable must be assigned at most once; it must be *definitely unassigned* when an assignment to it occurs. Such an assignment is defined to occur if and only if either the simple name of the variable, or its simple name qualified by `this`, occurs on the left hand side of an assignment operator. A Java compiler must carry out a specific conservative flow analysis to make sure that, for every assignment to a blank `final` variable, the variable is definitely unassigned before the assignment; otherwise a compile-time error must occur.

The remainder of this chapter is devoted to a precise explanation of the words "definitely assigned before" and "definitely unassigned before".

The idea behind definite assignment is that an assignment to the local variable or blank `final` field must occur on every possible execution path to the access. Similarly, the idea behind definite unassignment is that no other assignment to the blank `final` variable is permitted to occur on any possible execution path to an assignment. The analysis takes into account the structure of statements and expressions; it also provides a special treatment of the expression operators `!`, `&&`, `||`, and `? :`, and of boolean-valued constant expressions.

For example, a Java compiler recognizes that `k` is definitely assigned before its access (as an argument of a method invocation) in the code:

```
{
    int k;
    if (v > 0 && (k = System.in.read()) >= 0)
        System.out.println(k);
}
```

because the access occurs only if the value of the expression:

```
v > 0 && (k = System.in.read()) >= 0
```

is true, and the value can be `true` only if the assignment to `k` is executed (more properly, evaluated).

Similarly, a Java compiler will recognize that in the code:

```
{
    int k;
    while (true) {
        k = n;
        if (k >= 5) break;
        n = 6;
    }
    System.out.println(k);
}
```

the variable `k` is definitely assigned by the `while` statement because the condition expression `true` never has the value `false`, so only the `break` statement can cause the `while` statement to complete normally, and `k` is definitely assigned before the `break` statement.

On the other hand, the code

```
{
    int k;
    while (n < 4) {
        k = n;
        if (k >= 5) break;
        n = 6;
    }
    System.out.println(k);// k is not "definitely assigned" before this
}
```

must be rejected by a Java compiler, because in this case the `while` statement is not guaranteed to execute its body as far as the rules of definite assignment are concerned.

Except for the special treatment of the conditional boolean operators `&&`, `||`, and `? :` and of boolean-valued constant expressions, the values of expressions are not taken into account in the flow analysis.

For example, a Java compiler must produce a compile-time error for the code:

```
{
    int k;
    int n = 5;
```

```
    if (n > 2)
        k = 3;
    System.out.println(k);// k is not "definitely assigned" before this
}
```

even though the value of n is known at compile time, and in principle it can be known at compile time that the assignment to k will always be executed (more properly, evaluated). A Java compiler must operate according to the rules laid out in this section. The rules recognize only constant expressions; in this example, the expression n > 2 is not a constant expression as defined in §15.28.

As another example, a Java compiler will accept the code:

```
void flow(boolean flag) {
    int k;
    if (flag)
        k = 3;
    else
        k = 4;
    System.out.println(k);
}
```

as far as definite assignment of k is concerned, because the rules outlined in this section allow it to tell that k is assigned no matter whether the flag is `true` or `false`. But the rules do not accept the variation:

```
void flow(boolean flag) {
    int k;
    if (flag)
        k = 3;
    if (!flag)
        k = 4;
    System.out.println(k); // k is not "definitely assigned" before here
}
```

and so compiling this program must cause a compile-time error to occur.

A related example illustrates rules of definite unassignment. A Java compiler will accept the code:

```
void unflow(boolean flag) {
    final int k;
    if (flag) {
        k = 3;
        System.out.println(k);
    }
    else {
        k = 4;
        System.out.println(k);
    }
}
```

as far as definite unassignment of k is concerned, because the rules outlined in this section allow it to tell that k is assigned at most once (indeed, exactly once) no matter whether the flag is `true` or `false`. But the rules do not accept the variation:

```
void unflow(boolean flag) {
    final int k;
    if (flag) {
        k = 3;
        System.out.println(k);
    }
    if (!flag) {
        k = 4;          // k is not “definitely unassigned” before here
        System.out.println(k);
    }
}
```

and so compiling this program must cause a compile-time error to occur.

In order to precisely specify all the cases of definite assignment, the rules in this section define several technical terms:

- whether a variable is *definitely assigned before* a statement or expression;
- whether a variable is *definitely unassigned before* a statement or expression;
- whether a variable is *definitely assigned after* a statement or expression; and
- whether a variable is *definitely unassigned after* a statement or expression.

For boolean-valued expressions, the last two are refined into four cases:

- whether a variable is *definitely assigned after* the expression *when true*;
- whether a variable is *definitely unassigned after* the expression *when true*;
- whether a variable is *definitely assigned after* the expression *when false*; and
- whether a variable is *definitely unassigned after* the expression *when false*.

Here *when true* and *when false* refer to the value of the expression.

For example, the local variable k is definitely assigned a value after evaluation of the expression

```
a && ((k=m) > 5)
```

when the expression is `true` but not when the expression is `false` (because if a is `false`, then the assignment to k is not necessarily executed (more properly, evaluated)).

The phrase “*V* is definitely assigned after *X*” (where *V* is a local variable and *X* is a statement or expression) means “*V* is definitely assigned after *X* if *X* completes normally”. If *X* completes abruptly, the assignment need not have occurred, and the rules stated here take this into account. A peculiar consequence of this definition is that "*V* is definitely assigned after `break;`" is always true! Because a `break` statement never completes normally, it is vacuously true that *V* has been assigned a value if the `break` statement completes normally.

Similarly, the statement "*V* is definitely unassigned after *X*" (where *V* is a variable and *X* is a statement or expression) means "*V* is definitely unassigned after *X* if *X* completes normally". An even more peculiar consequence of this definition is that "*V* is definitely unassigned after `break;`" is always true! Because a `break` statement never completes normally, it is vacuously true that *V* has not been assigned a value if the `break` statement completes normally. (For that matter, it is also vacuously true that the moon is made of green cheese if the `break` statement completes normally.)

In all, there are four possibilities for a variable *V* after a statement or expression has been executed:

- *V* is definitely assigned and is not definitely unassigned.
  (The flow analysis rules prove that an assignment to *V* has occurred.)
- *V* is definitely unassigned and is not definitely assigned.
  (The flow analysis rules prove that an assignment to *V* has not occurred.)
- *V* is not definitely assigned and is not definitely unassigned.
  (The rules cannot prove whether or not an assignment to *V* has occurred.)
- *V* is definitely assigned and is definitely unassigned.
  (It is impossible for the statement or expression to complete normally.)

To shorten the rules, the customary abbreviation "iff" is used to mean "if and only if". We also use an abbreviation convention: if a rule contains one or more occurrences of "[un]assigned" then it stands for two rules, one with every occurrence of "[un]assigned" replaced by "definitely assigned" and one with every occurrence of "[un]assigned" replaced by "definitely unassigned".

For example:

- *V* is [un]assigned after an empty statement iff it is [un]assigned before the empty statement.

should be understood to stand for two rules:

- *V* is definitely assigned after an empty statement iff it is definitely assigned before the empty statement.
- *V* is definitely unassigned after an empty statement iff it is definitely unassigned before the empty statement.

The definite unassignment analysis of loop statements raises a special problem. Consider the statement `while (e) S`. In order to determine whether *V* is definitely unassigned within some subexpression of *e*, we need to determine whether *V* is definitely unassigned before *e*. One might argue, by analogy with the rule for definite assignment (§16.2.10), that *V* is definitely unassigned before *e* iff it is definitely unassigned before the `while` statement. However, such a rule is inadequate for our purposes. If *e* evaluates to true, the statement *S* will be executed. Later, if *V* is assigned by *S*, then in the following iteration(s) *V* will have already been assigned when *e* is evaluated. Under the rule suggested above, it would be possible to assign *V* multiple times, which is exactly what we have sought to avoid by introducing these rules.

A revised rule would be: "*V* is definitely unassigned before *e* iff it is definitely unassigned before the while statement and definitely unassigned after *S*". However, when we formulate the rule for *S*, we find: "*V* is definitely unassigned before *S* iff it is definitely unassigned after *e* when true". This leads to a circularity. In effect, *V* is definitely unassigned *before* the loop condition *e* only if it is unassigned *after* the loop as a whole!

We break this vicious circle using a *hypothetical* analysis of the loop condition and body. For example, if we assume that *V* is definitely unassigned before *e* (regardless of whether *V* really is definitely unassigned before *e*), and can then prove that *V* was definitely unassigned after *e* then we know that *e* does not assign *V*. This is stated more formally as:

Assuming *V* is definitely unassigned before *e*, *V* is definitely unassigned after *e*.

Variations on the above analysis are used to define well founded definite unassignment rules for all loop statements in the language.

Throughout the rest of this chapter, we will, unless explicitly stated otherwise, write *V* to represent a local variable or a blank `final` field (for rules of definite assignment) or a blank `final` variable (for rules of definite unassignment). Likewise, we will use *a*, *b*, *c*, and *e* to represent expressions, and *S* and *T* to represent statements. We will use the phrase *a* is *V* to mean that *a* is either the simple name of the variable *V*, or *V*'s simple name qualified by `this` (ignoring parentheses). We will use the phrase *a* is not *V* to mean the negation of *a* is *V*.

16.1 Definite Assignment and Expressions

> *Driftwood: The party of the first part shall be known in this contract as the party of the first part.*
> —Groucho Marx, *A Night at the Opera* (1935)

16.1.1 Boolean Constant Expressions

- *V* is [un]assigned after any constant expression whose value is `true` when false.
- *V* is [un]assigned after any constant expression whose value is `false` when true.

Because a constant expression whose value is `true` never has the value `false`, and a constant expression whose value is `false` never has the value `true`, the two preceding rules are vacuously satisfied. They are helpful in analyzing expressions involving the operators && (§16.1.2), `||` (§16.1.3), `!` (§16.1.4), and `? :` (§16.1.5).

- *V* is [un]assigned after any constant expression whose value is `true` when true iff *V* is [un]assigned before the constant expression.
- *V* is [un]assigned after any constant expression whose value is `false` when false iff *V* is [un]assigned before the constant expression.
- *V* is [un]assigned after a boolean-valued constant expression *e* iff *V* is [un]assigned after *e* when true and *V* is [un]assigned after *e* when false. (This is equivalent to saying that *V* is [un]assigned after *e* iff *V* is [un]assigned before *e*.)

16.1.2 The Boolean Operator &&

- *V* is [un]assigned after *a* && *b* when true iff *V* is [un]assigned after *b* when true.
- *V* is [un]assigned after *a* && *b* when false iff *V* is [un]assigned after *a* when false and *V* is [un]assigned after *b* when false.
- *V* is [un]assigned before *a* iff *V* is [un]assigned before *a* && *b*.
- *V* is [un]assigned before *b* iff *V* is [un]assigned after *a* when true.
- *V* is [un]assigned after *a* && *b* iff *V* is [un]assigned after *a* && *b* when true and *V* is [un]assigned after *a* && *b* when false.

16.1.3 The Boolean Operator `||`

- *V* is [un]assigned after *a* `||` *b* when true iff *V* is [un]assigned after *a* when true and *V* is [un]assigned after *b* when true.
- *V* is [un]assigned after *a* `||` *b* when false iff *V* is [un]assigned after *b* when false.
- *V* is [un]assigned before *a* iff *V* is [un]assigned before *a* `||` *b*.
- *V* is [un]assigned before *b* iff *V* is [un]assigned after *a* when false.
- *V* is [un]assigned after *a* `||` *b* iff *V* is [un]assigned after *a* `||` *b* when true and *V* is [un]assigned after *a* `||` *b* when false.

16.1.4 The Boolean Operator `!`

- *V* is [un]assigned after `!`*a* when true iff *V* is [un]assigned after *a* when false.
- *V* is [un]assigned after `!`*a* when false iff *V* is [un]assigned after *a* when true.
- *V* is [un]assigned before *a* iff *V* is [un]assigned before `!`*a*.
- *V* is [un]assigned after `!`*a* iff *V* is [un]assigned after `!`*a* when true and *V* is [un]assigned after `!`*a* when false. (This is equivalent to saying that *V* is [un]assigned after `!`*a* iff *V* is [un]assigned after *a*.)

16.1.5 The Boolean Operator `? :`

Suppose that *b* and *c* are boolean-valued expressions.

- *V* is [un]assigned after *a* `?` *b* `:` *c* when true iff *V* is [un]assigned after *b* when true and *V* is [un]assigned after *c* when true.
- *V* is [un]assigned after *a* `?` *b* `:` *c* when false iff *V* is [un]assigned after *b* when false and *V* is [un]assigned after *c* when false.
- *V* is [un]assigned before *a* iff *V* is [un]assigned before *a* `?` *b* `:` *c*.
- *V* is [un]assigned before *b* iff *V* is [un]assigned after *a* when true.
- *V* is [un]assigned before *c* iff *V* is [un]assigned after *a* when false.
- *V* is [un]assigned after *a* `?` *b* `:` *c* iff *V* is [un]assigned after *a* `?` *b* `:` *c* when true and *V* is [un]assigned after *a* `?` *b* `:` *c* when false.

16.1.6 The Conditional Operator ? :

Suppose that *b* and *c* are expressions that are not boolean-valued.

- V is [un]assigned after *a* ? *b* : *c* iff V is [un]assigned after *b* and V is [un]assigned after *c*.
- V is [un]assigned before *a* iff V is [un]assigned before *a* ? *b* : *c*.
- V is [un]assigned before *b* iff V is [un]assigned after *a* when true.
- V is [un]assigned before *c* iff V is [un]assigned after *a* when false.

16.1.7 Other Expressions of Type boolean

Suppose that *e* is a an expression of type boolean and is not a boolean constant expression, logical complement expression !*a*, conditional-and expression *a* && *b*, conditional-or expression *a* || *b*, or conditional expression *a* ? *b* : *c*.

- V is [un]assigned after *e* when true iff V is [un]assigned after *e*.
- V is [un]assigned after *e* when false iff V is [un]assigned after *e*.

16.1.8 Assignment Expressions

Driftwood: Would you like to hear it once more?
Fiorello: Just the first part.
Driftwood: What do you mean? The party of the first part?
Fiorello: No, the first part of the party of the first part.
—Groucho Marx and Chico Marx,
A Night at the Opera (1935)

Consider an assignment expression *a* = *b*, *a* += *b*, *a* -= *b*, *a* *= *b*, *a* /= *b*, *a* %= *b*, *a* <<= *b*, *a* >>= *b*, *a* >>>= *b*, *a* &= *b*, *a* |= *b*, or *a* ^= *b*.

- V is definitely assigned after the assignment expression iff either
  - *a* is V or
  - V is definitely assigned after *b*.
- V is definitely unassigned after the assignment expression iff *a* is not V and V is definitely unassigned after *b*.

- *V* is [un]assigned before *a* iff *V* is [un]assigned before the assignment expression.
- *V* is [un]assigned before *b* iff *V* is [un]assigned after *a*.

Note that if *a* is *V* and *V* is not definitely assigned before a compound assignment such as *a* &= *b*, then a compile-time error will necessarily occur. The first rule for definite assignment stated above includes the disjunct "*a* is *V*" even for compound assignment expressions, not just simple assignments, so that *V* will be considered to have been definitely assigned at later points in the code. Including the disjunct "*a* is *V*" does not affect the binary decision as to whether a program is acceptable or will result in a compile-time error, but it affects *how many* different points in the code may be regarded as erroneous, and so in practice it can improve the quality of error reporting. A similar remark applies to the inclusion of the conjunct "*a* is not *V*" in the first rule for definite unassignment stated above.

16.1.9 Operators ++ and --

- *V* is definitely assigned after ++*a*, --*a*, *a*++, or *a*-- iff either *a* is *V* or *V* is definitely assigned after the operand expression.
- *V* is definitely unassigned after ++*a*, --*a*, *a*++, or *a*-- iff *a* is not *V* and *V* is definitely unassigned after the operand expression.
- *V* is [un]assigned before *a* iff *V* is [un]assigned before ++*a*, --*a*, *a*++, or *a*--.

16.1.10 Other Expressions

> *Driftwood: All right. It says the, uh, the first part of the party of the first part, should be known in this contract as the first part of the party of the first part, should be known in this contract . . .*
>
> —Groucho Marx, *A Night at the Opera* (1935)

If an expression is not a boolean constant expression, and is not a preincrement expression ++*a*, predecrement expression --*a*, postincrement expression *a*++, postdecrement expression *a*--, logical complement expression !*a*, conditional-and expression *a* && *b*, conditional-or expression *a* || *b*, conditional expression *a* ? *b* : *c*, or assignment expression, then the following rules apply:

- If the expression has no subexpressions, *V* is [un]assigned after the expression iff *V* is [un]assigned before the expression. This case applies to literals, names, `this` (both qualified and unqualified), unqualified class instance creation expressions with no arguments, initialized array creation expressions whose initializers contain no expressions, unqualified superclass field access expressions, named method invocations with no arguments, and unqualified superclass method invocations with no arguments.

- If the expression has subexpressions, *V* is [un]assigned after the expression iff *V* is [un]assigned after its rightmost immediate subexpression.

There is a piece of subtle reasoning behind the assertion that a variable *V* can be known to be definitely unassigned after a method invocation. Taken by itself, at face value and without qualification, such an assertion is not always true, because an invoked method can perform assignments. But it must be remembered that, for the purposes of the Java programming language, the concept of definite unassignment is applied *only* to blank `final` variables. If *V* is a blank `final` local variable, then only the method to which its declaration belongs can perform assignments to *V*. If *V* is a blank `final` field, then only a constructor or an initializer for the class containing the declaration for *V* can perform assignments to *V*; no method can perform assignments to *V*. Finally, explicit constructor invocations (§8.8.7.1) are handled specially (§16.9); although they are syntactically similar to expression statements containing method invocations, they are not expression statements and therefore the rules of this section do not apply to explicit constructor invocations.

For any immediate subexpression *y* of an expression *x*, *V* is [un]assigned before *y* iff one of the following situations is true:

- *y* is the leftmost immediate subexpression of *x* and *V* is [un]assigned before *x*.
- *y* is the right-hand operand of a binary operator and *V* is [un]assigned after the left-hand operand.
- *x* is an array access, *y* is the subexpression within the brackets, and *V* is [un]assigned after the subexpression before the brackets.
- *x* is a primary method invocation expression, *y* is the first argument expression in the method invocation expression, and *V* is [un]assigned after the primary expression that computes the target object.
- *x* is a method invocation expression or a class instance creation expression; *y* is an argument expression, but not the first; and *V* is [un]assigned after the argument expression to the left of *y*.
- *x* is a qualified class instance creation expression, *y* is the first argument expression in the class instance creation expression, and *V* is [un]assigned after the primary expression that computes the qualifying object.

- *x* is an array instance creation expression; *y* is a dimension expression, but not the first; and *V* is [un]assigned after the dimension expression to the left of *y*.
- *x* is an array instance creation expression initialized via an array initializer; *y* is the array initializer in *x*; and *V* is [un]assigned after the dimension expression to the left of *y*.

16.2 Definite Assignment and Statements

Driftwood: The party of the second part shall be known in this contract as the party of the second part.
—Groucho Marx, *A Night at the Opera* (1935)

16.2.1 Empty Statements

- *V* is [un]assigned after an empty statement iff it is [un]assigned before the empty statement.

16.2.2 Blocks

- A blank final member field *V* is definitely assigned (and moreover is not definitely unassigned) before the block that is the body of any method in the scope of *V*.
- A local variable *V* is definitely unassigned (and moreover is not definitely assigned) before the block that is the body of the constructor, method, instance initializer or static initializer that declares *V*.
- Let *C* be a class declared within the scope of *V*. Then:
  - *V* is definitely assigned before the block that is the body of any constructor, method, instance initializer or static initializer declared in *C* iff *V* is definitely assigned before the declaration of *C*.

  Note that there are no rules that would allow us to conclude that *V* is definitely unassigned before the block that is the body of any constructor, method, instance initializer or static initializer declared in *C*. We can informally conclude that *V* is not definitely unassigned before the block that is the body of any constructor, method, instance initializer or static initializer declared in *C*, but there is no need for such a rule to be stated explicitly.
- *C* [un]assigned after an empty block iff it is [un]assigned before the empty block.

- *V* is [un]assigned after a nonempty block iff it is [un]assigned after the last statement in the block.
- *V* is [un]assigned before the first statement of the block iff it is [un]assigned before the block.
- *V* is [un]assigned before any other statement *S* of the block iff it is [un]assigned after the statement immediately preceding *S* in the block.

We say that *V* is definitely unassigned everywhere in a block *B* iff

- *V* is definitely unassigned before *B*.
- *V* is definitely assigned after e in every assignment expression *V* = *e*, *V* += *e*, *V* -= *e*, *V* *= *e*, *V* /= *e*, *V* %= *e*, *V* <<= *e*, *V* >>= *e*, *V* >>>= *e*, *V* &= *e*, *V* |= *e*, or *V* ^= *e* that occurs in *B*.
- *V* is definitely assigned before before every expression ++*V*, --*V*, *V*++, or *V*--. that occurs in *B*.

These conditions are counterintuitive and require some explanation. Consider a simple assignment V = e. If V is definitely assigned after e, then either:

1. The assignment occurs in dead code, and V is vacouusly definitely assigned. In this case, the assignment will not actually take place, and we can assume that V is not being assigned by the assignment expression.
2. V was already assigned by an earlier expression prior to e. In this case the current assignment will cause a compile-time error.

So, we can conclude that if the conditions are met by a program that causes no compile time error, then any assignments to V in B will not actually take place at run time.

16.2.3 Local Class Declaration Statements

- *V* is [un]assigned after a local class declaration statement iff it is [un]assigned before the local class declaration statement.

16.2.4 Local Variable Declaration Statements

- *V* is [un]assigned after a local variable declaration statement that contains no variable initializers iff it is [un]assigned before the local variable declaration statement.

- *V* is definitely assigned after a local variable declaration statement that contains at least one variable initializer iff either it is definitely assigned after the last variable initializer in the local variable declaration statement or the last variable initializer in the declaration is in the declarator that declares *V*.
- *V* is definitely unassigned after a local variable declaration statement that contains at least one variable initializer iff it is definitely unassigned after the last variable initializer in the local variable declaration statement and the last variable initializer in the declaration is not in the declarator that declares *V*.
- *V* is [un]assigned before the first variable initializer in a local variable declaration statement iff it is [un]assigned before the local variable declaration statement.
- *V* is definitely assigned before any variable initializer *e* other than the first one in the local variable declaration statement iff either *V* is definitely assigned after the variable initializer to the left of *e* or the initializer expression to the left of *e* is in the declarator that declares *V*.
- *V* is definitely unassigned before any variable initializer *e* other than the first one in the local variable declaration statement iff *V* is definitely unassigned after the variable initializer to the left of *e* and the initializer expression to the left of *e* is not in the declarator that declares *V*.

16.2.5 Labeled Statements

- *V* is [un]assigned after a labeled statement *L*:*S* (where *L* is a label) iff *V* is [un]assigned after *S* and *V* is [un]assigned before every `break` statement that may exit the labeled statement *L*:*S*.
- *V* is [un]assigned before *S* iff *V* is [un]assigned before *L*:*S*.

16.2.6 Expression Statements

- *V* is [un]assigned after an expression statement *e*`;` iff it is [un]assigned after *e*.
- *V* is [un]assigned before *e* iff it is [un]assigned before *e*`;`.

16.2.7 `if` Statements

The following rules apply to a statement `if (`*e*`)` *S*:

- *V* is [un]assigned after `if (`*e*`)` *S* iff *V* is [un]assigned after *S* and *V* is [un]assigned after *e* when false.
- *V* is [un]assigned before *e* iff *V* is [un]assigned before `if (`*e*`)` *S*.
- *V* is [un]assigned before *S* iff *V* is [un]assigned after *e* when true.

The following rules apply to a statement `if (`*e*`)` *S* `else` *T*:

- *V* is [un]assigned after `if (`*e*`)` *S* `else` *T* iff *V* is [un]assigned after *S* and *V* is [un]assigned after *T*.
- *V* is [un]assigned before *e* iff *V* is [un]assigned before `if (`*e*`)` *S* `else` *T*.
- *V* is [un]assigned before *S* iff *V* is [un]assigned after *e* when true.
- *V* is [un]assigned before *T* iff *V* is [un]assigned after *e* when false.

16.2.8 `assert` Statements

The following rules apply both to a statement `assert` *e1* and to a statement `assert` *e1 :e2* :

- *V* is definitely [un]assigned before *e1* iff *V* is definitely [un]assigned before the `assert` statement.
- *V* is definitely assigned after the `assert` statement iff *V* is definitely assigned before the `assert` statement.
- *V* is definitely unassigned after the `assert` statement iff *V* is definitely unassigned before the `assert` statement and *V* is definitely unassigned after *e1* when true.

The following rule applies to a statement `assert` *e1: e2* :

- *V* is definitely [un]assigned before *e2* iff *V* is definitely [un]assigned after *e1* when false.

16.2.9 `switch` Statements

- *V* is [un]assigned after a `switch` statement iff all of the following are true:
  - Either there is a `default` label in the `switch` block or *V* is [un]assigned after the switch expression.

  - Either there are no switch labels in the `switch` block that do not begin a block-statement-group (that is, there are no switch labels immediately before the "}" that ends the switch block) or *V* is [un]assigned after the switch expression.
  - Either the `switch` block contains no block-statement-groups or *V* is [un]assigned after the last block-statement of the last block-statement-group.
  - *V* is [un]assigned before every `break` statement that may exit the `switch` statement.
- *V* is [un]assigned before the switch expression iff *V* is [un]assigned before the `switch` statement.

If a switch block contains at least one block-statement-group, then the following rules also apply:

- *V* is [un]assigned before the first block-statement of the first block-statement-group in the switch block iff *V* is [un]assigned after the switch expression.
- *V* is [un]assigned before the first block-statement of any block-statement-group other than the first iff *V* is [un]assigned after the switch expression and *V* is [un]assigned after the preceding block-statement.

16.2.10 `while` Statements

- *V* is [un]assigned after `while (`*e*`)` *S* iff *V* is [un]assigned after *e* when false and *V* is [un]assigned before every `break` statement for which the `while` statement is the break target.
- *V* is definitely assigned before *e* iff *V* is definitely assigned before the `while` statement.
- *V* is definitely unassigned before *e* iff all of the following conditions hold:
  - *V* is definitely unassigned before the `while` statement.
  - Assuming *V* is definitely unassigned before *e*, *V* is definitely unassigned after *S*.
  - Assuming *V* is definitely unassigned before *e*, *V* is definitely unassigned before every `continue` statement for which the `while` statement is the continue target.
- *V* is [un]assigned before *S* iff *V* is [un]assigned after *e* when true.

16.2.11 do Statements

- *V* is [un]assigned after `do` *S* `while (`*e*`);` iff *V* is [un]assigned after *e* when false and *V* is [un]assigned before every `break` statement for which the `do` statement is the break target.
- *V* is definitely assigned before *S* iff *V* is definitely assigned before the `do` statement.
- *V* is definitely unassigned before *S* iff all of the following conditions hold:
  - *V* is definitely unassigned before the `do` statement.
  - Assuming *V* is definitely unassigned before *S*, *V* is definitely unassigned after *e* when true.
- *V* is [un]assigned before *e* iff *V* is [un]assigned after *S* and *V* is [un]assigned before every `continue` statement for which the `do` statement is the continue target.

16.2.12 for Statements

The rules herein cover the basic `for` statement (§14.14.1). Since the enhanced `for` (§14.14.2) statement is defined by traslation to a basic `for` statement, no special rules need to be provided for it.

- *V* is [un]assigned after a `for` statement iff both of the following are true:
  - Either a condition expression is not present or *V* is [un]assigned after the condition expression when false.
  - *V* is [un]assigned before every `break` statement for which the `for` statement is the break target.
- *V* is [un]assigned before the initialization part of the `for` statement iff *V* is [un]assigned before the `for` statement.
- *V* is definitely assigned before the condition part of the `for` statement iff *V* is definitely assigned after the initialization part of the `for` statement.
- *V* is definitely unassigned before the condition part of the `for` statement iff all of the following conditions hold:
  - *V* is definitely unassigned after the initialization part of the `for` statement.
  - Assuming *V* is definitely unassigned before the condition part of the `for` statement, *V* is definitely unassigned after the contained statement.

  - Assuming *V* is definitely unassigned before the contained statement, *V* is definitely unassigned before every `continue` statement for which the `for` statement is the continue target.

- *V* is [un]assigned before the contained statement iff either of the following is true:
  - A condition expression is present and *V* is [un]assigned after the condition expression when true.
  - No condition expression is present and *V* is [un]assigned after the initialization part of the `for` statement.
- *V* is [un]assigned before the incrementation part of the `for` statement iff *V* is [un]assigned after the contained statement and *V* is [un]assigned before every `continue` statement for which the `for` statement is the continue target.

16.2.12.1 *Initialization Part*

- If the initialization part of the `for` statement is a local variable declaration statement, the rules of §16.2.4 apply.
- Otherwise, if the initialization part is empty, then *V* is [un]assigned after the initialization part iff *V* is [un]assigned before the initialization part.
- Otherwise, three rules apply:
  - *V* is [un]assigned after the initialization part iff *V* is [un]assigned after the last expression statement in the initialization part.
  - *V* is [un]assigned before the first expression statement in the initialization part iff *V* is [un]assigned before the initialization part.
  - *V* is [un]assigned before an expression statement *E* other than the first in the initialization part iff *V* is [un]assigned after the expression statement immediately preceding *E*.

16.2.12.2 *Incrementation Part*

- If the incrementation part of the `for` statement is empty, then *V* is [un]assigned after the incrementation part iff *V* is [un]assigned before the incrementation part.
- Otherwise, three rules apply:
  - *V* is [un]assigned after the incrementation part iff *V* is [un]assigned after the last expression statement in the incrementation part.

- V is [un]assigned before the first expression statement in the incrementation part iff V is [un]assigned before the incrementation part.
- V is [un]assigned before an expression statement E other than the first in the incrementation part iff V is [un]assigned after the expression statement immediately preceding E.

16.2.13 `break`, `continue`, `return`, and `throw` Statements

> *Fiorello:* *Hey, look! Why can't the first part of the second party be the second part of the first party? Then you've got something!*
>
> —Chico Marx, *A Night at the Opera* (1935)

- By convention, we say that V is [un]assigned after any `break`, `continue`, `return`, or `throw` statement. The notion that a variable is "[un]assigned after" a statement or expression really means "is [un]assigned after the statement or expression completes normally". Because a `break`, `continue`, `return`, or `throw` statement never completes normally, it vacuously satisfies this notion.
- In a `return` statement with an expression *e* or a `throw` statement with an expression *e*, V is [un]assigned before *e* iff V is [un]assigned before the `return` or `throw` statement.

16.2.14 `synchronized` Statements

- V is [un]assigned after `synchronized (`*e*`) S` iff V is [un]assigned after S.
- V is [un]assigned before *e* iff V is [un]assigned before the statement `synchronized (`*e*`) S`.
- V is [un]assigned before S iff V is [un]assigned after *e*.

16.2.15 `try` Statements

These rules apply to every `try` statement, whether or not it has a `finally` block:

- V is [un]assigned before the `try` block iff V is [un]assigned before the `try` statement.
- V is definitely assigned before a `catch` block iff V is definitely assigned before the `try` block.

- *V* is definitely unassigned before a `catch` block iff all of the following conditions hold:
  - *V* is definitely unassigned after the `try` block.
  - *V* is definitely unassigned before every `return` statement that belongs to the `try` block.
  - *V* is definitely unassigned after *e* in every statement of the form `throw` *e* that belongs to the `try` block.
  - *V* is definitely unassigned after *e1* for every statement of the form `assert` *e1*, that occurs in the try block.
  - *V* is definitely unassigned after *e2* in every statement of the form `assert` *e1* : *e2* that occurs in the try block.
  - *V* is definitely unassigned before every `break` statement that belongs to the `try` block and whose break target contains (or is) the `try` statement.
  - *V* is definitely unassigned before every `continue` statement that belongs to the `try` block and whose continue target contains the `try` statement.

If a `try` statement does not have a `finally` block, then this rule also applies:

- *V* is [un]assigned after the `try` statement iff *V* is [un]assigned after the `try` block and *V* is [un]assigned after every `catch` block in the try statement.

If a `try` statement does have a `finally` block, then these rules also apply:

- *V* is definitely assigned after the `try` statement iff at least one of the following is true:
  - *V* is definitely assigned after the try block and *V* is definitely assigned after every `catch` block in the try statement.
  - *V* is definitely assigned after the `finally` block.
  - *V* is definitely unassigned after a `try` statement iff *V* is definitely unassigned after the `finally` block.
- *V* is definitely assigned before the `finally` block iff *V* is definitely assigned before the `try` statement.
- *V* is definitely unassigned before the `finally` block iff all of the following conditions hold:
  - *V* is definitely unassigned after the `try` block.

- V is definitely unassigned before every `return` statement that belongs to the `try` block.
- V is definitely unassigned after e in before every statement of the form `throw` e that belongs to the `try` block.
- V is definitely unassigned after $e1$ for every statement of the form `assert` $e1$, that occurs in the try block.
- V is definitely unassigned after $e2$ in every statement of the form `assert` $e1$: $e2$ that occurs in the try block.
- V is definitely unassigned before every `break` statement that belongs to the `try` block and whose break target contains (or is) the `try` statement.
- V is definitely unassigned before every `continue` statement that belongs to the `try` block and whose continue target contains the `try` statement.
- V is definitely unassigned after every `catch` block of the `try` statement.

16.3 Definite Assignment and Parameters

- A formal parameter V of a method or constructor is definitely assigned (and moreover is not definitely unassigned) before the body of the method or constructor.
- An exception parameter V of a `catch` clause is definitely assigned (and moreover is not definitely unassigned) before the body of the `catch` clause.

16.4 Definite Assignment and Array Initializers

- V is [un]assigned after an empty array initializer iff it is [un]assigned before the empty array initializer.
- V is [un]assigned after a nonempty array initializer iff it is [un]assigned after the last variable initializer in the array initializer.
- V is [un]assigned before the first variable initializer of the array initializer iff it is [un]assigned before the array initializer.
- V is [un]assigned before any other variable initializer I of the array initializer iff it is [un]assigned after the variable initializer to the left of I in the array initializer.

16.5 Definite Assignment and Enum Constants

The rules determining when a variable is definitely assigned or definitely unassigned before an enum constant are given §16.8.

DISCUSSION

This is because an enum constant is essentially a static final field (§8.3.1.1, §8.3.1.2) that is initialized with a class instance creation expression (§15.9).

- *V* is definitely assigned before the declaration of a class body of an enum constant with no arguments that is declared within the scope of *V* iff *V* is definitely assigned before the enum constant.
- *V* is definitely assigned before the declaration of the class body of an enum constant with arguments that is declared within the scope of *V* iff *V* is definitely assigned after the last argument expression of the enum constant

The definite assignment/unassignment status of any construct within the class body of an enum constant is governed by the usual rules for classes.

Let *y* be an argument of an enum constant, but not the first. Then:

- *V* is [un]assigned before *y* iff it is [un]assigned after the argument to the left of *y*

Otherwise:

- *V* is [un]assigned before the first argument to an enum constant iff it is [un]assigned before the enum constant

16.6 Definite Assignment and Anonymous Classes

- *V* is definitely assigned before an anonymous class declaration (§15.9.5) that is declared within the scope of *V* iff *V* is definitely assigned after the class instance creation expression that declares the anonymous class.

DISCUSSION

It should be clear that if an anonymous class is implicitly defined by an enum constant, the rules of section §16.5 apply.

16.7 Definite Assignment and Member Types

Let *C* be a class, and let *V* be a blank final member field of *C*. Then:

- *V* is definitely assigned (and moreover, not definitely unassigned) before the declaration of any member type of *C*.

Let *C* be a class declared within the scope of *V*. Then:

- *V* is definitely assigned before a member type (§8.5, §9.5) declaration of *C* iff *V* is definitely assigned before the declaration of *C*.

16.8 Definite Assignment and Static Initializers

Let *C* be a class declared within the scope of *V*. Then:

- *V* is definitely assigned before an enum constant or static variable initializer of *C* iff *V* is definitely assigned before the declaration of *C*.

Note that there are no rules that would allow us to conclude that *V* is definitely unassigned before a static variable initializer or enum constant. We can informally conclude that *V* is not definitely unassigned before any static variable initializer of *C*, but there is no need for such a rule to be stated explicitly.

Let *C* be a class, and let *V* be a blank `final static` member field of *C*, declared in *C*. Then:

- *V* is definitely unassigned (and moreover is not definitely assigned) before the leftmost enum constant, `static` initializer or `static` variable initializer of *C*.
- *V* is [un]assigned before an enum constant, `static` initializer or `static` variable initializer of *C* other than the leftmost iff *V* is [un]assigned after the preceding enum constant, `static` initializer or `static` variable initializer of *C*.

Let *C* be a class, and let *V* be a blank `final static` member field of *C*, declared in a superclass of *C*. Then:

- *V* is definitely assigned (and moreover is not definitely unassigned) before every enum constant of *C*.
- *V* is definitely assigned (and moreover is not definitely unassigned) before the block that is the body of a static initializer of *C*.
- *V* is definitely assigned (and moreover is not definitely unassigned) before every static variable initializer of *C*.

16.9 Definite Assignment, Constructors, and Instance Initializers

Let *C* be a class declared within the scope of *V*. Then:

- *V* is definitely assigned before an instance variable initializer of *C* iff *V* is definitely assigned before the declaration of *C*.

Note that there are no rules that would allow us to conclude that *V* is definitely unassigned before an instance variable initializer. We can informally conclude that *V* is not definitely unassigned before any instance variable initializer of *C*, but there is no need for such a rule to be stated explicitly.

Let *C* be a class, and let *V* be a blank `final` non-`static` member field of *C*, declared in *C*. Then:

- *V* is definitely unassigned (and moreover is not definitely assigned) before the leftmost instance initializer or instance variable initializer of *C*.
- *V* is [un]assigned before an instance initializer or instance variable initializer of *C* other than the leftmost iff *V* is [un]assigned after the preceding instance initializer or instance variable initializer of *C*.

The following rules hold within the constructors of class *C*:

- *V* is definitely assigned (and moreover is not definitely unassigned) after an alternate constructor invocation (§8.8.7.1).
- *V* is definitely unassigned (and moreover is not definitely assigned) before an explicit or implicit superclass constructor invocation (§8.8.7.1).
- If *C* has no instance initializers or instance variable initializers, then *V* is not definitely assigned (and moreover is definitely unassigned) after an explicit or implicit superclass constructor invocation.

* If *C* has at least one instance initializer or instance variable initializer then *V* is [un]assigned after an explicit or implicit superclass constructor invocation iff *V* is [un]assigned after the rightmost instance initializer or instance variable initializer of *C*.

Let *C* be a class, and let *V* be a blank `final` member field of *C*, declared in a superclass of *C*. Then:

* *V* is definitely assigned (and moreover is not definitely unassigned) before the block that is the body of a constructor, or instance initializer of *C*.
* *V* is definitely assigned (and moreover is not definitely unassigned) before every instance variable initializer of *C*.

CHAPTER 17

Threads and Locks

And oft-times in the most forbidding den
Of solitude, with love of science strong,
How patiently the yoke of thought they bear;
How subtly glide its finest threads along!
—William Wordsworth, *Monks and Schoolmen,*
in *Ecclesiastical Sonnets* (1822)

WHILE most of the discussion in the preceding chapters is concerned only with the behavior of code as executed a single statement or expression at a time, that is, by a single *thread*, each Java virtual machine can support many threads of execution at once. These threads independently execute code that operates on values and objects residing in a shared main memory. Threads may be supported by having many hardware processors, by time-slicing a single hardware processor, or by time-slicing many hardware processors.

Threads are represented by the `Thread` class. The only way for a user to create a thread is to create an object of this class; each thread is associated with such an object. A thread will start when the `start()` method is invoked on the corresponding `Thread` object.

The behavior of threads, particularly when not correctly synchronized, can be confusing and counterintuitive. This chapter describes the semantics of multithreaded programs; it includes rules for which values may be seen by a read of shared memory that is updated by multiple threads. As the specification is similar to the *memory models* for different hardware architectures, these semantics are known as the *Java programming language memory model*. When no confusion can arise, we will simply refer to these rules as "the memory model".

These semantics do not prescribe how a multithreaded program should be executed. Rather, they describe the behaviors that multithreaded programs are allowed to exhibit. Any execution strategy that generates only allowed behaviors is an acceptable execution strategy.

17.1 Locks

The Java programming language provides multiple mechanisms for communicating between threads. The most basic of these methods is *synchronization*, which is implemented using *monitors*. Each object in Java is associated with a monitor, which a thread can *lock* or *unlock*. Only one thread at a time may hold a lock on a monitor. Any other threads attempting to lock that monitor are blocked until they can obtain a lock on that monitor. A thread *t* may lock a particular monitor multiple times; each unlock reverses the effect of one lock operation.

The `synchronized` statement (§14.19) computes a reference to an object; it then attempts to perform a lock action on that object's monitor and does not proceed further until the lock action has successfully completed. After the lock action has been performed, the body of the `synchronized` statement is executed. If execution of the body is ever completed, either normally or abruptly, an unlock action is automatically performed on that same monitor.

A `synchronized` method (§8.4.3.6) automatically performs a lock action when it is invoked; its body is not executed until the lock action has successfully completed. If the method is an instance method, it locks the monitor associated with the instance for which it was invoked (that is, the object that will be known as `this` during execution of the body of the method). If the method is static, it locks the monitor associated with the `Class` object that represents the class in which the method is defined. If execution of the method's body is ever completed, either normally or abruptly, an unlock action is automatically performed on that same monitor.

The Java programming language neither prevents nor requires detection of deadlock conditions. Programs where threads hold (directly or indirectly) locks on multiple objects should use conventional techniques for deadlock avoidance, creating higher-level locking primitives that don't deadlock, if necessary.

Other mechanisms, such as reads and writes of volatile variables and classes provided in the `java.util.concurrent` package, provide alternative ways of synchronization.

17.2 Notation in Examples

The memory model specified herein is not fundamentally based in the object oriented nature of the Java programming language. For conciseness and simplicity in our examples, we often exhibit code fragments without class or method definitions, or explicit dereferencing. Most examples consist of two or more threads containing statements with access to local variables, shared global variables or instance fields of an object. We typically use variables names such as `r1` or `r2` to indicate variables local to a method or thread. Such variables are not accessible by other threads.

Restrictions of partial orders and functions. We use $f|_d$ to denote the function given by restricting the domain of f to d: for all x in d, $f|_d(x) = f(x)$ and for all x not in d, $f|_d(x)$ is undefined. Similarly, we use $p|_d$ to represent the restriction of the partial order p to the elements in d: for all x,y in d, $p(x, y)$ if and only if $p|_d(x, y) = p(x)$. If either x or y are not in d, then it is not the case that $p|_d(x, y)$.

17.3 Incorrectly Synchronized Programs Exhibit Surprising Behaviors

The semantics of the Java programming language allow compilers and microprocessors to perform optimizations that can interact with incorrectly synchronized code in ways that can produce behaviors that seem paradoxical.

Trace 17.1: Surprising results caused by statement reordering - original code

Thread 1	Thread 2
1: r2 = A;	3: r1 = B;
2: B = 1;	4: A = 2;

Trace 17.2: Surprising results caused by statement reordering - valid compiler transformation

Thread 1	Thread 2
B = 1;	r1 = B;
r2 = A;	A = 2;

Consider, for example, the example shown in Trace 17.1. This program uses local variables `r1` and `r2` and shared variables `A` and `B`. Initially, `A == B == 0`.

It may appear that the result `r2 == 2, r1 == 1` is impossible. Intuitively, either instruction 1 or instruction 3 should come first in an execution. If instruction 1 comes first, it should not be able to see the write at instruction 4. If instruction 3 comes first, it should not be able to see the write at instruction 2.

If some execution exhibited this behavior, then we would know that instruction 4 came before instruction 1, which came before instruction 2, which came before instruction 3, which came before instruction 4. This is, on the face of it, absurd.

However, compilers are allowed to reorder the instructions in either thread, when this does not affect the execution of that thread in isolation. If instruction 1 is reordered with instruction 2, as shown in Trace 17.2, then it is easy to see how the result `r2 == 2` and `r1 == 1` might occur.

To some programmers, this behavior may seem ``broken''. However, it should be noted that this code is improperly synchronized:

- there is a write in one thread,
- a read of the same variable by another thread,
- and the write and read are not ordered by synchronization.

This situation is an example of a *data race* (§17.4.5). When code contains a data race, counterintuitive results are often possible.

Several mechanisms can produce the reordering in Trace 17.2. The just-in-time compiler and the processor may rearrange code. In addition, the memory hierarchy of the architecture on which a virtual machine is run may make it appear as if code is being reordered. In this chapter, we shall refer to anything that can reorder code as *a compiler*.

Trace 17.3: Surprising results caused by forward substitution

Thread 1	**Thread 2**
r1 = p;	r6 = p;
r2 = r1.x;	r6.x = 3;
r3 = q;	
r4 = r3.x;	
r5 = r1.x;	

Trace 17.4: Surprising results caused by forward substitution

Thread 1	**Thread 2**
r1 = p;	r6 = p;
r2 = r1.x;	r6.x = 3;
r3 = q;	
r4 = r3.x;	
r5 = r2;	

Another example of surprising results can be seen in Trace 17.3. Initially: `p == q`, `p.x == 0`. This program is also incorrectly synchronized; it writes to shared memory without enforcing any ordering between those writes.

One common compiler optimization involves having the value read for `r2` reused for `r5`: they are both reads of `r1.x` with no intervening write. This situation is shown in Trace 17.4.

Now consider the case where the assignment to `r6.x` in Thread 2 happens between the first read of `r1.x` and the read of `r3.x` in Thread 1. If the compiler decides to reuse the value of `r2` for the `r5`, then `r2` and `r5` will have the value 0, and `r4` will have the value 3. From the perspective of the programmer, the value stored at `p.x` has changed from 0 to 3 and then changed back.

17.4 Memory Model

A *memory model* describes, given a program and an execution trace of that program, whether the execution trace is a legal execution of the program. The Java programming language memory model works by examining each read in an execution trace and checking that the write observed by that read is valid according to certain rules.

The memory model describes possible behaviors of a program. An implementation is free to produce any code it likes, as long as all resulting executions of a program produce a result that can be predicted by the memory model.

DISCUSSION

This provides a great deal of freedom for the implementor to perform a myriad of code transformations, including the reordering of actions and removal of unnecessary synchronization.

The memory model determines what values can be read at every point in the program. The actions of each thread in isolation must behave as governed by the semantics of that thread, with the exception that the values seen by each read are determined by the memory model. When we refer to this, we say that the program obeys *intra-thread semantics*. Intra-thread semantics are the semantics for single threaded programs, and allow the complete prediction of the behavior of a thread based on the values seen by read actions within the thread. To determine if the actions of thread *t* in an execution are legal, we simply evaluate the implementation of thread *t* as it would be performed in a single threaded context, as defined in the rest of this specification.

Each time the evaluation of thread *t* generates an inter-thread action, it must match the inter-thread action *a* of *t* that comes next in program order. If *a* is a read, then further evaluation of *t* uses the value seen by *a* as determined by the memory model.

This section provides the specification of the Java programming language memory model except for issues dealing with final fields, which are described in §17.5.

17.4.1 Shared Variables

Memory that can be shared between threads is called *shared memory* or *heap memory.*

All instance fields, static fields and array elements are stored in heap memory. In this chapter, we use the term *variable* to refer to both fields and array elements. Local variables (§14.4), formal method parameters (§8.4.1) or exception handler parameters are never shared between threads and are unaffected by the memory model.

Two accesses to (reads of or writes to) the same variable are said to be *conflicting* if at least one of the accesses is a write.

17.4.2 Actions

An *inter-thread action* is an action performed by one thread that can be detected or directly influenced by another thread. There are several kinds of inter-thread action that a program may perform:

- *Read* (normal, or non-volatile). Reading a variable.
- *Write* (normal, or non-volatile). Writing a variable.
- *Synchronization actions,* which are:
  - *Volatile read.* A volatile read of a variable.
  - *Volatile write.* A volatile write of a variable.
  - *Lock.* Locking a monitor
  - *Unlock.* Unlocking a monitor.
  - The (synthetic) first and last action of a thread
  - Actions that start a thread or detect that a thread has terminated, as described in §17.4.4.

- *External Actions.* An external action is an action that may be observable outside of an execution, and has a result based on an environment external to the execution.
- *Thread divergence actions* (§17.4.9). A thread divergence action is only performed by a thread that is in an infinite loop in which no memory, synchronization or external actions are performed. If a thread performs a thread divergence action, it will be followed by an infinite number of thread divergence actions.

DISCUSSION

Thread divergence actions are introduced to model how a thread may cause all other threads to stall and fail to make progress

---

This specification is only concerned with inter-thread actions. We do not need to concern ourselves with intra-thread actions (e.g., adding two local variables and storing the result in a third local variable). As previously mentioned, all threads need to obey the correct intra-thread semantics for Java programs. We will usually refere to inter-thread actions more succinctly as simply *actions*.

An action a is described by a tuple $< t, k, v, u >$, comprising:

- t - the thread performing the action
- k - the kind of action
- v - the variable or monitor involved in the action. For lock actions, v is the monitor being locked; for unlock actions, it is the monitor being unlocked. If the action is (volatile or non-volatile) read, v is the variable being read. If the action is a (volatile or non-volatile) write, v is the variable being written
- u - an arbitrary unique identifier for the action

An external action tuple contains an additional component, which contains the results of the external action as perceived by the thread performing the action. This may be information as to the success or failure of the action, and any values read by the action.

Parameters to the external action (e.g., which bytes are written to which socket) are not part of the external action tuple. These parameters are set up by other actions within the thread and can be determined by examining the intra-thread semantics. They are not explicitly discussed in the memory model.

In non-terminating executions, not all external actions are observable. Non-terminating executions and observable actions are discussed in §17.4.9.

17.4.3 Programs and Program Order

Among all the inter-thread actions performed by each thread *t*, the *program order* of *t* is a total order that reflects the order in which these actions would be performed according to the intra-thread semantics of *t*.

A set of actions is *sequentially consistent* if all actions occur in a total order (the execution order) that is consistent with program order and furthermore, each read *r* of a variable *v* sees the value written by the write *w* to *v* such that:

- *w* comes before *r* in the execution order, and
- there is no other write *w'* such that *w* comes before *w'* and *w'* comes before *r* in the execution order.

Sequential consistency is a very strong guarantee that is made about visibility and ordering in an execution of a program. Within a sequentially consistent execution, there is a total order over all individual actions (such as reads and writes) which is consistent with the order of the program, and each individual action is atomic and is immediately visible to every thread.

If a program has no data races, then all executions of the program will appear to be sequentially consistent.

Sequential consistency and/or freedom from data races still allows errors arising from groups of operations that need to be perceived atomically and are not.

DISCUSSION

If we were to use sequential consistency as our memory model, many of the compiler and processor optimizations that we have discussed would be illegal. For example, in Trace 17.3, as soon as the write of 3 to `p.x` occurred, subsequent reads of that location would be required to see that value.

17.4.4 Synchronization Order

Every execution has a *synchronization order*. A synchronization order is a total order over all of the synchronization actions of an execution. For each thread *t*, the synchronization order of the synchronization actions (§17.4.2) in *t* is consistent with the program order (§17.4.3) of *t*.

Synchronization actions induce the *synchronized-with* relation on actions, defined as follows:

- An unlock action on monitor *m* synchronizes-with all subsequent lock actions on *m* (where subsequent is defined according to the synchronization order).
- A write to a volatile variable (§8.3.1.4) *v* synchronizes-with all subsequent reads of *v* by any thread (where subsequent is defined according to the synchronization order).
- An action that starts a thread synchronizes-with the first action in the thread it starts.
- The write of the default value (zero, `false` or `null`) to each variable synchronizes-with the first action in every thread. Although it may seem a little strange to write a default value to a variable before the object containing the variable is allocated, conceptually every object is created at the start of the program with its default initialized values.
- The final action in a thread *T1* synchronizes-with any action in another thread *T2* that detects that *T1* has terminated. *T2* may accomplish this by calling `T1.isAlive()` or `T1.join()`.
- If thread *T1* interrupts thread *T2*, the interrupt by *T1* synchronizes-with any point where any other thread (including *T2*) determines that *T2* has been interrupted (by having an `InterruptedException` thrown or by invoking `Thread.interrupted` or `Thread.isInterrupted`).

The source of a synchronizes-with edge is called a *release*, and the destination is called an *acquire*.

17.4.5 Happens-before Order

Two actions can be ordered by a *happens-before* relationship. If one action happens-before another, then the first is visible to and ordered before the second.

If we have two actions *x* and *y*, we write *hb(x, y)* to indicate that *x* happens-before *y*.

- If x and y are actions of the same thread and x comes before y in program order, then *hb(x, y).*
- There is a happens-before edge from the end of a constructor of an object to the start of a finalizer (§12.6) for that object.
- If an action x synchronizes-with a following action y, then we also have *hb(x, y).*
- If *hb(x, y)* and *hb(y, z),* then *hb(x, z).*

It should be noted that the presence of a happens-before relationship between two actions does not necessarily imply that they have to take place in that order in an implementation. If the reordering produces results consistent with a legal execution, it is not illegal.

DISCUSSION

For example, the write of a default value to every field of an object constructed by a thread need not happen before the beginning of that thread, as long as no read ever observes that fact.

More specifically, if two actions share a happens-before relationship, they do not necessarily have to appear to have happened in that order to any code with which they do not share a happens-before relationship. Writes in one thread that are in a data race with reads in another thread may, for example, appear to occur out of order to those reads.

The `wait` methods of class `Object` have lock and unlock actions associated with them; their happens-before relationships are defined by these associated actions. These methods are described further in §17.8.

The happens-before relation defines when data races take place.

A set of synchronization edges, *S,* is *sufficient* if it is the minimal set such that the transitive closure of *S* with the program order determines all of the happens-before edges in the execution. This set is unique.

DISCUSSION

It follows from the above definitions that:

- An unlock on a monitor happens-before every subsequent lock on that monitor.
- A write to a volatile field (§8.3.1.4) happens-before every subsequent read of that field.
- A call to `start()` on a thread happens-before any actions in the started thread.
- All actions in a thread happen-before any other thread successfully returns from a `join()` on that thread.
- The default initialization of any object happens-before any other actions (other than default-writes) of a program.

When a program contains two conflicting accesses (§17.4.1) that are not ordered by a happens-before relationship, it is said to contain a *data race*.

The semantics of operations other than inter-thread actions, such as reads of array lengths (§10.7), executions of checked casts (§5.5, §15.16), and invocations of virtual methods (§15.12), are not directly affected by data races.

DISCUSSION

Therefore, a data race cannot cause incorrect behavior such as returning the wrong length for an array.

A program is *correctly synchronized* if and only if all sequentially consistent executions are free of data races.

DISCUSSION

A subtle example of incorrectly synchronized code can be seen below. The figures show two different executions of the same program, both of which contain conflicting accesses to shared variables `X` and `Y`. The two threads in the program lock and unlock a monitor `M1`. In execution (a), there is a happens-before relationship between all pairs of conflicting accesses. However, in execution (b), there is no happens-before ordering between the conflicting accesses to X. Because of this, the program is not correctly synchronized.

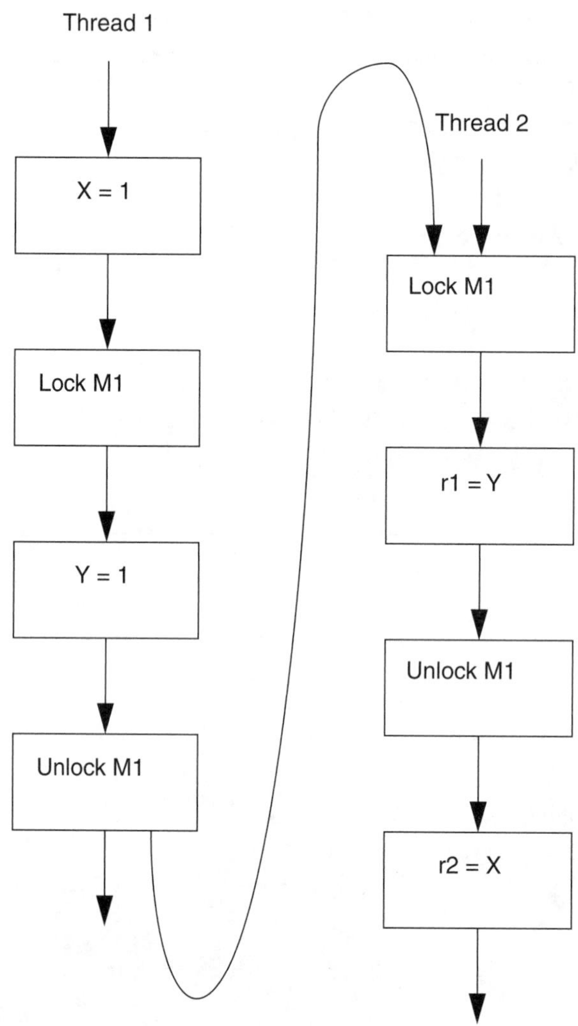

(a) Thread 1 acquires lock first; Accesses to X are ordered by happens-before

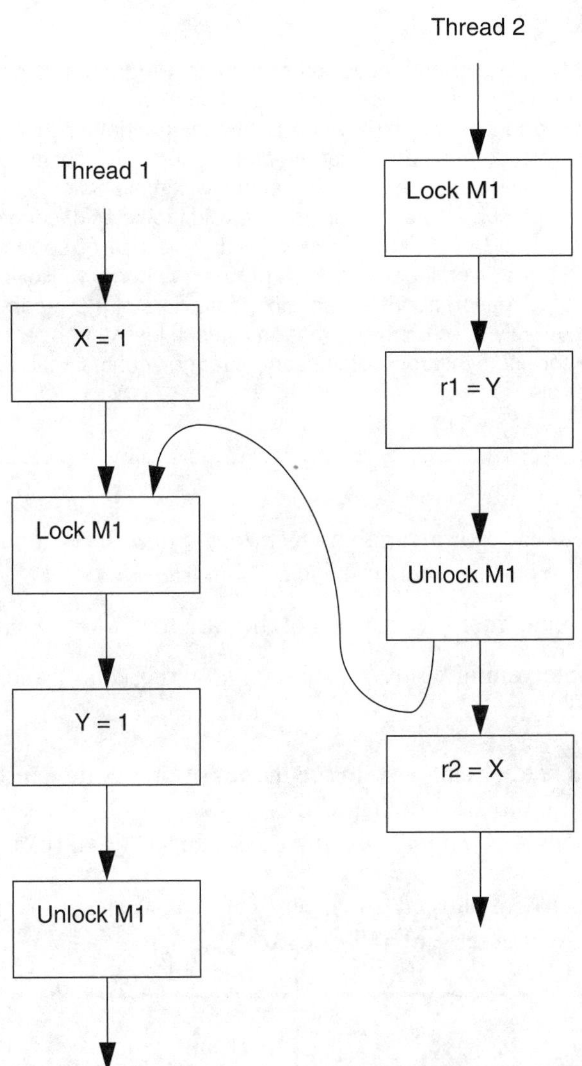

(b) Thread 2 acquires lock first; Accesses to X not ordered by happens-before

If a program is correctly synchronized, then all executions of the program will appear to be sequentially consistent (§17.4.3).

DISCUSSION

This is an extremely strong guarantee for programmers. Programmers do not need to reason about reorderings to determine that their code contains data races. Therefore they do not need to reason about reorderings when determining whether their code is correctly synchronized. Once the determination that the code is correctly synchronized is made, the programmer does not need to worry that reorderings will affect his or her code.

A program must be correctly synchronized to avoid the kinds of counterintuitive behaviors that can be observed when code is reordered. The use of correct synchronization does not ensure that the overall behavior of a program is correct. However, its use does allow a programmer to reason about the possible behaviors of a program in a simple way; the behavior of a correctly synchronized program is much less dependent on possible reorderings. Without correct synchronization, very strange, confusing and counterintuitive behaviors are possible.

We say that a read *r* of a variable *v* is *allowed to observe* a write *w* to *v* if, in the happens-before partial order of the execution trace:

- *r* is not ordered before *w* (i.e., it is not the case that *hb(r, w)*, and
- there is no intervening write *w'* to *v* (i.e., no write *w'* to *v* such that *hb(w, w')* and *hb(w', r)*.

Informally, a read r is allowed to see the result of a write *w* if there is no happens-before ordering to prevent that read.

A set of actions *A* is *happens-before consistent* if for all reads *r* in *A*, it is not

Trace 17.5 Behavior allowed by happens-before consistency, but not sequential consistency. May observe r2 ==0, r1 == 0

Thread 1	**Thread 2**
B = 1;	A = 2;
r2 = A;	r1 = B;

the case that either *hb(r, W(r))*, where *W(r)* is the write action seen by *r* or that there exists a write *w* in *A* such that *w.v* = *r.v* and *hb(W(r), w)* and *hb(w, r)*.

DISCUSSION

In a happens-before consistent set of actions, each read sees a write that it is allowed to see by the happens-before ordering.
For example, the behavior shown in Trace 17.5 is happens-before consistent, since there are execution orders that allow each read to see the appropriate write.

Initially, A == B == 0. In this case, since there is no synchronization, each read can see either the write of the initial value or the write by the other thread. One such execution order is

```
1: B = 1;
3: A = 2;
2: r2 = A; // sees initial write of 0
4: r1 = B; // sees initial write of 0
```

Similarly, the behavior shown in Trace 17.5 is happens-before consistent, since there is an execution order that allows each read to see the appropriate write. An execution order that displays that behavior is:

```
1: r2 = A; // sees write of A = 2
3: r1 = B; // sees write of B = 1
2: B = 1;
4: A = 2;
```

In this execution, the reads see writes that occur later in the execution order. This may seem counterintuitive, but is allowed by happens-before consistency. Allowing reads to see later writes can sometimes produce unacceptable behaviors.

17.4.6 Executions

An execution E is described by a tuple $< P, A, po, so, W, V, sw, hb >$, comprising:

- P - a program
- A - a set of actions
- po - program order, which for each thread t, is a total order over all actions performed by t in A
- so - synchronization order, which is a total order over all synchronization actions in A
- W - a write-seen function, which for each read r in A, gives $W(r)$, the write action seen by r in E.
- V - a value-written function, which for each write w in A, gives $V(w)$, the value written by w in E.

- *sw* - synchronizes-with, a partial order over synchronization actions.
- *hb* - happens-before, a partial order over actions

Note that the synchronizes-with and happens-before are uniquely determined by the other components of an execution and the rules for well-formed executions (§17.4.7).

An execution is *happens-before consistent* if its set of actions is happens-before consistent(§17.4.5).

17.4.7 Well-Formed Executions

We only consider well-formed executions. An execution *E* = < *P, A, po, so, W, V, sw, hb* > is *well formed* if the following conditions are true:

1. *Each read sees a write to the same variable in the execution.* All reads and writes of volatile variables are volatile actions. For all reads *r* in *A,* we have *W(r)* in *A* and *W(r).v* = *r.v.* The variable *r.v* is volatile if and only if *r* is a volatile read, and the variable *w.v* is volatile if and only if *w* is a volatile write.
2. *Happens-before order is a partial order.* Happens-before order is given by the transitive closure of synchronizes-with edges and program order. It must be a valid partial order: reflexive, transitive and antisymmetric.
3. *The execution obeys intra-thread consistency.* For each thread *t*, the actions performed by *t* in *A* are the same as would be generated by that thread in program-order in isolation, with each write *w* writing the value *V(w)*, given that each read *r* sees the value *V(W(r))*. Values seen by each read are determined by the memory model. The program order given must reflect the program order in which the actions would be performed according to the intra-thread semantics of *P*.
4. *The execution is happens-before consistent* (§17.4.6).
5. *The execution obeys synchronization-order consistency.* For all volatile reads *r* in *A*, it is not the case that either *so(r, W(r))* or that there exists a write *w* in *A* such that *w.v* = *r.v* and *so(W(r), w)* and *so(w, r).*

17.4.8 Executions and Causality Requirements

A well-formed execution *E* = < *P, A, po, so, W, V, sw, hb* > is validated by *committing* actions from *A*. If all of the actions in *A* can be committed, then the execution satisfies the causality requirements of the Java programming language memory model.

Starting with the empty set as C_0, we perform a sequence of steps where we take actions from the set of actions *A* and add them to a set of committed actions

C_i to get a new set of committed actions C_{i+1}. To demonstrate that this is reasonable, for each C_i we need to demonstrate an execution E_i containing C_i that meets certain conditions.

Formally, an execution *E satisfies the causality requirements of the Java programming language memory model* if and only if there exist

- Sets of actions C_0, C_1, ... such that
  - C_0 is the empty set
  - C_i is a proper subset of C_{i+1}
  - $A = \bigcup(C_0, C_1, C_2, \ldots)$

  If A is finite, then the sequence C_0, C_1, ... will be finite, ending in a set $C_n = A$. However, if A is infinite, then the sequence C_0, C_1, ... may be infinite, and it must be the case that the union of all elements of this infinite sequence is equal to A.
- Well-formed executions E_1, ..., where $E_i = < P, A_i, po_i, so_i, W_i, V_i, sw_i, hb_i, O_i >$.

Given these sets of actions C_0, ... and executions E_1, ... , every action in C_i must be one of the actions in E_i. All actions in C_i must share the same relative happens-before order and synchronization order in both E_i and E. Formally,

1. C_i is a subset of A_i
2. $hb_i|_{Ci} = hb|_{Ci}$
3. $so_i|_{Ci} = so|_{Ci}$

The values written by the writes in C_i must be the same in both E_i and E. Only the reads in C_{i-1} need to see the same writes in E_i as in E. Formally,

4. $\mathrm{V_i}|_{\mathrm{Ci}} = \mathrm{V}|_{\mathrm{Ci}}$
5. $W_i|_{Ci-1} = W|_{Ci-1}$

All reads in E_i that are not in C_{i-1} must see writes that happen-before them. Each read r in C_i - C_{i-1} must see writes in C_{i-1} in both E_i and E, but may see a different write in E_i from the one it sees in E. Formally,

6. For any read r in $A_i - C_{i-1}$, we have $hb_i(W_i(r), r)$
7. For any read r in $(C_i - C_{i-1})$, we have $W_i(r)$ in C_{i-1} and $W(r)$ in C_{i-1}

Given a set of sufficient synchronizes-with edges for E_i, if there is a release-acquire pair that happens-before (§17.4.5) an action you are committing, then that pair must be present in all E_j, where $j \geq i$. Formally,

8. Let ssw_i be the sw_i edges that are also in the transitive reduction of hb_i but not in po. We call ssw_i the *sufficient synchronizes-with edges for* E_i. If $ssw_i(x, y)$ and $hb_i(y, z)$ and z in C_i, then $sw_j(x, y)$ for all $j \geq i$.

If an action y is committed, all external actions that happen-before y are also committed.

9. If y is in C_i, x is an external action and $hb_i(x, y)$, then x in C_i.

DISCUSSION

Happens-Before consistency is a necessary, but not sufficient, set of constraints. Merely enforcing happens-before consistency would allow for *unacceptable* behaviors -- those that violate the requirements we have established for programs. For example, happens-before consistency allows values to appear ``out of thin air''. This can be seen by a detailed examination of Trace 17.6.

Trace 17.6 Happens-Before consistency is not sufficient

Thread 1	Thread 2
r1 = x;	r2 = y;
if (r1 != 0) y = 1;	if (r2 != 0) x= 1;

The code shown in Trace 17.6 is correctly synchronized. This may seem surprising, since it doesn't perform any synchronization actions. Remember, however, that a program is correctly synchronized if, when it is executed in a sequentially consistent manner, there are no data races. If this code is executed in a sequentially consistent way, each action will occur in program order, and neither of the writes will occur. Since no writes occur, there can be no data races: the program is correctly synchronized.

Since this program is correctly synchronized, the only behaviors we can allow are sequentially consistent behaviors. However, there is an execution of this program that is happens-before consistent, but not sequentially consistent:

```
r1 = x; // sees write of x = 1
y = 1;
r2 = y; // sees write of y = 1
x = 1;
```

This result is happens-before consistent: there is no happens-before relationship that prevents it from occurring. However, it is clearly not acceptable: there is no sequentially consistent execution that would result in this behavior. The fact that we allow a read to see a write that comes later in the execution order can sometimes thus result in unacceptable behaviors.

Although allowing reads to see writes that come later in the execution order is sometimes undesirable, it is also sometimes necessary. As we saw above, Trace 17.5 requires some reads to see writes that occur later in the execution order. Since the reads come first in each thread, the very first action in the execution order must be a read. If that read can't see a write that occurs later, then it can't see any value other than the initial value for the variable it reads. This is clearly not reflective of all behaviors.

We refer to the issue of when reads can see future writes as *causality*, because of issues that arise in cases like the one found in Trace 17.6. In that case, the reads cause the writes to occur, and the writes cause the reads to occur. There is no ``first cause'' for the actions. Our memory model therefore needs a consistent way of determining which reads can see writes early.

Examples such as the one found in Trace 17.6 demonstrate that the specification must be careful when stating whether a read can see a write that occurs later in the execution (bearing in mind that if a read sees a write that occurs later in the execution, it represents the fact that the write is actually performed early).

The memory model takes as input a given execution, and a program, and determines whether that execution is a legal execution of the program. It does this by gradually building a set of ``committed'' actions that reflect which actions were executed by the program. Usually, the next action to be committed will reflect the next action that can be performed by a sequentially consistent execution. However, to reflect reads that need to see later writes, we allow some actions to be committed earlier than other actions that happen-before them.

Obviously, some actions may be committed early and some may not. If, for example, one of the writes in Trace 17.6 were committed before the read of that variable, the read could see the write, and the ``out-of-thin-air'' result could occur. Informally, we allow an action to be committed early if we know that the action can occur without assuming some data race occurs. In Trace 17.6, we cannot perform either write early, because the writes cannot occur unless the reads see the result of a data race.

17.4.9 Observable Behavior and Nonterminating Executions

For programs that always terminate in some bounded finite period of time, their behavior can be understood (informally) simply in terms of their allowable executions. For programs that can fail to terminate in a bounded amount of time, more subtle issues arise.

The observable behavior of a program is defined by the finite sets of external actions that the program may perform. A program that, for example, simply prints "Hello" forever is described by a set of behaviors that for any non-negative integer *i*, includes the behavior of printing "Hello" *i* times.

Termination is not explicitly modeled as a behavior, but a program can easily be extended to generate an additional external action *executionTermination* that occurs when all threads have terminated.

We also define a special *hang* action. If behavior is described by a set of external actions including a *hang* action, it indicates a behavior where after the external actions are observed, the program can run for an unbounded amount of time without performing any additional external actions or terminating. Programs can *hang* if all threads are blocked or if the program can perform an unbounded number of actions without performing any external actions.

A thread can be blocked in a variety of circumstances, such as when it is attempting to acquire a lock or perform an external action (such as a read) that depends on external data. If a thread is in such a state, `Thread.getState` will return `BLOCKED` or `WAITING`.

An execution may result in a thread being blocked indefinitely and the execution's not terminating. In such cases, the actions generated by the blocked thread must consist of all actions generated by that thread up to and including the action that caused the thread to be blocked, and no actions that would be generated by the thread after that action.

To reason about observable behaviors, we need to talk about sets of observable actions.

If O is a set of observable actions foran execution E, then set O must be a subset of E's actions, A, and must contain only a finite number of actions, even if A contains an infinite number of actions. Furthermore, if an action y is in O, and either $hb(x, y)$ or $so(x, y)$, then x is in O.

Note that a set of observable actions are not restricted to external actions. Rather, only external actions that are in a set of observable actions are deemed to be observable external actions.

A behavior B is an allowable behavior of a program P if and only if B is a finite set of external actions and either

- There exists an execution E of P, and a set O of observable actions for E, and B is the set of external actions in O (if any threads in E end in a blocked state and O contains all actions in E, then B may also contain a *hang* action), or
- There exists a set O of actions such that B consists of a *hang* action plus all the external actions in O and for all $K \geq |O|$, there exists an execution E of P with actions A, and there exists a set of actions O' such that:
  - Both O and O' are subsets of A that fulfill the requirements for sets of observable actions.
  - $O \subseteq O' \subseteq A$
  - $|O'| \geq K$
  - $O' - O$ contains no external actions

DISCUSSION

Note that a behavior *B* does not describe the order in which the external actions in *B* are observed, but other (internal) constraints on how the external actions are generated and performed may impose such constraints.

17.5 Final Field Semantics

Fields declared `final` are initialized once, but never changed under normal circumstances. The detailed semantics of final fields are somewhat different from those of normal fields. In particular, compilers have a great deal of freedom to move reads of final fields across synchronization barriers and calls to arbitrary or unknown methods. Correspondingly, compilers are allowed to keep the value of a final field cached in a register and not reload it from memory in situations where a non-final field would have to be reloaded.

Final fields also allow programmers to implement thread-safe immutable objects without synchronization. A thread-safe immutable object is seen as immutable by all threads, even if a data race is used to pass references to the immutable object between threads. This can provide safety guarantees against misuse of an immutable class by incorrect or malicious code. Final fields must be used correctly to provide a guarantee of immutability.

An object is considered to be *completely initialized* when its constructor finishes. A thread that can only see a reference to an object after that object has been completely initialized is guaranteed to see the correctly initialized values for that object's final fields.

The usage model for final fields is a simple one. Set the final fields for an object in that object's constructor. Do not write a reference to the object being constructed in a place where another thread can see it before the object's constructor is finished. If this is followed, then when the object is seen by another thread, that thread will always see the correctly constructed version of that object's final fields. It will also see versions of any object or array referenced by those final fields that are at least as up-to-date as the final fields are.

DISCUSSION

The example below illustrates how final fields compare to normal fields.

```
class FinalFieldExample {
  final int x;
  int y;
  static FinalFieldExample f;
  public FinalFieldExample() {
    x = 3;
    y = 4;
  }

  static void writer() {
    f = new FinalFieldExample();
  }

  static void reader() {
    if (f != null) {
      int i = f.x; // guaranteed to see 3
      int j = f.y; // could see 0
    }
  }
}
```

The class `FinalFieldExample` has a final int field `x` and a non-final int field `y`. One thread might execute the method `writer()`, and another might execute the method `reader()`.

Because `writer()` writes `f` *after* the object's constructor finishes, the `reader()` will be guaranteed to see the properly initialized value for `f.x`: it will read the value 3. However, `f.y` is not final; the `reader()` method is therefore not guaranteed to see the value 4 for it.

DISCUSSION

Final fields are designed to allow for necessary security guarantees. Consider the following example. One thread (which we shall refer to as thread 1) executes

```
Global.s = "/tmp/usr".substring(4);
```

while another thread (thread 2) executes

```
String myS = Global.s;
if (myS.equals("/tmp"))System.out.println(myS);
```

`String` objects are intended to be immutable and string operations do not perform synchronization. While the `String` implementation does not have any data races, other code could have data races involving the use of `Strings`, and the memory model makes weak guarantees for programs that have data races. In particular, if the fields of the `String` class were not final, then it would be possible (although unlikely) that Thread 2 could initially see the default value of 0 for the offset of the string object, allowing it to compare as equal to `"/tmp"`.

A later operation on the `String` object might see the correct offset of 4, so that the `String` object is perceived as being `"/usr"`. Many security features of the Java programming language depend upon `Strings` being perceived as truly immutable, even if malicious code is using data races to pass `String` references between threads.

17.5.1 Semantics of Final Fields

The semantics for final fields are as follows. Let *o* be an object, and *c* be a constructor for *o* in which *f* is written. A *freeze* action on a final field *f* of *o* takes place when *c* exits, either normally or abruptly.

DISCUSSION

Note that if one constructor invokes another constructor, and the invoked constructor sets a final field, the freeze for the final field takes place at the end of the invoked constructor.

For each execution, the behavior of reads is influenced by two additional partial orders, the dereference chain *dereferences()* and the memory chain *mc()*, which are considered to be part of the execution (and thus, fixed for any particular execution). These partial orders must satisfy the following constraints (which need not have a unique solution):

- **Dereference Chain** If an action *a* is a read or write of a field or element of an object *o* by a thread *t* that did not initialize *o,* then there must exist some read *r* by thread *t* that sees the address of *o* such that *r dereferences(r , a).*
- **Memory Chain** There are several constraints on the memory chain ordering:
  - If *r* is a read that sees a write *w*, then it must be the case that *mc(w, r).*
  - If *r* and *a* are actions such that *dereferences(r , a),* then it must be the case that *mc(r, a).*
  - If *w* is a write of the address of an object *o* by a thread *t* that did not initialize *o*, then there must exist some read *r* by thread *t* that sees the address of *o* such that *mc(r, w)*.

Given a write *w*, a freeze *f*, action *a* (that is not a read of a final field), a read r_1 of the final field frozen by *f* and a read r_2 such that *hb(w, f)*, *hb(f, a)*, *mc(a,* r_1*)* and *dereferences(*r_1, r_2*)*, then when determining which values can be seen by r_2, we consider *hb(w,* r_2*)* (but these orderings do not transitively close with other happens-before orderings). Note that the *dereferences* order is reflexive, and r_1 can be the same as r_2.

For reads of final fields, the only writes that are deemed to come before the read of the final field are the ones derived through the final field semantics.

17.5.2 Reading Final Fields During Construction

A read of a final field of an object within the thread that constructs that object is ordered with respect to the initialization of that field within the constructor by the usual happens-before rules. If the read occurs after the field is set in the constructor, it sees the value the final field is assigned, otherwise it sees the default value.

17.5.3 Subsequent Modification of Final Fields

In some cases, such as deserialization, the system will need to change the final fields of an object after construction. Final fields can be changed via reflection and other implementation dependent means. The only pattern in which this has reasonable semantics is one in which an object is constructed and then the final fields of the object are updated. The object should not be made visible to other threads, nor should the final fields be read, until all updates to the final fields of the object are complete. Freezes of a final field occur both at the end of the constructor in which the final field is set, and immediately after each modification of a final field via reflection or other special mechanism.

Even then, there are a number of complications. If a final field is initialized to a compile-time constant in the field declaration, changes to the final field may not be observed, since uses of that final field are replaced at compile time with the compile-time constant.

Another problem is that the specification allows aggressive optimization of final fields. Within a thread, it is permissible to reorder reads of a final field with those modifications of a final field that do not take place in the constructor.

DISCUSSION

For example, consider the following code fragment:

```
class A {
  final int x;
  A() {
    x = 1;
  }
  int f() {
    return d(this,this);
  }
  int d(A a1, A a2) {
    int i = a1.x;
    g(a1);
    int j = a2.x;
    return j - i;
  }
  static void g(A a) {
    // uses reflection to change a.x to 2
  }
}
```

In the `d()` method, the compiler is allowed to reorder the reads of `x` and the call to `g()` freely. Thus, `A().f()` could return -1, 0 or 1.

An implementation may provide a way to execute a block of code in a *final field safe context*. If an object is constructed within a final field safe context, the reads of a final field of that object will not be reordered with modifications of that final field that occur within that final field safe context.

A final field safe context has additional protections. If a thread has seen an incorrectly published reference to an object that allows the thread to see the default value of a final field, and then, within a final-field safe context, reads a properly published reference to the object, it will be guaranteed to see the correct value of the final field. In the formalism, code executed within a final-field safe context is treated as a separate thread (for the purposes of final field semantics only).

In an implementation, a compiler should not move an access to a final field into or out of a final-field safe context (although it can be moved around the execution of such a context, so long as the object is not constructed within that context).

One place where use of a final-field safe context would be appropriate is in an executor or thread pool. By executing each `Runnable` in a separate final field safe context, the executor could guarantee that incorrect access by one `Runnable` to a object *o* won't remove final field guarantees for other `Runnable`s handled by the same executor.

17.5.4 Write Protected Fields

Normally, final static fields may not be modified. However `System.in`, `System.out`, and `System.err` are final static fields that, for legacy reasons, must be allowed to be changed by the methods `System.setIn`, `System.setOut` and `System.setErr`. We refer to these fields as being *write-protected* to distinguish them from ordinary final fields.

The compiler needs to treat these fields differently from other final fields. For example, a read of an ordinary final field is ``immune'' to synchronization: the barrier involved in a lock or volatile read does not have to affect what value is read from a final field. Since the value of write-protected fields may be seen to change, synchronization events should have an effect on them. Therefore, the semantics dictate that these fields be treated as normal fields that cannot be changed by user code, unless that user code is in the `System` class.

17.6 Word Tearing

One implementation consideration for Java virtual machines is that every field and array element is considered distinct; updates to one field or element must not interact with reads or updates of any other field or element. In particular, two threads that update adjacent elements of a byte array separately must not interfere or interact and do not need synchronization to ensure sequential consistency.

Some processors do not provide the ability to write to a single byte. It would be illegal to implement byte array updates on such a processor by simply reading an entire word, updating the appropriate byte, and then writing the entire word back to memory. This problem is sometimes known as *word tearing*, and on processors that cannot easily update a single byte in isolation some other approach will be required.

DISCUSSION

Here is a test case to detect word tearing:

```
public class WordTearing extends Thread {
    static final int LENGTH = 8;
    static final int ITERS = 1000000;
    static byte[] counts = new byte[LENGTH];
```

```
    static Thread[] threads = new Thread[LENGTH];
    final int id;
    WordTearing(int i) {
        id = i;
    }
    public void run() {
        byte v = 0;
        for (int i = 0; i < ITERS; i++) {
            byte v2 = counts[id];
            if (v != v2) {
             System.err.println("Word-Tearing found: " +
                        "counts[" + id
                           + "] = " + v2 + ", should be " + v);
                return;
            }
            v++;
            counts[id] = v;
        }
    }
    public static void main(String[] args) {
        for (int i = 0; i < LENGTH; ++i)
            (threads[i] = new WordTearing(i)).start();
    }
}
```

This makes the point that bytes must not be overwritten by writes to adjacent bytes

---

17.7 Non-atomic Treatment of `double` and `long`

Some implementations may find it convenient to divide a single write action on a 64-bit long or double value into two write actions on adjacent 32 bit values. For efficiency's sake, this behavior is implementation specific; Java virtual machines are free to perform writes to long and double values atomically or in two parts.

For the purposes of the Java programming language memory model, a single write to a non-volatile long or double value is treated as two separate writes: one to each 32-bit half. This can result in a situation where a thread sees the first 32 bits of a 64 bit value from one write, and the second 32 bits from another write. Writes and reads of volatile long and double values are always atomic. Writes to and reads of references are always atomic, regardless of whether they are implemented as 32 or 64 bit values.

VM implementors are encouraged to avoid splitting their 64-bit values where possible. Programmers are encouraged to declare shared 64-bit values as volatile or synchronize their programs correctly to avoid possible complications.

17.8 Wait Sets and Notification

17.8.1 Wait

Wait actions occur upon invocation of `wait()`, or the timed forms `wait(long millisecs)` and `wait(long millisecs, int nanosecs)`. A call of `wait(long millisecs)` with a parameter of zero, or a call of `wait(long millisecs, int nanosecs)` with two zero parameters, is equivalent to an invocation of `wait()`.

A thread *returns normally* from a `wait` if it returns without throwing an `InterruptedException`.

Let thread *t* be the thread executing the wait method on object *m*, and let *n* be the number of lock actions by *t* on *m* that have not been matched by unlock actions. One of the following actions occurs.

- If *n* is zero (i.e., thread *t* does not already possess the lock for target *m*) an `IllegalMonitorStateException` is thrown.
- If this is a timed wait and the nanosecs argument is not in the range of 0-999999 or the millisecs argument is negative, an `IllegalArgumentException` is thrown.
- If thread *t* is interrupted, an `InterruptedException` is thrown and *t*'s interruption status is set to false.
- Otherwise, the following sequence occurs:

1. Thread *t* is added to the wait set of object *m*, and performs *n* unlock actions on *m*.
2. Thread *t* does not execute any further instructions until it has been removed from *m*'s wait set. The thread may be removed from the wait set due to any one of the following actions, and will resume sometime afterward.
   - A *notify* action being performed on *m* in which *t* is selected for removal from the wait set.
   - A *notifyAll* action being performed on *m*.
   - An *interrupt* action being performed on *t*.
   - If this is a timed wait, an internal action removing *t* from *m*'s wait set that occurs after at least `millisecs` milliseconds plus `nanosecs` nanoseconds elapse since the beginning of this wait action.

- An internal action by the implementation. Implementations are permitted, although not encouraged, to perform ``spurious wake-ups'' -- to remove threads from wait sets and thus enable resumption without explicit instructions to do so. Notice that this provision necessitates the Java coding practice of using `wait` only within loops that terminate only when some logical condition that the thread is waiting for holds.

Each thread must determine an order over the events that could cause it to be removed from a wait set. That order does not have to be consistent with other orderings, but the thread must behave as though those events occurred in that order.

For example, if a thread *t* is in the wait set for *m*, and then both an interrupt of *t* and a notification of *m* occur, there must be an order over these events. If the interrupt is deemed to have occurred first, then *t* will eventually return from `wait` by throwing `InterruptedException`, and some other thread in the wait set for *m* (if any exist at the time of the notification) must receive the notification. If the notification is deemed to have occurred first, then *t* will eventually return normally from `wait` with an interrupt still pending.

3. Thread *t* performs *n* lock actions on *m*.
4. If thread *t* was removed from *m*'s wait set in step 2 due to an interrupt, *t*'s interruption status is set to false and the wait method throws `InterruptedException`.

17.8.2 Notification

Notification actions occur upon invocation of methods `notify` and `notifyAll`. Let thread *t* be the thread executing either of these methods on object *m*, and let *n* be the number of lock actions by *t* on *m* that have not been matched by unlock actions. One of the following actions occurs.

- If *n* is zero an `IllegalMonitorStateException` is thrown. This is the case where thread *t* does not already possess the lock for target *m*.
- If *n* is greater than zero and this is a `notify` action, then, if *m*'s wait set is not empty, a thread *u* that is a member of *m*'s current wait set is selected and removed from the wait set. (There is no guarantee about which thread in the wait set is selected.) This removal from the wait set enables *u*'s resumption in a wait action. Notice however, that *u*'s lock actions upon resumption cannot succeed until some time after *t* fully unlocks the monitor for *m*.

- If n is greater than zero and this is a `notifyAll` action, then all threads are removed from m's wait set, and thus resume. Notice however, that only one of them at a time will lock the monitor required during the resumption of `wait`.

17.8.3 Interruptions

Interruption actions occur upon invocation of method `Thread.interrupt`, as well as methods defined to invoke it in turn, such as `ThreadGroup.interrupt`. Let t be the thread invoking u`.interrupt`, for some thread u, where t and u may be the same. This action causes u's interruption status to be set to true.

Additionally, if there exists some object m whose wait set contains u, u is removed from m's wait set. This enables u to resume in a wait action, in which case this wait will, after re-locking m's monitor, throw `InterruptedException`.

Invocations of `Thread.isInterrupted` can determine a thread's interruption status. The static method `Thread.interrupted` may be invoked by a thread to observe and clear its own interruption status.

17.8.4 Interactions of Waits, Notification and Interruption

The above specifications allow us to determine several properties having to do with the interaction of waits, notification and interruption. If a thread is both notified and interrupted while waiting, it may either:

- return normally from `wait`, while still having a pending interrupt (in other works, a call to `Thread.interrupted` would return true)
- return from `wait` by throwing an `InterruptedException`

The thread may not reset its interrupt status and return normally from the call to `wait`.

Similarly, notifications cannot be lost due to interrupts. Assume that a set s of threads is in the wait set of an object m, and another thread performs a `notify` on m. Then either

- at least one thread in s must return normally from `wait`, or
- all of the threads in s must exit `wait` by throwing `InterruptedException`

Note that if a thread is both interrupted and woken via `notify`, and that thread returns from `wait` by throwing an `InterruptedException`, then some other thread in the wait set must be notified.

17.9 Sleep and Yield

`Thread.sleep` causes the currently executing thread to sleep (temporarily cease execution) for the specified duration, subject to the precision and accuracy of system timers and schedulers. The thread does not lose ownership of any monitors, and resumption of execution will depend on scheduling and the availability of processors on which to execute the thread.

Neither a sleep for a period of zero time nor a yield operation need have observable effects.

It is important to note that neither `Thread.sleep` nor `Thread.yield` have any synchronization semantics. In particular, the compiler does not have to flush writes cached in registers out to shared memory before a call to `Thread.sleep` or `Thread.yield`, nor does the compiler have to reload values cached in registers after a call to `Thread.sleep` or `Thread.yield`.

DISCUSSION

For example, in the following (broken) code fragment, assume that `this.done` is a non-volatile boolean field:

```
while (!this.done)
    Thread.sleep(1000);
```

The compiler is free to read the field `this.done` just once, and reuse the cached value in each execution of the loop. This would mean that the loop would never terminate, even if another thread changed the value of `this.done`.

CHAPTER 18

Syntax

Is there grammar in a title. There is grammar in a title. Thank you.
—Gertrude Stein, *Arthur a Grammar*, in *How to Write* (1931)

THIS chapter presents a grammar for the Java programming language.

The grammar presented piecemeal in the preceding chapters is much better for exposition, but it is not well suited as a basis for a parser. The grammar presented in this chapter is the basis for the reference implementation. Note that it is not an LL(1) grammar, though in many cases it minimizes the necessary look ahead.

The grammar below uses the following BNF-style conventions:

- *[x]* denotes zero or one occurrences of *x*.
- *{x}* denotes zero or more occurrences of *x*.

x | *y* means one of either *x* or *y*.

18.1 The Grammar of the Java Programming Language

Identifier:
    IDENTIFIER

QualifiedIdentifier:
    Identifier { . Identifier }

Literal:
IntegerLiteral
FloatingPointLiteral
CharacterLiteral
StringLiteral
BooleanLiteral
NullLiteral

Expression:
Expression1 [AssignmentOperator Expression1]]

AssignmentOperator:
=
+=
-=
*=
/=
&=
|=
^=
%=
<<=
>>=
>>>=

Type:
Identifier [TypeArguments]{ . Identifier [TypeArguments]} {`[]`*}*
BasicType

TypeArguments:
< *TypeArgument {* , *TypeArgument}* >

TypeArgument:
Type
`?` *[(* `extends` | `super` *) Type]*

StatementExpression:
Expression

ConstantExpression:
Expression

Expression1:
Expression2 [Expression1Rest]

Expression1Rest:
    ? *Expression* : *Expression1*

Expression2 :
    Expression3 [Expression2Rest]

Expression2Rest:
    {InfixOp Expression3}
    Expression3 instanceof *Type*

InfixOp:
    ||
    &&
    |
    ^
    &
    ==
    !=
    <
    >
    <=
    >=
    <<
    >>
    >>>
    +
    -
    *
    /
    %

Expression3:
    PrefixOp Expression3
    (*Expression | Type*) *Expression3*
    Primary {Selector} {PostfixOp}

Primary:
    ParExpression
    NonWildcardTypeArguments (ExplicitGenericInvocationSuffix | this
Arguments)
    this *[Arguments]*
    super *SuperSuffix*

Literal
new *Creator*
Identifier { . Identifier }[IdentifierSuffix]
BasicType {[]*}* .class
void.class

IdentifierSuffix:
[*(*] *{*[]*}*. class | *Expression*]*)*
Arguments
. *(* class | *ExplicitGenericInvocation* | this | super *Arguments* | new *[NonWildcardTypeArguments] InnerCreator)*

ExplicitGenericInvocation:
NonWildcardTypeArguments ExplicitGenericInvocationSuffix

NonWildcardTypeArguments:
< *TypeList* >

ExplicitGenericInvocationSuffix:
super *SuperSuffix*
Identifier Arguments

PrefixOp:
++
--
!
~
+
-

PostfixOp:
++
--

Selector: Selector:
. *Identifier [Arguments]*
. *ExplicitGenericInvocation*
. this
. super *SuperSuffix*
. new *[NonWildcardTypeArguments] InnerCreator*
[*Expression*]

SuperSuffix:
  Arguments
  . *Identifier [Arguments]*

BasicType:
  `byte`
  `short`
  `char`
  `int`
  `long`
  `float`
  `double`
  `boolean`

Arguments:
  (*[Expression { , Expression }]*)

Creator:
  [NonWildcardTypeArguments] CreatedName (ArrayCreatorRest | ClassCreatorRest)

CreatedName:
  Identifier [NonWildcardTypeArguments] {. Identifier [NonWildcardTypeArguments]}

InnerCreator:
  Identifier ClassCreatorRest

ArrayCreatorRest:
  [*(*] *{*[]*} ArrayInitializer | Expression*] *{*[*Expression*]*} {*[]*})*

ClassCreatorRest:
  Arguments [ClassBody]

ArrayInitializer:
  { *[VariableInitializer {, VariableInitializer} [,]]* }

VariableInitializer:
  ArrayInitializer
  Expression

ParExpression:
  (*Expression*)

Block:
  { *BlockStatements* }

BlockStatements:
  { BlockStatement }

BlockStatement :
  LocalVariableDeclarationStatement
  ClassOrInterfaceDeclaration
  [Identifier : *] Statement*

LocalVariableDeclarationStatement:
  [`final`*] Type VariableDeclarators* ;

Statement:
  Block
  `assert` *Expression [* : *Expression]* ;
  `if` *ParExpression Statement [*`else` *Statement]*
  `for` (*ForControl*) *Statement*
  `while` *ParExpression Statement*
  `do` *Statement* `while` *ParExpression* ;
  `try` *Block (Catches* | *[Catches]* `finally` *Block)*
  `switch` *ParExpression* { *SwitchBlockStatementGroups* }
  `synchronized` *ParExpression Block*
  `return` *[Expression]* ;
  `throw` *Expression* ;
  `break` *[Identifier]*
  `continue` *[Identifier]*
  ;
  StatementExpression ;
  Identifier : *Statement*

Catches:
  CatchClause {CatchClause}

CatchClause:
  `catch` (*FormalParameter*) *Block*

SwitchBlockStatementGroups:
  { SwitchBlockStatementGroup }

SwitchBlockStatementGroup:
  SwitchLabel BlockStatements

SwitchLabel:
  `case` *ConstantExpression* :
  `case` *EnumConstantName* :
  `default` :

MoreStatementExpressions:
  { , StatementExpression }

ForControl:
  ForVarControl
  ForInit; *[Expression]* ; *[ForUpdate]*

ForVarControl
  [`final`*] [Annotations] Type Identifier ForVarControlRest*

Annotations:
  Annotation [Annotations]

Annotation:
  `@` *TypeName [*`(` *[Identifier =] ElementValue*`)`*]*

ElementValue:
  ConditionalExpression
  Annotation
  ElementValueArrayInitializer

ConditionalExpression:
  Expression2 Expression1Rest

ElementValueArrayInitializer:
  `{` *[ElementValues] [*`,`*]* `}`

ElementValues:
  ElementValue [ElementValues]

ForVarControlRest:
  VariableDeclaratorsRest; *[Expression]* ; *[ForUpdate]*
  : *Expression*

ForInit:
  StatementExpression Expressions

Modifier:
  Annotation
  `public`
  `protected`
  `private`
  `static`
  `abstract`
  `final`

`native`
`synchronized`
`transient`
`volatile`
`strictfp`

VariableDeclarators:
VariableDeclarator { , VariableDeclarator }

VariableDeclaratorsRest:
VariableDeclaratorRest { , VariableDeclarator }

ConstantDeclaratorsRest:
ConstantDeclaratorRest { , ConstantDeclarator }

VariableDeclarator:
Identifier VariableDeclaratorRest

ConstantDeclarator:
Identifier ConstantDeclaratorRest

VariableDeclaratorRest:
{[]} [= VariableInitializer]

ConstantDeclaratorRest:
{[]} = VariableInitializer

VariableDeclaratorId:
Identifier {[]}

CompilationUnit:
[[Annotations] `package` QualifiedIdentifier   ;] {ImportDeclaration} {TypeDeclaration}

ImportDeclaration:
`import` [`static`] Identifier { . Identifier } [.   *] ;

TypeDeclaration:
ClassOrInterfaceDeclaration
;

ClassOrInterfaceDeclaration:
{Modifier} (ClassDeclaration | InterfaceDeclaration)

ClassDeclaration:
NormalClassDeclaration
EnumDeclaration

NormalClassDeclaration:
 `class` *Identifier [TypeParameters]* [`extends` *Type] [*`implements` *TypeList] ClassBody*

TypeParameters:
 < *TypeParameter {* , *TypeParameter}* >

TypeParameter:
 Identifier [`extends` *Bound]*

Bound:
 Type {& *Type}*

EnumDeclaration:
 `enum` *Identifier [*`implements` *TypeList] EnumBody*

EnumBody:
 { [EnumConstants] [,] [EnumBodyDeclarations] }

EnumConstants:
 EnumConstant
 EnumConstants , EnumConstant

EnumConstant:
 Annotations Identifier [Arguments] [ClassBody]

EnumBodyDeclarations:
 ; {ClassBodyDeclaration}

InterfaceDeclaration:
 NormalInterfaceDeclaration
 AnnotationTypeDeclaration

NormalInterfaceDeclaration:
 `interface` *Identifier [TypeParameters] [*`extends` *TypeList] InterfaceBody*

TypeList:
 Type { , *Type}*

AnnotationTypeDeclaration:
 @ interface Identifier AnnotationTypeBody

AnnotationTypeBody:
 { [AnnotationTypeElementDeclarations] }

AnnotationTypeElementDeclarations:
AnnotationTypeElementDeclaration
AnnotationTypeElementDeclarations AnnotationTypeElementDeclaration

AnnotationTypeElementDeclaration:
{Modifier} AnnotationTypeElementRest

AnnotationTypeElementRest:
Type Identifier AnnotationMethodOrConstantRest ;
ClassDeclaration
InterfaceDeclaration
EnumDeclaration
AnnotationTypeDeclaration

AnnotationMethodOrConstantRest:
AnnotationMethodRest
AnnotationConstantRest

AnnotationMethodRest:
( ) [DefaultValue]

AnnotationConstantRest:
VariableDeclarators

DefaultValue:
`default` *ElementValue*

ClassBody:
{ *{ClassBodyDeclaration}* }

InterfaceBody:
{ *{InterfaceBodyDeclaration}* }

ClassBodyDeclaration:
;
[`static`*] Block*
{Modifier} MemberDecl

MemberDecl:
GenericMethodOrConstructorDecl
MethodOrFieldDecl
`void` *Identifier VoidMethodDeclaratorRest*
Identifier ConstructorDeclaratorRest
InterfaceDeclaration
ClassDeclaration

GenericMethodOrConstructorDecl:
  TypeParameters GenericMethodOrConstructorRest

GenericMethodOrConstructorRest:
  (Type | `void`*) Identifier MethodDeclaratorRest*
  Identifier ConstructorDeclaratorRest

MethodOrFieldDecl:
  Type Identifier MethodOrFieldRest

MethodOrFieldRest:
  VariableDeclaratorRest
  MethodDeclaratorRest

InterfaceBodyDeclaration:
  `;`
  {Modifier} InterfaceMemberDecl

InterfaceMemberDecl:
  InterfaceMethodOrFieldDecl
  InterfaceGenericMethodDecl
  `void` *Identifier VoidInterfaceMethodDeclaratorRest*
  InterfaceDeclaration
  ClassDeclaration

InterfaceMethodOrFieldDecl:
  Type Identifier InterfaceMethodOrFieldRest

InterfaceMethodOrFieldRest:
  ConstantDeclaratorsRest `;`
  InterfaceMethodDeclaratorRest

MethodDeclaratorRest:
  FormalParameters {`[]`*} [*`throws` *QualifiedIdentifierList] (MethodBody* |
`;` *)*

VoidMethodDeclaratorRest:
  FormalParameters [`throws` *QualifiedIdentifierList] (MethodBody* | `;` *)*

InterfaceMethodDeclaratorRest:
  FormalParameters {`[]`*} [*`throws` *QualifiedIdentifierList]* `;`

InterfaceGenericMethodDecl:
  TypeParameters (Type | `void`*) Identifier InterfaceMethodDeclaratorRest*

VoidInterfaceMethodDeclaratorRest:
  FormalParameters [`throws` *QualifiedIdentifierList]* `;`

ConstructorDeclaratorRest:
FormalParameters [`throws` *QualifiedIdentifierList*] *MethodBody*

QualifiedIdentifierList:
QualifiedIdentifier { `,` *QualifiedIdentifier*}

FormalParameters:
`(` [*FormalParameterDecls*] `)`

FormalParameterDecls:
[`final`] [*Annotations*] *Type FormalParameterDeclsRest*]

FormalParameterDeclsRest:
VariableDeclaratorId [`,` *FormalParameterDecls*]
`...` *VariableDeclaratorId*

MethodBody:
Block

EnumConstantName:
Identifier

Index

A

D

F

G

H

I

J

K

L

M

N

O

P

Q

R

S

U

V

W

Y

Z

Credits

THE following organizations and copyright holders granted permission for quotations used in this book.

Time after Time. Words and Music by Cyndi Lauper and Rob Hyman © 1983 Rellla Music Co. and Dub Notes. All Rights Administered by Sony/ATV Music Publishing, 8 Music Square West, Nashville, TN 37203. International Copyright Secured. All Rights Reserved.

The Lion Sleeps Tonight. New lyric and revised music by George David Weiss, Hugo Peretti and Luigi Creatore. © 1961 Folkways Music Publishers, Inc. © Renewed 1989 by George David Weiss, Luigi Creatore and June Peretti. © Assigned to Abilene Music, Inc. All Rights Reserved. Used by Permission. WARNER BROS. PUBLICATIONS U.S. INC., Miami, FL 33014.

Lyric excerpt of *My Favorite Things* by Richard Rodgers and Oscar Hammerstein II. Copyright © 1959 by Richard Rodgers and Oscar Hammerstein II. Copyright Renewed. WILLIAMSON MUSIC owner of publication and allied rights throughout the world. International Copyright Secured. All Rights Reserved.

Up, Up and Away. Words and Music by Jimmy Webb. Copyright © 1967 (Renewed 1995) CHARLES KOPPELMAN MUSIC, MARTIN BANDIER MUSIC and JONATHAN THREE MUSIC CO. International Copyright Secured. All Rights Reserved.

Did You Ever Have to Make Up Your Mind? Words and Music by John Sebastian. Copyright © 1965, 1966 (Copyrights Renewed) by Alley Music and Trio Music, Inc. All rights administered by Hudson Bay Music, Inc. International Copyright Secured. All Rights Reserved. Used by Permission. WARNER BROS. PUBLICATIONS U.S. INC., Miami, FL 33014.

Way Down Yonder in New Orleans. Words and Music by Henry Creamer and J. Turner Layton. Copyright © 1922 Shapiro, Bernstein & Co., Inc., New York. Copyright Renewed. International Copyright Secured. All Rights Reserved. Used by Permission.

Lyric excerpt of *Space Oddity* by David Bowie. Used by Permission. © 1969 David Bowie.

"*From Arthur a Grammar*," HOW TO WRITE, Gertrude Stein, 1931. Republished by Dover Publications, 1975. Reprinted with permission.

A NIGHT AT THE OPERA, Groucho Marx 1935. © 1935 Turner Entertainment Co. All rights reserved.

Here Inside my Paper Cup, Everything is Looking Up. PAPER CUP. Words and Music by Jim Webb. © 1970 CHARLES KOPPELMAN MUSIC, MARTIN BANDIER MUSIC and JONATHAN THREE MUSIC CO. All Rights Reserved. International Copyright Secured. Used by Permission.

From Ira Forman, Michael Connor, Scott Danforth, and Larry Raper, RELEASE-TO-RELEASE BINARY COMPATIBILITY IN SOM, OOPSLA '95 Conference Proceedings, Austin, October 1995. Reprinted with permission.

The Name Game. Words and music by Lincoln Chase and Shirley Elliston. Copyright © 1964 renewed by Embassy Music Corporation (BMI) and EMI/Galico Music. International copyright secured. All rights reserved. Reprinted by permission.

Excerpt from "Too Many Daves," from "The Sneetches and Other Stories" by Dr. Suess. Copyright © 1961 Random House, Inc. Reprinted by permission.

Structure and Interpretation of Computer Programs, 2/e by Harold Abelson, Gerald Jay Sussman and Julie Sussman, foreward by Alan J. Perlis. Copyright © 1996 The MIT Press, Cambridge, MA. Reprinted by permission.

Dictionary of the Khazars (F) by Milorad Pavic. Copyright © 1989 Vintage Books. Reprinted by permission of Random House, Inc.

Colophon

CAMERA-READY electronic copy for this book was prepared by the authors using FrameMaker (release 6.0) on Sun workstations.

The body type is Times, set 11 on 13. Chapter titles, section titles, quotations, and running heads are also in Times, in various sizes, weights, and styles. The index is set 9 on 10.

Some of the bullets used in bulleted lists are taken from Zapf Dingbats. Greek and mathematical symbols are taken from the Symbol typeface.

The monospace typeface used for program code in both displays and running text is Lucida Sans Typewriter; for code fragments in chapter titles, section titles, and first-level index entries, Lucida Sans Typewriter Bold is used. In every case it is set at 85% of the nominal size of the surrounding Times text; for example, in the body it is 85% of 11 point.

Learning hath gained most by those books by which the printers have lost.
—Thomas Fuller (1608–1661), *Of Books*

Some said, "John, print it"; others said, "Not so."
Some said, "It might do good"; others said, "No."
—John Bunyan (1628–1688), *Pilgrim's Progress—Apology for his Book*

'T is pleasant, sure, to see one's name in print;
A book's a book, although there's nothing in 't.
—Lord Byron (1788–1824)

The Java™ Series

ISBN 0-201-63456-2

ISBN 0-201-70433-1

ISBN 0-201-31005-8

ISBN 0-321-24575-X

ISBN 0-201-70393-9

ISBN 0-201-48558-3

ISBN 0-201-74622-0

ISBN 0-201-75280-8

ISBN 0-201-76810-0

ISBN 0-201-31002-3

ISBN 0-201-31003-1

ISBN 0-201-48552-4

ISBN 0-201-71102-8

ISBN 0-201-70329-7

ISBN 0-201-30955-6

ISBN 0-201-31008-2

ISBN 0-201-78472-6

ISBN 0-201-78791-1

ISBN 0-201-31009-0

ISBN 0-201-70502-8

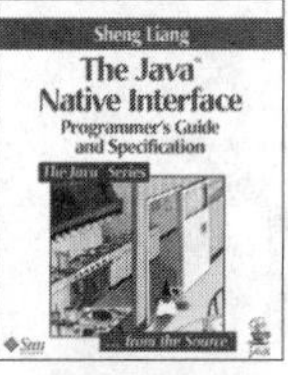

ISBN 0-201-32577-2

ISBN 0-201-43294-3

ISBN 0-201-91466-2

ISBN 0-321-19801-8

ISBN 0-201-74627-1

ISBN 0-201-70456-0

ISBN 0-201-77580-8

ISBN 0-201-78790-3

ISBN 0-201-77582-4

ISBN 0-201-91467-0

ISBN 0-201-70969-4

ISBN 0-321-17384-8

Visit www.awprofessional.com/javaseries for more information on these titles.